E9–1 (3) Gain on sale of investments, $50
E9–2 Loss on sale of investments, August 31, $28,000
E9–3 (4) Future amount, $13,151.25
E9–4 (4) Present value, $2,083
E9–5 (4) Future amount, $92,994.50
E9–6 (4) Present value, $22,548.20
E9–7 (3) Payment, $1,655.57
E9–8 (1) Rate of return, 16%
E9–9 (1) 4 years
E9–10 At 10%, $189,540
E9–11 (2) Payment, $34,464
E9–15 (5) Investment revenue reported each year, $120
P9–1 (3) Net loss from selling securities, $1,600
P9–2 (1) Loss on short-term investments, $950
P9–3 (4) Present value, $1,000.03
P9–4 No key figure
P9–5 (1b) Gain on sale of investments, equity method, $4,250
P9–6 (1) Loss on sale of bonds June 1, 1983, $1,171.51
P9–7 No key figure
P9–8 (2) Selling price, $217,061.60
P9–9 (1) Selling price, $21,493.50
P9–10 No key figure
P9–11 (3) Savings account balance, $114,913
P9–12 No key figure

E10–1 (2) Depreciation, $2,935
E10–3 (2a) Sum-of-the-years'-digits, $8,182
E10–6 (3) Double-declining-balance, 1981, $2,250
E10–7 (3) Sum-of-the-years'-digits, 1981, $17,333
E10–8 (4) Units-of-production, $1,000
E10–9 (2) Double-declining-balance, $4,934 in year 2
E10–10 (3) Gain of $7,000
E10–11 (3) $10,000 for 1993
E10–13 (2) Book value, $2,000
E10–14 (2) Loss of $3,070
P10–1 (2) Depreciation expense, $228
P10–2 (2b) Sum-of-the-years'-digits, $12,000
P10–3 (2) Book value at end of 1982, $7,875
P10–4 (1b) Sum-of-the-years'-digits, 1983, $11,250
P10–5 (1d) Units-of-production, 1982, $2,100

P10–6 (2) 1984; net income, $13,364
P10–7 No key figure
P10–8 No key figure
P10–9 (4b) Book value, $100,000
P10–10 (3) Book value of liquor license, $4,500

E11–5 (2) 1983 credit balance in Deferred Taxes Payable, $11,000
E11–13 Effective interest rate, Case C, $5\frac{1}{2}$%
E11–15 (3) Interest expense, year 4, $50
E11–16 Effective interest rate, $8\frac{1}{8}$%
E11–18 (1) Amount of payment, $8,870
P11–1 (4) Effective interest rate, 20%
P11–2 Credit to Deferred Income Taxes Payable in 1977, $4,000
P11–3 (1) Present value of lease payments, $33,901
P11–4 (1b) Debit to Bond Interest Expense, $2,880
P11–5 (2) Loss on retirement of bonds, $3,275
P11–6 No key figure
P11–7 (1) Issuance price, $93,373
P11–8 (2) Effective interest rate, 7.3%
P11–9 (2) Loss on retirement of bonds, $5,760
P11–10 (2) Loss on retirement of bonds, $12,600

E12–7 (3) Total stockholders' equity, $2,560,000
E12–8 (3) Paid-in Capital—Preferred Stock, $18,000
E12–9 (5) Legal capital, $1,400,000
E12–10 (1) Ending Retained Earnings Balance, $49,500
E12–11 (2) August price per share, $2.87
E12–13 Case B—Common Stock, $13,000
E12–14 (2) Dividends paid, $172,485
E12–18 Ending capital, $18,250
E12–19 (2) Ending capital, $89,500
E12–20 (2) Paolini, Capital, $102,680
E12–21 Madsen ending equity, $66,000
P12–1 (6b) Retained Earnings—Unappropriated, $226,000
P12–2 (2) Retained Earnings, Ending balance, $113,450
P12–3 (4) Dividends on preferred stock in 1981, $9,600
P12–4 (2) Total preferred stock dividend for the year, $9,016

P12–5 (2) Total ending stockholders' equity, $1,012,100
P12–6 (1) Appropriated Retained Earnings, $100,000
P12–7 (2) Ending capital, $22,000
P12–8 (2) Epsilon ending capital, $48,950
P12–9 (2) Ending stockholders' equity, $782,750
P12–10 (2) Ending stockholders' equity, $395,800

E13–1 (5) Decrease in current liabilities, $16,800
E13–2 Increase in working capital, $34,800
E13–3 Increase in working capital, $13,000
E13–4 (3) Net working capital provided, $3,340
E13–5 (2) Net cash provided, $2,400
E13–6 Working capital provided by operations, $25,700
E13–7 (2a) Working capital provided by sale of equipment, $1,000
E13–9 Working capital provided by operations, $630,000
E13–10 Decrease in working capital, $90,000
E13–11 Working capital provided by operations, $11,400
E13–12 Increase in working capital, $140,000
E13–13 Total sources of working capital, $1,000,000
E13–15 Working capital provided by operations, $628,000
P13–1 (1) Net increase in working capital, $11,000
P13–2 Total assets, December 31, 1981, $152,000
P13–3 Net increase in cash, $3,000
P13–4 Net increase in working capital, $286,000
P13–5 Net decrease in working capital, $736
P13–6 (1) Net increase in working capital, $442
P13–7 (1) Net increase in working capital, $8
P13–8 Net increase in working capital, $40,000
P13–9 (3) Net increase in working capital, Amalgamated Retail Corporation, $829
P13–10 (2) Decrease in working capital, 1982, $1,032

(Continued on back endpaper)

FINANCIAL ACCOUNTING

Financial Accounting

K. Fred Skousen
Brigham Young University

Harold Q. Langenderfer
University of North Carolina, Chapel Hill

W. Steve Albrecht
Brigham Young University

WORTH PUBLISHERS, INC.

Financial Accounting

Copyright © 1981 by Worth Publishers, Inc.

All rights reserved

Manufactured in the United States of America

Library of Congress Catalog Card Number 80-54177

ISBN: 0-87901-156-4

First printing, January 1981

Editor: Betty Jane Shapiro

Production: Kenneth R. Ekkens

Design: Malcolm Grear Designers

Composition: Syntax International

Printing and binding: Rand McNally & Company

Worth Publishers, Inc.

444 Park Avenue South

New York, New York 10016

To Julie, Joan, and LeAnn

PREFACE

A textbook preface is often nothing more than a review of the book's table of contents. We would like to do something a little different. We would like to tell you why we wrote this book as we did and, in the process, explain what we believe to be its distinctive features. We want you to see why we feel this book "works" as well as, or better than, any accounting textbook you may have used.

Most introductory accounting classes are made up of students with very different interests and backgrounds—ranging from high motivation to dread, from some knowledge of accounting to none. Recognizing this problem, we have deliberately tried to introduce subjects in a general manner before moving into any detail. We have found that, with the help of these initial overviews, students have a better appreciation of the "whys" of accounting and are better motivated to understand its "hows." For example, the Prologue and Chapter 1 set the stage for the study of accounting; Chapters 2, 3, and 4 then carefully explain the output and the mechanics of the accounting process. Similarly, Chapter 7, which provides an overview of the Balance Sheet, is followed by chapters covering specific Balance Sheet items and issues.

A related objective has been to create just the right mix of conceptual and procedural coverage. Not only do we carefully explain the important basic procedures, we also take great care to help students understand the underlying rationale. For example, a logical three-step method for determining and recording adjusting entries is described in Chapter 4. With this approach, students can easily see and perform the mechanics of adjusting entries, but the reasons for them—the need for a proper matching of revenues and expenses and for reporting accurate accrual amounts on the Balance Sheet—are presented with equal care.

As an extension of this philosophy, eight of the chapters are followed by supplements that provide more in-depth coverage of a topic—for example, the supplement on payroll tax accounting at the end of Chapter 8. These chapter supplements allow you more flexibility in choosing the amount of detail your students are to cover. The basic concepts and essential procedures are presented in the chapters; the supplements expand upon procedural aspects or describe more complex techniques, or simply provide additional coverage.

There is one exception to this approach; we have chosen to integrate the explanation of present value into Chapter 9 because it plays such a prominent role in accounting for investments and long-term liabilities (Chapter 11). Present value is introduced in a manner that is not mathematically demanding, and the simple examples enable students to grasp the concepts readily and to use the present value tables in a wide variety of applications.

Another objective in writing this book has been to streamline the coverage of certain topics, without sacrificing clarity or completeness. All important subjects are dealt with, but the number of chapters (in comparison to other texts) has been reduced by eliminating redundancies. Chapter 10, on long-term operational assets, illustrates this point: Many texts have a chapter on property, plant, and equipment, another on intangible assets, and sometimes one on natural resources. Each of these chapters deals primarily with the accounting for the same three basic events: acquisition of assets, expiration of asset costs, and disposal of assets. In this text, we clearly distinguish between the three classes of assets and then discuss and illustrate the accounting procedures in one chapter. Students have no trouble understanding that the same concepts and procedures apply to all three classes of assets.

As another example of this approach, in Chapter 1 we introduce students to the three basic forms of business: proprietorship, partnership, and corporation. We then focus on the corporation. The differences between the three forms of business in the handling of owners' equity are explained later in the book, when students have been given the background necessary to understand them fully. This approach does two things: it reduces the number of chapters needed to cover financial accounting, and it emphasizes the most important organizational form of business—the corporation.

By eliminating some duplications in this way, we were free to treat more fully some subjects that we consider to be of growing importance to contemporary accounting. For example, we provide chapters on not-for-profit accounting and internal control because we believe that introductory accounting students should be exposed to both topics. On the other hand, while we introduce consolidated statements, their procedural aspects are not covered; we feel these are better left to a more advanced course.

An important objective has been to organize the book so that learning is reinforced. Each chapter is carefully structured to help students focus on important ideas and remember them. First, an outline of major topics to be covered gives students a sense of the chapter's objectives. The definitions of key terms in the margins make it easier to learn terminology and later to review for exams. Similarly, several concise summaries within the chapter help students to assimilate the important terms and ideas just discussed. The end-of-chapter review and the list of key terms (with page references) serve as additional reinforcement.

Each chapter contains discussion questions, exercises, and problems. The discussion questions are designed to test the students' understanding of terms and concepts and to stimulate class discussion. The exercises are brief, dealing with single concepts and procedures. The problems take longer to complete and usually cover more than one concept. Several of the problems are designated as *unifying problems*; these require students to integrate several concepts. Some problems include *interpretive questions* that require students to analyze the computed results. These interpretive questions are optional: you can assign the first part of the problem and stop there.

We have designed the book for use in a one-semester or two-quarter sequence. A separate volume, entitled *Principles of Accounting*, is also available; it contains these chapters plus nine chapters covering topics related to managerial accounting.

Through their many revisions in manuscript, the text and end-of-chapter materials have been repeatedly reviewed and painstakingly checked by students, professors, and practicing accountants for accuracy, realism, and usefulness. In our opinion, the effectiveness of a textbook in fostering learning and understanding can only be reliably judged after it is used and the results measured. For this reason we class-tested a preliminary version of this book. The special characteristics we have described were well received by our students and were judged to be especially effective in teaching them the essentials of accounting.

LEARNING AND TEACHING AIDS
THAT ACCOMPANY THE TEXTBOOK

We have personally written all supplements that accompany the text. Our objective was to ensure that they were well coordinated with the text and were written with equal attention and care. We think the result is an integrated package that will be highly useful to students and instructors.

The *Study Guide* includes chapter outlines with textbook page references; detailed chapter reviews; demonstration problems with all important steps and calculations shown; self-tests, including matching, true-false, and multiple-choice questions, and computational exercises; and solutions to the self-test material. In effect, the *Study Guide* reviews the main concepts, chapter by chapter, from several different angles, each of which tends to reinforce the others, resulting in better student comprehension.

There are two *Practice Sets* that cover the accounting cycle and financial statement analysis. In a sense they are "mini" practice sets because they each require only 6 to 12 hours to complete. In addition, there is a set of *Working Papers* for student use in solving the problems in the book.

A complete set of pedagogical aids is available to instructors, including a *Solutions Manual* with answers to all discussion questions, detailed solutions to every exercise and problem, and solutions to the practice sets.

Also available are a computerized *Test Bank* (with over 900 multiple-choice, true-false, and matching questions) and easy-to-read overhead *Transparencies* of solutions to selected exercises and problems.

ACKNOWLEDGMENTS

We are deeply indebted to many people for their support and their help with the writing of this book, most notably our families, our colleagues, our students, and our publisher. We are especially grateful to the accounting educators listed below who critiqued the manuscript for content and accuracy during its development. Most of our reviewers did not know who the authors were, and, spurred on by our publisher, their comments have been candid, demanding, and extremely helpful.

Carl P. Allen, University of California, Long Beach
James A. Anderson, Washington University
Wilton T. Anderson, Oklahoma State University
Bruce P. Budge, Washington State University
Edwin H. Caplan, University of New Mexico
Robert W. Clark, University of Idaho
Richard K. Ferguson, Fairleigh Dickinson University, Madison
Martin L. Gosman, Boston University
Robert E. Hamilton, University of Minnesota, Minneapolis
James P. Mandel, Rice University
Franklin L. McCarthy, University of Pittsburgh
M. E. Moustafa, California State University, Long Beach
Rodney Redding, University of North Carolina, Chapel Hill
Judy Rosenberg, Wayne State University
Jack Shapiro, Loop College, Chicago
Karl M. Skousen, Brigham Young University
Curtis H. Stanley, Ohio State University, Columbus
Floyd W. Windal, University of Georgia
Leon W. Woodfield, Brigham Young University

We are particularly indebted to six of these professors who reviewed the entire manuscript in at least two stages, and, in some instances, galley proof as well. To this stalwart group goes a heartfelt message of appreciation: Bruce P. Budge, Edwin H. Caplan, Martin L. Gosman, Karl M. Skousen, Curtis H. Stanley, and Leon W. Woodfield.

We also wish to extend a special thanks to Ra Nae Allen, Mary Perry, Pat Penland, and Celeste Thompson, our typists, and to some dedicated students at Brigham Young University and the University of North Carolina who assisted us in many ways: Gary Blaylock, Richard Bloomfield, John Graden, Keith Griffiths, Warren Jenson, Chad Miller, Norman Nemrow, Scott Peterson, Bernard Vianes, Alan Wood, Glen Woods, and Mei-Ling Yang.

Finally, we have enjoyed an extraordinary working relationship with our publisher. Special recognition goes to Betty Jane Shapiro, whose editorial support and guidance have been invaluable. We sincerely appreciate the efforts of all our friends at Worth Publishers.

K. Fred Skousen
Harold Q. Langenderfer
W. Steve Albrecht

January 1981

TO THE STUDENT

Welcome to the study of introductory accounting. We know that many of you are seeking only a general understanding of accounting and have no intention of becoming an accountant. Others of you will seek careers as professionals in the field of accountancy and need a strong foundation upon which to build a knowledge of accounting principles and procedures. Regardless of your objective, if you will follow the suggestions here, you will be more successful in studying introductory accounting.

First, you should realize that accounting is as essential to commerce as language is to civilization. In fact, accounting is often called the language of business. Without accounting, we couldn't judge the success of economic activities. We wouldn't be able to plan our personal finances or our country's economic policies. Thus, accounting affects each of us. It provides the information upon which almost every financial decision is based. Recognizing its importance and far-reaching effects should motivate you to study hard, which is the key to your success in this course.

Second, accounting is best learned by doing. That is why so much homework is assigned and why it is essential that you do the homework regularly. Those accounting students who learn most are the ones who do not fall behind. Accounting concepts build upon each other, so it is difficult to understand concepts and applications in later chapters if the material in earlier chapters is not understood. Answering the discussion questions at the end of each chapter is a good way to review the chapter and to test your understanding of the topics covered. If you are not able to answer the questions, you probably do not understand the concepts and procedures well enough, which means you should restudy the appropriate sections of the chapter. Also, a *Study Guide* is available that highlights the major points of each chapter and provides questions and exercises (with solutions) for self-study. We believe you will find the *Study Guide* very helpful.

Finally, we have found that many students attempt to do well in this course by memorizing accounting details, including the solutions to specific problems. However, accounting problems tend to be unique, each with a slightly different twist; so a better approach is to try to understand the concepts and the reasoning underlying accounting rules, and then to apply this understanding to specific situations. Your emphasis should be on understanding and reasoning rather than on memorization.

Good luck!

KFS
HQL
WSA

CONTENTS IN BRIEF

CONTENTS

PROLOGUE

Whatever your motivation—career interest, university requirement, or parental suggestion—you are about to begin the study of accounting. At the outset you may have several questions: What is accounting and why is it important? How is it related to other areas of business? Why should I study accounting? This Prologue provides answers to these questions and thereby offers a perspective of the accounting profession, its nature and purposes. This background should make it easier for you to understand the concepts and techniques that will be explained in later chapters.

The Decision-Making Process

Every day you are required to make many decisions. For example, each morning you decide when to get up, what to wear, and whether or not to have breakfast. You make decisions like these routinely, without much thought, and sometimes by default (when, for example, the alarm doesn't go off). On the other hand, you may now be involved in selecting a college major and in determining the sort of contribution you want to make to society through your career. In making these and other important decisions throughout your life, you will need to consider carefully all available information and to use a rational decision-making process.

Some decisions, of course, are more crucial and complex than others, but the *decision-making process* is essentially the same. The problem or question is identified, the facts surrounding the situation are gathered and analyzed, several courses of action are considered, and a decision or judgment is reached. Making decisions that result in the wise use of resources—money or time, for example—is critical because individuals and businesses have only a limited amount of resources to be allocated among alternative uses.

The Role of Accounting

Accounting contributes to the decision-making process by providing some of the information needed in determining how to allocate limited resources as efficiently as possible. The information supplied by accounting is in the form of quantitative data, primarily financial in nature, and is concerned with organizational units called *economic entities*. An economic entity may be an individual; a business, such as a grocery store, a steel plant, or a car dealership; a government agency; a school; a hospital; or the total economy of a nation. Whether large or small, the economic entity is the unit for which we account. Through the accounting process, economic data are identified, measured, recorded, summarized, and communicated to decision makers, some of whom (management) work within the economic entity and some of whom do not (investors and creditors, for example).

Accounting information is used in making a wide variety of decisions. Investors use it to help them decide where to invest their money, which alternative investment to choose, and how otherwise to meet their financial objectives. Bankers use it to determine whether a loan should be approved. Corporate managers use accounting information to keep track of and control costs, to price products, and to prepare budgets for use in achieving long-term goals. And government officials use it to establish tax rates, set trade restrictions, and determine priorities for economic and social programs. Although these examples represent only a few of the many uses of accounting data, they illustrate the types of economic, social, and political decisions that make accounting necessary. To the extent that accounting information is used effectively as a basis for making decisions, limited resources are utilized efficiently. This results in an improved economy and a higher standard of living.

The Evolution of Accounting

Accounting is a service activity. It is not an end in itself but an integral part of the decision-making process and, as such, has evolved to meet the needs of those who use the information it provides. It can be argued that as a profession accounting is very young; however, as a service activity it dates back several thousand years. Among the earliest known records are those of the Egyptians and Babylonians (from approximately 3000 B.C.), who recorded on clay tablets such transactions as the payment of wages and taxes. During the Roman period (which lasted from approximately 500 B.C. to A.D. 500), detailed tax records were maintained. In England under Henry I (around 1100), investigations of financial records similar to contemporary audits were conducted. And as early as 1494, an Italian Franciscan monk, Luca Pacioli, published a treatise containing the essential elements of the "double-entry" accounting system that is still in use today.

In its early stages, business activity centered around a "barter" economy. Instead of using cash or credit cards as a medium of exchange, people traded goods and services. The emphasis was on accounting for the receipt and disposition of these goods and services. As the means of transacting business changed, accounting also changed. The essential elements of the accounting process were maintained, but certain concepts and procedures were modified in order to serve the users of accounting information better.

The Industrial Revolution brought about momentous changes in business, and therefore in accounting. Beginning in England in the mid-1800s, manufacturing processes started to change from individualized, handicraft systems to mass-production, factory systems. Technological advances provided not only new machinery, but new types of expenditures as well. Thus, cost accounting systems had to be developed to analyze and control the financial operations of these increasingly complex manufacturing processes.

Also important to the evolution of accounting was the development of the corporate form of business. In a "corporation," the owners of the business (the shareholders) often are not the managers of the business. This creates a need for accurate reporting of financial information to investors, creditors, security analysts, and the other external parties who have a direct interest in the company but who are not involved in its day-to-day management.

Governmental laws and requirements have caused further changes in the business environment and have stimulated the growth of accounting services. For example, the Companies Act in England in the 1850s established compulsory independent audits by chartered accountants. In the United States, the 1913 Revenue Act instituted the personal federal income tax, which created a need for income tax accounting. The 1934 Securities Exchange Act established the Securities and Exchange Commission (SEC), which monitors the reporting procedures of all companies that sell stock publicly.

These and other factors have produced changes in the types of accounting services needed and, in many instances, have affected the accounting procedures themselves. Thus, the profession of accounting has evolved to meet the needs of the people it serves in an ever-changing and increasingly complex business environment.

The Relationship of Accounting to Business

Business is the general term applied to the production and distribution of goods and services. Some of the specific functions of business are the manufacturing and marketing of goods, and the raising of capital by organizations that produce and sell those goods. Accounting is related to these functions because it is used to communicate financial information within a business and between businesses. As a result, accounting is often called the language of business; it provides the means of recognizing and recording the financial successes and failures of an organization.

All organizations, whether profit-oriented or not, have certain objectives. The term *business entity* is used to describe an organization that has as its primary objective the making of a profit—that is, the selling of goods or services at a price sufficient to more than cover all production, marketing, and operating costs. In a *not-for-profit organization*, such as a school, a hospital, or a government agency, the primary objective is to make sure the organization achieves its goals within its budgetary constraints and in an efficient and effective manner. A university, for example, tries to provide its students with the best education at the least cost possible.

Regardless of their type, size, or complexity, all organizations have some activities in common. As depicted in Exhibit P–1, all organizations begin with money resources. This money comes from investors and creditors, and from the business itself in the form of earnings that have been retained. For many not-for-profit organizations, the money comes from tax appropriations. These resources are used to buy land, buildings, and equipment, purchase materials, hire employees, and otherwise meet the expenses involved in the production and marketing of goods or services. When the product or service is sold, revenues are earned. If revenues exceed expenses, "income" results; if expenses exceed revenues, a "loss" is incurred. The net income generated by a business is converted to money resources that can be used to pay off loans, provide dividends to owners, and pay taxes, or they can be retained in the business and used to buy new materials, pay wages, and otherwise continue business activity. The results of these activities are measured and communicated by accountants, who thus provide a basis for judging whether the entity has attained its financial objectives.

In order to measure these results accurately, accountants follow a standard set of procedures, usually referred to as the *accounting process*, or the *accounting cycle*. The cycle includes several steps, which involve the recording, classifying, summarizing, reporting, and interpreting of accounting data.

At the end of the accounting process, various reports are supplied to the users of accounting information. As depicted in Exhibit P–2, there are at least four major categories of reports. The general-purpose financial statements are prepared for those individuals, basically investors and creditors, who are involved financially with an enterprise but are not a part of its management. This area is referred to as "financial accounting." In addition, income tax returns and other tax data are supplied to the Internal Revenue Service (IRS) and state and local governments. Special reports are provided to the government through various regulatory agencies, one of the most notable being the Securities and Exchange Commission (SEC). Detailed discussion of these last two categories—involving taxes and governmental reports, which are also considered financial accounting—are outside the scope of this text.

The accounting process also generates a number of internal reports for use by those who administer the daily affairs of an enterprise. These individuals are referred to collectively as management. All of this information is generated for what is basically the same purpose: to assist individuals in making decisions that maximize the use of limited resources.

EXHIBIT P–1   Activities Common to All Organizations

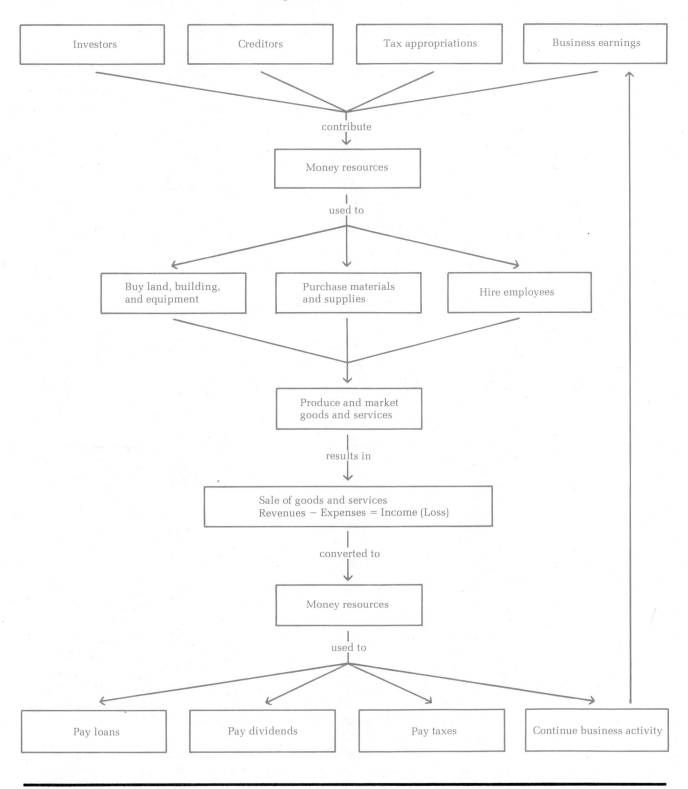

EXHIBIT P-2 Outputs of the Accounting Process

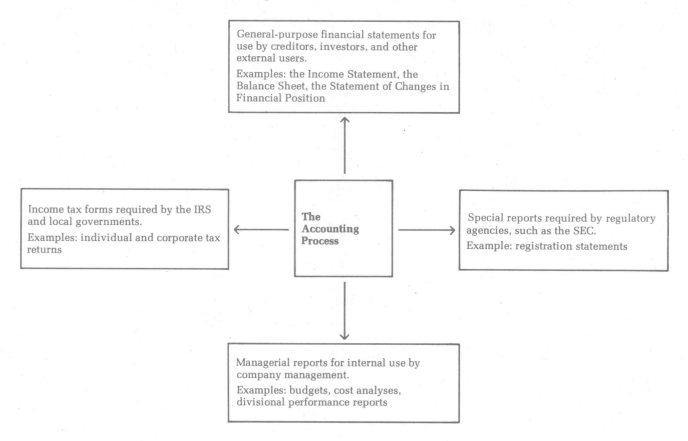

Career Opportunities in Accounting

Accounting is not only a field of study—an academic discipline—it is also one of the fastest growing professions in the United States and throughout the world, and it is playing an increasingly vital role in our economy. Accounting offers many attractive career opportunities. It also provides an excellent educational background for advanced study in business or law, as well as an avenue to leadership positions in the business world.

Students who choose accounting as their major field of study in college may select from among at least four career paths. These include working for a certified public accounting (CPA) firm, an industrial firm, or a not-for-profit organization, including the government, or using accounting as a background for other careers. The alternatives are shown in Exhibit P–3.

EXHIBIT P–3   Career Opportunities in Accounting

WORKING FOR A CPA FIRM

Most large certified public accounting firms provide four services to clients: (1) auditing, (2) tax consulting, (3) administrative services, and (4) small-business consulting. Small CPA firms also generally provide "write-up" services; that is, they handle some or all of their clients' bookkeeping in addition to preparing their financial statements.

Auditing is the term generally used to describe the verification of a company's general-purpose financial statements and accounting procedures. This review provides the basis for the auditor to issue a professional opinion as to the reliability of the information presented. Accountants employed by the company assist management in preparing financial statements for external use. Public accountants then carefully examine the company records, in effect giving their "stamp of approval" to management's financial statements. Thus, independent audits add credibility to the financial statements prepared by management.

The audit function, then, is not one of generating data but of investigating, inspecting, analyzing, testing, and checking as a basis for a professional opinion. Auditing deals with evidence and with judgments relating to the validity and reliability of that evidence. It is therefore an essential accounting service that provides about 60 percent of the total business of large CPA firms. It offers an attractive career opportunity in public accounting.

Tax accountants do much more than just prepare individual or corporate tax returns. A highly complex and technical field, *tax accounting* involves the use of data generated from the accounting process in the preparation of financial reports according to tax laws. These reports provide the basis for assessing an organization's tax liability. The tax revenues produced are used to establish and maintain the government's economic and social programs. In addition to preparing tax returns and reports, tax accountants become involved in estate and other forms of tax planning, and in analyzing the tax consequences of managerial decisions. Thus, another career possibility is to become a tax consultant, either within a CPA firm or as an independent practitioner.

A third main area of emphasis within CPA firms is *administrative services*, which is a consulting activity, generally provided on a project-by-project basis. For example, independent accountants may be asked by a client to analyze and make recommendations for improving a company's information system or its internal control procedures. Similarly, accountants performing administrative services may assist in installing a computer system, or they may conduct a study to determine the most efficient procedures for maintaining an inventory of essential materials. As these examples suggest, consultants in this field render a wide variety of services to clients—so wide, in fact, that the SEC has questioned whether some of them are appropriate for CPA firms to perform. This career alternative may be especially appealing to those who would like to combine accounting expertise with computer and mathematical skills.

Small-business consulting is another activity in which an accountant with a CPA firm might specialize. The accounting services provided may include some or all of the activities just described. In many ways, small-business consulting is similar to working as a general practitioner in medicine; that is, the accountant in this area must know something about all aspects of accounting and be able to perform a variety of jobs.

WORKING FOR AN INDUSTRIAL FIRM

Managerial accounting is concerned with the planning, budgeting, and controlling of activities within organizations. The reports generated are those needed by management. Increasingly, the managerial accountant performs a variety of information-generating and information-interpreting functions as a member of the managerial team.

In an industrial firm, there are four positions that offer major career opportunities: (1) controller, (2) chief financial executive, (3) internal auditor, and (4) operations executive.

As the title would indicate, a *controller* is an accountant who assists management in the planning and control functions of a business. The controller is usually responsible for determining the costs of operating the business and for making sure that those costs are not excessive. Specifically, he or she projects future costs and revenues, compares actual results with the projections, and determines whether and where the company controls need modification. The controller also normally assumes at least some of the responsibility of preparing the external financial reports.

Employment as an accountant within an industrial firm may eventually lead to becoming *chief financial executive* of the firm. As such, the accountant would be responsible for a broad range of activity—that is, for supervising all financial aspects of the company. More chief financial officers have backgrounds in accounting than in any other discipline.

Accountants employed by industrial firms also work as *internal auditors*. Generally only large firms have internal audit staffs to examine and test the reliability of the accounting information generated. Smaller firms usually rely only on annual audits by independent CPAs. Internal auditing includes some of the same types of audit activity and the same kinds of challenges that exist in external auditing. However, internal auditing usually involves a more detailed investigation of the operations of a company, a function called "operational auditing."

Another aspect of working as an accountant in an industrial firm is the opportunity to become an *operations executive*, such as a divisional or regional manager. As accountants progress and are given greater responsibilities, they become knowledgeable about almost every aspect of a business and its operations. Consequently, in a relatively short time (as compared with other experts), accountants often become operations managers. And although their technical accounting skills may decline because of lack of practice, their knowledge of accounting concepts and what accounting information conveys will almost certainly increase. It is this ability to understand and use accounting and other pertinent information in the decision-making process that has projected so many accountants into top positions as operations executives.

WORKING FOR THE GOVERNMENT AND OTHER NOT-FOR-PROFIT ORGANIZATIONS

There are numerous career opportunities for accountants in government. In the federal government, for example, many agencies and units—such as the military, the Environmental Protection Agency, and the Federal Power Commission—need audit staffs. Additional employers are the General Accounting Office (GAO), the Internal Revenue Service (IRS), and the Federal Bureau of Investigation (FBI). The GAO employs auditors to perform both internal operations audits and external financial audits of the various government agencies under its jurisdiction. The IRS hires accountants as agents to assist in determining appropriate tax revenues. For a number of years the FBI has sought individuals with accounting backgrounds, primarily to investigate financial frauds.

In addition, many accounting jobs are available in state and local government agencies and in not-for-profit organizations such as schools, hospitals, and universities. All the financial and managerial accounting activities discussed earlier are applicable to not-for-profit organizations. The reporting emphasis, however, is not on measuring income (or loss), but on determining how efficiently the organization is accomplishing its nonprofit objectives. Consequently, different accounting concepts may be used. Not-for-profit accounting is one of the fastest growing segments of accounting practice.

EDUCATIONAL PREPARATION

Some college students decide to earn an undergraduate degree in accounting, even though they have no intention of practicing as an accountant. This is particularly true for those who want to obtain a degree in law (J.D.) or a graduate degree in business administration (M.B.A.). Accounting is considered by many educators to be one of the two or three best prelaw majors. A person with an undergraduate major in accounting combined with an M.B.A. degree is much sought after by business firms.

Another alternative that should receive careful consideration is graduate study in accountancy. For those who would seek careers as professional accountants, a master's degree in accountancy (M.Acc.) is likely to provide an advantage. The expanding role of accounting and the increasing complexity of business require additional formal education and training in the field. To meet this need, professional schools of accountancy have been established at more than a dozen universities in the United States. These schools offer 5-year professional programs leading to the M.Acc. degree.

Some students may want to consider a teaching career in accounting. To teach at the college level generally requires a Ph.D. degree and an interest in conducting research. The shortage of qualified accounting professors, combined with increased enrollments in accounting, has resulted in excellent job opportunities for accounting teachers.

Each of the career opportunities described offers significant benefits, but none is without disadvantages. The practice of accounting is rigorous, often requiring long hours, sometimes under adverse circumstances as a result of financial and legal pressures. (Accounting is not usually considered the easiest major in school, either.) However, the financial rewards are attractive, the work is challenging, and accountants can feel a sense of accomplishment in belonging to a profession that provides useful services and makes a positive contribution to society.

FINANCIAL ACCOUNTING

SECTION 1

The Accounting Process

This cuneiform tablet from Babylonia is an example of an accounting record prepared during the reign of Bur-Sin, about 2400 B.C. (The Bettmann Archive)

CHAPTER 1

Accounting and Its Environment

THIS CHAPTER EXPLAINS: The differences between financial and managerial accounting.

Some of the basic assumptions and concepts that underlie financial accounting.

The structure and role of accounting theory, including the development of accounting principles.

The role of the Financial Accounting Standards Board and its Conceptual Framework Study.

---

business entity *an organization with a profit objective that derives its earnings by providing goods or services*

not-for-profit organization *an entity without a profit objective, oriented toward accomplishing nonprofit goals in an efficient manner*

Each member of society belongs to and interacts with organizations. These organizations, or entities, are defined by their objectives. That is, a business entity, such as a grocery store or a movie theater, strives to make a profit. A not-for-profit organization, such as a city planning commission or a hospital, has a goal of service and efficiency. And, on a fairly informal basis, a social organization, such as a family, also has certain goals—for example, to save enough money to enable the children to attend college.

Every organization, regardless of its size or purpose, should have a means of keeping track of its activities and measuring how well it is accomplishing its objectives. Accounting provides such a mechanism. It therefore has a major role to play in business and in each of our personal economic lives. For this reason, a basic knowledge of accounting is useful to everyone.[1]

Financial and Managerial Accounting

Economic organizations, like individuals, have limited resources that must be allocated among alternative uses. Accounting helps these organizations to determine the optimal use of their resources and thereby to accomplish

[1] The first few pages of Chapter 1 repeat information from the Prologue. The purpose of this repetition is to reinforce and expand upon your understanding of certain key terms and concepts.

their objectives. It does so by providing information, primarily financial in nature, about the organization's activities and goals. For example, suppose that you own an auto parts store. You may need to decide whether to purchase only new parts for resale or whether, in addition, to maintain a machine shop where certain used parts can be rebuilt and then resold. Accounting information about the costs of operating the machine shop compared with the expected sales of used parts would help you make that decision. Indeed, it would be virtually impossible to make a rational decision without such facts.

Thus, accounting is a service activity designed to accumulate, measure, and communicate economic information about organizations. Such information helps individuals make better economic decisions.

accounting   *a service activity designed to accumulate, measure, and communicate financial information about organizations for decision-making purposes*

MANAGERIAL ACCOUNTING

Accounting information is useful to a number of different groups. The primary "internal" user group is management, individuals who make the day-to-day operating decisions in an organization. These people use accounting information in deciding which products to produce, what prices to charge, how to market the products, which costs seem excessive, and what cost controls need to be tightened. Thus, managerial accounting focuses on the functions of planning, budgeting, cost determination, and the control of expenses—and, in general, on the accounting information used by management in making decisions.

management   *individuals who are responsible for overseeing the day-to-day operations of a business and who are the "internal" users of accounting information*

managerial accounting   *the area of accounting concerned with assisting managers in decision making, specifically with planning, budgeting, and controlling costs and revenues*

FINANCIAL ACCOUNTING

The primary "external" users of accounting information are those individuals who have an interest, financial or otherwise, in an organization but are not involved in its day-to-day management. Creditors and investors are considered the most important external users. They need accounting information to help them answer such questions as: Should a loan be made to a company and for how much? What company in an industry is likely to provide the best investment opportunity? Should a company's stock be held or sold? Is a certain return on an investment reasonable? The accounting concepts and financial information used by investors, creditors, and other external users in making decisions about an organization belong to the area referred to as financial accounting. This area is concerned with measuring and reporting the financial status and operating results of organizations.

Managers, investors, and creditors are but three groups of users of accounting information. There are others—for example, individuals in government agencies, labor union officials, economists, attorneys, and financial analysts. There are also other types of business decisions for which accounting information may be used. Many of these will be described and illustrated in this book. The main point to remember is that accounting is not an end in itself but a service activity designed to provide the financial information needed by decision makers.

financial accounting   *the area of accounting concerned with measuring and reporting on a periodic basis the financial status and operating results of organizations to interested external parties*

Accounting is not an exact science. It has evolved over several centuries, changing to meet the needs of users and adapting itself to the economic environment in which it operates. The balance of this chapter examines the basic accounting assumptions, concepts, and principles that form a theoretical foundation for current accounting practice. Do not be concerned if you do not fully understand at this first encounter all of the terms and concepts. Accounting is often called the language of business, and it takes time to learn a new language. The terms and concepts will become much more familiar to you as you study later chapters.

Basic Assumptions and Concepts Underlying Financial Accounting

accounting model   *the basic accounting concepts and assumptions that determine the manner of recording, measuring, and reporting an entity's transactions*

The basic assumptions of accounting are those propositions that are accepted as valid, although they are not necessarily proven facts. These assumptions, along with certain basic concepts, set the boundaries of accounting practice, indicating which events will be accounted for and in what manner. In total, they provide the essential characteristics of the traditional accounting model.

This section will cover several basic concepts and assumptions: the entity concept, the assumption of arm's-length transactions, the concept of money measurement, the going-concern assumption, and the double-entry concept of accounting. A few additional concepts and assumptions will be introduced in later chapters.

THE ENTITY CONCEPT

entity   *an organizational unit (a person, partnership, or corporation) for which accounting records are kept and about which accounting reports are prepared*

For accounting purposes, an entity is the organizational unit for which accounting records are maintained—for example, the XYZ Corporation. It is the focal point for identifying, measuring, and communicating accounting data.

An accountant records only those financial activities that occur between the entity being accounted for and other parties. The accountant for XYZ Corporation, for example, would record all sales of XYZ products to Companies A and B, but not those of Company A to Company B. Accountants for these other firms would keep track of their own companies' activities.

There are three major types of business entities: a proprietorship, a partnership, and a corporation. Although the emphasis in this book will be on accounting for corporations and other business entities, note that most of the same principles are applicable to not-for-profit organizations, discussed in Chapter 15.

Proprietorship

proprietorship   *an unincorporated business owned by one person*

A proprietorship is an unincorporated business enterprise owned by one person. Usually, the owner of the business is also the manager. For example, most farmers supervise the planting and harvesting of their crops and then receive the benefits that accrue from the sale of those crops. Similarly, many owners of small businesses—especially those that provide personal services—manage the day-to-day activities of, and receive the profits from, those businesses.

Because accountants view the business unit as a separate entity, care must be exercised to distinguish between the resources and records of the owner, or proprietor, and those of the accounting entity, the business. If the resources of the reporting entity are not separately accounted for, the financial success of the entity cannot be measured accurately. Although business records must be kept separate from the proprietor's personal records, the owner is ultimately responsible for all obligations of the business.

Partnership

partnership   an unincorporated business owned by two or more individuals or entities

A partnership is an unincorporated business owned by two or more individuals or entities. As in a proprietorship, the partners generally manage the business as well as own it. Sometimes, one partner takes the lead in managing the business and is considered the "general partner," while the other owners provide only financial support and are known as "limited partners."

A partnership agreement determines the ownership rights of the partners and specifies when and how the earnings of the business are to be distributed. Also, like a proprietorship, most partnerships are not legally separate from their owners, and the partners are ultimately responsible for any partnership obligations. For accounting purposes, however, the activities and records of the partnership are kept separate from the activities and records of the owners.

Corporation

corporation   a legal entity chartered by a state, with ownership represented by transferable shares of stock

stockholders (shareholders) individuals or organizations that own a portion (shares of stock) of a corporation

A corporation is a business that is chartered (incorporated) as a separate legal entity under the laws of a particular state. The by-laws of a corporation describe its scope of activity and specify the amount and type of ownership interests it can sell. Because these ownership interests are in the form of stock certificates, the owners of a corporation are called stockholders, or shareholders. Within the constraints of the by-laws, shareholders can freely buy and sell their interests, thus allowing the corporate ownership to change without the dissolution of the business.

The shareholders elect a board of directors, which, in turn, hires executives to manage the corporation. The management, as employees of the corporation, may or may not be shareholders. This separation of ownership from management illustrates the need for two kinds of accounting information. As noted earlier, the internal users, management, need managerial accounting information; the external users, investors as well as creditors, need financial accounting information.

In contrast to a proprietor and most partners, stockholders have only a "limited liability" for the obligations of the corporation. That is, they may lose their investment if the stock becomes worthless, but they cannot be held responsible for amounts in excess of their investment. Thus, the creditors of a corporation cannot recover monies owed them from the personal resources of the individual shareholders.

Corporations have become very popular in modern business. The limited liability feature and the potential for a reasonable return on investment make the corporate form of business attractive to shareholders. The corporate form also enables businesses to raise large amounts of capital through the sale of stock to many shareholders.

Because of its widespread use in the business world, and because it involves most major accounting concepts, the corporate form of business will be emphasized in this book.

TO SUMMARIZE The accounting information that is identified, measured, and communicated always concerns the transactions of a specific entity, which is considered separate from the individual owners. The entity may be small or large; a business or a not-for-profit organization; a proprietorship, a partnership, or a corporation; but it is the organizational unit about which accounting records are kept and financial reports prepared.

ARM'S-LENGTH TRANSACTIONS

transactions *exchanges of goods or services between entities (whether individuals, businesses, or other organizations), as well as events having an economic impact on a business*

Viewed broadly, transactions include not only exchanges of economic resources between separate entities but also events that have an economic impact on a business but do not involve other entities. The borrowing and lending of money and the sale and purchase of goods or services are examples of the former type. A fire loss or the deterioration of a piece of equipment are examples of the latter. Collectively, transactions provide the data that are included in accounting records and reports.

Accounting for economic transactions enables us to measure the success of an entity. The data for a transaction will not, however, accurately represent that transaction if any favoritism or irregularity is involved. Therefore, unless there is evidence to the contrary, accountants assume arm's-length transactions. That is, they make the assumption that both parties—for example, a buyer and a seller—are rational and free to act independently, each trying to make the best deal possible in establishing the price of the transaction. Arm's-length transactions provide the basis for valid accounting measurements because they offer objective evidence of economic activities.

arm's-length transactions *business dealings between independent and rational parties who are looking out for their own interests*

MONEY MEASUREMENT

money measurement *the idea that money, as the common medium of exchange, is the accounting unit of measurement, and that only economic activities measurable in monetary terms are included in the accounting model*

Accountants do not record all activities of economic entities. They record only those that can be measured in monetary terms. Thus, the concept of money measurement becomes another important characteristic of the accounting model. For example, employee morale cannot be directly measured in money amounts and is not reported in the accounting records. Wages, however, are quantifiable in money terms and are reported. In the accounting model all transactions are stated in monetary terms, whether or not cash is involved.

In the United States the dollar is the unit of exchange and so is the measuring unit for accounting purposes. For consistency, multinational U.S. companies must restate the results of overseas operations in terms of equivalent U.S. dollars.

In using the dollar as the measuring unit to account for transactions, accountants ignore the fact that its value is not stable. In other words, they behave as though the dollar has the same ability to purchase goods and services today as it had last year or as it will have next year. Traditionally, therefore, accountants have not reported the effects of inflation or deflation. However, current inflationary conditions in the United States— indeed, the rapid deterioration in the value of the U.S. dollar—have forced the accounting profession to question this procedure. As a result, most large companies are now required to provide with their financial statements selected supplemental information on the impact of changing prices.

THE GOING-CONCERN ASSUMPTION

going concern *the idea that an accounting entity will have a continuing existence for the foreseeable future*

Another characteristic of accounting is the assumption that the entity being accounted for—household, business, or governmental unit—is a going concern. This means that in the absence of evidence to the contrary, the entity is expected to continue in operation, at least for the foreseeable future. If accountants made the opposite assumption, that an entity was about to go out of business, they would record liquidation values (the generally lower prices that would be obtained if the entity were forced to sell all goods and resources) rather than the historical costs of transactions.

THE DOUBLE-ENTRY CONCEPT

The accounting model is built upon a basic equation, which is the foundation of double-entry accounting. Known as the accounting equation, it is

accounting equation *an algebraic equation that expresses the relationship between assets (resources), liabilities (obligations), and owners' equity (net equity, or the residual interest in a business after all liabilities have been met): Assets = Liabilities + Owners' Equity*

Assets	**=**	**Liabilities**	**+**	**Owners' Equity**
Resources $\begin{pmatrix} Property\ rights \\ of\ an\ entity \end{pmatrix}$		Obligations $\begin{pmatrix} Creditors' \\ claims\ against \\ assets \end{pmatrix}$		Net Equity $\begin{pmatrix} Resources\ less \\ obligations; \\ that\ is,\ owners' \\ claims\ against \\ assets \end{pmatrix}$

The accounting equation is presented here merely to give you a first glimpse of the double-entry concept. An in-depth discussion of the equation's characteristics and operations will be reserved for Chapter 2.

double-entry accounting *a system of recording transactions in which the equality of the accounting equation is maintained*

Since the accounting equation is an algebraic equation, both sides must always be equal. This is a very important point. An increase or decrease on one side of the equation must be exactly offset by an increase or decrease on the other side of the equation. To maintain this balance, accountants record all transactions with a double entry; that is, they show the offsetting effects of the entry on both sides of the equation. To illustrate, if a company were to borrow money from a bank, the transaction would be recorded on the company's books as an increase in the Cash account (an asset) and a corresponding increase in the company's obligation (a liability) to the bank. The mechanics of double-entry accounting are explained in considerable detail in Chapters 3 and 4.

TO SUMMARIZE   In conducting economic activities, entities enter into transactions that form the basis of accounting records. An accounting model has been developed for the recording, measuring, and reporting of an entity's transactions. This model is founded on certain basic concepts and several important assumptions. First, the organizational unit being accounted for is a separate entity. Second, accountants assume arm's-length transactions. Third, transactions must be measurable in money amounts. Fourth, the accounting entity is assumed to be a going concern. Fifth, the accounting model is based on a double-entry system represented by the fundamental accounting equation: Assets = Liabilities + Owners' Equity.

The Structure and Role of Accounting Theory

As noted in the Prologue, accounting can be traced to antiquity, wherever the need for economic data prompted the use of systematic methods of accumulating, measuring, and communicating relevant financial information. Although user needs were simple, the system elementary, and the means of recording primitive (for example, the number of sheep or baskets of grain was inscribed with a stylus on a soft clay tablet), the cornerstone for accounting theory had been laid. A need was felt, an objective established, and, in the existing environment, a systematic approach was developed to meet the need. Accounting theory has obviously surpassed the days of stylus and clay tablet, but the basic requirement that prompted the first step is still present: the need for reliable economic data.

AN OUTLINE OF THE STRUCTURE

Accounting has two broad functions: (1) measurement, or the accumulation of reliable economic data reflecting the financial progress and status of an enterprise's activities; and (2) communication, or the reporting and interpreting of these data in order to facilitate decision making. Accounting theory provides the framework for the measurement and communication functions of accounting.

The structure of accounting theory is depicted in Exhibit 1–1. The foundation is formed by certain accounting concepts and assumptions, such as the five we have introduced in this chapter.

accounting concepts and assumptions *fundamental ideas that provide the foundation upon which the principles and procedures of accounting theory rest*

Accounting concepts and assumptions are not natural laws; rather, they are man-made and are derived from the general business environment. Although they are subject to change—as the overall environment in which they operate evolves—such changes will be slow and infrequent.

accounting principles *broad guidelines that identify the procedures to be used in specific accounting situations*

Built upon the base of concepts and assumptions are accounting principles, broad guidelines or directives to action. Because they are directly related to specific accounting problems, principles are more numerous than concepts and are more subject to environmental changes. They find support in the concepts, but, more important, they find support in their acceptance by accountants and by users of economic information.

EXHIBIT 1–1   **A Structure of Accounting Theory**

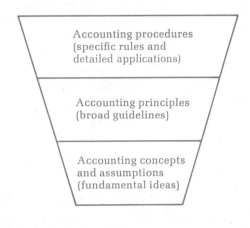

Accounting procedures
(specific rules and
detailed applications)

Accounting principles
(broad guidelines)

Accounting concepts
and assumptions
(fundamental ideas)

accounting procedures
*specific rules or methods for
applying accounting principles*

   Accounting procedures are the specific methods and means of applying accounting principles—for example, the LIFO (last-in, first-out) inventory method. They are the "rules" of accounting. Accounting procedures are pragmatic, more numerous than principles, and more readily susceptible to change. They often represent alternative ways of applying the same principle.

THE ROLE OF ACCOUNTING THEORY

Accounting theory provides an explanation of or justification for accounting practices. It is the rationale for action. Further, it provides a guide for developing new accounting practices and procedures. Such a frame of reference is indispensable if accounting is to respond effectively to environmental changes and new business conditions. Indeed, this frame of reference is the essence of professionalism in the field of accounting. Without it, the professional accountant would be little more than a robot, mechanically handling prescribed accounting situations and unable to adjust to circumstances that do not coincide precisely with predetermined criteria. Thus, despite some inherent weaknesses, accounting theory forms the basis for the critical judgments required in the practice of accounting.

   Although business activity has changed and accounting principles have been modified accordingly, you should not get the impression that accounting practice is subject to frequent and haphazard change. Accountants

generally accepted accounting
principles (GAAP)   *guidelines
that authoritatively define
accounting practice at a
particular time*

follow generally accepted accounting principles, those principles that are based upon fundamental, time-tested accounting concepts. Only as concepts and principles prove useful are they incorporated into the body of knowledge referred to as "generally accepted accounting principles" (GAAP).

HISTORICAL DEVELOPMENT OF GAAP

During the last 50 years, concerted efforts have been made to develop an authoritative, comprehensive code of generally accepted accounting principles. Significant progress has been made, but it is still a difficult and ongoing task.

There are several reasons for this continuing interest in a statement of GAAP. Many feel that more carefully specified GAAP would reduce the number of alternative accounting procedures and thus improve financial reporting. Others contend that a framework of GAAP is essential if accountants are to perform an ever-expanding role without undue legal risk. Still others see a formalized statement of GAAP as a natural conclusion to the evolution of a mature accounting profession.

The Early Period (1930–1959)

The first real period of interest in specifying GAAP began in the early 1930s. It was sparked by several events: (1) the passage of the 1933 and 1934 Securities Acts and the establishment of the Securities and Exchange Commission (SEC), (2) the reorganization of the American Accounting Association (AAA) and the renewed interest it took in accounting theory, and (3) the publication of several articles that attempted to set forth generally accepted accounting principles. As a part of this activity, the American Institute of CPAs (AICPA), through its Committee on Accounting Procedures, began publishing Accounting Research Bulletins (ARBs), each of which identified and explained specific accounting principles and rules. During the next 20 years, the AICPA published 51 ARBs and, in an independent effort, the AAA revised its statement on accounting principles three times.

The APB Period (1959–1973)

The Accounting Principles Board (APB) was established in 1959 by the AICPA. It replaced the Committee on Accounting Procedures and attempted to increase its research effort and to reduce the number of alternative reporting practices being followed at the time.

The APB consisted of 18 to 21 members, each of whom served on a part-time, nonsalaried basis. During its life, the APB issued 31 Opinions and 4 interpretive Statements. (The Opinions were authoritative and considered GAAP; the Statements were not considered GAAP but were expressions of the committee's position on an issue.) Also during this period, the AICPA published 15 Research Studies and the AAA published one major statement of accounting theory.

During the late 1960s and early 1970s, the APB was criticized severely, both within and outside the profession. Much of the criticism had to do with the APB's inability to respond quickly enough to the demands of the profession. In response to these criticisms, a committee of the AICPA recommended the establishment of the Financial Accounting Standards Board (FASB).

The FASB Period (1973–present)

In March 1973, the Financial Accounting Standards Board replaced the APB as the primary standard-setting body for accounting principles in the

Securities and Exchange Commission (SEC) *the government body responsible for regulating the financial reporting practices of most publicly owned corporations in connection with the buying and selling of stocks and bonds*

American Accounting Association (AAA) *the national organization representing accounting educators and practitioners; it serves as a forum for the expression of accounting ideas and encourages accounting research*

American Institute of CPAs (AICPA) *the national organization representing practicing certified public accountants in the United States*

Accounting Principles Board (APB) *the organization established by AICPA to set standards for financial accounting and reporting between 1959 and 1973*

Financial Accounting Standards Board (FASB) *the private organization in the United States responsible for establishing the standards for financial accounting and reporting*

private sector. It is important to note that the FASB is not a part of the AICPA, as the APB was. It is an independent body, and its members are appointed by the Financial Accounting Foundation (nine trustees representing a broad spectrum of the financial community). Furthermore, the seven members of the FASB are well-paid and work full-time on the Board. The FASB is assisted by a large staff and by the Financial Accounting Standards Advisory Council (FASAC). Members of the Advisory Council serve on a part-time, voluntary basis for a period of one year, which can be renewed. A more complete description of the FASB—its background and operating procedures—is provided in the Supplement to this chapter.

There are several advantages inherent in the organizational structure of the FASB. The standard-setting process remains in the private sector. The Board is independent of the AICPA and the interests of private companies. And it is a small board of highly qualified professionals who devote their full time and energy to the difficult task of developing a complete and authoritative set of accounting standards.

The FASB is currently recognized as the primary source of generally accepted accounting principles. Since its organization, it has issued more than 37 Statements, over 33 Interpretations of those Statements, and at least two Statements of Concepts.

Although the Board has a broad base of support, there are those who maintain that it is not moving fast enough. The development of GAAP is a challenging assignment, and it remains to be seen if the FASB is up to the task. The SEC and Congress are playing a more active role in the development of accounting principles and may take over that assignment should the FASB fail.

The FASB Conceptual Framework Study

Recognizing the importance of developing a framework of accounting principles, the FASB has undertaken a "Conceptual Framework Study." Completion of this project is viewed by many accountants as the most pressing task of the FASB and of the accounting profession. Until such a "constitution" is established, they maintain, the resolution of many individual accounting problems, such as how to account for leases or inflation, will not be possible except on a stopgap, temporary basis.

The FASB Conceptual Framework Study covers a broad range of issues. It is intended to build on work already completed (past Opinions, Statements, and Research Studies) and to reach conclusions about such fundamental questions as: What are the objectives of financial statements? To whom are they directed and for what purposes? What type of information should be reported? What are the trade-offs between relevancy, objectivity, and comparability? What are the basic elements of accounting? What is an asset? A liability? Should the measuring unit be adjusted for inflation?

To accomplish the enormous task of answering these questions and resolving difficult issues, the project has been divided into stages. During the first stage, which took over three years to complete, the FASB identified the objectives of financial statements and specified the basic elements of those statements. In this procedure, the FASB reached tentative conclusions, issued a proposed "Statement of Concepts," and then, after a discussion period, in December 1978 issued a final pronouncement, its first Statement of Concepts. The FASB is now studying such matters as the form and content of financial statements and how to measure the operating results of a company's activities.

Although a conceptual framework is necessary, it should not be viewed as a panacea. It will not solve all accounting problems. Judgments will still be required. The essential characteristics of accounting principles will not change and improvements will still have to be made. Such is the nature of accounting. It is a dynamic, service-oriented discipline continually evolving to meet the needs of the people it serves.

CHAPTER REVIEW

Accounting is a service activity designed to accumulate, measure, and communicate economic data about organizations. The information is supplied to managers, creditors, investors, and other users to assist in the decision-making process. Managerial accounting deals primarily with the internal accounting functions of cost determination, planning, and control. Financial accounting is concerned with reporting to external parties a firm's financial position, changes in that position, and results of the enterprise's operations for a period of time. The objectives of both divisions of accounting are measurement and communication.

The boundaries of accounting are established by basic concepts and assumptions. These concepts and assumptions include the entity concept, the assumption of arm's-length transactions, the concept of money measurement, the going-concern assumption, and the concept of double-entry accounting. Collectively, they determine the essential characteristics of the accounting model.

Accounting theory provides the rationale or justification for accounting practice. It also guides the development of new accounting procedures, and provides a frame of reference for the critical judgments required of accountants in meeting the responsibilities of their profession.

The structure of accounting theory rests on a foundation of basic concepts and assumptions, which are very broad, few in number, and derived from business practice. Accounting principles are based upon this foundation. The principles provide guidelines, or directives to action. Accounting procedures are applications of principles in specific circumstances.

Accounting principles have evolved over time to meet the changing demands of the business environment. They are, therefore, not absolute. Only if they prove useful do they become generally accepted. Accounting principles need to be applied with judgment so that the information presented will be useful.

The enormous range and the diverse nature of generally accepted accounting principles have prevented accountants from setting forth an authoritative statement of GAAP that is agreeable to all preparers and users. Some view this as a significant problem within the accounting profession. Others do not. They see the need for continually striving to improve accounting principles but are not sure that a statement of principles that covers all situations is possible, or even desirable. However, almost all accountants agree that financial reporting would be improved if the number of alternative accounting practices were reduced.

During the past 50 years, several organizations have been involved in the development of accounting principles. The American Institute of CPAs (AICPA), the American Accounting Association (AAA), the Securities and Exchange Commission (SEC), and the Financial Accounting Standards Board (FASB) are among the most prominent. The FASB is currently the primary standard-setting body for accounting principles in the private sector.

One of the most important FASB projects is the Conceptual Framework Study. It is hoped that this project will provide a basic framework for accounting and reporting practices for many years to come. However, given the complexities of business and the judgments required in accounting, no single statement of principles can be expected to provide conclusive solutions to all accounting problems.

KEY TERMS AND CONCEPTS

accounting (17)
accounting concepts
  and assumptions
  (22)
accounting equation
  (21)
accounting model (18)
accounting principles
  (22)
Accounting Principles
  Board (APB) (24)
accounting procedures
  (23)
American Accounting
  Association (AAA)
  (24)
American Institute of
  CPAs (AICPA) (24)

arm's-length
  transactions (20)
business entity (16)
corporation (19)
double-entry
  accounting (21)
entity (18)
financial accounting
  (17)
Financial Accounting
  Standards Board
  (FASB) (24)
generally accepted
  accounting
  principles (GAAP)
  (23)
going concern (21)
management (17)

managerial accounting
  (17)
money measurement
  (20)
not-for-profit
  organization (16)
partnership (19)
proprietorship (18)
Securities and
  Exchange
  Commission (SEC)
  (24)
stockholders
  (shareholders) (19)
transactions (20)

DISCUSSION QUESTIONS

(Note that some of the questions for this chapter also relate to material introduced in the Prologue.)

1. What is the nature of accounting?

2. What are the essential elements in decision making, and where does accounting fit into the process?

3. What types of personal decisions have required you to use accounting information?

4. What does the term "business" mean to you?

5. As you begin the study of accounting, what ideas do you have about its role and importance in the business world? Be specific by discussing your views of accounting in relation to marketing, finance, economics, and management.

6. Who are the primary users of accounting data?

7. Distinguish between financial accounting and managerial accounting.

8. List some of the basic concepts and assumptions that provide the foundation of accounting.

9. Explain why each of the following concepts or assumptions is important in accounting.
   (a) entity concept
   (b) assumption of arm's-length transactions
   (c) money measurement concept
   (d) going-concern assumption
10. What are the distinguishing features of a proprietorship, a partnership, and a corporation?
11. What is the purpose of accounting theory?
12. Why does the application of accounting principles require accountants to use professional judgment?
13. Define GAAP.
14. What is expected of the Conceptual Framework Study of the FASB?
15. Some argue that governmental regulation of accounting is needed. Do you agree or disagree? Why?
16. How would you recommend that the accounting profession solve the problem of establishing generally accepted accounting principles?

EXERCISES

E1-1 The Role and Importance of Accounting

You are applying for a part-time job as an accounting clerk in a retail clothing establishment. The store manager tells you that she feels accounting is of only marginal value in her business. Explain to the manager how accounting can be useful in her business and give examples of how accounting has helped others in positions of responsibility like hers.

E1-2 The Purposes of Accounting

As the owner of ASD (Accounting Systems Design, Inc.), you are repeatedly asked to explain the main purposes of setting up an accounting system. How do you respond?

E1-3 The Benefits of Studying Accounting

Assume that one of the following describes your future occupation. How would your knowledge of accounting benefit you?
1. financial executive
2. city manager
3. financial analyst
4. proprietor of a small business
5. politician planning to become a representative in Congress

E1-4 The Entity Concept

Delbert James lives in a small community and is involved in a number of different occupations. He is a real estate agent, a notary public, the mayor of the town, and he prepares tax returns during the tax season. Explain how the entity concept applies to Mr. James' business affairs and indicate how you would recommend that he account for his various activities.

E1-5 The Assumption of Arm's-Length Transactions

Susan Hamilton owns and manages a reception center. She has decided to build another reception center in a medium-sized town 50 miles away. Because of the short distance, she can manage both centers, and the new reception center can be built on some land she already owns. The land was purchased 10 years ago for $12,000 for personal use. Would $12,000 be the appropriate value at which to record the land if it is used for the new reception center?

E1-6 Money Measurement Concept

Identify the problems that arise from using the U.S. dollar as the measuring unit for recording transactions and indicate how these problems might be overcome. If a different unit of measure were used, would all measurement problems be eliminated? Discuss why or why not.

E1-7 The Going-Concern Assumption

Assume that you open an auto repair business. You purchase a building and buy new equipment. What difference does the going-concern assumption make with regard to how you would account for these assets?

E1-8 The Role of Accounting Theory

In a discussion with a friend, you explain that accounting is more like an art than a science and that accounting principles are not like the natural laws of science but are man-made and changeable. In reply, your friend asks why accountants are so concerned with accounting theory and with establishing accounting principles if they are so changeable. Briefly explain the role of accounting theory and the importance of developing a theoretical structure for accounting.

E1–9   The FASB

Soon after beginning a career with one of the large, international accounting firms, you are approached by a client who does not understand the objectives of the Financial Accounting Standards Board (FASB) and accuses it of being a puppet of the accounting profession and big business. Briefly explain the purpose of the FASB. (See the Supplement for additional information in answering this question.)

E1–10   Reporting Flexibility Versus Uniformity

During your first week as a management trainee you are asked by one of the accounting clerks why so many different procedures can be used in accounting for the same events. Explain to the clerk why this is so and what steps the FASB is taking to reduce the number of choices in any particular situation.

E1–11   The FASB Conceptual Framework Study

At a training seminar for new staff accountants in your firm, a debate arises over the "Conceptual Framework Study" of the FASB. Some argue that it will solve all of the profession's problems and others say that it is a waste of time. Briefly describe what the Conceptual Framework Study can be expected to accomplish, as well as its limitations.

SUPPLEMENT

The Financial Accounting Standards Board

This supplement, adapted from an FASB letter dated March 25, 1980, provides additional information concerning the FASB and explains the process used in establishing financial accounting standards.

DESCRIPTION AND BACKGROUND OF THE FASB

Since 1973, the Financial Accounting Standards Board has been the organization in the private sector with the responsibility for establishing standards of financial accounting and reporting. FASB standards are officially recognized as authoritative by the Securities and Exchange Commission and the American Institute of Certified Public Accountants.

The SEC has statutory authority to establish financial accounting and reporting standards under the Securities Acts of 1933 and 1934. Throughout its history, however, the Commission's policy has been to rely on the private sector for this function, to the extent that the private sector demonstrates the ability to fulfill this responsibility in the public interest. The FASB was conceived by a special study group headed by a former SEC commissioner and was carefully designed to carry out this responsibility.

The sponsoring organizations of the FASB are:

American Accounting Association (educators)
American Institute of Certified Public Accountants (public accountants)
Financial Analysts Federation (investors and investment advisors)
Financial Executives Institute (corporate executives)
National Association of Accountants (primarily management accountants)
Securities Industry Association (investment bankers, brokers)

There also is a trustee-at-large whose election is endorsed by the principal national associations in the banking industry.

The *Financial Accounting Standards Advisory Council* has responsibility for consulting with the Standards Board about major technical issues, the Board's agenda and the assigning of priorities to projects, those matters likely to require the attention of the FASB, the selection and organization of task forces, and such other matters as may be requested by its chairman or the FASB chairman. The Council has 37 members who are broadly representative of the relevant constituencies, including government, law, education, large and small businesses, large and small accounting firms, investors, creditors, and other users of financial information.

DUE PROCESS OF THE FASB

The FASB issues Statements of Financial Accounting Standards, Statements of Concepts, and Interpretations. Statements establish new standards or amend those previously issued. Concepts provide guidelines in solving problems and enable those who use financial reports to understand the context in which financial accounting standards are formulated. Interpretations clarify, explain, or elaborate on existing standards. The FASB staff issues Technical Bulletins to provide guidance on applying existing standards.

Before it issues a Statement, the FASB is required by its rules to follow extensive "due process" procedures. In connection with each of its major projects, the Board takes the following steps:

Appoints a task force of technical experts representing a broad spectrum of preparers, auditors, and users of financial information to advise on the project.

Studies existing literature on the subject and conducts such additional research as may be necessary.

Publishes a comprehensive discussion of issues and possible solutions (a discussion memorandum) as the basis for public comment.

Conducts a public hearing.

Gives broad distribution to an exposure draft of the proposed Statement for public comment.

Considers comments received and issues a Statement of Financial Accounting Standards.

The FASB technical staff works directly with the Board and task forces, conducts research, participates in public hearings, analyzes oral and written comments received from the public, and prepares recommendations and drafts of documents for consideration by the Board.

The Board's deliberations are open to the public, and a complete public record is maintained.

CHAPTER 2

Outputs of the Process:
The Financial Statements

The objectives of financial reporting.

The basic elements of general-purpose financial statements.

The purpose, format, and relationships of each major financial statement.

The importance of notes to financial statements and the independent auditor's report.

The concept of consolidated financial statements.

We have described accounting as a means of accumulating, measuring, and communicating financial information that is useful in making economic decisions. It follows, as we have shown, that the objective of the accounting process is to gather, organize, and transform accounting data into a useable form. The financial statements prepared for external users are among the most important outputs of the accounting process and are the subject of this chapter. An initial overview of these statements should help you put into context the related concepts and the mechanical aspects of accounting that will be explained in later chapters.

Objectives of Financial Reporting

Financial reports are designed to provide useful information about specific entities. As such, they must serve many purposes for a wide variety of users, including present and potential stockholders, creditors, financial analysts, and regulatory agency officials. Though each of these users has different needs, there is a common body of financial information about an entity that suits all of their purposes. This information is contained in the financial statements.

THE GENERAL-PURPOSE FINANCIAL STATEMENTS

general-purpose financial statements *the primary financial statements intended for general use by a variety of external groups; includes the Income Statement (Statement of Earnings), the Balance Sheet (Statement of Financial Position), and the Statement of Changes in Financial Position (Funds Statement)*

Because financial statements are used by so many different groups, they are called general-purpose financial statements.[1] They are also known as the primary financial statements and are described on pages 37 through 42. Before we discuss these statements, it will be useful to examine the kinds of information needed by external users.

Cash Flow and Earnings Potential

Investors in corporate stock want to know how much cash they eventually will receive as a result of their investment, that is, whether they will recover their original investment as well as earn a return, or profit, on that investment. This cash flow is derived from one of two sources: (1) periodic payments from a company, called dividends; and (2) proceeds from the sale of stock to another party. In the first instance, cash is received but the investment remains intact; in the latter situation, the investment itself is liquidated.

earnings potential *the ability of a company to generate positive future net cash flows from operations*

A company's earnings potential stems from its ability to generate from operations future cash inflows that will exceed future cash outflows. This concept relates to both current earnings and the expectations of future earnings. Current earnings provide the primary source of cash for dividend payments; anticipated earnings influence the market price of stock, and therefore the amount of cash investors will receive when they sell the stock.

Creditors are also interested in cash flows and the related concept of earnings potential. Obviously, creditors are primarily concerned with the repayment of loans or the payments for goods or services they have provided to an enterprise.

Liquidity, Solvency, and Profitability

liquidity *a company's ability to meet current obligations with cash or with other assets that can be quickly converted to cash*

In assessing the adequacy of a company's expected cash flows and earnings potential, investors and creditors should consider three related concepts: liquidity, solvency, and profitability. Liquidity generally refers to the ability of an enterprise to meet its current obligations. The basic question is whether an organization (or individual) has enough cash, or other assets that can be quickly converted to cash, to pay current bills. If a company cannot meet its short-term obligations, it may be forced into bankruptcy and never have a chance to prove its potential for long-term profitability.

solvency *a company's long-run ability to meet all financial obligations*

Solvency usually relates to the enterprise's long-term ability to meet its obligations. The question here is not only how much cash is readily available to pay current bills, but whether the future cash inflows are expected to be sufficient to meet all obligations as they come due over the life of the enterprise.

profitability *a company's ability to generate revenues in excess of costs incurred in producing those revenues*

Profitability has to do with the generation of revenues in excess of the costs incurred in producing those revenues. The excess is income, or earnings. Profitability is therefore directly related to an enterprise's ability to generate earnings and positive cash flows.

---

[1] The complete general-purpose financial statements for Armstrong World Industries (formerly Armstrong Cork Company) for 1979 are presented as the Supplement to this chapter.

THE CONCEPT OF FULL DISCLOSURE

For financial reporting to be most effective, all relevant information must be presented in an unbiased, understandable, and timely manner. This is sometimes referred to as the "full and fair disclosure standard." Achieving such a standard is not an easy task. Too much information can confuse; too little information can mislead. Even selecting the most appropriate format for presentation is a challenge.

To the extent that full disclosure is achieved, external decision makers are better able to evaluate alternative courses of action and the expected returns, costs, and risks associated with those alternatives. This should result in a better allocation of resources, and therefore a more efficient economy.

TO SUMMARIZE Potential investors and creditors, as well as other external users of financial information, need to assess the amounts, timing, and degree of certainty of an entity's prospective cash flows and earnings potential. Such information, which is related to a company's liquidity, solvency, and profitability, is found in large part in the general-purpose financial statements. Full and fair disclosure is the overall standard sought in financial reporting.

The Basic Elements of General-Purpose Financial Statements

The overall purpose of financial statements, and of financial reporting in general, is to provide information about an enterprise's economic resources, obligations, and results of operations. To introduce you to the distinctions and relationships between resources, obligations, and earnings, we will briefly describe the eight basic elements of general-purpose financial statements: assets, liabilities, owners' equity, revenues, expenses, gains, losses, and net income (or loss). The relationships of these elements are reflected in the basic accounting model—Assets = Liabilities + Owners' Equity—which will be discussed in Chapter 3.

ASSETS

assets economic resources that are owned or controlled by an enterprise as a result of past transactions or events, and that are expected to have future economic benefits (service potential)

In general terms, assets may be defined as economic resources that are owned or controlled by an enterprise as a result of past transactions or events, and that are expected to provide future economic benefits (have service potential) for that entity. Assets are financial representations and so are measured or estimated in monetary amounts. Thus, assets have four essential characteristics: (1) they represent potential future benefits; (2) the benefits will be secured to a particular entity, usually through ownership; (3) they can be measured in monetary terms; and (4) they result from past transactions. Assets include cash, accounts receivable, inventory (goods held for sale), land, buildings, equipment, and even intangible items, such as copyrights or patents.

LIABILITIES

liabilities   obligations of an enterprise to pay cash or other economic resources in return for past or current benefits; they represent claims against assets

The term liabilities is used to describe an enterprise's obligations to pay cash or other economic resources to other people or organizations. Liabilities represent claims against assets and are measured in monetary amounts. They generally indicate that cash, goods, or services (economic resources) will be transferred in the future to settle an obligation that has resulted from a past transaction. In summary, four conditions must be met if an item is to qualify as a liability: (1) it must involve a future sacrifice of resources; (2) it must be measurable in monetary terms; (3) the sacrifice must be an obligation of the enterprise; and (4) the obligation must have arisen from a past transaction. Some common liabilities are accounts payable, notes payable, and mortgages.

OWNERS' EQUITY

owners' equity (stockholders' equity)   the ownership interest in the assets of an enterprise; equals net assets (total assets minus total liabilities)

The remaining ownership interest in the assets of an enterprise, after the liabilities are deducted, is referred to as owners' equity (also called stockholders' equity for corporations). It does not represent a specific asset, such as cash; instead, it is a collective "net equity" concept that indicates the amount of assets available after all obligations are satisfied. Obviously, if there are no liabilities (an unlikely situation, except at the start of a business), then the total assets are represented by the owners' claims against those assets—the owners' equity.

Another distinguishing feature of owners' equity is that it changes in response to the profitability of the entity and the amount of dividends paid. In contrast, liability amounts are determined by contractual agreement and will not change unless a particular agreement is modified, the liability is paid, or a new liability is incurred. Thus, the total amount of liabilities will not automatically fluctuate with the overall profitability of an enterprise.

When viewed in terms of where assets came from, owners' equity and liabilities show the sources of assets committed to or invested in a business. Once resources are committed, those who made the commitment have claims against the business entity. Thus, stockholders have the right to receive dividends, if declared; creditors should be paid for their goods and services; and lenders should receive principal payments plus interest.

REVENUES

revenues   resource increases from the sale of goods or services derived from the normal operations and from other activities of an enterprise

The resource increases from the sale of goods or services derived from the normal operating and other activities of an enterprise are its revenues. It is important to note the difference between revenues and income (or loss). Revenues represent gross receipts from which expenses are subtracted to derive income or loss. Thus, revenue is a "gross" concept, while income (loss) is a "net" concept. The major revenue item for a manufacturing or merchandising entity is sales. A service enterprise (for example, a CPA firm) will generate revenues from the fees it charges for the services it has rendered. Companies might also earn revenues from other activities, for example, interest or royalties.

EXPENSES

expenses *costs of assets used up or additional liabilities incurred in the normal course of business to generate revenues*

The term expenses refers to the costs incurred in the normal operations of business to generate revenues. Thus, expenses represent the costs of benefits derived from the use of a company's resources (assets) or the incurrence of additional liabilities. For example, cash received from the sale of goods represents an asset that is used in part to pay salaries—an expense. Expenses, like revenues, represent flows of resources during a period of time, but in the opposite direction.

Some expenses can be easily assigned (allocated) to particular revenues in determining if an activity is profitable. For example, the cost of materials to manufacture a product can be matched directly to that product's sales price. Other expenses, such as the general and administrative expenses of corporate headquarters, are not so easily assigned to a particular product and may have to be charged to a period of time instead. Nevertheless, all items of expense must be covered by revenues if there is to be income for the period.

GAINS AND LOSSES

gains (losses) *net increases (decreases) in an entity's resources derived from peripheral activities or associated with nonrecurring, unusual events and circumstances*

A fine and sometimes arbitrary distinction is made between gains and losses, and revenues and expenses. As indicated, revenues and expenses are associated with the normal operating activities of an enterprise: producing, buying, selling, rendering services, and so on. Gains and losses are associated with peripheral, nonoperating activities of an enterprise and with nonrecurring and uncontrollable events affecting the enterprise. An example of a gain from a nonoperating activity might be the sale of land or a building for more than its cost by a company that is not in the real estate business. An example of a loss from a nonrecurring and uncontrollable event might be the loss of inventory as the result of a flooded warehouse or an earthquake. These and similar events are generally considered unusual, infrequent, and not within the control of the enterprise.

There is another distinction made between gains and losses, and revenues and expenses. Gains and losses are generally reported on a "net" basis. Either a net gain or a net loss is derived from some peripheral activity or unusual event. For example, referring again to the sale of land, the gain or loss to be reported is the excess, or deficiency, of receipts from its sale over its cost. Revenues and expenses, on the other hand, are accounted for on a "gross" basis and must be compared (matched) with each other to determine if there is a positive (income) or negative (loss) residual.

NET INCOME (LOSS)

net income (earnings) *a measure of the overall performance of a business entity; equal to revenues plus gains for a period minus expenses and losses for the period*

Net income, sometimes called earnings or profit, is an overall measure of the performance of a business entity's activities. As such, net income is a residual concept reflecting the business's accomplishments (revenues and gains) in excess of its efforts (expenses and losses) from normal operating activities as well as from peripheral or nonrecurring activities during a particular period of time. If the residual is positive, it is called net income; if the residual is negative, it is called net loss. However, a distinction is

operating income *a measure of the profitability of a business from normal operations; equals revenues minus operating expenses*

usually made between operating income, which is income before gains or losses, and net income. Thus, net income is equal to:

Revenues
− Expenses
―――――――――
Operating Income
+ Gains
− Losses
―――――――――
Net Income (Earnings)

Because it represents the results of an enterprise's activities, the income measurement is considered by many to be the single most important indicator for predicting future cash flows.

The Primary Financial Statements

As noted earlier, the accounting process can generate a number of different reports. However, most of the financial information needed by external users is contained in just three reports, the primary financial statements: (1) the Balance Sheet (Statement of Financial Position), (2) the Income Statement (Statement of Earnings), and (3) the Statement of Changes in Financial Position (Funds Statement). A fourth report, the Statement of Retained Earnings, may be presented as a separate, major statement or combined with the Income Statement. However, an increasing number of companies substitute a more comprehensive Statement of Changes in Owners' (Stockholders') Equity for the Statement of Retained Earnings. This statement is used because of the frequent changes in other owners' equity accounts in addition to the changes in the Retained Earnings account.

THE STATEMENT OF FINANCIAL POSITION

Balance Sheet (Statement of Financial Position) *the primary financial statement that shows the financial resources of an enterprise at a particular date and the claims against those resources, and therefore the relationships of assets, liabilities, and owners' equity*

The Statement of Financial Position, commonly called the Balance Sheet, provides a financial picture of an enterprise at a particular date. It shows a company's financial resources (assets) and the sources of, or claims against, those resources (liabilities and owners' equity). It is referred to as a Balance Sheet because assets always equal the total of liabilities and owners' equity. This, you will recall, is in keeping with the basic accounting equation: Assets = Liabilities + Owners' Equity.

The format of a Balance Sheet is shown in Exhibit 2–1. (Another example, from the 1979 annual report of Armstrong World Industries, is provided in the Supplement to this chapter.) At the top of the page is the name of the company and the title and date of the statement. The statement then lists all assets, generally in decreasing order of liquidity—for example, cash, accounts receivable, inventory, and long-term assets. Below the assets are the liabilities and, in a separate section, the owners' equity. Notice that the owners' equity section reports separately the proceeds from the issuance of

---

EXHIBIT 2–1   Fashion Fabrics, Inc.

Balance Sheet as of December 31, 1981

Assets

Cash..............................	$ 1,150	
Accounts Receivable	2,500	
Inventory..........................	12,000	
Furniture and Fixtures	10,000	
Building...........................	40,000	
Total Assets......................		$65,650

Liabilities and Owners' Equity

Accounts Payable.....................	$ 4,000	
Mortgage Payable....................	30,000	
Total Liabilities	$34,000	
Capital Stock (1,500 shares at $10)	$15,000	
Retained Earnings	16,650	
Total Owners' Equity	31,650	
Total Liabilities and Owners' Equity ...		$65,650

---

capital stock   *the portion of owners' equity contributed by investors (the owners) through the issuance of stock*

retained earnings   *the accumulated portion of owners' equity that has been earned and retained from profitable operations and not paid out in dividends or restricted for some other use; equal to owners' equity less contributed capital*

Income Statement (Statement of Earnings)   *the primary financial statement that summarizes the revenues generated, the expenses incurred, and any gains or losses of an entity during a period of time*

capital stock and the retained earnings of an enterprise. This is to distinguish the amounts invested by owners from the amounts earned and retained from profitable operations of the business.

TO SUMMARIZE   The Balance Sheet provides a capsule view at a particular date of the financial status of an enterprise. It helps external users assess the liquidity and solvency of the business. Chapters 7–12 analyze the Balance Sheet in detail.

THE STATEMENT OF EARNINGS

The Statement of Earnings, or Income Statement, shows the results of an entity's operations over a period of time (a month, a quarter, or a year). It is a summary of the revenues generated and expenses incurred by an entity, as well as its gains or losses.

A simple, but typical Income Statement is presented in Exhibit 2–2. (The 1979 Statement of Earnings for Armstrong World Industries is provided in the Supplement to this chapter.) The Income Statement, like the Balance Sheet, begins with the name of the company and the title of the report. Note that the Income Statement designates the period of time covered, for example, "the year ended," as contrasted to the Balance Sheet, which is "as of" a particular date.

gross margin   *the excess of net sales revenues over the cost of goods sold*

For most manufacturing and merchandising enterprises the first item on the Income Statement is sales revenue. The cost of goods sold—that is, the cost of inventory sold—is subtracted from sales to derive a gross margin (gross profit) measurement. From the gross margin are subtracted other expenses, such as advertising, employee salaries, utilities, and rent. After all operating expenses are subtracted from gross margin, the result is operating income (loss). Other revenues and expenses, any gains or losses,

---

EXHIBIT 2-2   **Fashion Fabrics, Inc.**

Income Statement for the Year Ended December 31, 1981

Sales Revenue		$52,000
Less Cost of Goods Sold		18,500
Gross Margin		$33,500
Less Selling and Administrative Expenses:		
Advertising	$ 800	
Salaries	12,000	
Rent	3,600	
Utilities	1,200	
Miscellaneous Expenses	1,700	19,300
Income Before Taxes		$14,200
Income Taxes		6,100
Net Income		$ 8,100

Earnings per share = $8,100 ÷ 1,500 shares = $5.40 per share.

---

earnings (loss) per share (EPS) *the amount of net income (earnings) related to each share of stock; computed by dividing net income by the weighted-average number of shares of stock outstanding during the period*

and the provision for income taxes are then added or subtracted. The "bottom line" is net income or net loss. Net income (loss) is used to compute earnings (loss) per share (EPS) of common stock and is added to (or, if a loss, is subtracted from) any past retained earnings to report the updated retained earnings figure on the next period's Balance Sheet.

The Income Statement tells investors and creditors how profitable an enterprise has been for the period. Comparative Income Statements (current and previous periods) will indicate trends and provide some basis for predicting future cash flows. Such relationships as the ratio of expenses to sales and of net income to stockholders' equity also provide useful information. These relationships are identified through financial statement analysis, which is covered in Chapter 14.

TO SUMMARIZE   The Income Statement provides a measure of the success of an enterprise over a specific period of time. It shows the major sources of revenues generated and the expenses incurred to produce those revenues. It matches efforts against accomplishments over a period of operating activity and helps external users evaluate the earnings potential of a company. Chapters 5 and 6 examine the Income Statement in detail.

THE STATEMENT OF CHANGES IN FINANCIAL POSITION

Statement of Changes in Financial Position (Funds Statement) *the primary financial statement that shows an entity's major sources and uses of financial resources (funds) during a period of time*

The Statement of Changes in Financial Position, also called the Funds Statement, shows the origin and disposition of an enterprise's financial resources. For this reason, the statement is also referred to as a Sources and Uses of Funds Statement.

The Funds Statement compares item amounts on successive Balance Sheets and explains why the individual items and balances changed as they did. For example, assume that the Furniture and Fixtures account for Fashion Fabrics was $3,000 on December 31, 1980, and $10,000 on December 31, 1981. The $7,000 increase reflects a use of resources to purchase furniture and fixtures. Similarly, assume that the balance in the company's

---

EXHIBIT 2–3 **Fashion Fabrics, Inc.**
Statement of Changes in Financial Position for the
Year Ended December 31, 1981

Sources of Funds

Operations	$14,200
Borrowing on Mortgage	5,000
Issuance of Capital Stock	4,000
Total Sources of Funds	$23,200

Uses of Funds

Purchase of Furniture and Fixtures	$ 7,000
Declaration of Cash Dividends	4,500
Increase in Net Working Capital	11,700
Total Uses of Funds	$23,200

Mortgage Payable account was $25,000 on December 31, 1980, and $30,000 on December 31, 1981. The $5,000 increase represents a source of funds obtained by borrowing money. Thus, the Funds Statement points out the reasons for changes in resources as indicated by increases or decreases in comparable account balances for successive periods.

The Funds Statement also relates to the Income Statement since a major source of funds is the amount of working capital or cash derived from operations. This amount is computed from the Income Statement and is reported as a major item on the Funds Statement. (In Exhibit 2–3 the amount is $14,200.)

Like the other two primary statements, the Funds Statement begins with the company name, the title of the statement, and the period of time covered, which is the same as for the Income Statement. The Funds Statement has two major sections, identifying "funds provided" (or simply sources of funds) and "funds applied" (or uses of funds), as shown in Exhibit 2–3. (Also see the Supplement to this chapter, which includes the Funds Statement for Armstrong World Industries.)

TO SUMMARIZE The Statement of Changes in Financial Position shows the major resource inflows (from operations, from external borrowing, and from equity financing) and the major uses of resources (for current operating purposes or to declare dividends, purchase furniture and fixtures, and so forth). Chapter 13 contains a discussion of the Funds Statement.

THE STATEMENTS OF RETAINED EARNINGS AND CHANGES IN OWNERS' EQUITY

Two other statements are sometimes included in the annual report to shareholders, although neither is considered one of the three primary financial statements. Because they are commonly found in practice, we will discuss each briefly.

The Statement of Retained Earnings identifies changes in the Retained Earnings account. It contains a beginning balance, the net income for the

Statement of Retained Earnings *a report that shows the changes in the Retained Earnings account during a period of time*

dividends   *the periodic distribution of earnings in the form of cash, stock, or other property to the owners (stockholders) of a corporation*

period, a deduction for any cash dividends declared, and an ending balance. Generally, then, the ending Retained Earnings balance is a cumulative figure, which equals the total amount of undistributed earnings since the business began operations. Assuming a beginning Retained Earnings amount of $13,050, net income of $8,100, and the declaration and payment of $4,500 in dividends by Fashion Fabrics, the Statement of Retained Earnings would be as follows:

Fashion Fabrics, Inc.
Statement of Retained Earnings for the
Year Ended December 31, 1981

Retained Earnings, January 1, 1981	$13,050
Add Net Income for the Year..................................	8,100
	$21,150
Less Dividends	4,500
Retained Earnings, December 31, 1981.............................	$16,650

The Statement of Retained Earnings may be combined with the Income Statement, as illustrated in Exhibit 2–4. This gives the reader a complete picture of current earnings and dividends, as well as the total earnings retained by the business over a period of years.

As noted earlier, there may be changes in owners' equity accounts in addition to those in Retained Earnings. Stock may have been issued, for example, or capital contributed through a donation of land. When all changes in owners' equity accounts are to be shown, the Statement of Changes in Owners' Equity replaces the Statement of Retained Earnings. A simple example is presented in Exhibit 2–5.

Statement of Changes in Owners' Equity   *a report that shows the total changes in owners' equity (including Retained Earnings) during a period of time*

EXHIBIT 2–4   **Fashion Fabrics, Inc.**

Combined Statement of Income and Retained Earnings for the
Year Ended December 31, 1981

Sales Revenue		$52,000
Less Cost of Goods Sold		18,500
Gross Margin		$33,500
Less Selling and Administrative Expenses:		
Advertising......................................	$ 800	
Salaries	12,000	
Rent..	3,600	
Utilities...	1,200	
Miscellaneous Expenses	1,700	19,300
Income Before Taxes		$14,200
Income Taxes		6,100
Net Income		$ 8,100
Add Retained Earnings at Beginning of Year		13,050
		$21,150
Less Dividends...................................		4,500
Retained Earnings at End of Year		$16,650

Earnings per share: $8,100 ÷ 1,500 shares = $5.40 per share
Dividends per share: $4,500 ÷ 1,500 shares = $3.00 per share

EXHIBIT 2–5   Fashion Fabrics, Inc.
Statement of Changes in Owners' Equity for the Year Ended December 31, 1981

	Capital Stock	Retained Earnings	Total Owners' Equity
Beginning Balances, December 31, 1980	$11,000	$13,050	$24,050
Add: Net Income for the Year		8,100	8,100
Issuance of Capital Stock	4,000		4,000
	$15,000	$21,150	$36,150
Less Dividends		4,500	4,500
Ending Balances, December 31, 1981 . .	$15,000	$16,650	$31,650

Notes to Financial Statements

notes to financial statements *explanatory information considered an integral part of the primary financial statements*

The notes to financial statements are considered an integral part of those statements because they provide vital information that cannot be captured solely by the descriptions and dollar amounts of statement items. For example, inventories are listed on the Balance Sheet at a certain amount, but a note is usually necessary to describe the contents of the inventory, how it was valued, and any special circumstances. Thus, explanatory notes are necessary to provide full disclosure and a better understanding of the information in the statements.

The notes generally follow a standard sequence. The first note describes the accounting policies and principles followed by the business. Other notes refer to specific items in the statements—usually being cross-referenced to those items—and are normally presented in the order in which the items appear in the statements. Generally, as illustrated in the Supplement to this chapter, a company will present the notes in a special section of the annual report adjacent to the statements themselves.

The Audit Report

audit report *a statement issued by an independent certified public accountant that expresses an opinion on the company's adherence to generally accepted accounting principles*

An audit report is issued by an independent certified public accountant (CPA). The report expresses an opinion as to the company's adherence to generally accepted accounting principles. Note that the financial statements themselves are the representations of a company's management, not of the CPA. Although not all companies have to be audited, audits are required for many purposes. For example, a banker generally will not make a commercial loan without first receiving audited financial statements from a prospective borrower. As another example, securities cannot be sold to the

certified public accountant (CPA)   *a special designation given to an accountant who has passed a national uniform examination and has met other certifying requirements; CPA certificates are issued and monitored by state boards of accountancy or similar agencies*

materiality   *the concept that accounting should disclose only those events important enough to have an influence on the decision maker*

general public until they are registered with the Securities and Exchange Commission, and the registration process requires inclusion of audited financial statements.

In conducting an audit, the CPA uses "generally accepted auditing standards" and measures the quality of reporting against "generally accepted accounting principles," as specified by the accounting profession (typically, the Financial Accounting Standards Board). Only when an auditor is satisfied that there are no material misleading representations in a company's statements is an audit report issued.

An audit report does not guarantee accuracy but it does provide added assurance that the financial statements are not misleading, inasmuch as they have been examined by an unbiased and independent professional. But because the CPA cannot examine every transaction upon which the summary figures in the financial statements are based, the accuracy of the statements must remain the responsibility of the company's management.

An audit report prepared by a CPA firm includes the following: a list of the statements examined and the periods covered by those statements, a general description of the auditing techniques used, and a dated and signed opinion concerning the appropriateness of the statements. An audit report is contained in the Supplement to this chapter (page 61).

Consolidated Financial Statements

subsidiary company   *a company owned or controlled by another company, known as the parent company*

parent company   *a company that owns or maintains control over other companies, known as subsidiaries, which are themselves separate legal entities; control generally refers to ownership of 50 percent or more of the stock of another company*

consolidated financial statements   *statements that show the operating results and financial position of two or more legally separate but affiliated companies as if they are one economic entity*

Obviously, financial statements are only useful if they clearly present the financial position and results of operations of the economic entity they represent. Where a single entity is involved there is no problem. However, many large corporations are the owners or part-owners of other companies, referred to as subsidiary companies. Generally, if the parent company has effective control over the subsidiary companies, the earnings and financial positions of the subsidiaries should be consolidated or combined with those of the parent company. In this way, the financial statements reflect the operating results and financial position of the total economic entity, which is what stockholders, creditors, and prospective investors are primarily interested in.

Consolidated financial statements are prepared by combining the individual statements of the entities, item by item, except for intercompany transactions—that is, transactions between the parent company and its subsidiaries, or between the subsidiaries. Thus, if Company A, the parent company, sells materials to its subsidiary, Company B, that transaction would not be included in the combined sales, purchases, or inventory figures in the consolidated financial statements for the two companies.[2]

---

[2] The technical details of consolidations are beyond the scope of this book. Further information about consolidation procedures can be found in advanced accounting texts.

Consolidated statements provide a means of aggregating accounting data for interrelated companies. However, for certain purposes, the disaggregation of accounting data by major segments of a company is also needed. Segment data are especially important when a company is diversified, that is, operating in several different lines of business. Suppose that a company has two main divisions, one producing household appliances and the other, men's clothing. Users of financial statements would want to know more than the results of total company activity; they would want to know how well each segment of the business is doing. The Supplement illustrates the breakdown of sales by segments of Armstrong World Industries.

CHAPTER REVIEW

The primary financial statements are designed to satisfy the needs for financial information of a variety of users: managers, creditors, stockholders, potential investors, financial analysts, and others. The information supplied for external users, primarily investors and creditors, is intended to help them assess the amounts, timing, and degree of certainty of an entity's prospective cash flows and earnings potential. In analyzing a company, investors and creditors should consider its liquidity, solvency, and profitability. Information relating to these concepts is found in the primary general-purpose financial statements: the Balance Sheet, the Income Statement, and the Funds Statement.

The basic elements of the Balance Sheet are the economic resources of an entity (assets) and the sources of, or claims against, those resources (creditor claims are called liabilities and ownership claims are referred to as owners' equity). On the Income Statement, revenues reflect resource increases from the sale of goods or services derived from normal operations during a period of time. Expenses refer to the costs of using resources (assets) or incurring additional liabilities during normal operations to generate revenues. Gains also represent net increases in resources but are derived from peripheral and nonrecurring activities. Similarly, net decreases in resources from peripheral and nonrecurring activities are known as losses. Net income, or earnings, is a basic element that represents the overall measure of performance of a business. Revenues less expenses is called operating income (loss); operating income plus gains minus losses results in net income (loss).

The Balance Sheet shows an entity's financial position at a particular date. It discloses the relationships among the firm's assets, liabilities, and owners' equity. The Income Statement reports the results of a company's operations, its overall income or loss, for a period of time. The Income Statement itemizes revenues, expenses, net gains or losses, and shows the resulting net income (net loss) and the amount of earnings per share of stock. The Funds Statement reports the major sources and uses of financial resources during a period. It helps explain the significant financing and investing activities of an entity and why the account balances on successive Balance Sheets have increased or decreased.

In analyzing financial statements, it is important to consider the accompanying notes. These explanatory notes provide additional information about certain items and dollar amounts in the statements. They are considered an integral part of the financial statements and should be given special care and attention in terms of the full-disclosure standard.

Another key item associated with financial statements is the independent audit report. This report contains the opinion of an independent CPA as to the company's adherence to generally accepted accounting principles. This professional opinion adds credence to management's representations.

Consolidated financial statements are the statements of related companies (parents and subsidiaries) combined to present the results of operations and the financial position as though all the separate legal entities were one single company—a total economic entity. Thus, intercompany transactions are not included in consolidated statements. The annual reports of most large companies include consolidated financial statements.

KEY TERMS AND CONCEPTS

assets (34)
audit report (42)
Balance Sheet
  (Statement of
  Financial Position)
  (37)
capital stock (38)
certified public
  accountant (CPA)
  (43)
consolidated financial
  statements (43)
dividends (41)
earnings (loss) per
  share (EPS) (39)
earnings potential (33)
expenses (36)
gains (losses) (36)

general-purpose
  financial statements
  (33)
gross margin (38)
Income Statement
  (Statement of
  Earnings) (38)
liabilities (35)
liquidity (33)
materiality (43)
net income (earnings)
  (36)
notes to financial
  statements (42)
operating income (37)
owners' equity
  (stockholders'
  equity) (35)

parent company (43)
profitability (33)
retained earnings (38)
revenues (35)
solvency (33)
Statement of Changes
  in Financial Position
  (Funds Statement)
  (39)
Statement of Changes
  in Owners' Equity
  (41)
Statement of Retained
  Earnings (40)
subsidiary company
  (43)

DISCUSSION QUESTIONS

1. What is the basic objective of financial reporting?

2. What factors determine the types of accounting reports generated?

3. Who are the primary users of general-purpose financial statements?

4. Why are investors and creditors interested in a company's earnings potential?

5. Distinguish between liquidity, solvency, and profitability.

6. What are the primary characteristics of assets?

7. Distinguish between:
  (a) assets and expenses
  (b) expenses and losses
  (c) revenues and gains

8. What are the primary characteristics of a liability?

9. What two features distinguish revenues and expenses from gains and losses?

10. Why is the measurement of earnings of a business considered useful information?

11. What is the major purpose of the:
  (a) Balance Sheet
  (b) Income Statement
  (c) Statement of Changes in Financial Position

12. Where does the name "Balance Sheet" come from?

13. What are the two main components of owners' equity? Why are they reported separately?

14. Some people feel that the Income Statement is more important than the Balance Sheet. Do you agree? Why or why not?

15. What are the main components of an Income Statement? Why is it important to list these major components separately?

16. How does the Funds Statement relate to both the Income Statement and the Balance Sheet?

17. What is the purpose of the notes to the financial statements?

18. Why is an audit report required in many instances?

19. Some people think that auditors are responsible for assuring the accuracy of financial statements. Do you agree? Why or why not?

20. What is the rationale for preparing consolidated financial statements?

EXERCISES

E2-1   General-Purpose Financial Statements

Ekhart Company's year-end is December 31. Company management is currently preparing the annual report to shareholders. Identify the complete title of each major financial statement that should be included in the annual report and describe each statement's basic purpose.

E2-2   Classification of Balance Sheet Items

Indicate for each of the following whether it is: an asset (A), liability (L), or an owners' equity item (OE).

1. Accounts Payable
2. Accounts Receivable
3. Cash
4. Advances to Employees
5. Land
6. Capital Stock
7. Equipment
8. Interest Receivable
9. Bonds Payable
10. Notes Payable
11. Buildings
12. Retained Earnings

E2-3   Accounting Equation—Simple Computations

Balance the following accounting equations.

Assets	= Liabilities	+ Owners' Equity
1. $20,000	$?	$15,000
2. 10,000	5,000	?
3. ?	2,000	8,000

E2-4   Accounting Equation

Compute the missing figures for firms A–D.

	A	B	C	D
Cash	$?	$12,000	$ 9,000	$ 7,500
Plant and Equipment .	35,000	?	31,000	22,500
Accounts Payable	10,000	5,000	?	6,000
Mortgage Payable	10,000	7,000	8,000	6,000
Owners' Equity	25,000	14,000	24,000	?

E2-5   Determining Profitability Measures

Quick-Stop Gas Company determined the following for the year ended December 31, 1981: sales revenues, $120,000; cost of goods sold, $65,000; selling and administrative expenses, $32,000; unusual fire loss, $7,500. Calculate the gross margin, operating income, and net income for the year (ignore taxes).

E2-6   Comprehensive Accounting Equation

Assuming that no stock was issued or dividends declared, compute the missing figures for these companies.

	Eaton Company	Richards Company
Assets: January 1, 1980	$180	$?
Liabilities: January 1, 1980	140	115
Owners' Equity: January 1, 1980	?	155
Assets: December 31, 1980	190	210
Liabilities: December 31, 1980	?	130
Owners' Equity: December 31, 1980 ..	?	180
Revenues in 1980	20	?
Expenses in 1980	24	29

E2-7   Retained Earnings Computations

During 1981, Zeno Company had revenues of $90,000 and expenses of $50,000. On December 31, 1980, Zeno had assets of $400,000, liabilities of $100,000, and capital stock of $250,000. Zeno declared and paid a cash dividend of $20,000 in 1981. No additional stock was issued. Compute the Retained Earnings amounts on December 31, 1980, and December 31, 1981.

E2–8   Earnings and Retained Earnings Relationships

Assume that Retained Earnings increased by $30,000 from December 31, 1980, to December 31, 1981, for Jones Manufacturing Company. During the year, a cash dividend of $5,000 was declared and paid.

1. Compute the net income for the year.

2. Assume that the revenues for the year were $180,000. Compute the expenses incurred for the year.

E2–9   Balance Sheet Relationships

Correct the following Balance Sheet.

Mountain View Company
Balance Sheet as of December 31, 1981

Assets		Liabilities and Owners' Equity	
Cash	$ 7,000	Land	$ 5,000
Accounts Payable	8,000	Accounts Receivable	3,000
Inventories	2,000	Capital Stock	10,000
Plant	10,000		
Retained Earnings	9,000		
	$36,000		$18,000

E2–10   Owner's Equity—Proprietorship

The accounting records of George's Hardware Company showed the following balances for assets and liabilities at the beginning and end of the year.

	January 1, 1981	December 31, 1981
Assets	$35,000	$45,000
Liabilities	25,000	30,000

Based on the above information and the additional information for each independent case presented below, compute the net income or loss from operations for the year. (Hint: First compute the change in capital during the year.)

1. The owner made no additional investments or withdrawals during the year.

2. The owner made an investment of $6,000 and no withdrawals during the year.

3. The owner made no additional investments and withdrew $15,000 during the year.

4. The owner made an additional investment of $12,000 and a withdrawal of $3,000.

E2–11   Income Statement Computations

You are given the following operating information about Sporting Goods, Inc. Determine:

1. The operating income and the net income for the year. (Ignore income taxes.)

2. The earnings per share.

Revenue from Sales of Inventory	$175,000
Cost of Inventory Sold	150,000
Salary Expense	12,000
Rent Expense	1,500
Administrative Expense	6,000
Gain on Sale of Land	2,300
Inventory Loss Due to Flood Damage	4,800
Average Number of Shares Outstanding—1,500	

E2–12   Preparation of an Income Statement

The following selected information is taken from the records of Allen Corporation. Prepare an Income Statement for the year ended December 31, 1981.

Accounts Receivable	$ 49,000
Advertising Expense	7,500
Capital Stock (10,000 shares outstanding)	50,000
Cash	15,500
Cost of Goods Sold	63,000
Dividends	5,000
Loss From Fire in Warehouse	9,500
Miscellaneous Operating Expenses	2,200
Income Taxes	17,320
Retained Earnings	75,000
Salaries	24,000
Sales Revenue	142,000

E2–13   Preparation of a Balance Sheet

From the following selected data, prepare a Balance Sheet for Good Time Corporation at December 31, 1981.

Accounts Payable	$ 6,200
Accounts Receivable	12,000
Advertising Expense	4,200
Buildings	60,000
Capital Stock (1,000 shares outstanding)	20,000
Cash	15,500
Dividends	2,500
Inventory	6,300
Land	22,000
Mortgage Payable	55,000
Net Income	15,700
Retained Earnings	34,600

E2–14   Preparation of a Statement of Retained Earnings

Prepare a Statement of Retained Earnings for Smith Ski Shop as of June 30, 1981, based upon the following information:

Net Income	$27,500
Retained Earnings, July 1, 1980	76,800
Dividends	16,700

E2–15   The Concept of Consolidated
Financial Statements

Builtmore Corporation owns controlling interest in
two other companies. One of its subsidiary companies
is Builtmore's primary supplier of wood, the main
material used by Builtmore in manufacturing a variety
of toys. The other subsidiary is a trucking company,
which Builtmore uses in transporting its products.
As the major stockholder of Builtmore, why might
you want to have the operating results of all three
companies combined in a consolidated Income
Statement?

PROBLEMS

P2–1   Balance Sheet Relationships

Pentration Company manufactures greeting cards. As
of December 31, 1981, its financial status is as follows:

Cash	$10,000
Accounts Receivable	10,000
Accounts Payable	7,000
Inventory	6,000
Land, Buildings, and Equipment	8,000
Notes Receivable	2,000
Notes Payable	2,000
Interest Receivable	1,000
Retained Earnings	9,000
Capital Stock	?

Required:

1. Compute the total amount of assets.
2. Compute the total amount of liabilities.
3. Compute the total amount of stockholders' equity.
4. Determine the amount of capital stock of Pentration
Company.

P2–2   Balance Sheet Preparation

The information presented below is taken from the
records of Hansen Cookie Company.

Building	$50,000
Accounts Payable	15,000
Retained Earnings	26,000
Cash	15,000
Capital Stock	80,000
Inventory	65,000
Accounts Receivable	10,000
Mortgage Payable	30,000
Temporary Investments	5,000
Land	6,000

Required:
Prepare a Balance Sheet for Hansen Cookie Company
as of March 31, 1981.

P2–3   Balance Sheet Preparation with a
Missing Element

The following data are available for Julie's Smart
Shop as of December 31, 1981.

Cash	$2,500
Accounts Payable	3,500
Capital Stock	?
Accounts Receivable	5,000
Building	7,000
Inventory	3,000
Retained Earnings	5,000
Land	2,500

Required:
1. Prepare a Balance Sheet for Julie's Smart Shop.
2. Determine the amount of capital stock at December
31, 1981.

P2–4   Income Statement Preparation

Use the following information for Tanaka Camera,
Inc., for the month of December, 1981.

Salary Expense	$1,200
Sales Revenue	7,800
Income Taxes	400
Miscellaneous Expense	200
Rent Expense	1,800
Cost of Goods Sold	3,100
Gain from Sale of Investments	1,200
Advertising Expense	400

Required:

1. Prepare an Income Statement for Tanaka Camera,
Inc., for the month ending December 31, 1981.
2. **Interpretive Question**   Of what significance is the
gross margin amount?
3. **Interpretive Question**   Why is the gain from sale
of investments shown separately from regular sales
revenues?

P2-5 Unifying Problem: Computation of Net Income and Preparation of a Statement of Retained Earnings

A summary of the operations of Construction Supply Company for the year ended May 31, 1981, is shown below:

Selling Expense	$ 2,760
Cost of Goods Sold	37,820
Loss Due to Flood Damage	4,900
Rent Expense	1,500
Salary Expense	18,150
Depreciation Expense	4,170
Dividends	12,400
Retained Earnings (6/1/80)	156,540
Gain on Sale of Land	5,100
Income Taxes	21,180
Sales Revenue	115,100
Administrative Expense	7,250

Required:

1. Determine net income for the year by preparing an Income Statement.

2. Prepare a Statement of Retained Earnings for the year ended May 31, 1981.

P2-6 Unifying Problem: Comprehensive Financial Statement Preparation

The following information was obtained from the records of Photo Supply Company as of December 31, 1981.

Land	$ 25,000
Buildings	96,700
Salary Expense	26,700
Utilities Expense	6,500
Accounts Payable	17,100
Sales Revenue	265,200
Inventory	46,300
Retained Earnings (1/1/81)	181,700
Capital Stock	30,000
Accounts Receivable	31,000
Cost of Goods Sold	138,600
Cash	38,900
Notes Payable	17,200
Gain on Sale of Land	2,300
Rent Expense	17,100
Dividends in 1981	42,800
Depreciation Expense	8,700
Income Taxes	35,200

Required:

1. Prepare an Income Statement for the year ended December 31, 1981.

2. Prepare a Statement of Retained Earnings for the year ended December 31, 1981.

3. Prepare a Balance Sheet as of December 31, 1981.

4. **Interpretive Question** Why is the balance in Retained Earnings so large as compared with the balance in Capital Stock?

P2-7 Unifying Problem: Financial Statement Preparation—Proprietorship

Jack Jones, a CPA, has worked for five years for a national CPA firm. On January 1, 1980, he began business as a single practitioner in his hometown. During the first year of operations he received professional fees of $68,500 for his services, and incurred the following expenses:

Secretarial Help	$20,000
Office Rent	6,000
Heat and Electricity	3,500
Telephone	750
Duplicating Services	500
Office Supplies	380
Professional Dues	220
Accounting and Tax Services	350
Travel and Entertainment	1,800
Total Expenses	$33,500

When Mr. Jones started his business, he invested $5,000 cash, a tax library worth $7,500, furniture valued at $15,000, and office equipment of different types with a value of $8,500. At the end of the year a note payable of $10,000, incurred to buy some of the furniture and office equipment, was still owed to the bank. During the year, Mr. Jones had withdrawn $25,000 for personal use. Cash amounting to $15,000 was on hand at the end of the year, as well as all the other assets invested by Jones. (You may assume that all revenue and expense items were cash transactions.)

Required:

1. Prepare an Income Statement for the year ended December 31, 1980. (Ignore depreciation and income taxes.)

2. Prepare a Balance Sheet as of December 31, 1980, including a schedule that shows the computation of proprietorship equity in support of the Jack Jones Capital account.

3. **Interpretive Question** Why isn't the $25,000 withdrawal listed among the expenses for Jack Jones' business?

P2-8 Unifying Problem: Elements of Comparative Financial Statements

Silverstein's Service Company
Comparative Balance Sheets as of December 31, 1981 and December 31, 1980

Assets	12/31/81	12/31/80
Cash	$ 6,000	$ 5,000
Accounts Receivable	12,000	11,000
Inventory	7,000	6,000
Total Assets	$25,000	$22,000

Liabilities and Stockholders' Equity	12/31/81	12/31/80
Liabilities:		
Accounts Payable..................	$ 2,000	$ 1,000
Stockholders' Equity:		
Capital Stock	11,000	11,000
Retained Earnings	12,000	10,000
Total Liabilities and Stockholders' Equity........................	$25,000	$22,000

The company paid office expenses of $500, salaries and wages of $4,700, miscellaneous expenses of $500, and a cash dividend of $1,200 in 1981.

Required:

1. Compute the total expenses incurred for 1981. (Assume that the accounts payable increase was offset by the increase in inventory.)

2. Compute the total revenue for 1981.

3. Compute the net income or net loss for 1981.

4. **Interpretive Question** Why are comparative financial statements generally of more value to users than statements for a single period?

SUPPLEMENT

The Financial Statements of Armstrong World Industries

Most corporations issue an annual report to shareholders every year. This report includes the primary financial statements, along with notes to the statements and supporting schedules. Following are the financial statements and related material from the 1979 annual report of Armstrong World Industries. Naturally, you will not understand all of the material at this early stage in your study of accounting. However, by examining this Supplement, you will have a better sense of what the major outputs of the accounting process are and a better perspective of external financial reporting. You may want to refer to this Supplement as you study the remaining chapters of the text; it will help illustrate and clarify the concepts and procedures you will be learning.

cost of goods sold   *the expenses incurred to purchase the merchandise sold during a period; equal to beginning inventory plus cost of goods purchased or manufactured less ending inventory*

gross profit (margin)   *the excess of net sales revenues over the cost of goods sold*

net income (earnings)   *a measure of the overall performance of a business entity; equal to revenues plus gains for a period minus expenses and losses for the period*

dividends   *the periodic distribution of earnings in the form of cash (or stock or other property) to the owners (stockholders) of a corporation*

preferred stock   *a class of stock issued by corporations, usually having dividend and liquidation preferences over common stock*

common stock   *the class of stock most frequently issued by corporations; it usually confers a voting right in the corporation; its dividend and liquidation rights are usually inferior to those of preferred stock*

Armstrong Cork Company and Subsidiaries

The Financial Review, pages 23–29, is an integral part of these statements.

Consolidated Statements of Earnings

Years ended December 31	1979	1978
	(000)	(000)
Current earnings		
Net sales	$1,341,067	$1,244,065
Cost of goods sold	975,709	892,845
Gross profit	365,358	351,220
Selling and administrative expense	227,474	209,703
Earnings before other income (expense) and income taxes	137,884	141,517
Other income (expense):		
Interest expense	(13,827)	(14,612)
Unrealized foreign exchange losses	(5,643)	(6,003)
Miscellaneous, net	7,447	7,425
	(12,023)	(13,190)
Earnings before income taxes	125,861	128,327
Taxes on income	59,817	67,195
NET EARNINGS	$ 66,044	$ 61,132
NET EARNINGS PER SHARE OF COMMON STOCK	$ 2.58	$ 2.36
Retained earnings		
Amount at beginning of year	$ 466,516	$ 431,574
Net earnings for year	66,044	61,132
	532,560	492,706
Less dividends:		
Preferred stock—$3.75 per share	443	443
Common stock: 1979—$1.075 per share; 1978—$1.00 per share	27,373	25,747
	27,816	26,190
Amount at end of year	$ 504,744	$ 466,516

20

current assets   *cash and other assets that may reasonably be expected to be converted to cash within one year or during the normal operating cycle*

current liabilities   *debts or other obligations that will be paid with current assets or otherwise discharged within one year or during the normal operating cycle*

stockholders' equity (owners' equity)   *the ownership interest in the assets of an enterprise; equals net assets (total assets minus total liabilities)*

retained earnings   *the accumulated portion of owners' equity that has been earned and retained from profitable operations and not paid out in dividends or restricted for some other use; equal to owners' equity less contributed capital*

Armstrong Cork Company and Subsidiaries

The Financial Review, pages 23–29, is an integral part of these statements.

Consolidated Balance Sheets

As of December 31	1979	1978
	(000)	(000)
Assets Current assets:		
Cash	$ 13,185	$ 8,481
Short-term securities	22,153	36,870
Accounts and notes receivable (less allowance for discounts and losses: 1979—$9,622,000; 1978—$9,020,000)	165,693	150,486
Inventories	235,813	204,846
Other current assets	10,419	13,783
Total current assets	447,263	414,466
Property, plant, and equipment (less accumulated depreciation and amortization: 1979—$352,186,000; 1978—$323,995,000)	419,418	406,734
Other noncurrent assets	9,631	22,852
	$876,312	$844,052

	1979	1978
Liabilities and stockholders' equity Current liabilities:		
Payable to banks	$ 22,858	$ 23,823
Current installments of long-term debt	2,720	2,431
Accounts payable and accrued expenses	105,280	88,980
Income taxes	8,328	16,364
Total current liabilities	139,186	131,598
Long-term debt	125,754	129,718
Deferred income taxes	40,406	32,849
Minority interest in foreign subsidiary	3,309	3,063
Other noncurrent liabilities	169,469	165,630
Stockholders' equity:		
Preferred stock, $3.75 cumulative, no par value. Authorized 161,821 shares; issued 161,522 shares (at redemption price of $102.75 per share)	16,596	16,596
Voting preferred stock. Authorized 1,500,000 shares	—	—
Common stock, $1.00 par value per share. Authorized 60,000,000 shares; issued 25,939,455 shares	25,939	25,939
Capital surplus	47,066	47,066
Retained earnings	504,744	466,516
	594,345	556,117
Less treasury stock, at cost: Preferred stock, $3.75 cumulative— 43,373 shares	3,986	3,986
Common stock: 1979—1,192,748 shares; 1978—192,748 shares	22,702	5,307
	26,688	9,293
Total stockholders' equity	567,657	546,824
	$876,312	$844,052

21

depreciation   *the portion of the original cost of plant and equipment that is recognized as an expense in a given period*

amortization   *the portion of the original cost of an intangible asset recognized as an expense in a given period*

working capital   *current assets minus current liabilities*

Armstrong Cork Company and Subsidiaries

The Financial Review, pages 23–29, is an integral part of these statements.

Consolidated Statements of Changes in Financial Position

Years ended December 31		1979	1978
		(000)	**(000)**
Funds became available from:	Operations:		
	Net earnings	**$ 66,044**	$ 61,132
	Add items not requiring funds:		
	Depreciation and amortization	**41,627**	42,745
	Increase in deferred income taxes	**7,557**	1,488
	Net unrealized loss on foreign exchange		
	related to long-term items	**3,443**	8,325
	Other	**246**	431
	Total from operations	**118,917**	114,121
	Redemption of Kerr Glass Manufacturing		
	Corporation preferred stock	**13,688**	—
	Other items	**390**	6,421
		$132,995	$120,542
These funds were used for:	Additions to property, plant, and equipment	**$ 56,076**	$ 43,749
	Dividends to stockholders	**27,816**	26,190
	Reduction in long-term debt	**6,499**	34,321
	Purchase of Company common stock for the		
	treasury (1,000,000 shares).......................	**17,395**	—
		107,786	104,260
	INCREASE IN WORKING CAPITAL	**$ 25,209**	$ 16,282
Changes in working capital consisted of:	Increase (decrease) in current assets:		
	Cash and short-term securities	**$ (10,013)**	$ (2,710)
	Receivables	**15,207**	22,942
	Inventories	**30,967**	9,334
	Other current assets	**(3,364)**	4,284
		32,797	33,850
	Decrease (increase) in current liabilities:		
	Payable to banks	**965**	(5,769)
	Current installments of long-term debt	**(289)**	(512)
	Accounts payable and accrued expenses	**(16,300)**	(10,013)
	Income taxes	**8,036**	(1,274)
		(7,588)	(17,568)
	INCREASE IN WORKING CAPITAL	**$ 25,209**	$ 16,282

Armstrong Cork Company and Subsidiaries # Financial Review

The consolidated financial statements and the accompanying data in this report include the accounts of the parent Armstrong Cork Company and its domestic and foreign subsidiaries. All significant inter-Company transactions have been eliminated from consolidated statements. Certain 1978 amounts have been reclassified to conform to current reporting formats.

To assist in understanding this financial review, the accounting policies and principles used are printed in *italics*.

Operating statement items

Net sales in 1979 totaled $1,341.1 million, 8% above the 1978 total of $1,244.1 million.

The amounts reported as net sales are the total sales billed during the year less the sales value of goods returned, trade discounts and customers' allowances, and freight costs incurred in delivering products to customers.

Net earnings of $66.0 million for 1979 are 8% above the $61.1 million reported for 1978.

Details of foreign exchange gains (losses)	1979	1978
	(000)	(000)
Realized, related to:		
Long-term debt	$ —	$ —
Other	102	(100)
Total before tax	102	(100)
Total after tax	3	(123)
Unrealized, related to:		
Long-term items	(3,443)	(8,325)
Effects of forward exchange contracts	(960)	2,263
	(4,403)	(6,062)
Other, primarily working capital items	(1,240)	59
Total before tax	(5,643)	(6,003)
Total after tax	(5,518)	(5,039)
Combined total before tax	$ (5,541)	$ (6,103)
Combined total after tax	$ (5,515)	$ (5,162)
Net earnings as reported	66,044	61,132
Earnings exclusive of foreign exchange losses	$71,559	$66,294

Unrealized foreign exchange losses, because of their significance, are reported in the Consolidated Statements of Earnings as separate items.

Earnings per common share were $2.58 compared with $2.36 per share in 1978.

During 1979 the Company purchased 1.0 million shares of its common stock in the open market and in negotiated transactions. The reduction in average common shares outstanding resulting from the purchases had the effect of increasing earnings per share by $.03.

Earnings per share are determined by dividing net earnings, after deducting preferred dividends, by the average number of common shares outstanding. Inclusion of shares issuable under stock options would not have reduced earnings per share in either year.

Depreciation and amortization amounted to $41.6 million in 1979 compared with $42.7 million in 1978.

Depreciation charges for financial reporting purposes are determined generally on the straight-line basis at rates calculated to provide for the retirement of assets at the end of their useful lives. Accelerated depreciation is generally used for tax purposes. When assets are disposed of or retired, their costs and related depreciation are removed from the books, and any resulting gains or losses are reflected in "Miscellaneous, net."

Employee compensation, including benefit costs, amounted to $440.8 million in 1979. Average employment of 23,835 persons during 1979 compares to 23,876 in 1978.

The Company and most of its subsidiaries have pension plans covering substantially all employees. Obligations of these plans are funded through trusts and insurance contracts. Pension costs charged to operations totaled $19.6 million in 1979 and $15.2 million in 1978. This increase resulted primarily from a full year's funding of 1978 plan enhancements, increases in members' earnings, and increases in benefits to retirees.

Pension costs consist of actuarially determined current service costs and amounts necessary to amortize prior service obligations over periods ranging up to 30 years. The Company generally funds these pension costs currently.

At the January 1, 1979, valuation date the actuarially computed value of vested benefits exceeded the market value of retirement fund assets by $28.0 million.

The unfunded prior service liability at December 31, 1979, amounted to approximately $68.0 million.

Employee compensation cost summary	1979	1978
	(000)	(000)
Wages and salaries, including vacations and holiday pay	$369,303	$334,710
Social security and other payroll taxes	29,418	26,405
Pension costs	19,612	15,205
Medical, hospitalization, accident, life insurance, and other benefit costs	22,461	17,707
	$440,794	$394,027

Armstrong Cork Company and Subsidiaries

Financial Review

Income taxes totaled $59.8 million in 1979 and $67.2 million in 1978.

Details of income taxes	1979	1978
	(000)	(000)
Federal: Current	$41,306	$54,383
Deferred	4,627	736
	45,933	55,119
Foreign: Current	3,904	2,195
Deferred	2,400	437
	6,304	2,632
State: Current	7,050	9,129
Deferred	530	315
	7,580	9,444
Total income taxes	$59,817	$67,195

No provision for U.S. income taxes has been made for the undistributed earnings of foreign subsidiaries because either these earnings have been permanently reinvested, or distribution would be largely offset by foreign tax credits.

Taxes deferred to future years represent principally timing differences resulting from the use of accelerated depreciation for tax purposes and straight-line depreciation for financial reporting.

Investment tax credits of $3.5 million in 1979 and $2.0 million in 1978 have been taken directly to income.

Reconciliation to U.S. statutory tax rate	1979	1978
Effective tax rates	47.5%	52.4%
Investment tax credits	2.8	1.6
State income taxes	(3.3)	(3.8)
Losses of British subsidiary without tax benefit	(.2)	(2.0)
Unrealized foreign exchange losses without tax benefit:		
British subsidiary	(1.9)	(1.3)
Others	—	(.2)
Other items	1.1	1.3
Statutory tax rate	46.0%	48.0%

Available loss carryforwards

At December 31, 1979, the Company's British subsidiary had loss carryforwards of $34.2 million available for financial reporting purposes and $73.5 million available to be used without time limit for British income tax purposes.

Available loss carryforwards (continued)

(Millions) Years	Financial reporting purposes	Differences: Accelerated depreciation	Differences: Inventory tax relief	Income tax purposes
1974–1977	£10.3	£15.4	£7.1	£32.8
1978	3.8	(1.0)	(2.0)	.8
1979	1.3	(0.8)	(1.0)	(0.5)
Total	£15.4	£13.6	£4.1	£33.1
Total*	$34.2	$30.2	$9.1	$73.5

*Total pounds sterling translated to dollars at year-end 1979 exchange rate of $2.22.

Balance sheet items

Cash and short-term securities decreased from $45.4 million at the end of 1978 to $35.3 million at the end of 1979. Operating and other factors associated with this decrease are detailed in the Consolidated Statements of Changes in Financial Position on page 22.

Short-term securities are carried at cost, which approximates market value.

Current receivables increased during the year 1979 by $15.2 million, as a result of higher sales.

Trade receivables are recorded in gross billed amounts as of date of shipment. Provision is made for estimated applicable discounts and losses.

Inventories	1979	1978
	(000)	(000)
Finished goods	$134,070	$115,678
Goods in process	32,186	29,143
Raw materials and supplies	69,557	60,025
	$235,813	$204,846

The ratio of inventories to net sales increased from 16.5% in 1978 to 17.6% at December 31, 1979. Inventories increased $31.0 million during the year 1979, primarily as a result of inventory associated with the usual requirements of sales activities and cost increases.

Inventories are valued at cost or market, whichever is lower. The materials portion of substantially all domestic inventories, except for furniture, is valued using the last-in, first-out (LIFO) method. Furniture inventories are valued on a LIFO basis. Other inventories are generally determined on a first-in, first-out (FIFO) method.

Inventory values at December 31, 1979 and 1978, were lower than would have been reported on a total FIFO basis by $75.4 million and $55.7 million, respectively.

Property, plant, and equipment values increased during 1979 as follows:

	1979	1978
	(000)	(000)
Land	$ 19,257	$ 19,149
Buildings	237,772	229,356
Machinery and equipment	487,988	454,661
Construction in progress	26,587	27,563
	771,604	730,729
Less accumulated depreciation and amortization	352,186	323,995
Net book value	$419,418	$406,734

The increase in fixed assets from $730.7 million to $771.6 million resulted from capital additions amounting to $56.1 million reduced by sales, retirements, and disposals of $15.2 million.

The unexpended cost of approved capital appropriations amounted to approximately $39.5 million at December 31, 1979, substantially all of which is scheduled to be expended during 1980.

Property, plant, and equipment values are stated at acquisition cost, with accumulated depreciation and amortization deducted to arrive at net book value.

Other noncurrent assets	1979	1978
	(000)	(000)
Kerr Glass Manufacturing Corporation 7% cumulative preferred stock	$ —	$15,291
Less current portion	—	1,520
	—	13,771
Miscellaneous	9,631	9,081
	$9,631	$22,852

The Kerr preferred stock was redeemed in total during December, 1979, for an aggregate redemption price of $15.2 million under Kerr's option to redeem all or part of the outstanding preferred stock.

Noncurrent assets are carried at cost or less. See also the notes on page 26, referring to parallel loan agreements.

Debt	1979	Average year-end interest rate	1978	Average year-end interest rate
	(000)	%	(000)	%
Payable to banks: (Foreign: 1979—63%; 1978—100%)	$ 22,858	11.90	$ 23,823	10.16
Long-term debt:				
8% sinking-fund debentures due 1996	$37,495	8.00	$41,377	8.00
8.45% notes due 1984	50,000	8.45	50,000	8.45
8¾% Swiss franc bonds due 1989	21,875	8.75	21,606	8.75
Pound sterling notes due through 1982	1,331	9.67	1,667	9.71
Other	17,773	5.82	17,499	6.45
Total long-term debt	128,474		132,149	
Less current installments	2,720		2,431	
Net long-term debt	$125,754	8.04	$129,718	8.10

The 8% sinking-fund debentures are redeemable at the Company's option at 104.8% prior to May 15, 1980, and at declining prices thereafter. Sinking-fund payments sufficient to retire $2.5 million principal amount of the debentures are due annually. At December 31, 1979, bonds having a face amount of $5.0 million were being held in anticipation of future sinking-fund requirements. At December 31, 1978, those bonds held amounted to $3.6 million.

The 8.45% notes are redeemable at the Company's option beginning on November 15, 1981, at par. There are no sinking-fund requirements.

The 8¾% Swiss franc bonds (totaling Sfr. 35 million) are redeemable at the Company's option at 102% after October 22, 1980, and at declining prices thereafter.

All obligations related to long-term debt have been satisfied through 1979.

Scheduled amortization of long-term debt

	(000)
1981	$ 2,735
1982	4,564
1983	4,395
1984	53,971
1985	3,999

The increased amortization of debt in 1984 represents scheduled redemption of the 8.45% notes maturing in that year.

Armstrong Cork Company and Subsidiaries

Financial Review

Debt (continued)

Under a parallel loan agreement, the Company's British subsidiary borrowed £11 million in 1974 from an unrelated British financial institution, and the Company loaned $25.6 million (the approximate equivalent of £11 million on the original date) to a U.S. affiliate of the British financial institution, with a net annual interest cost of 2¼%. Each loan matures in 1985 with a right to prepay without premium.

Under another parallel loan agreement, the Company borrowed £6 million in 1978 from the pension funds of an unrelated British company, and the Company loaned $11 million (the approximate equivalent of £6 million on the original date) to the same pension funds, with a net annual interest cost of 1⅜%. Each loan is to be repaid in equal installments in 1986, 1988, and 1990, with a right to prepay without premium.

For reporting purposes, the parallel loans are offset. Differences between the U.S. receivables and the current dollar values of the pound sterling loans are included in "Other noncurrent assets."

Stock options

Under the stock option plan approved by the stockholders in 1974, there were 224,180 shares reserved for future options at December 31, 1979, and 303,705 shares at December 31, 1978. The option prices are not less than the closing market price of the shares on the dates the options were granted. The stock options are nonstatutory, include provision for stock appreciation rights, and expire ten years from the date of grant.

Changes in option shares outstanding	1979	1978
Option shares outstanding at beginning of year	461,875	375,680
Options granted	127,150	120,000
	589,025	495,680
Less: Options exercised	—	34
Stock appreciation rights exercised	—	791
Options canceled	47,625	32,980
	47,625	33,805
Option shares outstanding at end of year	541,400	461,875
Average option price	$ 20.05	$ 21.08

Geographic areas

United States net trade sales include export sales to nonaffiliated customers of $62.9 million in 1979, $52.4 million in 1978, $45.2 million in 1977, $50.1 million in 1976, and $44.6 million in 1975.

"Europe" includes operations located primarily in England, Spain, Germany, France, and Italy. Operations in Canada, Australia, Japan, and Brazil are included in the "Other foreign" area.

Transfers between geographic areas and commissions paid to affiliates marketing exported products are accounted for by methods which approximate arm's-length transactions, after considering the costs incurred by the selling company and the return on assets employed of both the selling unit and the purchasing unit. Operating profits of a geographic area include profits accruing from sales to affiliates.

At December 31	1979	1978	1977	1976	1975
(millions)					
Net trade sales:					
United States	$1,098.5	$1,040.5	$ 917.0	$816.3	$702.0
Europe	177.7	145.4	116.1	106.0	105.5
Other foreign	64.9	58.2	56.3	58.9	51.9
Inter-area transfers:					
United States	13.3	10.4	16.4	19.3	10.2
Europe	1.4	1.2	.6	.6	.2
Other foreign	5.1	1.6	1.0	2.9	1.4
Eliminations	(19.8)	(13.2)	(18.0)	(22.8)	(11.8)
Consolidated net sales	$1,341.1	$1,244.1	$1,089.4	$981.2	$859.4
Operating profit: (Note 1, page 27)					
United States	$ 149.2	$ 159.1	$ 136.0	$128.0	$ 87.1
Europe	12.6	6.6	.1	(1.8)	2.3
Other foreign	8.4	3.6	3.5	3.4	2.7
Corporate items:					
Corporate expense, net	(26.1)	(20.3)	(20.3)	(15.6)	(13.2)
Interest expense	(13.8)	(14.6)	(15.0)	(13.1)	(16.6)
Foreign exchange gains (losses) (Note 2, page 27)	(4.4)	(6.1)	(9.0)	1.5	2.7
Earnings before income taxes	$ 125.9	$ 128.3	$ 95.3	$102.4	$ 65.0
Identifiable assets: (Notes 3 and 4, page 27)					
United States	$ 650.1	$ 603.5	$ 573.5	$551.9	
Europe	139.9	129.4	125.4	110.5	
Other foreign	43.8	38.3	40.0	41.3	
Corporate	51.7	77.7	83.5	87.2	
Eliminations	(9.2)	(4.9)	(6.6)	(6.7)	
Consolidated assets	$ 876.3	$ 844.0	$ 815.8	$784.2	

Industry segments

The Company operates worldwide in four reportable segments: floor coverings, ceilings, furniture, and industry products and other.

Operations in the floor coverings segment involve the production and sale of resilient floor coverings, carpet, and related installation accessories. Floor covering sales include sales of resilient floors and accessories of $482.9 million in 1979, $454.0 million in 1978, $404.6 million in 1977, $366.9 million in 1976, and $323.4 million in 1975. Sales of carpet and accessories included in floor covering sales were $241.7 million in 1979, $249.8 million in 1978, $241.9 million in 1977, $217.9 million in 1976, and $189.1 million in 1975.

The ceilings segment involves the production and sale of mineral-fiber and wood-fiber ceiling products and the sale of related installation and lighting accessories.

Operations in the furniture segment involve primarily production and sale of wood furniture, principally for bedroom, dining room, and occasional use.

Production and sale of pipe insulation, textile mill supplies, gasketing materials, industrial adhesives, and other miscellaneous products comprise the remaining segment.

Intersegment sales or transfers are immaterial.

Notes:

(1) *Operating profit of geographic areas and industry segments excludes general corporate expenses, interest expense, certain foreign exchange items, and taxes on income.*

(2) *Includes realized and unrealized losses before tax related to long-term items and forward exchange contracts; other exchange gains and losses are included in appropriate geographic or industry segments.*

(3) *Identifiable assets for geographic areas and industry segments exclude cash, marketable securities, and fixed assets of a corporate nature.*

(4) *Data for 1975 have not been calculated.*

At December 31 (millions)	1979	1978	1977	1976	1975
Net trade sales:					
Floor coverings	$ 724.6	$ 703.8	$ 646.5	$584.8	$512.5
Ceilings	279.8	237.6	193.2	177.9	162.7
Furniture	200.1	185.5	146.1	130.3	110.0
Industry products and other	136.6	117.2	103.6	88.2	74.2
Consolidated net sales	**$1,341.1**	$1,244.1	$1,089.4	$981.2	$859.4
Operating profit: (Note 1)					
Floor coverings	$ 91.4	$ 110.2	$ 94.7	$ 88.6	$ 67.7
Ceilings	39.4	31.7	22.1	18.4	12.1
Furniture	10.5	3.1	1.9	5.1	2.8
Industry products and other	28.9	24.3	21.0	17.5	9.5
Corporate items:					
Corporate expense, net	(26.1)	(20.3)	(20.3)	(15.6)	(13.2)
Interest expense	(13.8)	(14.6)	(15.0)	(13.1)	(16.6)
Foreign exchange gains (losses) (Note 2)	(4.4)	(6.1)	(9.0)	1.5	2.7
Earnings before income taxes	**$ 125.9**	$ 128.3	$ 95.4	$102.4	$ 65.0
Depreciation and amortization: (Note 4)					
Floor coverings	$ 22.8	$ 22.2	$ 19.5	$ 17.8	
Ceilings	8.0	8.0	7.8	7.1	
Furniture	6.0	6.7	5.5	5.0	
Industry products and other	4.2	5.2	4.3	4.9	
Corporate items, net	.6	.6	.6	.4	
Consolidated depreciation and amortization	**$ 41.6**	$ 42.7	$ 37.7	$ 35.2	
Capital additions: (Note 4)					
Floor coverings	$ 34.7	$ 25.9	$ 32.8	$ 42.2	
Ceilings	7.9	5.4	6.2	5.3	
Furniture	5.9	7.2	6.3	9.3	
Industry products and other	7.0	4.8	4.2	3.8	
Corporate items, net	.6	.4	1.2	1.8	
Total capital additions	**$ 56.1**	$ 43.7	$ 50.7	$ 62.4	
Identifiable assets: (Notes 3 and 4)					
Floor coverings	$ 442.6	$ 405.1	$ 398.1	$365.6	
Ceilings	153.0	145.8	134.3	139.1	
Furniture	128.1	123.0	113.7	111.5	
Industry products and other	100.9	92.4	86.2	80.8	
Corporate items, net	51.7	77.7	83.5	87.2	
Consolidated assets	**$ 876.3**	$ 844.0	$ 815.8	$784.2	

Armstrong Cork Company and Subsidiaries **Financial Review**

Internal Revenue Service examination

During 1979, all matters relating to the Internal Revenue Service examination of consolidated U.S. tax returns for 1972 and 1973 were substantially resolved with no material adjustments. Examinations for 1974 and 1975 have been completed, and no material adjustments are expected.

Litigation

Since 1970 the Company has been named as one of a number of defendants in lawsuits alleging injury to the health of individuals incurred in connection with the installation of asbestos insulation products manufactured or sold by the Company until mid-1969. Approximately 2,150 suits assert claims on behalf of approximately 2,950 individual plaintiffs. As of December 31, 1979, about 1,900 of such suits involving approximately 2,700 individuals remain pending, including one suit involving an unspecified number of individuals. The Company's products may not be involved in a number of these suits. The Company discontinued the sale of all asbestos insulation products in 1969. However, because of the time period prior to manifestation of injury

resulting from exposure to asbestos fibers and the inability to determine the number of future cases claiming that such injury arose from exposure to the Company's products, the number of potential unasserted claims and the potential liability therefrom with which the Company may be involved in the future cannot reasonably be ascertained. The extent of insurance coverage for the bulk of such lawsuits and potential unasserted claims is disputed by the insurance carriers of the Company and may require judicial determination to resolve the carriers' obligations. Based upon a review of the coverage issues by counsel for the Company, the Company believes it should prevail in establishing its rights to defense and indemnification from its carriers in respect of substantially all such suits and claims.

Even though the potential unasserted claims and liability therefrom cannot be ascertained and there is no assurance of prevailing in the dispute with the Company's insurance carriers, after consideration of the factors discussed above and the Company's experience with this litigation, the Company believes that its liability for these lawsuits and claims would have no material adverse effect on the Company's financial position.

Quarterly financial information (unaudited)
amounts (millions) except earnings per share, dividends, and stock prices

	First	Second	Third	Fourth	Total year
			1979		
Net sales	$326.7	$342.8	$341.3	$330.3	$1,341.1
Gross profit	92.4	98.7	93.7	80.6	365.4
Earnings exclusive of unrealized foreign exchange	17.7	21.2	19.3	13.4	71.6
Net earnings	16.9	18.1	18.3	12.7	66.0
Per share of common stock	$.65	$.70	$.72	$.51	$2.58
Dividend payments on common stock	.25	.275	.275	.275	1.075
Price range of common stock—Low	15⅜	16½	17¼	14⅝	
—High	17⅞	19	19	18⅛	
			1978		
Net sales	$293.1	$326.2	$312.1	$312.7	$1,244.1
Gross profit	81.3	94.9	90.3	84.7	351.2
Earnings exclusive of unrealized foreign exchange	14.3	20.3	17.0	14.7	66.3
Net earnings	14.5	20.7	13.3	12.6	61.1
Per share of common stock	$.56	$.80	$.51	$.49	$2.36
Dividend payments on common stock	.25	.25	.25	.25	1.00
Price range of common stock—Low	14⅜	15⅝	16½	14⅞	
—High	18⅛	19⅜	21⅜	20⅝	

Fourth quarter 1979 compared with third quarter 1979

Generally in line with the normal seasonal pattern of the Company, consolidated net sales declined in the fourth quarter of 1979 from the third quarter by 3.2%.

Net earnings declined $5.6 million, 30.6%. Excluding the effects of unrealized exchange losses, $0.7 million in the fourth quarter and $1.0 million in the third quarter, fourth-quarter earnings of $13.4 million were $5.9 million less than the previous quarter.

The earnings decline is the result of the decline in sales volume and escalating costs. Selling-price increases fell short of covering all of the cost increases.

Fourth quarter 1979 compared with fourth quarter 1978

Fourth-quarter 1979 sales of $330.3 million surpassed the $312.7 million of the fourth quarter 1978 by 5.6%. Much of this improvement was attributable to sales price increases.

Earnings after taxes of $12.7 million surpassed the 1978 level of $12.6 million and reflected the positive effect of a reduction in the effective tax rate in 1979 versus 1978. Excluding unrealized exchange, those earnings were $13.4 million and $14.7 million for 1979 and 1978, respectively. Reduced volume and increased cost of raw materials, energy, and employee compensation each had an influence on the decline in profit performance.

Report of management

The management of Armstrong Cork Company is responsible for the integrity of the financial statements of the Company and for ascertaining that these statements accurately reflect the financial position and results of operations of the Company. The Company's financial statements are prepared in accordance with generally accepted accounting principles and include management estimates and judgments, where appropriate.

Armstrong has a system of internal controls designed to provide reasonable assurance that the Company's assets are safeguarded and that the Company's records reflect the transactions of the Company accurately, fairly, and in reasonable detail. The internal control system provides for the careful selection and training of personnel, the delegation of management authority and responsibility, the dissemination of management and control policies and procedures, and an extensive internal audit program. The Internal Audit Department is staffed to perform audits covering all parent Company and subsidiary locations. A review of controls and practices to assure compliance with corporate ethical policy is performed as a part of each audit. The auditing procedures of the Internal Audit Department are coordinated with those of the independent accountants.

The Company's independent accountants, Peat, Marwick, Mitchell & Co., provide an objective review of management's reporting of operating results and financial condition. Working with our internal auditors and making tests as appropriate, Peat, Marwick, Mitchell & Co. has audited the data included in the financial statements of this Annual Report, and their opinion concerning these statements appears below.

An Audit Committee consisting of four nonemployee directors is appointed by the Company's Board of Directors. This Committee meets periodically with management, internal auditors, and independent accountants of the Company to discuss the scope and results of the internal and independent audits, financial and operating results, internal controls, Company policies, and other significant matters, including the financial statements accompanying this Annual Report.

Accountants' report

The Board of Directors and Stockholders,
Armstrong Cork Company:

We have examined the consolidated balance sheets of Armstrong Cork Company and subsidiaries as of December 31, 1979 and 1978 and the related consolidated statements of earnings and changes in financial position for the years then ended. Our examinations were made in accordance with generally accepted auditing standards, and accordingly included such tests of the accounting records and such other auditing procedures as we considered necessary in the circumstances.

In our opinion, the aforementioned consolidated financial statements present fairly the financial position of Armstrong Cork Company and subsidiaries at December 31, 1979 and 1978, and the results of their operations and the changes in their financial position for the years then ended, in conformity with generally accepted accounting principles applied on a consistent basis.

Philadelphia, Pa.
February 18, 1980

PEAT, MARWICK, MITCHELL & CO.

Management's analysis of operations

1979 compared with 1978

Consolidated results

The Company's 1979 sales of $1,341.1 million exceeded by 8% the previous record of $1,244.1 million set in 1978.

Record 1979 net earnings of $66.0 million surpassed by 8% the 1978 earnings of $61.1 million, even though earnings before taxes declined slightly. Net earnings include unrealized foreign currency translation losses of $5.5 million in 1979 and $5.0 million in 1978.

The 1979 results reflect an effective tax rate of 47.5%, compared with the 1978 rate of 52.4%. This reduction is due mainly to the change in the U.S. statutory tax rate from 48% to 46%, higher investment tax credits, and the beneficial tax effect of significantly reduced British company losses.

The principal reasons for the decline in earnings before taxes were rapidly escalating prices for raw materials and energy, strongly influenced by worldwide oil prices; unusually high new-product development and start-up costs; lower sales volume in some of the Company's businesses; and generally higher operating expenses.

Geographic areas (page 26)

The factors mentioned in the preceding paragraph had their greatest impact on United States-based operations, while the operating profit of foreign operations improved dramatically from 1978 levels. Throughout 1979, economic conditions overseas were stronger than in the United States, with notable demand for the Company's products in Western Europe, England, Canada, and Japan. Armstrong served these foreign markets with products from its factories abroad as well as through exports from the United States.

On a 22% sales increase in Europe, operating profit nearly doubled from 1978 to 1979, influenced particularly by improved performance of subsidiaries in Germany and England. As a result of sizable sales gains as well as improved manufacturing efficiency in the rotogravure sheet flooring plant at Teesside, England, British company results moved from a $2.1 million operating loss in 1978 to an operating profit of $2.7 million in 1979.

Operating profit in the other foreign areas improved 132% between 1978 and 1979 on a 12% sales increase. Largely responsible for the increased profits were stronger demand for Armstrong products, primarily in Canada and Japan, and effective cost-reduction and cost-containment programs.

Industry segments (page 27)

Sales increased in all industry segments, with operating profit improving in all but the floor coverings segment.

- Dollar sales of floor coverings increased over those of 1978. On a unit basis, resilient flooring products maintained the high levels of 1978, while carpet lagged the previous year. Operating profit of the floor coverings segment was adversely affected by substantial cost increases in petrochemical-based raw materials and by continuing inflationary pressures in other cost areas that could not be fully recovered through price increases. Other adverse factors include an overall decline in unit volume, production cost variances, and high new-product development and start-up costs. As a result, operating profit declined 17%.

- Sales and operating profit of the ceilings segment set new records, with profit improving 24% in 1979 versus 1978 on sales increases of 18%. Demand for the Company's architectural ceilings, tied principally to nonresidential construction and renovation, remained strong throughout the year; residential ceilings also exceeded their 1978 performance levels.

- New styling introductions, a restructured marketing approach, and improved manufacturing efficiency contributed to the substantial progress of the furniture segment in 1979. Sales in 1979 bettered those of 1978 by 8%, and operating profit more than tripled the depressed 1978 levels.

- The "Industry products and other" segment recorded sales improvement of 17% and an operating profit increase of 19%. Generally, demand for products in this segment was strong throughout the year, and profit margins were at record levels.

Performance of the British company

		(millions of dollars)		
	1979	1978	1977	1976
Profit (loss) from operations	$ 2.7	$(2.1)	$ (5.6)	$(6.2)
Interest expense	(3.3)	(3.2)	(4.0)	(2.9)
Income tax benefit	—	—	—	2.0
(Loss) before unrealized exchange adjustment	(0.6)	(5.3)	(9.6)	(7.1)
Unrealized exchange gain (loss)	(5.3)	(3.4)	(5.6)	4.1
Total (loss)	$(5.9)	$(8.7)	$(15.2)	$(3.0)

Management's analysis of operations (continued)

1978 compared with 1977

The Company's 1978 sales of $1,244.1 million were 14% above the previous high of $1,089.4 million set in 1977.

Consolidated net earnings of $61.1 million represented an improvement of 51% over the 1977 earnings of $40.4 million. These earnings include unrealized foreign currency translation losses of $5.0 million in 1978 and $7.3 million in 1977.

In 1978, all segments of the Company's business shared in the overall improvement from the depressed 1977 levels. Higher sales volume, more efficient manufacturing and cost-containment programs made the most notable contributions to this improvement.

Operating profit in Europe moved from essentially a break-even position in 1977 to a 1978 profit of $6.6 million, the result of reduced losses in the British company and improved profits in the other European companies. While the British company continued to experience losses, with no present tax benefit, such losses were reduced significantly from 1977's $9.6 million before unrealized exchange adjustments to $5.3 million in 1978, an improvement of $4.3 million. (See table on page 30.)

The 1978 effective tax rate of 52.4%, compared with a 57.6% rate in 1977, reflects the significantly reduced British losses and lower unrealized foreign exchange losses, both without tax effect.

Report of the impact of inflation upon the business

Introduction

Inflation has become an increasingly significant factor in the economic life of the United States during the last decade. Customary financial reports stated at historical costs do not reflect the effects of inflation on sales and earnings, or on assets and liabilities. In recognition of the need to provide users of financial statements with information intended to assist them in assessing the impact of inflation on business enterprises, the Financial Accounting Standards Board in September 1979 issued Statement No. 33, "Financial Reporting and Changing Prices." The statement establishes standards for reporting, on an experimental basis, the effects of changing prices on selected accounting data.

While the required information is designed to recognize the effects of inflation on a company's performance and financial position, such information should be used with caution. Many factors must be taken into consideration when a company's performance and prospects are being evaluated, and not all of these factors can be quantified. As the historical-cost-based financial statements cannot be expected to present all of the information necessary for such evaluation, the constant-dollar data in this report should not be expected to provide all the information needed to ascertain the impact of inflation upon Armstrong's results.

Operating policy

It is the Company's practice to recognize the effects of inflation in current and long-range planning. Product selling prices are established with consideration of current costs of materials and labor. Evaluations of proposed investments in property, plant, and equipment incorporate the effects of estimated future inflation on both costs and benefits. Annual operating budgets and longer-range plans reflect projected economic factors and consider future cash needs under inflationary conditions. As stated in the Financial Review, a major part of the Company's inventories is accounted for by the last-in, first-out (LIFO) method. The LIFO method of inventory valuation has the effect of assessing current costs against current revenues and therefore goes far toward recognizing the effect of inflation on cost of goods sold.

Replacement-cost reporting

The Company has continued to calculate the replacement-cost information required by the Securities and Exchange Commission (SEC) since 1976. Such data will be shown in the Company's Form 10-K report filed with the SEC. While similar in effect, replacement-cost information differs from the constant-dollar values, principally because of differences in prescribed methods of measurement.

Constant-dollar reporting

In compliance with the requirements of Statement No. 33, page 32 of this report includes schedules showing certain amounts adjusted to dollars of equivalent value or purchasing power (constant dollars). The average 1979 constant-dollar amounts have been derived by aging data reported on the historical basis and by applying the Consumer Price Index for All Urban Consumers (CPI-U) to such data. The adjusted data are intended to reflect the effects of general inflation or changes in purchasing power of the U.S. dollar and should be read in conjunction with the comparable historical financial statements and the notes incorporated therein.

Even though the validity of using the CPI-U for adjusting historical figures has been questioned by some authorities, it has been used here as required by Statement No. 33.

The *Schedule of operating results adjusted for general inflation* shown on page 32 provides a comparison of the adjusted 1979 results with those reported on an historical basis. The adjustments assume all assets used in production have been acquired with dollars measured in 1979 purchasing power.

Charges for the use of such higher-valued property, plant, equipment, and inventories would have increased depreciation and cost of goods sold significantly, reducing earnings before income taxes from almost $126 million to about $87 million. The constant-dollar earnings exclude any inflation adjustments to the provision for taxes on income. Consequently, about 69% of before-tax constant-dollar earnings would be needed to satisfy income tax requirements.

Report of the impact of inflation upon the business (continued)

Unrealized gain from decline in purchasing power of net amounts owed shows the effect of general inflation on the Company's net monetary position. It is generally understood that debts (monetary liabilities) incurred early in a period of inflation may be repaid in dollars of lower purchasing power. Conversely, cash and amounts receivable in fixed dollar terms (monetary assets) will be worth less in purchasing power as inflation rises. Like many companies, Armstrong has a favorable net monetary liability position. The gain reported in the schedule indicates that Armstrong will pay such net monetary liabilities in dollars of lower purchasing power.

Net assets at year-end, as adjusted, reflect the equivalent of stockholders' equity after upward revaluation of inventory and net property, plant, and equipment for the effects of general inflation.

Schedule of operating results adjusted for general inflation

For the year ended December 31, 1979 (millions, except Earnings per share)	As reported in the financial statements (historical cost)	Selected data adjusted for general inflation (constant dollar)
Net sales	$1,341.1	$1,341.1
Cost of goods sold*	941.1	955.4
Other operating expenses, net*	213.2	213.2
Depreciation and amortization	41.6	66.4
Interest expense	13.8	13.8
Unrealized foreign exchange losses	5.6	5.6
Earnings before income taxes................	$ 125.8	$ 86.7
Taxes on income	59.8	59.8
Net earnings	$ 66.0	$ 26.9
Earnings per share.............	$2.58	$1.04
Net assets at year-end	$ 567.7	$ 921.6
Unrealized gain from decline in purchasing power of net amounts owed		$ 11.0

*Excludes depreciation and amortization

Shown below is a *Schedule of selected financial data developed under the standards of Statement No. 33 to measure the impact of general inflation.* This schedule shows selected data for five years adjusted to a common unit of measure or purchasing power. The 1979 sales and dividend data are assumed to have occurred in average 1979 dollars and are the same as reported in the primary financial statements. The market price per common share at year-end has been adjusted to average 1979 constant dollars.

Prior-year data were developed by multiplying historical amounts by a restatement factor derived by dividing the CPI-U average for the respective year into the CPI-U average for 1979.

Schedule of selected financial data developed under the standards of Statement No. 33 to measure the impact of general inflation
(in average 1979 constant dollars)

For year	1979	1978	1977	1976	1975
Net sales (millions)	$1,341.1	$1,384.8	$1,305.5	$1,251.7	$1,159.6
Dividends per common share ...	$ 1.075	$ 1.11	$ 1.20	$ 1.16	$ 1.12
Market price per common share at year-end	15⅝	17¼	20¾	34⅜	31¾
Average consumer price index**	217.4	195.4	181.5	170.5	161.2

**1967 = 100

Armstrong Cork Company and Subsidiaries

Five-Year Summary

For year		1979	1978	1977	1976	1975
Net sales	$(000)	**1,341,067**	1,244,065	1,089,377	981,208	859,412
Cost of goods sold	$(000)	**975,709**	892,845	786,523	700,263	635,833
Selling and administrative expense	$(000)	**227,474**	209,703	190,090	172,661	149,754
Interest expense	$(000)	**13,827**	14,612	14,995	13,046	16,629
Other income (expense), net	$(000)	**1,804**	1,422	(2,433)	7,209	7,793
Earnings before income taxes and extraordinary gain	$(000)	**125,861**	128,327	95,336	102,447	64,989
As a percentage of sales		**9.4%**	10.3%	8.8%	10.4%	7.6%
Taxes on income	$(000)	**59,817**	67,195	54,961	50,197(b)	30,068
Effective income tax rate		**47.5%**	52.4%	57.6%	49.0%	46.3%
Earnings before extraordinary gain	$(000)	**66,044**	61,132	40,375	52,250	34,921
As a percentage of sales		**4.9%**	4.9%	3.7%	5.3%	4.1%
As a percentage of average total assets		**7.7%**	7.4%	5.0%	6.8%	4.7%
As a percentage of average invested capital (c)		**9.1%**	8.7%	5.9%	8.0%	5.6%
As a percentage of average common stockholders' equity (d)		**12.0%**	11.7%	8.1%	11.1%	7.9%
Extraordinary gain	$(000)	**—**	—	—	12,400	—
Net earnings	$(000)	**66,044**	61,132	40,375	64,650(a)	34,921
Net earnings applicable to common stock	$(000)	**65,601**	60,689	39,932	64,207(a)	34,478
Per common share	$	**2.58**	2.36	1.55	2.49(a)	1.34
Per common share before extraordinary gain	$	**2.58**	2.36	1.55	2.01	1.34
Dividends per common stock	$	**1.075**	1.00	1.00	.91	.83
Capital additions	$(000)	**56,076**	43,749	50,720	62,387	38,296
Total depreciation and amortization	$(000)	**41,627**	42,745	37,679	35,249	32,166
Total federal, foreign, state, and local taxes	$(000)	**97,848**	100,518	85,076	76,157(b)	52,424
Average number of employees		**23,835**	23,876	23,121	23,005	22,512
Average number of common shares outstanding	(000)	**25,395**	25,747	25,746	25,742	25,738
YEAR-END POSITION						
Working capital	$(000)	**308,077**	282,868	266,586	241,952	217,848
Net property, plant, and equipment	$(000)	**419,418**	406,734	406,599	395,098	369,266
Total assets	$(000)	**876,312**	844,052	815,786	784,142	740,733
Total invested capital (c)	$(000)	**736,537**	711,823	701,042	678,596	627,670
Stockholders' equity	$(000)	**567,657**	546,824	511,881	497,666	456,753
Book value per share of common stock	$	**22.45**	20.77	19.41	18.86	17.27
Number of stockholders		**16,992**	18,226	17,561	17,634	18,410
Common shares outstanding	(000)	**24,747**	25,747	25,747	25,745	25,738
Market value per common share		**16½**	16⅛	17¾	27½	24¼

Notes:

(a) Includes extraordinary gain of $12,400,000, or $.48 per common share, from the sale of excess woodlands.

(b) Excludes $6,400,000 of income taxes resulting from the sale of excess woodlands.

(c) Invested capital is defined as total stockholders' equity plus long-term debt including current maturities and deferred taxes.

(d) After deducting preferred dividend requirements.

CHAPTER 3

Transaction Analysis

The process of transforming transaction data into useful accounting information.

The basic accounting equation.

The steps in the accounting cycle.

The analysis of operating-cycle transactions in terms of the accounting equation.

In the first two chapters we provided an overview of financial accounting. We discussed the environment of accounting and its objectives, the basic concepts and principles underlying accounting practice, and the outputs of the accounting process. With this chapter, we begin our study of transaction analysis. This simply means that we will examine the procedures for analyzing, recording, summarizing, and reporting the transactions of an entity. Emphasis is placed on operating-cycle transactions.

In Chapter 4, we deal with the adjustments and closing entries required to complete what is commonly called the accounting cycle. An extended illustration is provided at the conclusion of that chapter to show the results of transaction analysis as related to the three major types of businesses: proprietorship, partnership, and corporation.

transaction analysis *the procedures for analyzing, recording, summarizing, and reporting transactions of an entity*

The Process of Transforming Transaction Data into Useful Accounting Information

Business entities buy and sell goods or services; borrow and invest money; pay wages to employees; purchase land, buildings, and equipment; distribute earnings to their owners; and pay taxes to the government. In order to determine how well an entity is managing its resources, the results

EXHIBIT 3–1   **The Accounting Process**

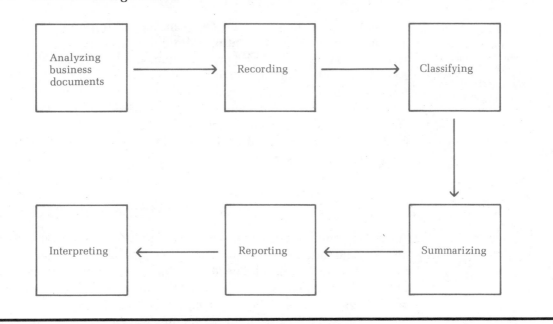

accounting process *the means of transforming accounting data into accounting reports that can be interpreted and used in decision making*

of these and similar types of transactions must be analyzed. The accounting process makes that analysis possible by recording, classifying, and summarizing an entity's transactions and preparing reports that present the summary results. Exhibit 3–1 is a diagram of the sequence, showing how the accounting process monitors the results of an entity's transactions. To fully understand how the inputs (transaction data) are transformed through the accounting process into the outputs (financial statements and reports), you should first learn the distinctions between certain key concepts.

DATA VERSUS INFORMATION

data *inputs to the accounting system that are derived from transactions*

information *data organized by the accounting system*

A basic distinction should be drawn between data and information. The inputs to an accounting information system are raw data, which are the result of transactions and are derived from an entity's business documents. These facts (data) are ordered, chronologically and topically, and put into a logical format via the accounting process. They are then summarized on various reports as information. Thus, accounting information may be viewed as organized data directed toward a specific objective; information in this form has increased communicative value to the person receiving it. Although the terms "data" and "information" are sometimes used interchangeably, they are distinguished here to show that the purpose of the accounting process is to transform financial data into useful information.

ACCOUNTING VERSUS MANAGERIAL INFORMATION SYSTEMS

accounting information system
a subset of the managerial information system whereby the financial data derived from recorded transactions are collected, processed, and reported

A second distinction is made between accounting and managerial information systems. The accounting information system is generally a highly formalized system within an organization. A relatively small but important part of the total managerial information system, the accounting system provides the financial information derived from transaction data. The managerial information system is the broader of the two systems; it encompasses all information related to the organization. For example, in addition to accounting information, it includes general market trends, economic indicators, and product-research reports.

managerial information system
the system whereby all information used by management is collected, processed, and reported

MANUAL VERSUS AUTOMATED ACCOUNTING SYSTEMS

A third distinction is that between a manually operated accounting system and an automated one. Historically, of course, all accounting systems had to be maintained by hand. The image of the accountant, with green eyeshade and quill pen, sitting on a high stool and meticulously maintaining the accounting records reflects those early manual systems. Today, few accounting systems are completely manual. Even small companies generally use some type of automated equipment—cash registers, adding machines, typewriters, calculators, bookkeeping machines. Such equipment helps to reduce the number of routine clerical functions and to improve the accuracy and timeliness of the accounting process.

automated accounting system
a system in which most of the data processing is performed by machines instead of people

An automated accounting system is one in which most of the data processing is performed by machines. Depending on the needs of the organization, the system may be as simple as an essentially manual system with several special-purpose business machines or as complex as an electronic data processing (EDP) system that utilizes the latest developments in computer technology. In a computerized accounting system, the accounting records are kept on punched cards, tapes, or discs, and displayed on computer printouts or cathode-ray-tube terminals. Although the accounting records and reports generated by a computerized system will usually look somewhat different from those of a manual system, the underlying accounting principles are the same. Because it is easier to understand and illustrate, a manual accounting system will be assumed in this text.

computerized accounting system   *a system in which most of the data processing is performed by computers*

The extent of automation depends not only on an organization's needs, but also on the costs of the system in relation to its benefits. For a small company with relatively few transactions each month and little need for frequent accounting reports, automation would be too expensive to be worthwhile. However, large complex organizations require more information and need to review it more often. For these companies, automation is practical because the costs of automated equipment, whether accounting machines or a full-fledged computer system, are outweighed by the benefits of more efficient performance of routine clerical functions and the production of more timely reports. Many small- to medium-sized companies use computers on a time-sharing basis, and in this way enjoy the advantages of automation while keeping costs at a reasonable level.

The Increasing Role of the Computer

A computer is a high-speed electronic device which, among other things, is capable of performing many of the routine recording and summarizing functions of the accounting process. Computers can also store and retrieve data quickly and can be programmed to follow instructions that enable them to perform designated operations without human intervention. Because of their speed and accuracy, computers can significantly reduce the accountant's clerical workload. The accountant can therefore devote more time to assisting management in the interpretation and decision-making functions.

Internal Controls

internal control *an organization's methods and procedures for safeguarding assets, checking on the accuracy and reliability of accounting data, and promoting operational efficiency and adherence to managerial policy*

Specific organizational needs, efficiency and effectiveness, costs and benefits, timeliness and completeness, all are important considerations in the design and implementation of an accounting information system. So too are the internal controls of the system. Internal control refers to a company's methods of safeguarding its assets, checking the reliability of the accounting data it produces, and promoting operational efficiency and adherence to managerial policies. Chapter 16 discusses internal controls in detail. The point to be made here is that internal controls are needed for automated accounting systems just as much as for manual systems. In fact, automation may increase the need for controls. In an EDP system, for example, many of the records exist on tapes or discs in a computer and are not available for physical inspection. One of the challenges facing the accounting profession today is to learn how to take advantage of the benefits of computerized accounting systems and still maintain the type of strong control characteristic of manual systems.

TO SUMMARIZE Accounting data are financial in nature and result from an entity's transactions. The accounting process is designed to accumulate and report the results of these transactions, to transform financial data into useful information. A company's need for financial information is generally satisfied by the accounting system, which is a subset of the managerial information system. Whether the accounting system is manually operated or automated—or, as is more likely, a combination of both—depends on a number of factors, particularly on the cost of automation in relation to its benefits for the enterprise.

General Business Activity

operating cycle *the general pattern of business activity whereby cash and other resources are converted to inventory and operational assets and eventually to a product or service that can be sold and for which cash and other resources are received*

As we explained in the Prologue, most businesses follow a basic pattern of activity whereby cash and other resources are converted to inventory and plant assets in order to produce a product or service that can be sold at a profit. This pattern is often referred to as the operating cycle. Although modifications are required for different types of businesses, the operating cycle is essentially a cash-to-cash cycle involving the investing, purchasing, selling, and collecting functions. Exhibit 3–2 illustrates this cycle for three types of businesses: service, merchandising, and manufacturing.

EXHIBIT 3–2 The General Pattern of Business Activity

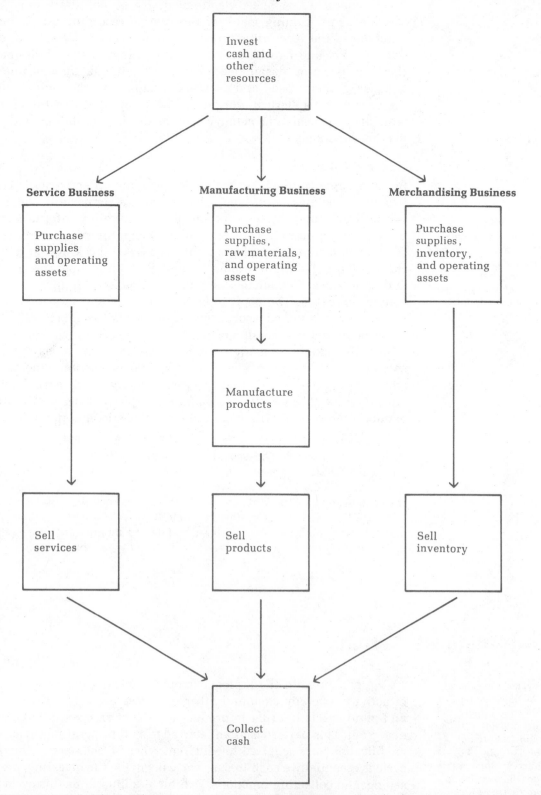

accounting cycle   *the sequence of procedures in the accounting process that includes analyzing business documents, journalizing, posting, balancing the accounts and preparing a trial balance and worksheet, journalizing and posting adjusting entries, preparing financial statements, closing nominal accounts, and balancing the accounts and preparing a post-closing trial balance*

To keep track of all the financial activities of an organization requires an accounting system tailor-made to the needs of a particular enterprise. Obviously, the accounting system in a large multinational corporation (a company with operations in several countries) with tens of thousands of business transactions each month will be much more complex than the system needed by a small grocery store. Regardless of the type or complexity of the business, however, all accounting systems include certain basic steps, referred to collectively as the accounting cycle.

Before you study the specific steps in the cycle, it is important that you understand double-entry accounting more fully. This concept was introduced briefly in Chapter 1. You will recall that the accounting model is built upon a basic equation. You now need to learn how to use this equation in accounting for business activities.

The Basic Accounting Equation

As you will recall, the fundamental accounting equation is

$$\textbf{Assets} \quad = \quad \textbf{Liabilities} \quad + \quad \textbf{Owners' Equity}$$

$$\text{(Resources)} \qquad \begin{pmatrix} Creditors'\ claims \\ against\ resources \end{pmatrix} \qquad \begin{pmatrix} Owners'\ claims \\ against\ resources \end{pmatrix}$$

Thus, the resources of a company are offset by claims against those resources, either creditor claims or owner claims. To determine the amount of ownership equity at any one time, the amount of creditor claims can be substracted from the assets. The difference is called net assets, or owners' equity. Thus, the equation can also be written:

net assets   *total assets less total liabilities; equal to owners' equity*

$$\text{Assets} - \text{Liabilities} = \text{Owners' Equity}$$

Since the accounting equation is an equality, it must always remain in balance. To see how this works, consider the following business activities.

Business Activity	Effect in Terms of the Accounting Equation
1. Borrow money	Increase asset (cash); increase liability (note payable)
2. Investment by owners	Increase asset (cash); increase owners' equity (capital stock)
3. Pay off note	Decrease asset (cash); decrease liability (note payable)
4. Purchase equipment for cash	Decrease asset (cash); increase asset (equipment)
5. Collect cash from customers	Increase asset (cash); decrease asset (accounts or notes receivable)
6. Give note to settle long-term debt	Increase liability (note payable); decrease liability (bond or mortgage payable)

In each case, the equation remains in balance because an identical amount is added to or subtracted from both sides of the equation, or it is added to and subtracted from the same side of the equation.

An efficient way to categorize transactions is to assign each type of asset, liability, or owners' equity item to a specific accounting record called an account. Thus, we may designate asset, liability, and owners' equity accounts. Examples of asset accounts are Cash, Inventory, and Equipment. Examples of liability accounts are Accounts Payable and Notes Payable, and examples of equity accounts are Capital Stock and Retained Earnings. Each account may be shown as follows:

account *an accounting record in which the results of similar transactions are accumulated; shows increases, decreases, and a balance*

These are called T-accounts. Note that every account has two sides. A debit represents an entry on the left side of the account; a credit represents an entry on the right side of the account. Thus, the appropriate debit (DR) and credit (CR) notations for the above accounts would be

T-account *a simplified depiction of an account in the form of a letter T, showing the debits on the left and credits on the right*

debit *an entry on the left side of an account*

credit *an entry on the right side of an account*

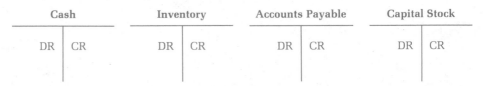

As shown, debits and credits represent the left and right sides of an account, respectively. Debits and credits also refer to the increases and decreases that result from each transaction, depending on the type of account. For liability and owners' equity accounts, credits refer to increases and debits to decreases. But for asset accounts, the opposite is true. Thus, to increase the Cash account, we debit it; to decrease the Cash account, we credit it. This debit–credit, increase–decrease relationship holds true for any asset account. The opposite relationship is true of liability and owners' equity accounts; they are increased by credits and decreased by debits.

Why is it, in accounting, that the meanings of the terms debit and credit switch from an increase to a decrease, and vice versa, as we go from one side of the accounting equation to the other? To explain this we need to keep three basic facts in mind: (1) For every transaction there must be a debit and a credit; (2) debits must always equal credits for each transaction; (3) debits are always entered on the left side of an account and credits are always entered on the right side. Now, notice what this means for the first example of a business transaction on page 71, borrowing money. We increase an asset account (Cash); in other words, we debit it. We increase a liability account (Note Payable); in other words, we credit it. So we have a debit and a credit for the transaction, even though we are increasing an account on either side of the equation. The effect of this system is shown on page 73, with an increase indicated by (+) and a decrease by (−).

Assets		=	Liabilities		+	Owners' Equity	
DR	CR		DR	CR		DR	CR
(+)	(−)		(−)	(+)		(−)	(+)

Be careful not to let the general, nonaccounting meanings of the words "credit" and "debit" confuse you here. In general conversation, credit has an association with plus and debit with minus. But on the asset side of the accounting equation, this association can lead you astray. To make sure you understand the relationship between debits and credits, the various accounts, and the accounting equation, let us reexamine the business activities listed on page 71.

Business Activity

Effect in Terms of the Accounting Equation

Assets		=	Liabilities		+	Owners' Equity	
1. Borrow money	DR(+)				CR(+)			
2. Investment from owners . . .	DR(+)							CR(+)
3. Pay off note		CR(−)		DR(−)				
4. Purchase equipment for cash	DR(+)	CR(−)						
5. Collect cash from customers	DR(+)	CR(−)						
6. Give note to settle long-term debt				DR(−)	CR(+)			

As observed, every time accounts are debited, other accounts have to be credited for the same amount. This is a major characteristic of a double-entry accounting system: The debits must always equal the credits.

TO SUMMARIZE   Debits are *always* entered on the left side of an account and credits are *always* entered on the right side. Debits increase asset accounts, the left side of the equation, and decrease liability and owners' equity accounts, the right side of the equation. Credits decrease asset accounts and increase liability and owners' equity accounts. Therefore, at any one time under a double-entry system of accounting, it is possible to check the accounting records to see that Assets = Liabilities + Owners' Equity, and that Debits = Credits.

The Steps in the Accounting Cycle

Although some of the procedures may be modified or combined, the accounting cycle generally consists of the specific steps shown in Exhibit 3–3. As we introduce each step in the cycle, you should try to understand the general concepts and terms. Do not be concerned about all the specifics, including the format used in recording transactions. More detailed illustrations and explanations will follow once the overall process is described.

EXHIBIT 3–3   The Accounting Cycle

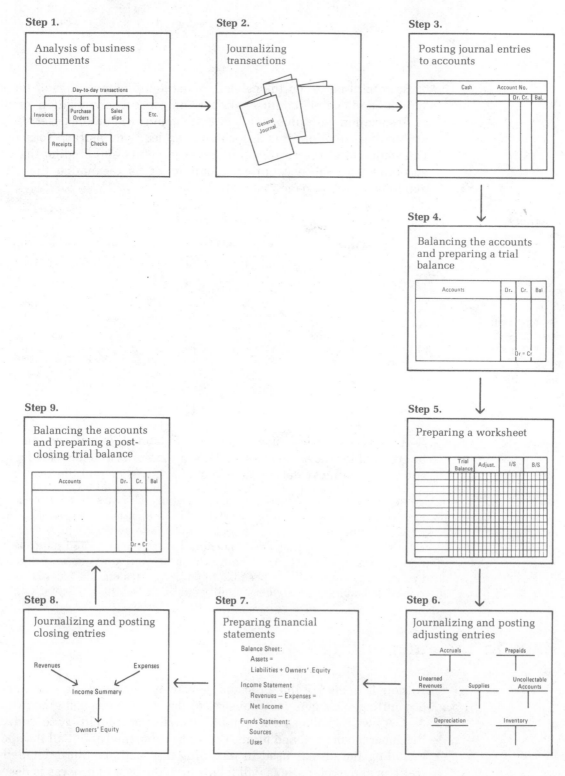

business documents *records of transactions used as the basis for recording accounting entries; includes invoices, check stubs, receipts, and similar business papers*

Step 1. Analysis of Business Documents

The first step is to analyze the business documents—the sales invoices, purchase orders, check stubs, and other records that are evidence of business transactions. Business documents confirm that a transaction has occurred and establish the amounts to be recorded. Exhibit 3–4 shows two examples of business documents: a sales invoice and a purchase order.

EXHIBIT 3–4 **Sales Invoice and Purchase Order**

NEPTCO

NEW ENGLAND PRINTED TAPE CO.
PAWTUCKET, RHODE ISLAND LENOIR, NORTH CAROLINA
P.O. BOX 2323 30 HAMLET STREET PAWTUCKET, RHODE ISLAND 02861 TELEPHONE 401-722-5500 TELEX 927625

Invoice

CUSTOMER NUMBER INVOICE NUMBER
INVOICE DATE SHIPPED FROM

SOLD TO SHIP TO

ORDER DATE	ORDER NUMBER	YOUR P O NUMBER	REL. NUMBER	TERMS	SHIP VIA

ITEM	PRODUCT NO	NO SHIPPED	DESCRIPTION	QUANTITY	U M	PRICE	AMOUNT

All bills not paid at maturity subject to interest.
"Seller warrants that all goods covered by this invoice were produced in compliance with the requirements of the FAIR LABOR STANDARDS ACT OF 1938, as amended."

NEPTCO

NEW ENGLAND PRINTED TAPE CO.
PAWTUCKET, RHODE ISLAND LENOIR, NORTH CAROLINA
P O BOX 2323 30 HAMLET STREET PAWTUCKET, RHODE ISLAND 02861 TELEPHONE 401-722-5500 TELEX 927625

Purchase Order

PURCHASE ORDER NUMBER
DATE DUE DATE
VENDOR NUMBER REQUISITION NUMBER

VENDOR SHIP TO

TERMS	F O B	SHIP VIA	DELIVER TO (DEPARTMENT)

ITEM	PART NO	DESCRIPTION	QUANTITY ORD	U M	PRICE	AMOUNT

Complete shipping information and return *this* copy.
It is essential that our Purchase Order and Part Number appear on all packing lists, invoices, etc.
Show terms and F.O.B. point on your invoices.
Please advise carrier of delivery hours, 9:00 am–1:00 pm only.
See reverse side for Terms and Conditions.
I hereby certify that the property herein described is purchased for the purpose of being manufactured in this state into a finished product for resale and becomes a recognizable, integral part of such finished product and is exempt from the sales or use tax pursuant to Chapter 18, Section 30H or W of the Rhode Island Sales and Use Tax Law.

WILL SHIP (DATE) FROM (CITY)
VIA
SIGNATURE
We hereby acknowledge and accept this order subject to the terms and conditions specified.

Step 2. Journalizing Transactions

The second step in the accounting cycle is to record the results of transactions in a journal. Known as books of original entry, journals provide a chronological record of all entity transactions. They show the dates of the transactions, the amounts involved, and the particular accounts affected by the transactions. Usually, an explanation of the transaction is also included. Exhibit 3–5 shows a partial page from a General Journal.

journal   the accounting record in which transactions are first entered; provides a chronological record of all business activities

Step 3. Posting Journal Entries to Accounts

Once transactions have been recorded in either the General Journal or various specialized journals, it is necessary to classify and group all similar items. This is accomplished by the bookkeeping procedure of posting all the journal entries to appropriate accounts. As indicated earlier, accounts are records of like items. They show transaction dates, increases and decreases, and account balances. For example, all items of cash, whether related to cash receipts or to cash disbursements (payments), are accumulated in one account called "Cash" and all sales transactions are grouped together in the "Sales" account. Exhibit 3–6 shows how the January 1 transaction from the General Journal (Exhibit 3–5) would appear in the Cash account.

posting   the process of classifying, grouping, and recording similar transactions in common accounts by transferring amounts from the journal to the ledger

All accounts are maintained in an accounting record called the General Ledger. A ledger, then, is a "book" of accounts. Exhibit 3–7 shows how the two cash transactions in the General Journal would be posted to the Cash account in the General Ledger, with arrows depicting the posting procedures. Observe that a number has been inserted in the "posting reference"

ledger   a book or grouping of accounts in which data from transactions recorded in journals are posted and thereby classified and summarized

---

EXHIBIT 3–5   General Journal

General Journal   Page 1

Date	Account Titles and Explanation	Post Ref.	Debit	Credit
19 81				
Jan. 1	Cash		5000	
	Notes Payable			5000
	Borrowed $5,000 from bank, securing loan with 1-year promissory note at 10% interest.			
4	Inventory		1500	
	Accounts Payable			1500
	Purchased inventory on account.			
10	Accounts Payable		1500	
	Cash			1500
	Paid amount owed on inventory purchase.			

EXHIBIT 3-6 **Cash Account**

General Ledger	Cash				Account No. 101
Date	Explanation	Post Ref.	Debit	Credit	Balance
1/1 81	Balance				10100
Jan 1	Note issued to bank		5000		15100

EXHIBIT 3-7 **Posting to the General Ledger**

General Journal				Page 1
Date	Account Titles and Explanation	Post Ref.	Debit	Credit
1981				
Jan 1	Cash	101	5000	
	Notes Payable			5000
	Borrowed $5,000 from bank, securing loan with 1-year promissory note at 10% interest.			
4	Inventory		1500	
	Accounts Payable			1500
	Purchased inventory on account.			
10	Accounts Payable		1500	
	Cash	101		1500
	Paid amount owed on inventory purchase.			

General Ledger	Cash				Account No. 101
Date	Explanation	Post Ref.	Debit	Credit	Balance
1/1 81	Balance				10100
Jan 1	Note issued to bank	GJ1	5000		15100
10	Payment for inventory purchase	GJ1		1500	13600

EXHIBIT 3–8   Chart of Accounts for a Merchandising Business

Assets (100–199)

Current Assets (100–120):
100   Petty Cash
101   Cash
102   Marketable Securities
103   Notes Receivable
105   Trade Accounts Receivable
106   Allowance for Doubtful Accounts
107   Inventory
108   Prepaid Rent
109   Prepaid Taxes
110   Prepaid Insurance
111   Other Prepaid Expenses

Funds and Investments (121–140):
121   Bond Sinking Fund
131   Investment in Stock of X Co.

Long-Term Operational Assets (141–160):
141   Land
142   Buildings
143   Accumulated Depreciation—Buildings
144   Store Equipment
145   Accumulated Depreciation—Store Equipment
146   Delivery Vehicles
147   Accumulated Depreciation—Delivery Vehicles
148   Office Furniture
149   Accumulated Depreciation—Office Furniture

Intangible Assets (161–180):
161   Patents
162   Franchises
163   Trademarks
164   Goodwill

Other Assets (181–199)

Liabilities (200–299)

Current Liabilities (200–219):
201   Notes Payable
202   Accounts Payable
203   Salaries Payable
204   Interest Payable
205   Payroll Taxes Payable
206   Income Taxes Payable
207   Rent Payable
219   Other Current Liabilities

Long-Term Liabilities (220–239):
221   Notes Payable
222   Bonds Payable
223   Mortgage Payable
224   Other Long-Term Liabilities

Stockholders' Equity (300–399)

301   Common Stock
302   Paid-in Capital in Excess of Par—Common Stock
303   Preferred Stock
304   Paid-in Capital in Excess of Par—Preferred Stock
310   Treasury Stock
330   Retained Earnings

---

column (also called the "folio" column). This number serves as a cross-reference between the General Journal and the accounts in the General Ledger. In the journal, it identifies the account to which the journal entry has been posted. In the account, it identifies the page on which the entry appears in the General Journal. For example, the GJ1 notation in the Cash account for the January 1 entry means that the $5,000 has been posted from page 1 of the General Journal.

Each organizational unit will have as many or as few accounts as it needs to provide a reasonable classification of its transactions. The list of accounts used by a company is known as its chart of accounts. Exhibit 3–8 shows a company's chart of accounts.

chart of accounts   *a systematic listing of all accounts used by a company*

Step 4. Balancing the Accounts and Preparing a Trial Balance

At the end of an accounting period, the accounts in the General Ledger

Sales (400–499)

400 Sales
402 Sales Returns and Allowances
404 Sales Discounts
451 Purchase Returns and Allowances
452 Purchase Discounts
453 Freight-In

Operating Expenses (500–599)

Selling Expenses (500–549):
501 Sales Salaries
505 Sales Commissions
510 Freight-Out
520 Payroll Taxes
521 Sales Supplies Expense
522 Fuel Expense
523 Utility Expense
524 Postage Expense
525 Travel Expense
526 Depreciation Expense—Delivery Vehicles
527 Equipment Rent Expense
528 Advertising Expense
529 Display Materials Expense
530 Sales Office Repair Expense
531 Depreciation Expense—Store Equipment

General and Administrative Expenses (550–599):
551 Officers' Salaries
552 Office Salaries
553 Administrative Salaries
570 Payroll Taxes
571 Office Supplies Expense
572 Fuel Expense
573 Utility Expense
574 Postage Expense
575 Travel Expense
576 Depreciation Expense—Buildings
577 Depreciation Expense—Office Furniture
578 Office Equipment Rent Expense
579 Legal Fees
580 Accounting Fees
581 Building Repair and Maintenance Expense
582 Charitable Contributions
583 Bad Debt Expense
584 Amortization of Goodwill
585 Amortization of Patents

Other Expenses (600–699)

601 Interest on Notes
602 Interest on Bonds
603 Interest on Mortgage

Other Income (700–799)

701 Interest Revenue
702 Revenue from Investments
703 Rental Income
704 Miscellaneous Income

---

trial balance   *a listing of all account balances; provides a means of testing whether debits equal credits for all accounts*

are reviewed to determine that each account has an updated balance—that is, to see that the difference between the total debits and total credits has been extended into the balance column. This is known as "balancing the accounts."

After the account balances are determined, and as a means of checking the accuracy of the recording and posting functions (steps 2 and 3), a trial balance is usually prepared as step 4 in the accounting cycle. A trial balance lists each account with its debit or credit balance (see Exhibit 3–9). If the debits equal the credits, there is some assurance that the recording and posting functions have been performed correctly. Even if the trial balance appears to be correct, there may be errors. A transaction may be omitted completely, or it may have been recorded incorrectly or posted to the wrong account. These types of errors will not be discovered by preparing a trial balance; they require additional analysis.

EXHIBIT 3–9   One-on-One Sports Company
Trial Balance as of March 31, 1981

	Debits	Credits
Cash	$ 1,421	
Accounts Receivable	1,050	
Supplies	1,450	
Prepaid Rent	1,500	
Photographic Equipment	12,000	
Accounts Payable		$ 2,000
Capital Stock		5,000
Retained Earnings		7,450
Service Fees		3,725
Salary Expense	550	
Miscellaneous Expense	204	
Totals	$18,175	$18,175

EXHIBIT 3–10   One-on-One Sports Company
Worksheet for the Month Ended March 31, 1981

Account Title	Trial Balance Debit	Trial Balance Credit
Cash	1421	
Accounts Receivable	1050	
Supplies	1450	
Prepaid Rent	1500	
Photographic Equipment	12000	
Accounts Payable		2000
Capital Stock		5000
Retained Earnings		7450
Service Fees		3725
Salary Expense	550	
Miscellaneous Expense	204	
	18175	18175
Supplies Expense		
Rent Expense		
Depreciation Expense		
Accumulated Depreciation		
Salaries Payable		
Net Income (to balance)		

Adjustments:
(a) Supplies Used (c) Depreciation Expense Recorded
(b) Rent Expense   (d) Salaries Payable Accrued

Step 5. Preparing a Worksheet

worksheet *a columnar schedule used to conveniently summarize accounting data*

Although financial statements can be prepared directly from the account balances, a worksheet provides a useful way to summarize data and indicate adjustments to the trial balance. If a worksheet is used, it will probably look something like the one shown in Exhibit 3–10. The accounts are listed on the left side of the worksheet and the trial balance amounts appear in the first two columns. Adjustments, such as recognizing any interest earned but not received or a decrease in asset values, are generally required at the end of each accounting period. These adjustments are included in the next two columns of the worksheet, with a transaction key explaining the adjustments. (All of this will be explained much more fully in later chapters.) The last four columns in our illustration include the adjusted amounts as they should be listed in the Income Statement and the Balance Sheet. Thus, these financial statements can be prepared directly from the worksheet.

Adjustments		Income Statement		Balance Sheet	
Debit	Credit	Debit	Credit	Debit	Credit
				1421	
				1050	
	(a) 760			690	
	(b) 500			1000	
				12000	
					2000
					5000
					7450
			3725		
(d) 55		605			
		204			
(a) 760		760			
(b) 500		500			
(c) 125		125			
	(c) 125				125
	(d) 55				55
1440	1440	2194	3725	16161	14630
		1531			1531
		3725	3725	16161	16161

Step 6. Journalizing and Posting Adjusting Entries

As we noted, adjustments are usually required at the end of every accounting period. These adjustments not only appear on a worksheet, if one is used, but also must be entered in the General Journal and posted to the proper accounts. For example, suppose that One-on-One Sports Company purchases an insurance policy for $900 on January 1, 1981. The transaction is recorded as an increase in the asset Prepaid Insurance and a decrease in the Cash account. If the premium ($900) provides three years' insurance coverage, at the end of 1981 the Prepaid Insurance account should be adjusted to show that one-third of that asset has been used up. Thus, $300 should be shown as an expense in 1981 and $600 should be the balance in Prepaid Insurance. To accomplish this, an adjusting entry would be recorded, showing the Insurance Expense of $300 and reducing Prepaid Insurance by the same amount. Once that journal entry is recorded and posted, the accounts will reflect proper balances. Adjusting entries are distinguished from other journal entries in that there are usually no current transactions or underlying documents that signal a need for them to be recorded. (Adjusting entries are discussed in Chapter 4.)

Step 7. Preparing Financial Statements

When all transactions have been journalized and posted and all adjusting entries made, the accounts can be summarized and presented as the general-purpose financial statements described in Chapter 2.

Step 8. Journalizing and Posting Closing Entries for Nominal Accounts

real accounts *the accounts appearing on the Balance Sheet; these accounts are not closed to a zero balance at the end of each accounting period*

Certain accounts are referred to as real accounts. These accounts report the cumulative additions and reductions in amounts from the date of organization of a company. They appear on the Balance Sheet and are permanent accounts; that is, they are not closed to a zero balance at the end of each accounting period. Balances that exist in these accounts at the end of a period are carried forward to the next period. Other accounts are known as nominal, or temporary, accounts. These accounts are reported on the Income Statement and, at the end of each period, are reduced to a zero balance through the closing process. Thus, nominal accounts begin with a zero balance at the start of each accounting cycle. During the period, the current transactions are recorded and posted to these accounts; prior to closing, the accounts show the results of operations for that period.

nominal accounts *the accounts appearing on the Income Statement; these accounts are closed to a zero balance at the end of each accounting period*

closing entries *entries that reduce all nominal, or Income Statement, accounts to a zero balance at the end of each accounting period, transferring their preclosing balances to permanent, Balance Sheet accounts*

The journal entries to close the nominal accounts, quite naturally called closing entries, must also be posted to the appropriate ledger accounts in order to get the books ready for the start of a new accounting cycle. Without closing entries, revenue and expense balances would extend from period to period, making it difficult to measure each period's results. The closing process is described briefly later in this chapter and explained in greater detail in Chapter 4.

Step 9. Balancing the Accounts and Preparing a Post-Closing Trial Balance

When the closing entries have been recorded and posted, the accounts can be balanced—that is, the debits and credits added and an account

post-closing trial balance *a*
listing of all real account
balances after the closing
process has been completed;
provides a means of testing
whether debits equal credits
for all real accounts prior to
beginning a new accounting
cycle

balance determined—and a post-closing trial balance can be prepared. This trial balance shows the account balances for all real accounts. The nominal accounts are not shown since they have been closed. This step is designed to provide some assurance that the previous steps in the cycle have been performed properly.

THE INTERPRETATION OF ACCOUNTING DATA

Although not usually considered one of the routine steps in the accounting cycle, interpretation of the products of the cycle—the accounting reports—is of utmost importance. Interpretation refers to the explanations, verbal or written, that accountants give to managers and external users to help them understand the information in accounting reports. For example, it would be useful not only to report an increase in total expenses but also to explain which individual expenses have increased, which have decreased, and why. Thus, interpretation is related to the full-disclosure standard mentioned in Chapter 2, and provides an opportunity for service by accountants. The procedures in the accounting cycle are only meaningful if the accounting information is relevant and is presented in a manner that assists users in making better decisions.

THE ACCOUNTING CYCLE: A SIMPLE ILLUSTRATION

The relationships of assets, liabilities, and owners' equity and the mechanics of double-entry accounting can be illustrated with the following simple example: Rick Jones set up R. J. Corporation in 1981 with an initial capital contribution of $20,000 for which he received capital stock. R. J. Corporation bought $10,000 worth of inventory and borrowed $50,000 from a bank to buy a building.

The purchase of inventory would be supported by invoices or other documentation showing the actual purchases, the dates, the amounts, and so forth. There would also be a bank note or mortgage for the $50,000 loan and a bill of sale for the purchase of the building. By analyzing these documents (step 1), the pertinent facts would be obtained and recorded in a General Journal.

A special format is used in journalizing transactions (step 2). The debit entry is always listed first; the credit entry is listed second and is indented to the right as shown below. Normally, the date and a brief explanation of the transaction are considered essential parts of the journal entry. Dollar signs generally are omitted.

General Journal Entry Format

```
Date   Debit Entry  ........................          xx
             Credit Entry  ...................................          xx
          Explanation
```

The journal entries to record the transactions for R. J. Corporation are as follows (note that letters are used in place of dates):

			Debit	Credit
asset (+)	**a**	Cash	20,000	
owners' equity (+)		Capital Stock		20,000
		Issued $20,000 of capital stock.		
asset (+)	**b**	Inventory	10,000	
asset (−)		Cash		10,000
		Purchased $10,000 of inventory for cash.		
asset (+)	**c**	Cash	50,000	
liability (+)		Notes Payable		50,000
		Borrowed $50,000 from the bank.		
asset (+)	**d**	Building	50,000	
asset (−)		Cash		50,000
		Purchased a building for cash.		

Next, the transactions would be posted to the ledger accounts (step 3). T-accounts are used to illustrate this process, with the letters **a**, **b**, **c**, and **d** showing the cross-references to the journal entry. A balance is shown for the end of the period.

Cash		Inventory		Building	
a .. 20,000	10,000 .. **b**	**b** .. 10,000		**d** .. 50,000	
c .. 50,000	50,000 .. **d**				
Bal...10,000		**Bal.**...10,000		**Bal.**...50,000	

Notes Payable		Capital Stock	
	50,000 .. **c**		20,000 .. **a**
	50,000..**Bal.**		20,000..**Bal.**

As a check on the accuracy of the journalizing and posting procedures, a trial balance may be prepared (step 4), as shown below.

R. J. Corporation
Trial Balance as of December 31, 1981

	Debit	Credit
Cash	$10,000	
Inventory	10,000	
Building	50,000	
Notes Payable		$50,000
Capital Stock		20,000
Totals	$70,000	$70,000

revenues *increases in resources from the sale of goods or services during the normal operations of a business*

expenses *costs of assets used up or additional liabilities incurred in the normal course of business to generate revenues*

At this point, we must digress slightly and bring <u>revenues</u> and <u>expenses</u> into the picture. Obviously, they are part of every ongoing business. Revenues provide resource inflows and expenses represent resource outflows (although some outflows are not expenses). The net result of revenues less expenses is income and is reflected in owners' equity. Revenues increase owners' equity; consequently, increases in revenues are recorded as credits. Expense accounts, which are in effect the opposite of revenue accounts, reduce owners' equity and are increased by debits. Recall that owners' equity is made up of the amount of capital contributed by owners (capital stock) plus the amount of earnings retained in the business (Retained Earnings). Revenues and expenses, in turn, determine the amount of periodic income and, through the closing process, have a direct impact on Retained Earnings.

Revenues and expenses may be thought of as subdivisions of owners' equity; that is, these two types of accounts are but temporary accumulation and storage compartments for operating transactions affecting Retained Earnings, a permanent account. The accounting equation may be expanded to include revenues and expenses as follows:

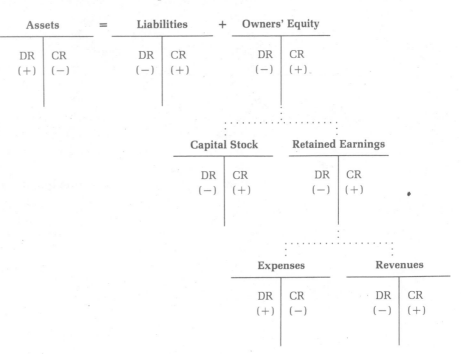

TO SUMMARIZE   Assets and expenses are increased by debits and reduced by credits; they usually have debit balances (that is, debits exceed credits). Liabilities, owners' equity, and revenues are increased by credits and reduced by debits; they generally have credit balances (that is, credits exceed debits).

To illustrate the accounting for revenues and expenses, we will assume that R. J. Corporation sold 10 percent, or $1,000 worth, of the inventory purchased. The company sold that inventory for $1,600, but to do so incurred $200 in selling expenses and $100 in miscellaneous expenses. The sale was originally made on credit, and the company later collected the cash. The journal entries to record these transactions would be as follows:

			Debits	Credits
asset (+)	**e**	Accounts Receivable	1,600	
revenues (+) [equity (+)]		Sales Revenue		1,600
		Sold $1,600 of merchandise on account.		
expense (+) [equity (−)]		Cost of Goods Sold	1,000	
asset (−)		Inventory		1,000
		To record the cost of goods sold.		
expense (+) [equity (−)]	**f**	Selling Expenses	200	
expense (+) [equity (−)]		Miscellaneous Expenses	100	
asset (−)		Cash		300
		Paid selling and miscellaneous expenses.		
asset (+)	**g**	Cash	1,600	
asset (−)		Accounts Receivable		1,600
		Collected accounts receivable.		

As with transactions **a–d**, illustrated on page 84, the journal entries that reflect the above transactions would be posted to the accounts. A trial balance would then be prepared.

To keep our example simple, we will make an unrealistic assumption that no year-end adjustments were required for R. J. Corporation and that a worksheet was not used. (Chapter 4 will cover this material.) Thus, an Income Statement and a Balance Sheet for R. J. Corporation, taken directly from the accounts, would be as shown in Exhibit 3–11 (step 7).

Regardless of whether a worksheet is used, at the end of each accounting cycle all revenue and expense accounts, the nominal accounts, must be closed (step 8), that is, reduced to a zero balance. Revenue accounts are closed by being debited; expenses are closed by being credited. The difference between the total revenue balances and the total expense balances

---

EXHIBIT 3–11   R. J. Corporation

Income Statement for the Year Ended December 31, 1981

Sales Revenue		$1,600
Less Cost of Goods Sold		1,000
Gross Margin		$ 600
Less: Selling Expense..........................	$200	
Miscellaneous Expense	100	300
Net Income		$ 300

Balance Sheet as of December 31, 1981

Assets		Liabilities and Owners' Equity	
Cash	$11,300	Notes Payable	$50,000
Inventory	9,000	Capital Stock.................	20,000
Building	50,000	Retained Earnings	300
Total	$70,300	Total	$70,300

is debited or credited to Retained Earnings. In our present example, sales and expenses would be closed to Retained Earnings as follows:

revenues (−) [equity (−)]	**h** Sales Revenue........................	1,600	
expense (−) [equity (+)]	Cost of Goods Sold............................		1,000
expense (−) [equity (+)]	Selling Expenses................................		200
expense (−) [equity (+)]	Miscellaneous Expenses		100
owners' equity (+)	Retained Earnings		300

To close sales and expenses to Retained Earnings.

As shown, the net result was to increase Retained Earnings by $300. This is the amount of income after appropriate expenses are recognized. After all entries are posted to the General Ledger, including the closing entries, the ledger accounts appear as follows:

Cash

a .. 20,000	10,000 .. **b**		
c .. 50,000	50,000 .. **d**		
g ... 1,600	300 .. **f**		
Bal...11,300			

Inventory

b .. 10,000	1,000 ... **e**
Bal... 9,000	

Building

d .. 50,000	
Bal....50,000	

Notes Payable

	50,000 .. **c**
	50,000..**Bal.**

Capital Stock

	20,000 .. **a**
	20,000..**Bal.**

Accounts Receivable

e ... 1,600	1,600 ... **g**

Sales Revenue

h ... 1,600	1,600 ... **e**

Cost of Goods Sold

e ... 1,000	1,000 ... **h**

Selling Expenses

f 200	200..... **h**

Miscellaneous Expenses

f 100	100..... **h**

Retained Earnings

	300..... **h**
	300 ....**Bal.**

An alternative to closing revenues and expenses directly to Retained Earnings is to close them to an Income Summary account. The balance in Income Summary would then be closed to Retained Earnings. Both procedures produce the same result.

Once revenues and expenses are closed to Retained Earnings, a post-closing trial balance for R. J. Corporation can be prepared (step 9). As you can see, the debits still equal the credits and the assets equal liabilities plus owners' equity (Exhibit 3–12). However, all nominal accounts are now closed and the books are ready for another accounting cycle to begin.

EXHIBIT 3–12   R. J. Corporation
Post-Closing Trial Balance as of December 31, 1981

	Debit	Credit
Cash	$11,300	
Inventory	9,000	
Building	50,000	
Notes Payable		$50,000
Capital Stock		20,000
Retained Earnings		300
Totals.......................................	$70,300	$70,300

TO SUMMARIZE   The accounting cycle is the process of analyzing, recording, classifying, summarizing, reporting, and interpreting the results of business activity. As illustrated in Exhibit 3–3 (page 74), the accounting cycle consists of nine steps in a well-defined sequence.

The bookkeeping procedures used in the accounting cycle are based upon the fundamental accounting equation: Assets = Liabilities + Owners' Equity. Revenues and expenses are subsets of owners' equity, with revenues increasing owners' equity and expenses decreasing it.

Transactions between business entities and related events provide the basis for all accounting records. For every transaction, a source document such as an invoice, a purchase order, or a check is prepared as a record of the essential data of the transaction. The data must be carefully analyzed to determine the proper entries in the entity's books. Through the accounting process, economic results are eventually reflected in the financial statements and other accounting reports. Interpretation of the data, while not considered a routine step in the accounting cycle, is an important responsibility of accountants. The information provided can then be used by people both inside and outside the company as the basis for better-informed decisions.

Analysis of Operating-Cycle Transactions

In this section, we examine the various transactions involved in the normal operating cycle of a business entity. These transactions are grouped according to type of activity: acquisition of cash, acquisition of other assets, utilization of assets to produce a product or service, and the collection of cash and payment of obligations and dividends. Obviously, we cannot present all possible transactions in this chapter. You should strive to understand the conceptual basis of transaction analysis rather than memorize particular journal entries. And that means understanding the dual effect of each transaction on the entity in terms of the basic accounting equation—that is, in terms of its impact on assets and on liabilities and owners' equity. Remember that the operating cycle naturally involves revenues and expenses as well, and that these nominal, or temporary, accounts will eventually be closed to an owners' equity account.

ACQUIRING CASH

One of the first tasks of any business is to acquire cash, either through owners' investment or by borrowing. Once a business is established, it normally generates cash from operations—by selling goods or services. The following transactions for two types of organizations—a proprietorship and a corporation—illustrate contributions by owners.

assets (+)
owner's equity (+)

| Cash .... | 10,000 | |
| J. Smith, Capital .... | | 10,000 |

Received $10,000 cash contribution from J. Smith, proprietor.

assets (+)
owners' equity (+)

| Cash .... | 50,000 | |
| Common Stock .... | | 50,000 |

Issued 5,000 shares of common stock at $10 per share.

These two transactions are similar in that each increased cash as a result of owners' contributions. In the first case, a proprietor contributed the cash; in the second case, capital stock of a corporation was issued, probably to several individuals. The economic impact of these situations may be summarized as

Assets   = Liabilities   + Owners' Equity
(increase $10,000   (no change)   (increase $10,000
or $50,000)   or $50,000)

(Actually, "proprietorship equity" is a more descriptive term than owners' equity for the first entry.)

In another example, cash is obtained by borrowing.

assets (+)
liabilities (+)

| Cash .... | 25,000 | |
| Notes Payable .... | | 25,000 |

Borrowed $25,000 from First National Bank, securing loan with 6-month note due January 1, 19XX, at 12% interest.

The accounting model would capture the economic impact as follows:

Assets   = Liabilities   + Owners' Equity
(increase $25,000)   (increase $25,000)   (no change)

In this last example, cash is increased by the sale of merchandise.

assets (+)
revenues (+) [equity (+)]

| Cash .... | 15,300 | |
| Sales Revenue .... | | 15,300 |

Sold merchandise for cash in November.

The accounting equation remains "in balance" because sales represent a revenue item, which will, when closed, increase owners' equity. Therefore,

Assets   = Liabilities   + Owners' Equity (Revenues)
(increase $15,300)   (no change)   (increase $15,300)

ACQUIRING OTHER ASSETS

Cash obtained from owners' contributions, borrowings, or sales can be used to acquire other assets needed to run the business. Such assets include inventory, buildings, equipment, and supplies. They may be obtained directly from investors or, as is more common, purchased with cash or on credit. Credit purchases require payment after a period of time, for example, 30 days. Normally, an interest expense is incurred when assets are bought on a time-payment plan that extends beyond two or three months. Examples of transactions involving the acquisition of noncash assets follow.

Example 1

Inventory costing $4,500 has been purchased "on account," which means that the buyer has used credit instead of cash to make the purchase and has an obligation (liability) to pay for the inventory at some future date.

assets (+)	Inventory	4,500	
liabilities (+)	Accounts Payable		4,500

Purchased inventory on account.

The accounting equation shows

Assets   = Liabilities   + Owners' Equity
(increase $4,500)   (increase $4,500)   (no change)

When the company pays for its inventory, cash will be reduced and the liability, Accounts Payable, will also be reduced, thus keeping the equation in balance. Inventory and similar items purchased on account are generally paid for within 30–90 days and normally do not require an interest charge.

Example 2

An asset has been acquired, a cash down payment has been made, and a long-term obligation has been incurred for the balance of the asset's cost. As the journal entry illustrates, more than two accounts can be involved in recording a transaction. This type of journal entry is called a compound entry.

assets (+)	Building 63,000		
liabilities (+)	Mortgage Payable	53,000
assets (−)	Cash	10,000

Purchased building for $63,000, making a $10,000 down payment and issuing a 10-year, 9% mortgage for the balance.

The accounting equation is

Assets   = Liabilities   + Owners' Equity
(increase $63,000;   (increase $53,000)   (no change)
decrease $10,000)

Example 3

An asset (for example, a machine) is given to a company by one of its owners. This is a valid transaction, but care must be exercised in determining a fair value for the asset. Since no arm's-length transaction is involved, the company must set a value based on the current market value of a similar asset.

asset (+)
owner's equity (+)

Equipment   5,500
   J. Smith, Capital   5,500

Acquired equipment valued at $5,500, contributed to the business by J. Smith, proprietor.

In the example given, the economic impact would be reflected in the equation as follows:

Assets   = Liabilities   + Owners' Equity
(increase $5,500)   (no change)   (increase $5,500)

Example 4

An increase in one asset is accompanied by a decrease in another asset.

assets (+)
assets (−)

Supplies   1,250
   Cash   1,250

Purchased supplies for cash.

The accounting equation is

Assets   = Liabilities   + Owners' Equity
(increase $1,250;   (no change)   (no change)
decrease $1,250)

PRODUCING GOODS OR PROVIDING SERVICES

The third step in the operating cycle is the use of a company's assets to produce goods or render services that can be sold to customers. Revenues are generated and expenses incurred during this process. Sometimes products or services are sold for cash; generally, however, a receivable is established and must be collected. Similarly, expenses may be incurred and paid for immediately by cash or they may be incurred on credit—that is, they may be "charged," with a cash payment to be made at a later date. Illustrative transactions follow.

Example 1

Cash has been received for services rendered.

assets (+)
revenues (+) [equity (+)]

Cash   17,000
   Consulting Fee Revenue   17,000

Received cash for consulting services.

Because revenues increase owners' equity, the accounting equation is

Assets   = Liabilities   + Owners' Equity (Revenues)
(increase $17,000)   (no change)   (increase $17,000)

Example 2

Merchandise is sold to customers on account, establishing a receivable. In this case, the company is allowing a customer 30 days to make payment. At the time payment is made, accounts receivable is reduced or eliminated and cash is increased by the same amount. Normally, no interest is charged on short-term credit sales or short-term credit purchases.

Sales, whether made on account or for cash, involve entries that reflect not only the sales but also the cost of the inventory sold. The cost of goods sold is an expense and, as such, is offset against the sales revenue to determine the profitability of sales transactions. The special procedures for handling inventory are described in Chapter 6. It is sufficient here to show an example of the impact of the transactions on the accounting equation.

assets (+)	Accounts Receivable	75,000	
revenues (+) [equity (+)]	Sales Revenue		75,000

Sold merchandise on account.

expenses (+) [equity (−)]	Cost of Goods Sold	60,000	
assets (−)	Inventory		60,000

To record the cost of goods sold and reduce inventory.

assets (+)	Cash	75,000	
assets (−)	Accounts Receivable		75,000

Collected receivables.

The effect on the accounting equation for each transaction would be as follows:

Sales on Account

Assets = Liabilities + Owners' Equity (Revenues)
(increase $75,000) (no change) (increase $75,000)

Cost of Goods Sold

Assets = Liabilities + Owners' Equity (Expenses)
(decrease $60,000) (no change) (decrease $60,000)

Collection of Receivables

Assets = Liabilities + Owners' Equity
(increase $75,000; (no change) (no change)
decrease $75,000)

Example 3

Expenses other than cost of goods sold are also incurred in operating a business. As entries for advertising and wages expenses illustrate, such expenses may involve either a cash transaction or the establishment of a liability, which will usually be eliminated at a later date by a cash payment.

expenses (+) [equity (−)]	Advertising Expense	500	
assets (−)	Cash		500

Paid advertising expense.

expenses (+) [equity (−)]	Wages Expense	22,500	
liabilities (+)	Wages Payable		22,500

To record employees' wages for September.

liabilities (−)	Wages Payable	22,500	
assets (−)	Cash		22,500

Paid (in October) wages earned in September.

COLLECTING CASH AND PAYING OBLIGATIONS

Obviously, once a product or service is sold on account, the receivable must be collected. The cash received generally is used to meet daily operating expenses and to pay other obligations. Excess cash can be reinvested in the business or distributed to the owners (in the form of dividends) as a return on their investment.

Example 1

The collection of accounts receivable is an important aspect of most businesses. Customers are allowed to purchase goods on charge accounts or with credit cards on the assumption that credit terms will increase total sales. If collections are not made, however, the seller may lose not only the cash but the merchandise as well. Even when the merchandise can be repossessed, it often cannot be resold at a price high enough to cover its cost. When receivables are collected, that asset is reduced and cash is increased.

assets (+)	Cash	150,000	
assets (−)	Accounts Receivable		150,000

Collected $150,000 of receivables.

liabilities (−)	Accounts Payable	80,000	
assets (−)	Cash		80,000

Paid $80,000 of obligations.

The effect on the accounting equation from recording the receivables collected is

Assets   = Liabilities   + Owners' Equity
(increase $150,000;   (no change)   (no change)
decrease $150,000)

After payment of accounts payable, the accounting equation is

Assets   = Liabilities   + Owners' Equity
(decrease $80,000)   (decrease $80,000)   (no change)

To help bring transaction entries into clearer focus, remember that two parties are always involved in exchange transactions on credit. What one buys, the other sells. Therefore, on one set of books (the seller's) a receivable will be recorded; on the books of the buyer a payable will be recorded. The two accounts are directly related. The seller of goods records a receivable and a sale (and simultaneously records an expense for the cost of goods sold and a reduction of inventory). The buyer records receipt of the merchandise as inventory and at the same time records an obligation to pay the seller at some future time. When payment is made, the buyer reduces accounts payable and cash while the seller increases cash and reduces accounts receivable.

Example 2

As the following entry shows, certain obligations require an additional cash payment for interest.

liabilities (−)	Notes Payable	7,000	
expenses (+) [equity (−)]	Interest Expense	800	
assets (−)	Cash		7,800

Paid $7,000 note with interest.

Analysis of this transaction reveals that assets have decreased for two reasons. First, a liability has been paid with cash; second, the interest expense associated with the note payable has also been paid. This relationship will generally be present in most long-term and some short-term liability transactions. Since the interest charge is an expense and decreases owners' equity, the impact of the entry on the accounting equation is

> Assets   = Liabilities   + Owners' Equity
> (decrease $7,800)   (decrease $7,000)   (decrease $800)

Example 3

Corporations that are profitable generally pay dividends to their shareholders. Put simply, dividends represent a distribution to the shareholders of part of the earnings of a company. Dividends are generally paid in cash, but can also be a distribution of stock. Note that cash dividends are required to be paid (that is, they become a liability) only after they are declared payable by the board of directors. The following entries illustrate the declaration and payment of a cash dividend.

owners' equity (−)	Dividends	12,000	
liabilities (+)	Dividends Payable		12,000

Declared a cash dividend of $12,000.

liabilities (−)	Dividends Payable	12,000	
assets (−)	Cash		12,000

Paid a $12,000 cash dividend.

Because dividends reduce the owners' claims against Retained Earnings, they are a reduction of owners' equity. Thus, the declaration and payment of dividends would affect the accounting equation as follows:

Dividend Declaration

> Assets   = Liabilities   + Owners' Equity
> (no change)   (increase $12,000)   (decrease $12,000)

Dividend Payment

Assets   = Liabilities   + Owners' Equity
(decrease $12,000)   (decrease $12,000)   (no change)

The above entries relate to corporations. The entry for a proprietorship or partnership would be

owners' equity (−)   Proprietorship (or Partnership) Withdrawal   12,000
assets (−)   Cash   12,000
                    Withdrew cash from proprietorship (or partnership).

The net effect on the accounting equation is the same. Withdrawals reduce the equity in proprietorships and partnerships, just as dividends reduce the equity in corporations.

CHAPTER REVIEW

The objective of the accounting process is to gather and transform raw data into useful information that measures and communicates the results of business activity. Financial data needed by individuals and external parties are obtained primarily from the accounting information system. Managers need additional information that is supplied by a broader managerial information system. An accounting system may be manual or automated, depending on the organization's requirements. In designing and implementing an accounting system, a company should consider the system's efficiency, the timeliness of the reports it produces, and its overall costs and benefits.

The accounting process is based on the fundamental accounting equation: Assets = Liabilities + Owners' Equity. Revenues and expenses, when closed, have a direct impact on the amount of equity. The double-entry system of accounting assures that the accounting equation will always balance because debit entries require equal credit entries; that is, debits must always equal credits when transactions are properly recorded.

In conducting economic activities, businesses and other types of entities enter into transactions. These transactions form the basis of accounting records. The procedures used in accounting for such transactions are known as the accounting cycle and include

1. Analyzing business documents.
2. Journalizing transactions.
3. Posting journal entries to accounts.
4. Balancing the accounts and preparing a trial balance.
5. Preparing a worksheet.
6. Journalizing and posting adjusting entries.
7. Preparing financial statements.
8. Journalizing and posting closing entries.
9. Balancing the accounts and preparing a post-closing trial balance.

The operating-cycle transactions of a business include acquiring cash, acquiring other assets, producing a product or a service, and collecting cash and paying obligations. Other types of transactions are covered in the next chapter, where we complete our analysis of the accounting cycle and explain the closing process more completely.

KEY TERMS AND CONCEPTS

account (72)
accounting cycle (71)
accounting information
   system (68)
accounting process (67)
automated accounting
   system (68)
business documents (75)
chart of accounts (78)
closing entries (82)
computerized
   accounting system
   (68)

credit (72)
data (67)
debit (72)
expenses (85)
information (67)
internal control (69)
journal (76)
ledger (76)
managerial information
   system (68)
net assets (71)
nominal accounts (82)
operating cycle (69)

post-closing trial
   balance (83)
posting (76)
real accounts (82)
revenues (85)
T-account (72)
transaction analysis
   (66)
trial balance (79)
worksheet (81)

DISCUSSION QUESTIONS

1. What is the basic objective of the accounting process?

2. Distinguish between the terms "data" and "information."

3. Distinguish between a managerial information system and an accounting information system.

4. What are the characteristics of a manual accounting system as compared with an automated accounting system?

5. Are internal controls needed in a computerized accounting system? Explain.

6. How does the operating cycle for a merchandising business differ from that of a manufacturing business? How does a service business differ?

7. In a double-entry system of accounting, why must debits always equal credits?

8. What types of accounts are increased by credits? What types of accounts are increased by debits?

9. List and briefly explain the major steps in the accounting cycle.

10. What purposes do business documents serve?

11. Distinguish between a journal and a ledger.

12. If a trial balance appears to be correct, does that guarantee complete accuracy in the accounting records? Explain.

13. What is the purpose of a worksheet?

14. Distinguish between real and nominal accounts.

15. Why is interpretation considered an important part of the accounting cycle?

16. What is the relationship of revenues and expenses to the basic accounting equation?

17. How are asset and expense accounts similar? How do they differ?

18. Does owners' equity represent cash? Why or why not?

19. Why must nominal accounts be closed at the end of each accounting cycle?

20. Indicate how each of the following transactions affects the accounting equation.
   (a) Purchase of supplies on account
   (b) Payment of wages
   (c) Cash sales
   (d) Payment of monthly utility bills
   (e) Purchase of another company's stock
   (f) Contribution of land by a shareholder
   (g) Payment of a cash dividend
   (h) Sale of goods for less than their cost

EXERCISES

E3-1   Operating Cycle

South African Diamond Store is an exclusive downtown operation that sells only high-quality cut diamonds on a retail basis. To encourage sales, generous credit terms are offered. Outline the operating cycle that is likely to be used in this business.

E3-2   Basic Accounting Equation

For each of the following general business activities, show how the fundamental accounting equation is kept in balance. Example: Borrowed money (increase asset, increase liability).

1. Purchased merchandise for resale by paying cash.
2. Paid off a note.
3. Collected a customer's account.
4. Sold merchandise on credit at a profit.
5. Paid the month's rent.

E3-3   Expanded Accounting Equation

Sofa City, a furniture store, had the following transactions during the year.

1. Purchased inventory on account.
2. Sold merchandise for cash, assuming no profit or loss on the sale.
3. Borrowed money from a bank.
4. Purchased land for cash down payment and a note.
5. Sold stock for cash.
6. Paid salaries for the year.
7. Paid vendor for inventory purchased on account.
8. Sold building for cash and notes receivable at no gain or loss.
9. Paid cash dividends to stockholders.

Using the following column headings, indicate the net effect of each transaction on the accounting equation (+ increase; − decrease; 0 no effect). Transaction 1 above has been completed as an example.

Transaction	Assets	=	Liabilities	+	Owners' Equity
1	+		+		0

E3-4   Journalizing Transactions

For each of the following transactions, make the entry in the company's General Journal.

1. Borrowed $10,000 from a bank. Signed a note to secure the debt.
2. Purchased inventory from a supplier on credit for $8,000.

3. Paid the supplier for the inventory received.
4. Sold inventory that cost $1,200 for $1,500 on credit.
5. Collected the $1,500 from the customer.

E3-5   Posting Journal Entries

For each of the transactions outlined in E3-4, draw T-accounts and post the journal entries to the T-accounts.

E3-6   Trial Balance

The account balances in M Company's ledger as of July 31, 1981, are listed below in alphabetical order. The balance of the Capital Stock account has been omitted. Prepare a trial balance, listing the accounts in proper sequence, and insert the missing amount for Capital Stock.

Accounts Payable	$ 4,300	Miscellaneous Expenses	$ 700
Accounts Receivable	1,000		
Buildings	10,000	Mortgage	
Capital Stock	?	Payable (due 1988)	12,000
Cash	7,000	Prepaid Insurance	800
Dividends	1,500	Retained Earnings	4,500
Equipment	8,000	Salary Expense	5,000
Fees Earned	11,000	Supplies on Hand	300
Insurance Expense	1,800	Utilities Expense	200
Land	9,500		

Hint: The Dividends account has a debit balance prior to being closed to Retained Earnings.

E3-7   Organization of a Worksheet

The trial balance at December 31, 1981, of Num Screwdriver Company is presented below. Use the trial balance to prepare an eight-column worksheet. Leave the "adjusting entries" columns blank.

	Debits	Credits
Sales Revenue		$150,000
Cash	$ 34,500	
Accounts Payable		65,000
Salary Expense	30,000	
Cost of Goods Sold	99,000	
Equipment	25,000	
Prepaid Insurance	2,500	
Accounts Receivable	25,000	
Capital, C. C. Num		43,000
Salaries Payable		5,000
Rent Expense	12,000	
Ending Inventory	35,000	
Totals	$263,000	$263,000

E3-8 Preparation of Financial Statements from a Worksheet

Use the worksheet from E3-7 to prepare an Income Statement for the year ended December 31, 1981, and a Balance Sheet at December 31, 1981, assuming no adjustments were necessary and ignoring income taxes.

E3-9 Real and Nominal Accounts

Classify each of the following accounts as either a real account (R) or a nominal account (N).

1. Cash
2. Sales
3. Accounts Receivable
4. Cost of Goods Sold
5. Prepaid Insurance
6. Capital Stock
7. Retained Earnings
8. Insurance Expense
9. Salaries Payable
10. Depreciation Expense
11. Insurance Premiums Payable
12. Salary Expense
13. Accounts Payable
14. Prepaid Salaries
15. Utility Expense
16. Notes Payable
17. Inventory
18. Property Tax Expense
19. Rent Expense
20. Equipment
21. Interest Payable
22. Income Taxes Payable
23. Land
24. Buildings
25. Office Supplies on Hand
26. Income Tax Expense

E3-10 Classification of Accounts

For each of the accounts listed in E3-9, indicate whether it is an asset (A), a liability (L), or owners' equity (OE). If it is a temporary owners' equity account, indicate whether it is a revenue (R) or an expense (E).

E3-11 Normal Account Balances

Refer to the list of accounts given in E3-9. For each account, indicate whether it would normally have a debit balance or a credit balance.

E3-12 Closing Entries

The balances in some of the accounts of Colin's Cat Food, Inc., are given below. Make all necessary journal entries to close the accounts on December 31, 1981. Use an Income Summary account in the closing process.

Sales Revenue	$96,320
Cost of Goods Sold	46,170
Salary Expense	12,500
Interest Expense	1,000
Utility Expense	1,250
Insurance Expense	1,750
Miscellaneous Expenses	30
Office Supplies Expense	720

E3-13 Journal Entries

Doug Jensen, owner of Doug's Dog Food Company, completed the following business transactions during March 1981. For each transaction, give the entry that Doug would make to record it in the company's General Journal (omit explanations).

March 1 Purchased inventory for $53,000 on credit.
 4 Collected $10,000 from customers as payments on their accounts.
 5 Paid a 3-year insurance premium for $3,000.
 6 Sold dog food that cost $30,000 to customers on account for $40,000.
 10 Paid the month's rent, $1,050.
 15 Paid the electricity bill, $100.
 17 Paid part-time helper's monthly salary of $300.
 20 Collected $33,000 from customers as payments on their accounts.
 22 Paid $53,000 to suppliers.
 25 Paid property taxes of $1,200.
 28 Sold merchandise that cost $20,000 to customers for $30,000 cash.

E3-14 Journalization

The following transactions for Karl's Kookie Company occurred during 1981.

Jan. 5 Purchased a new building for $10,000 down and a note of $25,000.
Feb. 7 Purchased $15,000 of inventory on account.
Mar. 8 Sold inventory costing $2,500 for $3,000 on account.
Mar. 31 Sold capital stock for $25,000.
Apr. 6 Collected $700 of accounts receivable.
Apr. 15 Paid utility bills totaling $120.
July 7 Sold old building for $27,000, receiving $10,000 cash and a $17,000 note (no gain or loss on the sale).
Sept. 1 Paid $2,000 cash dividends to stockholders (use a Dividends account).

Record the transactions above as you would in the General Journal (omit explanations).

E3-15 Compound Journal Entries

Barnes Merchandise Company had the following transactions during 1981. Record these transactions (omit explanations).

1. Paid off a note of $5,000 together with one year's interest at 8%.
2. Sold merchandise that cost $30,000 for a total of $45,000, of which $15,000 cash was received immediately. The other $30,000 will be collected in 30 days.

3. Purchased a machine costing $12,000, paying $2,000 cash and issuing a note for $10,000.
4. Exchanged $2,000 cash and $8,000 in capital stock for a piece of land costing $10,000.
5. Purchased an automobile for $15,000 with $3,000 down and the balance to be paid in one year with interest at 18%.

E3–16 Journal Entries from Ledger Analysis

T-accounts for Cooper Fence, Inc., are shown below. Analyze the accounts and prepare the journal entries from which the accounts were prepared (omit explanations).

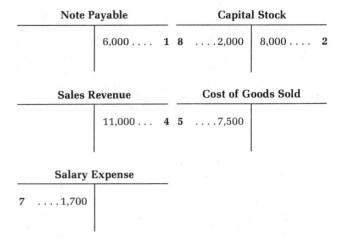

Cash		Accounts Receivable	
1 6,000	4,500 3	4 2,000	1,000 9
2 8,000	3,700 6		
4 9,000	1,700 7		
9 1,000	2,000 8		

Inventory		Accounts Payable	
3 9,000	7,500 5	6 3,700	4,500 3

Note Payable		Capital Stock	
	6,000 1	8 2,000	8,000 2

Sales Revenue		Cost of Goods Sold	
	11,000 ... 4	5 7,500	

Salary Expense	
7 1,700	

E3–17 Accounting for Dividends

The board of directors of Pro Enterprises declared a $40,000 cash dividend on March 8, 1981. The dividends will be paid on March 20. Give the entries to record both the declaration and the payment of the dividends to the stockholders. (Use a Dividends account.)

PROBLEMS

P3–1 Manual Versus Automated Accounting Systems

Alfred Holmes plans to open Holmes Sport Shop. The shop will be a medium-sized operation, specializing primarily in the sale of bicycle and ski equipment. Alfred also plans to service the types of equipment he sells. Although Alfred wants his accounting department to function smoothly and efficiently, he would like to keep expenditures to a minimum. He is considering the following accounting systems.

a. A system in which journal entries are performed manually, but adding machines and calculators are provided to assist in making calculations.

b. A system in which a minicomputer is used to store accounting records and make calculations.

c. A system in which a computer does all of the journalizing and posting of transactions. Results of individual transactions are recorded as input into the computer by a clerk.

Required:

1. List the advantages and disadvantages of each of the proposed accounting systems, keeping in mind the costs and benefits of each. Consider the following: personnel, accuracy, speed, initial purchase price, efficiency.

2. **Interpretive Question** Is the most advanced accounting system always the best one? What factors must be considered when selecting computer equipment in a business?

P3–2 General Pattern of Business Activity

Three businesses that are members of the Midtown Chamber of Commerce are described below.

Sam's Fix-it Shop is a medium-sized business that has a reputation for being able to fix any kind of appliance. Sam maintains an inventory of parts for various household appliances, such as toasters and washing machines. No credit terms are offered.

Dandy Department Store is a large store that has operated in Midtown for many years. In order to encourage sales, management has decided to extend credit terms to customers who have satisfactory credit ratings.

Maxwell Manufacturing Company makes high-quality waffle irons. These products are sold on credit to retail outlets.

Required:

1. For each business, outline the basic operating cycle.

2. Point out any similarities and differences between the business patterns of service, merchandising, and manufacturing businesses.

P3–3 Journalizing Entries and Preparing a Trial Balance

The following data describe the transactions of Jenkins Ice Cream Company in 1981.

a. Jane Jenkins' total ice cream sales for the year 1981 were $78,000, all cash.

b. The cost of the ice cream sold was $25,000.

c. Her electricity expense paid for the year 1981 was $8,000.

d. Jane paid three high school students $100 per month each to help out on a part-time basis.

e. Full-time employees earned and were paid $25,000 during the year.

f. Jane Jenkins withdrew $1,250 a month for 12 months for living expenses.

All expenses were paid in cash, unless otherwise stated. The balances in the company's ledger as of January 1, 1981 were

Cash	$18,000	
Accounts Receivable	200	
Inventory	26,000	
Equipment	3,000	
Salaries Payable		$ 4,000
Accounts Payable		2,500
Notes Payable		20,000
J. Jenkins, Capital		20,700
Totals	$47,200	$47,200

Required:

1. Prepare journal entries to record each of the above transactions (omit explanations).

2. Prepare a trial balance for Jenkins Ice Cream Company at December 31, 1981.

3. **Interpretive Question** If the debit and credit columns of the trial balance are equal, does this mean that no errors have been made in journalizing the transactions? Why or why not?

P3–4 Journalizing Entries from Ledger Analysis

Given below are a number of T-accounts. Transactions have been posted to the accounts and given a letter to indicate each transaction.

Cash					**Accounts Payable**	
a ..100,000	40,000 ... b		k ...10,000		850 ...	f
d .. 500	1,000 ... c		l ... 1,200		10,000 ...	h
i .. 12,400	3,000 ... g				650 ...	j
	10,000 ... k					
	1,200 ... l					

Accounts Receivable			**Capital Stock**	
e ...15,700	12,400 ... i		100,000 ..	a

Delivery Equipment		**Salaries Expense**	
b ...40,000		g 3,000	
h ...10,000			

Delivery Revenues			**Delivery Expenses**	
	500 ... d	f	850	
	15,700 ... e			

Rent Expense		**Heating Expense**	
c 1,000		j 300	

Utilities Expense		**Telephone Expense**	
j 200		j 150	

Required:

Describe the likely event that is being recorded with each entry.

P3–5 Correcting a Trial Balance

The following trial balance for Miami Company as of December 31, 1981, does not balance because of a number of errors.

	Debits	Credits
Cash............................	$ 2,000	
Accounts Receivable	1,500	
Supplies........................	700	
Prepaid Insurance	140	
Equipment (net)	5,700	
Inventory.......................	3,000	
Notes Payable....................		$ 900
Accounts Payable.................		650
Mike Johnson, Capital		13,500
Mike Johnson, Withdrawals	150	
Sales Revenue		9,800
Cost of Goods Sold	5,600	
Wages Expense	3,800	
Rent Expense	520	
Advertising Expense	41	
	$23,151	$24,850

In the process of comparing the trial-balance amounts with the balances in the General Ledger, recomputing the balances of the accounts, and comparing the postings with the journal entries, the following errors were discovered.

a. The balance in the Cash account is understated by $200.

b. A cash disbursement of $210 was posted as a credit to Cash of $120. The debit side of the entry was posted correctly.

c. A debit of $50 to Accounts Receivable was not posted. The $50 credit was posted correctly.

d. An insurance policy acquired at a cost of $120 was posted as a credit to Prepaid Insurance. The cash portion of this entry was recorded correctly.

e. A return of $230 of defective supplies was erroneously posted as a $320 credit to Supplies. The debit side of the entry was recorded correctly.

f. A debit of $100 in Notes Payable was overlooked when determining the balance of the account.

g. The balance of Accounts Payable was overstated by $150.

h. A debit of $200 for a withdrawal by the owner was posted as a credit to the Capital account.

i. The balance of $410 in Advertising Expense was entered as $41 in the trial balance.

j. Miscellaneous Expense, with a balance of $190, was omitted from the trial balance.

k. Cash sales of $400 were overlooked and not recorded. The related cost of goods sold was properly recorded.

Required:
Prepare a corrected trial balance as of December 31, 1981.

P3–6   Unifying Problem: Journalizing, Posting, Preparing a Trial Balance and a Balance Sheet

The following transactions of Alexander Company (a proprietorship) occurred during May 1981.

May 1   Received $100,000 cash from the owner, John Alexander, as an investment in the company.

10   Purchased land and a building for $20,000 cash and a 10-year $40,000 mortgage. The land was appraised at $15,000 and the building at $45,000.

15   Purchased service supplies from Baltzer Company for $5,000 on account.

31   Sold half of the land purchased on May 10 for $7,500, paying $2,500 cash and issuing a 60-day note in the amount of $5,000.

Required:
1. Journalize the above transactions.
2. Post to T-accounts.
3. Prepare a trial balance.
4. Prepare a Balance Sheet.

P3–7   Preparation of a Worksheet and Financial Statements

The year-end trial balance of Carrie's Calculators, Inc., is presented below.

Carrie's Calculators, Inc.

Trial Balance as of December 31, 1981

	Debits	Credits
Cash............................	$ 25,000	
Accounts Receivable	7,500	
Inventory	38,500	
Equipment.......................	26,000	
Accumulated Depreciation—Equip....		$ 8,000
Land............................	85,000	
Prepaid Insurance	500	
Prepaid Rent	1,100	
Notes Payable....................		25,000
Accounts Payable.................		12,500
Salaries Payable		1,500
Capital Stock		50,000
Retained Earnings		61,600
Sales Revenue....................		320,000
Cost of Goods Sold	210,000	
Salary Expense...................	48,000	
Rent Expense	12,000	
Insurance Expense................	3,000	
Property Tax Expense	2,500	
Office Supplies Expense	1,500	
Income Tax Expense	18,000	
Totals	$478,600	$478,600

Required:

1. Prepare a worksheet from the trial balance. Assume that there are no adjusting entries.

2. Using your worksheet, prepare an Income Statement for the year ended December 31, 1981, and a Balance Sheet as of December 31, 1981.

3. **Interpretive Question** In what ways does a worksheet facilitate the preparation of financial statements?

P3−8 Journalizing and Posting

Bertha's Bowling Ball Company had the following transactions in July 1981.

July 1   Issued capital stock for $15,000 cash.
3   Paid a note of $10,000 owed since January 1, 1981, together with interest at 12%.
5   Paid $12,000 to employees for their June 1981 wages.
9   Paid yearly property taxes of $1,800.
17   Purchased $15,000 worth of bowling balls on credit for resale.
21   Sold all of the bowling balls purchased on July 17 for $22,500. Customers paid $7,500 cash. The remainder of the $22,500 was on credit.
25   Paid $14,500 of the accounts payable.
29   Received $10,300 from customers as payments on their accounts.

Required:

1. Journalize each of the transactions for July.

2. Set up T-accounts and post each of the journal entries that you made in (1).

3. **Interpretive Question** If an owner of a business wanted to know at any given moment how much cash or inventory the company had on hand, where would the owner look? Why?

P3−9 Unifying Problem: Journal Entries; T-accounts; Trial Balance

Paperpro Company, a manufacturer of paper products, had the following account balances as of April 30, 1981.

Cash	$ 4,100	
Accounts Receivable	7,900	
Inventory	16,000	
Land	26,000	
Building	24,000	
Furniture	4,000	
Accounts Payable		$12,000
Notes Payable		25,000
Common Stock		30,000
Retained Earnings		15,000
Totals	$82,000	$82,000

During May the company had the following transactions.

May 3   Paid one-half of 4/30/81 accounts payable.
6   Collected all of 4/30/81 accounts receivable.
7   Sold $7,700 of inventory for $6,000 cash and $4,000 on account.
8   Sold one-half the land for $13,000, receiving $8,000 cash plus a note issued for $5,000.
10   Purchased inventory on account, $10,000.
15   Paid installment of $5,000 on note payable.
21   Issued additional capital stock for $2,000 cash.
23   Sold $4,000 of inventory for $7,500 cash.
25   Paid salaries of $2,000.
26   Paid rent of $500.
29   Purchased desk for $500 cash.

Required:

1. Prepare the journal entry for each transaction.

2. Post the entries to T-accounts.

3. Prepare a trial balance as of May 31, 1981.

P3−10   Closing Entries and Accounting for Dividends

The Income Statement for Edwards Eraser Company for the year ended December 31, 1982, is presented below.

Edwards Eraser Company
Income Statement for the Year Ended December 31, 1982

Sales Revenue		$512,000
Less Cost of Goods Sold		363,000
Gross Margin		$149,000
Operating Expenses:		
Salary Expense	$72,000	
Interest Expense	5,250	
Office Supplies Expense	3,820	
Insurance Expense	4,930	
Property Tax Expense	11,200	
Total Operating Expenses		97,200
Net Income		$ 51,800

Dividends of $40,000 were declared by the board of directors on December 30, 1982.

Required:

1. Give the entries required on December 31, 1982, to properly close the nominal accounts using an Income Summary account.

2. Give the entry required to record the declaration of dividends by the board of directors.

3. **Interpretive Question** Is the Dividend account closed? If so, to which account?

P3—11 Unifying Problem: Analysis and Correction of Errors

At the end of November 1981, the General Ledger of Maynard Pool Supply Company showed the following amounts.

Assets	$64,250
Liabilities..............................	28,800
Owners' Equity	62,000

The company's bookkeeper is new on the job and does not have a lot of accounting experience. Because he has made numerous errors, total assets do not equal liabilities plus owners' equity. The following is a list of errors made.

a. Inventory that cost $21,000 was sold, but the entry to record cost of goods sold was not made.

b. Sales of $12,100 were posted to the General Ledger as $21,100.

c. $12,500 of inventory was purchased on account and received before the end of November, but no entry to record the purchase was made until December.

d. November salaries payable of $2,500 were not recorded until paid in December.

e. Common stock was sold for $18,500 and credited to Accounts Payable.

f. Inventory purchased for $31,050 was incorrectly posted to the asset account as $13,500.

Required:
Determine the correct balances of assets, liabilities, and stockholders' equity.

P3—12   Unifying Problem: The Accounting Cycle

The post-closing trial balance of Simson Company at December 31, 1980, is presented below.

Simson Company
Post-Closing Trial Balance at December 31, 1980

	Debits	Credits
Cash............................	$ 15,000	
Accounts Receivable	20,000	
Inventory........................	30,000	
Land............................	25,000	
Buildings	75,000	
Equipment.......................	50,000	
Accounts Payable..................		$ 25,000
Notes Payable....................		35,000
Capital Stock		100,000
Retained Earnings		55,000
Totals	$215,000	$215,000

During 1981, the company had the following transactions.

a. Inventory purchases were $80,000, all on credit.

b. An additional $10,000 of capital stock was issued.

c. Merchandise that cost $100,000 was sold for $180,000. Of the $180,000, $100,000 were credit sales; the balance were cash sales.

d. The notes were paid, including $7,000 interest.

e. $105,000 was collected from customers.

f. $95,000 was paid to reduce accounts payable.

g. Salary expenses were $30,000, all paid in cash.

h. A $10,000 cash dividend was declared and paid (use a Dividends account).

Required:

1. Prepare journal entries to record each of the 1981 transactions.

2. Set up T-accounts with the proper balances at January 1, 1981, and post the journal entries to the T-accounts.

3. Prepare a worksheet beginning with a trial balance as of December 31, 1981. Assume no adjusting entries.

4. Using your worksheet, prepare an Income Statement for the year ended December 31, 1981, and a Balance Sheet as of that date.

5. Prepare the entries necessary to close the nominal and dividend accounts.

6. Post the closing entries to the ledger accounts and prepare a post-closing trial balance at December 31, 1981.

CHAPTER 4

Completing the Accounting Cycle

THIS CHAPTER EXPLAINS: Some important additional characteristics of the accounting model.

The adjustments required to complete the accounting cycle.

How to use a worksheet.

The closing process in the accounting cycle.

In Chapter 3 we explained transaction analysis—the process of analyzing, recording, summarizing, and reporting financial information. The emphasis was on operating-cycle transactions and the first four steps of the accounting cycle: (1) analyzing business documents, (2) journalizing transactions, (3) posting journal entries, and (4) balancing the accounts and preparing a trial balance. In this chapter we discuss the analyses and adjustments required to complete the accounting cycle. Of particular importance are the adjusting and closing entries, and the rationale for making them. The use of a worksheet is also highlighted.

Characteristics of the Accounting Model—Continued

In Chapter 1 we described several characteristics of the accounting model. These include the assumptions that an accounting entity is a separate economic unit and a going concern, that entities enter into arm's-length transactions which become the basis for accounting entries, and that the dollar is the common unit used in the United States to measure and communicate the results of business transactions.

Another characteristic of the accounting model is that it is essential to report accounting information on a timely basis. To be useful, information must be received in time to be taken into account in making decisions. Thus, the financial statements of a business entity need to be issued periodically so that interested parties can review the company's status and progress on a continuing, timely basis. This basic accounting assumption is called the time-period assumption, or the periodicity concept. It has as its basis the idea that an accounting entity's life can be divided into distinct and regular reporting periods, such as a year or a quarter or a month. The importance of periodic reporting and its relationship to accrual accounting are described below.

time-period assumption (periodicity concept) *the idea that the life of a business is divided into distinct and relatively short time periods so that accounting information can be timely*

PERIODIC REPORTING

Current owners, prospective investors, bankers, and others need to know periodically what economic events have taken place in a company and whether those events have had a positive or a negative impact. In brief, they need to know the financial position of the entity (from the Balance Sheet), significant changes in that financial position (from the Statement of Changes in Financial Position), and the relative success or failure of current operations (from the Income Statement).

The financial picture of an entity, its success or failure in meeting its economic objectives, cannot really be complete until the "life" of a business is over. However, managers, owners, creditors, and others cannot wait 10, 20 or 100 years to receive an exact accounting of a business. They must have timely information in order to make ongoing economic judgments. Accordingly, the life of an enterprise is divided into distinct accounting periods, each generally covering 12 months or less. The 12-month accounting period is referred to as the fiscal year. When an entity closes its books on December 31, it is said to be reporting on a calendar year basis.

fiscal year *an entity's reporting year covering a 12-month accounting period*

calendar year *an entity's reporting year ending on December 31 and covering 12 months*

Most corporations, and even many small companies, issue a report to shareholders as of a fiscal year-end. This annual report includes the primary financial statements (the Balance Sheet, Income Statement, and Statement of Changes in Financial Position) and other financial data, such as a 5-year summary of operations. Other financial reports are prepared more frequently, perhaps quarterly or monthly. Indeed, some reports, such as sales reports for use by management, may be prepared on a daily basis.

Although periodic reporting is vital to a firm's success, such frequency of reporting forces accountants to use tentative data that are based on judgments and estimates. As you will see, the shorter the reporting period (for example, a month instead of a year), the less exact are the measurements of assets and liabilities and the recognition of revenues and expenses. Ideally, accounting judgments are carefully made and estimates are based on reliable evidence. Even so, the limitations of accounting reports should be recognized.

ACCRUAL ACCOUNTING

cash-basis accounting *a system of accounting in which transactions are recorded, and revenues and expenses are recognized, only when payment is received or made*

In some small businesses, entries are recorded, and revenues and expenses are recognized, only when payment is received or made. This is referred to as cash-basis accounting. Most people prepare their income tax returns on a cash basis.

accrual-basis accounting *a system of accounting in which revenues and expenses are recorded as they are earned and incurred, not necessarily when payment is received or made*

On a cash basis, income is cash receipts during the period less cash disbursements of the period. For most accounting purposes, however, accrual-basis accounting is more appropriate. This important characteristic of the traditional accounting model simply means that revenues are recognized when earned without regard to when payment is received, and expenses are recorded as incurred without regard to when they are paid. For example, under accrual accounting, if XYZ Company sold $80,000 of goods in 1981, but did not receive the cash proceeds until 1982, the $80,000 would still be recognized as revenue in 1981, when it was earned. The same is true of expenses; they are recognized when incurred, not when paid. Therefore, income under accrual accounting is equal to earned revenues minus incurred expenses as a measurement of the change in net assets. It is not revenues minus expenses in the sense of cash receipts less cash disbursements.

The concept of accrual accounting is closely related to the time-period assumption. That is, not until the life of a business has been divided into time periods does it become necessary for revenues and expenses to be properly assigned to each period. In determining income on an accrual basis, only those revenues that have actually been earned during a period are reported. This is sometimes referred to as the revenue recognition principle, or realization principle. Similarly, all expenses incurred to generate those revenues should be associated with that same period. This is called the matching principle. It is this matching process that determines income when accrual-basis accounting is used.

revenue recognition principle *the idea that revenues should be recorded when (1) the earnings process has been substantially completed, and (2) an exchange has taken place*

matching principle *the idea that all costs and expenses incurred in generating revenues must be recognized in the same reporting period as the related revenues*

For revenues to be recognized in the accounting records, two main criteria have to be met.

1. The earnings process must be substantially complete, which generally means that a sale has been made or services have been performed.
2. An exchange must have taken place.

The first criterion ensures that the parties to the transaction have fulfilled their commitment, or are formally obligated to do so. For example, a company generally records sales revenues when goods are shipped or when services are performed. If a buyer were to pay in advance for goods not yet received, the seller should not record those payments as revenues until the goods are made available to the buyer. The second criterion ensures that there is objective evidence by which to measure the amount of revenue involved. The subject of revenue recognition is an important one and is discussed more completely in later chapters.

Once a company determines which revenues should be recognized during a period, all expenses incurred to generate those revenues should also be associated, or matched, with that period. Sometimes, however, expenses cannot be associated with particular revenues, so they have to be assigned according to particular periods of time. As an example, the exact amount of electricity used to produce a particular product generally cannot be determined, but the amount used for a month or a year is known and can be matched to the revenues earned during that same period. This recognition and matching process, as shown in Exhibit 4–1, determines the income reported on the Income Statement.

EXHIBIT 4–1   **Determining Accrual Income**

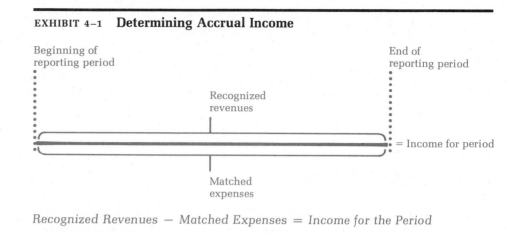

Recognized Revenues — Matched Expenses = Income for the Period

Not only is accrual-basis accounting important for proper income determination, it is also needed for the assignment of appropriate Balance Sheet values at a particular date. This is illustrated by the time line in Exhibit 4–2. As the time line shows, and as we discussed in Chapter 2, at the end of each accounting period a Balance Sheet is prepared *as of* that date and an Income Statement is prepared for the period ending *on* that date. Before any data can be reported in the financial statements, however, it is necessary to make sure that all accounts have appropriate balances and that all revenues and expenses have been properly recognized. This is accomplished by making adjusting entries. For example, accounts that involve estimates of future amounts may need adjustment at the end of a period on the basis of existing facts or more current estimates. Similarly, earned revenues and incurred expenses for which no journal entries have been made must be recognized prior to the preparation of the financial reports. Thus, in order to report all asset, liability, and owners' equity amounts properly, and to recognize all revenues and expenses for the period on an accrual basis, adjustments are required at the end of each accounting period.

adjusting entries *entries required at the end of each accounting period to recognize on an accrual basis revenues and expenses for the period and to report proper amounts for assets, liabilities, and owners' equity accounts*

EXHIBIT 4–2   **Relationship Between Income Statements and Balance Sheets**

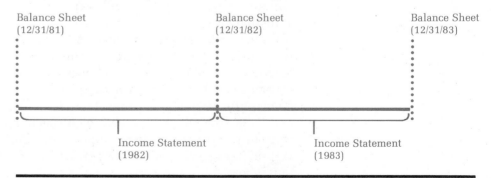

TO SUMMARIZE   Users of accounting information need timely, periodic financial reports in order to make appropriate decisions. The recognition and matching principles provide guidelines for assigning the appropriate amounts of revenues and expenses to each accounting period. At the end of each period, some accounts must be adjusted so that the Balance Sheet will reflect appropriate account balances and the Income Statement will show a proper measurement of earnings.

Adjusting Entries

In Chapter 3 we indicated that step 5 of the accounting cycle is the preparation of a worksheet, with adjusting entries being step 6. If a worksheet is used in preparing the periodic financial statements, the normal order followed in accounting practice is to journalize and post the adjusting entries after the worksheet has been completed and the financial statements prepared. We will discuss steps 5 and 6 in reverse order, however, because you need to understand adjusting entries before you can use them on a worksheet.

As we have just noted, adjusting entries are made at the end of each accounting period, after the trial balance has been taken and the financial statements prepared but before the books are closed. For many accounts, adjusting entries provide periodic updating. Adjusting entries are recorded in the General Journal and posted to the accounts in the General Ledger in the same manner as other journal entries. If a worksheet is used, the entries are included in the adjustments columns and carried forward to the appropriate columns on the Income Statement and the Balance Sheet. If a worksheet is not used, financial statements are prepared directly from the adjusted accounts in the General Ledger.

The accounts that generally need adjustments may be classified under four headings.

1. Unrecorded revenues.
2. Unrecorded expenses.
3. Unearned revenues.
4. Prepaid expenses.

Before illustrating and discussing the categories of accounts that usually require adjustments, we will explain the general process of making adjusting entries. Remember that the basic purpose of adjustments is to periodically bring certain account balances to their correct amounts. In this way, the Income Statement will reflect appropriate operating results for the period and the Balance Sheet will show the proper financial status at the end of the period. To accomplish this requires a three-step analysis: (1) identify the original entries, (2) determine the correct account balances, and (3) determine what adjusting entries are needed to bring the amounts originally recorded to their appropriate balances. T-accounts are often helpful in analyzing adjusting entries and will be used in the illustrations that follow.

UNRECORDED REVENUES

unrecorded revenues and accrued assets   *revenues not previously recognized, and companion receivable accounts, earned during a period but not received by the end of that period*

Those revenue items that have not been collected or recorded but were earned during a particular period (that is, those that have met the revenue recognition criteria) are referred to as <u>unrecorded revenues</u> and the companion receivable accounts as <u>accrued assets</u>. Even though cash payments have not been received, the revenues are earned and should be reported as such. Thus, an adjustment is required at the end of an accounting period to recognize the actual revenues earned and to report the corresponding receivables as assets.

To illustrate, we will assume that Alfie's, Inc., reports on a calendar year basis and has determined the following on December 31, 1981.

1. Rental revenues of $500 earned in 1981 will not be received until January 10, 1982.

2. Interest revenue of $400 has been earned on a $24,000 note. The interest rate is 10 percent with interest payments due April 30 and October 31 of each year.

Following the three-step analysis for item 1, we observe that no original entry has been made. The accounts involved, in T-account form, and the correct balances as of December 31, 1981, are shown below.

	Accrued Rent Receivable		Rental Revenue	
Original Entry	none			none
Correct Balances (12/31/81)	500			500

Therefore, the adjusting journal entry required at December 31 to reflect the accounts properly would be

Adjusting Entry

Accrued Rent Receivable	500	
Rental Revenue		500

To record accrual of rent not yet received.

Item 2 has not yet been recorded either. Unless an adjusting entry is made, the applicable revenue and asset accounts will be understated and the resulting financial statements will not be accurate. The appropriate adjusting entry may be determined by following the same process as for item 1, as follows:

	Accrued Interest Receivable		Interest Revenue	
Original Entry	none			none
Correct Balances (12/31/81)	400			400

The proper adjusting entry is

Adjusting Entry

Accrued Interest Receivable   400
   Interest Revenue   400

To record accrual of interest on a $24,000 note at 10%, payments due April 30 and October 31: $24,000 × 10% = $2,400 ÷ 12 = $200 × 2 months (November, December) = $400.

After the adjusting entries are journalized and posted, the receivables appear as assets on the Balance Sheet, and the rent and interest revenues are reported on the Income Statement. Through the adjusting entries, the accounts are properly stated and revenues are appropriately reported in the year earned.

UNRECORDED EXPENSES

Those expenses incurred in a particular period but not recorded during that time are referred to as unrecorded expenses and their companion payable accounts are called accrued liabilities. When goods or services are received and used, even though they have not yet been paid for, valid expenses have been incurred. These expenses should be recorded in the period of incurrence, along with the corresponding obligations, or liabilities, to pay for the goods or services. Thus, adjusting entries are required at the end of an accounting period to recognize any unrecorded expenses in the proper period of incurrence and to accrue the corresponding liabilities. If such adjustments were not made, the income for the period would be overstated because of the omission of certain expenses, and the liabilities on the Balance Sheet would be understated.

Again to illustrate, we will assume that on December 31, 1981, the following information for Alfie's, Inc., has been determined.

1. Salaries of $1,500 earned by employees will not be paid until January 3, 1982.

2. Interest expense of $300 is owed on a bank loan of $12,000. The interest rate is 10 percent and payments are due twice a year, March 31 and September 30.

To represent its financial position and earnings accurately, Alfie's has to record the impact of these events in the accounts, even though cash transactions have not yet occurred. The analysis and resulting adjusting journal entries required at year-end for item 1 would be

unrecorded expenses and accrued liabilities *expenses not previously recognized, and companion payable accounts, incurred during a period but not paid for by the end of that period*

	Salaries Expense		Accrued Salaries Payable	
Original Entry	none		none	
Correct Balances (12/31/81)	1,500		1,500	

Adjusting Entry

Salaries Expense   1,500

    Accrued Salaries Payable.   1,500

To record accrual of salaries not yet paid.

Item 2 would require the following.

	Interest Expense		Accrued Interest Payable
Original Entry	none		none
Correct Balances (12/31/81)	300		300

Adjusting Entry

Interest Expense   300

    Accrued Interest Payable   300

To record interest accrual on a bank loan of $12,000 at 10% = $1,200 ÷ 12 = $100 × 3 months (October, November, December) = $300.

The salaries and interest expenses would be reflected on the Income Statement for the year ended December 31, and the accrued payables—salaries and interest—would be shown on the Balance Sheet as of December 31. Because of the adjusting entries, both statements would more accurately reflect the financial situation of Alfie's, Inc.

UNEARNED REVENUES

unearned revenues   *amounts received before they have been earned*

Amounts received in advance of the actual earning of revenue are known as <u>unearned revenues</u>. They arise when customers pay in advance of the receipt of goods or services. For example, a building contractor may require a deposit before proceeding to construct a house. Upon receipt of the deposit, the contractor has unearned revenue; that is, he must construct the house to earn the revenue. If he does not build the house, he would be obligated to repay the deposit.

The analysis that we have used for unrecorded revenues and expenses applies equally well to the adjustments for unearned revenues and prepaid expenses to be discussed next. The proper amounts of revenues and expenses must be recognized during the period and the appropriate liability and asset account balances should be shown on the Balance Sheet. There is one difference which is sometimes confusing. For unrecorded items there is no original entry and so, in determining the adjustments, the correct year-end balance becomes the amount of the adjusting entry. For unearned revenues and prepaid expenses, this is not the case. An original entry has been made. Therefore, the amount of the adjusting entry is the difference between what the correct balance should be and the original entry.

To illustrate the adjustments for unearned revenues, we will assume the following about Alfie's, Inc.

1. On June 1, a tenant pays $3,600 for rent one year in advance.

2. On October 1, a client pays $1,800 as consulting fees for regular monthly services to be rendered by Alfie's during the next 12 months.

3. As before, Alfie's books are closed on December 31.

In considering the $3,600 of rent received in advance, we need to make one further assumption concerning how the original entry was recorded. It could have been recorded as a debit to Cash and a credit to Rental Revenue, showing the total amount of revenue that will eventually be earned. This is sometimes called the <u>revenue approach</u>. On the other hand, the original entry could have been made as a debit to Cash and a credit to Unearned Rent, or Rent Received in Advance, showing the actual liability that currently exists. Technically, until the revenue is earned by allowing the tenant to use the facility, the amount of rent received in advance is a liability. Thus, this approach is referred to as the <u>liability approach</u>. The amount of the adjusting entry will differ, depending on which approach is taken in recording the original entry. However, the end result—the correct balances—will be the same after the adjusting entry is journalized and posted. We will illustrate both the revenue and liability approaches, so you can see that the final results are identical.

revenue approach *an accounting procedure whereby unearned revenues are originally credited to a revenue account, even though the amount is not yet earned; a year-end adjustment is required to record the revenue actually earned during the period and to establish a corresponding liability for the amount not earned at year-end*

liability approach *an accounting procedure whereby unearned revenues are originally credited to a liability account; a year-end adjust-ment is required to record the revenue earned during that period and to reduce the companion liability account*

Original Entries to Revenue Accounts (Revenue Approach)

In using the revenue approach, the entry to record the $3,600 of rental revenue received in advance would be

```
June 1
Cash ......................................     3,600
   Rental Revenue ....................................         3,600
```
Received 12 months' rent in advance: $300 × 12 = $3,600.

At year-end the correct balances would determine the appropriate amount of the adjusting entry as follows:

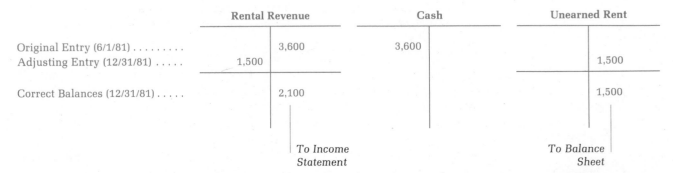

	Rental Revenue	Cash	Unearned Rent
Original Entry (6/1/81)	3,600	3,600	
Adjusting Entry (12/31/81)	1,500		1,500
Correct Balances (12/31/81)	2,100		1,500
	To Income Statement		To Balance Sheet

Of the $3,600 received on June 1, Alfie has earned $2,100; that is, by December 31, seven months of rental revenue, at $300 per month, should be shown as earned revenue on the Income Statement. The difference—in this case, $1,500—should be shown on the Balance Sheet as a liability: Unearned Rent or Rent Received in Advance. The adjusting entry required to bring the accounts to their proper balances would be

Adjusting Entry

Rental Revenue	1,500	
Unearned Rent		1,500

To adjust for proper rental revenue earned for 7 months and to record the remaining obligation due: $300 × 5 = $1,500.

Again assuming that the original entry was to a revenue account, the analysis of the consulting transaction would be the same as for the rental transaction. The entries may be summarized in T-accounts as follows:

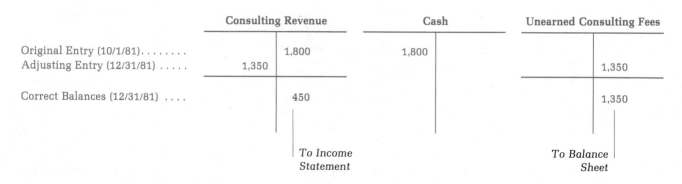

The amount of consulting revenue earned by December 31 is $450 ($150 per month × 3 months) and that amount should be shown on the Income Statement. The difference of $1,350 is to be earned during the next nine months and should be reported on the Balance Sheet as an existing liability. The actual adjusting entry, then, would be

Adjusting Entry

Consulting Revenue........................	1,350	
Unearned Consulting Fees.............................		1,350

To adjust for proper consulting revenue earned for 3 months and to record the remaining obligation due: $1,800 ÷ 12 = $150 × 9 months = $1,350.

Original Entries to Liability Accounts (Liability Approach)

Assuming that the entries for the two previous transactions were originally made to liability accounts rather than to revenue accounts, the amounts required for the year-end adjustments would be different, as shown below. However, note that the process of analysis and the end result are exactly the same.

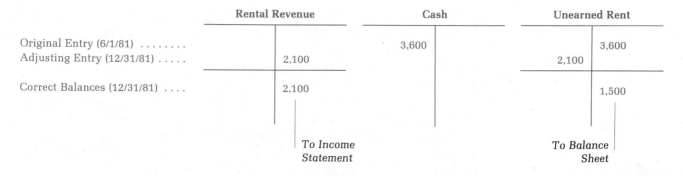

In the example, the original entry was made to Unearned Rent, a liability account.

June 1
Cash 3,600
   Unearned Rent 3,600
Received 12 months' rent in advance: $300 × 12 = $3,600.

Then, at year-end, an adjusting entry is required to bring the accounts to their correct balances. Of the total $3,600 received in advance, $2,100 has now been earned and should be so reported on the Income Statement. The difference, $1,500, is still a liability and must be reported on the Balance Sheet. The adjusting entry would be

Adjusting Entry

Unearned Rent 2,100
   Rental Revenue 2,100
To establish rental revenue for 7 months to reduce the liability amount: $300 × 7 months = $2,100.

The same process of analysis can be used for the consulting transaction. The entries are summarized in T-account form as follows:

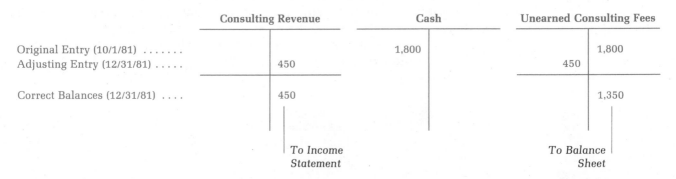

The adjusting entry—debiting Unearned Consulting Fees and crediting Consulting Revenue—is needed to make the account balances current. After the adjusting entry is journalized and posted, the proper amount of consulting revenue ($150 × 3 months, or $450) will be shown on the Income Statement. The liability, Unearned Consulting Fees or Consulting Fees Received in Advance, will also be reported at its correct amount ($1,350, or $1,800 ÷ 12 = $150 × 9 months' interest yet to be earned).

Liability Approach Versus Revenue Approach

The liability approach recognizes that the seller is obligated to either return the asset received (usually cash) or deliver the goods or services promised. It has theoretical merit because, until the revenue is earned, the amount of revenue received in advance is technically a liability and should be accounted for as such. The revenue approach is justified on the grounds of expediency and on the assumption that the revenue will be earned during the coming period. Regardless of which approach is used, the final result will be the same. Therefore, the important concept to master is the analysis process for adjusting entries. First, determine what original entries have been made, if any. Second, analyze the accounts to determine the correct end-of-year balances. Third, make the adjusting entries needed to bring the accounts up-to-date, that is, from the original entry amounts to the correct balances as of the end of the year.

PREPAID EXPENSES

prepaid expenses *payments made in advance for items normally charged to expense*

Payments made in advance for items normally charged to expense are known as prepaid expenses. An example would be the payment of an insurance premium for three years. Theoretically, every resource acquisition is an asset, at least temporarily. Thus, the entry to record an advance payment should be a debit to an asset (Prepaid Expense) account and a credit to Cash, showing the exchange of cash for another asset.

Business enterprises do not acquire expenses. Expenses emerge as benefits are received from the assets acquired. Therefore, an expense is a "used-up" asset, a resource whose service potential has been at least partly realized. However, when it is apparent that the benefits of an expenditure will all be received within the current accounting period, the expenditure is usually recorded initially as an expense. Thus, a payment in advance, as a matter of expediency, may be initially recorded as an expense instead of as an asset.

asset approach *an accounting procedure whereby prepaid expenses are originally debited to an asset account; a year-end adjustment is required to record the asset value used up as an expense of the period, and to adjust the related asset account to its proper balance*

expense approach *an accounting procedure whereby prepaid expenses are originally debited to an expense account, even though future benefits exist; a year-end adjustment is required to record the actual expense incurred during the period and to establish a companion asset account equal to remaining future benefits*

As with unearned revenues, the nature of the adjusting entries for prepaid expenses at the end of a period will depend on how the original prepayment was recorded—as an asset (the asset approach) or as an expense (the expense approach). If adjusting entries are analyzed and recorded correctly, regardless of which approach is used, the final result will be the same—that is, accurate recognition of expenses on the Income Statement and proper reporting of assets on the Balance Sheet.

If the expense approach is used for the original entry, the adjusting entry will reduce the expense to a proper amount and establish a companion asset account. If the original entry is to an asset account, the adjusting entry reduces the asset to an amount that reflects its remaining future benefit, and at the same time recognizes the actual expense for the period. The objective of these adjustments is to recognize the complete or partial expiration of an asset's ability to help generate future revenues.

To illustrate, we will assume that on September 1, 1981, Alfie's, Inc., rents office space in a building. The rent is $150 a month, and Alfie's is required to pay 6 months' rent in advance. Then, on November 1, Alfie's purchases a 2-year insurance policy, paying a $2,400 premium. These items can be recorded as expenses or as assets (prepaid expenses). The type of adjusting entry required will depend on whether the asset or expense approach is used for the original entry. However, the process of analysis is the same. Assuming a calendar year-end, the entries for both alternatives are illustrated below.

Original Entries to Expense Accounts (Expense Approach)

In applying the expense approach, the original entry to record the $900 advance payment of rent expense would be

September 1
Rent Expense   900
  Cash   900
Paid 6 months' rent in advance: 6 × $150 = $900.

At December 31, Alfie's must recognize that not all of the $900 is an expense of this accounting period. A portion of the 6-month advance payment—2 months' worth to be exact—will benefit the company during the next accounting period and should be reported as an asset: Prepaid Rent or Rent Paid in Advance. The benefit of 4 months' worth of the $900 prepayment has been received and the rent is properly recognized as an expense of the current period. The T-accounts shown below reflect this information and identify the proper adjusting entry to be made.

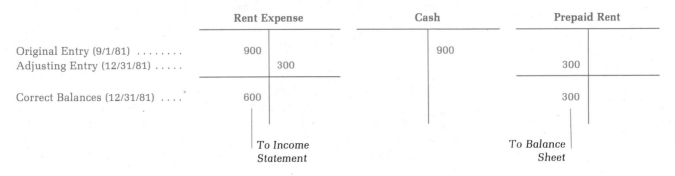

Original Entry (9/1/81) . . . .
Adjusting Entry (12/31/81) . . . . .
Correct Balances (12/31/81) . . . .

As journalized, the adjusting entry would be

Adjusting Entry

Prepaid Rent   300
  Rent Expense   300
To adjust for proper rent expense for 4 months and record the remaining asset amount: 2 × $150 = $300.

After the adjustment, $600 would be properly shown as an expense on the Income Statement and $300 would be carried forward to the next period as an asset on the Balance Sheet.

The entries and analysis for the insurance transaction are similar. The original prepayment entry is debited to Insurance Expense. At year-end, an adjustment must be made to reflect the proper insurance expense for the period and the amount of prepaid insurance to be shown on the Balance Sheet as an asset. The entries, in T-account form, are

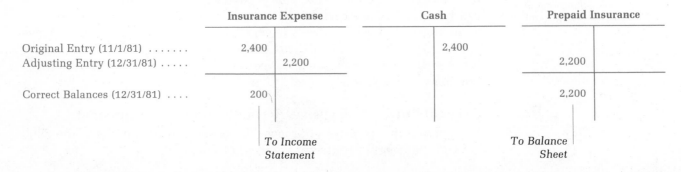

Original Entry (11/1/81) . . . .
Adjusting Entry (12/31/81) . . . . .
Correct Balances (12/31/81) . . . .

Thus, the adjusting entry would update the accounts so that 2 months' worth of insurance expense ($200) would be reported on the Income Statement. The remaining 22 months' worth of insurance benefits ($2,400 ÷ 24 months = $100 × 22 = $2,200) would be shown as an asset, Prepaid Insurance, on the Balance Sheet.

Original Entries to Asset Accounts (Asset Approach)

In using the asset approach, the prepayment of rent would have been recorded originally as

September 1
Prepaid Rent.............................. 900
  Cash 900
Paid 6 months' rent in advance: 6 × $150 = $900.

At year-end, only the amount of assets that still offers future benefits to the company should be reported on the Balance Sheet. Thus, an adjustment is required to reduce the Prepaid Rent account and to establish the amount of rent expense for the period. In this example, 4 months' rent has been used, so the rent expense should be $600 (4 months at $150 a month) and the balance in the asset account should be $300 (2 months' rent at $150 per month). As shown in the T-accounts, the adjusting entries would be

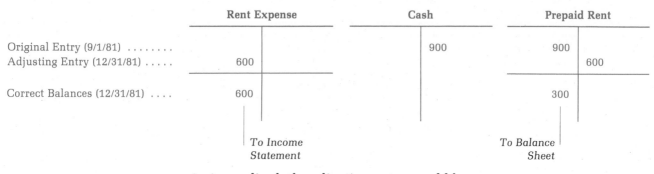

As journalized, the adjusting entry would be

Adjusting Entry

Rent Expense 600
  Prepaid Rent 600
To adjust rent expense for 4 months to the proper asset amount: 4 × $150 = $600.

The analysis of the insurance transaction under the asset approach is the same as for prepaid rent. Therefore, it will not be explained in detail. The entries are summarized in T-account form as follows:

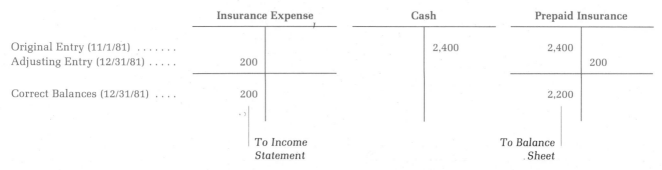

Under either the asset or the expense approach, the objective remains: to report the proper amount of insurance expense on the Income Statement (2 months × \$100 = \$200) and to show the appropriate balance in the asset account on the Balance Sheet (22 months of insurance protection remaining × \$100 = \$2,200).

TO SUMMARIZE   In order to present financial statements that report accurately the financial position and the results of operations on an accrual basis and for specific periods of time, adjusting entries must be made. The four main categories of adjustments are unrecorded revenues, unrecorded expenses, unearned revenues, and prepaid expenses. In analyzing accounts at the end of an accounting cycle adjusting entries are made in order to increase or decrease any account to recognize all earned revenues and all incurred expenses, and to report the proper balances in the asset, liability, and owners' equity accounts. This requires a three-step analysis: (1) identifying the original entries; (2) determining the correct year-end balances; and (3) preparing adjusting entries, to bring the original account balances to their proper end-of-year amounts. Exhibit 4–3 summarizes these adjustments and the Supplement to this chapter discusses reversing entries and other means of disposing of adjusting entry amouunts.

EXHIBIT 4–3   **Summary of Adjustments**

Type of Adjusting Entry	Result of Adjusting Entry	Where Item Is Included on Financial Statements
Unrecorded revenue/accrued asset	Increases asset (DR) Increases revenue (CR)	Asset on Balance Sheet Revenue on Income Statement
Unrecorded expense/accrued liability	Increases expense (DR) Increases liability (CR)	Expense on Income Statement Liability on Balance Sheet
Unearned revenue		
Initially recorded as a revenue	Reduces revenue (DR)	Net amount as revenue on Income Statement
	Increases liability (CR)	Total amount as liability on Balance Sheet
Initially recorded as a liability	Reduces liability (DR)	Net amount as liability on Balance Sheet
	Increases revenue (CR)	Total amount as revenue on Income Statement
Prepaid expense		
Initially recorded as an expense	Increases asset (DR)	Total amount as asset on Balance Sheet
	Reduces expense (CR)	Net amount as expense on Income Statement
Initially recorded as an asset	Increases expense (DR)	Total amount as expense on Income Statement
	Reduces asset (CR)	Net amount as asset on Balance Sheet

Using a Worksheet

worksheet *a columnar schedule used to conveniently summarize accounting data*

trial balance *a listing of all account balances; provides a means of testing whether debits equal credits for all accounts*

As we explained in Chapter 3, accountants often use a worksheet to facilitate the preparation of financial statements. Columns (1) and (2) of a worksheet usually list the account balances prior to adjustments. This set of columns contains the unadjusted trial balance. Columns (3) and (4) are for adjusting entries. Columns (5) through (8) are used for extending the unadjusted trial balance figure, plus or minus adjustments, into the appropriate set of financial statement columns. Revenue and expense accounts are extended into the Income Statement columns, and asset, liability, and owners' equity accounts are extended into the Balance Sheet columns. There are no columns for the Statement of Changes in Financial Position (Funds Statement). This statement is a summary of elements already included on the Balance Sheet and Income Statement. However, other columns can be added; for example, an adjusted trial balance set of columns can be included. The exact form of a worksheet is flexible and should reflect the needs of the business.

To illustrate the use of a worksheet, we will examine the operating activities of Yang Company for one month. To make the example realistic, we have included some transactions and adjustments that will be explained in later chapters. However, our present purpose is to show you how a worksheet is used. Do not be concerned if you do not understand every adjustment. The worksheet for Yang Company, Exhibit 4–4, is based on the following transactions (note that the company was organized on January 1, 1981).

January	1	Issued capital stock for cash, $20,000.
	2	Bought a truck for $4,800 cash.
	3	Received 6 months' rental revenue from tenant, $600.
	4	Paid $480 for a 1-year insurance policy.
	8	Purchased $250 of office supplies for cash.
	10	Purchased inventory for $10,000 on account.
	14	Sold $8,000 of inventory for $15,000 on account.
	18	Collected $12,000 cash from customers' accounts receivable.
	20	Paid $7,000 cash for inventories bought on January 10.
	23	Paid $1,500 for sales representatives' salaries.
	27	Purchased $14,000 of inventory for cash.
	31	Sold $13,000 of inventory for cash, $19,700.

After all of these transactions have been journalized and posted, the balances in the accounts can be listed in the first two columns of the worksheet as the unadjusted trial balance. Assuming an accounting period of one month, the following data are applicable to the necessary adjusting entries at January 31.

(a) Accrued sales salaries, $700.

(b) Expired insurance, $40.

(c) Monthly rental revenue earned, $100.

(d) Supplies on hand, $110.

(e) Depreciation rate, 10% a year.

EXHIBIT 4–4   Yang Company
Worksheet for the Month Ended January 31, 1981

Account Titles	Trial Balance Debit	Trial Balance Credit	Adjustments Debit	Adjustments Credit
Cash	24270			
Capital Stock		20000		
Truck	4800			
Rent Received in Advance		600	(c) 100	
Prepaid Insurance	480			(b) 40
Office Supplies	250			(d) 140
Inventory	3000			
Accounts Payable		3000		
Accounts Receivable	3000			
Sales		34700		
Cost of Goods Sold	21000			
Salaries Expense	1500		(a) 700	
	58300	58300		
Accrued Salaries Payable				(a) 700
Insurance Expense			(b) 40	
Rental Revenue				(c) 100
Supplies Expense			(d) 140	
Depreciation			(e) 40	
Accumulated Depreciation—Truck				(e) 40
			1020	1020
Net Income (to balance)				

Adjustments:
(a) Accrued Salaries, $700
(b) Insurance Expense, $40 ($480 ÷ 12 = $40 a month)
(c) Rental Revenue Earned, $100
(d) Office Supplies Used, $140 ($250 − $110)
(e) Depreciation of Truck, $40 (10% × $4,800 = $480 ÷ 12 = $40 a month)

Adjusted Trial Balance		Income Statement		Balance Sheet	
Debit	Credit	Debit	Credit	Debit	Credit
24270				24270	
	20000				20000
4800				4800	
	500				500
440				440	
110				110	
3000				3000	
	3000				3000
3000				3000	
	34700		34700		
21000		21000			
2200		2200			
	700				700
40		40			
	100		100		
140		140			
40		40			
	40				40
59040	59040	23420	34800	35620	24240
		11380			11380
		34800	34800	35620	35620

The adjustments appear in the adjustments columns, identified as entries (a)–(e). The remaining columns on the worksheet show the adjusted trial balance, the Income Statement, and the Balance Sheet, respectively. The financial statements, which are prepared directly from the worksheet, are presented as Exhibits 4–5 and 4–6. (Note that taxes have been ignored to simplify the example.)

EXHIBIT 4–5   **Yang Company**
Income Statement for the Month Ended January 31, 1981

Sales Revenue		$34,700
Cost of Goods Sold		21,000
Gross Margin		$13,700
Operating Expenses:		
Insurance	$ 40	
Salaries	2,200	
Supplies	140	
Depreciation	40	2,420
Operating Income		$11,280
Rental Revenue		100
Net Income		$11,380

EXHIBIT 4–6   **Yang Company**
Balance Sheet as of January 31, 1981

Assets

Cash		$24,270
Accounts Receivable		3,000
Inventory		3,000
Office Supplies		110
Prepaid Insurance		440
Truck	$4,800	
Less Accumulated Depreciation	40	4,760
Total Assets		$35,580

Liabilities and Owners' Equity

Liabilities:		
Accounts Payable	$3,000	
Salaries Payable	700	
Rent Received in Advance	500	
Total Liabilities		$ 4,200
Owners' Equity:		
Capital Stock	$20,000	
Retained Earnings	11,380	
Total Owners' Equity		31,380
Total Liabilities and Owners' Equity		$35,580

TO SUMMARIZE   A worksheet is often used to analyze year-end adjustments and to facilitate the preparation of financial statements. At a minimum, a worksheet will usually have eight columns: two for the unadjusted trial balance, two for adjusting entries, two for the Income Statement, and two for the Balance Sheet.

Closing Entries

closing entries   entries that reduce all nominal, or Income Statement, accounts to a zero balance at the end of each accounting period, transferring their preclosing balances to permanent, Balance Sheet accounts

You have almost reached the end of the accounting cycle. As you recall, the cycle includes journalizing transactions, posting to the ledger accounts, balancing the accounts and preparing a trial balance, setting up a worksheet, making adjusting entries, and producing the financial statements. Just one final step needs to be taken, and that is the journalizing and posting of closing entries. These entries close all nominal, or Income Statement, accounts and leave only the real, or Balance Sheet, accounts with balances at the start of the new accounting cycle.

Let us review and expand upon the concept of closing the accounts that was introduced in Chapter 3. The Income Statement accounts are used to accumulate and classify all revenue and expense items for a period of time, generally a year. They are temporary accounts, which at the beginning of each period have a zero balance. Transactions throughout the period are journalized and posted to these accounts and, at the end of the period, adjustments are made, the Income Statement is prepared, and the balances are then closed to an owners' equity account. The closing entries bring the Income Statement accounts back to a zero balance, which makes the accounting records ready for a new cycle of transactions.

Income Summary account   a clearing account used to close all revenues and expenses at the end of an accounting period; the balance of the Income Summary account before it is closed represents the operating results (income or loss) of a given accounting period

clearing account   a temporary account, such as Income Summary, that is used only at the end of an accounting period to collect the debit and credit balances from other accounts as they are closed; the clearing account balance is then closed to a permanent account

As a means of facilitating the closing process and preparing the books for a new accounting cycle, an Income Summary account (also called a Revenue and Expense Summary account) may be used. This is a temporary, clearing account, the function of which is to facilitate the collection of data. An Income Summary account works in the following manner. All items of revenue are debited, with the total credited to Income Summary. All items of expense are credited, with the total debited to Income Summary. The balance in the Income Summary account, which is the income or loss for the period (the difference between revenues and expenses), is in turn closed to the appropriate permanent owners' equity account. As mentioned, use of an Income Summary account is a facilitating procedure; it is not required. Revenues and expenses can be closed directly to the equity account, as was illustrated in Chapter 3.

You should note that the Balance Sheet accounts are not closed at the end of the cycle. Through the adjusting entries, they are modified to reflect appropriate balances that are then carried forward to the next accounting cycle.

The closing process, when an Income Summary account is used, is illustrated on the basis of the facts given for Yang Company in Exhibit 4–4. The closing journal entries (remember that the period covered was January 1–31) would be

January 31
Sales Revenue   34,700
Rental Revenue   100
    Income Summary   34,800

To close revenues to Income Summary.

January 31
Income Summary   23,420
    Cost of Goods Sold   21,000
    Salaries Expense   2,200
    Insurance Expense   40
    Supplies Expense   140
    Depreciation Expense   40

To close expenses to Income Summary.

January 31
Income Summary   11,380
    Retained Earnings   11,380

To close Income Summary to Retained Earnings.

The last entry, which is the difference between revenues and expenses, or the income for the period, is a credit to Retained Earnings if a corporate form of business is assumed. However, if the business is a proprietorship or a partnership, the credit portion of the entry would be to Proprietorship or Partnership Capital. (The owners' equity section of the Balance Sheet is explained fully in Chapter 12.)

Note that dividends are not generally declared or paid on a monthly basis. However, if Yang Company had paid dividends during January, the amount in the Dividends account should be closed to Retained Earnings on January 31 by crediting Dividends and debiting Retained Earnings.

The closing procedure above requires three entries. To save time, the first two could be combined as a compound entry.

January 31
Sales Revenue   34,700
Rental Revenue   100
    Cost of Goods Sold   21,000
    Salaries Expense   2,200
    Insurance Expense   40
    Supplies Expense   140
    Depreciation Expense   40
    Income Summary   11,380

To close revenues and expenses to Income Summary.

The final step again would be to close the Income Summary account to Retained Earnings. If a clearing account had not been used, Retained Earnings would have been credited directly for $11,380. No matter how many entries are made, the effect is the same. All nominal accounts will have a zero balance. Correspondingly, all real accounts, including the owners' equity accounts, will be stated at their appropriate balances. The books are now ready for a new accounting cycle. The closing process for a corporation is shown schematically in Exhibit 4–7.

EXHIBIT 4–7   **The Closing Process**

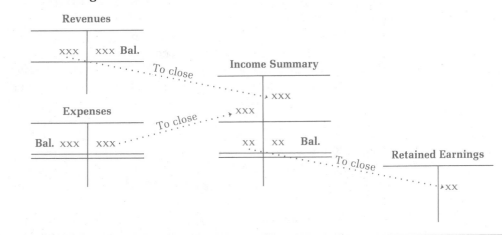

TO SUMMARIZE   The last step in the accounting cycle is to close all nominal, or Income Statement, accounts to a zero balance. All real, or Balance Sheet, accounts are carried forward to the new reporting period. Revenue accounts are closed by being debited; expense accounts are closed by being credited. If an Income Summary account is used as a clearing account, total debits from revenues are credited to Income Summary and total credits from expenses are debited to Income Summary. The balance in Income Summary is then closed to Retained Earnings.

CHAPTER REVIEW

In conducting economic activities, businesses or other types of entities enter into transactions. These transactions form the basis of accounting records and must be analyzed, classified, recorded, summarized and reported.

To facilitate the accounting process, an accounting model has been established. This model has several important characteristics, including the notion of a separate accounting entity that is a going concern and that enters into arm's-length transactions. In the United States these transactions are measured in money amounts using the U.S. dollar as the unit of measurement.

The model further assumes that accounting information is needed on a timely basis for decision-making purposes. This requires that the total life of a business be divided into accounting periods, generally a year or less, for which reports are prepared. Although periodic reporting is a necessity, some of the data presented in such reports must be tentative because of the allocations and estimates involved in dividing an entity's life into relatively short reporting periods.

Finally, it is assumed that accrual accounting is needed to provide accurate statements of financial position and results of operations for the accounting period. Accrual-basis accounting means that revenues are recognized as earned, not necessarily when payments are received, and expenses are recognized as incurred, not necessarily when payments are made.

One of the most important functions that accountants perform is the proper matching of the revenues recognized during a reporting period with the expenses incurred to generate those revenues. This requires that adjusting entries be made at the end of each accounting period. Adjusting entries are the means of increasing or decreasing accounts so as to report proper year-end revenue and expense amounts on the Income Statement and appropriate balances for Balance Sheet accounts.

Generally, a worksheet is used to facilitate the preparation of financial statements. The accounts and their balances are listed on a worksheet, the adjustments are then shown, and the adjusted balances are transferred to the appropriate financial statement.

Once the adjusting entries have been journalized and posted to the accounts and the financial statements have been prepared, the accounting records should be made ready for the next accounting cycle. This is accomplished by journalizing and posting closing entries for all nominal accounts.

A case study is presented on pages 141 to 159 as a review of the first four chapters of the text, and specifically to help solidify your understanding of the accounting cycle.

KEY TERMS AND CONCEPTS

accrual-basis accounting (106)	account (123)	trial balance (119)
adjusting entries (107)	liability approach (112)	unearned revenues (111)
asset approach (115)	matching principle (106)	unrecorded expenses and accrued liabilities (110)
calendar year (105)	prepaid expenses (115)	
cash-basis accounting (105)	revenue approach (112)	unrecorded revenues and accrued assets (109)
clearing account (123)	revenue recognition (106)	
closing entries (123)	reversing entry (139)	worksheet (119)
expense approach (115)	time-period assumption (periodicity concept) (105)	
fiscal year (105)		
Income Summary		

DISCUSSION QUESTIONS

1. What are the objectives of periodic financial reporting?

2. Distinguish between reporting on a calendar year and a fiscal year basis.

3. Why do you think the numbers in the financial statements are often rounded to thousands of dollars?

4. Explain why accrual-basis accounting is more appropriate than cash-basis accounting for most businesses.

5. What is a significant disadvantage of accrual-basis accounting?

6. When are revenues generally recognized?

7. What is the matching principle?

8. Why are adjusting entries necessary?

9. Identify four categories for which adjusting entries are commonly required prior to the preparation of financial statements.

10. Describe the three-step process used in determining the appropriate amounts for adjusting entries.

11. Distinguish between the revenue approach and the liability approach in adjusting for unearned revenues. Which do you think is the better approach, and why?

12. In making adjusting entries for prepaid expenses, why will the final result be the same, regardless of whether the expense or the asset approach is used?

13. Why is preparing a worksheet considered a useful but not a required step in the accounting cycle?

14. What purpose do closing entries serve?

15. Which types of accounts remain "open" after the closing process?

16. What is the purpose of the Income Summary account? Is its use required?

17. How would a corporation's closing process differ from that of a partnership or a proprietorship?

EXERCISES

E4–1   Cash-Basis Accounting

In which year would John Johnson recognize the transaction for each situation below if his accounting records are kept on a cash basis?

1. On January 5, 1983, John received and paid the December 1982 electricity bill.

2. On December 30, 1982, he paid an insurance premium for the year 1983.

3. John received a notice from his bank on January 3, 1983, informing him that his savings account had earned interest of $100 during the last quarter of 1982.

4. John paid his state property taxes on January 10, 1983. The taxes were assessed on his property for the year 1982.

E4–2   Accrual-Basis Accounting

Refer to the preceding problem. Assume that Mr. Johnson keeps his records on an accrual basis. For each situation, in which year would he recognize the transaction?

E4–3   Cash- and Accrual-Basis Accounting

Watkins Company had the following transactions during the first month of its operations in 1981.

January	1	Purchased $500 of supplies on account.
	9	Billed Hawkins Company $1,500 for services performed during this month.
	15	Received $1,200 from Hawkins for services performed.
	20	Paid $400 for supplies purchased on account on January 1.

1. Prepare journal entries using accrual-basis accounting.

2. Prepare journal entries using cash-basis accounting.

3. Which basis of accounting is generally more appropriate, and why?

E4–4   Classifications of Accounts Requiring Adjusting Entries

For each item listed, indicate whether it is an unrecorded revenue, an unrecorded expense, an unearned revenue, or a prepaid expense at December 31, 1982.

1. Property taxes for the year 1982 not to be paid until 1983.

2. Rent revenue earned during 1982, but not collected until 1983.

3. Salaries earned by employees in December 1982, but not to be paid until January 5, 1983.

4. A payment received from a customer in December 1982 for services that will not be performed until February 1983.

5. An insurance premium paid on December 29, 1982, for the period January 1, 1983, to December 31, 1985.

6. Gasoline charged on a credit card during December 1982. The bill will not be received until January 15, 1983.

7. Interest on a certificate of deposit held during 1982. The interest will not be received until January 7, 1983.

E4–5   Balances in Expense Accounts at Year-End

Assuming accrual-basis accounting for each of the following situations, state how much expense should be reported by Rhonda Roads for 1983.

1. On January 1, 1983, Rhonda borrowed $1,000 from her bank. The note is due, with annual interest at 8%, on January 1, 1985.

2. Rhonda paid in advance her car insurance premium of $120 on October 1, 1983. The premium is for a 6-month period of insurance coverage.

3. Rhonda paid her babysitter $300 on December 1, 1983. This amount represents salary for December and January.

4. Rhonda subscribed to a magazine on August 1, 1983. She paid $24 on that date for a 2-year subscription.

5. Rhonda rented a storage shed. She paid $120 on November 1, 1983, for the next year's rent.

E4–6 Balances in Revenue Accounts at Year-End

Frank Furter, a businessman, receives his income from many sources. In preparing his year-end financial statements at December 31, 1982, he had trouble deciding how much revenue to report on the 1982 Income Statement. Assuming accrual-basis accounting, for each revenue listed below indicate how much Frank should include in his 1982 Income Statement.

1. Will receive interest revenue of $12,000 on some of his savings accounts on February 1, 1983, for the 3-month period ending January 31, 1983.

2. Rented an office building that he owns to the McCord Corporation. On July 1, 1982, McCord paid Frank $100,000 rent for the year ended June 30, 1983.

3. Will receive his December 1982 salary on January 10, 1983. His salary as president of Frankco, Inc., is $20,000 per month.

4. Will receive a dividend check from Locke Company on January 22, 1983. He owns 20,000 shares of Locke Company stock. On December 30, 1982, Locke company declared a cash dividend of $2 per share payable to persons who owned its stock on that date.

5. Received a check from a client on December 1, 1982, for $36,000. The payment is for professional advice and counseling for the 12-month period ending November 30, 1983.

E4–7 Year-End Analysis of Account Balances

Account balances for City Electric Supply at the beginning and end of 1981 are shown below.

	1/1/81	12/31/81
1. Prepaid Insurance	$3,200	$4,600
2. Wages Payable	1,700	1,200
3. Prepaid Rent	700	500

Expense accounts for the year associated with the above accounts are listed below.

1. Insurance Expense	$ 4,400
2. Wages Expense	26,000
3. Rent Expense	2,100

Determine the amount of cash paid out during the year for each type of expense, (1) through (3).

(**Note:** Unless otherwise indicated, assume accrual-basis accounting for all exercises and problems from this point on.)

E4–8 Adjusting Entries: Unrecorded Revenues

Patty Sloan is a professional investor. During 1981, she had the following economic transactions. For each transaction, give the entry that Patty would make on December 31, 1981, to record the proper balance at year-end.

1. Patty leased the Goodnight Hotel to Frank Goodwin on July 1, 1981, for $18,000 per year. Frank will pay the first year's rent on July 1, 1982.

2. Martha Higbee, Patty's aunt, borrowed $20,000 from Patty on September 1, 1981. Martha will repay the $20,000 with interest at 12% on March 1, 1982.

3. Patty's certificates of deposit earn 18% interest per year. Her bank will pay her the interest for the year November 1, 1981, to November 1, 1982, on November 1, 1982. Patty has $20,000 in certificates of deposit.

4. Patty owns 10,000 shares of Oklahoma Drilling Company common stock. On November 15, 1981, the company declared a dividend of $5 per share to stockholders of record on that date. Patty will receive her dividend check on January 15, 1982.

E4–9 Adjusting Entries: Unrecorded Expenses

Gary Blaylock owns Blaylock Safety-Pin Company. In 1982, Gary had the following economic transactions. For each transaction, give the adjusting entry that Gary would make to record the account balances properly at December 31, 1982.

1. Gary has not yet paid his November and December utility bills. He will pay $450 on January 15 ($150 a month for November, December, and January).

2. Gary borrowed $10,000 from his bank on July 1, 1982. He will repay the loan, together with interest at 15%, on July 1, 1983.

3. Gary will pay his employees their December salaries on January 5, 1983. The monthly salary expense is $10,000. (Ignore payroll taxes.)

4. Gary charged $500 per month in gasoline expenses on his credit card in 1982. He has not yet received his bill for the charges made in December.

5. Gary will pay his December rent on January 5, 1982. The rent is $2,500 per month.

E4–10 Adjusting Entries: Unearned Revenues Using the Revenue Approach

Gail Hopkins is the owner/operator of Hopkins Consulting Company. Gail uses the revenue approach in recording all unearned revenues. Give the entry that Gail would make to record each of the following transactions on the date of occurrence and, assuming accrual-basis accounting, give the adjusting entries needed at December 31, 1982.

1. Gail received $1,800 on September 15, 1982, in return for which she agreed to provide consulting services for 18 months beginning immediately.

2. Gail rents part of her office space to the Bristle Brush Company. Bristle paid her $1,200 on November 1, 1982, for the next 6 months' rent.

3. Gail received $12,000 on November 1, 1982, in return for which she agreed to provide consulting for the next 18 months to a client who wants to install a new computer system.

4. Gail received $10,000 on September 1, 1982, from a client who wants advice on investing in certain securities. In return for this sum, Gail agreed to provide consulting services for the next 10 months, including September.

5. Gail loaned $100,000 to a neighbor several years ago. On November 1, her neighbor paid $24,000, which represented 2 years' interest in advance (November 1, 1982 through October 31, 1984).

E4–11   Adjusting Entries: Unearned Revenues Using the Liability Approach

Refer to the transactions outlined in E4–10. Assume now that Gail Hopkins uses the liability approach in recording all unearned revenues. Give the entry that Gail would make to record each of the transactions on the date it occurred, as well as the adjusting entries she would need to make on December 31, 1982.

E4–12   Adjusting Entries: Prepaid Expenses Using the Expense Approach

Simon Simson owns and operates SS Signs, Inc. Simon uses the expense approach in recording all prepaid expenses. Give the entry that Simon would make to record each of the following transactions on the date it occurred, and prepare the adjusting entries needed on December 31, 1982.

1. On July 1, 1982, Simon paid a 3-year premium of $7,200 on an insurance policy that is effective July 1, 1982, and expires June 30, 1985.

2. On February 1, 1982, Simon paid his property taxes for the year February 1, 1982, to January 31, 1983. His tax bill was $1,800.

3. On May 1, 1982, Simon paid $180 for a 3-year subscription to an advertising journal. The subscription starts May 1, 1982, and expires April 30, 1985.

4. On August 1, 1982, Simon paid $36,000 rent for the year August 1, 1982, to July 31, 1983.

5. On December 1, 1982, Simon paid his utility bills totaling $300 for December 1982 and January 1983. The amount for each month was $150.

E4–13   Adjusting Entries: Prepaid Expenses Using the Asset Approach

Refer to the transactions outlined in E4–12. Assume now that Simon uses the asset approach in recording all prepaid expenses. Give the entry that Simon would make on the date of each transaction's occurrence, as well as the adjusting entries he would make on December 31, 1982.

E4–14   Adjusting Entries

The information presented below is from Julian Company. Prepare the adjusting entries that should be made on December 31, 1980.

1. Accrued salaries for the period 12/26/80 through 12/31/80 amounted to $7,120. (Ignore payroll taxes.)

2. Interest is payable for 3 months on a 10% $80,000 loan.

3. Rent of $12,000 was paid for 6 months in advance on December 1 and charged to expense.

4. Rental revenue received in advance is $16,700. Rent is credited to a revenue account when received.

5. The unexpired portion of the insurance policy is $500. The Insurance Expense account was originally debited.

6. Interest revenue from a $1,000 note has been earned, but has not been collected or recorded.

E4–15   Classifying Account Balances

For each of the following accounts, indicate whether it would be found in the Income Statement or the Balance Sheet columns of a company's worksheet.

1. Cash
2. Inventory
3. Salary Expense
4. Prepaid Salaries
5. Retained Earnings
6. Office Supplies Expense
7. Accounts Receivable
8. Cost of Goods Sold
9. Maintenance Expense
10. Interest Receivable
11. Common Stock
12. Accounts Payable
13. Plant
14. Accumulated Depreciation—Machinery
15. Interest Expense
16. Accounts Payable
17. Notes Receivable
18. Office Supplies on Hand
19. Sales Revenue
20. Insurance Expense
21. Machinery
22. Land
23. Salaries Payable
24. Prepaid Insurance
25. Notes Payable
26. Depreciation Expense

E4–16 Companion Accounts—Debits and Credits

Following are two lists of accounts. Match each account in list (1) with an account in list (2) that would normally be credited when the account in list (1) is debited. Example: _f_ Accounts Receivable (where f = Sales).

(1)	(2)
__ Accounts Receivable	a. Supplies on Hand
__ Cost of Goods Sold	b. Interest Payable
__ Insurance Expense	c. Dividends
__ Salary Expense	d. Inventory
__ Interest Expense	e. Accumulated
__ Inventory	Depreciation
__ Interest Receivable	f. Sales Revenue
__ Depreciation Expense	g. Prepaid Insurance
__ Supplies Expense	h. Accounts Payable
__ Retained Earnings	i. Salaries Payable
	j. Interest Revenue

E4–17 Closing Entries

Mike's Bike Shop reported the following revenue and expense items on its 1982 Income Statement. Prepare all necessary entries to close the account balances.

Revenues:

Gross Bicycle Sales Revenue	$100,000
Revenue from Bicycle Repairs	50,000
Total Revenues	$150,000

Expenses:

Rent	$ 20,000
Utilities	5,000
Salaries	30,000
Depreciation	5,000
Property Taxes	1,000
Oil and Grease	250
Cost of Goods Sold	70,000
Total Expenses	$131,250

E4–18 Closing Entries

Income and expense accounts of Hair Supply Company for September 1980 are presented below. Prepare the entires required to close the income and expense accounts to retained earnings.

	DR	CR
Sales Revenue		$27,000
Cost of Goods Sold	$13,000	
Salary Expense	2,700	
Rent Expense	500	
Supplies Expense	100	
Depreciation Expense	700	
Interest Expense	400	

PROBLEMS

P4–1 Cash- and Accrual-Basis Accounting

In the course of your examination of the books and records of Flexo Rubber Company, you find the following data.

Salaries Accrued	$ 53,000
Salaries Paid	55,000
Total Sales	838,000
Cash Collected from Sales	900,000
Utilities Expense Accrued	5,000
Utility Bills Paid	4,800
Cost of Goods Sold	532,000
Cash Paid on Purchases in 1982	411,000
Inventory at December 31, 1982	320,000
Tax Assessment for 1982	5,000
Taxes Paid in 1982	4,900
Rent Expense for 1982	30,000
Rent Paid in 1982	25,000

Required:

1. Compute Flexo's net income for 1982 using cash-basis accounting.

2. Compute Flexo's net income for 1982 using accrual-basis accounting.

3. **Interpretive Question** Why is accrual-basis accounting usually used? Can you see any opportunities for improperly reporting income under cash-basis accounting? Explain.

P4–2 Calendar Year Versus Fiscal Year

Benson Company reports its income on a quarterly basis. Quarterly revenues and expenses for the years 1980 and 1981 are shown below.

	First Quarter	Second Quarter	Third Quarter	Fourth Quarter
1980				
Total revenues	$50,000	$100,000	$76,000	$89,000
Total expenses....	60,000	75,000	43,000	57,000
1981				
Total revenues	$60,000	$110,000	$91,000	$81,000
Total expenses....	68,000	82,000	46,000	62,000

Required:

1. Determine Benson Company's annual net income if it uses as its fiscal year the 12 months ended March 31, 1981.

2. Determine Benson Company's net income if it uses as its fiscal year the 12 months ended September 30, 1981.

3. Determine Benson Company's net income if it uses as its fiscal year the calendar year ended December 31, 1981.

P4–3 Determining Adjusting Entries from General Journal Entries

George Wilde, the bookkeeper of Morton Company, thinks that the following journal entries may lead to adjusting entries at December 31, 1981.

February 1	Prepaid Insurance	1,200	
	Cash		1,200
March 31	Cash	18,000	
	Rent Revenue		18,000
May 1	Legal Service Expense...	1,800	
	Cash		1,800
August 1	Property Tax Expense...	12,000	
	Cash		12,000
October 31	Prepaid Interest	600	
	Cash		600

George has discovered the following additional information.

a. The insurance premium is for the 12-month period ending February 1, 1982.

b. The rent revenue represents rent received from a tenant for the period March 31, 1981, to September 30, 1981.

c. The legal service expense is for the services of Angus M. Cartwright, attorney-at-law, for the 12-month period ending April 30, 1982.

d. The property tax expense is for the state's fiscal year, which ends June 30, 1982.

e. The prepaid interest represents interest on a loan for the last 3 months of 1981.

Required:

Make adjusting entries required at December 31, 1981.

P4–4 Examination of Accounts and Adjusting Entries

During the course of your review of Grandy Company at December 31, 1981, you find that the company owes the following notes to its bank.

a. A 2-year, $20,000, 6% note dated January 1, 1981, due December 31, 1982. Grandy Company is required to make semiannual interest payments to the bank on July 1 and December 31 of each year.

b. A 6-month, 12% note dated November 1, 1981, due April 30, 1982. The face value of the note, $3,000, is payable on April 30, together with the interest.

Required:

1. For the first note, give the entries necessary to record the interest payments on July 1 and December 31, 1981; any adjusting entry that may be required on December 31; the interest payments on July 1, 1982, and December 31, 1982; and the payment of the note in full on December 31, 1982.

2. For the second note, give the entries necessary to record the receipt of the proceeds of the note on November 1, 1981; any adjusting entry that may be required on December 31, 1981; and the payment of the note in full on April 30, 1982.

3. What is Grandy Company's total interest expense for the calendar year 1981?

P4–5 Unifying Problem: Adjusting Entries and Financial Statements

The 1981 year-end financial statements of Allen Company, a service business, are shown below. The company's accountant prepared the statements before making the necessary adjustments.

Allen Company
Income Statement for the Year Ended December 31, 1981

Revenue from Services..............		$75,960
Operating Expenses:		
Insurance Expense..................	$ 2,740	
Rent Expense	250	
Office Supply Expense..............	1,480	
Salaries Expense	27,500	31,970
Net Income		$43,990

Allen Company
Balance Sheet as of December 31, 1981

Assets

Cash	$ 11,000
Accounts Receivable	20,000
Notes Receivable	6,400
Machinery	90,000
Total Assets	**$127,400**

Liabilities and Owner's Equity

Accounts Payable	$ 27,400
Mark Allen, Capital	100,000
Total Liabilities and Owner's Equity	**$127,400**

The following items lead to adjusting entries.

a. Salaries earned but not recorded or paid were $2,500. (Ignore payroll taxes.)

b. Unexpired insurance premiums were $975. Insurance Expense was originally debited for the full amount.

c. Interest earned but not received or recorded was $350.

d. Service revenue collected but not earned was $2,090.

Required:

1. Give the required adjusting entries.

2. Prepare a revised Income Statement and Balance Sheet.

3. Prepare a schedule reconciling the revised amount of owner's equity with the amount shown on the original statement.

P4–6 Adjusting Entries

You have just completed the trial balance and an analysis of the accounts of Vallo, Inc., at December 31, 1981. Your analysis reveals the following information.

a. The Prepaid Rent account shows a zero balance. Included in the Rent Expense account is an amount of $9,000, a payment of one year's rent for the period October 1, 1981, to September 30, 1982.

b. The Prepaid Insurance account was debited as the following insurance was bought.

Policy No.	Purchase and Effective Date of Policy	Life of Policy	Premiums
1AX	Jan. 1, 1980	3 years	$2,400
2BX	June 1, 1980	2 years	960
3CX	Sept. 1, 1980	1 year	480
4DX	Sept. 1, 1981	1 year	600

c. The balance in the Prepaid Advertising account is $3,600. This amount is for a series of radio spot announcements to be run for a 6-month period, beginning November 1, 1981.

d. At the close of the year, the company had two notes receivable. The first, a 90-day, 8% note for $7,200, was dated December 16, 1981. The second, a 60-day, 9% note for $6,000, was dated December 1, 1981.

e. At the close of the year, three short-term notes were outstanding.

Date of Note	Face Amount	Note Period	Interest Rate
October 17	$ 8,100	90 days	8%
November 1	12,000	4 months	10%
November 16	6,600	120 days	6%

f. Property taxes not yet recorded at December 31, 1981, amount to $2,275.

g. $10,800 was received on a one-year equipment lease, effective August 1, 1981. The receipt was credited to Equipment Rental Revenue.

h. Salaries and wages incurred but not yet recorded at December 31, 1981, total $3,500.

Required:

Prepare the adjusting journal entries required at December 31, 1981, assuming a 360-day year.

P4–7 Adjustment of Accounts to Reflect Yearly Expenses

Several of the account balances at January 1, 1981, for Don's Dry Cleaners are listed below.

Rent Payable	$ 500
Salaries Payable	1,300
Interest Payable	100
Utilities Payable	50

The following information is pertinent to 1981.

a. For the year 1981, Don's rent was $600 per month. At December 31, 1981, he had not yet paid his December 1981 rent. Rent payments are debited to Rent Expense.

b. Don's monthly salary expense is $1,200. Workers are paid each month's wages on the fifth day of the next month. Salaries paid are debited to Salaries Expense.

c. Don paid off a bank loan during the year 1981. He debited the interest that he paid on the loan to Interest Expense. He had no loans outstanding on December 31, 1981.

d. Don's utility expense in 1981 was $100 per month. On December 29, 1981, Don paid his December 1981 utility bill. During 1981, he debited all utility payments to Utility Expense.

Required:

1. For each transaction, give the entry that Don would make on December 31, 1981, to properly record the expenses for the calendar year 1981.

2. **Interpretive Question** Why is it important to know both the amount of an expense and the method used to record its payment in order to properly make an adjusting entry?

P4–8 Unifying Problem: Adjusting and Closing Entries

Two trial balances of Staley Company as of December 31, 1981, are presented below. One is before adjustments and the other is after adjustments.

Staley Company
Trial Balance as of December 31, 1981

	Unadjusted		Adjusted	
	DR	CR	DR	CR
Cash	$ 1,820		$ 1,820	
Supplies	585		600	
Prepaid Rent	1,350		745	
Prepaid Insurance	380		148	
Building	12,500		12,500	
Accumulated Depreciation— Building		$ 2,500		$ 2,500
Equipment	8,700		8,700	
Accumulated Depreciation— Equipment		3,000		3,000
Accounts Payable		750		865
Salaries Payable		—		250
Taxes Payable		—		148
Capital Stock		16,245		16,245
Service Fees Earned ...		11,750		11,750
Salaries Expense	2,750		3,000	
Rent Expense.........	—		605	
Supplies Expense	1,880		1,865	
Depreciation Expense— Equipment	1,000		1,000	
Depreciation Expense— Building	1,250		1,250	
Utilities Expense	470		585	
Taxes Expense........	1,000		1,148	
Insurance Expense	—		232	
Miscellaneous Expense	560		560	
Totals	$34,245	$34,245	$34,758	$34,758

Required:

1. Prepare the entries that were required to adjust the accounts at December 31, 1981.

2. Prepare the journal entries that are required to close the accounts at December 31, 1981.

P4–9 Closing Entries

Astro Company's trial balances as of August 31, 1981 and 1982 are shown below.

Astro Company
Trial Balance as of August 31, 1982 and 1981

	1982		1981	
Cash.................	$16,700		$ 6,250	
Accounts Receivable ...	3,200		3,750	
Inventory.............	1,400		4,300	
Accounts Payable......		$ 700		
Land.................			7,400	
Capital Stock		18,300		$18,300
Dividends		250		
Retained Earnings		3,400		
Sales Revenue........		11,000		17,000
Cost of Goods Sold	6,000		8,200	
Rent Expense	700		700	
Advertising Expense ...	400		250	
Salaries Expense	5,000		4,200	
Totals	$33,400	$33,400	$35,300	$35,300

Required:

1. Prepare journal entries to close the books as of August 31, 1981.

2. In 1982, the company suffered a net loss, which reduced Retained Earnings accordingly. Prepare closing entries as of August 31, 1982.

P4–10 Unifying Problem: Preparation of Worksheet and Financial Statements

Jones Supply Company has the following balances in its accounts at the end of 1981.

	Debit	Credit
Cash...........................	$ 51,000	
Accounts Receivable	22,500	
Accounts Payable.................		$ 12,500
Inventory.......................	63,250	
Salary Expense...................	50,000	
Depreciation Expense	2,500	
Sales Revenue		300,000
Cost of Goods Sold	150,000	
Office Supplies Expense	2,500	
Interest Expense..................	1,000	
Retained Earnings		36,450
Interest Payable..................		0
Salaries Payable		0
Insurance Expense................	0	
Rent Expense	45,000	
Property Tax Expense	3,000	
Prepaid Insurance	1,200	
Accumulated Depreciation—Fixtures .		12,500
Common Stock		50,000
Premium on Common Stock		30,000
Rent Payable.....................		500
Fixtures	55,000	
Notes Payable....................		5,000
Totals	$446,950	$446,950

The following information is provided for your use.

a. An insurance premium of $1,200 was paid on July 1, 1981, for the period July 1, 1981, to June 30, 1982.

b. No entry has been made to record the interest expense on a $5,000 note. The note was signed on October 1, 1981, and is due with interest at 12% on April 1, 1982.

c. The salaries earned by company personnel in December have not yet been recorded. These salaries, totaling $5,000, will be paid on January 5, 1982.

Required:

1. Prepare an 8-column worksheet. (Omit the adjusted trial balance columns.)

2. Make any necessary adjusting entries.

3. Prepare a year-end Income Statement and Balance Sheet.

P4–11   Closing Entries at Year-End

Rainy Umbrella Company's Income Statement is given below.

Rainy Umbrella Company
Income Statement for the Year Ended December 31, 1981

Gross Sales Revenue		$800,000
Less Cost of Goods Sold		500,000
Gross Margin		$300,000
Operating Expenses:		
Selling Expenses:		
Sales Salaries	$ 50,000	
Sales Supplies Expense	500	
Depreciation Expense—		
Sales Vehicles	1,000	
Total Selling Expenses		$ 51,500
General and Administrative		
Expenses:		
Officers' Salaries	$100,000	
Office Supplies Expense . . .	1,000	
Postage Expense	50	
Total General and		
Administrative Expenses	101,050	
Total Operating Expenses		152,550
Income from Operations		$147,450
Other Revenues and Expenses:		
Interest Revenue	$ 5,000	
Rental Revenue	3,000	
Total Other Revenues		
and Expenses.		8,000
Pretax Income		$155,450
Income Tax Expense		55,780
Net Income.		$ 99,670

Required:

1. Give the journal entries necessary to close the revenue and expense accounts to an Income Summary account.

2. Give the entries required to close the Income Summary account to Retained Earnings.

3. **Interpretive Question**   Some companies prepare what is called a post-closing trial balance after the accounts have been closed at year-end. What would be some of the advantages of a post-closing trial balance?

P4–12   Ten-Column Worksheet

The following trial balance is taken from the records of Mansion Company.

Mansion Company
Trial Balance as of December 31, 1981

	Debit	Credit
Cash.	$ 2,115	
Accounts Receivable	3,245	
Notes Receivable	2,400	
Office Supplies on Hand	160	
Land.	3,700	
Notes Payable		$ 1,540
Capital Stock		7,500
Dividends	30	
Retained Earnings, December 31, 1980		2,010
Fees Earned		2,437
Rent Earned		143
Advertising Expense	146	
Office Expense	134	
Wages Expense	1,700	
Totals	$13,630	$13,630

Data for adjustments:

a. Earned fees not yet recorded, $74

b. Interest on notes receivable not yet recorded, $24

c. Liability for office expense, $30

d. Interest on notes payable not yet recorded, $18

Required:

Using a worksheet, make any necessary adjustments and extend the adjusted trial balance figures to the Income Statement and Balance Sheet columns.

P4–13   Unifying Problem: Analysis of Accounts

The following summary totals were taken from the accounting records of Toy Products Company for the year ended December 31, 1981.

Assets $62,700
Liabilities 26,500
Equity 36,200
Income.................................... 26,900

The controller overlooked the following information and did not make the necessary adjustments as of 12/31/81.

1. On July 1, 1981, the company loaned $12,000 to the president. The president gave the company a 1-year note with a 10% interest rate. The loan was recorded properly on July 1. The president has not paid anything in 1981.

2. An insurance policy was purchased on November 1, 1981. The premium of $1,200 for the first year was pre-paid and charged to Prepaid Insurance.

3. On June 1, 1981, the company received one year's advance rent of $2,100 and credited Rent Revenue.

4. Interest on a 10%, $10,000 note payable to the bank is due every July 1. (The interest was last paid on July 1, 1981.)

5. Accrued salaries for the period 12/29/81 to 12/31/81 were $2,524.

6. Income taxes of 30% were overlooked by the controller.

Required:

Determine the proper balances of assets, liabilities, owners' equity, and income as of December 31, 1981. Use the following format in working this problem.

Item	Assets	= Liabilities +	Owners' Equity	Income
Beg. Bal.	$62,700	$26,500	$36,200	$26,900
1.				
2.				
3.				
4.				
5.				
Subtotal				
6.				
Correct Balances	$	$	$	$

SUPPLEMENT

Disposal of Amounts from Adjusting Entries

Adjusting entries at the end of an accounting period affect both the Income Statement and the Balance Sheet. All of the Income Statement accounts are reduced to a zero balance through the closing process. However, the Balance Sheet accounts are not closed. So what happens to the adjustment amounts posted to Balance Sheet accounts? When and how are these amounts cleared from the accounts? This Supplement is intended to answer these questions, and to explain where reversing entries, which are sometimes considered a part of the accounting cycle, fit in.

Methods of Accounting for Adjustments to Balance Sheet Items

There are four methods that can be used to account for the year-end adjustments to Balance Sheet accounts. First, leave the amount as it is; do nothing! The amount remains in the account as a "permanent" adjustment. Second, remove the amount as part of a "split" entry in the ensuing accounting period. Third, readjust to a new balance as part of the adjusting entry process at the *end* of the next accounting period. Fourth, readjust at the *beginning* of the next accounting period by reversing the adjusting entry made. Examples of each of the four methods follow.

LEAVE AS IS

Assume that following salary arrangement was made by Jerry's Garage with an employee, Dan Jones. Dan is to receive $2,000 on the fifteenth of each month for work performed during the month ending on that day. Jerry's Garage closes its books on December 31 each year. The normal journal entry to record Dan's last salary payment for 1981 (ignoring payroll taxes) would be

December 15
Salary Expense   2,000
   Cash   2,000
Paid monthly salary to Dan Jones for the period ending December 15, 1981.

At the end of December, an adjusting entry would be needed to properly record the salary expense for the period and to accrue the liability as of December 31. The adjusting entry would be

December 31
Salary Expense   1,000
   Accrued Salaries Payable.   1,000
To record the accrual of salaries payable for Dan Jones for one-half month.

At the end of 1981, the Salary Expense account would be closed. On January 15, 1982, when the regular payroll is paid, the entry would be the same as that made on December 15, 1981: a debit to Salary Expense and a credit to Cash for $2,000. This same entry would be made for each month of the year. As the debit to Salary Expense is made each month, the correct amount of expense, $2,000, is recorded including that for the month of December. The total 12 months' salary expense for Dan Jones is $24, 000, the correct amount. As of December 31, 1982, the liability account, Accrued Salaries Payable, is also correctly stated as $1,000—the amount accrued at December 31, 1981, and left in the account throughout the year 1982. Furthermore, as long as Dan Jones' salary arrangement and pay period remain unchanged, the accounts will be properly maintained by recording the monthly salary expense as cash is paid on the fifteenth of each month.

Some of the most common adjusting entries that use this method are for the depreciation of tangible operational assets (machinery, for example), the amortization of intangible operational assets (goodwill, for example), and bond interest accrual on long-term bonds payable in instances where the interest period and accounting period do not coincide. Adjustments for these types of items, as well as others, will be covered in later chapters and in more advanced accounting texts. It is sufficient at this point for you to understand that for some types of adjusting entries, Balance Sheet amounts may not require readjustment until years later, if at all.

SPLIT ENTRY

Again take the example of Dan Jones and Jerry's Garage. In using the split-entry approach, the adjusting entry on December 31 would be unchanged. When payment to Dan is made on January 15, 1982, however, the entry would be

Salary Expense   1,000
Accrued Salaries Payable   1,000
   Cash   2,000
Paid monthly salary to Dan Jones for the period ending January 15, 1981, a portion of the salary expense previously recorded.

This entry splits the payment into two parts—one part to account for the expense for the 15-day period since December 31, and the other to pay the accrual for the last half of December. This method requires additional analysis but is commonly used in accounting practice.

READJUST AT THE END OF THE NEXT YEAR

Again referring to the Dan Jones example, we have explained that with the "leave as is" method the $1,000 remains in the account called Accrued Salaries Payable, and it is correctly stated. Since salary expense is also correctly stated, no adjusting entry is required. However, some accounts need readjustment at the end of the next year. One such account is office supplies. Assume that office supplies of $940 were on hand at the end of 1981. If more or less than this amount is in the account at year-end, the account would need to be adjusted to the correct amount of $940.

To illustrate, we will assume that the Office Supplies account showed a balance before adjustment of $480 at the end of 1981, even though $940 of supplies were actually on hand. A total of $1,290 was spent for supplies during 1981 and $1,430 during 1982, all charged to Office Supplies Expense, an Income Statement account. Furthermore, after a physical count and pricing, Office Supplies on Hand is determined to be $750 at the end of 1982. Entries based upon these assumptions and T-accounts reflecting the effect of these entries on the two companion accounts would be

1981
Office Supplies Expense   1,290
    Cash   1,290
Purchased office supplies, 1981.

December 31
Office Supplies on Hand   460
    Office Supplies Expense   460
To adjust office supplies to inventory left at December 31, 1981.

December 31
Income Summary   830
    Office Supplies Expense   830
To close Office Supplies Expense to Income Summary.

1982
Office Supplies Expense   1,430
    Cash   1,430
Purchased office supplies, 1982.

December 31
Office Supplies Expense   190
    Office Supplies on Hand   190
To adjust office supplies to inventory left at December 31, 1982.

December 31
Income Summary   1,620
    Office Supplies Expense   1,620
To close Office Supplies Expense to Income Summary.

	Office Supplies on Hand	
Balance (12/30/81)...	480	
Adjusting Entry (12/31/81).........	460	
Balance (12/31/81) ..	940	
		190 Adjusting Entry ....(12/31/82)
Balance (12/31/82) ..	750	

	Office Supplies Expense	
Purchases (1981)....	1,290	
		460 Adjusting Entry ....(12/31/81)
		830 .. To close (12/31/81)
Balance (12/31/81) ..	0	
Purchases (1982)....	1,430	
Adjusting Entry (12/31/82).........	190	
		1,620 .. To close (12/31/82)
Balance (12/31/82) ..	0	

REVERSING ENTRIES (READJUSTMENT AT THE BEGINNING OF THE NEXT YEAR)

reversing entry   *a type of adjusting entry made at the beginning of a year that exactly reverses the adjusting entry made at the end of the previous year*

A reversing entry is an adjusting entry made at the beginning of a year that exactly reverses the adjusting entry made at the end of the previous year. Reversing entries are never required; they are always optional. In some instances, they facilitate the recording of expenses and revenues with routine entries. Thus, they may reduce the need for account analysis to determine how much of a payment is expense and how much is settlement of a liability, and how much is revenue or asset collection.

To illustrate reversing entries, we will again assume that Dan Jones receives a $2,000 monthly salary payment on the fifteenth of each month. The adjusting entry at December 31, 1981, would be the same as previously shown.

December 15
Salary Expense 2,000
   Cash 2,000
Paid monthly salary to Dan Jones for the period ended December 15, 1981.

December 31
Salary Expense 1,000
   Accrued Salaries Payable................ 1,000
To record the accrual of salaries payable for Dan Jones for one-half month.

A reversing entry could be made as of January 1, 1982, as follows:

January 1
Accrued Salaries Payable 1,000
   Salary Expense 1,000
To reverse the adjusting entry made on December 31, 1981.

Note the effect on the companion accounts from these entries. The Balance Sheet account, Accrued Salaries Payable, set up to show the liability for Balance Sheet presentation purposes as of December 31, 1981, has now been canceled. The expense account shows a credit balance of $1,000. This amount will be deducted from the 12 monthly payments of $2,000 each plus a $1,000 accrual at December 31, 1982, a total of $25,000. Thus, the correct amount of expense for 1982 ($24,000) will automatically be shown in the Salary Expense account, just as it was for 1981.

	Salary Expense	
Payments (Jan.–Nov. 1981) 22,000		Reversing Entry (1/1/81, from previous
Payment (12/15/81) .. 2,000	1,000 .... period)	
Adjusting Entry (12/31/81) 1,000		
		Closing Entry
	24,000 .... (12/31/81)	
Balance (12/31/81) .. 0		Reversing Entry
	1,000 .... (1/1/82)	

	Accrued Salaries Payable	
		Adjusting Entry
	1,000 .... (12/31/81)	
	1,000 .. Balance (12/31/81)	
1,000		
	0 .. Balance (1/1/82)	

Reversing entries are appropriate for transactions that involve un-recorded revenues, unrecorded expenses (such as our example), unearned revenues that are originally credited to a revenue account, and prepaid expenses that are originally debited to an expense account. If reversing entries are not used, these transactions must be accounted for by one of the other methods described in this Supplement.

SUPPLEMENT
(Chapters 1–4)

A Case Study

In these first four chapters, we have laid a foundation for the study of accounting. The purpose of this Supplement is to help you solidify your understanding of the basic accounting cycle by providing a case study of the recording process. The three major types of businesses are highlighted; that is, the company depicted here begins as a proprietorship, expands to a partnership, and finally becomes a corporation.

As you follow the evolution of a small business through the proprietorship, partnership, and corporate stages, you should be able to recognize the accounting similarities and differences. The main differences arise in accounting for the equity of the individuals involved. Additional differences and complexities will be explored in later chapters. Most of the legal and tax implications for different forms of business are beyond the scope of this book. But, in brief, it might be stated that a corporation is a taxable entity, whereas a partnership and a proprietorship are not, although a partnership is required to file an "information" tax return.

Obviously, our example has to be a simple one, with many details summarized or omitted. In the "real world," transactions are more numerous and complex, and, for a large business, require an automated accounting system that includes high-speed data processing equipment, specialized journals, and a well-designed internal control system. Nonetheless, the basic steps in the accounting cycle and the essential record-keeping procedures will be similar to those illustrated, and need only be adapted to specific business environments.

The setting for the case study is a relatively small university town of 70,000 people, 20,000 of whom are students. Other than the university, the local economy in Mountain View is supported by some small industry, tourism (there are excellent facilities in the area for skiing in the winter and for a variety of recreational activities in the summer), and a farily large steel plant located nearby.

Dixon Able was a junior in college, majoring in business management. An enterprising young man with a desire to run his own business, Dixon observed a need for "homelike" housing for parents who came to Mountain View to bring entering students to the university, for friends and relatives who wanted to visit students enrolled in the university, and for the students themselves. There also appeared to be a market among vacationers for this type of housing.

EXHIBIT 4A–1   **Layout for One-Bedroom Apartment**

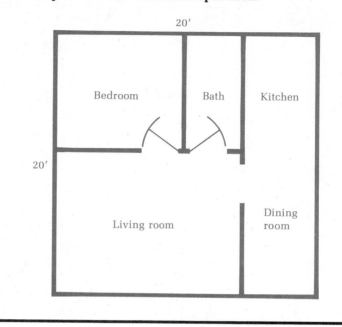

In checking with professors, other students, and his father (who is in the real estate and home construction business), and after conducting a market survey, Dixon decided that a one-bedroom unit with a small living room, a dining room–kitchen combination, and a bath would be most popular (see layout in Exhibit 4A–1). There also appeared to be some demand for two- and three-bedroom units. The construction costs for a 20-foot by 20-foot one-bedroom unit ran between $25 and $27 per square foot. Common walls for multiple units kept those costs to a minimum. Land costs near the university were high, but this area was considered most desirable because of the favorable location.

On the basis of the information above, and with the encouragement of his father, Dixon decided to start his business with a four-unit complex (three one-bedroom units and a two-bedroom unit). During the first six months, Dixon engaged in the following transactions.

1. Invested $4,000 of personal savings in the business.

2. Borrowed $15,000 from his father, Charles Able, on a 2-year note at 6% interest.

3. Purchased a lot near the university for $7,000 down and a 10-year contract for the $20,000 balance of the purchase price. The interest rate on the contract was 9%.

4. Constructed a building complex containing 2,000 square feet at a cost of $26.25 per square foot. Landscaping and other exterior building improvements cost an additional $5,200. The construction was financed

by a loan from First National Bank on a 25-year mortgage at $9\frac{1}{2}$% interest. Dixon's father cosigned the mortgage.

5. Purchased furnishings for the rental units at a cost of $4,300. Paid half in cash, with the balance due in 60 days at no interest.

6. Paid advertising and promotion expenses of $475.

7. Paid two friends a total of $300 for helping with the clean-up work.

8. Paid $400 for utility hook-ups and deposits.

9. Withdrew $500 from the business for school-related expenses.

The demand for Dixon's "home-style" rental units was impressive. During the first month, the occupancy rate was 60 percent, and for the next five months, the rate never fell below 80 percent, and usually averaged about 85 percent. Dixon rented the one-bedroom units for $30 a day, or $180 a week, and the two-bedroom unit for $40 a day, or $240 a week. Additional transactions for this 6-month period were

10. Cash revenues were $4,400. The balance of the $18,900 total revenues were credit card sales. Of the $14,500 total receivables, three-fourths had been remitted, less the 3% service charge retained by the credit card companies.

11. Paid an average of $240 per month for utilities. Maintenance costs were $460 for the 6-month period. Advertising amounted to $300.

12. Recorded depreciation on the building, furnishings, and building improvements in the amounts of $1,312, $860, and $520, respectively.

13. Paid interest of $8,182 on notes ($900 + $1,800 + $5,482 = $8,182 interest expense).

14. Made principal payments of $4,000 on the land note and $2,500 on the building note.

15. Withdrew $1,000 for additional school expenses. Any remaining profits were closed to Dixon's Proprietor's Capital account.

Dixon's accounting records consisted of a General Journal and a General Ledger. Anxious to know the results of his first year in business, Dixon journalized the transactions above; posted them to the ledger accounts; prepared a trial balance, and financial statements consisting of an Income Statement, Balance Sheet, and Statement of Changes in Financial Position (see Exhibits 4A–2 through 4A–7).

As you review Dixon's records, remember that for a proprietor the owner's equity account is simply Dixon Able, Capital. This account shows the amount remaining after all liabilities (creditor claims) are subtracted from the assets. It represents the original investment of the proprietor less any withdrawals plus any additions to capital from further investments and from earnings of the business. Also note the cross-referencing between the ledger accounts and the journal. The post reference column is designed for this purpose. Note also that all figures have been rounded to the nearest dollar. Finally, observe that instead of using dates, the transactions are identified by the numbers in parentheses—for example, transaction (1), (2), and so forth.

EXHIBIT 4A–2   General Journal—Dixon Able, Proprietor

Page 1

Date	Account Titles and Explanation	Post Ref.	Debit	Credit
(1)	Cash	100	4000	
	Dixon Able, Capital	220		4000
	Invested $4,000 in company.			
(2)	Cash	100	15000	
	Notes Payable	211		15000
	Issued note to Charles Able (terms: 2 years, 6%).			
(3)	Land	112	27000	
	Cash	100		7000
	Notes Payable	211		20000
	Purchased land for $7,000 cash and issued note of $20,000 (terms: 10 years, 9%).			
(4)	Building	113	52500	
	Building Improvements	114	5200	
	Notes Payable	211		57700
	Constructed building financed by 25-year note at 9½%.			
(5)	Furnishings	115	4300	
	Cash	100		2150
	Accounts Payable	200		2150
	Purchased furnishings, ½ down and balance in 60 days at no interest.			
(6)	Advertising Expense	501	475	
	Cash	100		475
	Paid advertising and promotion expenses.			
(7)	Cleaning Expense	502	300	
	Cash	100		300
	Paid clean-up expenses.			

Page 2

Date	Account Titles and Explanation	Post. Ref.	Debit	Credit
(8)	Utility Expense	503	400	
	Cash	100		400
	Paid utility hook-up charge.			
(9)	Dixon Able, Capital	220	500	
	Cash	100		500
	Withdrew cash from the business.			
(10)	Cash	100	4400	
	Accounts Receivable	101	14500	
	Revenues	401		18900
	Received service revenues.			
	Cash	100	10549	
	Financing Expense	504	326	
	Accounts Receivable	101		10875
	Collected accounts receivable, less			
	finance expense ($14,500 × 3/4 =			
	$10,875 × 3% = $326.25).			
(11)	Utilities Expense	503	1440	
	Cash	100		1440
	Paid utilities expense for 6			
	months ($240 × 6 = $1,440).			
	Maintenance Expense	505	460	
	Cash	100		460
	Paid for maintenance for 6 months.			
	Advertising Expense	501	300	
	Cash	100		300
	Paid advertising expenses.			
(12)	Depreciation Expense	506	2692	
	Accumulated Depreciation—Building	113A		1312
	Accumulated Depreciation—Improvements	114A		520
	Accumulated Depreciation—Furnishings	115A		860
	To record depreciation for the year.			

(handwritten marginal notes by the collection entry: "40,000 ×", ".80", "× 3%")

(continued on the next page)

Page 3

Date	Account Titles and Explanation	Post Ref.	Debit	Credit
(13)	Interest Expense	507	8182	
	Cash	100		8182
	Paid interest on notes			
	for first year.			
(14)	Notes Payable	211	6500	
	Cash	100		6500
	Paid principal on notes.			
(15)	Dixon Able, Capital	220	1000	
	Cash	100		1000
	Withdrew cash from the business.			
	Income Summary	305	14575	
	Advertising Expense	501		775
	Cleaning Expense	502		300
	Utility Expense	503		1840
	Financing Expense	504		326
	Maintenance Expense	505		460
	Depreciation Expense	506		2692
	Interest Expense	507		8182
	To close expense accounts to			
	Income Summary.			
	Revenues	401	18900	
	Income Summary	305		18900
	To close Revenues to Income			
	Summary.			
	Income Summary	305	4325	
	Dixon Able, Capital	220		4325
	To close Income Summary to			
	Dixon Able, Capital.			

EXHIBIT 4A–3   General Ledger—Dixon Able, Proprietor

Cash   Account No. 100

Date	Explanation	Post Ref.	Debit	Credit	Balance
	Beginning Balance				-0-
		GJ1	4000		4000
		GJ1	15000		19000
		GJ1		7000	12000
		GJ1		2150	9850
		GJ1		475	9375
		GJ1		300	9075
		GJ2		400	8675
		GJ2		500	8175
		GJ2	4400		12575
		GJ2	10549		23124
		GJ2		1440	21684
		GJ2		460	21224
		GJ2		300	20924
		GJ3		8182	12742
		GJ3		6500	6242
		GJ3		1000	5242

Accounts Receivable   Account No. 101

Date	Explanation	Post Ref.	Debit	Credit	Balance
	Beginning Balance				-0-
		GJ2	14500		14500
		GJ2		10875	3625

Land   Account No. 112

Date	Explanation	Post Ref.	Debit	Credit	Balance
	Beginning Balance				-0-
		GJ1	27000		27000

(continued on the next page)

Building — Account No. 113

Date	Explanation	Post Ref.	Debit	Credit	Balance
	Beginning Balance				-0-
		GJ1	52500		52500

Accumulated Depreciation—Building — Account No. 113A

Date	Explanation	Post Ref.	Debit	Credit	Balance
	Beginning Balance				-0-
		GJ2		1312	< 1312 >

Building Improvements — Account No. 114

Date	Explanation	Post Ref.	Debit	Credit	Balance
	Beginning Balance				-0-
		GJ1	5200		5200

Accumulated Depreciation—Building Improvements — Account No. 114A

Date	Explanation	Post Ref.	Debit	Credit	Balance
	Beginning Balance				-0-
		GJ2		520	< 520 >

Furnishings   Account No. 115

Date	Explanation	Post Ref.	Debit	Credit	Balance
	Beginning Balance				-0-
		GJ1	4300		4300

Accumulated Depreciation-Furnishings   Account No. 115A

Date	Explanation	Post Ref.	Debit	Credit	Balance
	Beginning Balance				-0-
		GJ2		860	< 860 >

Accounts Payable   Account No. 200

Date	Explanation	Post Ref.	Debit	Credit	Balance
	Beginning Balance				-0-
		GJ1		2150	< 2150 >

Notes Payable   Account No. 211

Date	Explanation	Post Ref.	Debit	Credit	Balance
	Beginning Balance				-0-
		GJ1		15000	< 15000 >
		GJ1		20000	< 35000 >
		GJ1		57700	< 92700 >
		GJ3	6500		< 86200 >

(continued on the next page)

Dixon Able, Capital — Account No. 220

Date	Explanation	Post Ref.	Debit	Credit	Balance
	Beginning Balance				—0—
		GJ1		4000	< 4000 >
		GJ2	500		< 3500 >
		GJ3	1000		< 2500 >
		GJ3		4325	< 6825 >

Income Summary — Account No. 305

Date	Explanation	Post Ref.	Debit	Credit	Balance
		GJ3	14575		14575
		GJ3		18900	< 4325 >
		GJ3	4325		—0—

Revenues — Account No. 401

Date	Explanation	Post Ref.	Debit	Credit	Balance
		GJ2		18900	< 18900 >
		GJ3	18900		—0—

Advertising Expense — Account No. 501

Date	Explanation	Post Ref.	Debit	Credit	Balance
		GJ1	475		475
		GJ2	300		775
		GJ3		775	—0—

Cleaning Expense   Account No. 502

Date	Explanation	Post Ref.	Debit	Credit	Balance
		GJ1	300		300
		GJ3		300	—0—

Utility Expense   Account No. 503

Date	Explanation	Post Ref.	Debit	Credit	Balance
		GJ2	400		400
		GJ2	1440		1840
		GJ3		1840	—0—

Financing Expense   Account No. 504

Date	Explanation	Post Ref.	Debit	Credit	Balance
		GJ2	326		326
		GJ3		326	—0—

Maintenance Expense   Account No. 505

Date	Explanation	Post Ref.	Debit	Credit	Balance
		GJ2	460		460
		GJ3		460	—0—

(continued on the next page)

Depreciation Expense   *Account No. 506*

Date	Explanation	Post Ref.	Debit	Credit	Balance
		GJ2	2692		2692
		GJ3		2692	—0—

Interest Expense   *Account No. 507*

Date	Explanation	Post Ref.	Debit	Credit	Balance
		GJ3	8182		8182
		GJ3		8182	—0—

EXHIBIT 4A–4   **Dixon Able, Proprietor**
Trial Balance as of December 31, 19X1

Number	Account	Debits	Credits
100	Cash	$ 5,242	
101	Accounts Receivable	3,625	
112	Land	27,000	
113	Building	52,500	
113A	Accumulated Depreciation—Building		$ 1,312
114	Building Improvements	5,200	
114A	Accumulated Depreciation—Building Improvements		520
115	Furnishings	4,300	
115A	Accumulated Depreciation—Furnishings		860
200	Accounts Payable		2,150
211	Notes Payable		86,200
220	Dixon Able, Capital		2,500
401	Revenues		18,900
501	Advertising Expense	775	
502	Cleaning Expense	300	
503	Utility Expense	1,840	
504	Financing Expense	326	
505	Maintenance Expense	460	
506	Depreciation Expense	2,692	
507	Interest Expense	8,182	
		$112,442	$112,442

EXHIBIT 4A–5 Dixon Able, Proprietor
Income Statement for the Year Ended December 31, 19X1

Revenues		$18,900
Less Expenses:		
Advertising	$ 775	
Cleaning	300	
Utility	1,840	
Financing	326	
Maintenance	460	
Depreciation	2,692	
Interest	8,182	14,575
Net Income		$ 4,325

EXHIBIT 4A–6 Dixon Able, Proprietor
Balance Sheet as of December 31, 19X1

Assets

Cash		$ 5,242
Accounts Receivable		3,625
Land		27,000
Building	$52,500	
Building Improvements	5,200	
Furnishings	4,300	
Subtotal	$62,000	
Less Accumulated Depreciation	2,692	59,308
Total Assets		$95,175

Liabilities and Proprietorship Capital

Accounts Payable		$ 2,150
Notes Payable		86,200
Dixon Able, Capital		6,825
Total Liabilities and Proprietorship Capital		$95,175

EXHIBIT 4A-7 **Dixon Able, Proprietor**

Statement of Changes in Financial Position for the Year Ended December 31, 19X1

Sources of Funds

Operations:	Net Income	$ 4,325	
	Add Depreciation	2,692	$ 7,017
Investment by Dixon in Business			4,000
Long-Term Note from Dixon's Father			15,000
Long-Term Note on Land			20,000
Long-Term Note on Building			57,700
Total Sources of Funds			$103,717

Uses of Funds

Purchase of Land	$27,000	
Purchase of Building	57,700	
Purchase of Furnishings	4,300	
Payment of Principal on Notes	6,500	
Withdrawal of Cash from Business	1,500	
Total Uses of Funds		97,000
Increase in Working Capital		$ 6,717

Schedule of Changes in Working Capital

	Beginning of Operation	End of First Year of Operation
Current Assets:		
Cash	0	$5,242
Accounts Receivable	0	3,625
	0	$8,867
Current Liabilities:		
Accounts Payable	0	2,150
Net Working Capital	0	$6,717

Increase in Net Working Capital = $6,717

The financial statements were impressive, especially for the first year of operation, and Dixon was excited about future prospects. In fact, Dixon was convinced that expansion held the key to even greater earnings. Specifically, he wanted to build more four-unit complexes, but that would require additional outside capital, as well as extra help in managing the units. Dixon convinced his close friend, John Graden, who was a graduate student in accounting, to enter into a partnership with him. John agreed to invest $7,500. Dixon's father and John's uncle, Sam Graden, were also brought in as partners, with Sam Graden contributing $15,000 and Charles Able investing the principal amount on the note owed him as his share of the partnership interest. Since only Dixon and John contributed to the management of the business, profits were distributed 30 percent each to Dixon and John and 20 percent each to Charles and Sam.

As soon as the partnership agreement was finalized, Dixon and John arranged for the purchase of additional land and the construction of two new four-unit complexes. The following transactions took place during the next year.

1. Collected the balance of accounts receivable, $3,625 less a 3% finance charge.

2. Made the second payment on furnishings purchased for the first rental unit, $2,150.

3. Purchased two adjacent building lots for $10,000 down plus a 5-year note payable for $45,000 at an interest rate of 9%.

4. Constructed two building complexes of 2,000 square feet each at a cost of $32 per square foot. Building improvements were an additional $12,000. The construction was financed by a 10-year loan of $140,000 from City Bank at an interest rate of $9\frac{1}{4}\%$.

5. Purchased furnishings for the new units at a cost of $9,200. $6,000 was paid in cash with the balance due in 6 months with no interest.

6. Paid clean-up expenses of $700.

7. Paid utility hook-up expenses of $800.

8. Earned revenues of $62,600. Of this amount, $22,600 was received in cash and the balance was credit card sales. Of the $40,000 total receivables, 80% were collected, less the 3% service charge retained by the credit card companies.

9. Paid an average of $250 per month for utilities for the first 6 months, and $700 per month for the last 6 months. Maintenance costs amounted to $1,200. Cleaning costs totaled $1,600. Advertising and promotion costs were $850.

10. Paid interest and principal on notes. The amount of interest expense incurred was $23,684 and the amount of principal paid was $21,100.

11. Recorded depreciation for the year: buildings, $4,512; building improvements, $1,720; and furnishings, $2,700.

12. Distributed one-half of the year's income to the partners.

Dixon and John journalized the transactions for the second year of operation, posted them to the ledger accounts, and prepared a trial balance and selected financial statements (see Exhibits 4A–8 through 4A–10).

EXHIBIT 4A-8 **Able & Graden, Partnership**
Trial Balance as of December 31, 19X2

Number	Account	Debits	Credits
100	Cash	$ 11,114	
101	Accounts Receivable	8,000	
112	Land	82,000	
113	Buildings	180,500	
113A	Accumulated Depreciation—Buildings		$ 5,824
114	Building Improvements	17,200	
114A	Accumulated Depreciation—Building Improvements		2,240
115	Furnishings	13,500	
115A	Accumulated Depreciation—Furnishings		3,560
200	Accounts Payable		3,200
211	Notes Payable		235,100
220	Dixon Able, Capital		6,825
221	John Graden, Capital		7,500
222	Charles Able, Capital		15,000
223	Sam Graden, Capital		15,000
401	Rent Revenues		62,600
501	Advertising Expense	850	
502	Cleaning Expense	2,300	
503	Utility Expense	6,500	
504	Financing Expense	1,069	
505	Maintenance Expense	1,200	
506	Depreciation Expense	8,932	
507	Interest Expense	23,684	
		$356,849	$356,849

EXHIBIT 4A-9 **Able & Graden, Partnership**
Income Statement for the Year Ended December 31, 19X2

Revenues		$62,600
Less Expenses:		
Advertising	$ 850	
Cleaning	2,300	
Utility	6,500	
Financing	1,069	
Maintenance	1,200	
Depreciation	8,932	
Interest	23,684	44,535
Net Income		$18,065

EXHIBIT 4A–10   Able & Graden, Partnership
Balance Sheet as of December 31, 19X2

Assets

Cash		$ 2,080
Accounts Receivable		8,000
Land		82,000
Buildings	$180,500	
Building Improvements	17,200	
Furnishings	13,500	
Subtotal	$211,200	
Less Accumulated Depreciation	11,624	199,576
Total Assets		$291,656

Liabilities and Partnership Capital

Accounts Payable	$ 3,200
Notes Payable	235,100
Dixon Able, Capital	9,535
John Graden, Capital	10,209
Charles Able, Capital	16,806
Sam Graden, Capital	16,806
Total Liabilities and Partnership Capital	$291,656

Everyone was pleased with the results of the first operating year of the partnership. They decided to continue the operations on a part-time basis, although Dixon and John had been graduated and had accepted full-time positions with a consulting firm and a CPA firm, respectively.

Because of the increasing demand for temporary housing in Mountain View, the profitability of the business grew substantially over the next two years, and Dixon and John decided that they would have to run the business on a full-time basis. The partners further decided to incorporate the business in order to raise additional capital to finance expansion into nearby markets. The following entries illustrate the conversion of the partnership into the Valley Housing Corporation, and the sale of 20,000 shares of common stock, $10 par value, for $10 per share. (The numbers here and in some of the exhibits that follow are assumed.)

Dixon Able, Capital	$50,500	
John Graden, Capital	47,500	
Charles Able, Capital	46,000	
Sam Graden, Capital	46,000	
Common Stock		$190,000

Converted partners' capital to common stock; 19,000 shares of stock were issued.

Cash	$200,000	
Common Stock		$200,000

Issued 20,000 shares of common stock, $10 per share.

During the following two years, additional buildings were constructed, several full-time and part-time employees were hired, and expansion into nearby markets proceeded smoothly. At the end of the second year of operation as a corporation, the company's accountant journalized the transactions, including the adjustments listed below, posted them to the ledger accounts, and prepared an adjusted trial balance, an Income Statement, and a Balance Sheet (see Exhibits 4A–11 through 4A–13).

1. Salaries unpaid for the last 4 days of the year amounted to $1,000.

2. Supplies on hand totaled $2,600. (Supplies are charged to expense when purchased.)

3. Rent received in advance as of the end of the year amounted to $1,100. (A Revenue account is credited when cash is received.)

4. Taxes of $7,000 for the next 6 months have already been paid and charged to Income Tax Expense.

Note that the capital accounts of the corporation include Common Stock and Retained Earnings. Retained Earnings shows the amount of net income accumulated in a business since incorporation after dividends are distributed to the stockholders.

EXHIBIT 4A–11 **Valley Housing Corporation**
Trial Balance as of December 31, 19X6

Number	Account	Debits	Credits
100	Cash	$ 78,780	
101	Accounts Receivable	75,600	
102	Supplies	2,600	
103	Prepaid Taxes	7,000	
112	Land	215,000	
113	Buildings	317,000	
113A	Accumulated Depreciation—Buildings		$ 27,950
114	Building Improvements	42,100	
114A	Accumulated Depreciation—Building Improvement		8,210
115	Furnishings	22,600	
115A	Accumulated Depreciation—Furnishings		6,300
200	Accounts Payable		2,500
201	Salary Payable		1,000
202	Rent Received in Advance		1,100
211	Notes Payable		190,000
220	Common Stock		390,000
221	Retained Earnings		37,600
401	Rent Revenues		314,180
501	Advertising Expense	2,300	
503	Utility Expense	24,600	
504	Financing Expense :	7,560	
505	Maintenance Expense	8,600	
506	Depreciation Expense	24,200	
507	Interest Expense	45,700	
508	Salary Expense	93,000	
509	Income Tax Expense	7,000	
510	Supplies Expense	5,200	
		$978,840	$978,840

EXHIBIT 4A–12   Valley Housing Corporation
Income Statement for the Year Ended December 31, 19X6

Revenues		$314,180
Less Expenses:		
Advertising	$ 2,300	
Utility	24,600	
Financing	7,560	
Maintenance	8,600	
Depreciation	24,200	
Interest	45,700	
Salary	93,000	
Income Taxes	7,000	
Supplies	5,200	218,160
Net Income		$ 96,020
EPS ($96,020 ÷ 39,000 shares outstanding)		$2.46

EXHIBIT 4A–13   Valley Housing Corporation
Balance Sheet as of December 31, 19X6

Assets

Cash	$ 78,780
Accounts Receivable	75,600
Supplies	2,600
Prepaid Taxes	7,000
Land	215,000
Buildings (Net of Accumulated Depreciation of $27,950)	289,050
Building Improvements (Net of Accumulated Depreciation of $8,210)	33,890
Furnishings (Net of Accumulated Depreciation of $6,300)	16,300
Total Assets	$718,220

Liabilities and Stockholders' Equity

Accounts Payable	$ 2,500
Salaries Payable	1,000
Rent Received in Advance	1,100
Notes Payable	190,000
Common Stock	390,000
Retained Earnings	133,620
Total Liabilities and Stockholders' Equity	$718,220

EXERCISES

E4A–1   Journalizing and Posting

Several transactions for Able & Graden partnership are identified on page 155. Journalize these transactions and post to appropriate ledger accounts. (Hint: If you account for the transactions properly, you should end up with the trial balance amounts on page 156.)

E4A–2   Worksheet and Closing Entries

From the information presented on page 158 and in Exhibits 4A–11 through 4A–13, prepare a worksheet that shows the adjustments required at the end of the year. Also prepare the closing journal entries for Valley Housing Corporation at year-end.

Income Determination

Obverse and reverse of a silver coin issued between 274 and 216 B.C. The obverse shows Hiero II of Syracuse and the reverse is Victory driving a four-horse chariot. (The Bettmann Archive)

CHAPTER 5

Income Measurement and Reporting

THIS CHAPTER EXPLAINS: What income is.

Alternative ways of measuring income.

The recognition of revenues.

How cost of goods sold and other expenses are measured.

The Income Statement.

In Chapter 2 we introduced the Income Statement, the Balance Sheet, and the Statement of Changes in Financial Position as the end products, or outputs, of the accounting cycle. Each of these statements plays a significant role in informing interested investors and others about the financial condition of a firm. The next nine chapters will help you understand the primary financial statements. Specifically, this and the next chapter analyze the Income Statement. Chapters 7 through 12 cover the Balance Sheet, and Chapter 13 considers the Statement of Changes in Financial Position.

This chapter will first describe different ways of measuring income and then will explain the currently used method in some detail. The explanation will include discussions of the recognition and nature of (1) revenues, (2) cost of goods sold, and (3) other expenses, as well as an explanation of the Income Statement.

While only one method of reporting income is currently used in the primary financial statements, an understanding of alternative income concepts is important because supplementary disclosures using other methods are required of some firms. In addition, there is considerable controversy about the adequacy of the currently accepted method. Many experts believe that it is only a matter of time until one of the alternatives is selected as the required method for reporting purposes.

Definition of Income

In an economic sense, income can be thought of as the increase in wealth experienced during a period. One well-known economist defined income essentially as the maximum amount a person or firm can consume during an accounting period and still be as well off at the end of the period as at the beginning.[1] In other words, if a firm has $1,000 at the beginning of an accounting period, its income would be the amount it could spend during the period and still have $1,000 at the end of the period (assuming no investments or withdrawals). Conceptually, this definition of income is excellent; in practice, economic income is difficult to measure.

To illustrate the complexity of measuring economic income, we will assume that three individuals decide to open a clothing store and that each contributes $17,000 to the business. We will also assume that they use their $51,000 (3 × $17,000) to purchase a building for $50,000 and an inventory of ten coats for a total cost of $1,000, or $100 each. If, during their first month of business, they sell all ten coats at a price of $200 each and have no other operating expenses, how much income did they earn? Your first reaction is probably to say that their income is $1,000 (10 coats × $100 profit on each coat). This answer may or may not be correct. If, in fact, the building is still worth exactly $50,000, their economic income is $1,000. If, however, the building's value has increased or decreased, income may be something more or less than $1,000. How much more or less cannot be exactly determined because the owners chose not to sell the building at the end of the month.

Some accounting theorists would argue that income could be determined by valuing the building at either its replacement cost (the amount it would cost to purchase a similar building) or the amount at which it could be sold. In reality, the only sure measure of the building's value is its sales price when it is actually sold.

When this single complication is considered in relation to an actual business with numerous assets and transactions, the problems of measuring income multiply considerably. In fact, the income of a business can only be accurately and objectively determined at the end of the firm's life, after it has sold or otherwise disposed of all its operating and other assets and when cash is the only remaining asset. At that time cash can be counted, and the increase over the beginning amount, adjusted for subsequent owner withdrawals and contributions, is income.

Since stockholders and others are unwilling to wait until the end of a firm's life to find out how well it has performed, firms compute and report estimates of net income at regular intervals (at least annually, and often monthly or quarterly). These periodic estimates are reported on the Income Statement. Although the Income Statement reports a precise net income number, there are usually several estimates included in the calculation of this number.

---

[1] J. R. Hicks, *Value and Capital*, 2nd ed. (New York: Oxford University Press, 1946).

Alternative Ways of Measuring Income

Various methods have been proposed for measuring income. Four of these will be considered here: (1) the cash-basis method, (2) the currently used accrual-basis historical cost method, (3) the general price-level-adjusted (constant dollar) historical cost method, and (4) the current-value method. In reading about these methods, you should note that this discussion is at an elementary level and that each method involves complexities and has variations not mentioned here.

CASH-BASIS INCOME

cash-basis method   *the method of measuring income in which income is defined as cash receipts less cash disbursements during an accounting period*

Probably the simplest and most objective measure of income results from using the cash-basis method. With this approach, income is the difference between a business's cash receipts and its cash disbursements during an accounting period. Cash receipts and disbursements can be measured with a high degree of objectivity. In fact, it is only after we have determined our cash-basis income that most of us make such personal decisions as whether or not we can afford to buy a new or used car. Most individuals also pay taxes on the amount of their cash-basis income.

To illustrate the cash-basis method of measuring income, we will assume the following data for Fox Sporting Goods.

inventory   *goods held for sale*

1. Started business on January 1, 1981. On that day Fox purchased a building for $100,000 as well as $50,000 of sporting goods inventory. The building is expected to have a useful life of 20 years.

2. During 1981, Fox sold one-half of the inventory for $60,000.

3. The only other expense incurred during 1981 was $20,000 paid for salaries.

Given these data and assuming that all of the above are cash transactions, the cash-basis loss might be computed as follows:

Cash Receipts		$ 60,000
Cash Disbursements:		
Purchase of Sporting Goods Inventory	$ 50,000	
Purchase of Building	100,000	
Payment of Salaries	20,000	
Total Cash Disbursements		170,000
Net Loss		($110,000)

As you can see, there are some problems when income is computed on a cash basis. First, did Fox really lose $110,000? Certainly, cash outflows exceeded cash inflows by $110,000. However, the major reason for the loss was a $100,000 expenditure for a building that will benefit the company for many years and is more of an investment than an expense. Wouldn't it be better to allocate or assign a portion of the cost of the building to each of the periods in which it is used by the company? For example, if the

expenses   *costs of assets used up or additional liabilities incurred in the normal course of business to generate revenues*

building can be used effectively for 20 years, wouldn't it be preferable to charge only one-twentieth of the cost against income in the current year?

Also, only half the inventory was actually sold. Shouldn't only the cost of the portion that was sold be an expense? And, what if additional sporting goods had been sold on credit, with payment yet to be received? Shouldn't such sales be recognized? And what if new sporting goods inventory had been bought on credit near the fiscal year-end, with payment to be made 60 days later? Shouldn't such purchases be recognized? Because of these and other questions, the cash-basis income measurement method may not be useful for determining income in many companies. However, some government and other not-for-profit organizations, as well as many small businesses, rely on this type of accounting.

ACCRUAL-BASIS HISTORICAL COST INCOME

accrual-basis historical cost method *the method of measuring income in which income is defined as revenues earned minus expenses incurred during a period without regard to changes in the values of assets or liabilities or in the general price level*

The second alternative, and the one currently used for the primary financial statements, is the accrual-basis historical cost method. Under this approach, the historical costs of assets are allocated (depreciated) over their useful lives and only the cost of inventory actually sold is charged as an expense. Net income is equal to revenues earned minus expenses incurred. To illustrate the accrual-basis historical cost method, we again calculate the net income of Fox Sporting Goods for 1981.

Revenues		$60,000
Expenses:		
Cost of Inventory Sold	$25,000	
Salary Expense	20,000	
Depreciation Expense ($100,000 ÷ 20 years)	5,000	50,000
Net Income		$10,000

GENERAL PRICE-LEVEL-ADJUSTED HISTORICAL COST INCOME

general price-level-adjusted historical cost method *the method of measuring income in which income is defined as revenues less expenses as adjusted by a general (economy-wide) price index, plus any purchasing power gains or losses due to changes in the general price level*

A third alternative is the general price-level-adjusted historical cost method. With this approach, which can be complicated, the original costs of assets, liabilities, and owners' equity are adjusted upward or downward according to some economy-wide price index (such as the Consumer Price Index). Because this method merely adjusts historical costs, it is not a valuation approach. Rather, it is a reporting scheme that attempts to measure financial statement information of different periods in constant dollars— that is, dollars of equivalent purchasing power.

To illustrate, we will again use the Fox Sporting Goods example. To remind you:

1. Fox started business on January 1, 1981. On that date, the company purchased a building for $100,000 and bought $50,000 of sporting goods inventory. The building is expected to have a useful life of 20 years.
2. During 1981, Fox sold one-half of the inventory for $60,000.
3. The only other expense during 1981 was $20,000 paid for salaries.

In addition, we will assume that on December 31, 1981, an economy-wide index indicated that, on the average, prices had risen 20 percent during the year.

Given these data, the amount of price-level-adjusted historical cost net income could be computed as follows:

Increases:
Revenues ($60,000 × 1.10) $66,000

Decreases:
Cost of Inventory Sold ($25,000 × 1.10) $27,500
Salary Expense ($20,000 × 1.10)   22,000
Depreciation Expense
[($100,000 × 1.20) ÷ 20 years]   6,000   55,500
Net Income $10,500

In this example, revenues, cost of inventory sold, and salary expense were adjusted by an index of 1.10. The 1.10 was used because it is assumed that the 20 percent inflation occurred evenly throughout the year and thus the average increase for the year was 10 percent. The depreciation expense was adjusted by 1.20 because the building was purchased on January 1 and was used for the full year. These assumptions were made to keep the example simple—otherwise these elements would have to be adjusted at the varying rates that existed on the specific dates the transactions occurred. Also, note that this approach does not include in income any changes in the values of the assets. Rather, it adjusts historical costs to constant dollars.

Several technical adjustments have been eliminated here to keep the example as simple as possible. For example, monetary gains and losses would be computed on assets and liabilities, such as accounts and notes payable. Since these types of assets and liabilities are fixed in total dollars, inflation, which reduces the purchasing power of the dollar, reduces their value. Thus, a holder of a note payable gains (through the decreased value of the debt) during a period of inflation, whereas a holder of cash loses purchasing power. These types of monetary gains and losses must also be included in the calculations of net income.

The price-level-adjusted alternative has received significant support in the profession. Its advantage is that indexes are readily available from the government and can be mechanically applied to any set of numbers. Its major disadvantage is that the specific assets and liabilities often do not increase or decrease in value at the same rate as economy-wide inflation. In fact, inflation is only one factor that affects price. Others are increases or decreases in productivity and technology and changes in supply or demand. An example of an asset that would be adversely affected by this method is a computer. With this method, the historical cost of computers would be adjusted upward because of inflation, whereas, in fact, due to technological advances their prices have dropped significantly in recent years. Nevertheless, in most cases this alternative works quite well and selected supplementary disclosure of the impact of general price changes on assets, liabilities, owners' equity, and income is currently required of many large companies by the Financial Accounting Standards Board (FASB).

CURRENT-VALUE INCOME

current-value method *the method of measuring income in which income is defined as the excess of revenues over expenses plus the net increases or decreases in the values of specific assets and liabilities during a period*

A fourth alternative is the current-value method. With this approach, all elements of the financial statements (assets, liabilities, revenues, expenses, and so forth) are recorded at their current values. The net income for a period, then, is the increase in net assets (assets minus liabilities) adjusted for any contributions or withdrawals by the owners of the business. For example, suppose that a company's total assets and total liabilities at the beginning and the end of a year were

	Current Values at Beginning of Year	Current Values at End of Year
Total Assets	$60,000	$80,000
Total Liabilities	30,000	34,000
Net Assets	$30,000	$46,000

If no additional investments or withdrawals were made during the year, current value net income would be $16,000 ($46,000 − $30,000).

To further illustrate, we will refer back to the data for Fox Sporting Goods. In addition, we will assume that on December 31, 1981, the values of the building and remaining inventory had increased to $125,000 and $35,000, respectively.

Given these data, current-value net income might be computed as follows:

Increases:		
Revenues (Sale of Goods)	$60,000	
Increase in Value of Building	25,000	
Increase in Value of Inventory	10,000	$95,000
Decreases:		
Current Cost Depreciation—Building		
($125,000 ÷ 20 years)	$ 6,250	
Current Cost of Inventory Sold	35,000	
Salary Expense	20,000	61,250
Net Income		$33,750

In this example, the increased value of the building is allocated (depreciated) over its useful life (20 years). Also, the cost of inventory sold is expensed at its replacement cost of $35,000. (Since the remaining half of the inventory has a current value of $35,000, it can be assumed that the replacement cost of the half that was sold is also $35,000.) Revenues and salary expense are already stated at their current costs and require no adjustment.

The current-value approach has received a significant amount of support in recent years because it is an attempt to measure the increase in the wealth of a business. In fact, in the mid-1970s, the SEC required approximately 100 of the largest companies in the United States to provide current-value data (as estimated by replacement costs) on most of their assets. In 1979, the FASB required that many firms provide both current-value and constant-dollar data[2] as supplementary information in their financial reports.

The major disadvantage of this method is the subjectivity of the current-value numbers. Unless the company's inventory and building, for example, are actually sold, it is difficult to know their exact current values. Nevertheless, this method is theoretically sound and may be the required reporting alternative of the future.

TO SUMMARIZE Four of the most common methods of measuring income are (1) cash-basis, (2) accrual-basis historical cost, (3) general price-level-adjusted historical cost, and (4) current-value. Each has advantages and disadvantages. The second method is required for the primary financial statements, while the third and fourth methods are required as supplementary disclosures for some companies.

The currently required accrual-basis historical cost income method will be used throughout this text.

Accrual-Basis Historical Cost Income

Net income under the accrual-basis historical cost method is equal to revenues earned minus expenses incurred. We will therefore first discuss and illustrate the issues relating to revenue recognition. Then we will describe how expenses are measured and recognized.

THE MEASUREMENT OF REVENUES

revenues *increases in resources from the sale of goods or services during the normal operations of a business*

revenue recognition principle *the idea that revenues should be recorded when (1) the earnings process has been substantially completed, and (2) an exchange has taken place*

Revenues, as you will recall from Chapter 2, are the increases in assets derived from the normal operating activities of an enterprise. According to the revenue recognition principle, revenues are usually recorded when two important criteria have been met: (1) the earnings process has been substantially completed, generally meaning that a sale has been made or a service has been performed, and (2) an exchange has taken place.[3] Thus, credit sales are recognized as revenues before cash is collected, and revenue from services performed is usually recognized when the service is performed and billed, not when cash is collected.

To illustrate this principle, we will assume that on a typical business day Gro Rite Products sells 30 sacks of fertilizer for cash and 20 sacks on credit, all at $10 per sack. Given these data, the revenue would be $500, and would be recorded as follows:

---

[2] The requirements of both the SEC and the FASB are far more complex than indicated by the simple examples used here. The illustrations are only intended to show the general nature of the various alternatives.

[3] There are cases in which revenue is recognized according to other criteria, such as upon production (when there is a ready market) or upon partial completion of the earnings process. However, these are exceptions to the rule.

Cash	300	
Accounts Receivable	200	
Sales Revenue		500

Sold 30 sacks of fertilizer for cash and 20 sacks on credit.

Although the debit entries are made to different accounts, the credit entry is always to a revenue account. Thus, accrual-basis accounting allows the recognition of $500 in revenue instead of the $300 that would be recognized with the cash-basis method.

The example given above is a simple illustration of how sales are recorded and revenue is recognized. In reality, sales transactions are usually more complex, involving such things as discounts for prompt payment, returns of merchandise sold, and losses from uncollectable credit sales. Before we discuss these complexities, one note is appropriate. In many companies, the most frequent types of journal entries are those to record sales, cash collections, purchases, and payments to suppliers. Because such transactions are so frequent, most firms maintain four separate special journals. These are: (1) the sales journal, (2) the cash receipts journal, (3) the purchases journal, and (4) the cash disbursements journal. In our analysis of transactions, we will use only a few selected journal entries and so we will continue to use the General Journal format. We discuss these special journals in the Supplement to this chapter.

Recognizing Revenue on Credit Sales

Most sales do not involve cash. Instead, they are on credit, with the buyer usually having from 10 days to 2 months in which to pay the seller for the merchandise purchased. The asset that arises from this kind of transaction is called an <u>accounts receivable</u>. An entry to record such a transaction and recognize the sales revenue might be

accounts receivable   *money due from rendering services or selling merchandise on credit; a current asset*

Accounts Receivable—Adam Smith	1,000	
Sales Revenue		1,000

Sold $1,000 of merchandise to Adam Smith.

This entry shows that a customer, Adam Smith, purchased $1,000 of merchandise on credit. When Adam Smith pays the full amount, the entry to record the receipt of cash and the canceling of the receivable would be

Cash	1,000	
Accounts Receivable—Adam Smith		1,000

Received payment in full from Adam Smith for merchandise purchased.

Complexities of Revenue Recognition

The two entries above are typical of those used to recognize sales revenue and record and cancel accounts receivable when the sales or collections transactions are simple. In many cases, however, there are complexities, such as sales discounts, returns of merchandise, or nonpayment by customers, that need to be considered.

Sales Discounts In many sales transactions the buyer is given a small discount if the bill is paid promptly. Such incentives to pay quickly are called sales, or cash, discounts and are typically expressed in abbreviated form. For example, 2/10, n/30 means that a buyer will receive a 2 percent discount from the purchase price (less any returns) if payment is made within 10 days of the date of purchase, but the net amount must be paid within 30 days or it will be considered past due. (Other common terms are 1/10, n/30, or 2/10, EOM, which means that a 2 percent discount is granted if payment is made within 10 days after the end of the month.) A 2 percent discount is a strong incentive to pay within 10 days because it is equal to an annual interest rate of about 36 percent.[4] In fact, if the amount owed is substantial, most firms will borrow from a bank or some other source at a lower rate in order to take advantage of the sales discount.

sales discount   a reduction in the sales price, allowed if payment is received within a specified period

If an account receivable is paid within a discount period, the entry to record the receipt of cash is different from the cash receipt entry shown earlier. Thus, if Adam Smith had purchased the $1,000 of merchandise on credit with terms 2/10, n/30 and had paid within the discount period, the entry to record the receipt of cash would be

Cash	980	
Sales Discounts	20	
Accounts Receivable—Adam Smith		1,000

Received payment from Adam Smith within the discount period.

Sales Discounts is a contra-revenue account, which means that it is deducted from Sales on the Income Statement. This account is included with other revenue accounts in the General Ledger but, unlike other revenues, has a debit balance. Exhibit 5–1 summarizes the entries for sales discounts, using the Adam Smith example.

contra account   an account that is offset or deducted from another account

Sales Returns and Allowances A customer often returns merchandise either because the item is defective or for more personal reasons, such as a change of heart. Whatever the reason, most companies generally accept

[4] This is calculated by computing an annual interest rate for the period that the money is "sacrificed." With terms 2/10, n/30, a buyer who pays on the 10th day instead of the 30th sacrifices the money for 20 days. Since 2 percent is earned in 20 days and there are almost 18 periods of 20 days in a year, earnings would be 18 times 2 percent, or approximately 36 percent annual interest.

EXHIBIT 5–1   Accounting for Sales Discounts

Transaction	Journal Entry		
Sale	Accounts Receivable	1,000	
	Sales Revenue		1,000
Payment (if within discount period)	Cash.......................	980	
	Sales Discounts ($1,000 × 2%) ..	20	
	Accounts Receivable....................		1,000
Payment (if not within discount period)	Cash.......................	1,000	
	Accounts Receivable....................		1,000

the merchandise in order to maintain good customer relations. When merchandise is returned, the company must make additional entries to correct both the Accounts Receivable and Sales Revenue accounts. A similar adjustment is required when the sales price is reduced because the merchandise was defective or damaged during shipment to the customer.

To illustrate the type of adjustment that would be needed, we will assume that Adam Smith returned $200 of the $1,000 of merchandise he had purchased. The entry to record the return of merchandise would be

Sales Returns and Allowances	200	
Accounts Receivable—Adam Smith		200

Received $200 of merchandise back from Adam Smith.

Adam Smith would be sent a "credit memorandum" for the return, stating that credit had been granted and that the balance of his account is now $800. The Sales Returns and Allowances account is a contra account similar to Sales Discounts.

It might seem that the use of offsetting contra accounts (Sales Discounts and Sales Returns and Allowances) involves extra steps that would not be necessary if returns of merchandise were deducted directly from the Sales Revenue account. Although such deductions would have the same final effect on net income, the separation of initial sales from all returns and allowances and discounts permits a company's management to analyze the extent to which customers are returning merchandise and taking advantage of discounts. If they find that excessive amounts of merchandise are being returned, they may decide that the company's sales returns policy is too liberal or that the quality of its merchandise needs improvement.

Losses from Uncollectable Accounts   The third kind of complication that can arise in the sales and collections cycle is the nonpayment of accounts. When companies sell goods and services on credit (as most do), there are usually some customers who do not pay for the merchandise they purchase. In fact, most businesses expect a certain percentage of their sales to be uncollectable. If a firm tries too hard to eliminate all losses from nonpaying customers, it usually makes its credit policy so restrictive that valuable sales are lost. On the other hand, if a firm extends credit too easily or to everyone, it may have so many uncollectable sales that it goes bankrupt. Because of this dilemma, most firms carefully monitor their credit sales to ensure that their policies are neither too restrictive nor too liberal.

When an account receivable becomes uncollectable, a firm incurs a bad-debt loss. This loss must be recognized as a cost of doing business and so is classified as an operating expense. There are two ways to account for losses from uncollectable accounts: the direct write-off method and the allowance method.

With the direct write-off method, an uncollectable account is recognized as an expense at the time it is deemed to be uncollectable. For example, assume that during the month of July, a certain store had credit sales of $30,000. These sales would be recorded as a debit to Accounts Receivable and a credit to Sales Revenue. If payments for all of the sales except one for $150 to R. Reynolds are received in August, the total of the entries to record collections is $29,850 in debits to Cash and credits to Accounts

---

Sales Returns and Allowances *a contra-sales account in which the return of or allowance for merchandise previously sold is recorded*

bad debt *an uncollectable account receivable*

direct write-off method *the recording of actual losses from uncollectable accounts as expenses during the period in which accounts receivable are determined to be uncollectable*

Receivable. If after receiving several past-due notices Reynolds still does not pay, the company will probably turn the account over to an attorney or an agency for collection. Then, if collection attempts fail, the company may decide that the R. Reynolds account will not be collected and write it off as a loss. The entry to record the loss under the direct write-off method would be

Doubtful Accounts Expense[5]   150
   Accounts Receivable—R. Reynolds   150
To write off the uncollectable account of R. Reynolds.

Although the direct write-off method is objective, it often violates the matching principle, which requires that all costs and expenses incurred in generating revenues be identified with those revenues, period by period. Thus, with the direct write-off method, sales made near the end of an accounting period may not be recognized as uncollectable until later periods. As a result, expenses are understated and net income is overstated in the earlier period and expenses are overstated in the later period. This makes the direct write-off method unacceptable to accounting policy makers unless bad debts are immaterial in amount.

The allowance method, on the other hand, satisfies the matching principle since it accounts for uncollectables during the period in which the sale takes place. With this method, a firm uses its experience or industry statistics to estimate the amount of each period's receivables that will become uncollectable. That estimate is recorded as a Doubtful Accounts Expense in the period of sale. Although the use of estimates may result in a rather imprecise expense figure, this is generally thought to be a less serious problem than the understatement of expenses created by the direct write-off method. In addition, with experience, these estimates tend to be quite accurate.

To illustrate the allowance method, we will assume that during 1980 total credit sales for a small appliance store were $200,000. If management estimated that one-half of 1 percent (0.005) of these sales would be uncollectable, the entry to record the doubtful accounts expense would be

Doubtful Accounts Expense   1,000
   Allowance for Doubtful Accounts   1,000
Estimated 1980 uncollectable accounts based on one-half of 1 percent of credit sales.

The Doubtful Accounts Expense is an account on the Income Statement, and Allowance for Doubtful Accounts (sometimes called Allowance for Bad Debts) is a contra account that is offset against Accounts Receivable on the Balance Sheet. In 1981, as actual losses are recognized, the balance in Allowance for Doubtful Accounts is written off. For example, if in 1981 a receivable of $150 could not be collected, the entry would be

Allowance for Doubtful Accounts   150
   Accounts Receivable   150
To write off an uncollectable account.

matching principle *the idea that all costs and expenses incurred in generating revenues must be recognized in the same reporting period as the related revenues*

allowance method *the recording of estimated losses due to uncollectable accounts as expenses during the period in which the sales occurred*

Doubtful Accounts Expense *an account that represents the current period's receivables estimated to become uncollectable*

Allowance for Doubtful Accounts *a contra account, deducted from Accounts Receivable, that shows the estimated losses from uncollectable accounts*

[5] It is recognized that the account is more than just doubtful; it is uncollectable. However, to keep the terminology consistent with the next section, the term Doubtful Accounts Expense will be used.

Because both Allowance for Doubtful Accounts and Accounts Receivable are Balance Sheet accounts, the write-off entry does not affect net income in 1981. Instead, the net income in 1980 (when the sale was actually made) already reflected the bad-debt expense. The net amount in Accounts Receivable after the write-off is exactly the same as it was before the entry, as shown below.

Before Write-off Entry		After Write-off Entry	
Accounts Receivable	$200,000	Accounts Receivable	$199,850
Less Allowance for Doubtful		Less Allowance for Doubtful	
Accounts	1,000	Accounts	850
Net Balance	$199,000	Net Balance	$199,000

book value of accounts receivable   *the net amount that would be received if all collectable receivables were collected; equal to total accounts receivable less the allowance for doubtful accounts*

This net balance of $199,000 is sometimes called the book value of accounts receivable (the amount that would be realized if all receivables were collected).

Occasionally, a customer whose account has been written off as uncollectable pays the outstanding balance. When this happens, the company reverses the entry that was used to write off the account and then recognizes the payment. For example, if the $150 were collected, the entries to correct the accounting records would be

Accounts Receivable	150	
Allowance for Doubtful Accounts......................		150

To reinstate the balance previously written off as uncollectable.

Cash	150	
Accounts Receivable..................................		150

Received payment in full of previously written-off accounts receivable.

It is extremely important to have good control over both the cash-collection procedures and the accounting for accounts receivable because subsequent payments could easily be pocketed by the person who received the cash. Since in this example the $150 had previously been written off as uncollectable, it would probably never be missed. For this reason, most companies separate cash handling from recording cash transactions in the accounts.

Estimating the Allowance for Doubtful Accounts   Because the amount recorded as Doubtful Accounts Expense affects net income directly, it is important that good estimation procedures be used. There are several methods of estimating uncollectable receivables.

1. As a percentage of total sales (usually credit sales).
2. As a percentage of total accounts receivable.
3. As a percentage based on an "aging" of accounts receivable.

To use these methods, a company must estimate the aggregate amount of the loss on the basis of experience. Obviously, a company that has been in business for several years should be able to make more accurate estimates than a new company. Many established companies will use a 3- or 5-year average as the basis for estimating current losses from uncollectable accounts.

If a company were to use credit sales as a basis for its estimate, the amount of uncollectables would be a straight percentage of the current year's credit sales. That percentage would be a projection based on experience and modified for the current period. For example, if credit sales for the year were $300,000 and if recent experience indicated that 1 percent of all credit sales would be uncollectable, the entry to record the estimate would be

Doubtful Accounts Expense   3,000
   Allowance for Doubtful Accounts   3,000
To record the doubtful accounts expense for the current year.

When this method is used, the balance, if one exists, in Allowance for Doubtful Accounts is ignored. The 1 percent of the current year's sales that is estimated to be uncollectable is calculated separately and then added to that balance. The rationale for not considering the existing balance in Allowance for Doubtful Accounts is that it relates to previous periods' sales and, as a strict interpretation of the matching principle suggests, should not affect the current period's estimate.

If a company bases its estimate of losses on total accounts receivable, the amount of uncollectables is a percentage of the total balance. Thus, if Meyers and Company has a balance of $90,000 in Accounts Receivable and its management determines that 3 percent of the receivables will be uncollectable, the balance in Allowance for Doubtful Accounts should be $2,700. However, if the account has an existing balance, only the net amount needed to bring the balance to $2,700 would be added. For example, as shown in the margin, a credit balance of $500 in Allowance for Doubtful Accounts would require the following entry.

Allowance for Doubtful Accounts

	500 . . . . Existing Balance
	2,200 . . . . Adjust- ment Needed
	2,700 Desired Balance

aging accounts receivable *the process of categorizing each account receivable by the number of days it has been outstanding*

Doubtful Accounts Expense   2,200
   Allowance for Doubtful Accounts   2,200
To record the doubtful accounts expense for the year.

When uncollectable accounts are estimated as a percentage of accounts receivable, the matching principle is not a consideration because, theoretically, the balance in the receivables could relate to any period.

The third method of estimating bad-debt losses requires that a company analyze the age of its receivables. With this procedure, called aging accounts receivable, each receivable is categorized according to age, such as current, 1–30 days past due, 31–60 days past due, 61–90 days past due, 91–120 days past due, and over 120 days past due. Once the receivables in each age classification are totaled, the totals are multipled by the appropriate uncollectable rate (as determined by experience). Exhibit 5–2 is a typical aging of accounts receivable analysis; it shows how a company with $90,000 in Accounts Receivable determines that $3,600 of its current receivables are likely to be uncollectable.

EXHIBIT 5–2 **Aging of Accounts Receivable**

| Customer | Balance | Current | Days Past Due | | | | |
			1–30	*31–60*	*61–90*	*91–120*	*Over 120*
A. Abel	1,000	1,000					
R. Beatty	150						150
F. Brock	625	500	125				
G. Dick	726			726			
M. Edwin . . .	400	400					
G. Ely	225				225		
R. Farmer . . .	100					100	
T. Fisher	200		200				
E. Williams . .	400	400					
Totals	90,000	70,000	15,000	1,500	2,000	1,000	500

Estimate of Losses from Uncollectable Accounts

Age	Balance	Percentage Estimated To Be Uncollectable	Amount
Current	$70,000	1.5	$1,050
1–30 days past due	15,000	3.0	450
31–60 days past due . . .	1,500	20.0	300
61–90 days past due . . .	2,000	40.0	800
91–120 days past due . .	1,000	60.0	600
Over 120 days past due .	500	80.0	400
Totals	$90,000		$3,600

NOTE: Wavy lines through a listing indicates that items have been omitted.

If the existing credit balance in Allowance for Doubtful Accounts is $500, the entry would be

Doubtful Accounts Expense	3,100	
Allowance for Doubtful Accounts . . . . . . :		3,100

To record the doubtful accounts expense for the year.

The aging of accounts receivable is probably the most accurate method of estimating uncollectable accounts. It is also a means whereby a company can quickly identify its problem customers. And because the method can identify such customers, even those companies that base their estimate of bad debts on total credit sales or outstanding receivables often also age their receivables as a way of monitoring the individual Accounts Receivable balances.

TO SUMMARIZE Revenue is generally accounted for according to the revenue recognition principle. The entries to record revenue from the sale of merchandise or the performance of a service involve debits to Cash or Accounts Receivable and credits to Sales or Service Revenue. Revenue transactions can be complicated by (1) sales discounts, (2) sales returns, or (3) the uncollectability of receivables that result from credit sales. There are two ways of accounting for losses from uncollectable receivables: the direct write-off method and the allowance method. The allowance method is required because it is consistent with the matching principle. The three ways of estimating losses from uncollectable receivables are: (1) as a percentage of sales, (2) as a percentage of total outstanding receivables, and (3) as a percentage based on an aging of accounts receivable.

THE MEASUREMENT OF EXPENSES

Thus far, the focus has been on the importance of carefully and correctly measuring revenues. Expenses are equally important and should also be carefully accounted for. They are often referred to as revenue deductions, which means that they are subtracted from revenues in computing net income. As a general rule, revenue deductions are recognized according to the matching principle; that is, they are recorded during the same time period that the revenues they make possible are recognized.

While most revenue deductions can be classified as expenses, the format of Income Statements usually separates the expenses of purchasing or manufacturing inventory from other operating expenses. The amount expended for inventory sold is usually called cost of goods sold and it appears as a separate calculation on the Income Statement immediately following the revenue section. As an example, consider a typical retail grocery store. The cost of goods sold would be the costs incurred in purchasing all vegetables, meat, canned goods, and other merchandise sold during the period. The other expenses would be the amounts incurred for rent, utilities, telephone, salaries, property taxes, and other operating items.

cost of goods sold *the expense incurred to purchase the raw materials and manufacture the products sold during a period, or to purchase the merchandise sold during a period; equal to beginning inventory plus cost of goods purchased or manufactured less ending inventory*

Cost of Goods Sold Expense

The measurement of cost of goods sold differs according to the type of business. In a retail business, such as a clothing store, the cost of goods sold is simply the expense incurred in purchasing the clothing sold during that period. In a manufacturing firm, however, goods are produced and so cost of goods sold must include all manufacturing costs of the products sold. Because the differences between accounting for purchased versus produced goods are significant, and because it is much easier to understand the concept of cost of goods sold in the context of a retail firm, manufacturing firms will not be considered here but will be discussed briefly in later chapters.

Even in retail and wholesale firms, the measurement of cost of goods sold is complicated by the fact that not all inventory on hand is sold before new inventory is purchased. Indeed, a company's management would be foolish to deplete all inventory before ordering new merchandise. Such a practice would result in frequent out-of-stock situations, thus drastically reducing income because of lost sales.

In any given accounting period, a firm may purchase more inventory than it sells, sell more inventory than it purchases, or buy and sell exactly the same amount of inventory. No matter which situation occurs, a company records inventory as an expense only when it is sold. Until it is sold, inventory is classified as an asset on the Balance Sheet. Thus, it is possible for the cost of goods sold to be higher, lower, or the same as the amount of inventory purchased in an accounting period.

There are two principal methods of accounting for inventory and cost of goods sold: (1) the perpetual method and (2) the periodic method.

Perpetual Inventory Method

perpetual inventory method *a system of recording inventory in which detailed records of the number of units and cost of each purchase and sales transaction are prepared throughout the accounting period*

The perpetual inventory method requires a company to maintain inventory records that identify the number and cost of all units purchased and sold each day. Accounting for inventory with the perpetual method is similar to accounting for cash. Because every inventory transaction is recorded in detail, the balance in the inventory account should at all times represent the amount of inventory actually on hand.

To illustrate a perpetual inventory accounting system, we will consider the case of Rainy Day Lawn Mower Company, which sells lawn mowers, snowblowers, and gardentillers, and maintains a separate inventory record for each product. The inventory record for the snowblower line for 1981 is shown in Exhibit 5–3.

EXHIBIT 5–3   Perpetual Inventory Record—Snowblowers, 1981

Date	Explanation	Purchased — Number of Units	Cost per Unit	Total Cost	Sold — Number of Units	Price per Unit	Total Price	Balance in Inventory — Number of Units	Cost per Unit	Total Cost
Jan. 1	Beginning inventory							32	$200	$ 6,400
Jan. 28	Sold				20	$300	$ 6,000	12	$200	$ 2,400
Mar. 3	Sold				8	$300	$ 2,400	4	$200	$ 800
Aug. 2	Purchased	100	$250	$25,000				104	4 at $200 / 100 at $250	$25,800
Aug. 8	Purchased	30	$250	$ 7,500				134	4 at $200 / 130 at $250	$33,300
Sept. 4	Purchased	10	$250	$ 2,500				144	4 at $200 / 140 at $250	$35,800
Sept. 6	Returned to manufacturer	(5)	$250	$ (1,250)				139	4 at $200 / 135 at $250	$34,550
Sept. 20	Sold				15	$350	$ 5,250	124	$250	$31,000
Sept. 30	Returned from customer				(1)	$350	$ (350)	125	$250	$31,250
Nov. 20	Sold				81	$350	$28,350	44	$250	$11,000
Dec. 15	Sold				24	$350	$ 8,400	20	$250	$ 5,000
Dec. 31	Ending inventory							20	$250	$ 5,000

The mechanics of a perpetual system can be illustrated by examining the September transactions. The first transaction, on September 4, involved the purchase of 10 snowblowers and would be accounted for as follows:

Inventory	2,500	
Accounts Payable		2,500

Purchased 10 snowblowers at $250 each.

Rainy Day Lawn Mower Company then decided to return five defective snowblowers to the manufacturer. If the snowblowers had not yet been paid for, the entry would be

Accounts Payable	1,250	
Inventory		1,250

Returned 5 defective snowblowers to the manufacturer.

When a company is using the perpetual inventory method, the entries to record sales transactions are slightly more complicated than those for purchase transactions. Since a sales transaction involves both the recognition of a sale and a reduction of inventory, two entries are needed. Thus, the two entries that would be made to account for the sale of 15 snowblowers on September 20 at $350 each would be

Accounts Receivable (or Cash)	5,250	
Sales Revenue		5,250
Cost of Goods Sold (4 at 200, 11 at 250)	3,550	
Inventory		3,550

Sold 15 snowblowers.

This entry illustrates that cost of goods sold expense is incurred only when merchandise is sold. In this case, the merchandise that was sold for $5,250 cost the company $3,550. The difference between the revenue of $5,250 and the cost of goods sold of $3,550 is $1,700 gross margin, which is the amount the company can use to cover its operating expenses and to provide profit to its owners.

Finally, the entry to account for the return of one snowblower from a customer on September 30 would be

Sales Returns and Allowances	350	
Accounts Receivable (or Cash)		350
Inventory	250	
Cost of Goods Sold		250

Received 1 snowblower back from a customer.

When using the perpetual method, at year-end a company can quickly determine its cost of goods sold as well as the amount of its ending inventory by examining the Inventory and Cost of Goods Sold accounts. In theory, the perpetual inventory method should eliminate the need to physically count the inventory. However, because of the possibility of clerical errors, spoilage, and theft, even firms that maintain perpetual inventory records usually count their inventory at least once a year. After the inventory is counted, the perpetual inventory records are adjusted to correct the balance in Inventory.

If a count were to reveal two snowblowers missing from inventory, the entry needed to account for the shortage would be

Inventory Shrinkage   500
   Inventory   500

To adjust the inventory balance to the physical count, 18 snowblowers.

For many companies, the perpetual method involves too many clerical transactions. Imagine keeping track of every item of inventory on a perpetual basis for General Motors Corporation. However, with the advent of computers to handle these repetitive transactions, use of the perpetual inventory method has become feasible for many companies. Department stores and other businesses can often maintain perpetual records by coding each inventory item and programming the cash register to adjust the records as an item is sold.

Periodic Inventory Method

Although a perpetual inventory system provides excellent control over merchandise and allows for a quick determination of the amount of inventory on hand at all times, many businesses do not use this system. For these firms, there is an alternative known as the periodic inventory method. It allows a company to determine Inventory and Cost of Goods Sold balances without keeping detailed records of every sale and purchase transaction. Because a firm that uses a periodic inventory system does not record the effect on inventory of each transaction, it can only find out how much inventory it has remaining at the end of the period by physically counting and pricing its entire stock.

When using a periodic inventory system, a company initially records all purchases of inventory in a Purchases account. During the period, the effects of sales are not reflected in either the Inventory or Purchases account. At the end of the period, the company takes a physical count of all inventory on hand and determines the cost of goods sold for the period by making the following calculation.

Beginning Inventory, January 1, 1981	$ 800
+ Purchases for the Year	2,200
= Cost of Goods Available for Sale During 1981	$3,000
− Ending Inventory, December 31, 1981	700
= Cost of Goods Sold for 1981	$2,300

The first item in this calculation is the dollar cost of the beginning inventory, which is the ending inventory balance of the previous year as determined by a physical count. The second item is the total amount of inventory purchased during the year. This is added to the beginning inventory and the total is the third item, the cost of goods available for sale during the period. The label "goods available for sale" is a useful one since all the inventory a firm sells must come either from units it had on hand at the beginning of the period or from units it purchased during the period. Fourth is the ending inventory,

periodic inventory method a system of recording inventory in which cost of goods sold is determined and inventory is adjusted at the end of the accounting period, not when merchandise is purchased or sold

Purchases *under a periodic inventory system, the account in which all inventory purchases are recorded*

which is determined by a physical count. This amount is subtracted from the cost of goods available for sale and the result is the cost of goods sold expense. Since inventory available for sale has to be either included in the ending inventory or sold during the period, the ending inventory and cost of goods sold are complementary amounts and their sum must always equal the total cost of goods available for sale.

Although the simple periodic system outlined here is correct, it is not complete. For example, purchase discounts, returns of merchandise purchased, and the cost of transporting merchandise into the firm all require adjustments to the amount purchased.

Purchase Discounts Purchases are simply sales viewed from the other side of the fence. That is, many purchase transactions include terms (such as 2/10, n/30) to encourage prompt payment. And, just as sales discounts reduce the net amount of sales, so purchase discounts reduce the net cost of purchases. When a company uses a periodic inventory system, it subtracts purchase discounts from purchases in the cost of goods sold calculation. The Purchase Discounts account is a contra account: it is deducted from Purchases and has a credit balance.

Purchase Returns and Allowances A firm may purchase merchandise for resale that is defective, does not meet specifications, or is otherwise unacceptable. This merchandise will be returned to the supplier, either for credit or a cash refund. The company will then account for the return by crediting a contra account in the General Ledger called Purchase Returns and Allowances, which reduces the amount of purchases in the cost of goods sold calculation for an Income Statement.

Freight-In The third adjustment to purchases is the cost of transporting merchandise *into* a firm (freight-in). When merchandise is sold, if the selling firm pays the cost of delivering it to customers, it is a delivery expense and is separately recognized on the Income Statement. This is not true of the cost of transporting purchased merchandise into a firm. Because merchandise cannot usually be sold until it is on location, the cost of transporting it into a firm is considered an addition to the net amount of the purchase. If, for example, an appliance dealer in Salt Lake City purchases dishwashers from a firm in Chicago for $200 each, with transportation costs of $30 per unit, the cost of the dishwashers is $230, not $200.

Now that you are familiar with these three adjustments, you can understand the expanded version of the cost of goods sold calculation. With arbitrary numbers, this calculation is

purchase discount *a reduction in the purchase price, allowed if payment is made within a specified period*

Purchase Returns and Allowances *a contra-Purchases account in which the return of or allowances for previously purchased merchandise are recorded*

Freight-In *an account used to record the costs of transporting into a firm all purchased merchandise or materials intended for resale; added to Purchases in calculating cost of goods sold*

Beginning Inventory, January 1, 1981		$ 8,000
Purchases	$20,000	
Add Freight-In	500	
Deduct:		
Purchase Discounts	(700)	
Purchase Returns and Allowances	(800)	
Net Purchases		19,000
Cost of Goods Available for Sale During 1981		$27,000
Less Ending Inventory, December 31, 1981		6,000
Cost of Goods Sold for 1981		$21,000

To illustrate accounting for merchandise in a periodic inventory system, we will refer again to Rainy Day Lawn Mower Company. As you will recall, Exhibit 5–3 showed perpetual inventory records for snowblowers. Here is a summary of that information, presented in the form needed to make periodic inventory calculations.

Beginning Inventory, January 1, 1981		32 units
Purchases	140 units	
Less Purchase Returns (to Manufacturers)	5 units	135 units
Goods Available for Sale		167 units
Units Sold	148 units	
Less Sales Returns (from Customers)	1 unit	147 units
Ending Inventory, December 31, 1981		20 units
		at $250 = $5,000

Although individual entries would usually be made for each transaction, in summary form, the General Journal entries to account for these data would be

Purchases	35,000	
Accounts Payable (or Cash)		35,000

Purchased 140 snowblowers.

Accounts Payable (or Cash)	1,250	
Purchase Returns and Allowances		1,250

Returned 5 defective snowblowers.

Accounts Receivable (or Cash)	50,400	
Sales Revenue		50,400

Sold 148 snowblowers: 28 at $300 each and 120 at $350 each.

Sales Returns and Allowances	350	
Accounts Receivable (or Cash)		350

Received 1 snowblower back from a dissatisfied customer.

As you can see, several accounts were affected by these transactions. However, no adjustments were made to Inventory. In fact, the balance in the Inventory account at any time during the year is the same as it was at the beginning of the year. Adjustments are made to that account only when a physical count is taken at the end of an accounting period. At that time, the adjusting entries are made as a debit to Inventory to set up the new amount and a credit to eliminate the old, now incorrect, balance. The offsetting debits and credits are made to Cost of Goods Sold. In the case of Rainy Day Lawn Mower, the entries to adjust Inventory at the end of 1981 would be

Cost of Goods Sold	6,400	
Inventory (amount of beginning inventory,		
32 units at $200)		6,400
Inventory (amount of ending inventory, 20 units		
at $250)	5,000	
Cost of Goods Sold		5,000

To adjust the balance in the inventory account to the 12/31/81 physical count.

Finally, if there had been either a cost for transporting the snowblowers into the firm or discounts when the snowblowers were purchased, the entries to record these items would have been

Freight-In 300
   Cash 300
Transported into company 50 snowblowers. (Numbers are arbitrary.)

Accounts Payable (Cash) 180
   Purchase Discounts 180
Received purchase discounts from suppliers. (Numbers are arbitrary.)

Closing Entries for Cost of Goods Sold In Chapter 4, we discussed the closing entries for several revenue and expense accounts. Since cost of goods sold is also an Income Statement account, it must be closed at the end of each accounting period. If a perpetual inventory system is being used, the amount is already summarized in a Cost of Goods Sold account, which can be closed simply by crediting the account for its balance and debiting Retained Earnings directly or by debiting Income Summary, which is later closed to Retained Earnings for the same amount. Thus, if in 1981, Rainy Day Lawn Mower Company had used a perpetual inventory system as shown in Exhibit 5–3 on page 177, the closing entry would be

Income Summary (Retained Earnings) 35,150
   Cost of Goods Sold 35,150
To close the Cost of Goods Sold account for 1981.

This amount represents the sale of 32 snowblowers, which cost $200 each, and 115 snowblowers (116 less one returned), which cost $250 each. Note that the amount in this entry assumes no shortage of snowblowers when the physical inventory count was made.

With a periodic inventory system, the closing entries for Cost of Goods Sold are somewhat more complex. You will recall that, with the periodic system, when sales or purchases are recorded, no adjustment is made to the inventory account. Instead, purchases of merchandise are recorded in an account called Purchases and the entries to record sales of merchandise include only an entry for Accounts Receivable and Sales Revenue.

Therefore, the net amount of purchases (gross purchases minus returns and discounts) must be added to Cost of Goods Sold. This account, which was created when the inventory balance was adjusted (see page 181), will then reflect the correct amount of cost of goods sold and can be closed to Income Summary. The closing entries for the snowblower line of Rainy Day Lawn Mower Company would be

Cost of Goods Sold 35,000
   Purchases 35,000
To close the Purchases account for 1981.

Purchase Returns and Allowances 1,250
   Cost of Goods Sold 1,250
To close the Purchase Returns and Allowances account for 1981.

An examination of the Cost of Goods Sold account now shows that the balance is $35,150, or the same as when the perpetual inventory method was used.

Snowblowers
Cost of Goods Sold (1981)

Purchases; see entry on page 182 .. 35,000	1,250 ... Purchase Returns and Allowances; see entry on page 182
Beginning Inventory; see entry on page 181 6,400	5,000 ... Ending Inventory; see entry on page 181
$35,150	

Finally, you should note that balances in Freight-In and Purchase Discounts, when they exist, also have to be closed to Cost of Goods Sold. The entries to close these accounts would be

Cost of Goods Sold	300	
Freight-In..		300
Purchase Discounts	180	
Cost of Goods Sold		180

To close the Freight-In and Purchase Discounts accounts in 1981. (Numbers are arbitrary.)

The next entry is the one that closes the Cost of Goods Sold account. This entry, which is the same as that used with the perpetual inventory method, is

Income Summary (Retained Earnings)	35,150	
Cost of Goods Sold		35,150

To close the Cost of Goods Sold account for 1981.

From the snowblower example, you can see that at the end of an accounting period both the perpetual and periodic inventory systems produce equal amounts of cost of goods sold and inventory. In both systems, inventory is recognized as an expense only when it is sold, and the ending inventory balances will always be the same. The difference between the two methods is in the timing of the adjustments to inventory. With the perpetual method, adjustments are made with each purchase and sales transaction; with the periodic method, they are made only at the end of the period.

The importance of properly accounting for all purchases and sales transactions cannot be emphasized too strongly. Both affect cost of goods sold and the result is that an error in accounting for these transactions affects net income by the same amount. To make sure that the amounts in the Inventory and Cost of Goods Sold accounts are proper, most firms close their warehouses while they take a physical count of inventory. By not allowing any merchandise to enter or leave the warehouse during this period, they attempt to ensure that all inventory counted is actually recorded in the accounting records and that all inventory recorded is actually in the warehouse.

Other Operating Expenses

Thus far, we have shown that revenues are recognized when earned and that inventory becomes an expense only when it is sold. Other business operating expenses—such as payments for salaries, advertising, rent, and insurance—must also be accounted for.

As we have already noted, expenses are recognized in accordance with the matching principle; that is, all expenses incurred in producing revenues should be identified with the revenues generated, period by period. Obviously, the matching principle is easier to apply to some expenses than others. For example, sales commissions are easily associated with sales revenue, but the allocation of a building's cost over its useful life is not so closely tied to sales revenue. To solve this problem and still apply the matching principle, companies usually record amounts as expenses as their asset value is used up. For example, prepaid rental fees would be classified as an expense of the period to which they apply. Similarly, the cost of supplies would be recognized as an expense as the supplies are used up. To consider another example not necessarily involving asset value, if Century Metal rented a building for the month of December, at a monthly rental fee of $500, the rental expense would be incurred and should be recognized in December, no matter when Century Metal pays the December rent.

Monies that are paid before expenses are incurred are called prepaid expenses (sometimes prepaid assets or prepayments) and are classified as assets until used. Expenses that are incurred before they are paid for result in accrued liabilities until paid. Thus, in any given accounting period, a firm can pay for expenses not yet incurred (prepaid expenses), incur expenses not yet paid for (accrued liabilities), and both incur and pay for expenses. The important point is that only expenses actually incurred should be reflected on the Income Statement. Both prepaid expenses and accrued liabilities are discussed in more detail in Chapter 8.

TO SUMMARIZE   Expenses are recognized according to the matching principle; that is, they are recorded at the same time that the associated revenues are recognized. Operating expenses are separated into cost of goods sold expense and other operating expenses. There are two common methods of accounting for inventory and cost of goods sold: periodic and perpetual. With the perpetual method, a running account of actual inventory is maintained; with the periodic method, inventory adjustments are made only at year-end. Other adjustments are required for purchase discounts, purchase returns, and the cost of transporting goods. The entries made under the two methods are summarized in Exhibit 5-4. (Note that the numbers do not relate to prior examples.) In addition to cost of goods sold, a firm has many other operating expenses. Monies expended prior to the incurrence of an expense are called prepaid expenses and are classified as assets. Expenses incurred before they are paid for result in accrued liabilities until paid.

EXHIBIT 5–4   **Comparison of Periodic and Perpetual Inventory Methods**

Event	Periodic Inventory System	Perpetual Inventory System

Purchased merchandise on credit (terms 2/10, n/30)	Purchases. 2,000
	    Accounts Payable 2,000
		Inventory 2,000
		    Accounts Payable 2,000

Returned merchandise to supplier	Accounts Payable . . . 100
	    Purchase Returns and
	    Allowances 100
		Accounts Payable . . . 100
		    Inventory 100

Paid for merchandise (not within discount period)	Accounts Payable . . . 1,900
	    Cash 1,900
		Accounts Payable . . . 1,900
		    Cash 1,900

Sold merchandise on credit (terms 2/10, n/30)	Accounts Receivable. 4,000
	    Sales Revenue 4,000
		Accounts Receivable. 4,000
		    Sales Revenue 4,000
		Cost of Goods Sold . . 2,400
		    Inventory 2,400

Received merchandise back from customer	Sales Returns and
	Allowances 200
	    Accounts Receivable 200
		Sales Returns and
		Allowances 200
		    Accounts Receivable 200
		Inventory 120
		    Cost of Goods Sold 120

Adjusted for inventory (assumes a beginning inventory of $8,000). The ending inventory would be determined by a physical count.	Cost of Goods Sold . . 8,000
	    Inventory 8,000
	Inventory 7,620
	    Cost of Goods Sold 7,620
		No entry

To close Cost of Goods Sold account	Cost of Goods Sold . . 2,000
	    Purchases 2,000
	Purchase Returns and
	Allowances. 100
	    Cost of Goods Sold 100
	Income Summary . . . 2,280
	    Cost of Goods Sold 2,280
		Income Summary . . . 2,280
		    Cost of Goods Sold 2,280

The Income Statement

Having separately reviewed the accounting for revenues and expenses, you are now ready to examine more knowledgeably an accrual-basis historical cost Income Statement, such as Exhibit 5–5.

Revenues, cost of goods sold, and operating expenses (which are separated into selling and general and administrative expenses on the Income Statement) have already been explained. The other revenues and expenses, extraordinary items, and earnings per share of common stock need some clarification. Other revenues and expenses (sometimes called financial revenues and expenses) are those items incurred or earned from activities that are outside of, or peripheral to, the normal operations of a firm. The most common entries in this section are interest and investment revenues and expenses.

EXHIBIT 5-5   Aslaw Company
Income Statement for the Year Ended December 31, 1981

Gross Sales Revenue		$2,500,000	
Less: Sales Returns and Allowances		(12,000)	
Sales Discounts		(13,000)	
Net Sales Revenue			$2,475,000
Cost of Goods Sold:			
Beginning Inventory		$ 800,000	
Purchases	$1,200,000		
Add Freight-In	36,000		
Deduct: Purchase Returns and			
Allowances	(26,000)		
Purchase Discounts	(24,000)		
Net Purchases		1,186,000	
Goods Available for Sale		$1,986,000	
Less Ending Inventory		(900,000)	
Cost of Goods Sold			1,086,000
Gross Margin			$1,389,000
Operating Expenses:			
Selling Expenses:			
Sales Salaries	$ 200,000		
Advertising Expense	45,000		
Depreciation, Stores	78,000		
Warranty Expense	14,000		
Total Selling Expenses		$ 337,000	
General and Administrative Expenses:			
Administrative Salaries	$ 278,000		
Depreciation—Office Equipment	18,000		
Property Taxes	22,000		
Miscellaneous Expense	8,000		
Total General and Administrative Expenses		326,000	
Total Operating Expenses			663,000
Income from Operations			$ 726,000
Other Revenues and Expenses:			
Interest Expense	$ 81,000		
Interest Revenue	(5,000)		
Net Other Expenses			76,000
Pretax Income			$ 650,000
Income Tax on Operations (50%)			325,000
Net Income Before Extraordinary Items			$ 325,000
Extraordinary Items:			
Flood Loss	$ 100,000		
Less Income Tax Effect	50,000		50,000
Net Income			$ 275,000
Earnings Per Share of Common Stock:			
Income Before Extraordinary Items			$3.25
Extraordinary Items			(0.50)
Net Income			$2.75

EXTRAORDINARY ITEMS

extraordinary items   special nonoperating gains and losses that are unusual in nature, infrequent in occurrence, and material in amount

The extraordinary items section of an Income Statement is reserved for reporting special nonoperating gains and losses. This category is restrictive and includes only those items that are (1) unusual in nature, (2) infrequent in occurrence, and (3) material in amount. They are separated from other revenues and expenses so that readers can identify them as one-time, or nonrecurring, events. The most common types of extraordinary items are losses or gains from floods, fires, earthquakes, and so on. If a firm has an extraordinary loss (such as the flood loss in this example), the amount of taxes it pays is less than it would have paid on the basis of ordinary operations. On the other hand, if a firm has an extraordinary gain, its taxes are increased. So that the full effect of the gain or loss can be presented, extraordinary items are always shown at their net-of-tax amounts. Thus, an income tax expense may appear in two places on the Income Statement: below pretax income and in the extraordinary items section.

EARNINGS PER SHARE

earnings per share   net income divided by the weighted-average number of shares of stock outstanding during the period

A company is required to show earnings per share (EPS) on the Income Statement. Usually, a firm will report EPS figures on income before extraordinary items, on extraordinary items, and on net income. Earnings per share is calculated by dividing a firm's income by the average number of shares of stock outstanding during the period. In Exhibit 5–5 it has been assumed that 100,000 shares of stock are outstanding. Earnings-per-share numbers are important because they allow potential investors to compare the profitability of all firms, whether large or small. Thus, the performance of a company earning $200,000 and having 200,000 shares of stock outstanding can be compared with the performance of a company that earns $60,000 and has 30,000 shares outstanding.

CHAPTER REVIEW

The four major ways of measuring income are: cash-basis, accrual-basis historical cost, general price-level-adjusted historical cost, and current-value. Each has its advantages and disadvantages, but the accrual-basis historical cost method is the one currently used for preparing the primary financial statements. The Income Statement is the means of reporting net income. Its major sections are revenues, cost of goods sold, operating expenses, other revenues and expenses, extraordinary items, net income, and earnings per share.

In general, revenues are recognized when the earnings process has been substantially completed and when an exchange has taken place. Revenue transactions can be straightforward or can involve complications, such as sales discounts, sales returns and allowances, or bad debts.

The cost of goods sold section of an Income Statement reports the cost of the merchandise sold during a period. Inventory and cost of goods sold can be accounted for using either of two methods: perpetual or periodic. While the accounting for each method is different, both produce the same ending balances for inventory and cost of goods sold. The differences between the two methods are in the control they provide over inventory and the amount of clerical effort required to maintain the inventory records. No adjustments are made to the inventory records during the year when a periodic inventory system is used, but inventory is adjusted for every sales or purchase transaction with a perpetual inventory system. Both methods take into consideration such things as purchase discounts, purchase returns and allowances, and freight-in.

In addition to cost of goods sold expense, businesses incur many other expenses. With accrual accounting, these are recognized as they are incurred, not when they are paid for. Monies paid prior to the incurrence of an expense are called prepaid expenses. Expenses incurred before they are paid for give rise to accrued liabilities. On the Income Statement, financial and other nonoperating revenues and expenses are classified separately. The Income Statement is not complete until extraordinary items and earnings-per-share amounts have been included.

KEY TERMS AND CONCEPTS

accounts receivable (169)

accrual-basis historical cost method (165)

aging accounts receivable (174)

Allowance for Doubtful Accounts (172)

allowance method (172)

bad debt (171)

book value of accounts receivable (173)

cash-basis method (164)

contra account (170)

control account (196)

cost of goods sold (176)

current-value method (167)

direct write-off method (171)

Doubtful Accounts Expense (172)

earnings per share (187)

expenses (164)

extraordinary items (187)

Freight-In (180)

general price-level-adjusted historical cost method (165)

inventory (164)

matching principle (172)

periodic inventory method (179)

perpetual inventory method (177)

purchase discount (180)

Purchase Returns and Allowances (180)

Purchases (179)

revenue recognition principle (168)

revenues (168)

sales discount (170)

Sales Returns and Allowances (171)

special journals (196)

subsidiary ledger (196)

DISCUSSION QUESTIONS

1. Why is economic income so difficult to measure?

2. When is it theoretically possible to precisely determine the income of a firm?

3. What are the major problems in measuring income on a cash basis?

4. When should revenues be recognized?

5. When should expenses be recognized?

6. Why is it usually important to take advantage of purchase discounts?

7. Why is it important to have separate accounts for Sales Returns and Allowances and Sales Discounts? Wouldn't it be much easier to directly reduce the Sales Revenue account for these adjustments?

8. Why do most companies tolerate a small percentage of their accounts receivable becoming uncollectable?

9. Why does the accounting profession prefer the allowance method of accounting for losses due to uncollectable accounts to the direct write-off method?

10. What type of an account is Inventory?

11. Under what conditions will the dollar amount of cost of goods sold for a period be equal to the dollar purchases made during that period?

12. Why is it necessary to take a physical count of inventory when a perpetual inventory system is being used?

13. Which inventory method (perpetual or periodic) provides the best control over a firm's inventory?

14. Is the accounting for purchase discounts and purchase returns the same with both the perpetual and periodic inventory methods? If not, what are the differences?

15. Are the costs of transporting inventory in and out of a firm treated the same way? If not, what are the differences?

16. What adjusting entries are required to Inventory when a perpetual inventory system is used?

17. What is the difference between a prepaid expense and an expense?

EXERCISES

E5–1   Recording Sales Transactions

On May 24, 1981, N and N Company sold $10,000 worth of merchandise to Fred Jones with terms of 2/10, n/30. Assuming that N and N Company uses a periodic inventory system, prepare journal entries to record the following:

1. The initial sale.

2. The payment of $4,900 by Jones on May 30 on his account.

3. The payment of $3,000 by Jones on June 20 on his account. Also, on June 20, Jones returned $2,000 of merchandise claiming that it malfunctioned and did not meet contract terms.

E5–2   Recording Sales Transactions

Sunshine Company sold $2,000 of merchandise on account to Atlantic Company on June 3, 1981, with terms of 2/10, n/30. On June 7, 1981, Sunshine Company received $100 of merchandise back from Atlantic Company and issued a credit memorandum for the appropriate amount. Sunshine Company received payment for the balance of the bill on June 21, 1981. Record these events on Sunshine Company's books, assuming that the company uses a periodic inventory system.

E5–3   Recording Sales Transactions

Record the events, assuming the same facts as in E5–2, except that Sunshine Company uses a perpetual inventory system and that the costs of the merchandise are 60 percent of the selling prices.

E5–4   Computing and Recording Doubtful Accounts Expense

During 1981, Abco Corporation had a total of $2,500,000 in sales, of which 80 percent were on credit. Also in 1981, $30,000 of accounts receivable were written off as uncollectable. At year-end the Accounts Receivable balance showed a total of $1,150,000, which was aged as follows:

Age	Amount
Current	$ 950,000
1–30 days past due	100,000
31–60 days past due	50,000
61–90 days past due	35,000
Over 90 days past due	15,000
	$1,150,000

Prepare the journal entry required at year-end to properly record doubtful accounts expense under each of the following methods. Assume, where applicable, that Allowance for Doubtful Accounts has a credit balance of $2,750 at year-end.

1. Use the direct write-off method. (Assume that all accounts determined to be uncollectable are written off in a single year-end entry.)

2. Based on experience, annual uncollectable accounts are estimated to be approximately 1.4 percent of total credit sales for the year.

3. Based on experience, uncollectable accounts for the year are estimated to be approximately 3 percent of total accounts receivable.

4. Based on experience, uncollectable accounts are estimated to be the sum of:

　　1 percent of current accounts receivable
　　6 percent of accounts 1–30 days past due
　　10 percent of accounts 31–60 days past due
　　20 percent of accounts 61–90 days past due
　　30 percent of accounts over 90 days past due

E5–5   Aging of Accounts Receivable and Uncollectable Accounts

XYZ Company has found that, historically, $\frac{1}{2}$ percent of its current accounts receivable, 1 percent of accounts 1 to 30 days past due, $1\frac{1}{2}$ percent of accounts 31 to 60 days past due, 3 percent of accounts 61 to 90 days past due, and 10 percent of accounts over 90 days past due are uncollectable. The following schedule shows an aging of the accounts receivable as of December 31, 1981.

	Days Past Due				
	Current	1 to 30	31 to 60	61 to 90	Over 90
Balance	$89,200	$19,700	$8,200	$1,700	$390

The balances at December 31, 1981, in certain selected accounts are as follows (assume that the allowance method is used):

Sales Revenue $240,192
Sales Returns   2,418
Allowance for Doubtful Accounts.   226 (credit balance)

1. Given the data above, make the necessary adjusting entry (entries) for uncollectable accounts on December 31, 1981.

2. On February 14, 1982, Jason Marks, a customer, informed XYZ Company that he was going bankrupt and would not be able to pay his account of $92. Make the appropriate entry (entries).

3. On June 29, 1982, Jason Marks was able to pay the amount he owed in full. Make the appropriate entry (entries).

4. Assume that Allowance for Doubtful Accounts at December 31, 1981, had a debit balance of $226 instead of a credit balance of $226. Make the necessary adjusting journal entry that would be needed on December 31, 1981. (The entry should be similar to that in question 1, except for the amount.)

E5–6   Cost of Goods Sold Calculations

Complete the following cost of goods sold calculations by filling in all missing numbers.

	Company A	Company B	Company C	Company D
Sales Revenue . .	500	(4) ____	480	1,310
Beginning Inventory	50	76	0	600
Purchases	(1) ____	423	480	249
Purchase Returns and Allowances . .	5	19	0	(8) ____
Ending Inventory	75	110	(6) ____	195
Cost of Goods Sold	300	370	(7) ____	(9) ____
Gross Margin . .	(2) ____	(5) ____	155	(10) ____
Expenses	27	22	34	129
Income (Loss) . .	(3) ____	107	121	546

E5–7   Estimating Cost of Goods Sold

PDQ Company is located in Los Angeles, California. During 1981, an earthquake demolished its building and most of the accounting records. The president of the company has requested that you reconstruct an Income Statement for the year ended December 31, 1981. In doing so, you have been able to gather the following information. (Ignore income taxes.)

Inventory Balance, January 1, 1981 . . . . $ 28,600
Purchases Made During 1981   62,400
Sales Made During 1981 100,000
Operating Expenses Incurred During 1981 (other than Cost of Goods Sold)   10,000

PDQ Company's cost of goods sold is normally 75 percent of sales; 1981 was a normal year.

E5–8   Cost of Goods Sold Calculations

ABC Company has provided the following information for the calendar year 1981.

Inventory Balance, January 1, 1981 . . . . $ 50,000
Total Goods Available for Sale 150,000
Sales Returns and Allowance   6,500
Purchase Returns and Allowances   2,500
Freight-In   1,000
Sales (Net of Returns and Allowances) 153,500
Operating Expenses   13,500

The gross sales of ABC Company are 160 percent of cost of goods sold. Using the available information, compute the following (ignore income taxes).

1. Gross sales for 1981.
2. Cost of goods sold for 1981.
3. Inventory balance at December 31, 1981.
4. Net income for 1981.
5. Net purchases for 1981.

E5–9   Cost of Goods Sold Calculations and Income Statement Preparation

The following account balances were included in the ledger of John R. Emerson Company on December 31, 1981.

Name of Account	Balance
Cash	$ 400
Freight-In	960
Beginning Inventory, Balance Carried from January 1, 1981	6,500
Purchases	82,000
Purchase Discounts	200
Purchase Returns and Allowances	1,120
Sales Revenue	93,000
Sales Discounts	300
Sales Returns and Allowances	1,400

The amount of inventory on hand on December 31, 1981, was $14,500. Prepare a partial Income Statement (through gross margin) from the available data for Emerson Company for the year ended December 31, 1981.

E5–10   Cost of Goods Sold Calculation

The accounts of Aquarius Company had the following balances for 1981.

Purchases	$130,000
Inventory, January 1, 1981	20,000
Purchase Returns and Allowances	3,820
Purchase Discounts	440
Freight-In	6,200
Freight-Out (Selling Expense)	1,200
Cash	2,000

The inventory balance on December 31, 1981, is $24,000. Using the information above, construct the Cost of Goods Sold section of the Income Statement for Aquarius Company for 1981.

E5–11   The Effect of Inventory Errors

The following are the abbreviated Income Statements for Blue Sky Corporation for the last two periods.

	Period 1	Period 2
Net Sales	$20,000	$25,000
Cost of Goods Sold:		
Beginning Inventory	$ 5,000	$ 4,000
Net Purchases	13,000	15,000
Cost of Goods Available for Sale	$18,000	$19,000
Ending Inventory	4,000	5,000
Cost of Goods Sold	$14,000	$14,000
Gross Margin	$ 6,000	$11,000
Operating Expenses	7,000	7,000
Net Income (Loss)	$ (1,000)	$ 4,000

Answer each of the following *unrelated* questions.

1. If the beginning inventory in period 1 ($5,000) is overstated by $2,000 (it should be $3,000), what is the correct net income (loss) for that period?

2. If the beginning inventory in period 2 ($4,000) is understated by $2,000 (it should be $6,000), what is the correct amount of net income for period 2?

3. If the ending inventory in period 1 ($4,000) is overstated by $2,000 (it should be $2,000), what is the correct cost of goods sold for the two periods combined?

4. If the cost of goods sold in period 2 ($14,000) is understated by $1,000 (ending inventory was overstated), what is the correct net income for period 2?

5. If the ending inventory in period 2 ($5,000) is understated by $2,000 (it should be $7,000), what is the total correct cost of goods sold for the two periods combined?

E5–12   Inventory: Adjusting and Closing Entries

In 1981, Bjorn Company had the following account balances.

Inventory, January 1, 1981	$ 60,000
Purchases	110,000
Cost of Goods Sold	120,000
Purchase Returns and Allowances	2,000

Assuming that a physical count of inventory on December 31, 1981, showed $46,000 of ending inventory, complete the following.

1. Adjust the inventory records and close the related purchases accounts, assuming that a periodic inventory system is used.

2. Adjust the inventory records and close the appropriate accounts, assuming that a perpetual inventory system is used.

E5–13   The Effect of Errors in Recording Expenses

An examination of the records of Treadwell Company early in 1981 revealed that the following errors and omissions had occurred during 1980 and 1981.

a. Wages of $600 owed to employees at December 31, 1980, were not recognized as an expense in 1980 and were recorded as an expense when paid in 1981.

b. All office supplies were charged to expense when purchased. Supplies on hand of $300 were overlooked when the appropriate December 31, 1980, adjusting entries were made.

c. A customer's payment of $400 in December 1980 for merchandise to be delivered in 1981 was recorded as a sale in 1980. No entry was made in 1981 when the goods were actually sold.

d. Rent for January 1981 of $450 was paid in advance during 1980 and was charged to expense when paid.

Given the information above, complete the following two requirements:

1. For each of the above four errors state (a) whether 1980 net income would be under- or overstated and by how much; and (b) whether 1981 net income would be under- or overstated and by how much.

2. If the reported net incomes for 1980 and 1981 were $10,000 and $15,000, respectively (before adjustments for the above items), what should have been the amount of net income for each of the two years?

E5–14   Completing an Income Statement

Randy Forgetful, the accountant for Swenson Supplies Company, forgot where he put the accounting records. After searching the premises, he did manage to find the following information for 1980 and 1981. The president of the company has requested comparative financial statements and Randy needs your help in determining the missing numbers before he turns in his report to Mr. Swenson.

	1980	1981
Sales Revenue	$276,000	$(5) ——
Beginning Inventory	65,000	(6) ——
Purchases	(1) ——	214,000
Goods Available for Sale	273,000	(7) ——
Ending Inventory	(2) ——	57,000
Cost of Goods Sold	224,000	(8) ——
Gross Margin	(3) ——	61,000
Expenses	30,000	(9) ——
Pretax Income	(4) ——	24,000

The foregoing table represents portions of the Income Statements of Atlas Company for the years 1980–1982. Fill in the missing numbers. Assume that gross margin is 40 percent of net sales.

E5–16 Preparing an Income Statement

Big Company is preparing financial statements for the calendar year 1981. The totals given below for each account have been verified as correct.

Office Supplies on Hand	$ 75
Insurance Expense	30
Gross Sales Revenue	1,500
Equipment	80
Cost of Goods Sold	805
Sales Returns and Allowances	50
Interest Expense	25
Accounts Payable	30
Accounts Receivable	65
Extraordinary Loss	270
Selling Expenses	90
Office Supplies Used	20
Cash	75
Revenue from Investments	70
Common Stock ($1 par value)	45

Prepare an Income Statement. Assume a 20 percent income tax rate on both income from operations and extraordinary items.

E5–15 Income Statement Analysis

	1980	1981	1982
Gross Sales Revenue	$ 25,800	$(9) ——	$ 42,000
Sales Discounts	100	100	0
Sales Returns and Allowances	700	200	0
Net Sales	(1) ——	(10) ——	42,000
Beginning Inventory	(2) ——	8,000	(15) ——
Purchases	15,000	(11) ——	24,800
Purchase Discounts	500	300	700
Freight-In	500	0	(16) ——
Goods Available for Sale	(3) ——	25,000	29,000
Ending Inventory	(4) ——	(12) ——	3,800
Cost of Goods Sold	(5) ——	(13) ——	(17) ——
Gross Margin	(6) ——	14,000	(18) ——
Selling Expenses	(7) ——	(14) ——	4,000
General and Administrative Expenses	3,000	3,200	(19) ——
Income Before Taxes	4,000	8,000	9,000
Income Tax Expense	(8) ——	4,000	4,500
Net Income	2,000	4,000	(20) ——

PROBLEMS

P5–1 Different Concepts of Income

Maryland Retail Association is a new store in Cambridge, Md., that sells hardware and other merchandise. During 1981, the store had the following information in its accounting and other records.

a. Started business on January 2, 1981. On that date, the company purchased a store building at a cost of $80,000. The building is expected to have a 20-year life.

b. On January 3, 1981, inventory was purchased for $50,000. No other inventory purchases were made during the year.

c. During the year, the store had the following transactions:

(1) Sold merchandise that cost $30,000 for $70,000.
(2) Paid $22,000 in salaries and other expenses.

d. All the above were cash transactions.

e. On December 31, 1981, it was determined that the current values of the store building and remaining inventory were $100,000 and $26,000, respectively.

Required:

1. Compute the following:
   (a) Cash-basis income (loss).
   (b) Accrual-basis historical cost income (loss).

2. **Interpretive Question** Which of these net income numbers provides better information regarding the performance of the store during 1981? Why?

3. **Interpretive Question** Do either of these alternatives reflect the effect of increases or decreases in the values of assets and liabilities caused by inflation, technological advances, and so forth? If not, what methods could be used to account for these factors?

4. **Interpretive Question** Briefly, what are the major differences between the general price-level-adjusted and current-value approaches to measuring income?

P5–2 Different Concepts of Income

RPA Corporation is a retail firm that sells video discs in the new and emerging home movie market. The company was formed on January 3, 1981, and during 1981 had the following cash transactions:

a. On January 3, purchased a new building at a cost of $100,000, some furniture at a cost of $40,000, and inventory at a cost of $20,000. The building has a 50-year life and the furniture a 10-year life.

b. During the year, sold $10,000 (one-half) of its inventory for $25,000, and paid salaries of $10,000. (No other expenses were recorded during the year.)

Required:

1. Given the above data, compute the following.
   (a) Cash-basis income (loss).
   (b) Accrual-basis historical cost income (loss).

2. **Interpretive Question**   Other than at the time of an exchange (sale or other arm's-length transaction), do either of these methods recognize changes in the value of assets and liabilities?

3. **Interpretive Question**   Explain why the general price-level method does not account for all changes in the values of the assets and liabilities.

P5-3   Concepts of Income—Cash and Accrual Accounting

During its initial year of operation in 1981, Johnson Manufacturing Company had the following transactions.

Sales Revenue	$80,000 ($60,000 of which has been collected and $20,000 of which is still in receivables)
Purchases of Merchandise	$40,000 ($36,000 of which has been paid for, the remainder of which is still owed at year-end)
Expenses:	
Salaries	$32,000 ($30,000 of which has been paid)
Utilities Expense	$ 2,000 (All of which has been paid)
Rent Expense	$10,000 (All of which has been paid)
Other Purchases (On December 31, 1981):	
Building	$22,000 ($5,000 of which has been paid)
Land	$ 6,000 ($2,000 of which has been paid)

Required:

1. Assuming that the amount of ending inventory is $4,000 and that there was no beginning inventory, compute the following.
   (a) Net income (using the currently required method) for 1981 (ignore income taxes, depreciation, and interest expense).
   (b) Net cash inflow (outflow) for 1981.

2. **Interpretive Question**   Which of the statements better indicates the performance of the company during 1981?

P5-4   Net Income and Cash Flows

As the controller for Sherwood Enterprises, you have just completed the annual report for 1981 and determined that net income for the year was $20,000. Notwithstanding the company's profitable operations, it is being plagued by a severe cash shortage. Helen Sherwood, the company president, has asked you to find the reasons for the company's cash problems. In preparing your report, you discover the following with respect to the year's operations.

a. Clock Corporation, a customer, was unable to pay for merchandise purchased during 1981. As a result, on November 1, 1981, Sherwood accepted a 90-day, 6 percent note from Clock in the amount of $8,000.

b. Trade accounts receivable were $24,000 on January 1, 1981, and $32,000 on December 31, 1981.

c. Accounts payable were $18,000 on January 1, 1981, and $12,000 on December 31, 1981.

d. During 1981, the company purchased a new building costing $200,000. Twenty percent of the purchase price was paid in cash and the balance was borrowed from a local bank. (Ignore interest.) The building has a 40-year life.

e. Inventory on hand totaled $42,000 on January 1, 1981, and $48,000 on December 31, 1981.

f. Other payables totaled $2,000 on January 1, 1981, and $0 on December 31, 1981.

g. Prepaid expenses increased $12,000 during 1981.

h. Depreciation expense for 1981 was $7,000.

i. Dividends paid during 1981 totaled $3,000.

Required:

1. Using the above information, compute the net amount of cash inflow or outflow for 1981.

2. **Interpretive Question**   Does the company have critical cash problems or does it appear that its negative cash position is only a short-run problem?

P5-5   Selling and Purchase Transactions

Hopkins Bicycle Shop had the following transactions during the first nine days of March 1981.

March 1   Purchased 20 bicycles at $100 each, terms 2/10, n/30.

     2   Returned 2 bicycles to suppliers because the frames were bent; received credit memorandum for $200.

     5   Sold 10 bicycles for $200 each to a local cycling club for cash.

     8   One of the bicycles sold on March 5 was returned because of a defective tire; refunded the cash.

     9   Paid supplier the net amount owed for the bicycles purchased on March 1.

Required:

1. Journalize the above transactions using:
   (a) A periodic inventory system.
   (b) A perpetual inventory system.
2. **Interpretive Question** What types of companies are more likely to use a perpetual inventory system?

P5-6 Income Statement Analysis

The following information is available for Yellow Jacket Corporation for the year 1981.

	First Quarter	Second Quarter	Third Quarter	Fourth Quarter	Annual State-ment
Revenues ...	$3,000	$4,000	$4,000	$?	$15,000
Beginning Inventory ..	____	____	300	?	____
Purchases ...	1,000	1,500	2,000	?	6,500
Purchase Discounts ..	15	____	____	?	100
Purchase Returns and Allowances.	____	25	15	?	100
Net Purchases	960	1,450	____	?	6,300
Total Goods Available for Sale	____	____	2,250	?	6,600
Ending Inventory ..	____	300	250	?	____
Cost of Goods Sold .	1,110	____	2,000	?	6,200
Other Expenses ..	1,500	1,500	____	?	5,200
Net Income ..	390	____	1,000	?	3,600

Required:

1. Complete the Income Statement entries given above by filling in all missing numbers in each quarter and in the annual statement.
2. **Interpretive Question** Ignoring the numbers above and in general terms, if the beginning inventory of the first quarter were overstated by $100, what would be the amount and direction of the over- or understatement of net income in the second quarter?
3. **Interpretive Question** Again, in general terms, if the ending inventory of the second quarter were understated by $200, what would be the amount and direction of the over- or understatement of net income in the third quarter?

P5-7 Estimating Uncollectable Accounts

The Jason Corporation makes and sells athletic equipment to sporting goods stores throughout the country. On December 31, 1981, before adjusting entries were made, it had the following account balances on its books.

Accounts Receivable	$ 580,000
Sales—1981 (60% were credit sales)	$4,000,000
Allowance for Doubtful Accounts	$ 1,000 (credit balance)
Doubtful Accounts Expense	$ 32,000

Required:

1. Make the appropriate adjusting entry on December 31, 1981, to record the allowance for doubtful accounts if uncollectable accounts are estimated to be 1 percent of credit sales.
2. Make the appropriate adjusting entry on December 31, 1981, to record the allowance for doubtful accounts if uncollectable accounts are estimated to be 3 percent of accounts receivable.
3. Make the appropriate adjusting entry on December 31, 1981, to record the allowance for doubtful accounts if uncollectable accounts are estimated on the basis of an aging of accounts receivable and the aging schedule revealed the following.

Balance of Accounts Receivable	Percent Estimated to Become Uncollectable
Not yet due $300,000	$\frac{1}{2}$ of 1 percent
1–30 days past due $200,000	1 percent
31–60 days past due .... $ 50,000	4 percent
61–90 days past due .... $ 20,000	10 percent
Over 90 days past due .... $ 10,000	30 percent

4. Now assume that on March 3, 1982, it was determined that a $16,000 account receivable from Outdoors Unlimited is uncollectable. Record the bad debt, assuming
   (a) The direct write-off method is used.
   (b) The allowance method is used.
5. Further assume that on June 4, 1982, Outdoors Unlimited paid this previously written off debt of $16,000. Record the payment assuming
   (a) The direct write-off method had been used on March 3 to record the bad debt.
   (b) The allowance method had been used on March 3 to record the bad debt.
6. **Interpretive Question** Which method of accounting for uncollectable accounts, direct write-off or allowance, is preferred? Why?

P5-8 Unifying Problem: The Income Statement

Use the following information to prepare an Income Statement for General Electronics Corporation for the year ending December 31, 1981. You should show separate classifications for revenues, cost of goods sold, gross margin, selling expenses, general and administrative expenses, income from operations, other revenue and expenses, pretax income, income tax, and net income. (Hint: Net income is $13,638.)

Sales Returns and Allowances	$ 2,140
Income Tax Expense	13,000
Interest Revenue	1,200
Office Supplies Expense (General and	
Administrative)	200
Depreciation Expense—Building (General and	
Administrative)	1,990
Office Salaries (General and Administrative)	6,032
Miscellaneous Selling Expense	230
Insurance Expense (Selling)	580
Advertising Expense	3,461
Sales Salaries	20,044
Inventory, December 31, 1981	22,150
Purchases................................	115,280
Sales Discounts...........................	1,822
Interest Expense	585
Miscellaneous General and Administrative	
Expense.................................	310
Insurance Expense (General and Administrative).	300
Payroll Tax Expense (General and	
Administrative)	1,800
Store Supplies Expense	400
Depreciation Expense—Store Equipment	
(Selling)	1,099
Purchase Discounts........................	1,525
Inventory, January 1, 1981	39,700
Sales Revenue	197,736
Accounts Receivable.......................	25,000
Average Number of Shares of Stock Outstanding.	10,000

P5–9   Unifying Problem: The Income Statement

From the following information prepare an Income Statement for Reynolds Incorporated for the year ended December 31, 1981. (Hint: Net income is $119,100.) Assume there are 10,000 shares of common stock outstanding.

Gross Sales Revenue	$3,625,000
Income Tax Expense (on operations)	140,000
Cost of Goods Sold........................	2,415,000
Sales Salaries	410,000
Depreciation Expense—Store Equipment	
(Selling)	16,000
Payroll Tax Expense (Selling)	3,100
Amortization of Trademarks (Selling)	2,000
Miscellaneous Selling Expense	7,800
Miscellaneous General and Administrative	
Expense..................................	5,400
Bad-Debt Expense (General and Administrative) .	3,500
Insurance Expense (General and Administrative)	1,900
Interest Expense...........................	46,000
Interest Revenue	3,000
Sales Returns and Allowances	10,000
Advertising and Promotion	199,000
Insurance Expense (Selling)	17,000
Warranty Expense (Selling)..................	3,100
Office Supplies Used (General and	
Administrative)...........................	8,000
Depreciation—Office Equipment (General and	
Administrative)...........................	1,100
Accounts Receivable	25,000
Administrative Salaries	180,000
Fire Loss (net of tax).......................	40,000

SUPPLEMENT

Special Journals

special journals   books of
original entry for recording
similar transactions that occur
frequently

So far, we have shown all journal entries in General Journal format. In practice, however, most firms use special journals *to record common transactions, such as credit sales, cash receipts, purchases, and cash disbursements. The use of such journals reduces the amount of posting and other clerical work necessary to account for these activities.*

Rather than use one continuous example to illustrate these journals, we will develop a different example for each journal.

The Sales Journal

A typical page from a sales journal and the posting of that journal, in T-account form, are illustrated in Exhibit 5–6.

The sales journal shows 10 transactions during the month of January, each with terms n/30. These are added and the total posted to the Accounts Receivable and Sales Revenue accounts in the General Ledger. The numbers in parentheses below the total in the sales journal indicate the accounts to which the total has been posted in the General Ledger. In the General Ledger accounts, the reference is the number of the sales journal page from which the entries came (in this case, 6). The use of a sales journal saves considerable time and effort because each individual entry does not have to be separately posted to the General Ledger.

Exhibit 5–6 also gives, in T-account form, the entries in the accounts receivable subsidiary ledger. This subsidiary ledger is needed by a business to help monitor customers' balances. At all times, the cumulative total of all subsidiary ledger accounts must equal the Accounts Receivable balance in the General Ledger. Therefore, Accounts Receivable is called the control account for the subsidiary ledger. When the individual sales are posted to the accounts receivable subsidiary ledger, the account numbers (in this case, 15.1 to 15.10) are entered in the sales journal. Similarly, in the subsidiary accounts, the number of the sales journal page is also referenced. This system of cross-referencing helps an accountant to check his or her work and minimizes the chances of mistakes.

subsidiary ledger   a grouping
of individual accounts that in
total equal the balance of a
control account in the General
Ledger

control account   a summary
account in the General Ledger
that is supported by detailed
individual accounts in a
subsidiary ledger

EXHIBIT 5-6   **Sales Journal and Posting to Ledger Accounts**

Sales Journal   *Page 6*

Date	Sales Invoice Number	Customer Name	Terms	Customer Account Number	Amount
19 81					
Jan. 2	125	Roger Jameson	N/30	15.5	600
3	126	Lee Smith	N/30	15.7	250
6	127	Ralph Smith	N/30	15.8	315
8	128	John Anderson	N/30	15.1	216
9	129	Carl Hartford	N/30	15.4	822
10	130	Mike Taylor	N/30	15.9	610
16	131	Marvin Brinkerhoff	N/30	15.3	545
23	132	Roy Avondet	N/30	15.2	125
27	133	Jay Rasmussen	N/30	15.6	312
31	134	Jerry Woolsey	N/30	15.10	816
					4611
					(15) (51)

General Ledger

Accounts Receivable (15)

6 1/81 4,611

Sales Revenue (51)

4,611 .... 1/81 6

Accounts Receivable Subsidiary Ledger (15)

John Anderson 15.1
6 1/81 .. 216

Roy Avondet 15.2
6 1/81 .. 125

Marvin Brinkerhoff 15.3
6 1/81 .. 545

Carl Hartford 15.4
6 1/81 .. 822

Roger Jameson 15.5
6 1/81 .. 600

Jay Rasmussen 15.6
6 1/81 .. 312

Lee Smith 15.7
6 1/81 .. 250

Ralph Smith 15.8
6 1/81 .. 315

Mike Taylor 15.9
6 1/81 .. 610

Jerry Woolsey 15.10
6 1/81 .. 816

EXHIBIT 5–7   Purchases Journal and Posting to Ledger Accounts

Purchases Journal   *Page 9*

Date	Creditor's Account	Sub. Account Number	Accounts Payable (CR)	Purchases (DR)	Supplies (DR)	Other Accounts Account	Post Ref.	Amount
1981								
Jan. 1	B. Cotton Betteridge	212.1	616	616				
2	D. Skinner	212.6	222		222			
6	R. Dudley	212.3	485	485				
12	S. Davies	212.2	690	690				
15	D. Handy	212.4	810	810				
22	B. Talbot	212.7	700	700				
29	R. Parsons	212.5	525	525				
	Totals		4048	3826	222			
			(212)	(411)	(125)			

General Ledger

Accounts Payable (212)   *Supplies* (125)
4,048...1/81 9   9 1/81 222

Purchases (411)
9 1/81 3,826

Accounts Payable Subsidiary Ledger (212)

B. Cotton Betteridge 212.1   *S. Davies*   212.2   *R. Dudley*   212.3
9 1/81... 616   9 1/81... 690   9 1/81... 485

D. Handy   212.4   *R. Parsons*   212.5   *D. Skinner*   212.6
9 1/81... 810   9 1/81... 525   9 1/81... 222

B. Talbot   212.7
9 1/81... 700

The Purchases Journal

When a firm purchases merchandise for resale, it usually records the cost of those purchases in a separate purchases journal. Just as the use of a sales journal saves considerable time and effort by minimizing the posting effort required, so does the purchases journal. A typical page from a purchases journal and the posting of that journal are illustrated, in T-account form, in Exhibit 5–7.

The relationships between the purchases journal and the General Ledger and the accounts payable subsidiary ledgers are similar to those between the sales journal and the General Ledger and the subsidiary accounts receivable ledger. Thus, as shown in Exhibit 5–7, the seven purchases made during January are recorded chronologically in the purchases journal. Then, the totals of the accounts payable (credit), purchases (debit), and supplies (debit) columns are posted to their respective General Ledger accounts. Finally, the individual purchases are posted to the separate creditor accounts in the subsidiary ledger. Again, as with the sales journal, the purchases journal is cross-referenced to the General Ledger and subsidiary ledgers, and the cumulative total of all balances in the accounts payable subsidiary ledger equals the balance in the Accounts Payable control account.

The Cash Receipts Journal

The third special journal is the one in which all cash receipts are recorded. A typical page from a cash receipts journal is displayed in Exhibit 5–8 and the posting of the entries to the General Ledger account is illustrated in Exhibit 5–9.

A page in the cash receipts journal includes a Sales (CR) column, in which all cash sales are recorded; Accounts Receivable (CR) and Sales Discount (DR) columns, in which the payments from the credit customers are recorded; a column called Cash (DR), which is a record of actual cash received; and a Miscellaneous Accounts (CR) column, in which are recorded all other "irregular" cash transactions—for example, collections of interest, rents, or notes receivable. The cash receipts journal always contains Cash (DR) and Miscellaneous Accounts (CR) columns; the other columns will depend on the frequency of the different types of transactions generated in a firm.

EXHIBIT 5–8 **Cash Receipts Journal**

Page 8

Date	Accounts Credited	Post Ref.	Cash (DR)	Misc. Accts. (CR)	Sales (CR)	Accts. Receivable (CR)	Sales Discount (DR)
July 1	Lewallyn & Sons	✓	6 8 6			7 0 0	1 4
2	Notes Receivable	113	1 5 0	1 5 0			
3	Sales	✓	1 2 5		1 2 5		
5	James Mann Company	✓	8 8 2			9 0 0	1 8
6	Interest Revenue	513	5 0	5 0			
7	Sales	✓	3 0		3 0		
9	EmCo Trucking	✓	3 9 2			4 0 0	8
31	Morrison Associates	✓	5 8 8			6 0 0	1 2
	Totals		2 5 2 0 0	3 0 0	4 0 0	2 5 0 0 0	5 0 0
			(1 1 1)	✓	(5 1 1)	(1 1 2)	(5 1 2)

In reading Exhibit 5–8, you can see that on July 1, Lewallyn and Sons made a cash payment of $686 to satisfy a $700 bill (debit Cash; credit Accounts Receivable). Because they paid promptly, they received a 2 percent cash discount (debit Sales Discounts by $14). The $125 cash sale on July 3 was credited to Sales and the interest revenue collected on July 6 was credited to Miscellaneous Accounts.

In posting the entries from the cash receipts journal to the General Ledger, only those amounts in the Miscellaneous Accounts (CR) column are handled individually, with the number of each ledger account appearing in the Post Reference column. For example, when the $150 payment was collected on July 2 and posted to Notes Receivable, the account number 113 was entered in the Post Reference column. All other columns are posted as totals at the end of each month. The individual entries in the Accounts Receivable (CR) column are posted to the individual customer accounts in the accounts receivable subsidiary ledger. Checkmarks are placed in the Post Reference column to indicate that these subsidiary postings have been made. Finally, at the end of a month, when the Accounts Receivable (CR), the Sales Discount (DR), and Cash (DR) columns are each totaled, they are checked to ensure that total debits equal total credits.

The totals are then posted to their respective accounts in the General Ledger. As the totals are posted, their account numbers are entered just below the column totals. The posting of the cash receipts journal is displayed in Exhibit 5–9.

EXHIBIT 5–9   **Posting from the Cash Receipts Journal**

Cash Receipts Journal   *Page 8*

Date	Accounts Credited	Post Ref.	Cash (DR)	Misc. Accts. (CR)	Sales (CR)	Accts. Receivable (CR)	Sales Discounts (DR)
July 1	Lewallyn & Sons	✓	686			700	14
2	Notes Receivable	113	150	150			
3	Sales	✓	125		125		
31	Morrison Associates	✓	588			600	12
	Totals		25,200	300	400	25,000	500
			(111)	✓	(511)	(112)	(512)

General Ledger

Accounts Receivable (112)
25,000..7/81 8

Notes Receivable (113)
150...7/81 8

Sales Discounts (512)
8 7/81...500

Sales (511)
400...7/81 8

Cash (111)
8 7/81..25,200

Accounts Receivable Subsidiary Ledger (112)

Lewallyn & Sons (112.1)
700..7/81 8

Morrison Associates (112.2)
600..7/81 8

The Cash Disbursements Journal

The cash payments of a business are usually recorded in a separate cash disbursements journal. A typical page from a cash disbursements journal is shown in Exhibit 5–10 and the postings from that journal are shown in Exhibit 5–11. The cash disbursements journal contains Miscellaneous Accounts (DR), Accounts Payable (DR), and Purchase Discounts (CR) columns, into which payments are recorded, and a Cash (CR) column, which is a record of all cash paid. The Miscellaneous Accounts (DR) column is used to record cash purchases of merchandise, and sometimes even the payments of salaries, rents, or notes. In all other respects, the recording, posting, and referencing of this journal is similar to that for the cash receipts journal.

EXHIBIT 5–10   Cash Disbursements Journal

Page 5

Date	Check	Payee	Post Ref.	Misc. Accts. (DR)	accts. Payable (DR)	Purchase Discounts (CR)	Cash (CR)
July 1	801	United Co.	✓		600	12	588
3	802	First Fed. Sav.	214	3000			3000
3	803	Johnson Co.	✓		800	16	784
4	804	Midwest Util.	614	350			350
5	805	United Co.	✓		300	6	294
6	806	Anderson Co.	✓		2500	50	2450
7	807	Davis Co.	✓				
31	896	Bell Telephone	615	225			225
		Totals		7220	16000	320	22900
				(✓)	(211)	(412)	(111)

EXHIBIT 5–11   Posting from the Cash Disbursements Journal

Cash Disbursements Journal   Page 5

Date	Check	Payee	Post Ref.	Misc. Accts. (DR)	Accts. Payable (DR)	Purchase Discounts (CR)	Cash (CR)
July 1	801	United Co.	✓		600	12	588
3	802	First Fed. Sav.	214	3000			3000
31	896	Bell Telephone	615	225			225
		Totals		7220	16000	320	22900
				(√)	(211)	(412)	(111)

General Ledger

Accounts Payable (211)   Notes Payable (214)   Telephone Expense (615)
5 7/81..16,000   5 7/81..3,000   5 7/81...225

        Cash (111)   Purchase Discounts (412)
        22,900..7/81 5   320...7/81 5

Accounts Payable Subsidiary Ledger (211)

        Davis Co. 211.1   Johnson Co. 211.2   United Co. 211.3
                                                                    5 7/81..600

CHAPTER 6

Inventory and Cost of Goods Sold

Chapter 5 was an introduction to the Income Statement. It focused on the major elements of net income, including revenues, cost of goods sold (including the periodic and perpetual inventory methods), and other expenses. Here, inventories and cost of goods sold will be examined in more detail by discussing: (1) what items belong in inventory, (2) the effects of errors in accounting for inventory, (3) different inventory costing methods, (4) the valuation of inventories, and (5) methods of estimating inventories and cost of goods sold.

The Proper Measurement of Inventory

A typical company's inventories are constantly in flux; at any given time, they are being bought, sold, and returned. As a result, it is sometimes difficult to keep track of which inventories on hand are owned, which are owned but not in stock, which have been sold but not yet shipped, and which have been purchased but have not yet arrived. Indeed, for many companies the key problem in computing net income is the proper measurement of inventory and cost of goods sold.

INVENTORY CUTOFF

Although inventory is physically counted at the end of each accounting period, determining how much inventory is on hand is similar in many ways to measuring the amount of water in a sink that has the drain open and the tap on. The guidelines for determining the inventory to be included in the account balance for a period is called inventory cutoff. This is shown in Exhibit 6–1.

inventory cutoff *the determination of which items should be included in the year-end inventory balance*

When inventory is purchased, the entry to record the purchase (assuming a periodic inventory method) is

Purchases	800	
Accounts Payable		800

Purchased $800 of inventory.

Since cost of goods sold is equal to beginning inventory plus purchases minus ending inventory, these purchases have the effect of increasing the amount of cost of goods sold. If a purchase has been entered in the accounting records but not physically counted and included in the ending inventory balance, the cost of goods sold will be overstated and net income will be understated. On the other hand, if a purchased item has been counted and included in the inventory balance but has not yet been recorded as a purchase, cost of goods sold is understated and net income is overstated. To examine the effects of these types of inventory errors, we will assume that J. C. Sears Company had the following inventory records for 1981.

Inventory Balance, January 1, 1981..................................	$ 8,000
Purchases through December 30, 1981	20,000
Inventory Balance, December 30, 1981	12,000

We will further assume that on December 31 the company purchased another $1,000 of inventory. The following comparison shows the kinds of inventory situations that can exist.

	Incorrect[1]	Incorrect	Incorrect	Correct
The $1,000 of merchandise was....	not recorded as a purchase and not counted as inventory	recorded as a purchase but not counted as inventory	not recorded as a purchase but counted as inventory	recorded as a purchase and counted as inventory
Beginning inventory .	$ 8,000	$ 8,000	$ 8,000	$ 8,000
Purchases..........	20,000	21,000	20,000	21,000
Goods Available for Sale	$28,000	$29,000	$28,000	$29,000
Ending inventory ...	12,000	12,000	13,000	13,000
Cost of Goods Sold ..	$16,000	$17,000	$15,000	$16,000

[1] This calculation produces the correct cost of goods sold but by an incorrect route.

From this example you can see the extent to which cost of goods sold (and net income) can be misstated by the improper recording and counting of inventory.

EXHIBIT 6–1   Inventory Cutoff

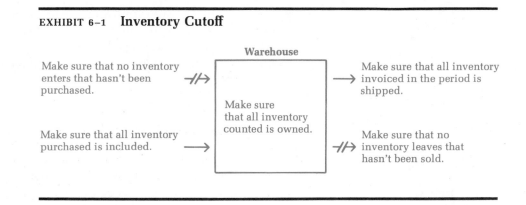

A similar situation can occur when merchandise is sold. If a sale is recorded but the merchandise remains in ending inventory, gross margin and net income will be overstated. If a sale is not recorded but inventory is shipped, gross margin and net income will be understated.

To illustrate these potential inventory errors, we will again consider the data of J. C. Sears Company. Note that sales figures have been added and the ending inventory and 1981 purchases now include the $1,000 purchase of merchandise made on December 31, 1981.

gross margin   *the excess of net sales revenues over the cost of goods sold*

net income   *a measure of the overall performance of a business entity; equal to revenues plus gains for a period minus expenses and losses for the period*

Sales During 1981 (before $2,000 sale)	$32,000 (200% of cost)
Inventory Balance (January 1, 1981)	8,000
Purchases During 1981	21,000
Inventory Balance (December 31, 1981)	13,000

In addition, assume that on December 31, inventory that cost $1,000 was sold for $2,000. The merchandise was delivered to the buyer on December 31. The following comparison shows the kind of situations that can exist.

	Incorrect	Incorrect	Incorrect	Correct
	Sale not recorded and merchandise counted as inventory	*Sale recorded and merchandise counted as inventory*	*Sale not recorded but merchandise excluded from inventory*	*Sale recorded and merchandise excluded from inventory*
Sales Revenue	$32,000	$34,000	$32,000	$34,000
Cost of Goods Sold:				
Beginning Inventory .	$ 8,000	$ 8,000	$ 8,000	$ 8,000
Purchases	21,000	21,000	21,000	21,000
Goods Available for Sale	$29,000	$29,000	$29,000	$29,000
Ending Inventory . . .	13,000	13,000	12,000	12,000
Cost of Goods Sold . .	16,000	16,000	17,000	17,000
Gross Margin	$16,000	$18,000	$15,000	$17,000

Because inventory cutoff errors cause such severe problems, most businesses close their warehouses for two or three days at year-end while they count inventory. During this period they do not accept or ship merchandise nor do they enter purchase or sales transactions in their accounting records.

OTHER FACTORS IN ACCOUNTING FOR INVENTORY

consignment *an arrangement whereby merchandise owned by one party (the consignor) is sold by another party (the consignee), usually on a commission basis*

consignor *the owner of merchandise sold by someone else, known as the consignee*

consignee *a vendor who sells merchandise owned by another party, known as the consignor, usually on a commission basis*

In addition to inventory cutoff, at least two other factors complicate a company's attempts to determine the proper amount of inventory. One factor involves the issuing of goods on consignment. Often, the inventory a firm stocks in its warehouse has not actually been purchased from suppliers. With this arrangement, suppliers, known as the consignors, retain ownership of the inventory until it is sold, and the firm selling the merchandise, known as the consignee, merely stocks and sells the merchandise for the consignor, and receives a commission on any sales as payment for services rendered. Some farm implement dealers, for example, do not actually own the tractors and other equipment they stock and sell.

It is extremely important that goods being held on consignment not be included in the inventory of the consignee, even though they are physically on the premises. It is equally important that consignors properly include all such inventory in their records, even though it is not on their premises.

FOB (free-on-board) destination *business term meaning that the seller of merchandise bears the shipping costs and maintains ownership until the sales destination is reached*

FOB (free-on-board) shipping point *business term meaning that the buyer of merchandise bears the shipping costs and acquires ownership at the point of shipment*

Another factor that complicates the accounting for inventory has to do with shipping. The question is: Who owns inventory that is on a truck or railroad car, the seller or the buyer? If the seller is bearing the shipping costs, the arrangement is known as FOB destination (free-on-board), and the seller owns the merchandise from the time it is shipped until it is delivered to the buyer. If the buyer is bearing the shipping costs, the arrangement is known as FOB shipping point, and the buyer owns the merchandise during transit. Thus, in determining which inventory should be counted and included in the inventory balance for a period, a company must note the amount of inventory in transit and the terms under which it is being shipped.

MANUFACTURING VERSUS NONMANUFACTURING FIRMS

Thus far, we have discussed factors that affect inventory accounting in all types of businesses. But we should also note that accounting for inventory in a manufacturing company is quite different from that in a retail or wholesale firm. The inventory of the latter types of firms is merchandise purchased from suppliers, whereas in manufacturing companies inventory is produced, and thus the accounting for it is much more complex.

raw materials *goods purchased for use in manufacturing products*

work-in-process *partially completed units in production*

finished goods *manufactured products ready for sale*

In a manufacturing firm, three types of inventory must be accounted for: (1) raw materials, (2) work-in-process, and (3) finished goods. Raw material inventories are goods purchased from suppliers for use in the manufacturing process. In a tire manufacturing firm, for example, raw materials would include rubber, steel, and other items used in making a tire. Work-in-process inventories are those production units that are in the process of being manufactured, together with their related manufacturing costs. For the tire manufacturer, the work-in-process inventory would include raw materials, factory labor (called direct labor), and other production costs (called overhead). Finally, finished goods inventories represent those units that are completed and ready for sale.

TO SUMMARIZE   It is important to account for all inventory properly because inventory errors can have a significant effect on the cost of goods sold, and thus on net income. Three factors that affect the measurement of inventory are (1) inventory cutoff, (2) consignments, and (3) shipping costs. In addition, manufacturing companies have three different types of inventory to account for.

ANALYZING THE EFFECTS OF INVENTORY ERRORS

In Chapter 5, we introduced the calculation for determining the cost of goods sold for a period. That calculation (with numbers from the first J. C. Sears Company example) is

Beginning Inventory	$ 8,000
+ Net Purchases	21,000
= Goods Available for Sale	$29,000
− Ending Inventory	13,000
= Cost of Goods Sold	$16,000

We further noted that a firm's gross margin is net sales less cost of goods sold.

The beginning inventory for any year, say 1981, is the amount of inventory counted and determined to be owned at the end of the previous year. The ending inventory is also determined by a physical count, this time at the end of the current year, 1981. If inventory is not counted correctly, gross margin and net income will be misstated by the same amount as the inventory error, not only in the current year, but in the following year as well. An overstatement of one year results in an understatement of the next year, and vice versa. The effect of inventory errors on gross margin and net income are illustrated in the following data from Quality Corporation.

	1980		1981	
Sales Revenue		$50,000		$40,000
Cost of Goods Sold:				
Beginning Inventory	$10,000		$ 5,000	
Purchases (Net)	20,000		25,000	
Goods Available for Sale	$30,000		$30,000	
Ending Inventory	5,000		10,000	
Cost of Goods Sold		25,000		20,000
Gross Margin		$25,000		$20,000
Expenses		10,000		10,000
Net Income		$15,000		$10,000

Now, suppose that ending inventory in 1980 was overstated. That is, instead of the correct amount of $5,000, the count erroneously showed $7,000 of inventory on hand. The following analysis shows the effect of the error on net income in both 1980 and 1981.

	1980		1981	
Sales Revenue		$50,000		$40,000
Cost of Goods Sold:				
Beginning Inventory	$10,000		$ 7,000	
Purchases (Net)	20,000		25,000	
Goods Available for Sale . .	$30,000		$32,000	
Ending Inventory	7,000		10,000	
Cost of Goods Sold		23,000		22,000
Gross Margin		$27,000		$18,000
Expenses		10,000		10,000
Net Income		$17,000		$ 8,000

This example shows that when the amount of ending inventory is overstated (as it was in 1980), both gross margin and net income are overstated by the same amount ($2,000 in 1980). If the ending inventory amount had been understated, net income and gross margin would also have been understated, again by the same amount.

Since the ending inventory in 1980 becomes the beginning inventory in 1981, the net income and gross margin for 1981 are also misstated. In 1981, however, beginning inventory is overstated, so net income and gross margin are understated, again by $2,000.

TO SUMMARIZE   Inventory errors affect cost of goods sold, gross margin, and net income on a dollar-for-dollar basis. That is, a $1 error in inventory results in a $1 error in the cost of goods sold, gross margin, and net income. Second, the misstatement of an ending inventory balance affects net income, both in the current year and in the next year. Third, errors in beginning and ending inventory have the opposite effect on cost of goods sold, gross margin, and net income. Finally, errors in inventory correct themselves after two years because a new count at the end of the second year should reveal the correct amount of ending inventory for that period.

Inventory Cost Flows

Merchandise is purchased or manufactured, stocked, and then sold. In most companies, the inventory purchased first is sold first to avoid problems of spoilage, obsolescence, or changing consumer demands. However, the specific physical flow of inventory depends on the nature of a firm's business.

To illustrate why it is so important to choose the appropriate inventory flow assumption, we will consider the September 1981 records of McDermitt Company (which sells one type of lawn mower).

Beginning inventory	10 lawn mowers, cost $200 each
September 3	Purchased 8 lawn mowers, cost $250 each
5	Sold 12 lawn mowers at $400 each
18	Purchased 16 lawn mowers, cost $300 each
20	Purchased 10 lawn mowers, cost $320 each
25	Sold 16 lawn mowers at $400 each

These inventory records show that during September the company had 44 lawn mowers (10 from beginning inventory and 34 that were purchased), which it could have sold. However, only 28 lawn mowers were sold, leaving a balance of 16 on hand at the end of September. Since the lawn mowers cost different amounts (probably because of inflation), the company, in order to correctly calculate the cost of goods sold and ending inventory, must know which lawn mowers were sold and which are still in inventory.

Actually, there are four patterns in which the lawn mowers could have flowed through the firm: (1) The oldest units could have been sold first, (2) the most recently purchased units could have been sold first, (3) the units could have been sold in a random sequence, or (4) specifically identified units could have been sold.

Each of these inventory flow assumptions is appropriate for certain businesses. For example, a grocery store usually tries to sell the oldest units first so that spoilage will not occur, whereas a company that stockpiles coal must first sell the coal purchased last, as it is on the top of the pile. Automobile dealers usually specifically identify the cars sold. And, in yet another type of company, say one that mixes chocolate in large vats and then sells it as candy bars, the units sold are a mixture of all ingredients purchased, and so some kind of weighted-average flow is used. These four types of inventory flows are shown in Exhibit 6–2.

PERIODIC INVENTORY COST FLOW METHODS

Just as the actual merchandise flows through a firm, the costs of that merchandise must flow from the Inventory account to Cost of Goods Sold. The four patterns previously identified provide the basis for this cost flow accounting. The names of these inventory costing methods are: FIFO (first-in, first-out), LIFO (last-in, first-out), weighted average, and specific identification.

Before explaining each of these methods, we should note that firms can, and do, use methods for inventory costing that may not represent the actual physical flow of their merchandise. Thus, if the coal company decided to use FIFO as an inventory costing method, even though the physical flow of its coal more correctly matches the LIFO assumption, it could do so. Similarly, a grocery store could use LIFO as an inventory costing assumption, even though most of its merchandise generally flows on a FIFO basis. When the cost of each inventory item is the same, all of these assumptions result in the same amounts for cost of goods sold and ending inventory. On the other hand, if inventory costs are rising, falling, or fluctuating during the year, the four different cost flow assumptions will generally result in different numbers for ending inventory and cost of goods sold. Con-

EXHIBIT 6–2 **Types of Inventory Flow**

Grocery store (oldest milk sold first)

Coal pile (most recently purchased coal sold first)

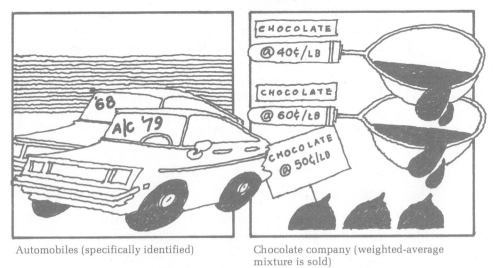

Automobiles (specifically identified)

Chocolate company (weighted-average mixture is sold)

sequently, in a period of nonstable prices (which has been the case in most countries in recent years), firms can, to some extent, influence the amount of cost of goods sold, gross margin, and net income they will report—as well as the amount of taxes they will pay—by choosing a particular inventory costing procedure. The only current requirement is that firms be consistent and use the same costing method each year.

In the next few sections, we will show how the four inventory costing methods are calculated. We will analyze each method first under the assumption of a *periodic inventory system* and then under the assumption of a *perpetual inventory system*. Data for McDermitt Company will again be used in illustrating the different methods.

McDermitt Company
Inventory Data as of September 30, 1981

Beginning Inventory . . . .   10 lawn mowers, cost $200 each

Purchases:
September 3   . . . .   8 lawn mowers, cost $250 each
    18 . . . .   16 lawn mowers, cost $300 each
    20 . . . .   10 lawn mowers, cost $320 each

Sales:
September 5   . . . .   12 lawn mowers
    25 . . . .   16 lawn mowers

FIFO Periodic Inventory Costing Method

FIFO (first-in, first-out) *an inventory cost flow assumption whereby the first goods purchased are assumed to be the first goods sold and the ending inventory consists of the most recently purchased goods*

The FIFO inventory costing method assumes that those units purchased first are sold first, and a periodic inventory system requires that all calculations be made at the end of a period. Thus, the FIFO periodic inventory and cost of goods sold amounts would be computed as follows:

	Lawn Mowers	Costs
Beginning Inventory	10	$ 2,000
Purchases	34	10,000*
Goods Available for Sale	44	$12,000
Ending Inventory	16	5,000 (a)
Cost of Goods Sold	28	$ 7,000 (b)

```
*  8 at $250 = $ 2,000
  16 at $300 =   4,800
  10 at $320 =   3,200
                $10,000
```

The 16 units on hand at the end of the period must be the last ones purchased, since FIFO assumes that the first ones purchased were the first ones sold. In order to determine which 16 units are on hand at the end of the period, McDermitt Company will simply identify the last 16 lawn mowers purchased during the month. These were

10 lawn mowers purchased on September 20 at $320 each = $3,200
6   lawn mowers purchased on September 18 at $300 each =   1,800
Total ending inventory cost = $5,000 (a)

Accordingly, the 28 lawn mowers sold were the first ones purchased, or

10 lawn mowers of beginning inventory at $200 each   = $2,000
8   lawn mowers purchased on September 3 at $250 each   =   2,000
10 lawn mowers purchased on September 18 at $300 each =   3,000
Total cost of goods sold = $7,000 (b)

LIFO Periodic Inventory Costing Method

LIFO (last-in, first-out) *an inventory cost flow assumption whereby the last goods purchased are assumed to be the first goods sold and the ending inventory consists of the first goods purchased*

The LIFO inventory costing method is the opposite of FIFO. Instead of assuming that the first units purchased are the first ones sold, LIFO assumes that the last units purchased are the first ones sold. If prices are rising, as they have in recent years, the LIFO assumption tends to leave old inventory costs on the Balance Sheet. Often, these costs are completely unrelated to the current cost of replacing the inventory. The Income Statement, however, is generally more realistic with LIFO. Since the most recent inventory costs are charged against sales as cost of goods sold, the LIFO method is better than FIFO in matching current costs with current revenues.

With the LIFO periodic inventory costing method, the cost of goods sold and ending inventory for the McDermitt Company would be computed as follows:

	Lawn Mowers	Costs
Beginning Inventory	10	$ 2,000
Purchases	34	10,000
Goods Available for Sale	44	$12,000
Ending Inventory	16	3,500 (c)
Cost of Goods Sold	28	$ 8,500 (d)

The 16 lawn mowers on hand at the end of the period must be from the beginning inventory and the first lawn mowers purchased.

10 lawn mowers of beginning inventory at $200 each   = $2,000
6 lawn mowers purchased on September 3 at $250 each = 1,500
                         Total ending inventory cost = $3,500 (c)

Accordingly, the 28 lawn mowers sold were the last ones purchased, or

10 lawn mowers purchased on September 20 at $320 each = $3,200
16 lawn mowers purchased on September 18 at $300 each = 4,800
2 lawn mowers purchased on September 3 at $250 each =   500
                          Total cost of goods sold = $8,500 (d)

Weighted-Average Periodic Inventory Costing Method

weighted average   *a periodic inventory cost flow assumption whereby the cost of goods sold and the cost of ending inventory are determined by using a weighted-average cost of all merchandise available for sale during the period*

A third costing assumption is weighted average. This method assumes that the costs of neither the first inventory nor the last purchased should be the first recognized as cost of goods sold. Instead, a weighted-average cost of all units then in inventory is charged against revenues each time a unit is sold. This assumption probably points up most clearly the difference between the flow of costs and the flow of goods through the firm. Although it may not be possible to mix the actual inventory items being sold (for instance, lawn mowers), it is perfectly acceptable to mix their costs to find the weighted-average cost of each item. The total cost of goods sold and ending inventory for McDermitt Company would then be computed as follows:

	Lawn Mowers	Costs
Beginning Inventory	10	$ 2,000
Purchases	34	10,000
Goods Available for Sale	44	$12,000
Ending Inventory	16	4,364 (rounded)
Cost of Goods Sold	28	$ 7,636

In this case, a weighted-average cost per lawn mower of $272.73 was used in computing both the ending inventory and cost of goods sold. This weighted-average cost per unit is the total number of units available for sale divided into the total cost of goods available for sale, or

$$\frac{\text{cost of goods available for sale}}{\text{total number of units available for sale}} = \frac{\$12,000}{44} = \frac{\$272.73}{\text{per lawn mower}}$$

The cost of the ending inventory is the weighted-average cost per unit multiplied by the number of units on hand at the end of a period, or 16 units × $272.73 = $4,364. And the cost of goods sold is the weighted-average cost per unit multiplied by the number of units sold, or $272.73 × 28 units = $7,636.

Specific-Identification Inventory Costing Method

specific identification   a method of valuing inventory and determining cost of goods sold whereby the actual costs of inventory items are assigned to specific units on hand and to those units that have been sold

Thus far, we have focused on inventory costing methods that involve cost flow assumptions. Specific identification is more precise; it requires that the individual costs of the actual units sold be charged against revenue as cost of goods sold. In order to compute cost of goods sold and ending inventory amounts with this method, a company must know which units were actually sold and the unit cost of each.

Suppose that of the 12 lawn mowers sold by McDermitt on September 5, 8 came from the beginning inventory and 4 from the September 3 purchase, and that all of the 16 units sold on September 25 came from the September 18 purchase. With this information, cost of goods sold and ending inventory would be computed as follows:

	Lawn Mowers	Costs
Beginning Inventory	10	$ 2,000
Purchases	34	10,000
Goods Available for Sale	44	$12,000
Ending Inventory	16	4,600 (f)
Cost of Goods Sold	28	$ 7,400 (e)

The cost of goods sold is the total of the costs of the specific lawn mowers sold, or

8 lawn mowers of beginning inventory at $200 each	=	$1,600
4 lawn mowers purchased on September 3 at $250 each	=	1,000
16 lawn mowers purchased on September 18 at $300 each	=	4,800
Total cost of goods sold	=	$7,400 (e)

Similarly, the cost of ending inventory is the total of the individual costs of the lawn mowers still on hand at the end of the month, or

2 lawn mowers of beginning inventory at $200 each	=	$ 400
4 lawn mowers purchased on September 3 at $250 each	=	1,000
10 lawn mowers purchased on September 20 at $320 each	=	3,200
Total ending inventory	=	$4,600 (f)

Comparison of Costing Methods Under the Periodic Inventory System

The cost of goods sold and ending inventory under each of the four periodic methods are

	FIFO	LIFO	Weighted Average	Specific Identification
Ending Inventory ...	$ 5,000	$ 3,500	$ 4,364	$ 4,600
Cost of Goods Sold ..	7,000	8,500	7,636	7,400
Total	$12,000	$12,000	$12,000	$12,000

This comparison shows that the two extremes are FIFO and LIFO. This is always the case when the cost of inventory items is either continually increasing (as in the example) or decreasing. Since in times of increasing prices, FIFO assumes the highest value of ending inventory, a firm that wishes to show the highest possible net income would employ that method. Many firms, however, choose to report the lowest possible net income since a higher net income results in higher income taxes. Accordingly, they elect to use LIFO in a period of rising prices in order to minimize tax payments in the current year. You should recognize, however, that over the life of a firm (as all inventory is eventually sold), total net income will be the same regardless of the method used.

Although in most instances where alternatives exist, firms are allowed to use one accounting method for tax purposes and another for financial reporting, such is not the case in accounting for inventory costs. The Internal Revenue Service (IRS) has ruled that firms may use LIFO for tax purposes, but if they do so, they must also use LIFO for financial reporting purposes. Therefore, companies must choose between reporting high profits and paying high taxes or reporting low profits and paying low taxes. In recent years, many organizations have switched from FIFO to LIFO, a trend that has been accelerated by the high rate of inflation. While FIFO and LIFO are the two most common methods of accounting for inventory, the specific-identification method is often used by companies with high-value inventory items, such as airplanes or diamonds, and the weighted-average method is used by firms that have numerous small-value inventory items.

PERPETUAL INVENTORY COST FLOW METHODS

The four inventory cost flow methods have been illustrated only in the context of a periodic inventory system. These same cost flow assumptions must also be made when a perpetual system is used. The specific-identification method will not be analyzed again because it is identical under either system. The basic difference between the two systems, you may recall, is that under a periodic system all calculations are made at the end of a period, while with a perpetual system inventory costs are calculated continuously throughout the period as inventory is purchased or sold.

FIFO Perpetual Inventory Costing Method

The ending inventory and cost of goods sold for McDermitt Company using the FIFO perpetual inventory method would be

	Lawn Mowers	Costs
Beginning Inventory	10	$ 2,000
Purchases	34	10,000
Goods Available for Sale	44	$12,000
Ending Inventory	16	5,000
Cost of Goods Sold	28	$ 7,000

The amount of ending inventory would be calculated as follows:

Date	Purchased — Number of Units	Purchased — Unit Cost	Purchased — Total Cost	Sold — Number of Units	Sold — Unit Price	Sold — Total Price	Remaining — Units	Remaining — Unit Cost	Remaining — Total Cost
Beginning inventory							10	$200	$2,000
Sept. 3	8	$250	$ 2,000				18	{ 10 at $200 / 8 at $250 }	$4,000
5				12	{ 10 at $200 / 2 at $250 }	$2,500	6	$250	$1,500
18	16	$300	$ 4,800				22	{ 6 at $250 / 16 at $300 }	$6,300
20	10	$320	$ 3,200				32	{ 6 at $250 / 16 at $300 / 10 at $320 }	$9,500
25				16	{ 6 at $250 / 10 at $300 }	$4,500	16	{ 6 at $300 / 10 at $320 }	$5,000
Totals	34		$10,000	28		$7,000			

This calculation shows that the ending inventory of **16 lawn mowers** at a cost of $5,000 is the same amount as that obtained with the FIFO periodic method. This is not a coincidence. While the analytic process is different, the amount of ending inventory, and thus the cost of goods sold, will always be the same under the FIFO costing assumption, no matter which inventory system is used. This is not true of the other assumptions.

LIFO Perpetual Inventory Costing Method

LIFO perpetual (like LIFO periodic) provides ending inventory and net income figures that are lower than those of FIFO when prices are rising. The difference between the two is usually not so large as with the periodic system, however. The amount of ending inventory using a LIFO perpetual inventory costing method would be determined as follows:

Date	Purchased Number of units	Unit Cost	Total Cost	Sold Number of Units	Unit Price	Total Price	Remaining Units	Unit Cost	Total Cost
Beginning inventory							10	$200	$2,000
Sept. 3	8	$250	$ 2,000				18	{ 10 at $200 8 at $250	$4,000
5				12	{ 8 at $250 4 at $200	$2,800	6	$200	$1,200
18	16	$300	$ 4,800				22	{ 6 at $200 16 at $300	$6,000
20	10	$320	$ 3,200				32	{ 6 at $200 16 at $300 10 at $320	$9,200
25				16	{ 10 at $320 6 at $300	$5,000	16	{ 6 at $200 10 at $300	$4,200
Totals	34		$10,000	28		$7,800			

The ending inventory amount of $4,200 is different from the $3,500 computed with the LIFO periodic costing method, as shown below.

Ending Inventory

LIFO Periodic		LIFO Perpetual	
10 at $200 =	$2,000	6 at $200 =	$1,200
6 at $250 =	1,500	10 at $300 =	3,000
	$3,500		$4,200

Since the LIFO perpetual method requires that computations be made as lawn mowers are sold or purchased, only the costs of those lawn mowers actually on hand can be recognized. Consider, for example, the September 5 sale of 12 units. On that date, only the units from beginning inventory and the September 3 purchase were available, and so all of the September 3 units purchased at $250 each were sold (because they were the last ones in). Under the LIFO periodic method, no calculations are made until the end of the month, so the unit costs that remain in inventory are the oldest ones, no matter which units were actually available for sale on which dates.

With the LIFO perpetual method, the calculation for cost of goods sold would be

	Lawn Mowers	Costs
Beginning Inventory	10	$ 2,000
Purchases	34	10,000
Goods Available for Sale	44	$12,000
Ending Inventory	16	4,200
Cost of Goods Sold	28	$ 7,800

Moving-Average Inventory Costing Method

moving average *a perpetual inventory cost flow assumption whereby the cost of goods sold and the cost of ending inventory are determined by using a weighted-average cost of all merchandise on hand after each purchase*

As the name implies, the weighted-average perpetual costing method involves the computation of weighted averages at different times throughout the period. (Under a periodic system, the average is taken only once, at the end of the period.) It is, therefore, referred to as the moving-average method. A company using this method would compute a new weighted average after each purchase transaction and would derive its ending inventory as follows:

	Purchased			Sold			Remaining		
Date	Units	Unit Cost	Total Cost	Units	Unit Cost	Total Costs	Units	Unit Cost	Total Cost
Beginning									(rounded)
inventory							10	$200.00	$2,000
Sept. 3	8	$250.00	$ 2,000				18	$222.22	$4,000
5				12	$222.22	$2,667	6	$222.22	$1,333
18	16	$300.00	$ 4,800				22	$278.77	$6,133
20	10	$320.00	$ 3,200				32	$291.67	$9,333
25				16	$291.67	$4,667	16	$291.67	$4,667
Totals	34		$10,000	28		$7,333*			

* rounding error.

The moving-average price of $222.22 on September 3, for example, is the total cost of all units available on that date divided by the total number of units available, or $4,000/18 units = $222.22. The calculations for the two other moving-average prices are as follows:

September 18 Average Price	September 20 Average Price
$6,133/22 units = $278.77 per unit	$9,333/32 units = $291.67 per unit

With the moving-average method, cost of goods sold is calculated as follows:

	Units	Costs
Beginning Inventory	10	$ 2,000
Purchases	34	10,000
Goods Available for Sale	44	$12,000
Ending Inventory	16	4,667
Cost of Goods Sold	28	$ 7,333

COMPARISON OF ALL INVENTORY COSTING METHODS

All of the ending inventory and cost of goods sold amounts that we have calculated in the chapter are summarized on the next page.

	FIFO		LIFO		Weighted Average (Periodic)	Moving Average (Perpetual)	Specific Identification
	Periodic	Perpetual	Periodic	Perpetual			
Ending inventory	$5,000	$5,000	$3,500	$4,200	$4,364	$4,667	$4,600
Cost of goods sold ...	7,000	7,000	8,500	7,800	7,636	7,333	7,400

This comparison points up several interesting facts. First, no matter which inventory system a company uses, during a period of rising prices cost of goods sold is always highest (and net income lowest) with LIFO and lowest with FIFO. Second, the difference between FIFO and LIFO cost of goods sold is usually greater with a periodic system than with a perpetual system. Third, perpetual and periodic cost of goods sold amounts are always the same when FIFO is used.

It is impossible to conclude that any one of these methods is best, even though in most circumstances there will be one method that is theoretically most appropriate, given a company's physical flow of goods. In practice, however, smaller owner-operated businesses are interested in paying less taxes and will usually choose LIFO in periods of rising prices, whereas larger, publicly owned firms have more incentive to show high profits. As the inflationary economy continues, however, more and more firms tend to switch to LIFO.

TO SUMMARIZE   There are four principal inventory costing methods: FIFO, LIFO, weighted average, and specific identification. Any of these methods can be used with either a perpetual or a periodic inventory system. During periods of inflation, the LIFO periodic inventory method results in the lowest net income and the FIFO method results in the highest net income.

Reporting Inventory at Amounts Below Cost

All the inventory costing methods we have discussed have one thing in common—they report inventory at cost. Occasionally, however, it becomes necessary to report inventory at an amount that is less than cost. This happens when inventory items are damaged or obsolete, or when inventory can be replaced new at a price that is less than its original cost.

INVENTORY VALUED AT NET REALIZABLE VALUE

net realizable value   *the selling price of an item less reasonable selling costs*

When inventory is damaged or becomes obsolete, it should be reported at no more than its <u>net realizable value</u>. This is the amount that the inventory can be sold for minus any selling costs. Suppose, for example, that an automobile dealer has a demonstrator car that originally cost $6,000, and can now be sold for $5,000. The car should be reported at its net realizable value. If a commission of $500 must be paid to sell the car, then the net realizable value is $4,500, or $1,500 less than cost. This loss is calculated as follows:

Cost		$6,000
Estimated Selling Price	$5,000	
Less Selling Commission	500	4,500
Loss		$1,500

In order to satisfy the matching rule, this estimated loss must be recognized as soon as it is known that a loss will be realized (even before the car is sold). The journal entry required to recognize the loss and reduce the inventory amount of the car would be

Loss on Write-Down of Inventory (Expense)	1,500	
Inventory		1,500

To write down demonstrator car to a net realizable value of $4,500.

By writing down inventory to its net realizable value, a company recognizes a loss when it happens and is thus able to break even when the inventory is finally sold. Using net realizable values means that assets are not being carried at amounts which exceed their future economic benefits.

INVENTORY VALUED AT LOWER OF COST OR MARKET

The other circumstance that requires inventory to be written down to an amount below cost arises when the inventory can be replaced new at a price that is less than its original cost. Although the replacement cost of inventory seldom falls below original cost in an inflationary environment, this has happened in certain industries. In the electronics industry, for instance, the costs of computers and electronic calculators have fallen drastically in recent years.

To illustrate the accounting for inventories using the lower-of-cost-or-market rule, we will consider the following situation. You own an office supply store; 10 calculators that cost you $200 each six months ago are to be sold for $250 each. However, these same calculators would now cost you only $125 each. Since the competition is selling the $125 calculators for $175, you drop your price to the market price of $175 and your inventory carrying cost to $125. You have experienced a loss of $75 ($200 − $125) per calculator, which must be recognized immediately. In this way you have preserved the $50 profit margin that will be recognized when the calculators are actually sold and at the same time you have written off the expired portion ($75) of the assets. The journal entry to recognize this loss would be

lower-of-cost-or-market rule *a basis for valuing certain assets at the lower of original cost or market value (current replacement cost), provided that the replacement cost is not higher than net realizable value or lower than net realizable value minus normal profit*

Loss on Write-Down of Inventory (Expense)   750
    Inventory   750

To write down inventory of calculators to lower of cost or market (10 × $75).

Note that market in this context means the price that would have to be paid to purchase or replace the item in inventory. When applying the lower-of-cost-or-market rule, in no case should inventory be carried at an amount greater than the net realizable value or at an amount less than net realizable value minus a normal profit.

Both the lower-of-cost-or-market and the net-realizable-value rules have gained wide acceptance because they place inventory on the Balance Sheet at amounts that are in keeping with future economic benefits. With both methods, losses are recognized when they occur, not necessarily when a sale is made.

TO SUMMARIZE   There are two cases in which inventory should be written down: (1) when it is damaged or obsolete, and (2) when it can be replaced (purchased new) at an amount that is less than its original cost. In the first case, inventory is reported at no more than net realizable value, an amount that allows a company to break even when the inventory is sold. In the second case, inventory is written down to the lower of cost or market, an amount that may restore a normal profit margin for the firm when the item is sold. In no case, however, should inventory be carried at an amount that exceeds the net realizable value. Both reporting alternatives are attempts to show assets at amounts that reflect realistic future economic benefits.

Methods of Estimating Inventories

We have assumed thus far that the number of inventory units on hand is known, generally by a physical count that takes place at the end of each accounting period. As we indicated, for a periodic inventory system this physical count is the only way to determine how much inventory is on hand at the end of a period. For a perpetual inventory system, the physical count provides a verification of the quantity on hand. There are times, however, when a company needs to know the dollar amount of ending inventory, but a physical count is either impossible or impractical. For example, many firms prepare quarterly, or even monthly, financial statements, but it is too expensive and time consuming to count the inventory at the end of each period. In such cases, if a perpetual inventory system is being used, the balance in the Inventory account is usually assumed to be correct. With a periodic inventory system, however, some estimate of the Inventory balance must be made.

There are two common methods of estimating the dollar amount of ending inventory. The first, the gross margin method, is used by all types of firms; the second, the retail inventory method, is used primarily by department stores and other retail businesses.

THE GROSS MARGIN METHOD

gross margin method   a procedure for estimating the amount of ending inventory; the historical relationship of cost of goods sold to sales is used in computing ending inventory

With the gross margin method, a firm uses its knowledge of the dollar amounts of beginning inventory and purchases and its historical gross margin percentage to estimate the dollar amounts of cost of goods sold and ending inventory.

To illustrate, we will assume the following data for Jason Brick Company.

Sales Revenue (January 1 to March 31)	$100,000
Inventory Balance (January 1)	15,000
Purchases (January 1 to March 31)	65,000
Gross Margin Percentage (historically determined percentage of sales price)	40%

With this information, the dollar amount of inventory on hand on March 31 can be estimated as follows:

		Dollars	Percentage of Sales
Sales Revenue		$100,000	100%
Cost of Goods Sold:			
Beginning Inventory................	$15,000		
Purchases	65,000		
Goods Available for Sale	$80,000		
Ending Inventory	20,000 (3)*		
Cost of Goods Sold		60,000 (2)*	60%
Gross Margin		$ 40,000 (1)*	40%

* The numbers indicate the order of calculation.

In this example, the amount of gross margin was first determined by calculating 40 percent of sales (step 1). Next, the cost of goods sold was found by subtracting gross margin from sales (step 2). Finally, the dollar amount of ending inventory was obtained by subtracting cost of goods sold from total goods available for sale (step 3). Obviously, the gross margin method of estimating cost of goods sold and ending inventory assumes that the historical gross margin percentage is appropriate for the current period. This assumption is a realistic one in many fields of business. In cases where the gross margin percentage has changed, either because of higher selling prices, higher inventory costs, or for other reasons, this method should be used with caution.

The gross margin method of estimating ending inventories is also useful when a fire or other calamity destroys a company's inventory. In these cases, the dollar amount of inventory lost must be determined before insurance claims can be made. The dollar amounts of sales, purchases, and beginning inventory can be obtained from prior years' financial statements, and from customers, suppliers, and other sources, so the gross margin method can be used to estimate the dollar amount of inventory lost.

THE RETAIL INVENTORY METHOD

The retail method of estimating the dollar amount of ending inventory is similar to the gross margin method. It is widely used by department stores, chain stores, and other retail businesses. In these types of organizations, all inventory is marked at selling prices. When a physical count of inventory is taken, retail (sales) prices are applied to all inventory items. Inventory at retail prices is then converted to inventory at cost by applying the appropriate ratio between costs and sales. For example, if a store's markup is 100 percent of cost, and if the retail inventory records showed a balance of $40,000, the cost of the inventory would be $20,000.

The retail method may also be used to estimate the dollar cost of inventory on hand when a physical count is not taken. When used, it requires that beginning inventory and purchases be recorded on both a cost and a selling price basis. Then, total goods available for sale can be calculated at both cost and selling price. By deducting sales for the period from the goods available for sale at selling price, the ending inventory at selling price is derived. This number is converted to ending inventory at cost by using the appropriate markup ratio.

To illustrate, we will consider the following data for Macey's Hardware Store.

	Cost	Selling Price
Beginning Inventory	$ 42,000	$ 63,000
Net Purchases During the Month	105,900	154,500
Goods Available for Sale	$147,900	$217,500
Less Net Sales for the Month		160,000
Ending Inventory at Selling Price		$ 57,500
Cost-to-Selling-Price Ratio ($147,900 ÷ $217,500)		68%
Ending Inventory at Cost (68% of $57,500)	$ 39,100	

In this case, the cost-to-selling-price ratio of goods available for sale is 68 percent. This percentage is applied to the ending inventory at selling price to determine the cost of the ending inventory.

The major difference between the retail inventory and the gross margin methods is that the former uses the percentage markup—that is, the cost-to-selling-price ratio for goods available for sale—*from the current period* (by keeping current records at both cost and retail), whereas the latter uses the *historical* gross margin rates. To the extent that the gross margin percentages change over time, inventory estimates based on the retail method should be more accurate.

In practice, the use of the retail method is often complicated by frequent price changes.

TO SUMMARIZE   There are two common methods of estimating the dollar amount of inventory: (1) the gross margin method, and (2) the retail inventory method. The former uses a historical gross margin percentage to estimate the cost of ending inventory; the latter uses the cost-to-selling-price ratio to estimate inventory levels in retail firms.

CHAPTER REVIEW

The three major factors affecting inventory measurement are inventory cutoff, consignments, and shipping costs. When inventory is not correctly accounted for, both cost of goods sold and net income will be incorrect. Inventory errors affect net income on a dollar-for-dollar basis and usually counter balance after two periods.

The four major cost flow assumptions used in accounting for inventories are: FIFO, LIFO, weighted average, and specific identification. Each of these results in different dollar amounts of ending inventory, cost of goods sold, and net income. A firm may choose any method without regard for the way goods physically flow through that firm. Often, the method selected will depend on tax considerations. During an inflationary period, LIFO provides the lowest net income and thus results in lower taxes. Because of this tax advantage, the LIFO method is currently very popular. All of these inventory methods can be used with either a periodic or perpetual inventory system.

Sometimes inventory must be reported at amounts below cost. This occurs (1) when inventory is damaged or obsolete, and (2) when the replacement price drops below inventory cost. In the first case, inventory is valued at net realizable value, and in the second, it is valued at the lower of cost or market. When the second approach is used, market is taken to mean the replacement cost of the inventory, but in no case can it be greater than the item's net realizable value, or less than net realizable value minus a normal profit.

Although most firms take a physical count of inventory at the end of each year, there may be other times when the dollar amount of inventory must be estimated. There are two common methods of estimating ending inventories: the gross margin method, which can be used in almost any situation, and the retail inventory method, which is limited to retail firms, such as chain or department stores. The gross margin method estimates the amount of inventory on the basis of historical gross margin percentages; the retail method uses the cost-to-selling-price ratio from the current period.

KEY TERMS AND CONCEPTS

consignee (208)
consignment (208)
consignor (208)
FIFO (213)
finished goods (208)
FOB destination (208)
FOB shipping point (208)
gross margin (207)
gross margin method (223)

inventory cutoff (206)
LIFO (213)
lower-of-cost-or-market rule (221)
moving average (219)
net income (207)
net realizable value (220)
raw materials (208)
retail inventory method (224)

specific identification (215)
weighted average (214)
work-in-process (208)

DISCUSSION QUESTIONS

1. When does the cost of inventory change from an asset to an expense?

2. What is the effect on net income when purchased merchandise is counted and included in the inventory balance but not recorded as a purchase?

3. What is the effect on net income of inventory sold and shipped but not recorded as a sale?

4. What is the effect on net income when goods held on consignment are included in the ending inventory balance?

5. Who owns merchandise during shipment under the terms FOB shipping point?

6. Why is it more difficult to account for the inventory of a manufacturing firm than for that of a merchandising firm?

7. If an ending inventory amount in period 1 were understated by $200, what would be the effect on reported net income in period 2?

8. Explain the difference between cost flows and the movement of goods.

9. Why have many firms switched to the LIFO inventory costing method in recent years?

10. Which inventory costing method results in paying the least amount of taxes when prices are falling?

11. Why is the weighted-average perpetual inventory cost assumption referred to as the moving-average method?

12. Why might you expect to see a different inventory costing method used in smaller, owner-operated firms than in larger, publicly owned companies?

13. When would a firm be prohibited from using one method of costing inventories for tax purposes and another for financial reporting purposes?

14. When should inventory be valued at its net realizable value?

15. When should inventory be valued at the lower of cost or market?

16. Why is the gross margin method of estimating dollar amounts of inventory more useful when using a periodic inventory system than when using a perpetual inventory system?

17. Why is it necessary to know which inventory cost flow methods are being used before the financial performances of different firms can be compared?

EXERCISES

E6–1 What Should Be Included in Inventory?

Pierre is trying to compute the inventory balance for the December 31, 1980, financial statements of his cutlery shop. He has computed a tentative book balance of $26,300 but suspects that several adjustments still need to be made. In particular, he believes the following could affect his inventory balance.

a. A shipment of goods that cost $1,700 was received on December 28, 1980. It was properly recorded as a purchase in 1980 but not counted with the ending inventory.

b. Another shipment of goods (FOB destination) was received on January 2, 1981, and cost $400. It was properly recorded as a purchase in 1981 but not counted with 1980's ending inventory.

c. A $1,400 shipment of goods to a customer on January 3 was recorded as a sale in 1981 but was deducted from the December 31, 1980, ending inventory balance. The goods cost $900.

d. The company had $3,000 of goods on consignment with a customer and $2,500 of merchandise was on consignment from a vendor. Neither amount was included in the $26,300 figure.

e. The following amounts represent merchandise that was in transit on December 31, 1980, and was recorded as purchases and sales in 1980 but not included in the December 31 inventory.

  (1) Ordered by Pierre, $900, FOB destination
  (2) Ordered by Pierre, $300, FOB shipping point
  (3) Sold by Pierre, $2,000, FOB shipping point
  (4) Sold by Pierre, $2,300, FOB destination

1. What is the proper amount of ending inventory at December 31, 1980?

2. If purchases (before any adjustment from above, if any) totaled $43,200 and beginning inventory (January 1, 1980) totaled $15,800, what is the cost of goods sold in 1980?

E6–2 Goods on Consignment

Company A has consignment arrangements with Supplier B and also with Customer C. In particular, Supplier B ships some of its goods to Company A on consignment while Company A ships some of its goods to Customer C on a consignment basis. At the end of 1981, Company A's accounting records showed:

Goods on consignment from Supplier B $12,000
Goods on consignment to Customer C $16,000

1. If a physical count of all inventory revealed that $60,000 of goods were on hand, what amount of ending inventory should be reported?

2. If the amount of the beginning inventory for the year was $54,000 and purchases during the year were $118,000, what is the cost of goods sold for the year? (Assume the ending inventory from question 1.)

3. If, instead of the above facts, Company A had only $8,000 of the goods on consignment with Customer C and $20,000 of consigned goods from Supplier B, and if physical goods on hand totaled $72,000, what would be the correct amount of the ending inventory?

4. With respect to question 3, if beginning inventory totaled $48,000 and the cost of goods sold was $95,000, what were the purchases?

E6–3   Transportation Terms (FOB)—Ownership of Inventory

1. In the following four cases, who would pay the freight charges?

The ABC Company buys goods from Supplier X with terms:
   (a) FOB shipping point
   (b) FOB destination

The ABC Company sells goods to Customer Y with terms:
   (c) FOB shipping point
   (d) FOB destination

2. The ABC Company has $15,300 of goods on hand, with a shipment of $2,300 in transit from Supplier X (FOB destination), and a shipment of $3,000 in transit to Customer Y (FOB shipping point). What is the proper amount of inventory of the ABC Company?

3. If the shipment from Supplier X described in question 2 was FOB shipping point and the shipment to Customer Y was FOB destination, what would be the proper amount of inventory?

E6–4   The Effect of Inventory Errors

As the accountant for Kelly Boutique, you are in the process of preparing its Income Statement for the year ended December 31, 1981. In doing so, you have noticed that a shipment of merchandise that cost $2,000 was received on December 24, 1981.

1. Prepare an Income Statement through gross margin under each of the following four assumptions.
   (a) The shipment is recorded as a purchase in the accounting records and is also counted in the ending physical inventory.
   (b) The shipment is recorded as a purchase but is not counted in ending inventory.

(c) The shipment is not recorded as a purchase in the accounting records but is counted in ending inventory.

(d) The shipment is not recorded as a purchase in the accounting records and is not counted in the ending inventory.

Before the effects of the $2,000 transaction were taken into account, the relevant Income Statement figures were

Sales Revenue $74,000
Beginning Inventory $18,000
Purchases. $44,000
Ending Inventory $13,000

2. Under the given circumstances, which of the four assumptions is correct?

3. Which assumption overstates gross margin (and therefore net income)?

4. Which assumption understates gross margin (and therefore net income)?

E6–5   The Effect of Inventory Errors

Mildred, the accountant for XYZ Company, reported the following accounting treatments for several purchase transactions that took place near December 31, 1980, the company's year-end.

Purchase Date	Was the purchase recorded in the company's books on or before December 31, 1980?	Amount	Was the inventory counted and included in the inventory balance at December 31, 1980?
1980:			
Dec. 26	Yes	$1,300	Yes
29	Yes	900	No
31	No	1,900	Yes
1981:			
Jan. 1	No	200	Yes
1	Yes	2,900	No
2	No	700	No
2	Yes	1,600	Yes

1. If XYZ Company's records reported purchases and ending inventory balances of $36,400 and $12,900, respectively, for 1980, what should have been the proper amounts in these accounts?

2. What would be the correct amount of cost of goods sold for 1980 if the beginning inventory balance on January 1, 1980, was $10,100?

3. By how much would the cost of goods sold be over- or understated if the corrections in question 1 were not made?

E6–6   The Effect of Inventory Errors

1. If the current year's accounting records of EMCO Manufacturing Company included an overstatement of purchases of $1,900, an understatement of beginning inventory of $2,400, and an understatement of ending inventory of $300, by how much would the cost of goods sold be misstated and would the misstatement be an overstatement or an understatement?

2. Given these same errors, what will be the amount and direction (overstatement or understatement) of the misstatement in the current year's net income?

3. What effect will these errors have on net income of the next period, assuming that purchases are stated correctly in the next period?

E6–7   FIFO, LIFO, and Weighted-Average Calculations (Periodic Inventory System)

The following transactions took place in the Century 21 Sporting Goods Store during April 1981.

April 1	Beginning Inventory	24 suits at $12.00
5	Purchase of Jogging Suits	15 suits at 13.00
11	Purchase of Jogging Suits	16 suits at 13.50
19	Sale of Jogging Suits	20 suits at 30.00
24	Purchase of Jogging Suits	10 suits at 14.00
30	Sale of Jogging Suits	12 suits at 30.00

Assuming a periodic inventory system, compute the cost of goods sold and ending inventory balances using the following inventory costing methods.

1. Weighted average
2. FIFO
3. LIFO

E6–8   Specific-Identification Inventory Costing Method

Decker's Diamond Shop is computing its inventory and cost of goods sold for November 1981. At the beginning of the month, the following jewelry items were in stock.

Ring A	8 at $600 =	$ 4,800
Ring A	10 at 650 =	6,500
Ring B	5 at 300 =	1,500
Ring B	6 at 350 =	2,100
Ring B	3 at 450 =	1,350
Ring C	7 at 200 =	1,400
Ring C	8 at 250 =	2,000
		$19,650

During the month, the following rings were purchased: four type A rings at $600, two type B rings at $450, and five type C rings at $300. Also during the month, the following sales were made.

Ring Type	Quantity Sold	Sales Price	Cost
A	2	$1,000	$600
A	3	1,050	600
A	1	1,200	650
B	2	850	450
B	2	800	350
C	4	450	200
C	3	500	250
C	1	550	250

Because of the high cost per item, Decker uses the specific-identification method of costing inventory.

1. Calculate cost of goods sold and ending inventory balances for November.

2. Calculate gross margin for the month.

E6–9   FIFO, LIFO, and Weighted-Average Calculations (Periodic Inventory System)

Bernardo's Bookstore has just closed its operations on the last day of July 1981. On that date, the inventory records showed the following.

July 1	Beginning Inventory	10,000 at $4.00 = $40,000
5	Sold	2,000
13	Purchased	3,000 at 4.50 = 13,500
17	Sold	1,500
25	Purchased	4,000 at 5.00 = 20,000
27	Sold	2,500
		$73,500

Assuming a periodic inventory system, compute Bernardo's cost of goods sold and ending inventory balances for July using the following methods.

1. FIFO
2. LIFO
3. Weighted average

E6–10   FIFO, LIFO, and Moving-Average Calculations (Perpetual Inventory System)

1. Using the figures in E6–9, compute the ending inventory and cost of goods sold balances with (1) FIFO, (2) LIFO, and (3) moving average, under a perpetual inventory system. Compute unit costs to the nearest tenth of a cent.

2. Why are the LIFO periodic and LIFO perpetual cost of goods sold amounts different?

3. Which of the three methods is best? Why?

E6–11   Tax Effects of FIFO, LIFO, and Weighted Average (Periodic)

James Corporation shows the following transactions in its 1981 books.

Beginning Inventory .	700 units at $3	= $2,100
Purchase	300 units at 4	= 1,200
Sale	400 units at 8 (sales price)	
Purchase	200 units at 5	= 1,000
Sale	300 units at 9 (sales price)	
		$4,300

1. If James is taxed at 19 percent, what is its 1981 tax liability under each of the following three inventory methods (assume that the only expense during 1981, other than cost of goods sold, was a $1,500 administrative expense).

(a) FIFO (periodic)
(b) LIFO (periodic)
(c) Weighted average (periodic)

2. Which method results in the lowest tax liability? Why?

E6–12   Various Inventory Costing Methods

The records of Samson Company showed the following with regard to one of the major inventory items being sold. Assume the transactions occurred in the order given.

	Units	Unit Cost
Beginning Inventory	50	$1.00
Purchase No. 1	50	2.00
Sale No. 1	20	
Purchase No. 2	100	3.00
Sale No. 2	110	

Compute the value of the *ending inventory* under each of the following assumptions (round to nearest dollar).

1. Weighted-average cost with periodic inventory procedures.
2. Weighted-average cost with perpetual inventory procedures (moving average).
3. FIFO cost with periodic inventory procedures.

E6–13   Cost of Goods Sold Calculations

The management of Huey's Discount Store wants to minimize its income taxes and intends to use the inventory method that best meets this objective. Prices in the economy are currently falling and Huey's tax rate is 40 percent.

1. Which method should Huey use to minimize income tax?
2. Concerning inventory and purchases, the following information is available.

(a) Beginning inventory consisted of 100 units at $23.
(b) The last purchase of 150 units cost $3,000 in total.

(c) There was only one additional purchase (besides the 150 units) during the period.
(d) 370 units were sold during the period.
(e) The ending inventory is 80 units.
(f) The total cost of goods available for sale for the period is $9,500.

Given this information, what were the number of units purchased and the price per unit of the one additional purchase?

3. Assuming a periodic inventory system, what are the dollar amounts of the ending inventory and cost of goods sold under the FIFO and LIFO methods?

4. How much tax is saved by using the method you suggested in answer to question 1 instead of the less favorable method?

E6–14   Cost of Goods Sold Calculations

Complete the Cost of Goods Sold section for the following five companies.

	Company A	Company B	Company C	Company D	Company E
Beginning Inventory .	$14,000	$24,800	$(5) _____	$(7) _____	$19,200
Purchases . . .	26,500	(3) _____	43,000	89,500	(9) _____
Purchase Returns and Allowances	(1) _____	1,000	1,800	200	2,200
Goods Available for Sale . . .	40,100	(4) _____	56,300	(8) _____	81,500
Ending Inventory .	(2) _____	22,200	15,200	28,800	(10) _____
Cost of Goods Sold	31,400	67,200	(6) _____	93,400	68,400

E6–15   Lower of Cost or Market

Prepare the necessary General Journal entries to account for the purchases and year-end adjustments of the inventory of ABC Manufacturing Company (periodic inventory system).

1. Purchased 50 standard widgets for $4.00 each to sell at $7 per unit.
2. Purchased 15 deluxe widgets at $9.00 per unit to sell for $15 per unit.
3. At the end of the year, the standard widgets could be purchased for $4.50 and are selling for $7.50.
4. At the end of the year, the deluxe widgets could be purchased for $5.00 and are selling for $8.00 per unit.
5. At the end of the second year, standard widgets could be purchased for $3.00 and are selling for $4.00.
6. At the end of the second year, the deluxe widgets could be purchased for $4.50 and are selling for $10.00.

E6–16   Valuation of Inventory

A flood recently damaged a warehouse of Jason and Company. After the flood, an examination and valuation of the inventory showed the following.

Item No.	Quantity	Original Unit Cost	Current Replacement Cost	Net Realizable Value
1062	50	$14	$14	$12
3095	40	16	17	10
4348	86	8	6	7
5326	24	32	25	15

1. By what amount, if any, should each item be written down?

2. Make the appropriate journal entry (entries).

E6–17   Gross Margin Method of Estimating Inventory

Smith Corporation is interested in estimating the inventory balance for its quarterly financial statements. A periodic inventory system is used. Records show that quarterly sales totaled $300,000, beginning inventory was $45,000, purchases totaled $140,000, and the historical gross margin percentage has averaged approximately 50 percent.

1. What is the approximate amount of ending inventory?

2. What could be the explanation for the difference if a physical count shows only $25,000 in inventory?

E6–18   Retail Inventory Estimation Method

Merchant Department Store uses the retail inventory method. During the first three months of 1981, the store had the following balances.

	At Cost	At Selling Price
Beginning Inventory................	$40,000	$ 62,000
Purchases	75,000	112,000
Sales Revenue....................		118,000

Given these data, what is the cost of the inventory that Merchant should report on its March 31 quarterly financial statements?

PROBLEMS

P6–1   The Effect of Inventory Errors

You have been hired as the accountant for Milky Way Seed Company, which uses a periodic inventory system. In reviewing the firm's records, you have noted what you think are several accounting errors made during the current year, 1981. These potential mistakes are listed below.

a. A $3,000 purchase of merchandise was properly recorded in the Purchases account but the related Accounts Payable account was credited for only $2,000.

b. A $4,300 shipment of merchandise received just before the end of the year was properly recorded in the Purchases account but was not counted in the inventory and hence was excluded from the ending inventory balance.

c. A $6,700 purchase of merchandise was erroneously recorded as a $7,600 purchase.

d. A $500 purchase of merchandise was not recorded either as a purchase or an account payable.

e. During the year, $1,200 of defective merchandise was sent back to a supplier. The original purchase entry had been recorded but the merchandise return entry wasn't recorded.

f. During the physical inventory count, inventory that cost $400 was counted twice.

Required:

1. If the previous accountant had tentatively computed the 1981 gross margin to be $10,000, what would be the correct gross margin for the year?

2. If the company was taxed at 40 percent, how much additional tax would it have to pay when these errors were corrected?

3. If these mistakes are not corrected, how much will the 1982 net income be in error?

P6–2   Cost of Goods Sold Calculations

Desoto Corporation had the following transactions and balances in its January 1981 accounting records.

Jan. 1	Beginning Inventory	100 units
3	Purchase..........................	50 units
11	Sale	40 units
14	Sale	20 units
20	Purchase..........................	60 units
26	Sale	30 units

Required:

Assuming that the total cost of goods available for sale at the end of January (beginning inventory plus purchases) was $1,430 and that the ending inventory for January 1981 was $890 on a FIFO basis and $740 on a LIFO (periodic) basis, compute the following.

1. The cost per unit of the beginning inventory and the January 3rd and January 20th purchases.

2. The cost of goods sold for January using both the FIFO and LIFO methods.

3. The weighted-average cost per unit of cost of goods sold and ending inventory for January (periodic).

P6–3   Perpetual and Periodic Inventory Systems

Required:

1. Journalize the following transactions of Mason Ice Cream Company, assuming a periodic inventory system.

   (a) Purchased 40 units of product x at $18/unit.
   (b) Purchased 50 units of product y at $46/unit.
   (c) Sold 15 units of product z at $8/unit (cost = $5/unit).
   (d) Sold 25 units of product x at $30/unit (cost = $16/unit).
   (e) Purchased 40 units of product y at $48/unit.
   (f) Closed the nominal accounts relating to the inventory system.

   Beginning inventory consisted of: 30 units of x at $16; 40 units of z at $5.

2. Journalize the above transactions assuming a perpetual inventory system.

3. **Interpretive Question**   Which inventory cost flow method is being used by Mason Company?

P6–4   Inventory Cost Flow Methods

The sales and inventory records of Harker Golf Sales, Inc., were as follows for January through March 1981.

	Clubs	Unit Cost	Total Cost
Beginning Inventory, January 1, 1981	460	$15	$6,900
Purchase, January 16, 1981	110	16	1,760
Sale, January 25 ($22.50/unit)	216		
Purchase, February 16	105	18	1,890
Sale, February 27 ($20.00/unit)	307		
Purchase, March 10	150	14	2,100
Sale, March 30 ($25.00/unit)	190		

Required:

1. Find the amounts for the ending inventory, cost of goods sold, and gross margin under the following costing methods: (a) FIFO, (b) LIFO, and (c) weighted average, all under a periodic inventory system.

2. **Interpretive Question**   Which method results in the highest amount of gross margin? Why?

P6–5   Inventory Cost Flow Methods

Village Hardware Company sells two products: hammers and saws. Beginning inventory for March 1, 1981, is as follows:

Item	No. of Units	Unit Cost
Hammers	100	$8.00
Saws	300	7.00

Purchases during March were as follows:

Date	Item	No. of Units	Unit Cost
March 5	Hammers ...	100	$8.30
5	Saws	200	7.10
16	Hammers ...	100	7.90
28	Saws	100	6.80

During March, the firm sold 150 hammers at $11 each and 350 saws at $10 each.

Required:

1. Assuming a periodic inventory system, calculate separately for hammers and saws the sales, cost of goods sold, ending inventory, and gross margin as of March 31, 1981, using the following cost flow assumptions.

   (a) FIFO
   (b) LIFO
   (c) Weighted average

2. **Interpretive Question**   Which method would result in paying the lowest taxes? Why?

P6–6   Effects of Different Inventory Cost Flow Assumptions on Gross Margin and Net Income

RAC Company uses a periodic inventory system. The following data are available.

	Date	No. of Units	Cost/ Unit	Total
Beginning inventory .	Jan. 1	20	$11	$ 220
Purchases	Jan. 10	7	11	77
	Feb. 24	18	12	216
	June 12	9	13	117
	Aug. 30	25	14	350
	Sept. 20	14	15	210
	Dec. 30	8	15	120
Total Purchases		81		$1,090
Sales.............	Jan. 5	20		
	Mar. 10	10		
	Sept. 13	35		
	Sept. 21	10		
	Nov. 15	5		
Total Sales		80		

Required:

1. Compute the ending inventory at December 31, 1981, using the FIFO method.

2. Assume that your answer to question 1 was $315 and that the gross margin using this figure for ending inventory was $700. What would be the ending inventory using the LIFO method? What would be the gross margin using the LIFO method?

3. Again, assume ending inventory was $315 using FIFO and the net income using that figure was $500. What would be the amount of net income using the weighted average method? (Ignore taxes and round to nearest dollar.)

4. **Interpretive Question** Which method would a company use if it wanted to report the highest net income possible?

P6–7 Gross Margin Method of
Estimating Inventory

On December 20, 1981, a major fire destroyed the contents of Jacobsen Furniture Company's warehouse. In order to file a claim for an insurance reimbursement, the company needs to estimate the amount of inventory lost in the fire. In an attempt to estimate the fire loss, the following information has been discovered.

a. By consulting with vendors, it was found that total purchases to the date of the fire amounted to $645,000.

b. The December 31, 1980, Balance Sheet noted an inventory balance of $125,000.

c. Sales commissions for the year (for the sales staff) totaled $80,000. Of the $80,000 in commissions, 40 percent was paid at a commission rate of 5 percent, and the balance was paid at a rate of 10 percent. Gross margin rates during the past several years have averaged about 45 percent.

Required:

1. What is the estimated amount of the inventory destroyed in the fire?

2. **Interpretive Question** If the insurance company thought the claim was too high, on what basis might it argue that your calculations are not valid?

3. What would the estimate of the loss be if the appropriate gross margin rate were 35 percent instead of 45 percent?

P6–8 Cost of Goods Sold Calculations

On July 1, 1981, the main warehouse of Johnson Manufacturing Company, a producer of outboard engines for boats, was destroyed by fire. In the fire, almost all of the inventory was destroyed. Fortunately, however, the company carried insurance on the ware-

house and its contents and will be reimbursed for its loss by the insurance company. Your job is to estimate the amount of inventory destroyed so that the insurance proceeds can be collected. In attempting to estimate the amount of inventory destroyed, you have gathered the following data.

From the financial statements as of December 31, 1980:

Net Sales Revenue........................	$1,000,000
Gross Margin............................	350,000
Inventory Balance........................	80,000
Net Income, 1980........................	25,000

From customers:

Sales from January 1, 1981, to June 30, 1981	$600,000
Accounts Receivable on June 30, 1981	75,000

From suppliers:

Net Purchases for the first six months of 1981 ..	$480,000
Amount owed on June 30, 1981	65,000

Required:

1. Assuming that 1980 results were typical of those in 1981, determine the cost of the inventory lost in the fire.

2. **Interpretive Question** What is the major assumption of this type of estimate? What would cause this assumption to be violated?

P6–9 Unifying Problem: Inventory Cost
Flow Methods

Molly's Wholesale buys canned peaches from canneries and sells them to retail markets. During August 1981 Molly's inventory records showed the following.

Aug. 1	Beginning inventory	4,100 cases	at	$10.50
4	Purchase	1,500 cases	at	11.00
9	Sale....................	950 cases	at	19.95
13	Purchase	1,000 cases	at	11.00
19	Sale....................	1,450 cases	at	19.95
26	Purchase	1,700 cases	at	11.50
30	Sale....................	1,900 cases	at	19.95

Even though it requires more computational effort, Molly uses the perpetual inventory method because she feels the extra cost is justified by always having current knowledge of inventory levels.

Required:

1. Calculate the cost of goods sold and ending inventory using the following cost flow assumptions (calculate costs to the nearest tenth of a cent).

    (a) FIFO
    (b) LIFO
    (c) Moving average

2. **Interpretive Question**   Why are the cost of goods sold amounts the same under the FIFO perpetual and FIFO periodic costing methods?

3. Calculate the ending inventory and cost of goods sold using the LIFO periodic system.

4. **Interpretive Question**   In this particular case, why does the LIFO method result in the same amounts under both inventory systems?

P6–10   Unifying Problem: Inventory Estimation Methods

Monterey Department Store has the following information available.

	At Cost	At Selling Price	Other
Purchases During January 1981	$60,000	$85,000	
Inventory Balance, January 1, 1981	24,000	31,000	
Sales During January 1981		90,000	
Average Gross Margin Rate for the Last Three Years			25%

Required:

1. On the basis of this information, estimate the cost of inventory on hand at January 31, 1981, using:

   (a) The gross margin method.

   (b) The retail inventory method.

2. **Interpretive Question**   Which method is probably the most accurate? Why?

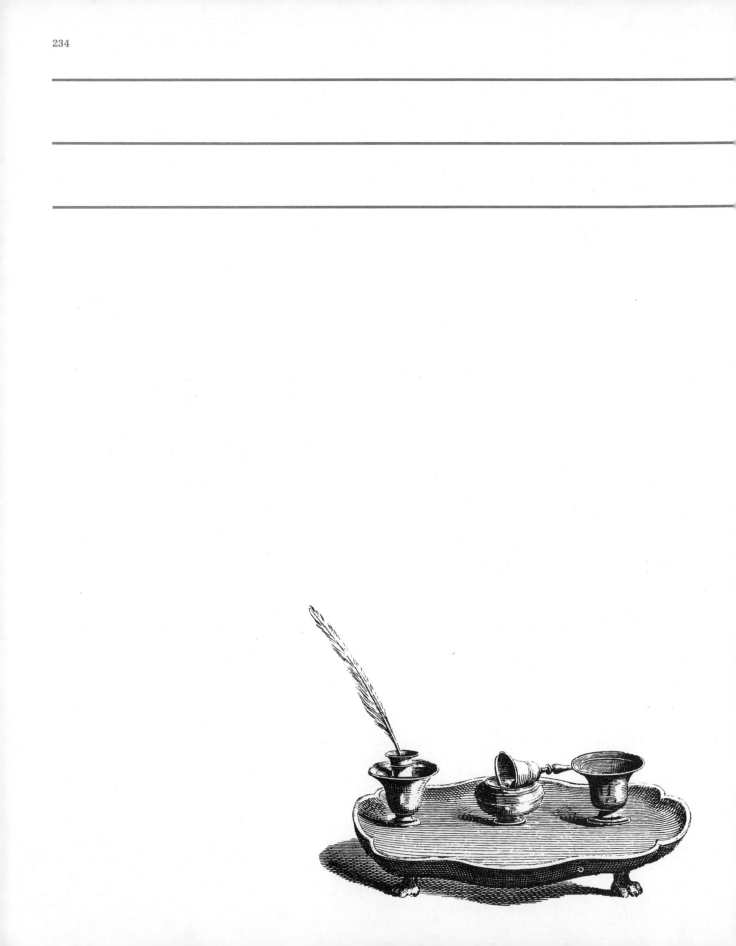

SECTION 3

Reporting Assets, Liabilities, and Owners' Equity

During the eighteenth century, all ledgers were maintained by accountants using quill pens, such as the one shown in this French line engraving. (The Granger Collection)

CHAPTER 7

The Balance Sheet

The function and structure of the Balance Sheet.

The classification of Balance Sheet items by age, use, and source.

Some limitations of the Balance Sheet.

Every day thousands of real estate investors shop for apartment buildings and other rental property. Almost without exception they ask the following two questions: (1) How much income will there be from this investment? (2) How much is this building worth? In answering the first question, realtors consider such things as rental revenues and the likely expenses for interest, property taxes, repairs, maintenance, and utilities. In answering the second question, they consider the square footage of the building, number of rooms, location, repairs needed, and similar factors.

Although a business is usually much more complex than an apartment building, it too can be considered a salable asset; and every day thousands of people invest in businesses. In contrast to rental properties, where a single investor may buy an entire complex, investors in corporations usually buy only a relatively small percentage of ownership through the purchase of stock. Despite this difference, investors in corporate stocks are basically interested in the same two items of information: (1) how much income the firm makes (and is likely to make in the future), and (2) how much the firm is worth.

Historically, two basic financial statements have been used to answer these questions. As discussed in Chapters 5 and 6, the Income Statement reports the results of operations. The Statement of Financial Position, or Balance Sheet,[1] is the report that comes closest to answering the second question: How much is a firm worth?

Balance Sheet (Statement of Financial Position) *the primary financial statement that shows the financial resources of an enterprise at a particular date and the claims against those resources, and therefore the relationships of assets, liabilities, and owners' equity*

This chapter is an overview of the Balance Sheet. It focuses on (1) valuation problems of the Balance Sheet—that is, the degree to which it presents a realistic and current assessment of the worth of a firm, (2) classifications of Balance Sheet accounts, and (3) limitations of the Balance Sheet.

[1] The official literature now calls this report the Statement of Financial Position. Because it is more concise, however, the term "Balance Sheet" will be used in this text.

Valuation Problems of the Balance Sheet

operating cycle   *the general pattern of business activity whereby cash and other resources are converted to inventory and operational assets and eventually to products or services that can be sold for cash and other resources*

The operating cycle of a typical merchandising business is summarized by the flow chart in Exhibit 7–1. Despite the orderly and sequential appearance of the flow chart, the normal operating cycle of a business is not necessarily so uncomplicated a process. At any particular time, most businesses are involved in all of the operating-cycle activities. For example, a firm will have purchased but not yet paid for inventory, it will have sold inventory but not yet collected the proceeds, and it will have purchased but not yet completely used up equipment and furniture. Because of these incomplete cycles and activities, it is usually difficult to determine the value of a firm at any particular time.

It is due to this inherent difficulty that a Balance Sheet cannot be said to be a current-value statement. Instead, it presents a firm's assets, liabilities, and owners' equity stated at their historical costs. If land originally cost $10,000, say in 1975, but has a current value of $20,000, it would be reported on the Balance Sheet at $10,000 (perhaps with the current value shown in parentheses). With this historical cost approach, Balance Sheet amounts are stated at their current values only in the period when they were originally acquired and placed on the Balance Sheet. Subsequently, the amounts reported can be quite close to or very different from current values, depending on many factors—one of which is the length of time the item has been carried on the Balance Sheet.

With this historical cost approach, the Balance Sheet discloses a mixture of items: short-term assets and liabilities closely approximating

EXHIBIT 7–1   Operations of a Business

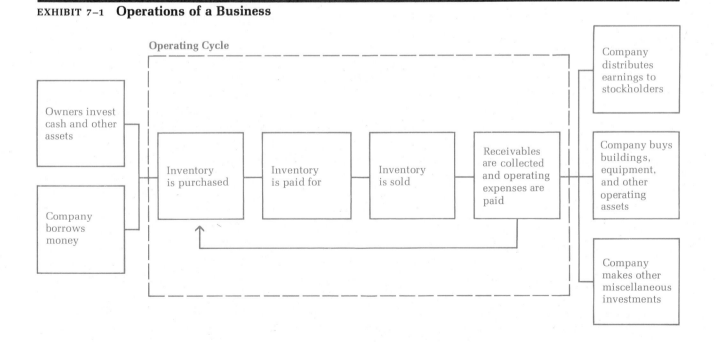

current values, and older assets representing only historical costs. Specifically, since the costs of buildings, equipment, and similar assets are usually depreciated over their estimated useful lives, the carrying amounts for these items represent only undepreciated original costs, which may be far different from the current values of these assets.

Accountants who support the historical cost Balance Sheet maintain that even though it is not a current-value statement, it is still very useful. Their arguments usually include the following points. First, the statement provides for the accountability of the dollars invested by the owners. That is, the actual dollars invested can be traced through operations or to residual valuations. With this accountability, fraud and embezzlement can be detected more readily than if historical costs were abandoned and current values were substituted. Second, the process of determining current values is too subjective and only the historical cost method provides a reliable summary of the operations and assets of a business. Third, the historical cost Balance Sheet provides a necessary bridge between two Income Statements by indicating which asset values will be carried forward to future periods.

Finally, the Balance Sheet traditionally has reported historical costs because of accounting's insistence upon linking it to the Income Statement—that is, Retained Earnings is the account into which net income is closed. If a Balance Sheet were to report current values and still be tied to an Income Statement, income would reflect changes in net asset values in addition to realized revenues less matched expenses from transactions. Thus, as long as conventional income determination concepts are used and the Balance Sheet is tied to the Income Statement, the Balance Sheet accounts will not reflect current values.

THE EFFECT OF INFLATION ON MONETARY AND NONMONETARY ITEMS

One of the largest single factors causing the current values of assets to differ from their historical costs is inflation. The extent to which inflation affects assets, liabilities, and owners' equity can best be understood by considering the monetary and nonmonetary nature of these accounts. Monetary assets are those items, such as cash, receivables, and payables, which involve dollar amounts that are fixed in the future either by contract or by nature. That is, these items are always equal to a specific number of dollars no matter what happens to the inflation rate or the purchasing power of the dollar. In contrast, nonmonetary items, such as inventories, buildings, equipment, or capital stock are items that fluctuate in value according to the changing purchasing power of the dollar, the demand for them in the marketplace, and other related factors.

Since the absolute dollar amounts of monetary assets and liabilities are fixed, companies having these items generally gain or lose purchasing power during periods of inflation or deflation. For example, a 1980 note payable (a liability) due in 1985 will be satisfied with the payment of 1985 dollars, regardless of whether a 1985 dollar is equivalent in purchasing

monetary items   those assets or liabilities fixed either by nature or contract as to the amount of future dollars they can command in the marketplace

nonmonetary items   those assets or equities that are not fixed as to the amount of future dollars they can command and hence fluctuate in value according to their demand in the marketplace

power to a 1980 dollar. Similarly, cash (an asset) held for several years during a period of inflation loses purchasing power. Although the cash involved always represents the same number of dollars, cash spent later will buy much less. Thus, during a period of inflation, companies holding monetary assets such as cash or receivables lose purchasing power, and companies with monetary liabilities such as accounts or notes payable gain purchasing power.

This phenomenon does not occur with nonmonetary assets and liabilities. Whereas the future dollar amount of monetary items is fixed, the value of nonmonetary items increases or decreases in response to demand in the marketplace. Thus, the price of such items as inventories, buildings, and equipment will generally rise in inflationary periods and fall during deflationary periods. In most countries inflation has been substantial over the last several years, and the result of using historical costs is that many inventories, buildings, and other assets are worth more than their reported historical costs.

ALTERNATIVE VALUATION AND REPORTING METHODS

Because a Balance Sheet's historical cost reporting does not reflect either current values or the general price-level-adjusted historical costs, critics argue that some other method of valuation and measurement should be used. The two most popular alternatives are general price-level-adjusted statements and current-value statements. Both of these were considered in the context of income measurement in Chapter 5; here we will discuss their effect on the Balance Sheet.

general price-level adjustments *restatement of historical costs on the basis of a general price-level index, which represents the impact of inflation*

As indicated in Chapter 5, the general price-level alternative suggests that historical costs be adjusted upward or downward by some general economy-wide price index. This index, which would measure the rate of inflation (or deflation), would adjust historical costs from nominal dollars to constant dollars. Thus, if an adding machine or other asset were purchased for $100 at a time when the general price index was 100 percent and a year later the general price index had increased to 110 percent, the asset's historical cost would be adjusted to $110. This method has the advantage of converting the dollar costs of transactions entered into at different times into comparable measurements that reflect units of equivalent purchasing power.

One of the major disadvantages of this approach is that it considers only changes caused by inflation and not changes in value that result from increases or decreases in such factors as supply, demand, and productivity. Clearly, some assets increase in value faster than others, and, in some cases, asset values actually decline during inflationary periods. Thus, using a general index to adjust historical costs may result in reporting assets at figures that are further from their current values than would be the case if unadjusted historical costs had been used. The general price-level approach can also become quite complicated, perhaps even to the extent that many people would probably not understand it.

current values *the amounts that assets or liabilities are presently worth in the marketplace; generally equal to replacement costs, net realizable values, or present values of items*

The second approach is to abandon historical cost valuation completely and adopt current-value accounting. Using the current-value approach, assets, liabilities, and stockholders' equity would be reported at their values as of the dates of the financial statements. These values would be reported on the Balance Sheet and the difference between the valuations at successive reporting dates would be considered income (or loss) to the business. Conceptually, this approach is very appealing, but implementing it presents many problems. The major difficulty is in obtaining accurate valuations that can be verified objectively. For example, the current values of stocks and bonds can be readily obtained because their prices are quoted daily on national stock exchanges. But how do you determine the current value of a plant that is 30 years old and still servicing the needs of a particular firm? To replace that facility would cost the company more money; however, the advantage of being able to install modern machinery in a new building or the chance to move to a different location might outweigh the cost. It is difficult to assess the ongoing value of such a facility. In fact, many accountants are concerned that the valuations required in order to use this approach would not always be objective and therefore the Balance Sheet might present misleading information to the public.

It is difficult to decide which method—historical cost, general price-level, or current-value—is preferable. Because there are significant advantages and disadvantages to each, in 1979 the FASB issued Statement No. 33, which requires that certain large companies report, as supplementary information to their primary historical cost financial statements, inventories and most plant assets on both a general price-level-adjusted and a current-value basis. In requiring all three types of disclosures, the FASB concluded that experimentation is necessary before the most effective reporting method can be selected.

TO SUMMARIZE Currently, the primary financial statements are prepared on a historical cost basis. However, because inflation and other factors cause these historical costs to be significantly different from current values, two reporting alternatives have been proposed. The general price-level alternative modifies historical costs by restating all costs as constant dollars. The current-value method abandons historical costs completely. Supplementary disclosures incorporating both methods are required of selected firms by the FASB.

What's in a Balance Sheet?

As noted in Chapter 2, the Balance Sheet is divided into three major sections: assets, liabilities, and owners' equity. The first section, while it does not report the current values of individual assets, shows what types of assets a firm owns and the amounts paid for those assets. Further, by categorizing the assets as current, or short-term, and noncurrent, or long-term, the composition of assets and their liquidity is disclosed.

The liability section informs readers of the extent and nature of a firm's borrowings, and provides a measure of its financial stability. By reading this section, together with the owners' equity and assets sections, one can see how an entity is financed (whether by borrowings or by owner contributions) and whether or not there are sufficient assets to pay off debts.

Finally, the owners' equity section completes the Balance Sheet by identifying the amount of a firm's resources that were contributed by owners and how much undistributed earnings a firm has had since inception. People often think that since this section represents the residual portion of the Balance Sheet equation—the remainder after liabilities have been subtracted from assets—it refers to the net worth of a firm. If the assets and liabilities were stated at current market values, this would be the case. As it now stands, however, owners' equity merely shows two of the ways in which resources are brought into a firm (owner contributions and retained earnings). The only source not shown in this section is borrowings, which are included in the liabilities section.

The Classified Balance Sheet

Thus far, the Balance Sheet has been discussed in an abstract and general manner. We will now review the detailed Balance Sheet of Radio Tune-Up Company, as shown in Exhibit 7–2.

Within the major categories of assets, liabilities, and owners' equity are several subcategories. The most common are

Balance Sheet

Assets	Liabilities	Owners' Equity
Current Assets	Current Liabilities	Contributed Capital
Long-Term Investments	Long-Term Liabilities	Retained Earnings
Property, Plant, and Equipment		
Intangible Assets		

classified Balance Sheet   a Balance Sheet on which assets, liabilities, and owners' equity are subdivided by age, use, and source

When subdivided into these categories, the statement is called a classified Balance Sheet. The purpose of these classifications is to provide order, allow comparisons, and save readers valuable time in comprehending the statements. Certainly, if companies reported all assets together or arranged the items on the Balance Sheet according to their own whims and desires, readers would have a difficult time understanding the statements.

CURRENT ASSETS

current assets   cash and other assets that may reasonably be expected to be converted to cash within one year or during the normal operating cycle

Current assets include cash and other short-term assets that may reasonably be expected to be converted to cash, sold, or consumed either within one year from the Balance Sheet date or during the normal operating cycle of a business. As shown in Exhibit 7–1, the operating cycle of most businesses involves three types of current assets: cash, inventory, and accounts receivable.

EXHIBIT 7–2 **Radio Tune-Up Company**
Balance Sheet as of December 31, 1981

Assets

Current Assets:			
Cash...........................		$ 300,000	
Short-Term Investments		50,000	
Accounts Receivable	$ 675,000		
Less Allowance for Doubtful Accounts	20,000	655,000	
Notes Receivable		15,000	
Inventory........................		300,000	
Prepaid Expenses.................		6,000	
Total Current Assets			$1,326,000
Long-Term Investments:			
Stock of Y Company		$ 20,000	
Bonds of Z Company		30,000	
Total Long-Term Investments			50,000
Property, Plant, and Equipment:			
Land............................		$ 100,000	
Store Equipment and Furniture	$ 300,000		
Less Accumulated Depreciation	50,000	250,000	
Building........................	$2,600,000		
Less Accumulated Depreciation	125,000	2,475,000	
Total Property, Plant, and			
Equipment...................			2,825,000
Intangible Assets:			
Patents.........................		$ 20,000	
Franchises......................		25,000	
Total Intangible Assets			45,000
Total Assets..................			$4,246,000

short-term investments *non-operational assets that a business intends to hold only for a short period of time, usually less than a year*

In addition, current assets include such nonoperational items as short-term investments, notes receivable, and prepaid expenses. Short-term investments are marketable securities (stocks or bonds of other companies) that a business plans to hold for a period shorter than the normal operating cycle. A company will make such investments when there is a temporary surplus of cash. Investments that are to be held for periods longer than one year or the normal operating cycle are reported as long-term investments.

Notes receivable are claims against debtors, evidenced by written promises to pay amounts of money on or before specified future dates. Like short-term investments, these notes must be collectable within one year in order to be classified as current assets. As you will recall from Chapters 4 and 5, prepaid expenses are payments made in advance for the use of goods and services, such as insurance, property taxes, and interest. Office supplies are also often classified as prepaid expenses until they are used.

Liabilities and Stockholders' Equity

Current Liabilities:

Accounts Payable	$ 200,000	
Notes Payable	70,000	
Wages Payable.................................	7,000	
Current Portion of Mortgage Payable	26,000	
Income Taxes Payable...........................	29,000	
Estimated Warranty Obligation....................	14,000	
Total Current Liabilities		$ 346,000

Long-Term Liabilities:

Mortgage Payable (final payment due 1988)	$ 300,000	
Bonds Payable (8%, maturity 1992)	600,000	
Total Long-Term Liabilities.....................		900,000
Total Liabilities		$1,246,000

Stockholders' Equity:

Contributed Capital:

Preferred Stock, 6%, 10,000 shares outstanding, $70 par	$ 700,000	
Common Stock, 160,000 shares outstanding, $10 par ...	1,600,000	
Paid-in Capital in Excess of Par, Common Stock.......	160,000	
Total Contributed Capital......................	$2,460,000	
Retained Earnings..............................	540,000	
Total Stockholders' Equity		3,000,000
Total Liabilities and Stockholders' Equity		$4,246,000

Current assets are usually presented in the order of their liquidity; that is, those that are most easily and quickly converted to cash are listed first and those most difficult and/or requiring the most time to convert are listed last. In Exhibit 7–2, current assets total $1,326,000 and comprise cash, short-term investments, accounts receivable, notes receivable, inventory, and prepaid expenses.

LONG-TERM INVESTMENTS

long-term investments *non-operational assets that a business intends to hold for more than a year or the normal operating cycle*

All investments that a company intends to hold for more than a year (or the normal operating cycle) are considered long-term investments. The most common types are stocks and bonds of other companies, real estate, and government bonds. Also included in this category are monies set aside for special purposes, such as to purchase land for a new plant site. Exhibit 7–2 indicates that Radio Tune-Up Company has two long-term investments: stock of Y Company and bonds of Z Company.

PROPERTY, PLANT, AND EQUIPMENT

property, plant, and equipment *tangible, long-lived assets acquired for use in the business rather than for resale*

depreciation *the process of cost allocation that assigns the original cost of plant and equipment to the periods benefited*

All assets that are tangible and of a permanent, or at least a long-term, nature and that were acquired for use by the business rather than for resale are grouped as property, plant, and equipment. The most common long-term assets are land, buildings, furniture, and equipment. With the exception of land, which usually increases in value, these assets gradually wear out or become obsolete and must be depreciated; that is, their cost must be written off as an expense over their useful lives. Depreciation is only an estimate; it is impossible to know exactly how long an asset will benefit a company or how much, if anything, it can be sold for at the end of its useful life. The amount of depreciation taken during the year is reported as an expense on the Income Statement and the cumulative amount of depreciation since the acquisition of an asset is reported on the Balance Sheet in an account called Accumulated Depreciation. The Accumulated Depreciation account is a contra account that is deducted from the asset account to produce the book, or carrying, value of the asset. As shown in Exhibit 7–2, land, store equipment and furniture, and buildings are the only property, plant, and equipment items owned by Radio Tune-Up Company.

accumulated depreciation *the total depreciation charged against an asset since acquisition; a contra account deducted from the original cost of an asset on the Balance Sheet*

book, or carrying, value *the net amount shown in the accounts for an asset, liability, or owners' equity item*

INTANGIBLE ASSETS

intangible assets *long-lived assets that do not have physical substance and are not held for resale*

This classification includes long-lived assets that are useful in the operation of a business, are not held for resale, and do not have physical substance. Intangible assets include patents, copyrights, goodwill, franchises, trademarks, and other such assets that provide competitive advantages to the company. Intangible assets can only be reported when they have been purchased or when cash has been expended for their development. The belief that one of these assets exists is not sufficient reason to include it as an asset.

The accounting for intangible assets is very similar to that for property, plant, and equipment. For both, the cost of the asset is apportioned over its estimated life and charged as an expense on the Income Statement. This process is called amortization and is similar to the depreciation process of tangible assets. The two intangible assets held by Radio Tune-Up (in Exhibit 7–2) are patents and franchises. A patent is an exclusive protection of an invention granted by the government and a franchise is a right to sell a product or offer a service in a certain geographical area.

patent *an exclusive right granted for up to 17 years by the federal government to an inventor to manufacture and sell an invention*

franchise *an exclusive right to sell a product or offer a service in a certain geographical area*

CURRENT LIABILITIES

current liabilities *debts or other obligations that will be paid with current assets or otherwise discharged within one year or the normal operating cycle*

This category includes those obligations or debts of a company that will be paid within a short time (one year or the normal operating cycle) and that are expected to be paid with current assets. The most common current liabilities are near-term cash obligations, such as accounts payable (amounts owed for the purchase of inventory and other items), short-term notes payable (obligations to pay certain amounts on or before a specified future date), wages payable, interest payable, rent payable, and income taxes payable. However, not all current liabilities are obligations to pay cash. Obligations to perform future services, such as warranty services, are also liabilities, and if services are to be performed within one year, the warranty is recorded as a current liability at the time it is issued.

The difference between total current assets and total current liabilities is called working capital and the ratio of current assets to current liabilities is the current ratio. This ratio is a measure of the short-term liquidity of a firm. For example, the total working capital of Radio Tune-Up Company is $980,000 ($1,326,000 − $346,000) and the current ratio is approximately 3.83 to 1 ($1,326,000 ÷ $346,000). Certainly, with 3.83 times as much in current assets as in current liabilities, Radio Tune-Up Company should have no problem paying off its current liabilities.

LONG-TERM LIABILITIES

Debts or other obligations that will not be paid within one year are called long-term liabilities. As they come within one year of payment, they are reclassified as current liabilities. Typical accounts in this section are long-term notes payable, mortgages payable, and bonds payable. Exhibit 7−2 shows that Radio Tune-Up has $900,000 of long-term liabilities, which includes a mortgage payable (probably on a building) and bonds payable.

OWNERS' EQUITY

Because Radio Tune-Up is a corporation, its owners' equity section is called stockholders' equity. Stockholders' equity represents the owners' interests in and claims to net assets and is usually subdivided into contributed capital and retained earnings. Contributed capital represents that portion of the equity provided from investments by the owners (usually through the purchase of stock). Retained earnings represents the amount of undistributed earnings (earnings not paid out to the owners) accumulated since the business was organized. Retained earnings is not the same as cash. In fact, in most companies, cash coming into the firm through operations is used to purchase other current and noncurrent assets, such as land, buildings, and inventories. The use of cash to purchase such assets does not reduce retained earnings. Retained earnings can be reduced only by the return of these earnings to owners, usually in the form of cash dividends, or by the company having sustained losses during a year. Thus, when a firm has income, both cash and retained earnings are usually increased.

An examination of the stockholders' equity section of Radio Tune-Up shows that two types of stock have been issued by the company: preferred and common. These types of stock are discussed in Chapter 12. For now, all you need to know is that when dividends are paid, preferred stockholders usually receive an amount equal to 6 percent of the $700,000 of preferred stock before common stockholders receive anything. Common stockholders, on the other hand, usually elect the board of directors and vote on other important matters concerning the corporation.

In addition to the two stock accounts, another account, Paid-in Capital in Excess of Par, has a balance of $160,000. This means that when the

---

working capital   *the funds (or resources) available to finance current operations; equal to current assets minus current liabilities*

current ratio   *current assets divided by current liabilities*

long-term liabilities   *debts or other obligations that will not be paid within one year or the normal operating cycle*

stockholders' equity   *the ownership interest in an enterprise's assets; equals net assets (total assets minus total liabilities)*

contributed capital   *that portion of stockholders' equity provided by the owners of the business, usually through the purchase of stock*

retained earnings   *the accumulated portion of owners' equity that has been earned and retained from profitable operations and not paid out in dividends or restricted for some other use; equal to owners' equity less contributed capital*

par (face) value   *the nominal value printed on the face of a share of stock*

common stock was sold, although it had a par (face) value of $10 per share, it was actually sold for an average price of $11 per share ($1,600,000 + $160,000 ÷ 160,000 shares).

Finally, Radio Tune-Up has a retained earnings balance of $540,000. In other words, since incorporation this company has retained in the business $540,000 of its earnings. Taking into account the probability that dividends were distributed to stockholders over the period, total earnings would have been more than $540,000.

TO SUMMARIZE   The most common Balance Sheet classifications involve separating assets into current assets, long-term investments, property, plant, and equipment, and intangible assets; dividing liabilities into current and long-term liabilities; and dividing owners' equity into contributed capital and retained earnings. The categorization of accounts by age (such as long-term and short-term), by use (such as investments and property, plant, and equipment), and by source (such as retained earnings and contributed capital) helps make the Balance Sheet easy to read and understand.

Limitations of the Balance Sheet

The valuation problem discussed earlier presents one limitation of the Balance Sheet: It may not reflect the current value of the company. Two other limitations should also be noted: (1) The Balance Sheet only reports resources that can be expressed in monetary (dollar) terms, which means that many items often considered assets or liabilities are not included on the Balance Sheet, and (2) companies may use different accounting methods for similar types of accounts, thus making comparisons between companies difficult.

Regarding the first limitation, consider the value of an efficient management team to a business organization. Certainly, most people would agree that sound management is as much an asset as a piece of machinery. Yet, because it is difficult to quantify the value of the management team, no appropriate asset is reported on the Balance Sheet. Other unreported nonmonetary items include major discoveries of new products or new sources of materials, strategic locations, and loyal and valued employees. Likewise, an event such as the emission of pollutants into the air or water is not recorded on the statements but could be considered a liability.

As another example, if a company purchases another business for more than the value of its assets, the excess cost is called goodwill and is classified as an intangible asset. On the other hand, if a company develops goodwill through good customer relations, a quality product, or some other means, the goodwill cannot be reported as an asset on the Balance Sheet. This is because it was not purchased in an arm's-length transaction and its value cannot be objectively determined.

With respect to the second limitation, firms are allowed to use alternative methods of accounting for several assets (for example, the various inventory cost flow methods discussed in Chapter 6). When companies use different reporting methods, comparisons are difficult, and sometimes meaningless.

CHAPTER REVIEW

Historically, the primary purpose of the Balance Sheet has been to report the financial position of a business enterprise. However, because Balance Sheet items are not adjusted for inflation and other factors affecting their current values, the statement does not show the worth of a firm. Instead, it reports assets, liabilities, and owners' equity at their original costs or carrying values. This lack of valuation information has caused many accountants to suggest alternative measurement methods, including general price-level and current-value.

Notwithstanding this deficiency, the Balance Sheet aids readers in understanding the financial position of a business. In fact, when Balance Sheet accounts are classified by age (short-term and long-term), by use, and by source, the statement provides a relatively clear picture of a business's financial position.

In addition to the valuation question, the Balance Sheet has two other limitations: (1) It only reports resources that can be expressed in monetary terms, omitting many items often considered assets or liabilities, and (2) companies may use different accounting methods for the same accounts, thus making comparisons difficult.

KEY TERMS AND CONCEPTS

accumulated depreciation (244)
Balance Sheet (236)
book, or carrying, value (244)
classified Balance Sheet (241)
contributed capital (245)
current assets (241)
current liabilities (244)
current ratio (245)
current values (240)

depreciation (244)
franchise (244)
general price-level adjustments (239)
intangible assets (244)
long-term investment (243)
long-term liabilities (245)
monetary items (238)
nonmonetary items (238)
operating cycle (237)

par (face) value (246)
patent (244)
property, plant, and equipment (244)
retained earnings (245)
short-term investment (242)
stockholders' equity (245)
working capital (245)

DISCUSSION QUESTIONS

1. What can be learned about a company by studying its Balance Sheet?

2. Why are Balance Sheet accounts separated into current, noncurrent, and other categories?

3. What characteristics differentiate depreciation from most other expenses?

4. Why is the periodic depreciation expense only an estimate?

5. What is the difference between the book and market value of an asset?

6. What is the basis for including as assets those items that have no physical substance (intangible assets)?

7. What types of obligations other than those requiring cash payments are liabilities?

8. Why are stockholders' equity and liabilities considered the "sources" of assets?

9. Distinguish between retained earnings and cash.

10. Why is it important to understand the monetary and nonmonetary nature of Balance Sheet accounts? Does inflation affect both monetary and nonmonetary items in the same way? Explain.

11. What is the effect on purchasing power of holding cash during a period of inflation?

12. Why do critics argue that financial statements adjusted by a general price-level index would not

necessarily represent current market values?

13. What are some of the practical problems involved in adopting the current-value method of preparing financial statements? Would current-value statements be as objective as historical cost statements?

14. When can a patent, goodwill, or other intangible assets be reported as an asset on the Balance Sheet?

EXERCISES

E7–1   The Balance Sheet Equation

Complete the financial statements of Johnson and McDermitt Companies by filling in the blanks. (Note: No stock was sold by either company during 1981.)

	Johnson Company	McDermitt Company
Assets, January 1, 1981	$ 490	$ (4)
Liabilities, January 1, 1981	210	320
Owners' Equity, January 1, 1981 . . .	(1)	170
Assets, December 31, 1981	500	(5)
Liabilities, December 31, 1981	(2)	300
Owners' Equity, December 31, 1981	(3)	200
Revenues in 1981	70	(6)
Operating Expenses in 1981	60	60

E7–2   General Balance Sheet

Fill in the blanks in each of the following statements.

1. The _____ is an asset's original cost less its accumulated depreciation.

2. _____ is the difference between total current assets and total current liabilities.

3. The accumulated earnings of a firm less all dividends paid to shareholders is its _____ .

4. _____ are payments for goods and services in advance of their use.

5. The accounting equation for the Balance Sheet is _____ .

6. _____ represents the owners' interest and claims to the net assets of a corporation.

7. Liabilities are increased by _____ entries.

8. Long-lived assets that usually provide a competitive advantage to a firm but have no physical substance are _____ .

E7–3   Effect of Transactions on the Balance Sheet

Capital Reef Company had the following transactions.
1. Issued stock for $500.

2. Purchased supplies on account for $750.

3. Paid a secretary's salary of $800.

4. Paid the current month's rent of $350.

5. Collected $325 for services performed.

6. Paid dividends of $600.

7. Paid a $300 note.

Using the column heads below, indicate the effect on total assets, total liabilities, and total stockholders' equity for each transaction. Your solutions should indicate both amount and direction (increase or decrease). Transaction (1) has been completed as an example.

Transaction	Total Assets	Total Liabilities	Total Stockholders' Equity
Issued stock for $500	+500	0	+500

E7–4   Effect of Transactions on the Balance Sheet

Thousand Lake Corporation had the following transactions.

1. Paid an account payable.

2. Billed a customer for services performed.

3. Declared a cash dividend that is payable 15 days after the close of the current accounting period.

4. A customer paid in advance for repair work to be completed while he is on vacation next month. The advance was accounted for using the liability approach.

5. Purchased a new service truck. Paid 10 percent down and issued a note for the balance.

6. Purchased supplies for cash.

7. Paid a loan in full.

Indicate the effect of each of the above transactions on total assets, total liabilities, and total stockholders' equity. Transaction (1) has been completed as an example.

Transaction	Total Assets	Total Liabilities	Total Stockholders' Equity
Paid an account	Decrease	Decrease	No effect

E7–5 Monetary and Nonmonetary Items

Selected accounts and balances from Jefferson Company's Balance Sheet appear in the following.

Cash	$ 800
Accounts Receivable......................	1,200
Inventory	2,000
Property, Plant, and Equipment (Net)..........	10,000
Accounts Payable	1,500
Notes Payable	2,200

1. What is the total amount of the monetary assets?
2. What is the total amount of the monetary liabilities?
3. How would the effect of inflation on this company's financial position compare with that of a company whose monetary liabilities were less than its monetary assets?

E7–6 Balance Sheet Analysis and the Effects of Inflation on Monetary and Nonmonetary Items

Victory Company has an extremely conservative management and has the following Balance Sheet as of December 31, 1981.

Victory Company
Balance Sheet as of December 31, 1981

Cash		$ 20,000
Accounts Receivable......................		40,000
Notes Receivable.........................		25,000
Inventory		60,000
Property, Plant, and Equipment (Net)..........		100,000
Total Assets		$245,000
Accounts Payable.................	$ 2,000	
Notes Payable...................	4,000	
Total Liabilities		$ 6,000
Common Stock	$ 80,000	
Retained Earnings	159,000	
Total Stockholders' Equity		239,000
Total Liabilities and Stockholders' Equity.....................................		$245,000

1. Why do you think this company is described as a conservative company?
2. How has this company primarily financed its operations?
3. What are the company's total monetary assets and total monetary liabilities?
4. Is this company's financial position one that will be adversely or positively affected by inflation? Why?

E7–7 Working Capital and Current Ratios

Madison and Macon Companies both operate in the same industry. At December 31, 1981, their respective Balance Sheets contained the following data.

	Madison Company	Macon Company
Cash	$ 800	$1,200
Accounts Receivable	1,200	2,400
Inventory	2,000	3,000
Property, Plant, and Equipment (Net)	6,000	5,000
Accounts Payable	500	600
Notes Payable (due in 6 months)	1,500	1,200
Notes Payable (due in 4 years)	4,000	4,000
Stockholders' Equity	4,000	5,800

1. Determine the amount of working capital for each firm.
2. Compute the current ratio for each company.

E7–8 Working Capital and Current Ratios

Summarized Balance Sheet information for Mayberry and Roseberry Companies is presented in the following.

	Mayberry Company	Roseberry Company
Current Assets...............	$ 800	$2,100
Property, Plant, and Equipment (Net)	1,200	6,000
Current Liabilities	400	1,400
Long-Term Liabilities	400	3,000
Stockholders' Equity	1,200	3,700

1. Determine the amount of working capital for each company.
2. Compute the current ratios of each company.

E7–9 Balance Sheet Classification—Matching

Selected Balance Sheet classifications for MBA Company as of December 31, 1981, are given on the right. Match each of the accounts on the left with the proper Balance Sheet classification.

MBA Company

Balance Sheet Accounts of December 31, 1981

1. Equipment
2. Goodwill
3. Prepaid Rent
4. Accrued Wages Payable
5. Building
6. Accumulated Depreciation—Building
7. Patents
8. Advances from Customers
9. Retained Earnings
10. Common Stock
11. Accounts Receivable
12. Income Taxes Payable
13. Cash
14. Notes Payable, due 1985
15. Mortgage Payable, due 2001
16. Land

a. Current Assets
b. Long-Term Investments
c. Property, Plant, and Equipment
d. Intangible Assets
e. Current Liabilities
f. Long-Term Liabilities
g. Contributed Capital
h. Retained Earnings

E7–10 Classified Balance Sheet Preparation

Using the accounts listed below, prepare, in good form, a classified Balance Sheet for Red Company as of December 31, 1981. The company was established January 1, 1981.

Account	Amount
Depreciation Expense	$ 200
Prepaid Insurance	200
Estimated Utilities Payable	50
Office Equipment	1,000
Common Stock	4,000
Miscellaneous Expense	150
Rental Fees Receivable	100
Note Payable (due 12/31/85)	2,000
Dividends	100
Unearned Rental Fees	100
Cash	500
Accumulated Depreciation—Furniture and Fixtures	150
Utilities Expense	100
Rental Revenue	1,000
Accounts Payable	150
Furniture and Fixtures	5,000
Insurance Expense	150
Accumulated Depreciation—Office Equipment	50

E7–11 Balance Sheet and Income Statement Classification

Some of the Balance Sheet and Income Statement accounts from Door Manufacturing Company are given. For each numbered item, identify the classification to which it belongs.

Accounts:
1. Accounts Receivable
2. Patents
3. Dividends Payable
4. Cash
5. Sales Revenue
6. Short-Term Investments
7. Depreciation Expense
8. Franchises
9. Office Supplies on Hand
10. Purchases
11. Note Payable (5-year maturity)
12. Estimated Warranty Obligation
13. Paid-in Capital in Excess of Par
14. Income Taxes Payable
15. Salary Expense

Classifications:
a. Current Assets
b. Long-Term Investments
c. Property, Plant, and Equipment
d. Intangible Assets
e. Current Liabilities
f. Long-Term Liabilities
g. Stockholders' Equity
h. Revenue
i. Cost of Goods Sold
j. Operating Expenses

E7–12 Balance Sheet Classification

Milato Corporation had the following Balance Sheet accounts on December 31, 1981.

Short-Term Investments	$ 6,000
Accounts Payable	2,000
Accounts Receivable	4,000
Wages Payable	3,000
Cash	1,500
Retained Earnings	12,000
Stock of Z Company	4,500
Accumulated Depreciation—Building	2,000
Patent	42,000
Land	9,000
Building	26,200
Inventory	9,000
Common Stock	30,000
Income Taxes Payable	1,800
Prepaid Expenses	600
Bonds Payable (mature in 1990)	10,000

Given this information, determine:

1. Current assets.
2. Long-term investments.
3. Property, plant, and equipment.
4. Current liabilities.
5. Long-term liabilities.
6. Stockholders' equity.

E7-13   Relationships Between a Balance Sheet and an Income Statement

The total amount of assets and liabilities of Edgewood Company at January 1, 1981, and December 31, 1981, are presented below.

	January 1	Post-Closing Trial Balance, December 31
Assets	$19,000	$28,000
Liabilities	6,500	7,200

Determine the correct amount of net income or loss for 1981, applying each of the following assumptions concerning the additional issuance of stock and dividend declarations by the firm. Each case is independent of the others.

1. Dividends of $2,700 were declared (no additional stock was issued) during the year.

2. Additional stock of $1,200 was issued (no dividends declared) during the year.

3. Additional stock of $15,500 was issued and dividends of $3,900 were declared during the year.

E7-14   Interpreting Balance Sheet Items—Property, Plant, and Equipment

ABC Pharmaceutical Company was established on January 1, 1980. XYZ Pharmaceutical Company was established in 1912. At the end of 1981, selected items from the financial statements of the two companies were as follows:

	ABC Company	XYZ Company
Property, Plant, and Equipment (net of accumulated depreciation)	$800,000	$100,000
Patents	160,000	12,000

1. From this information, can you conclude that ABC is a much larger company than XYZ? What could account for the reported differences in the amounts of property, plant, and equipment?

2. What could account for the low amount in the Patents account of XYZ Company? Does this information indicate that ABC has more patents?

PROBLEMS

P7-1   Classification of Accounts

Required:

Following are the titles of 25 accounts. For each account, identify: (1) the financial statement on which it would appear; (2) whether it is an asset, liability, stockholders' equity, expense, or revenue account; and (3) whether it would usually have a debit or credit balance. For example, for Accounts Receivable your answer would be as follows:

Account	Financial Statement	Classification	Normal Balance
Accounts Receivable	Balance Sheet	Asset	Debit

1. Cash
2. Notes Payable
3. Sales Returns and Allowances
4. Purchases
5. Gas, Oil, and Repairs Expense
6. Accrued Wages Payable
7. Unearned Service Fees
8. Prepaid Insurance
9. Interest Revenue
10. Furniture and Fixtures
11. Sales Discounts
12. Depreciation Expense—Delivery Equipment
13. Accrued Service Fees Receivable
14. Accumulated Depreciation—Delivery Equipment
15. Accounts Payable
16. Capital Stock
17. Freight-Out
18. Delivery Equipment
19. Supplies on Hand
20. Supplies Used
21. Retained Earnings
22. Allowance for Doubtful Accounts
23. Purchase Returns and Allowances
24. Purchase Discounts
25. Patent

P7-2   Classification of Balance Sheet Accounts

Maestro Corporation has the following Balance Sheet accounts as of December 31, 1981.

Land	$ 69,000
Cash	26,000
Short-Term Investments	12,000
Building	178,000
Accounts Payable	100,000
Common Stock	335,000
Accounts Receivable	88,000
Notes Payable (Short-Term)	105,000
Equipment	350,000
Patent	30,000
Bonds Payable, due 1990	300,000
Retained Earnings	58,000
Franchise	10,000
Inventory	170,000
Prepaid Expenses	15,000
Accumulated Depreciation—Building	20,000
Accumulated Depreciation—Equipment	30,000

Required:

1. Compute the total amount of
   (a) Current assets.
   (b) Property, plant, and equipment.
   (c) Intangible assets.
   (d) Current liabilities.
   (e) Long-term liabilities.
   (f) Stockholders' equity.

2. What is Maestro's current ratio?

P7–3   Current-Ratio and Balance
Sheet Interpretation

McDonald Company had the following unclassified
Balance Sheet as of December 31, 1981.

McDonald Company
Balance Sheet as of December 31, 1981

Assets

Cash	$ 8,500
Accounts Receivable	4,000
Inventory	16,000
Prepaid Expenses	1,500
Land	15,000
Building (net of depreciation)	40,000
Equipment (net of depreciation)	50,000
Patent	3,000
Total Assets	$138,000

Liabilities and Stockholders' Equity

Liabilities:

Notes Payable (Short-Term)	$ 8,000	
Accounts Payable	4,500	
Wages Payable	2,500	
Income Taxes Payable	3,000	
Bonds Payable (due 1983)	25,000	
Total Liabilities		$43,000

Stockholders' Equity:

Common Stock	$80,000	
Retained Earnings	15,000	
Total Stockholders' Equity		95,000
Total Liabilities and Stockholders' Equity		$138,000

Required:

1. Compute McDonald's current ratio.

2. **Interpretive Question** McDonald is presently applying for a 4-year bank loan of $30,000. The bank is only willing to loan the money if McDonald can achieve and maintain a current ratio of 2 to 1. Which of the following actions would give McDonald the needed ratio?
   (a) Paying all wages.
   (b) Paying all accounts.
   (c) Paying all income taxes and accounts.

3. **Interpretive Question** Will anything happen in the next couple of years that will probably put McDonald in violation of the debt requirement? Explain.

P7–4   Interpreting the Balance Sheet

The Balance Sheet for RTV Corporation as of December 31, 1981, is as follows:

Assets

Cash		$13,600
Accounts Receivable		13,000
Land		20,000
Office Equipment	$ 6,000	
Less Accumulated Depreciation	600	5,400
Total Assets		$52,000

Liabilities and Stockholders' Equity

Liabilities:

Accounts Payable	$ 900	
Income Taxes Payable	1,100	
Interest Payable	200	
Notes Payable (payable in 1 year)	2,000	
Total Liabilities		$ 4,200

Stockholders' Equity:

Common Stock (Par Value, $10)	$30,000	
Paid-in Capital in Excess of Par	3,000	
Retained Earnings	14,800	
Total Stockholders' Equity		47,800
Total Liabilities and Stockholders' Equity		$52,000

Required:

1. When was the office equipment purchased if it is expected to have a useful life of 10 years and no salvage value, assuming straight-line depreciation?

2. What is the annual interest rate on the note if it has been outstanding for six months and no interest has yet been paid?

3. If the company has been in existence since January 1, 1981, and if $3,000 of dividends were declared during 1981, what was 1981's net income?

4. How many shares of common stock are outstanding at December 31, 1981?

5. At what price was the stock issued if it was all issued at one time at the same price?

6. What is RTV's current ratio?

P7–5 Analysis of a Balance Sheet

Minnimart Corporation had the following Balance Sheet as of December 31, 1981.

Assets

Cash		$ 5,000
Accounts Receivable	$28,000	
Less Allowance for Doubtful Accounts	560	27,440
Land		20,000
Building	$50,000	
Less Accumulated Depreciation	5,000	45,000
Total Assets		$97,440

Liabilities and Stockholders' Equity

Liabilities:		
Accounts Payable	$20,000	
Income Taxes Payable	12,840	
Interest Payable	1,600	
Notes Payable	20,000	
Total Liabilities		$54,440
Stockholders' Equity:		
Common Stock (Par Value $20)	$20,000	
Paid-in Capital in Excess of Par	2,000	
Retained Earnings	21,000	
Total Stockholders' Equity		43,000
Total Liabilities and Stockholders' Equity		$97,440

Required:

1. If Minnimart Company estimates its bad debts on the basis of total receivables and has just made its adjusting entry, what percentage of accounts receivable has it estimated to be uncollectable?

2. If the company was started on January 1, 1980, and the building was purchased on that date, what is the useful life of the building? (The estimated salvage value of the building is zero.)

3. If the note has been outstanding for eight months and no interest has yet been paid, what is the interest rate of the loan?

4. What was the market price of the stock when it was issued to shareholders?

5. How many shares of common stock are outstanding?

P7–6 Preparation of a Classified Balance Sheet

Following are the December 31, 1981, account balances for E-Z Rental Company. The inventory balance on December 31, 1981, was $1,500.

Cash	$ 2,700
Accounts Receivable	2,500
Supplies on Hand	1,800
Prepaid Insurance	1,000
Equipment	11,275
Accounts Payable	3,450
Accrued Wages Payable	250
Dividends Payable	1,750
Common Stock	6,225
Retained Earnings, January 1, 1981	12,000
Sales	15,000
Purchases	11,000
Freight-In	200
Dividends Declared	1,750
Other Operating Expenses	1,550
Inventory, January 1, 1981	3,700
Wages Expense	2,200
Accumulated Depreciation—Equipment	1,000

Required:

1. Prepare a classified Balance Sheet as of December 31, 1981.

2. **Interpretive Question** On the basis of its 1981 earnings, was this company's decision to pay dividends of $1,750 a sound one?

P7–7 Preparation of a Classified Balance Sheet

Following are the account balances as of December 31, 1981, for Johnson Manufacturing Corporation.

Retained Earnings	$45,734
Mortgage Payable (current portion)	600
Mortgage Payable (noncurrent portion)	7,500
Accounts Receivable	7,880
Cash	7,590
Building	50,000
Accumulated Depreciation—Building	10,900
Office Equipment	4,570
Accumulated Depreciation—Office Equipment	2,720
Store Equipment	12,200
Accumulated Depreciation—Store Equipment	5,700
Salaries Payable	196
Land	6,000
Common Stock	30,000
Accounts Payable	8,420
Office Supplies on Hand	830
Prepaid Insurance	700
Inventory	22,000

Required:

1. Prepare a classified Balance Sheet as of December 31, 1981.

2. **Interpretive Question**   Does it appear that Johnson is a financially sound company?

P7–8   Preparation of a Classified Balance Sheet

Following are the account balances for Jason Corporation as of December 31, 1981.

Land	$ 90,000
Accumulated Depreciation—Building	26,000
Accumulated Depreciation—Equipment	43,000
Equipment	180,000
Prepaid Insurance	5,000
Building	180,000
Accounts Payable	50,000
Bonds Payable—Long-Term	120,000
Retained Earnings	262,500
Income Taxes Payable	7,500
Common Stock	230,000
Paid-in Capital in Excess of Par	10,000
Dividends Payable	10,000
Inventory	171,000
Accounts Receivable	84,000
Cash	39,000
Patent	10,000

Required:

1. Prepare a classified Balance Sheet as of December 31, 1981.

2. **Interpretive Question**   Is Jason Corporation a financially sound company?

P7–9   Unifying Problem: A Classified Balance Sheet

Marco Company has the following Balance Sheet accounts as of December 31, 1981.

Notes Payable (Short-Term)	$ 20,000
Accounts Payable	170,000
Land	40,000
Cash	58,000
Prepaid Expenses	27,000
Bonds Payable (mature in 1990)	250,000
Common Stock	150,000
Retained Earnings	50,000
Inventory	155,000

Building	110,000
Accumulated Depreciation—Equipment	30,000
Accumulated Depreciation—Building	10,000
Equipment	330,000
Mortgage Payable (due 1984)	40,000

Required:

1. Prepare a classified Balance Sheet for Marco Company as of December 31, 1981.

2. Compute Marco Company's current ratio.

3. Compute Marco Company's total monetary assets and monetary liabilities.

4. **Interpretive Question**   Is Marco's financial position one that will be eased or made more difficult by inflation?

P7–10   Unifying Problem: The Balance Sheet

McNichols Company has the following Balance Sheet accounts at December 31, 1981.

Common Stock	$200,000
Bonds Payable (mature in 1998)	230,000
Notes Payable (6 months)	18,000
Cash	32,900
Inventory	37,000
Land	28,000
Building	102,000
Accumulated Depreciation—Building	52,000
Equipment	369,000
Accumulated Depreciation—Equipment	20,000
Accounts Payable	9,700
Mortgage Payable (due 1990)	60,000
Retained Earnings	10,000
Income Tax Payable	12,000
Prepaid Expenses	24,800
Accounts Receivable	8,000
Patent	10,000

Required:

1. Prepare a classified Balance Sheet as of December 31, 1981.

2. Compute McNichols' current ratio.

3. Compute McNichols' total monetary assets and total monetary liabilities.

4. **Interpretive Question**   How has this company acquired most of its financial resources?

CHAPTER 8

Current Assets and Current Liabilities

THIS CHAPTER EXPLAINS: Accounting for cash, including cash control, petty-cash funds, and the reconciliation of bank accounts.

Accounting for receivables, including the discounting of notes receivable.

Accounting for prepaid expenses.

Accounting for current liabilities, including accounts payable, notes payable, accrued liabilities, payroll-related liabilities, and noncash liabilities.

Accounting for contingent liabilities.

The concepts of working capital and the current and acid-test ratios.

working capital the funds (or resources) available to finance current operations; equal to current assets minus current liabilities

With this chapter, we begin our detailed examination of the Balance Sheet. Current assets and current liabilities are covered together because they involve similar accounting procedures and because they are generally considered as a unit for planning purposes. Most of the funding for day-to-day business operations must come from working capital (the excess of total current assets over total current liabilities). For this reason, business managers, as well as those who monitor business reports (security analysts, investors, bankers, and so on), tend to pay special attention to current asset and liability ratios.

The current assets discussed here include cash, accounts receivable, notes receivable, and prepaid expenses. Inventories and short-term investments are examined in Chapters 6 and 9, respectively. Current liabilities include accounts payable, notes payable, accrued liabilities (such as payroll liabilities), and noncash liabilities. Contingent liabilities are also touched upon briefly.

Current Assets

current assets *cash and other assets that may reasonably be expected to be converted to cash within one year or during the normal operating cycle*

liquidity *a company's ability to meet current obligations with cash or other resources that can be quickly converted to cash*

Current assets are cash and other assets that can reasonably be expected to be converted to cash or used within one year or during the normal operating cycle. Since current assets are listed on the Balance Sheet in order of liquidity, we will follow that sequence in describing the individual accounts.

Accounting for Cash

Cash is obviously the most liquid asset. It includes coins, paper money, money orders or checks (made payable or endorsed to the company), and money on deposit with banks or savings institutions. All of the various transactions involving these forms of cash are usually reported under a single Balance Sheet caption, Cash. This category does not, however, include postage stamps (prepaid expenses), IOUs (receivables), or postdated checks. Only the amount of cash restricted for a special purpose (such as the repayment of a bond payable), or restricted by law or contract, is excluded from the cash balance.

The major elements of accounting for cash are (1) recording and processing cash transactions, (2) accounting for petty cash, and (3) bank reconciliations.

In many companies, cash transactions are journalized, posted, and summarized by a computer. The duties of accounting personnel are then reduced to "inputting" the original data (keypunching journal entries), while the computer performs most of the accounting functions, including the preparation of special journals and the financial statements. In relatively small businesses, cash transactions are entered manually in separate cash receipts and cash disbursements journals. These journals were discussed in the Supplement to Chapter 5.

CONTROL OF CASH

Because of its value, and because it is the most liquid asset, cash must be carefully safeguarded. In particular, management must attempt to

1. Prevent losses of cash by theft or fraud.

2. Provide accurate accounting of all the inflows, outflows, and balances of cash.

3. Maintain a sufficient balance of cash on hand to provide for day-to-day requirements, finance current operations, and satisfy maturing liabilities.

4. Prevent large amounts of excess or idle cash from accumulating on hand or in checking accounts.

Several control procedures have been developed to help management meet these objectives. The first is that the handling of cash be separated from accounting for cash. The purpose of this separation of duties is to make it difficult for theft to occur unless at least two people are involved. Without such collusion, if the employee who receives the cash tries to commit fraud, the accounting clerk will usually discover it, and vice versa.

To illustrate what can happen without this safeguard, we will consider the employee who pockets the cash payment of an account receivable from a first customer and then records the payment by that customer only when a second customer pays. The second customer's payment is recorded when a third customer pays, and so on. This type of lagged recording of payments is called lapping and allows an employee to use company money for extended periods of time.

lapping   *a procedure used to conceal the theft of cash by crediting the payment from one customer to another customer's account on a delayed basis*

Separation of duties involves three other procedures: (1) the separation of cash receiving from cash disbursing, (2) the clear identification and use of specific routines for cash receiving and cash disbursing, and (3) the assignment to different individuals of each aspect of cash handling and accounting.

A second cash-control feature is the requirement that all cash receipts be deposited daily in bank accounts. Most cash comes from over-the-counter sales or orders received in the mail. To ensure that all such sales are properly accounted for, businesses use cash registers, which provide a tape of the day's sales. At the end of the day, all cash is counted, compared with the amount on the tape, and deposited in the bank. Payments received through the mail are controlled by separating the receiving, recording, and depositing functions. The person who receives the cash and checks makes a list, then forwards the cash and checks to the cashier for deposit. The list is also sent to the accounting department to be compared with the actual receipted deposit slip from the bank and entered in the cash receipts journal. If all cash receipts are deposited on the day they are received, the likelihood of cash being lost or misused is minimized.

A third cash-control feature is the requirement that all cash expenditures (except those paid out of petty cash) be made with prenumbered checks. In addition, the person or persons who approve payment should be different from those who actually sign the checks. In companies where this system is used, no checks can be signed unless they are accompanied by an approved invoice, which gives the purpose of the check and the justification and verification for the expenditure. Any check not actually used should be clearly marked "void," mutilated, and filed in sequence in the checkbook so all checks can be accounted for.

While the use of these three control features—separation of duties, daily deposits of all cash receipts, and prenumbered checks—can help a business reduce the misuse of cash, it is difficult to prevent theft or fraud if collusion exists. Another difficulty in controlling cash results from the use of computers. Large businesses computerize cash transactions and, by so doing, sometimes eliminate one or more of the control features just described. For example, with computers it is sometimes difficult to have a meaningful separation of duties; thus, a deceptive and intelligent computer operator can steal cash in ways that are almost impossible to detect. Even with this potential for misuse, many businesses have found that the benefits of a computer—the reduced accounting costs and the efficiency it can provide—far outweigh the disadvantages.

In addition to safeguarding and protecting cash, a business must ensure that cash is wisely managed. In fact, many businesses establish elaborate control and budgeting procedures for monitoring cash balances, working capital ratios, and future cash needs.

ACCOUNTING FOR PETTY CASH

For control purposes, it makes sense to pay everything by check, since the check provides a permanent record of each transaction. However, most businesses find it too expensive and inconvenient to write checks for all miscellaneous cash expenditures. Instead, they usually pay for items such as minor delivery charges, stamps, and inexpensive supplies out of cash kept on hand in what is called a petty-cash fund. The size of a petty-cash fund depends on the number, magnitude, and frequency of these miscellaneous expenditures. Obviously, the combined petty-cash fund of a multinational corporation will be much larger than that of a small business. Businesses want the fund to be large enough so that it does not have to be replenished too often but not so large that it tempts theft or misuse. Most firms keep enough cash on hand to cover about one month's miscellaneous expenditures. It is also common for firms to limit the amount that can be taken from the petty-cash fund for a single expenditure.

petty-cash fund a small amount of cash kept on hand for making miscellaneous payments

Although a petty-cash fund is more difficult to control than checks, misuse can be minimized by handling the petty-cash fund on an imprest basis. That is, any cash removed from the fund must be replaced by a prenumbered petty-cash voucher accompanied by a receipt or invoice from the supplier of the item or service purchased. The receipt or invoice validates the type and amount of the expenditure. Thus, with an imprest petty-cash fund, the balance can easily be checked. The total of unused cash and vouchers should always equal the balance. Exhibit 8–1 is a voucher showing that a $42 delivery bill from EmCo Trucking Company was paid from petty cash.

imprest petty-cash fund a petty-cash fund in which all expenditures are documented by vouchers or vendors' receipts or invoices

EXHIBIT 8–1 **Petty-Cash Voucher**

		No. 22
Payment made to: *EmCo Trucking*		Date *July 17*
Description	Account to be charged	Amount
Delivery Bill	*616 (Freight-In)*	*$42.00*
Signature of person using funds	*John Doe*	

To illustrate the accounting for an imprest petty-cash fund, we will assume that on July 1, Miller Company decided to establish a petty-cash fund of $200. A check was made out to petty cash and cashed at the bank. The $200 was placed in a convenient but safe place. The entry in the cash disbursements journal would be

July 1
Petty Cash................................. 200
   Cash 200
Established a $200 petty-cash fund.

For each expenditure, a voucher (accompanied by a receipt) is prepared to account for the money spent. For example, if Miller paid $40 for office supplies, $42 for freight, and $30 for postage, three vouchers would be placed in the fund. Petty-cash expenditures are not accounted for as they occur; instead, a single entry is made when the petty-cash fund is replenished. The entry to replenish Miller's petty-cash fund would be

August 1
Office Supplies 40
Freight-In 42
Postage 30
   Cash 112
Replenished the petty-cash fund.

As this entry indicates, when the petty-cash fund is replenished, a check is written for the total amount of all expenditures, Cash is credited, and the affected expense accounts are debited individually. The items in this entry are then posted to their respective accounts. At no time is the petty-cash fund replenished by debiting or crediting the Petty Cash account. The only entries ever made to that account are those which either permanently increase it or permanently decrease it.

For control purposes, one person should have complete responsibility for the petty-cash fund. A different person should be authorized to write the checks that replenish the fund. The custodian of the petty-cash fund should be responsible for maintaining the fund's balance and should make sure that all petty-cash vouchers are prenumbered and used only once.

If the actual balance is ever different from the amount that should be in the fund (usually because of an error in making change), the discrepancy should be noted in an account called Cash Over and Short. This account, which is used only to correct small errors, is debited when there is a shortage and credited when there is an excess of cash. For example, if Miller Company had found on August 1 that the petty-cash fund had only $82 in cash (instead of a correct amount of $88) and $112 in validated expenditures, the entry to replenish the petty-cash fund would have been

Cash Over and Short *an account used to record overages and shortages in petty cash*

August 1
Office Supplies 40
Freight-In 42
Postage 30
Cash Over and Short........................ 6
   Cash 118
Replenished the petty-cash fund and recognized a shortage of $6.

A debit balance in Cash Over and Short is posted to a Miscellaneous Expense account, and a credit balance in the account is posted to a Miscellaneous (or Other) Revenue account. Entries to replenish a petty-cash fund are recorded in the cash disbursements journal.

RECONCILING THE BANK ACCOUNT

With the exception of petty cash, most cash is kept in checking accounts at one or more banks. Generally, only a few employees are authorized to sign checks and they must have their signatures on file with the bank.

Every month, the bank sends the business a statement, which shows the cash balance at the beginning of the period, the deposits, the amounts of the checks processed, and the cash balance at the end of the period. With the statement, the bank includes all of that month's canceled checks, as well as debit and credit memos (for example, an explanation of charges for NSF checks and services fees).

NSF check *a check that is not honored by a bank because of insufficient cash in the customer's account*

Miller Company's bank statement for July is presented in Exhibit 8–2. This statement includes two bank adjustments to Miller's balance—a bank service charge of $7 (the bank's monthly fee) and a $3,200 automatic deposit apparently made by a customer who regularly deposits payments directly to Miller's bank account. Several other adjustments are commonly made to a company's bank account. These adjustments, with their common codes, are

EC (Error Correction): This identifies arithmetic and other errors and corrections made by the bank.

NSF (Not Sufficient Funds): This reverses a prior deposit of a check for which there was not a sufficient balance in the writer's account to cover the withdrawal.

MS (Miscellaneous): This code is used to cover other adjustments made by a bank.

It is unusual for the ending balance on the bank statement to be equal to the amount of cash recorded in a company's Cash account. The most common reasons for differences are

1. *Time period differences*: The time period of the bank statement does not coincide with the company's posting to the Cash account.

2. *Deposits in transit*: These are deposits that have not yet reached the bank for processing, usually because they were made during the last days of the month.

3. *Outstanding checks*: These are checks that have been written and deducted from a company's Cash account but have not yet reached the bank for processing.

4. *Bank charges*: These are bank fees and other bank charges that have not yet been recorded by the company. The most common are monthly service charges and NSF checks.

EXHIBIT 8–2 **Bank Statement**

First Security Bank
Palo Alto, California

Statement of Account

Miller Company
110 El Camino Real
Palo Alto, CA 94305

Account Number   325-78126

Date of Statement   July 31, 1981

CHECKS	DEPOSITS	DATE	BALANCE
		6/30	13,000
140		7/01	12,860
250	1,500	7/03	14,110
860		7/05	13,250
210		7/08	13,040
	2,200	7/09	15,240
205		7/10	15,035
310		7/14	14,725
425		7/15	14,300
	3,200 A	7/18	17,500
765		7/19	16,735
4,825		7/22	11,910
420		7/24	11,490
326	1,600	7/25	12,764
	2,100	7/26	14,864
210		7/29	14,654
225		7/31	14,422
7SC			
9,171	10,600	Service Charge $7	14,422

EC = Error Correction   A = Automatic Deposit   MS = Miscellaneous
NSF = Not Sufficient Funds   SC = Service Charge

5. *Bank credits:* These are credits made by a bank to a company's account that have not yet been recorded by the company. The most common are notes that have been collected for the depositor by the bank and automatic deposits.

6. *Accounting errors:* These are numerical errors made by either the company or the bank. The most common are transpositions of numbers.

bank reconciliation *the process of systematically comparing the cash balance as reported by the bank and as recorded on the company's books and explaining any differences*

The process of determining the reasons for the differences between the bank balance and the company's Cash account balance is called reconciling the bank account. This usually results in adjusting both the bank statement and the book (Cash account) balances.

We will use Miller Company's bank account to illustrate a bank reconciliation. The statement shown in Exhibit 8–2 indicates an ending balance of $14,422 for the month of July. After arranging the month's checks in numerical order and examining the bank statement, Miller's accountant notes the following.

1. A deposit of $3,100 on July 31 was not shown on the bank statement.

2. Checks #625 for $326, #701 for $426, and #702 for $185 are outstanding.

3. The bank service charge for the month is $7.

4. An automatic deposit of $3,200 was made by Joy Company, a regular customer.

5. Check #694 for John Jones' wages was recorded in the accounting records as $240 instead of the correct amount, $420.

6. The Cash account in the General Ledger shows an ending balance of $13,572.

Given these data, the bank reconciliation would be as shown in Exhibit 8–3.

If adjusted book and bank balances do not agree the first time a reconciliation is attempted, the accountant will look for errors in bookkeeping, in back-up calculations, or in the bank's figures. When the balances finally agree, any necessary adjustments are made to the Cash account to bring it to the correct balance. The entries to correct the balance include debits to Cash for all reconciling additions to the book balance and credits to Cash for all reconciling deductions from the book balance. Additions and deductions from the bank balance do not require adjustments to the company's books, since the deposits in transit and the outstanding checks have already been recorded by the company and bank errors are corrected by notifying the bank. The adjustments required to correct Miller's Cash

---

EXHIBIT 8–3   Miller Company Bank Reconciliation
July 31, 1981

Ending Balance on Bank Statement.............	$14,422	Balance Per Books............................		$13,572
Reconciling Items		**Reconciling Items**		
Additions to Bank Balance:		*Additions to Book Balance:*		
Deposits in Transit	3,100	Automatic Deposit...........................		3,200
Total..................................	$17,522	Total..................................		$16,772
Deductions from Bank Balance:		*Deductions from Book Balance:*		
Outstanding Checks: 625 .... $326		Service Charge...................... $ 7		
701 426		Error in Recording Check 180		(187)
702 185				
	(937)			
Adjusted Bank Balance.....................	$16,585	Adjusted Book Balance......................		$16,585

account would be

Cash	3,200	
Accounts Receivable.................................		3,200

To record the additions due to the July bank reconciliation (a $3,200 deposit made by Joy Company).

Miscellaneous Expense	7	
Wages Expense	180	
Cash		187

To record the deductions due to the July bank reconciliation (service charge of $7 and a $180 error in recording check #694).

TO SUMMARIZE   Cash is a company's most liquid asset and is always the first current asset listed on its Balance Sheet. Companies must carefully monitor and control the way cash is handled and accounted for. Common controls include: (1) separation of duties in the handling of and accounting for cash, (2) daily deposits of all cash receipts, and (3) payment of all expenditures by prenumbered checks, except for the small miscellaneous ones paid from petty-cash funds. The petty-cash fund is usually maintained on an imprest basis.

Because most payments are made by check, companies need to reconcile monthly bank statements with the cash balance reported on the company's books. This reconciliation process involves determining reasons for the differences and bringing the book and bank balances into agreement. Adjusting entries are then made for additions to and deductions from the book balance.

Receivables

receivables   claims for money, goods, or services

The term receivables refers to all claims for money, goods, or services by a company. Receivables are created through various kinds of transactions, the two most common being the sale of inventory on credit and the lending of money. A company may have several other kinds of receivables: from officers or employees of the company (a loan to an employee, for example), from interest, and from affiliated (parent or subsidiary) companies. In order to identify and maintain the distinctions between these receivables, businesses establish a separate General Ledger account for each one. And, if the amount of a receivable is material, it is separately identified on the Balance Sheet. When receivables are to be converted to cash in a relatively short period of time, they are classified as current assets and listed on the Balance Sheet just below cash and short-term investments.

ACCOUNTS RECEIVABLE

accounts receivable   money due from rendering services or selling merchandise on credit

Many sales involve credit, and the buyer usually has from 10 days to 2 months to pay the seller for merchandise purchased. The receivable that arises from the sale of merchandise or services is called an account receivable (also often called a trade receivable). Since we discussed accounts receivable in Chapter 5 in connection with the measurement and reporting of revenues, we now focus on other types of receivables.

NOTES RECEIVABLE

note receivable *a claim against a debtor, evidenced by an unconditional written promise to pay a certain sum of money on or before a specified future date*

A note receivable is an unconditional written promise to pay a sum of money on or before a specified future date. Depending on the length of time between the end of the accounting period and the due date, the note may be classified as a current or a long-term asset. In addition, it may be either a trade note receivable (that is, one due from a customer who purchased merchandise) or a nontrade note receivable. Exhibit 8–4 shows a typical note receivable.

maker *a person (entity) who signs a note to borrow money and who assumes responsibility to pay the note at maturity*

payee *the person (entity) to whom payment on a note is to be made*

principal *the face amount of a note; the amount (excluding interest) that the maker agrees to pay the payee*

maturity date *the date on which a note or other obligation becomes due*

interest rate *the cost of using money, expressed as an annual percentage*

interest *the amount charged for using money*

There are several key terms associated with a note receivable. The maker of a note is the person who signs the note and who is responsible for its payment. The payee is the person to whom payment will be made. The principal is the face amount of the note. The maturity date is the date the note becomes due. Notes can either be interest- or non-interest-bearing. For example, a bank note to borrow money for the purchase of an automobile or furniture is usually interest-bearing. The interest rate is the percentage of the principal that the payee annually charges the maker for the loan and the interest is the dollar amount paid by the maker in accordance with this rate. Interest can also be thought of as the service charge for the use of money. The formula for computing the interest on a note is

$$\text{principal} \times \text{interest rate} \times \text{time (fraction of a year)} = \text{interest}$$

For example, if Miller Company accepted from Sherwood Company a 12 percent, 60-day, \$2,000 note receivable, the interest would be calculated as follows:

$$\$2{,}000 \times 12\% \times 60/360 = \$40$$

In calculating the time, 360 days is often used to represent a business year.

EXHIBIT 8–4 Note Receivable

__________ DATE   __________ CITY $__________

PAY TO THE ORDER OF __________

__________ DOLLARS

VALUE RECEIVED AND DEBIT THE SAME TO THE ACCOUNT OF

TO: FIRST SECURITY BANK
National Association
POST OFFICE BOX 6004
PALO ALTO, CA 94304

If the $2,000 note were accepted in settlement of an account because Sherwood Company could not pay its account receivable with Miller Company on time, the journal entry to record the note in Miller's books would be

Notes Receivable—Sherwood Company   2,000
    Accounts Receivable—Sherwood Company   2,000
Accepted note from Sherwood Company in lieu of payment of its account receivable.

When the collection is made on the maturity date of the note (60 days later), the entry to record the receipt of cash is

Cash   2,040
    Notes Receivable—Sherwood Company   2,000
    Interest Revenue   40
Received payment from Sherwood Company for $2,000 note plus interest.

Principal plus interest, or $2,040 in this example, is known as the maturity value of the note. If the note is not paid by the maturity date, negotiations with the maker usually result in the company's extending the grace period for payment, issuing a new note, or retaining an attorney or collection agency to collect the note. If the note eventually proves to be worthless, it is written off against Allowance for Doubtful Accounts.

Often, notes receivable are classified on the Balance Sheet as special receivables when an agency or attorney is attempting to make collection.

maturity value   *the amount of an obligation to be collected or paid at maturity date; equal to principal plus any interest*

Non-Interest-Bearing Notes

Occasionally, a company will accept a non-interest-bearing note. The advantage of this type of note over an account receivable is that it is a written promise to pay. The accounting for a short-term non-interest-bearing note is similar to that for an interest-bearing one—except, of course, there is no stated interest. If the note is long-term, generally accepted accounting principles require that the principal be reduced in amount, using an implicit interest rate to reflect the real interest that is probably already included in the face amount. Since money has a time value, the accounting profession argues that no rational person or business would accept a real non-interest-bearing, long-term note that does not have some interest built into the principal amount.

Discounting Notes Receivable

discounting a note receivable   *the process of the payee's selling notes to a financial institution for less than the maturity value*

Because notes receivable are promises to pay money in the future, they are negotiable. They can be sold, or discounted, to banks and other financial institutions. This means that a holder of a note who needs cash before a note will mature sells the note to a financial institution (simply by endorsing the note). The maker of the note, therefore, owes the money to the new payee.

To financial institutions, the purchase of a note for cash is just like making a loan; that is, cash is given out now in return for repayment of principal with interest in the future. To a company selling a note, discounting is a way of receiving cash earlier than otherwise would be possible.

Several key terms are associated with the discounting of notes. The discount rate is the rate (percentage of maturity value) charged by the financial institution for buying the note, the discount is the actual amount the bank will receive on the transaction, and the discount period is the length of time for which the note is discounted. The formula for computing discount is

maturity value × discount rate × discount period = discount

To illustrate the discounting of a note, we refer to the 60-day, 12 percent note for $2,000 that Miller accepted from Sherwood Company. After holding the note for 15 days, Miller decides to discount it at 16 percent at First Security Bank. The discount would be $40.80, which is computed as follows:

$2,040 × 16% × 45/360 = $40.80

maturity value × discount rate × discount period = discount

Since the note that Sherwood Company will now pay to the bank is worth $2,040 at maturity, Miller will receive $1,999.20 ($2,040.00 − $40.80), called net proceeds, from the bank for the note. The entry to record the discounting of the note would be

Cash	1,999.20	
Interest Expense	.80	
Notes Receivable—Sherwood Company		2,000.00

To record the discounting of $2,000 note from Sherwood Company.

The net effect of this transaction on Miller Company is a cost of $0.80. Since the bank's 16 percent discount rate is higher than the note's 12 percent interest rate, Miller Company has no interest revenue on the note, even though the note was held for 15 days. If Miller had held the note for 45 days and then discounted it, the amount of discount would have been $13.60 ($2,040 × 16% × 15/360), leaving $26.40 interest. The entry to record the transaction would have been

Cash	2,026.40	
Interest Revenue		26.40
Notes Receivable—Sherwood Company		2,000.00

To record the discounting of $2,000 note from Sherwood Company.

In this case, Miller has $26.40 of interest revenue, which was earned by holding the Sherwood Company note for 45 days.

In most cases, notes are discounted with recourse. That is, if the maker of a note does not pay the bank on the maturity date, the firm discounting the note is responsible for payment. Thus, if Sherwood Company does not pay its note, Miller has to reimburse First Security Bank. The amount due is usually the maturity value of the note plus a handling fee charged by the bank.

discount rate *the interest rate charged by a financial institution for buying a note receivable*

discount *the amount paid to a bank when selling, or discounting, a note receivable; calculated as maturity value times discount rate times discount period*

discount period *the time between the date a note is sold to a financial institution and its maturity date*

recourse *the right to seek payment on a discounted note from the payee if the maker defaults*

OTHER RECEIVABLES

Besides accounts and notes receivable, a firm may have other kinds of receivables. The most common are receivables from employees, interest receivables, and receivables from affiliates (subsidiary or parent companies). The accounting for these receivables presents no new problems. If short-term, they are included with the accounts and notes receivable under current assets on the Balance Sheet. If long-term, they are usually included as other long-term assets on the Balance Sheet. Whatever their nature, these other receivables, if material, should be kept separate from accounts and notes receivable and should bear appropriate descriptive titles when shown on the Balance Sheet.

TO SUMMARIZE A company can have several types of receivables. Accounts receivable, which arise from credit sales, are the most common. Notes receivable, which are unconditional written promises to pay specific amounts in the future, may also be included. Notes receivable that result from sales or loans are negotiable, and so can be discounted with banks. Any other receivables that are material should be carefully labeled and separately accounted for.

Prepaid Expenses

prepaid expenses *payments made in advance for items normally charged to expense*

Prepaid expenses (sometimes called prepayments or prepaid assets) are payments made for goods and services in advance of their use. Because they represent a company's claim to the future use of goods or services, they are classified as assets until consumed or used. The most common prepaid expenses include insurance premiums, rent, and interest paid in advance. Office supplies purchased prior to their use are sometimes included in this category. Prepaid expenses are classified as current assets, since they usually will be consumed within the next year.

Although prepaid expenses were discussed in Chapter 4, a short review is included here. Most prepaid expenses are recorded initially as assets and then expensed as used, but the accounting can be accomplished in any one of three different ways. Two of these methods, the asset and expense approaches, were discussed in Chapter 4. The third method is a combination of the other two.

To illustrate, we will assume that on April 1, Miller paid a $360 premium for a 1-year (April 1 to March 31) fire insurance policy. Since coverage is for the coming year, the $360 is a prepaid expense. Assuming an accounting year-end of December 31, this payment could be handled in any one of the three ways shown in Exhibit 8–5.

It should be apparent that, under all three methods, the amounts in Prepaid Insurance (a current asset) and Insurance Expense on December 31 are the same. Prepaid Insurance always has an ending balance of $90, which represents that portion of the premium covering January, February, and March of the next year. Insurance Expense has a balance of $270, which represents the premiums for the first nine months.

The accounting procedures for supplies, prepaid rent, prepaid interest, and other prepaid expenses are essentially the same.

EXHIBIT 8–5   **Three Ways of Accounting for Prepaid Expenses**

	Asset Approach	Expense Approach	Combination
			Assume that the $360 is originally classified as both an asset and an expense.
	Assume that the $360 is originally classified as an asset.	*Assume that the $360 is originally classified as an expense.*	

Entry when paid (April 1)	Prepaid Insurance . . 360
	  Cash 360
	Purchased a 1-year insurance policy.
		Insurance Expense . 360
		  Cash 360
		Purchased a 1-year insurance policy.
			Prepaid Insurance . . 90
			Insurance Expense . 270
			  Cash 360
			Purchased a 1-year insurance policy.

Entry to adjust the accounts on December 31 (year-end)	Insurance Expense . 270
	  Prepaid Insurance 270
	To adjust for proper insurance expense (9/12 × $360).
		Prepaid Insurance . . 90
		  Insurance Expense . . . 90
		To adjust for proper prepaid insurance (3/12 × $360).
			No Entry Needed

Prepaid Insurance account after both entries	**Prepaid Insurance**	**Prepaid Insurance**	**Prepaid Insurance**
	(4/1) . . . . 360 | 270 . . (12/31) **Bal.** 90	**Bal.** 90	**Bal.** 90

Insurance Expense account after both entries	**Insurance Expense**	**Insurance Expense**	**Insurance Expense**
	Bal. 270	(4/1) . . . . 360 | 90 . . . (12/31) **Bal.** 270	**Bal.** 270

TO SUMMARIZE   Prepaid expenses are payments made for goods and services in advance of their use. Because they represent a company's claims to the future use of goods or services, they are classified as assets until used. There are three ways to account for prepaid expenses: (1) asset approach, (2) expense approach, or (3) a combination of the two. With all three, the relevant asset and expense accounts have proper balances at year-end.

Current Liabilities

current liabilities   *debts or other obligations that will be paid or otherwise discharged within one year or the normal operating cycle*

Current liabilities are obligations that can reasonably be expected to be paid or satisfied within one year or during the normal operating cycle. They can be obligations either to pay cash or to perform services. The most common cash obligations are accounts payable, short-term notes payable, and accrued liabilities (including payroll-related liabilities). The most common noncash obligations are those to deliver goods to customers (in return for advances received) or to perform a future service, such as the repair of an automobile or stereo under a warranty agreement.

Accounts Payable

accounts payable   money owed to creditors

Accounts payable (sometimes called trade payables) are amounts owed for credit purchases. The accounting for accounts payable is fairly simple: Accounts Payable is increased, or credited, when inventory is purchased on credit, and decreased, or debited, when cash is paid to vendors.

Notes Payable

note payable   a debt owed to a creditor, evidenced by an unconditional written promise to pay a sum of money on or before a specified future date

Notes payable differ from accounts payable in that they usually represent written obligations to pay certain amounts of money on or before some future date. If a note is short-term, that is, if the business signs a note in order to borrow money from a bank or financial institution for only two or three months, it is considered a current liability. On the other hand, if it has a term that extends beyond the current operating cycle, it is classified as a long-term liability.

Notes payable are usually interest-bearing and interest is computed in the same way it is for notes receivable.

principal × interest rate × time (fraction of a year) = interest

For example, if Miller Company borrows $2,000 from the First Security Bank for two months at 10 percent interest, the calculation would be

$2,000   ×   10%   ×   60/360   = $33.33

principal × interest rate × time (fraction of a year) = interest

The entries to record the borrowing and the repayment two months later of the $2,000 by Miller would be

Cash 2,000.00
   Notes Payable—First Security Bank 2,000.00
Borrowed $2,000 from First Security Bank.

Notes Payable—First Security Bank 2,000.00
Interest Expense 33.33
   Cash 2,033.33
Repaid $2,000, 10% note to First Security Bank with interest.

As we explained earlier, notes are negotiable and can be transferred to a third party by endorsement. Therefore, it is not uncommon to find that a note payable has been discounted or transferred by the original payee to a third party, usually a bank. (See pages 265–266 for a discussion of discounting notes.)

Accrued Liabilities

accrued liability *an obligation for benefits received but not yet paid for*

Accrued liabilities are obligations that have been incurred but not yet paid. For example, taxes on wages are accumulated during a period but not paid until the next period. Thus, at the end of the accounting period, adjusting entries must be made to recognize the amount of these liabilities. If not properly recorded, expenses and liabilities are understated and net income is overstated.

To illustrate the accounting for a typical accrued liability, we will assume that Miller pays its annual property taxes of $3,600 (for the period July 1, 1980, through June 30, 1981) on June 30, 1981. Although the company does not pay the property taxes until June 30, 1981, the estimated property tax expense and liability for the month must be recorded at the end of each month, beginning in July 1980. The monthly entry would be

Property Tax Expense.   300
   Accrued Property Taxes Payable   300
To record property tax expense and liability for one month.

Because these types of liabilities usually accumulate on a day-to-day basis but are not recorded until the end of the period, the word "accrued" is often used in the liability account titles. The word "accrued" distinguishes these liabilities from others, which are created by economic transactions. The use of the word "accrued" is optional, however, and some companies prefer to omit it. Thus, Miller's monthly allocation of $300 for property taxes could be labeled either Accrued Property Taxes Payable or just Property Taxes Payable. Similar labeling options exist for other accrued items.

Payroll Liabilities

The accounting for accrued rent, utilities, and interest is exactly the same as for property taxes. However, the accounting for salaries and related payroll taxes is somewhat more complex, primarily because every business is legally required to withhold certain taxes from employees' salaries.

Very few people receive their full salary as take-home pay. For example, an employee who earns $25,000 a year would probably take home between $15,000 and $20,000. The balance would be withheld by the employer to pay the employee's federal and state income taxes, social security (FICA) taxes, and other voluntary or contractual withholdings that the employee has authorized (such as union dues, medical insurance premiums, and charitable contributions). Thus, the accounting entry to record the liability

social security (FICA) taxes *Federal Insurance Contributions Act taxes imposed on employee and employer; used mainly to provide retirement benefits*

for an employee's monthly salary (computed as one-twelfth of $25,000) might be

Salary and Wages Expense....................	2,083.34	
FICA Taxes Payable—John Doe		125.00
State Withholding Taxes Payable.....................		166.67
Federal Withholding Taxes Payable....................		375.00
Union Dues Payable		50.00
Salary and Wages Payable		1,366.67

To record John Doe's salary expense for July.

All of the credit amounts (which are arbitrary in this example) are liabilities that must be paid by the employer to the federal and state governments, the union, and the employee.

In addition to serving as a government agent by collecting employee taxes, companies must also pay certain payroll-related taxes on each employee. The two most common payroll taxes levied on corporations are the employer's portion of the FICA taxes (an amount equal to the employee's portion) and state and federal unemployment taxes. These taxes are included in the operating expenses of a business, and an illustrative entry to record the payroll taxes relating to John Doe would be

Payroll Tax Expense	195.65	
FICA Taxes Payable—Employer.........................		125.00
Federal Unemployment Taxes Payable....................		14.41
State Unemployment Taxes Payable.....................		56.24

To record the payroll tax liabilities associated with John Doe for July.

Again, the numbers in this entry are arbitrary and were chosen for illustrative purposes only. The eight different liabilities listed in the above two entries for payroll would be eliminated as payments are made. The entries to account for the payments would be

FICA Taxes Payable	250.00	
Federal Withholding Taxes Payable	375.00	
Federal Unemployment Taxes Payable	14.41	
Cash		639.41

Paid July federal withholding and payroll taxes on John Doe.

State Withholding Taxes Payable	166.67	
State Unemployment Taxes Payable	56.24	
Cash		222.91

Paid July state withholding and payroll taxes on John Doe.

Union Dues Payable	50.00	
Cash		50.00

Paid July union dues for John Doe.

Salaries and Wages Payable	1,366.67	
Cash		1,366.67

Paid July salary to John Doe.

If you are interested in learning more about payroll accounting, you should read the Supplement to this chapter.

Noncash Current Liabilities

Noncash current liabilities are obligations to perform future services or to supply goods. The most common noncash performance obligations are due to advances from customers (sometimes called unearned revenues) and warranties or guarantees. With advances from customers, the company has an obligation to ship a product or perform a service. With warranties, the company has to repair or replace defective parts of merchandise sold.

To illustrate advances, we assume that Jason Company pays Miller $300 for goods to be shipped in the future. Miller thus has a liability until the time of shipment. When the goods are shipped, revenue is earned and the liability is eliminated. The entry to record this advance from Jason would be

```
Cash ......................................          300
     Advances from Customers (liability)......................          300
Received an advance payment from Jason Company.
```

When the goods are delivered, the liability is eliminated with the following entry.

```
Advances from Customers (liability) ...........          300
     Sales Revenue  .......................................          300
To recognize revenue on the shipment of goods to Jason Company.
```

The performance liability created when a firm offers a warranty or guarantee involves a similar recording process. For example, some major automobile manufacturers offer a 12,000-mile, 12-month warranty on new cars. Because warranties create obligations to perform repair services free of charge, they must be recognized as current liabilities at the time of sale. Obviously, the amount of a warranty liability can only be estimated since the actual repair expenditures will not be known until the services have been performed. Accounting principles require that a period's expenses be matched with its revenues, and so it is better to make a timely but somewhat imprecise estimate than to record no expense at all. A typical warranty liability entry would be

```
Warranty Expense.........................        15,000
     Provision for Warranties ..............................        15,000
Estimated warranty costs on 1980 sales.
```

The credit entry, Provision for Warranties, is a current liability. When actual expenses are incurred in servicing the warranties, the liability is eliminated with the following type of entry.

```
Provision for Warranties ...................        15,000
     Cash ...............................................        10,000
     Wages Payable (to service employees) ....................         4,000
     Supplies ...........................................         1,000
Paid service costs of the warranties.
```

This entry shows that supplies, labor, and cash were required to honor the warranty agreement.

Contingent Liabilities

contingent liability   *a potential obligation, dependent upon the occurrence of future events*

In addition to actual obligations to pay cash or perform services, a company often has potential obligations to do so. These contingent liabilities are usually tied to the occurrence of some future event, and so are paid only when that event takes place (if it does). Examples of liabilities that qualify as contingent liabilities are notes receivable discounted with recourse (for which the payee is obligated to pay if the maker of the note defaults), lawsuits (in which the company is obligated to pay if the lawsuit is lost), and cosigned notes (for which the company is obligated to pay if the signer does not). Potential obligations that qualify as contingent liabilities can be recorded as actual liabilities, disclosed in the notes to the financial statements, or ignored, depending on their materiality and probability of occurrence.

TO SUMMARIZE   Current liabilities are obligations that can reasonably be expected to be paid or satisfied within one year or during the normal operating cycle. The most common types of current liabilities are (1) accounts payable; (2) notes payable; (3) accrued liabilities, including payroll-related liabilities; and (4) obligations to perform future services. Contingent liabilities are potential obligations, which will be paid only if specific future events occur.

Analyzing Current Assets and Current Liabilities

current (working capital) ratio   *a measure of the liquidity of a business; equal to current assets divided by current liabilities*

Current assets and current liabilities have been discussed separately. However, it is important to consider these accounts together because that is how management and investors usually examine them when planning and evaluating short-run strategy and liquidity. The relationship between these accounts is best analyzed in terms of working capital, which is the excess of total current assets over total current liabilities (see Chapter 7), and the current, or working capital, ratio, which is current assets divided by current liabilities. For example, if total current assets are $500,000 and total current liabilities are $200,000, working capital is $300,000 and the current ratio is 2.5, or $500,000/$200,000. The concepts of working capital and current ratio are extremely important because they probably provide the best single barometer of a company's liquidity, as well as of the shrewdness with which current assets have been managed. If a current ratio is too low, investors and creditors may fear that a company will have difficulty meeting its current obligations. If a current ratio is too high, they may be concerned that management is not taking sufficient advantage of current assets that could be reinvested in the business and earn a higher return. Because the current ratio is closely monitored, there is great pressure on businesses to maintain ratios close to an industry average. These averages vary from industry to industry and are usually taken to indicate the most efficient level of operations.

acid-test (quick) ratio *a measure of the liquidity of a business; equal to cash plus short-term investments and receivables divided by current liabilities*

Another ratio often used to measure a firm's liquidity is the acid-test, or quick, ratio. It is defined as cash, accounts receivable, and short-term investments divided by total current liabilities. Since the numerator of the ratio excludes inventory and prepaid expenses, the ratio measures a firm's ability to meet its current obligations with cash and near-cash items. In those industries with large inventories that turn over slowly, the acid-test ratio is probably a better barometer of liquidity than the working capital ratio.

CHAPTER REVIEW

Current assets and current liabilities include those accounts that are of a short-term nature. Some current assets are cash, short-term investments, accounts receivable, notes receivable, inventories, and prepaid expenses. Current liabilities include accounts payable, notes payable, accrued liabilities, payroll taxes, and obligations to perform future services.

Cash is the most liquid of all current assets. Therefore, stringent procedures for controlling cash must be established and maintained. Most cash is kept in bank accounts, which are reconciled each month. One exception is the petty-cash fund, which is maintained to meet small, miscellaneous expenditures.

A note receivable is an unconditional written promise to pay a sum of money on or before a future specified date. Notes receivable are usually interest-bearing and the interest equals principal times the interest rate times the time period of the note. Notes can be discounted at a bank or other financial institution. Discounting allows the original payee of a note to receive money prior to the maturity date.

Prepaid expenses are payments made for goods or services in advance of their use. Common prepaid expenses are insurance, rent, and interest. Office supplies purchased prior to their use are sometimes included as prepaid expenses. Prepaid expenses must be adjusted at year-end so that the related asset and expense accounts will be properly stated.

Accounting for current liabilities is similar to accounting for current assets. Notes payable are the reverse of notes receivable. Accrued liabilities are usually recorded as adjusting entries at the end of an accounting period. Payroll accounting is complicated because of federal and state requirements to withhold employee taxes and to pay both employee and employer taxes. Contingent liabilities are potential obligations tied to the occurrence of some future event. Contingent liabilities can be included with other liabilities on the Balance Sheet, disclosed in the footnotes to the financial statements, or ignored, depending on their materiality and probability of occurrence.

Current assets and current liabilities are considered together by managers, investors, and creditors in their financial planning and analyses. Working capital, which is total current assets less total current liabilities, and the related current and acid-test ratios are measures of the liquidity of a firm.

KEY TERMS AND CONCEPTS

accounts payable (269)
accounts receivable (263)
accrued liability (270)
acid-test (quick) ratio (274)
bank reconciliation (262)
Cash Over and Short (259)
contingent liability (273)
current assets (256)
current liabilities (268)
current ratio (273)
discount (266)

discount period (266)
discount rate (266)
discounting a note receivable (265)
imprest petty-cash fund (258)
interest (264)
interest rate (264)
lapping (257)
liquidity (256)
maker (264)
maturity date (264)
maturity value (265)

note payable (269)
note receivable (264)
NSF check (260)
payee (264)
petty-cash fund (258)
prepaid expenses (267)
principal (264)
receivables (263)
recourse (266)
social security (FICA) taxes (270)
unearned revenues (272)
working capital (255)

DISCUSSION QUESTIONS

1. Why do companies usually have more control features for cash than for other assets?

2. What are three generally practiced controls for cash and what are their purposes?

3. What is an imprest petty-cash fund, and why is it important that petty cash be handled this way?

4. What are the major reasons that the balance of a bank statement is usually different from the Cash book balance (Cash per the General Ledger)?

5. Why don't the additions and deductions from the bank balance on a bank reconciliation require adjustment by the company?

6. What is the difference between a note receivable and an account receivable?

7. Why would a company accept a non-interest-bearing note?

8. What is the difference between an asset and an expense?

9. What information is conveyed by the "current" and "quick" ratios?

10. Why are obligations to perform services considered liabilities?

11. What types of financial statement disclosures are required for contingent liabilities?

12. Which payroll-related taxes are usually paid by employers and which are usually paid by employees?

EXERCISES

E8-1   Definition of Cash

For each of the following separate cases, compute the amount that would be reported as cash on the Balance Sheet.

1. Balance in general checking account at Bank A, $10,000; IOU from company employee, $200; balance in savings account at Bank C, $2,000; balance in fund which is to be used to repay a bond debt, $7,000; balance in bank account in South Korea, $5,000 (restricted).

2. Cash on hand, $850; petty-cash fund, $250; overdraft in special checking account at Bank A, $100; NSF check for $500; postage stamps, $85; undeposited checks of $1,025.

3. Money orders, $200; certificates of deposit, $5,000; money advanced to company president, $2,000; note receivable left with bank for collection, $2,500.

E8-2   Control for Cash

Jack Kane is an employee of Grow Big Company, a small manufacturing concern. His responsibilities include opening the daily mail, depositing the cash and checks received in the bank, and making the accounting entries to record the receipt of cash and the reduction of receivables.

Explain briefly how Mr. Kane might be able to misuse some of Grow Big's cash receipts. As a consulting accountant, what control procedures would you recommend?

E8–3 Accounting for Petty Cash

The following transactions relating to petty cash were completed by Williams Corporation, a firm with a December 31 year-end.

Dec. 19   Established a petty-cash fund for $25 with check #1135.

20   Paid Great Southern Railroad delivery bill of $24.60 for freight on merchandise purchased—used petty-cash voucher #1.

21   A count of cash in the petty-cash fund revealed $0.50. Replenished the fund with check #1240.

23   Decided to increase the fund permanently to $50 with check #1290.

27   Purchased stamps, $24 (petty-cash voucher #2); paid newspaper carrier, $2.50 (petty-cash voucher #3); purchased office supplies, $21.50 (petty-cash voucher #4).

31   Replenished the fund with check #1335 for $48.00.

Prepare General Journal entries where appropriate.

E8–4 Accounting for Petty Cash

Patty McClintock is interested in setting up a petty-cash fund to handle the small-cash transactions of her new company. She has heard that you have experience in accounting matters and asks you to handle the accounting for the fund. Prepare appropriate journal entries for the following January 1981 transactions.

Jan. 1   Transferred $250 from the checking account to a petty-cash fund.

10   Purchased $10 of postage stamps.

12   Purchased $25 of office supplies.

18   Patty was short of cash and borrowed $50 from the fund for personal use.

19   Replenished the petty-cash fund by depositing a check for $90. (The $90 includes an amount sufficient to make up any discovered shortage.)

31   Permanently reduced the fund to $150.

E8–5 Bank Reconciliation Computations

Jamison Corporation has the following financial information (assume that all receipts and payments are in check form).

March 31, 1981, Bank Reconciliation

Balance per Bank	$12,000
Add Deposits in Transit	2,550
	$14,550
Deduct Outstanding Checks	3,250
Balance per Books	$11,300

April Results	**Per Bank**	**Per Books**
Balance, April 30	$14,220	$17,230
April deposits	8,600	12,500
April checks	12,450	11,650
April note collected by bank	1,000	—
April bank charges	10	—

From the information provided, compute the amount of:

1. Deposits in transit on April 30, 1981.
2. Outstanding checks on April 30, 1981.

E8–6 Bank Reconciliation

The July 1981 bank statement for Berg Corporation shows an ending cash balance of $7,642. The cash balance in Berg's books is $7,526 at the end of July. Based on the following items, prepare a bank reconciliation for Berg for the month of July.

1. Deposit of July 31 not recorded on bank statement—$1,052.

2. Checks outstanding as of July 31—$658.

3. Non-interest-bearing note collected by bank not yet recorded in the books—$1,000.

4. A check written for $750 was improperly recorded as $75 in the books.

5. Bank service charges not recorded in the books—$15.

6. Automatic deposit by Jason Caloma, a customer—$200.

E8–7 Bank Reconciliation

From the following information for Baker Manufacturing Company, prepare a bank reconciliation and any journal entries needed to adjust the Cash account as of August 31, 1981.

1. August 1, 1981, cash balance per books—$6,246.

2. Net increase in cash balance per books for the month of August—$2,039.

3. Balance per bank statement as of August 31, 1981—$7,887.

4. Deposits in transit as of the end of August—$2,649.

5. Checks outstanding as of August 31, 1981—$2,355.

6. Bank improperly recorded a $650 deposit by Baker as $560.

7. A check of $45 payable to the EmCo Trucking Company for delivery charges was mistakenly recorded in the books at $54.

8. Bank service charges—$23.

E8–8 Bank Reconciliation

Using the following information, prepare a bank reconciliation for Wilcox Company at September 30, 1981, and make any necessary adjusting journal entries.

1. At September 30, cash per books was $17,798; per bank statement, $16,427.
2. Deposits in transit totaled $2,122.
3. Service charges for the month were $38.
4. Checks outstanding: #284 for $548, #291 for $607, and #293 for $496.
5. NSF check—Jesse James, $378.
6. Among the checks returned by the bank was a check paid in error by the bank for $484 after Wilcox Company had issued a stop payment and had voided the check in the cash disbursements journal.

E8–9 Bank Reconciliation

Wilson Company has just received the September 30, 1981, bank statement summarized in the following schedule.

	Charges	Deposits	Balance
Balance, September 1			$ 5,100
Deposits recorded during September		$27,000	32,100
Checks cleared during September	$27,300		4,800
NSF Check—J. J. Jones	50		4,750
Bank Service Charges	10		4,760
Balance, September 30			4,760

Cash on hand (booked but not deposited) on September 1 and September 30 amounted to $200. There were no deposits in transit or checks outstanding at September 1, 1981. The Cash account for September reflected the following.

Cash

Sept. 1 balance ...	5,300	28,000	...... Sept. checks
Sept. deposits	29,500		

Answer the following questions. (Hint: It may be helpful to prepare a complete bank reconciliation.)
1. What is the ending balance per the Cash account before adjustments?
2. What adjustments should be added to the depositor's books?
3. What is the total amount of the deductions from the depositor's books?
4. What is the total amount to be added to the bank's balance?
5. What is the total amount to be deducted from the bank's balance?

E8–10 Bank Reconciliation

On the basis of the following information, prepare a bank reconciliation for Pratt Company.

1. The June 30, 1981, bank statement showed the following.

Balance, June 1	$11,000.00
Canceled Checks	13,904.20
Deposits	16,500.40
Balance, June 30	13,596.20

2. The Cash account showed the following for the month of June.

Balance, June 1	$11,000.00
Debits	22,700.40
Credits	22,886.34
Ending Balance, June 30	10,814.06

3. A service charge on the bank statement was $18.00.
4. Outstanding checks totaled $9,100.14.
5. Deposits in transit totaled $8,000.00.
6. The bank statement reveals that the company's account has been reduced by $100.00. The company had deposited a $100 check from one of its customers, which was subsequently returned to the company's bank and marked "Not Sufficient Funds."
7. The bank collected $1,800 for the company. The company was not aware of this collection until now.

E8–11 Note Receivable—Journal Entries

As the accountant for Music Man Company, prepare General Journal entries for the following events.

Apr. 1 Professor Harold Hill purchased band uniforms costing $8,000 for a small-town band in Indiana on credit terms of 2/10, n/30.

May 1 A letter from Professor Hill included an explanation of his inability to pay immediately and a note promising payment in three months with interest at 7 percent compounded annually.

June 30 A check from Professor Hill was received, which included the total amount of principal and accrued interest.

July 5 The check from Professor Hill was returned by the bank because of insufficient funds.

Dec. 31 Professor Hill seems to have disappeared from the area. The debt was determined to be uncollectable. Ignore interest from June 30 and assume that the allowance method of accounting for bad debts is being used.

E8–12 Discounting Notes Receivable

Assume the same facts as in E8–11, except that on May 31 Music Man Company discounted the note at a local bank at an 8 percent discount rate (with recourse).

1. As the accountant for the company, prepare an appropriate journal entry to record the discounting of the note.

2. Prepare the appropriate entry assuming that at maturity (July 31) Hill defaulted on the note. The bank charges a penalty fee of 0.25 percent of maturity value for all defaulted notes discounted with recourse.

E8–13 Discounting Notes Receivable

You are the accountant for Lowe Finance Company. The following transactions and events occurred in June 1981 and 1982.

1981: June 1   Lowe made a $15,000 loan to Henry Leggs, who signed a note promising to pay the loan plus interest at 9 percent in one year.

June 16   Due to excessive loans made in the month of June, Lowe Finance discounted Mr. Leggs' note at a local bank at 12 percent (with recourse).

1982: June 1   The local bank notified Lowe of the default by Mr. Leggs and demanded immediate payment of the principal, accrued interest, and a $50 penalty fee.

July 1   Lowe collected the entire receivable from Mr. Leggs plus 9 percent interest on the receivable, interest, and the penalty fee from June 1, 1982.

1. Prepare journal entries for the above, assuming a a 360-day year.

2. Should any disclosure of the discounted liability on the note be made on Lowe Finance Company's financial statements for December 31, 1981? If so, what type of disclosure?

E8–14 Accounting for Prepaid Expenses

During 1981 Jagger Corporation had the following transactions.

Apr. 1   Purchased a 2-year fire insurance policy for $600; policy effective immediately.

June 30   Purchased on account (on credit) office supplies costing $150.

July 10   Paid the $150 due for the June 30 purchase of supplies.

Sept. 30   Paid the $15,000 annual rent for the warehouse and plant facilities. (The rental payment covers the period of October 1, 1981, to October 1, 1982.)

Assuming that Jagger Corporation's fiscal year ends March 31, prepare:

1. Journal entries for all of the transactions.

2. The adjusting entries as of March 31, 1982.

Assume that Jagger Corporation originally classifies all prepaid expenses as assets. On March 31, 1982, there were $45 worth of office supplies on hand.

E8–15 Accounting for Prepaid Expenses

With the information and transactions described in E8–14, prepare original journal entries and adjusting entries for Jagger Corporation based upon the following two assumptions.

1. Jagger Corporation originally records all prepayments as expenses.

2. Jagger Corporation records all prepayments as both assets and expenses. The original entries are made this way in order to eliminate the need for adjusting entries whenever possible.

E8–16 Accounting for Prepaid Expenses

1. On December 31, 1981, the following information is available.

Office supplies on hand, January 1, 1981	$ 5,000
1981 cash purchases of office supplies	50,000
1981 credit purchases of office supplies	150,000
Office supplies on hand, December 31, 1981	25,000

(a) What is the total office supplies expense for 1981?

(b) Give the adjusting entry on December 31, 1981, assuming that Office Supplies Expense was debited for all purchases.

(c) Give the adjusting entry on December 31, 1981, assuming that Office Supplies on Hand was debited for all purchases.

2. On September 1, 1980, a 3-year insurance premium of $1,080 was paid. At the time of payment, Prepaid Insurance was debited for the full amount. Give the December 31, 1981, adjusting entry.

E8–17 Accounts and Notes Payable

Jimbo Bubble Gum Company purchases raw materials on credit with terms of 2/10, n/30. Occasionally, a short-term note payable is executed to obtain cash for current operations. The following two transactions were selected from the many 1981 transactions for your analysis.

August 10, 1981   Purchased materials on credit, $7,000; terms, 2/10, n/30. (Assume that the company uses a periodic inventory system.)

August 31, 1981   Borrowed $15,000 cash from a local bank in return for a six-month note with 8 percent annual interest payable at maturity.

1. Prepare the original journal entry for each of the foregoing transactions.

2. Prepare an entry to record the payment of the August 10 account payable within the discount period.

3. Prepare the same entry as in (2) but assume that the payment was not made within the discount period.

4. Prepare the entry to record the accrued interest on the $15,000 note as of December 31, 1981.

5. Prepare the entry to record the payment of the note in (4) plus interest at maturity.

E8–18   Accounting for Notes Payable

Blue Corporation borrowed $4,000 on a 9 percent, 1-year note dated October 1, 1981. Its annual accounting period ends on December 31. Give entries on the following dates (assuming that all interest is paid on September 30, 1982): October 1, 1981, December 31, 1981, and September 30, 1982.

E8–19   Accrued Liabilities (Including Simple Payroll Entries)

December 31, 1981, is a Thursday. As the accountant for B.I.G. Industries, you are to make all necessary adjusting journal entries on that date. The following information (assume a calendar year) is available.

1. B.I.G. Industries pays salaries weekly, with the payroll for the five-day workweek distributed on the following Monday. The payroll is fairly consistent from week to week and usually includes the following items and amounts.

Salaries Expense	$80,000
Income Taxes Withheld from Employees	16,000
FICA Taxes Withheld from Employees	4,800
Union Dues Withheld from Employees	300
Cash Distributed	58,900

2. On November 1, 1981, rent revenue of $5,000 was collected in advance. The payment was for the period November 1, 1981, to October 31, 1982, on an apartment held as an investment. The original entry included a credit to Unearned Rent Revenue for the full amount of the cash received.

3. Assume the same facts as in (2), except that the credit in the original entry was to Rent Revenue instead of Unearned Rent Revenue.

E8–20   Accounting for Warranties

Jim E. Carter, president of Reliable Television Stores, has been concerned recently with declining sales due to increased competition in the area. Jim has noticed that many of the national stores selling television sets and appliances have been placing heavy emphasis in their marketing programs on warranties. In an effort to revitalize his sales, Jim has decided to offer free service and repairs for one year as a warranty on his television sets. Based on past experience, Jim has incurred first-year service and repair costs on his television sets of approximately 5 percent of sales. The first month of operations following the initiation of Jim's new marketing plan showed significant increases in sales of TV sets. Total sales of TV sets for the first three months under the warranty plan were $10,000, $8,000, and $12,000, respectively.

1. Assuming that Jim prepares adjusting entries and financial statements for his own use at the end of each month, prepare the appropriate entry to recognize warranty expense for each of these first three months.

2. Prepare the appropriate entry to record services provided to repair sets under warranty in the second month, assuming that the following costs were incurred: labor (paid in cash), $550; supplies, $330.

E8–21   Current and Acid-Test Ratios

As a financial analyst, you are interested in the liquidity position of Orton Tool Company. The following Balance Sheet shows the financial position of Orton Tool Company as of December 31, 1981.

Orton Tool Company
Balance Sheet as of December 31, 1981

Assets

Current Assets:			
Cash		$ 30,900	
Accounts Receivable		1,800	
Inventory		55,100	
Prepaid Insurance		2,000	
Total Current Assets			$ 89,800
Property, Plant, and Equipment:			
Land		$150,000	
Plant and Equipment	$559,700		
Less Accumulated Depreciation	100,000	459,700	
Total Property, Plant, and Equipment			609,700
Other Assets:			
Land Held as Investment			25,000
Total Assets			$724,500

Liabilities and Stockholders' Equity

Current Liabilities:

Accounts Payable	$ 34,000	
Property Taxes Payable	4,500	
Accrued Wages Payable	6,000	
Total Current Liabilities		$ 44,500

Long-Term Liabilities:

Notes Payable	200,000	
Total Liabilities		$244,500

Stockholders' Equity:

Capital Stock, par $10 (40,000 shares)................	$400,000	
Paid-in Capital in Excess of Par..................	50,000	
Retained Earnings	30,000	480,000
Total Liabilities and Stockholders' Equity		$724,500

1. Based on the information provided in this Balance Sheet, compute the following.

    (a) Working capital

    (b) Current ratio

    (c) Acid-test ratio

2. Assuming that the average current ratio in Orton's industry is approximately 1.5, evaluate the company's current position.

E8–22 Payroll Accounting (Supplement)

IMB Corporation has four employees, W, X, Y, and Z. During 1981, these employees made $22,000, $30,000, $26,000, and $40,000, respectively. During 1981, the FICA tax rate is 6 percent of the first $27,000, federal and state unemployment taxes (FUTA and SUTA) are 0.7 and 2.7 percent of the first $6,000, respectively, and the employees paid federal and state income taxes as follows:

Employee	Federal Income Tax	State Income Tax
W	$ 3,500	$ 700
X................	4,600	900
Y...............	2,500	500
Z...............	5,100	1,000
Totals	$15,700	$3,100

Given this information, record the following entries for the full year.

1. Salaries expense.

2. Employer's payroll taxes.

3. Payment of salaries to employees.

4. Payment of all payroll-related taxes and withholdings.

E8–23 Payroll Accounting (Supplement)

Johnson Electric Company has three employees, John Baker, Max Able, and Mary Johnson. Summaries of their 1981 salaries and withholdings are as follows:

Employee	Gross Salary	Federal Income Taxes Withheld	State Income Taxes Withheld
John Baker	$ 40,000	$ 4,200	$ 600
Max Able	36,000	2,800	500
Mary Johnson	39,000	4,600	700
Totals...............	$115,000	$11,600	$1,800

Also during 1981, the FICA and Unemployment Tax rates were

FICA tax rate	7 percent of first $30,000
FUTA tax rate	0.7 percent of first $ 6,000
SUTA tax rate	2.7 percent of first $ 6,000

Given this information, record for Johnson Electric the following summary entries for 1981.

1. Salaries expense.

2. Employer's payroll taxes.

3. Payment of salaries to employees.

4. Payment of all appropriate payroll liabilities to the state.

5. Payment of all appropriate payroll liabilities to the federal government.

PROBLEMS

P8–1   Definition of Cash

Required:

1. Determine which of the following items should be included in the cash balance of a company.
   (a) Check returned by bank (NSF).
   (b) Postage stamps.
   (c) IOUs signed by employees.
   (d) Money orders on hand (made payable to the company).
   (e) Petty cash on hand.
   (f) Deposit made with a utility company.
   (g) Deposit in a foreign bank (unrestricted).
   (h) Postdated checks.
   (i) Money advanced to officers.
   (j) Note receivable left with bank for collection.
   (k) Bank account balance at City Bank.
   (l) Checks payable to the company.
2. State how each of the noncash items would be accounted for.

P8–2   Accounting for Petty Cash

The Johnson Company uses an imprest petty-cash fund to pay for small, miscellaneous expenditures.

Required:

1. Assuming that you are the accountant, prepare the necessary journal entries to record the following events.
   (a) Establishment of a petty-cash fund of $1,000 on January 1, 1981.
   (b) On January 12, a disbursement of $65 is made to Coca-Cola to pay for office drinks.
   (c) On January 15, $30 is taken from the fund to pay for postage stamps.
   (d) On January 18, because the company is short of cash, $600 of the fund is used to meet payroll expenses.
   (e) On January 25, with the company cash position restored, the petty-cash fund is replenished.
   (f) On January 26, it is decided that only $500 is needed in the fund, and it is reduced accordingly.
2. **Interpretive Question** Explain why a petty-cash fund should be handled on an imprest basis.
3. **Interpretive Question** Explain why one person is usually given complete responsibility for handling a petty-cash fund. Doesn't that make it easy to steal from the fund?

P8–3   Bank Reconciliation

Eldon Company has just received the following monthly bank statement for June.

Date	Debits	Credits	Balance
June 1			$25,000
2	$ 150		24,850
3		$ 6,000	30,850
4	750		30,100
5	1,500		28,600
7	8,050		20,550
9		8,000	28,550
10	3,660		24,890
11	2,690		22,200
12		9,000	31,200
13	550		30,650
17	7,500		23,150
20		5,500	28,650
21	650		28,000
22	700		27,300
23		4,140[†]	31,440
25	1,000		30,440
31	50*		30,390
Total	$27,250	$32,640	

* Bank service charge.
[†] Note collected, including $140 interest.

The Cash account of Eldon Company for June is as follows:

Cash

June 1 Balance....	20,440	Checks written:		
Deposits:		1,500	..........June 1	
June 2	6,000	8,500	....	4
5	8,000	2,690	....	6
10	9,000	550	....	8
18	5,500	7,500	....	9
30	6,000	650	....	12
	34,500	700	....	19
		1,000	....	22
		1,300	....	26
		1,360	....	27
		25,750		

At the end of May, Eldon had four checks outstanding for a total of $4,560. All four checks were processed by the bank during June. There were no deposits outstanding at the end of May. It was discovered during the reconciliation process that a check for $8,050 written on June 4 for supplies was improperly recorded on the books at $8,500. The imprest petty-cash fund balance is $500, of which $200 has been spent and is evidenced by petty-cash vouchers.

Required:

1. Determine the amount of deposits in transit at the end of June.
2. Determine the amount of outstanding checks at the end of June.

3. Prepare a June bank reconciliation.

4. Prepare the journal entries to correct the Cash account.

5. **Interpretive Question** Why is it important that the Cash account be reconciled on a timely basis?

P8–4 Bank Reconciliation

The records of Pertech Corporation show the following information for December.

Bank Statement Information

a.	Bank Balance, December 31	$43,700
b.	Service charges for December.............	25
c.	Rent collected by bank	500
d.	Note receivable collected by bank (including $150 interest)	1,150
e.	December check returned marked NSF (check was a payment of an account receivable).............................	100
f.	Bank erroneously reduced Pertech's account for a check written by the Pert Company	500
g.	Cash account balance, December 31	40,600
h.	Outstanding checks......................	4,600
i.	Deposits in transit	2,500

1. Prepare a bank reconciliation for December. Other than the error identified in (f) above, the bank statement has been verified to be correct.

2. Prepare the entry to correct the cash account as of December 31.

3. **Interpretive Question** Why is it important for you to know that the bank statement was verified as correct?

P8–5 Discounting Notes Receivable

On May 1, 1981, Grover Company sold $5,000 of merchandise to Jim Dandy on credit terms of 2/10, n/30. On June 1, 1981, Jim Dandy was unable to pay the $5,000. Instead, Grover Company agreed to accept a 90-day note for $5,000 at 15 percent. On July 15, Grover needed cash and decided to discount the note at 20 percent at a local bank. Upon maturity of the note, Jim Dandy defaulted and the bank subsequently collected from Grover the amount due plus a $10 handling fee. A month later, Grover decided that the debt was uncollectable and wrote it off.

Required:

1. Prepare journal entries to record in Grover Company's books the following.
   (a) Sale of the merchandise (assume a periodic inventory system).
   (b) Acceptance of the note.
   (c) Discounting of the note.
   (d) Payment to the bank upon default.

(e) Write-off of Jim Dandy account (assume Grover uses the allowance method of recording bad-debt expense).

2. How would you account for the transaction if Jim Dandy six months later paid $5,197.50?

3. **Interpretive Question** How would Grover Company account for the note during the period July 15 to the maturity date?

P8–6 Discounting Notes Receivable

Required:

1. Record the following transactions in General Journal form in the books of Home Drilling Company. Assume that Home Drilling closes its books monthly.

March 1	Sold 100 barrels of oil to Shellaco Oil for $2,000, terms 2/10, n/30 (periodic inventory system).
March 12	Accepted a $2,000, 90-day, 10 percent note from Shellaco Oil in payment of its account.
April 11	Discounted the note with recourse at the bank at a 14 percent discount rate.
June 10	On the maturity date of the note, Shellaco Oil paid the amount due.
June 15	Notified by bank that Shellaco Oil defaulted; the check was returned marked NSF. Give the necessary entries in Home's books to record its payment of the note to the bank.
June 30	Wrote off the Shellaco note as uncollectable.

2. **Interpretive Question** Why did Home have to pay off Shellaco's note?

3. How would the note receivable have been accounted for on Home's April 30 financial statements?

4. How would Home account for the note if on July 7, Shellaco paid the amount in full?

P8–7 Accounting for Payables and Prepaid Expenses

Required:

1. Prepare journal entries to record the following events in the books of Joe's Drug Store.
   (a) On January 17, 1981, Joe purchased $500 of drugs for resale. The terms of payment were 2/10, n/30. A perpetual inventory system is used.
   (b) On March 1, 1981, Joe paid the semiannual interest on a $1,000, 9 percent, 2-year note. The note had been outstanding since September 1, 1980, and an adjusting entry for the 1980 interest expense had been made on December 31, 1980.
   (c) On March 16, 1981, Joe paid the full $500 due on the January drug purchase.

(d) On April 1, 1981, Joe paid $2,000 of insurance premiums, effective immediately, to cover his delivery truck for a full year. (Any prepayments are generally recorded as assets by Joe.)

(e) On September 1, 1981, Joe paid semiannual interest on the 9 percent $1,000 note.

(f) On December 31, 1981, properly record:

(1) Accrual of interest expense on the note payable.

(2) Accrual of salary expense, assuming that salaried employees are paid every Monday for the previous week's work. This year, December 31 is a Wednesday. The weekly payroll totals $5,000. (Assume that there are no voluntary or involuntary withholdings and that employees work a 5-day workweek starting Monday.)

(3) The appropriate insurance expense on the delivery truck.

(4) Accrual of annual property taxes of $4,000 for the period ending June 30, 1982. (Assume that no other accrual entries have been made for property taxes during 1981.)

2. The insurance paid for in item (d) could have been recorded in two other ways. Show these other possible entries.

P8–8 Unifying Problem: Payables, Prepaid Expenses, and Their Effect on Net Income, Total Liabilities, and Total Assets

Jensen Bookkeeping Agency is making adjusting entries on December 31.

Required:

1. Prepare the necessary December 31 adjusting entries in General Journal form to account for the following transactions.

(a) Weekly salaries total $1,500 for a five-day workweek and are payable on Fridays. December 31 of the current year is a Thursday. (Ignore payroll taxes.)

(b) The firm paid $3,600 for a 2-year insurance policy on September 1 of the current year, effective the same date. The entire amount of the premium was debited to Prepaid Insurance and no subsequent adjustments have been made.

(c) During December, Jensen provided $2,000 worth of bookkeeping services to clients whom it will bill on January 2.

(d) The prior year's property tax expense was $2,000. The tax assessment for the current year (January 1 through December 31) has not yet been received, and no amount had been recorded for this year's expense. It is estimated that the assessment will be 30 percent higher this year.

(e) In December, Jensen received $500 to complete a tax return for Art Jacobs. At the time the money was received, Cash was debited and Service Fees Revenue credited. The tax work will be performed in January.

(f) The Supplies on Hand account has a balance of $960 on December 31. However, $200 of supplies purchased on December 21 were debited to Supplies Expense, which now has a balance of $200 for the year. A count of supplies on December 31 indicates that $970 of supplies are still on hand.

(g) On September 1, Jensen borrowed $3,000 from the City National Bank at 12 percent for one year. Record the accrued interest as of December 31.

(h) Jensen's lease calls for rent at $200 per month to be paid in advance on the first of each month. The next payment is due January 1 of next year.

(i) The agency estimates that its utility expense for December will be $90.

2. If, before considering these adjustments, Jensen had a reported net income of $60,000, what would the agency's correct income be for the year?

3. How much would liabilities have been understated if the foregoing adjusting entries had not been made?

4. **Interpretive Question**   How do you explain the fact that the understatement of liabilities is greater than the resulting decrease in net income?

P8–9   Unifying Problem: Current Assets and Current Liabilities

Miranda Corporation is applying to the First National Bank for a loan. As part of the application, Miranda provided the following Balance Sheet.

Miranda Corporation
Balance Sheet as of December 31, 1981

Assets

Cash...........................	$ 6,000	
Accounts Receivable	14,000	
Inventory........................	45,000	
Prepaid Insurance	9,000	
Total Current Assets		$ 74,000
All Other Assets...................		193,000
Total Assets		$267,000

Liabilities and Stockholders' Equity

Accounts Payable..................	$13,000	
Short-Term Notes Payable...........	8,000	
Income Taxes Payable	6,000	
Total Current Liabilities..........		$ 27,000
Long-Term Bonds Payable...........		100,000
Stockholders' Equity		140,000
Total Liabilities and Stockholders' Equity		$267,000

In reviewing the Balance Sheet, the First National Bank computed Miranda's current ratio and agrees that it meets the bank's minimum established criterion of 2 to 1 for making loans. However, to be safe, the bank decides to audit Miranda's books to see if they are accurate. During the audit, the following information is discovered.

a. The Cash account includes $3,000 that was restricted for the purpose of retiring the bonds in six years.

b. $5,000 of the accounts receivable are over 200 days old and should be written off as uncollectable. Miranda also does not maintain an Allowance for Doubtful Accounts account. The auditor believes that 2 percent of the remaining receivables is a good estimate of the amount that will be uncollectable.

c. The inventory contains $22,000 of damaged or obsolete inventory that has no value.

d. No interest has been accrued on either the short-term note or the bonds payable. The short-term note is an 8 percent note that has been outstanding for six months and three months' interest has accrued on the 10 percent bonds.

e. Accrued wages totaling $2,000 should have been recorded. (Ignore payroll taxes.)

f. Accrued property taxes totaling $2,500 should have been recorded.

g. The prepaid insurance was purchased on May 1 and is a 2-year policy on the office building. The $9,000 represents the total cost of the policy.

Required:

1. Make the necessary General Journal entries to account for the new information discovered by the auditor.

2. Prepare a new Balance Sheet (in the same format) for Miranda Corporation.

3. Compute Miranda's old and new current ratios.

4. **Interpretive Question** State why you would or would not make the loan to Miranda.

P8–10 Payroll Accounting (Supplement)

Lexington Bank has three employees, Mrs. T, Miss V, and Mr. W. During July 1981, these three employees made $2,500, $3,000, and $3,500, respectively. The following table summarizes their earnings and withholdings to date.

Employee	Annual Salary	Salary Received Through June 30, 1981	Federal Income Tax Withholdings	State Tax Withholdings
Mrs. T ...	$30,000	$15,000	9%	3%
Miss V ...	36,000	18,000	10%	4%
Mr. W ...	42,000	21,000	12%	5%

In addition, during 1981 FICA taxes are 6 percent of the first $20,000 and FUTA and SUTA tax rates are 0.7 percent and 2.7 percent, respectively, of the first $6,000.

Required:

1. Given these data, record the following for July 1981.
   (a) Salaries expense.
   (b) Employer's payroll-tax expenses.
   (c) Payment of salaries.
   (d) Payment of withholdings and payroll taxes.

2. **Interpretive Question** Why were the July FICA taxes so low and why weren't any unemployment taxes paid?

Payroll Accounting

Salaries and the related payroll taxes are major expenses in most businesses. Many large corporations have tens of thousands of employees and labor costs are their largest single operating expense. Accounting for salaries and the related payroll taxes creates several types of current liabilities.

Legislation and Payroll Taxes

Payroll accounting is constantly changing because, almost every year, state and federal governments pass legislation that revises the amounts and the nature of the taxes that employees and employers must pay. Although some payroll-related taxes are paid by employers and some by employees, the employer is responsible for reporting and remitting all payroll taxes to the government. Thus, employers withhold certain taxes from employees' salaries and make timely deposits of these withholdings to the government. Companies that fail to report and remit taxes are subject to severe fines and penalties. Because of these requirements, it is important that companies have accurate and timely systems of accounting for payroll. First we will examine the various kinds of taxes and other items that affect payroll accounting, and then we will study the accounting for these transactions.

FICA (SOCIAL SECURITY) TAXES

The Federal Insurance Contributions Act (FICA), which became effective in 1937, established a national social security program through which older people would be provided with a continuing source of income during their retirement years. Originally, this Act demanded only small taxes from employees, and payments to retired persons were correspondingly small. Thus, it required payment of 1 percent of the first $3,000 of wages. Subsequent Acts, however, have increased the payments, and hence the social security taxes. For example, the 1965 Medicare law raised taxes in order to provide medical protection to individuals 65 and over. The 1977 law again

EXHIBIT 8–6   **Sample FICA Tax Rates and Amounts**

Year	Tax Rate	Salary Base	Maximum Tax Withheld
1937	1.00%	$ 3,000	$ 30
1951	1.50	3,600	54
1959	2.50	4,800	120
1966	4.20	6,600	277
1972	5.20	9,000	468
1975	5.85	14,100	825
1976	5.85	15,300	895
1977	5.85	16,500	965
1978	6.05	17,700	1,071
1979	6.13	22,900	1,404
1980	6.13	25,900	1,588
1981	6.65	29,700	1,975
1982	6.70	31,800	2,131
1983	6.70	33,900	2,271
1984	6.70	36,000	2,412
1985	7.05	38,100	2,686
1986	7.15	40,200	2,874
1987	7.15	42,600	3,046

increased social security taxes and is, in the increases it effected for the following ten years, the single largest peacetime tax increase in the history of the United States. Today, in addition to providing benefits to retirees, social security makes payments to disabled persons and to dependents of deceased workers.

The current FICA tax rate schedule (established in December 1977), together with a sample of those used in previous years, is shown in Exhibit 8–6. FICA taxes have increased dramatically in recent years. Approximately 31 percent of all federal receipts now come from FICA taxes. Because of these high rates, there is considerable political pressure to reduce some of the tax rates that were established in 1977.

In computing FICA taxes, an employer multiplies the current rate by the salary earned, up to the current yearly ceiling. The product is the amount of taxes to be paid by the employee and matched by the employer. For example, an employee who earned $28,000 in 1980 paid FICA taxes of $1,588 (6.13% × $25,900) and the employer paid an equal amount. Had the employee made only $20,000, the FICA tax payments would have been $1,226 (6.13% × $20,000) for both the employee and employer. Thus, you see that there are maximum bases beyond which these taxes are not paid. Once an employee's salary goes above the base, FICA taxes are no longer withheld and paid on the excess. In paying the FICA taxes, employers deduct the employee's portion of the tax from their paychecks and remit it, together with the company's share, to the federal government. Self-employed persons also pay FICA taxes, but at rates approximately $1\frac{1}{2}$ times higher than those of employed persons.

Obviously, these scheduled FICA tax rates are subject to change. Taxpayers appear to be becoming less tolerant of heavy tax burdens. In addition, many businesspeople and government leaders feel that because the number of retired persons is increasing while the work force remains fairly stable, major changes in the structure of the social security system are necessary if it is to remain solvent. A likely change might involve differential FICA payments for employers and employees, with the employer paying a higher tax.

FEDERAL AND STATE INCOME TAXES

In addition to FICA taxes, employees must also pay federal and state income taxes. Although these taxes are actually paid by employees, it is the employer who is responsible for making the payment with regard to salary income. By law, employers are required to withhold income taxes from each employee's paycheck and then deposit them directly with the respective state and federal governments. (Governments believe that this system results in a higher compliance rate than if employees were allowed to remit their own taxes.)

The amount of state and federal income tax withheld from each employee's paycheck depends on three factors: income level, marital status, and number of dependents. In general, the higher the income, the higher the percentage of salary that is withheld. Obviously, the lower the income level and the more dependents an employee has, the lower the tax. Presently, federal income tax rates range from 14 to 70 percent of a person's income. States have no standard rates; in fact, a few states have no individual income tax. When a person starts a new job, he or she is required to fill out a W-4 form (Employee's Withholding Allowance Certificate). Along with income level, the information provided on this form—the number of exemptions (dependents) and marital status—determines the amount of income tax to be withheld from an employee's paycheck.

OTHER WITHHOLDINGS

In addition to withholding the FICA and federal and state income taxes from an employee's paycheck, employers may be authorized by an employee to withhold other amounts. The most common types of nontax withholdings are payments for life or medical insurance coverage, contributions to firm retirement plans, company credit union payments, purchases of savings bonds, union dues, and contributions to charitable organizations (such as United Way). Of course, once a firm withholds amounts from an employee's paycheck, it has an obligation to make prompt payment on behalf of the employee.

FEDERAL AND STATE UNEMPLOYMENT TAXES

Another kind of payroll tax is the unemployment tax levied on employers by both federal and state governments. Federal unemployment taxes (FUTA) are used by the federal government primarily to pay the administrative costs of unemployment programs. Only a small percentage of these taxes is paid out directly as unemployment compensation. The present FUTA rate is 0.7 percent of the first $6,000 of annual wages paid to each employee.

States use unemployment taxes to make payments to unemployed persons, usually for approximately one year after they become unemployed. Although each state sets its own unemployment tax rate, the rates tend to be similar: about 2.7 percent of the first $6,000 of annual wages paid to each employee. However, in most states, employers with a good employee-retention record are rewarded with a decrease from the standard 2.7 percent rate.

REPORTING AND REMITTING PAYROLL TAXES TO THE GOVERNMENT

Generally, every employer who is liable for social security tax or who is required to withhold income tax and social security tax from wages must file a quarterly return on Form 941. Employers are also required to make periodic deposits of taxes withheld and payable to a Federal Reserve Bank or authorized commercial bank. The timing and frequency of the deposits depend on the amounts payable. For example, cumulative undeposited taxes exceeding $2,000 by the 7th, 15th, 22nd, or last day of a month must be deposited within 3 banking days. Cumulative undeposited taxes of $200 or more but less than $2,000 at the end of the first or second month of the calendar quarter must be deposited within 15 days after the end of the month. Smaller amounts can be deposited less frequently. Receipts are received for deposits made (Federal Tax Deposit Form 501) and are remitted with Form 941, along with any balance payable.

Federal unemployment taxes are reported annually on Form 940. State unemployment taxes are generally reported on a quarterly basis, although state requirements may differ.

Illustration of Payroll Accounting

To illustrate the accounting for payroll, we assume that, in 1980, three employees of Miller Company, Mr. X, Mr. Y, and Mr. Z, earned $16,200, $24,000, and $32,000, respectively. Table 8–1 summarizes their salary withholding information for the year.

Although these three employees would probably be paid on a semi-monthly basis, for simplicity it is assumed that they are paid only once a year. The debits and credits would be handled in exactly the same manner (not the amounts, of course) no matter how often they were paid.

The entries to account for payroll can be divided into those that recognize the payroll expense and those that record the payments of the payroll-tax liabilities. The entry to record the salary expense for Employees X, Y, and Z is shown on the next page.

Table 8−1   Earnings and Deductions of Three Employees in 1980

Employee	Salary	FICA Base	Unemployment Tax Base	FICA (6.13%)	Federal Withholding	State Withholding	Medical Insurance	United Way	Net Pay
		Taxable Earnings			*Taxes*		*Other Deductions*		
Mr. X	$16,200	$16,200	$ 6,000	$ 993	$ 2,400	$ 600	$ 360	$120	$11,727
Mr. Y	24,000	24,000	6,000	1,471	3,800	925	360	72	17,372
Mr. Z	32,000	25,900	6,000	1,588	5,600	1,330	360	144	22,978
Totals	$72,200	$66,100	18,000	$4,052	$11,800	$2,855	$1,080	$336	$52,077

Salary Expense	72,200	
FICA Taxes Payable—Employees......................		4,052
Federal Income Tax Withholding Payable................		11,800
State Income Tax Withholding Payable..................		2,855
Medical Insurance Payable		1,080
United Way Payable................................		336
Salaries Payable		52,077

To record salary expense for Employees X, Y, and Z for 1980.

In addition to the salary expense, paid partly to the three employees directly, and partly to others on their behalf, the employer must also pay the associated payroll-tax expense, which includes the federal and state unemployment taxes and the employer's share of the FICA taxes. The entry to record these payroll-related taxes would be

Payroll Tax Expense	4,664	
Federal Unemployment Tax Payable ($6,000 × 3 × 0.007)................................		126
State Unemployment Tax Payable ($6,000 × 3 × 0.027)................................		486
FICA Taxes Payable—Employer.........................		4,052

To record the payroll-tax liabilities associated with Employees X, Y, and Z for 1980.

The entries to record the payment of the payroll and payroll-related taxes would be

Salaries Payable...........................	52,077	
Cash		52,077

Paid wages to Employees X, Y, and Z in 1980.

FICA Taxes Payable (2 × $4,052)	8,104	
Federal Income Tax Withholding Payable	11,800	
Federal Unemployment Tax Payable...........	126	
Cash		20,030

Paid federal withholding and payroll taxes on Employees X, Y, and Z for 1980.

State Income Tax Withholding Payable	2,855	
State Unemployment Tax Payable.............	486	
Cash		3,341

Paid state payroll-tax liabilities on Employees X, Y, and Z for 1980.

Medical Insurance Payable   1,080

    Cash   1,080

Paid medical insurance withholdings on Employees X, Y, and Z for 1980.

United Way Payable   336

    Cash   336

Paid contributions to the United Way for Employees X, Y, and Z for 1980.

These payments are all shown as being made at year-end; however, each of the withholdings may have a different payment date depending, to a great extent, on the magnitude of the gross withholdings by the company. As mentioned earlier, companies in which the withholdings involve large amounts of money must make more frequent deposits than those whose withholdings are relatively small.

At the end of each year, the employer summarizes each employee's earnings and tax withholdings on a W-2 form, which is submitted to the government and to the employee (see Exhibit 8–7). Employees must attach a copy of their W-2 forms to their income tax returns as proof of earnings for the year.

EXHIBIT 8–7 W-2 Form

1 Control number		2 Employer's State number			
	222				

3 Employer's name, address, and ZIP code	4 Subtotal ☐ Correction ☐ Void ☐

Grayson Company
13 Main Street
Provo, UT 84601

5 Employer's identification number
13-2473504

6 Advance EIC payment	7

8 Employee's social security number	9 Federal income tax withheld	10 Wages, tips, other compensation	11 FICA tax withheld	12 Total FICA wages
152-64-5986	6250.03	25000.00	1167.50	19000.00

13 Employee's name (first, middle, last) and address	14 Pension plan coverage? Yes/No	15	16 FICA tips
George Rafferty 178 South Emerson Orem, UT 84057	YES		

18 State income tax withheld	19 State wages, tips, etc.	20 Name of state
845.00	25000.00	Utah

21 Local income tax withheld	22 Local wages, tips, etc.	23 Name of locality
100.00	25000.00	UT-R

Copy B To be filed with employee's FEDERAL tax return
This information is being furnished to the Internal Revenue Service.

Form **W–2 Wage and Tax Statement**

Department of the Treasury—Internal Revenue Service

CHAPTER 9

Investments, and Present and Future Value

In order to engage effectively in the sale of goods or services, a company must usually purchase inventories, land, buildings, and equipment. However, a business may also find it advantageous to invest a portion of its available resources in assets not directly related to its primary operations. These may be long-term investments in assets that are expected to contribute to the success of the business—for example, purchasing the business of a key customer. Or they may be long-term investments that independently contribute to earnings. And sometimes they are short-term investments that make use of temporarily idle funds.

investment   an expenditure to acquire assets that are expected to produce future earnings

In general, the higher the potential return on an investment, the riskier the investment. Exhibit 9–1 presents in a general way how this relationship applies to a few types of investments.

The investments shown in Exhibit 9–1 can be either short-term or long-term, depending on how long management intends to hold them. Certainly, a wise investment, if it could be found, would be one that was relatively short-term and provided both low risk and high return. (In recent years, real estate has often been such an investment.)

In this chapter, both short- and long-term investments are discussed. The chapter is divided into three sections: (1) short-term investments, (2) present and future values, and (3) long-term investments. Present and future value concepts and procedures are included because they play an integral part in accounting for long-term investments. They will be essential also to an understanding of material in later chapters.

EXHIBIT 9–1 **A Classification of Investments by Risk and Potential Return**[1]

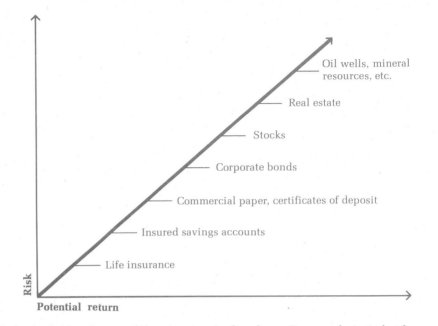

[1] The levels of risk and return of these investments often change. For example, in the last few years, some certificates of deposit have paid higher earnings than many stocks and bonds.

Short-Term Investments

Most businesses are cyclical or seasonal; that is, their cash inflows and outflows vary significantly throughout the year. At certain times (particularly when inventories are being purchased), a company's cash supply is low. At other times (usually during heavy selling seasons), there is excess cash on hand. A typical cash flow pattern for a firm is shown in Exhibit 9–2.

To ensure that there is always cash available to meet current obligations, most firms have a line of credit with their bank. Such an arrangement allows them to borrow up to a certain amount of cash on a short-term basis—usually for less than a year. Thus, companies should maintain only enough cash on hand to meet their average cash needs. Having a line of credit to fall back on also enables firms to invest in long-term high-income-yielding investments when operations generate funds in excess of average cash needs.

Even though a company will try to keep a minimum of cash on hand, it will usually have excess cash at least some time during a year. Because money has a time value and can earn a return, these temporary excesses of cash are usually invested, in some cases for as few as only three or four days. Typical short-term investments include stocks and bonds of other companies, commercial paper (an investment contract at a guaranteed

line of credit *an arrangement whereby a bank agrees to loan an amount of money (up to a certain limit) on demand for short periods of time*

short-term investment *an expenditure for nonoperating assets that a business intends to hold for a short period of time, usually less than a year*

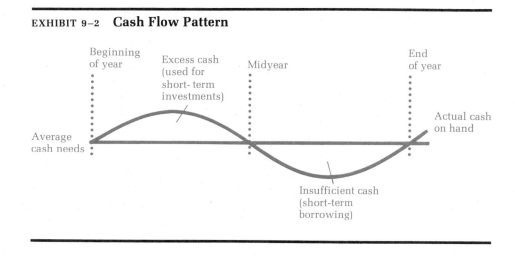

EXHIBIT 9–2   **Cash Flow Pattern**

interest rate for a specific investment period), certificates of deposit, savings accounts, and government bonds and treasury bills.

Also referred to as <u>marketable securities</u>, short-term investments are classified as current assets because they are extremely liquid and can be readily sold for cash at any time (although an early withdrawal penalty may be assessed). Investments must be properly classified as either short-term or long-term because there are important differences in the way they are accounted for.

ACCOUNTING FOR SHORT-TERM INVESTMENTS

Short-term investments, like all other assets, are recorded at cost when purchased. For accounting purposes, this includes the market price of the asset, as well as the cost of making the purchase (such as a broker's fee).

To illustrate, we will assume that during a period of excess cash, Bicknell Incorporated has purchased 100 shares of Mohawk stock at $171 per share and has paid a broker's commission of $500. The entry to record the investment would be

Short-Term Investments—Mohawk Stock   17,600
   Cash   17,600
Purchased 100 shares of Mohawk stock as a short-term investment at $171 per share plus $500 in commissions.

Obviously, Bicknell's managers invested in Mohawk because they thought it would earn a good return. Such returns are earned either from dividends or through a gain made on the sale of the stock.

The accounting entry for the receipt of a dividend of $1.40 per share of Mohawk's stock would be

Cash   140
   Dividend Revenue   140
Received dividends on the investment in Mohawk stock.

marketable securities
short-term investments that can be readily sold in established markets

The entry to account for a gain on the sale of Mohawk stock would be

Cash 18,000
    Short-Term Investments—Mohawk Stock. 17,600
    Gain on Sale of Short-Term Investments 400
Sold 100 shares of Mohawk stock at $185 per share, less a $500 sales commission.

In this case, the market price at the time of the sale is $185 per share but the company only receives $18,000 because a sales commission of $500 must be paid. Note that increases in market price above the cost of a stock are not recognized until the stock is actually sold.

The last entry, Gain on Sale of Short-Term Investments, would be included on the Income Statement with Other Revenues and Expenses. The investment has been written off and the proceeds are included in Cash on the Balance Sheet. Accounting for investments in bonds or commercial paper is the same as for stock.

SHORT-TERM INVESTMENTS AT LOWER OF COST OR MARKET

lower of cost or market *a basis for valuing certain assets at the lower of original cost or market value (current replacement cost)*

Although investments are initially recorded at cost and are never written up to recognize increases in market prices, investments in marketable equity securities (primarily common stock) must be written down to market value if it drops below the original cost. This practice of recording short-term investments at the lower of cost or market (LCM) represents an important departure from the usual procedure of reporting assets at cost. Technically, only marketable equity securities must be reported at lower of cost or market; however, this procedure is appropriate and followed by many companies for all marketable securities, whether equity or debt. In this book, we will apply the lower-of-cost-or-market rule to all marketable securities.

In deciding whether short-term investments should be written down, a company should consider all marketable securities (its entire portfolio) as a unit. When the selling price of a stock investment drops below its original cost, it is not written down if the market value of the company's total portfolio of all marketable securities is still equal to or greater than the original cost.

To illustrate, we will assume that Bicknell's portfolio of short-term investments includes the following.

	Cost	Market	Unrealized Gain (Loss)
Common stock of Mohawk Company .	$17,600	$18,500	$ 900
U.S. government bonds	21,000	19,000	(2,000)
Bonds of MMM Company	26,500	25,000	(1,500)
Other marketable securities	13,200	14,100	900
Total	$78,300	$76,600	($1,700)

Because the portfolio's market value is $1,700 less than its original cost, short-term investments should be written down to $76,600. The entry to recognize this loss is

Loss on Short-Term Investments   1,700
      Allowance To Reduce Investments to LCM   1,700
To reduce short-term investments to lower of cost or market ($78,300 − $76,600).

Loss on Short-Term Investments[2] appears on the Income Statement under Other Revenues and Expenses, and Allowance to Reduce Short-Term Investments to LCM is a contra-short-term investments account on the Balance Sheet. An accepted alternative is to credit the Short-Term Investment account directly.

If the market prices of previously written-down short-term investments subsequently rise above cost, such investments should be written back up to, but never to more than, their original cost. However, because these investments are usually held only for short periods of time, such subsequent fluctuations in the market price seldom occur, and adjustments to their carrying values are not required.

TO SUMMARIZE   Short-term investments are extremely liquid, so they are listed just below Cash on the Balance Sheet. Revenue from short-term investments usually takes the form of dividends, interest, or capital gains and is included under Other Revenues and Expenses on the Income Statement. Marketable securities should be written down to the lower of cost or market if the company's entire portfolio drops below cost.

The Present and Future Value of Money

Present and future values have to do with the time value of money, that is, why a dollar today is worth more than a dollar received at some future date. Thus, they are essential for evaluating long-term investments. In addition, present and future values are useful in accounting for long-term liabilities and in capital budgeting.

There are two major reasons for current dollars being more valuable than future dollars: inflation and interest. Because of inflation, $100 will buy more today than it will a year from now. Similarly, today's $100 could be earning interest and amount to more than $100 a year from now, possibly enough to offset inflation. In this discussion of present and future values, only the effects of interest will be considered; the discussion of inflation will be left to other chapters.

Any one of four concepts may be used in calculating differences in the value of money over time.

---

[2] Losses incurred in writing down short-term investments to a market price that is lower than cost are not deductible for tax purposes.

1. Future amount of $1.
2. Present value of $1.
3. Future amount of an annuity of $1.
4. Present value of an annuity of $1.

THE FUTURE AMOUNT OF $1

future amount of $1 *the amount to which $1 will increase if invested for a certain number of periods at a specified interest rate*

simple interest *interest calculated only on the principal amount each period*

compound interest *interest calculated on the principal amount plus any previously earned interest*

compound period *period of time for which interest is calculated*

The future amount of $1 is the amount to which $1 will increase if it is invested for a certain number of periods at a specified interest rate. For example, if $1,000 were invested for 4 years at 6 percent, the future amount of the $1,000 would be $1,000 + ($1,000 × 6% × 4) = $1,000 + $240 = $1,240. This calculation assumes simple interest, which means that interest earned in earlier years does not earn additional interest in later years. The assumption of simple interest is usually not realistic. Instead, most investments pay on a compound-interest basis; that is, interest is earned not only on the principal amount but also on any interest earned and retained prior to the current period.

An important consideration in the calculation of compound interest is the compound period, the period for which interest is calculated. The length of the period determines the frequency with which earned interest is added to the principal in calculating the new amount of interest earned. To illustrate, we again assume that $1,000 is invested at 6 percent interest for 4 years and that interest is compounded annually. The computation of the interest would be

Time Period	Beginning Amount	Interest						Ending Amount
Year 1	$1,000.00	+	$1,000	× 0.06 =	$60.00	=	$1,060.00
Year 2	1,060.00	+	1,060	× 0.06 =	63.60	=	1,123.60
Year 3	1,123.60	+	1,123.60	× 0.06 =	67.42	=	1,191.02
Year 4	1,191.02	+	1,191.02	× 0.06 =	71.46	=	1,262.48

The difference between simple and compound interest on $1,000 over 4 years is $22.48 ($1,262.48 − $1,240.00), which represents interest earned on prior interest. This $22.48 can be validated as follows:

$$1\text{st year's interest} = \$60.00 \times 0.06 \times 3 \text{ years} = \$10.80$$
$$2\text{nd year's interest} = 63.60 \times 0.06 \times 2 \text{ years} = 7.63$$
$$3\text{rd year's interest} = 67.42 \times 0.06 \times 1 \text{ year} = \underline{4.05}$$
$$\underline{\underline{\$22.48}}$$

In this example, if the interest had been compounded semiannually (a compound period of 6 months) instead of annually, the future amount would be $1,266.78, which is computed as follows (note that an interest rate of 6% × ½, or 3%, is used, but the number of interest periods doubles from 4 to 8):

Time Period	Beginning Amount	Interest			Ending Amount
Year 1, 1st period	$1,000.00 +	$1,000.00 × 0.03 =	$30.00 =		$1,030.00
Year 1, 2nd period	1,030.00 +	1,030.00 × 0.03 =	30.90 =		1,060.90
Year 2, 1st period	1,060.90 +	1,060.90 × 0.03 =	31.83 =		1,092.73
Year 2, 2nd period	1,092.73 +	1,092.73 × 0.03 =	32.78 =		1,125.51
Year 3, 1st period	1,125.51 +	1,125.51 × 0.03 =	33.77 =		1,159.28
Year 3, 2nd period	1,159.28 +	1,159.28 × 0.03 =	34.78 =		1,194.06
Year 4, 1st period	1,194.06 +	1,194.06 × 0.03 =	35.82 =		1,229.88
Year 4, 2nd period	1,229.88 +	1,229.88 × 0.03 =	36.90 =		1,266.78

The future amount of $1,266.78 is $4.30 greater than the $1,262.48 that resulted from annual compounding. Future amounts are always greater with more frequent compounding. And, of course, the higher the interest rate, the greater the future amount.

As you can see from even this simple example, future value computations can become quite involved. Because of this, there are prepared tables that give the future amounts of $1 for various compound periods and interest rates (see page 322).

An examination of Table I shows that the future value of $1 compounded annually for four periods at 6 percent is 1.2625. When you multiply this by $1,000, you get $1,262.50, a figure very close to the $1,262.48 found earlier ($0.02 is a rounding difference).

Future values can also be computed with the formula for compound interest. That formula is

$$FV = P(1 + i)^n$$

where

FV = future value of the principal amount

P = principal amount

i = interest rate

n = number of periods

Applying the formula to the example above, we again find that the future value of $1,000 invested for 4 years at 6 percent is $1,262.48, or $1,000 (1 + 0.06)^4. The availability of hand calculators has made the formula method of calculation quite simple.

THE PRESENT VALUE OF $1

present value of $1   *the value today of $1 to be received at some future date, given a specified interest rate*

The present value of $1 is the value today of a dollar to be received at some date in the future. Money in hand now could be earning interest, so it is more valuable than the same amount of money received in the future. A dollar received at some future date must be discounted by this interest rate to determine its present value. Present value is the reciprocal of future value and is calculated by discounting the future sum back to the present. This may be accomplished with compound discounting, which means that the compound interest is subtracted from the future amount.

To illustrate the calculation of present values, we will assume that $10,000 is to be received 4 years in the future. If interest is 6 percent compounded annually, the value today of the $10,000 to be received in 4 years is $7,921. This amount can be extracted from Table II on page 323, which shows that the present value of $1 for 4 years at 6 percent is 0.7921. Multiplying 0.7921 by $10,000 gives you $7,921. Or it can be calculated with the formula for present values.

$$PV = F \frac{1}{(1 + i)^n}$$

where

PV = present value

F = future amount to be discounted

i = interest rate

n = number of periods

Applying this formula to the example, we have

$$PV = \$10,000 \ \frac{1}{(1 + 0.06)^4}$$

$$= \$10,000(0.7921)$$

$$= \$7,921$$

When using the tables, you should bear in mind that the present and future value factors are for $1. Thus, when calculating the present or future value of a sum other than $1, you should multiply the factor found in the table by the number of dollars being discounted or compounded.

As present value is the inverse of future value, it follows that the more frequently the future value is discounted, or the higher the interest rate, the lower the present value. For example, the present value of the $10,000 to be received in 4 years would have been $7,894 if 6 percent interest had been compounded semiannually instead of annually. You can check this by looking under 3 percent (6 percent ÷ 2) for eight periods (4 years × 2) in the present value table.

THE FUTURE AMOUNT OF AN ANNUITY OF $1

ordinary annuity   *a series of equal amounts to be received or paid at the end of equally spaced time intervals*

In discussing present and future values, we have considered only lump-sum payments or receipts of money. An <u>ordinary annuity</u> is a series of equal amounts to be received or paid at the end of equally spaced intervals

future amount of an annuity of $1 *the amount to which a series of equally spaced payments of $1 will accumulate if invested for a certain number of periods at a specified interest rate*

of time. The future amount of an annuity of $1 is the amount that a series of equally spaced payments of $1 earning a specified rate of interest will accumulate to at some date in the future.

In calculating the future and present values of annuities, the compounding of interest is again used. To illustrate, suppose that an investor is willing to pay, in return for an asset, $1,000 at the end of each of 4 years. If those amounts are deposited in a savings account that pays interest at 6 percent compounded annually, the future value of the four $1,000 payments plus interest is $4,374.61, which is calculated as follows:

Time	Payment	Interest			Total
End of Year 1.............	$1,000.00				$1,000.00
End of Year 2.............	1,000.00	$1,000.00 × 0.06 =	$60.00		2,060.00
End of Year 3.............	1,000.00	2,060.00 × 0.06 =	123.60		3,183.60
End of Year 4.............	1,000.00	3,183.60 × 0.06 =	191.02		4,374.62
	$4,000.00 +		$374.62	=	$4,374.62

Like the future amount of $1, the future amount of an annuity of $1 increases as the number of compound periods or the interest rate increases. For example, if a series of eight $500 payments were received, one at the end of each 6-month period, instead of four $1,000 payments, the future amount of the annuity would be $4,446.15. The formula for computing the future value of an annuity is

$$FV = R\left(\frac{(1+i)^n - 1}{i}\right)$$

where

FV = future value of an annuity

R = periodic payment to be accumulated

i = interest rate

n = number of periods

Using this formula, the future value of $1,000 received each year for 4 years at 6 percent compounded annually is

$$FV = \$1,000\left(\frac{(1+0.06)^4 - 1}{0.06}\right)$$

$$= \$1,000(4.3746)$$

$$= \$4,374.60$$

Although these calculations are easily computed with a hand calculator, you could refer instead to Table III on page 324. From the table, the future value factor for $1 received or paid every year for 4 years at 6 percent interest compounded annually is 4.3746.

THE PRESENT VALUE OF AN ANNUITY OF $1

The present value of an annuity of $1 is the amount that a future series of equally spaced payments of $1 is worth today. Due to the time value of money, these future payments must be discounted at the prevailing interest rate to determine their present values. The calculation of the present value of an annuity of $1 is the inverse of the calculation of the future amount of an annuity of $1.

To illustrate, we will assume that $1,000 will be received at the end of each of 4 years. If interest is 6 percent compounded annually, the present value of the four $1,000 payments is $3,465.10. This present value can be computed either by using the formula or Table IV on page 325. The formula, which is somewhat more complicated than the earlier ones, is

$$PV = R \left(\frac{1 - \frac{1}{(1 + i)^n}}{i} \right)$$

where

PV = present value of an annuity

R = periodic payment to be discounted

i = interest rate

n = number of discount periods

Applying this formula to the example, we have

$$PV = \$1,000 \left(\frac{1 - \frac{1}{(1 + 0.06)^4}}{0.06} \right)$$

$$= \$1,000(3.46511)$$

$$= \$3,465.10$$

As with the present value of $1, the higher the interest rate or the more often compounding takes place, the lower the present value of an annuity.

TO SUMMARIZE Four present and future value concepts are commonly used in calculating the time value of money. Which one to use in a given situation can be found in the answers to two questions:

1. Is a lump sum or a series of equal payments involved?

2. Are you interested in the value today (present value) of a payment(s) to be received in the future or the amount that this payment(s) will accumulate to in the future (future value) at a specified interest rate?

If a series of equal payments is involved, it is an annuity and Table III or IV should be used. If a lump-sum payment is involved, there is no annuity and Table I or II should be used.

If present values are involved, Table II or IV is appropriate. If it is the amount that a future payment(s) at a specified rate of interest will accumulate to, the computation involves future values and the use of either Table I or III. These various combinations are summarized below.

Payment	Future Values	Present Values
Lump sum	Table I	Table II
Series of equal payments (annuity)	Table III	Table IV

Finally, because present and future values are widely used, the formulas are stored in many calculators. If you have such a calculator, you may prefer it to the tables. You should note that because most calculators carry formulas to several decimal points, results may differ slightly from those derived from the tables.

Long-Term Investments

long-term investments *non-operational assets that a business intends to hold for more than a year or the normal operating cycle*

There are many types of <u>long-term investments</u>, including investments in real estate, life insurance, and corporate stocks and bonds. The accounting for real-estate and life-insurance investments is relatively simple. The accounting for long-term investments in stocks and bonds, however, can be complicated and will be the focus of this last section.

ACCOUNTING FOR LONG-TERM INVESTMENTS IN STOCKS

Like all other assets, long-term investments in stocks are initially accounted for on a cost basis. That is, the total paid to acquire the stocks (market price plus commission) is recognized as the cost of the long-term investment.

To illustrate, we again assume that Bicknell Incorporated purchased 300 shares of Davis Company stock at $10 a share. In addition, Bicknell paid $200 in commissions. The entry to record the long-term investment would be

Long-Term Investment—Davis Stock   3,200
  Cash   3,200
Purchased 300 shares of Davis stock [(300 × $10) + $200 commission].

There are several reasons for a company to purchase, on a long-term basis, the stock of another company. The two most common reasons are

1. To receive the dividends paid on the stock (and, ideally, to realize additional earnings when the stock is eventually sold).

2. To purchase a significant or controlling interest in another company.

EXHIBIT 9–3 **Methods of Accounting for Long-Term Investments in Stocks**

Accounting Method	Circumstances
Cost	The cost method is to be used when the number of shares of stock owned is so small that the investor can exercise *no significant influence on or control over* the company. The inability to exercise influence or control is presumed to exist if an investor owns less than 20 percent of the outstanding voting stock.
Equity	The equity method is to be used when one company's investment in the stock of another company is large enough that the investor can exercise a *significant influence* on the operations of that company. The ability to exercise significant influence is presumed to exist if an investor owns 20 percent or more of the outstanding voting stock of another company. A controlling interest exists if over 50 percent is owned.

---

subsidiary company *a company owned or controlled by another company, known as the parent company*

parent company *a company that owns or maintains control over other companies, known as subsidiaries, which are themselves separate legal entities*

As you may recall, companies owned and controlled by other companies are called subsidiary companies, or subsidiaries, and the companies exercising the ownership and control are called parent companies.

The amount of stock one company owns in another is an important determinant of the degree of influence the first company has on the second; it also affects the accounting records of both companies. This is so because the accounting profession requires that different accounting methods for long-term investments be employed for different amounts of ownership. Exhibit 9–3 outlines the circumstances under which either the cost or the equity method of accounting for long-term stock investments should be used.

If one company owns over 50 percent of the outstanding stock of another company, a controlling interest obviously exists. In this case, the companies' financial statements are usually combined as consolidated financial statements. Basically, consolidation involves preparing financial statements of two or more associated enterprises as if they were one organization. Some accounts would be combined (such as cash of the parent company and cash of the subsidiary) and some would be eliminated (such as intercompany sales and purchases, the parent company account covering investments in the subsidiary, and the subsidiary's owners' equity accounts).

consolidated financial statements *statements that show the operating results and financial position of two or more legally separate but affiliated companies as if they were one economic entity*

To illustrate the cost and equity methods of accounting for long-term investments in stock, we will assume that Bicknell Incorporated plans to purchase some stock in Blue Ridge Company. Blue Ridge has 1,000 shares of outstanding stock, currently selling at $10 a share. The accounting for the purchase of shares of stock would be as shown in Exhibit 9–4 (assuming that no commissions are paid).

The Cost Method

cost method of accounting for investments in stocks *accounting for an investment in another company where less than 20 percent of the outstanding voting stock is owned, by recording the initial acquisition at cost and recognizing dividends as revenue earned*

The cost method of accounting for long-term equity investments is essentially the same as the method used in accounting for short-term equity investments. That is, the original investment is recorded at cost and is

EXHIBIT 9–4   Long-Term Investments in Stock

	Cost Method	Equity Method
Event:	*Bicknell purchases 150 shares of Blue Ridge Company stock (15% ownership):*	*Bicknell purchases 400 shares of Blue Ridge Company stock (40% ownership):*
Accounting for the initial purchase	Investment in Blue Ridge Stock . . 1,500 Cash . . . . 1,500 *Purchased 150 shares of Blue Ridge Company stock (15% ownership).*	Investment in Blue Ridge Stock . 4,000 Cash . . . . 4,000 *Purchased 400 shares of Blue Ridge Company stock (40% ownership).*
Payment of 80¢-per-share dividend by Blue Ridge Company	Cash . . . . 120 Dividend Revenue—Blue Ridge Stock . . . . 120 *Received 80¢-per-share dividend from Blue Ridge Company.*	Cash . . . . 320 Investment in Blue Ridge Stock . . . . 320 *Received 80¢-per-share dividend from Blue Ridge Company.*
Announcement by Blue Ridge Company of earnings of $6,000 for the year	No entry	Investment in Blue Ridge Stock . 2,400 Revenue from Investments . . . . 2,400 *To recognize proportionate share of Blue Ridge Company earnings for the year (40% of $6,000).*

carried on a lower-of-cost-or-market basis. Generally, if the market value of a company's portfolio of long-term equity investments falls below its original cost, the long-term investments are written down to the market price. The entry to recognize the lower market price, however, is different from the one used to write down short-term investments. It would be

Unrealized Loss on Long-Term Investments   8,000
   Allowance to Reduce Long-Term Investments
   to Market   8,000
To recognize investments at lower of cost or market. (Numbers are arbitrary.)

The debit entry "Unrealized Loss on Long-Term Investments" is a contra-owners' equity account and the credit entry, "Allowance to Reduce Long-Term Investments to Market," is a contra-long-term investment account. Neither account appears on the Income Statement, so there is no loss recognized when the market price of long-term investments drops below cost.[3] The rationale for not taking these declines into current income is that the investments will be held for a long time and the price may rise before the stock is sold.

---

[3] However, if the decline in the market value of a long-term equity security is judged to be other than temporary, the cost basis should be written down and the write-down should be recorded as a loss on the Income Statement. In such cases, the new cost basis is not to be changed for subsequent increases in market value.

As was the case with short-term investments, if the market price of a written-down portfolio of long-term investments subsequently rises, it should be written up to the new market price, as long as that price does not exceed the original cost. Under no circumstances are investments written up to a market price that exceeds cost. The entry to recognize a subsequent recovery in the market price of long-term investments that have previously been written down is the reverse of the previous entry and would be

Allowance To Reduce Long-Term Investments
to Market 4,000
    Unrealized Loss on Long-Term Investments 4,000
To recognize partial recovery in the market price of long-term investments. (Numbers are arbitrary.)

The Equity Method

When a stock investment involves significant influence (20 percent or more ownership), it is presumed that the investor can influence the timing and extent of dividend payments by the subsidiary. If the cost method were used, the parent company would be allowed to report revenues when dividends were received and so could increase its income merely by requiring the investee to pay larger and more frequent dividends. Because of this potential for abuse, where significant influence exists, the equity method is required.

Under the equity method, dividend payments represent a return of investment, and revenue is recognized only when the investee company has earnings. When earnings are announced, the amount of the investment is increased because the investor now owns a significant portion of a company that is worth more than it was when the investment was originally made.

In accounting for investments with the equity method, the original investment is first recorded on the books at cost and is subsequently modified to reflect the investor's share of the investee's reported incomes and losses. In this way, book value is increased to recognize the investor's proportionate share of earnings or decreased to recognize losses and dividends received. Unless a permanent decline in the value of an investment is considered to have occurred, the lower-of-cost-or-market rule is not applied under the equity method.

There is one exception to the rule that the equity method must be used when 20 percent or more of a subsidiary's stock is owned. If the purchased stock does not possess voting rights in the company, the investment is accounted for with the cost method, no matter what the percentage of ownership. The reason the cost method is used in these circumstances is that a nonvoting investor has much less influence on the operating and dividend policies of a subsidiary.

When a stock is sold, any proceeds that exceed its book value (under either the cost or equity method) are recognized as a gain. The entry to record the sale of a stock held as a long-term investment would be

Cash 10,000
    Long-Term Investment 9,000
    Gain on Sale of Investments 1,000
Sold long-term investments at more than book value. (Numbers are arbitrary.)

equity method of accounting for investments in stocks
accounting for an investment in another company where significant influence can be imposed (presumed to exist when 20 or more percent of the outstanding voting stock is owned), by recording the initial acquisition at cost but recognizing dividends as return of investment and the proportionate share of earnings as revenue

TO SUMMARIZE   All long-term investments in stock are initially accounted for on a cost basis. However, because different levels of investment provide different degrees of influence over investee companies, two methods of accounting for long-term investments are used. If an investor company owns less than 20 percent of the voting stock of another company, the cost method is used. With the cost method, revenue is recognized when dividends are received and the investment is accounted for at the lower of cost or market. (Note that when long-term investments are written down to the lower of cost or market, the adjustment reduces owners' equity and investments; it does not affect the Income Statement. This is not true of short-term investments.) If 20 percent or more of the total outstanding voting stock is owned (which is presumed to represent significant influence), the equity method is used. This method involves increasing the investment balance for earnings and decreasing it for losses and dividends.

LONG-TERM INVESTMENTS IN BONDS

bonds   *documents evidencing a long-term obligation of a company or government agency; usually bonds bear interest at stated rates, mature at specified future dates, and are issued in units of $1,000*

Another common type of long-term investment involves one company's purchase of another company's bonds. Essentially, bonds are long-term borrowings by a company or government agency. (See Chapter 11 for a discussion of the nature and issuance of bonds.) For example, in order to raise money for new schools, school districts often sell bonds to the public. Similarly, corporations issue bonds to finance plant expansions or for other reasons. Such bonds are usually sold in denominations of $1,000. A typical bond is shown in Exhibit 9–5.

An investment in bonds does not confer upon the purchaser the same privileges that an investment in stock does—for example, bond owners have no voting rights and receive no dividends. However, bonds do provide important benefits: periodic interest payments at a stated rate and a specified principal payment (face, or maturity, value) at some future date (the maturity date). Like stocks, bonds are traded on major exchanges and their prices fluctuate from day to day. Investors often find it profitable to sell bonds before their maturity date. Thus, there are two ways of earning a return on an investment in bonds: (1) by receiving the periodic interest payments made on the bonds, and (2) by selling the bonds at a profit.

face (maturity) value of a bond   *the amount of principal that will be paid on the maturity date*

bond maturity date   *date at which a bond principal or face amount becomes payable*

The market price of bonds in most cases is influenced by (1) the risk factor of the bonds and (2) the interest rate at which the bonds are issued. The first factor, riskiness of the bonds, is determined by general economic conditions and the financial status of the company selling the bonds, as measured by organizations that regularly assign a rating, or a grade, to all corporate bonds.

Companies strive to earn as high a bond rating as possible because the higher the rating, the lower the interest rate their bonds will have to pay to attract buyers. A high-risk bond, on the other hand, will have a low rating and will have to offer a higher rate of interest to attract buyers.

Interest rates affect the market prices of bonds according to the following general rule: If the stated interest rate of a particular bond is higher than the current market interest rate for similar investments (bonds with identical ratings, for example), the bond will sell at a price above its face value. If the interest rate on the bond is lower than the prevailing market rate for equivalent investments, the bond will sell for less than its face

EXHIBIT 9–5 **Sample Bond with Coupons**

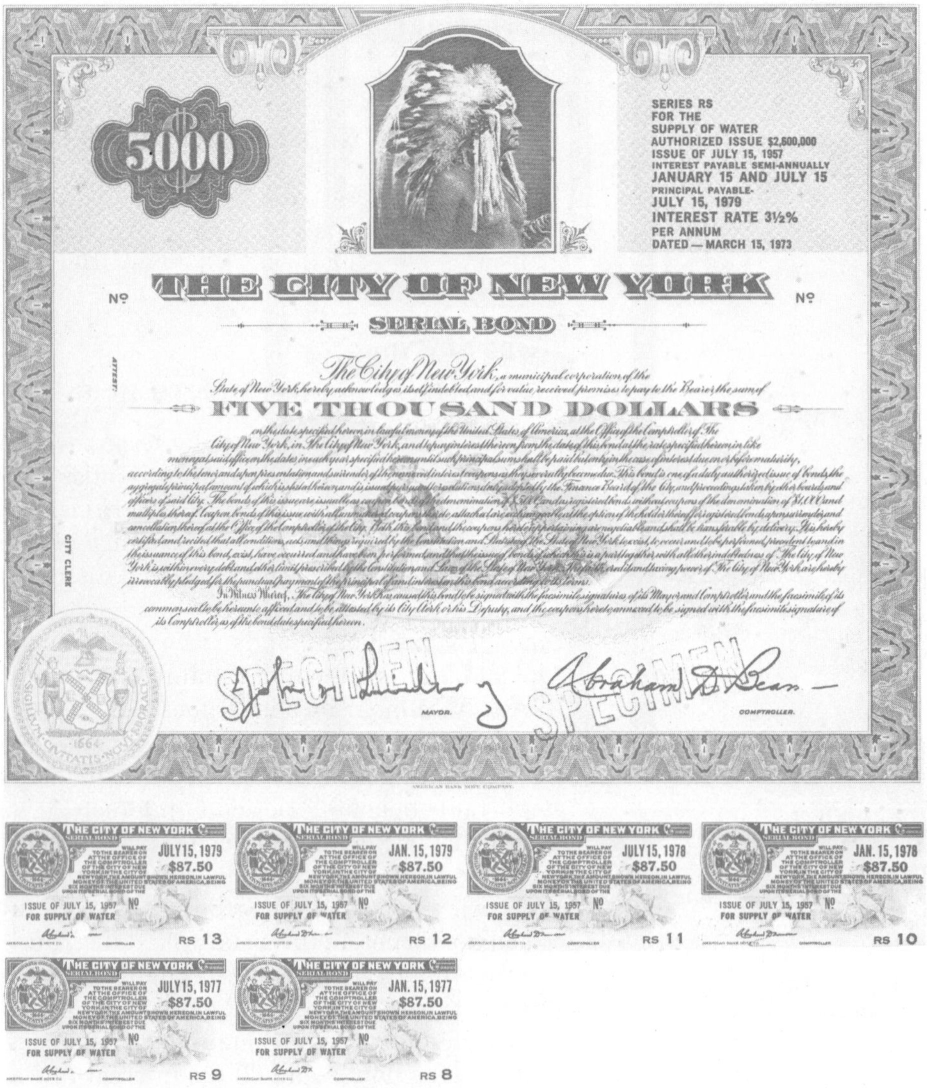

value. Once bonds have been issued and their stated interest rates have been fixed, their prices usually increase when market interest rates fall and decrease when market interest rates rise. For example, a $1,000, 10 percent bond may sell at a price of $960 while the market rate of interest for bonds of the same grade is 12 percent but may increase to $1,040 if the market interest rate drops to 8 percent. To see why this happens, assume the following: You own a 10 percent bond but have an opportunity to buy a 12 percent bond with a similar rating. If you, along with many other investors, decide to sell the former and buy the latter, the price of the 10 percent bond is very likely to drop and the price of the 12 percent bond is likely to increase.

Bond Price Determination

Before investing in bonds, individual or corporate investors should decide on the minimum rate of return they want to earn, and then determine the price that will bring them that rate. The concepts of present value are helpful in this regard. In using these concepts, an investor should first recognize that buying a bond involves the purchase of two separate elements: the right to receive interest payments of a fixed amount at equal intervals over the life of the bond, and the right to receive a fixed sum—the maturity value of the bond—at the maturity date.

To illustrate how an investor uses present value concepts to determine how much to pay for a bond, we will assume that Bicknell Incorporated plans to purchase twenty $1,000 bonds of the Sunglow Corporation as a long-term investment. These bonds mature in 5 years (in reality, most bonds have a life of 20–25 years) and pay an annual interest rate of 12 percent, with payments every 6 months. In purchasing 20 bonds, Bicknell has the right to receive the following.

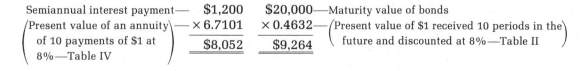

Thus, Bicknell would be purchasing 10 semiannual interest payments of $1,200 each ($20,000 × 0.12 × $\frac{1}{2}$ year) and a lump-sum payment of $20,000 (the maturity value) at the end of the 5 years.

In calculating how much to pay for this investment, Bicknell must decide what rate of return it wants to earn. For example, if 16 percent is needed to justify the investment, then no more than $17,316 should be paid for the $20,000 bonds. The $17,316 purchase price is obtained by adding the present value of $20,000 (received 10 periods in the future and discounted at 8 percent) to the present value of the annuity of the 10 interest payments of $1,200 each (discounted at 8 percent). The calculations are

Semiannual interest payment— **$1,200**   **$20,000**—Maturity value of bonds
$\begin{pmatrix}\text{Present value of an annuity}\\ \text{of 10 payments of \$1 at}\\ \text{8\%—Table IV}\end{pmatrix}$ — × 6.7101   × 0.4632— $\begin{pmatrix}\text{Present value of \$1 received 10 periods in the}\\ \text{future and discounted at 8\%—Table II}\end{pmatrix}$
  $8,052 $9,264

$$\$8,052 + \$9,264 = \$17,316$$

Note that since the interest is received semiannually, the rate used to discount the interest and lump-sum payments is 8 percent (16 percent ÷ 2) and the number of periods is 10 (5 × 2).

This $17,316 is the amount that earns Bicknell exactly 16 percent; anything less returns more than 16 percent and anything more returns less than 16 percent. If Bicknell could purchase Sunglow's bonds for $17,316 or less, the investment would be worthwhile. If not, Bicknell should probably look elsewhere for investment opportunities. The one exception, of course, would be if Bicknell expected the market rate of interest to drop, which would result, as noted earlier, in an increase in the value of the bonds.

Accounting for Long-Term Investments in Bonds

Regardless of the price at which bonds are originally purchased, if held to maturity, the investor receives the principal, or face value, of the bonds from the issuing company. Because the difference between the principal and the cost represents earnings (or loss) that occur during the period the bonds are held, investments in bonds must be written up or down to their face, or maturity, value over the life of the bonds. This process is shown in Exhibit 9–6. Accounting for long-term investments in bonds involves four major steps:

1. Accounting for the acquisition of bonds.

2. Accounting for the interest received on bonds.

3. Accounting for the write-up or write-down of bonds from their original acquisition cost to their face value.

4. Accounting for the sale of bonds, if sold before their maturity date, or the receipt of their face value.

EXHIBIT 9–6 **The Writing Up or Down of Bond Investments**

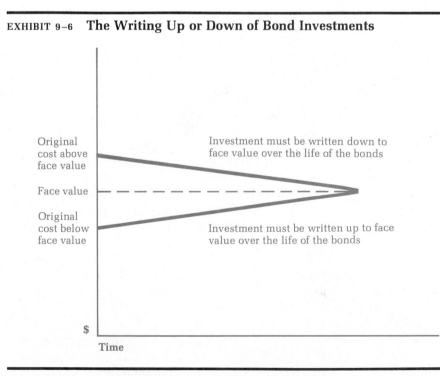

bond premium   *the difference between the face value and the sales price of a bond when it is sold above its face value*

bond discount   *the difference between the face value and the sales price of a bond when it is sold below its face value*

Accounting for the Acquisition of Bonds   Bonds can be purchased either above face value (at a <u>premium</u>), below face value (at a <u>discount</u>), or at face value (at par). Regardless of the purchase price, like all other assets, bonds are initially recorded at cost. The cost is the total amount paid to acquire the bonds, which includes the price of the bonds and any other purchasing costs, such as commissions or broker's fees. The entry to record an investment in bonds would be

Investment in Bonds—Sunglow Company   17,316
   Cash   17,316
Purchased $20,000 of Sunglow bonds at a discount.

The only possible complication to this entry occurs when bonds are purchased between interest dates. Every 6 months (or however often the bonds pay interest), each bondholder is paid the full period's interest. Therefore, an investor purchasing bonds between interest dates must also pay the previous owner for the interest earned (called accrued interest) between the last interest payment date and the purchase date.

To illustrate this concept, we will assume that Bicknell purchased the Sunglow bonds on May 1 and that the bonds ($20,000 at 12 percent) pay interest every January 1 and July 1. On July 1, Bicknell will receive $1,200 ($20,000 × 12 percent × $\frac{1}{2}$), even though the bonds were purchased only 2 months ago. Since the previous owner is entitled to 4 months' interest on May 1, Bicknell would have to pay that company—which could be the issuing corporation or some other intermediate investor—the interest for the period January 1 to May 1. This is illustrated in Exhibit 9–7.

The entry to record the investment in bonds on May 1 (between interest dates) would be

Investments in Bonds—Sunglow Company   . . .   17,316
Bond Interest Revenue   800
   Cash   18,116
Purchased $20,000 of Sunglow bonds at discount and paid accrued interest.

EXHIBIT 9–7   Investing Between Interest Dates

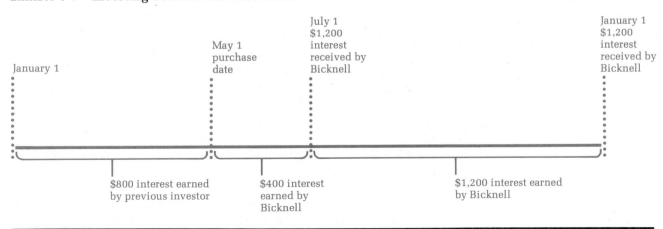

Accounting for Interest Earned on Bond Investments   When the $1,200 interest is received on July 1, the entry to record its receipt is

Cash   1,200
    Bond Interest Revenue   1,200
Received the first interest payment from Sunglow bonds.

As shown here, on July 1, the Bond Interest Revenue account has a credit balance of $400, which represent Bicknell's earnings for the 2 months.

Bond Interest Revenue

amount paid with purchase on May 1...800	1,200 . . . . amount received on July 1
	400 . . . . Balance—amount earned

An alternative method of recording interest on bonds purchased between interest payment dates is to debit Bond Interest Receivable instead of Bond Interest Revenue. When this alternative is used, the entry on the interest payment date (in this case, July 1) will include two credits: one to Bond Interest Receivable ($800), and one to Bond Interest Revenue ($400). Both methods produce the same balance in the Bond Interest Revenue account after the interest payment date. In the examples and problems in this book we will use the revenue approach.

Whichever method is used, the entry to record subsequent receipts of interest would be

Cash   1,200
    Bond Interest Revenue   1,200
Received interest on Sunglow bonds.

Bond Interest Revenue is a revenue account and, if material in amount, is shown separately on the Income Statement under the caption "Other Revenues and Expenses."

Accounting for the Amortization of Bond Discounts and Premiums   As indicated previously, bonds are not always purchased at their face value. In fact, only in those rare instances when the interest rate of a bond is exactly equivalent to the prevailing market rate for similar investments is a bond purchased at its face value. At all other times, bonds are purchased either at a discount (below face value) or at a premium (above face value). Because the face amount, or principal, of a bond is received at maturity, discounts and premiums must be written off over the period that a bond is held. This writing off of bond premiums and discounts is referred to as amortization.

There are two common methods of amortizing discounts and premiums on bonds; the simpler is straight-line interest amortization. With straight-line amortization, a company writes off the same amount of premium or discount each period the bonds are held.

amortization of bonds   *the systematic writing off of a bond discount or premium over the life of the bond*

straight-line interest amortization   *a method of systematically writing off a bond discount or premium, in equal amounts each period until maturity*

To illustrate this method of amortizing a bond discount, we will assume again that Bicknell purchased the Sunglow $20,000, 12 percent, 5-year bonds for $17,316, that is, at a discount. The entry to record this investment was given on page 309. If the bonds were purchased on the issuance date, Bicknell would amortize the $2,684 discount ($20,000 face amount − $17,316 purchase price) at the rate of $536.80 a year ($2,684 ÷ 5 years). Each year for 5 years an amortization entry would be made. At the end of 5 years, the Investments in Bonds—Sunglow Company would have a balance of $20,000. These annual entries would be

Investment in Bonds—Sunglow Company 536.80
    Bond Interest Revenue 536.80
To record the annual straight-line amortization of Sunglow bonds.

Note that with the straight-line amortization method, bond premiums and discounts can be amortized annually, as illustrated, or on each interest payment date.

The $536.80 in bond discount amortization is revenue earned on the bonds because, when the bonds mature, Bicknell will receive $20,000, or the face value, in return for an original investment of $17,316. It is this additional revenue of $2,684 that increases the return the investor actually earns from the 12 percent stated interest rate to the effective rate of 16 percent.

When accounting for the amortization of a bond discount, a company must be careful to amortize the discount only over the period the bonds are actually held. For example, if Bicknell had purchased the Sunglow bonds 4 months after the issuance date, the discount would have been amortized over a period of 56 months (4 full years plus 8 months of the first year). The amortization for the first year would then have been approximately $383.43 ($2,684 × 8/56) and the amortization for each of the succeeding 4 years would be approximately $575.14 ($2,684 × 12/56).

Accounting for the amortization of a premium on investments is essentially the opposite of that for a discount. Basically, amortization of a premium results in a decrease in revenue earned, and the effect of the amortization entry is to reduce Investments in Bonds to the face value of the bonds by maturity date.

To illustrate the accounting for amortization of a bond premium, we will assume that Bicknell purchased ABC Company's $20,000, 18 percent, 5-year bonds for $21,800 on the issuance date. The entries to record the purchase of bonds at a premium and receipt of interest on bonds are similar to those for bonds purchased at a discount. However, the annual entry to record amortization of the bond premium is different and results in a decrease in both revenues earned and the investment balance, as shown here.

Bond Interest Revenue   360
    Investment in Bonds—ABC Company   360
To record the annual straight-line amortization of one-fifth of the $1,800 premium on ABC Company bonds ($1,800 ÷ 5 years).

Bicknell would be willing to pay such a premium only when the stated interest rate on bonds is higher than the prevailing market interest rate for similar investment opportunities. The effect of the amortization entries is to reduce the return earned on the bonds from the stated interest rate of 18 percent to the rate actually earned on the investment (approximately 16 percent).

Effective-Interest Amortization   Another common method of amortizing bond premiums and discounts is the <u>effective-interest amortization</u> method. This method is more theoretically correct than the straight-line method because it takes into consideration the time value of money. Rather than amortizing the same amount each year, as does the straight-line method, the effective-interest method recognizes a varying amount of amortization each year, which is the difference between the actual interest earned and the interest received on the bonds.

effective-interest amortization a method of systematically writing off a bond premium or discount that takes into consideration the time value of money; results in an equal rate of amortization for each period

To illustrate the computations involved in using the effective-interest amortization method, we will again consider Bicknell's purchase of 12 percent, 5-year, $20,000 bonds of Sunglow Company for $17,316. The amount of discount amortized in each of the 5 years using the effective-interest method would be

(1) Time Period	(2) Interest Received	(3) Interest Actually Earned (16% × ½)	(4) Amount of Amortization (3) − (2)	(5) Investment Balance
Acquisition date				$17,316
Year 1, 1st 6 months	$1,200	(8% × $17,316) = $1,385	$185	17,501
Year 1, 2nd 6 months	1,200	(8% × 17,501) = 1,400	200	17,701
Year 2, 1st 6 months	1,200	(8% × 17,701) = 1,416	216	17,917
Year 2, 2nd 6 months	1,200	(8% × 17,917) = 1,433	233	18,150
Year 3, 1st 6 months	1,200	(8% × 18,150) = 1,452	252	18,402
Year 3, 2nd 6 months	1,200	(8% × 18,402) = 1,472	272	18,674
Year 4, 1st 6 months	1,200	(8% × 18,674) = 1,494	294	18,968
Year 4, 2nd 6 months	1,200	(8% × 18,968) = 1,517	317	19,285
Year 5, 1st 6 months	1,200	(8% × 19,285) = 1,543	343	19,628
Year 5, 2nd 6 months	1,200	(8% × 19,628) = 1,572	372	20,000
			$2,684	

In this computation, column (2) represents the interest payment received at the end of each period; column (3) shows the amount of effective interest earned, which is the amount that will be reported on the Income Statement each period; column (4) is the difference between columns (3) and (2) and so represents the amortization; and column (5) shows the investment balance that will be reported on the Balance Sheet at the end of each period. Note that the interest rate used to compute the actual interest earned is the effective rate of 8 percent (16 percent ÷ 2) and not the stated rate of 12 percent. Also note that the total discount is the same as it was when the straight-line method was used—$2,684.

When bonds are purchased at a discount, the amount of amortization increases each successive period. This is so because the investment balance of the bonds increases, and a constant interest rate times an increasing balance results in an increasing amount of interest. If the bonds had been purchased at a premium, the effective-interest amortization method would involve a constant interest rate being multiplied by a declining investment balance each period. The result would be a decline in actual interest earned each period.

Since the effective-interest amortization method takes into account the time value of money and thus shows the true revenue earned each period, whereas the straight-line method represents only approximations, the accounting profession requires companies to use the effective-interest amortization method. As an exception to this rule, however, companies are allowed to use the straight-line method when the two methods produce amortization amounts that are not significantly different. Because this is often the case, both methods continue to be used.

Accounting for the Sale of Bonds or the Receipt of Their Maturity Value
If bonds are held until their maturity date, the accounting for the proceeds at maturity is simple. For example, if Bicknell were to hold the $20,000, 12 percent bonds from Sunglow until they mature, the entry to record the receipt of the bond principal on the maturity date would be

Cash   20,000
    Investment in Bonds—Sunglow Company   20,000
Received the principal of Sunglow bonds at maturity.

This entry assumes, of course, that all previous receipts of interest and bond amortizations have been properly recorded.

Bonds are accounted for as though they will be held until maturity. However, because they are usually traded on major exchanges that provide a continuous and ready market, they are often sold to other investors prior to that time. When bonds are sold prior to their maturity, the difference between the sales price and the investment balance is recognized as a gain or loss on the sale of investments.

To illustrate, we will assume that Bicknell purchased ten $1,000, 8 percent, 5-year bonds of RTA Company. We will also assume that the bonds were originally purchased on January 1, 1978, at 101 percent of face value (at 101) for $10,100, and that on January 1, 1981, Bicknell showed an unamortized balance of $10,040 for these bonds. If the bonds were sold on that day for $10,300, the entry to record the sale and recognize the gain would be (assuming no sales commission)

Cash   10,300
    Gain on Sale of Bonds   260
    Investment in Bonds—RTA Company   10,040
Sold the RTA bonds for $10,300.

When bonds are sold prior to their maturity date, it is important that the amortization of bond premiums or discounts be current at the date of sale.

If the amortization of disounts or premiums is not updated, the gains or losses recognized on the sale will be incorrect.

TO SUMMARIZE   Companies often make long-term investments in bonds issued by other companies or organizations. The price paid for a bond usually depends on the risk involved (reflected in its rating) and the bond interest rate. If the stated interest rate of a bond is less than the current market rate of similar investments, bonds usually sell at a discount. If the stated interest rate is higher than the market rate, a premium is usually paid. Companies investing in bonds purchase two elements: the right to receive interest payments at regular intervals over the life of the bond, and the face amount of the bond at maturity. Accounting for investments in bonds involves four steps: (1) accounting for the purchase of bonds, (2) accounting for interest received on bonds, (3) accounting for premium or discount amortization, and (4) accounting for the sale or maturity of the bonds. Amortization of premiums and discounts is usually accounted for by (1) the simple straight-line amortization method, or (2) the more theoretically correct effective-interest amortization method.

CHAPTER REVIEW

In addition to purchasing inventories, land, buildings, and equipment, firms often invest in other assets not directly related to their primary operations. These investments are classified as short-term assets if they are readily marketable and if management intends to hold them for one year or less, and as long-term assets if management does not intend to dispose of them within one year.

Short-term equity investments are accounted for on a lower-of-cost-or-market basis. That is, they are carried at cost unless the market price of a firm's total portfolio of short-term investments drops below cost, at which time the investments are written down to market. Gains and losses resulting from either the sale or the reduction to the lower of cost or market of short-term investments are included in a firm's net income.

Long-term investments in stocks can be accounted for by using either the cost or the equity method, depending on the degree of ownership in the investee company. If less than 20 percent of the outstanding stock of another company is owned, the cost method is used. If the level of ownership is at least 20 percent, the equity method is used. With the cost method, dividends received from investee companies are recorded as revenue. With the equity method, the investment balance is decreased by dividends and increased by the proportionate share of investee company earnings.

Long-term investments in bonds are initially recorded at cost. Cost is adjusted over the life of the bonds as discounts or premiums are amortized. The amortization of premiums and discounts adjusts the interest earned on bonds from the stated to the effective rate and writes up or down the book value of bonds to face value at maturity. Bond discounts and premiums can be amortized using either the straight-line or the effective-interest method. The latter is more theoretically correct and is required by current accounting standards, but since the differences between the two are usually insignificant, both are widely used.

KEY TERMS AND CONCEPTS

amortization of bonds (310)

bonds (305)

bond discount (309)

bond maturity date (305)

bond premium (309)

compound interest (296)

compound period (296)

consolidated financial statements (302)

cost method of accounting for investments in stocks (302)

effective-interest amortization (312)

equity method of accounting for investments in stocks (304)

face (maturity) value of a bond (305)

future amount of an annuity of $1 (299)

future amount of $1 (296)

investment (291)

line of credit (292)

long-term investment (301)

lower of cost or market (294)

marketable securities (293)

ordinary annuity (298)

parent company (302)

present value of an annuity of $1 (300)

present value of $1 (297)

short-term investment (292)

simple interest (296)

straight-line interest amortization (310)

subsidiary company (302)

DISCUSSION QUESTIONS

1. Why do firms invest in assets that are not directly related to their primary operations?

2. Describe the risk and return trade-off of investments.

3. What is the difference between simple and compound interest?

4. Why is a dollar received today generally worth more than a dollar received in the future?

5. Why is it especially important to use the concepts of present and future values during inflationary periods?

6. Why do more frequent compound periods result in greater future values (for example, quarterly compounding versus annual compounding)?

7. Why does the discounting of future sums with higher interest rates result in lower present values?

8. What is the primary basis for classifying investments as short- or long-term?

9. Why are short-term investments in stocks written down if cost exceeds market price, but not written up if the market price exceeds cost?

10. What is meant by a portfolio of stocks?

11. Are losses resulting from the write-down of long- and short-term investments to market treated the same? If not, how does the accounting differ?

12. Define a subsidiary and a parent company.

13. Why is the equity method required when accounting for investments in which an investor has 20 percent or more ownership of voting stock?

14. Do you think the "less than 20" and "more than 20" percent classifications of stock ownership correctly identify situations of little or no control or significant influence? Why?

15. What are bonds, and why are they issued?

16. What future cash inflows is a company buying when it purchases a bond?

17. When would a company be willing to pay more than the face amount (that is, a premium) for a bond?

18. What factors cause the prices of bonds to fluctuate in the marketplace?

19. Why does the amortization of a bond discount increase the amount of interest revenue earned on a bond?

20. Why is the effective-interest amortization method theoretically superior to the straight-line method?

21. Why must an investor purchasing bonds between interest payment dates pay the previous owner for accrued interest on those bonds?

22. In which direction would the market interest rate have to move in order for an investor in bonds to be able to sell the bonds at a price that is higher than the acquisition cost?

EXERCISES

E9-1 Short-Term Investments—Journal Entries

Prepare journal entries to record the following short-term investment transactions.

1. Purchased 100 shares of Langden Corporation stock at $32 per share, and paid brokerage costs of $200.

2. Received a cash dividend of 75 cents per share on Langden Corporation stock.

3. Sold 50 shares of Langden Corporation stock at $35 per share.

E9-2 Short-Term Investments in Stock

In December 1981, the treasurer of Beacon Company discovered that the company had excess cash on hand and decided to invest in Stewart Corporation stock. He intended to hold the stock for a period of 6 to 12 months. The following transactions took place.

January 1	Purchased 5,500 shares of Stewart Corporation stock for $82,500.
April 15	Received a cash dividend of 65 cents per share on the Stewart Corporation stock.
May 22	Sold 1,500 shares of the Stewart Corporation stock at $20 per share for cash.
July 15	Received a cash dividend of 45 cents per share on the Stewart Corporation stock.
August 31	Sold the balance of the Stewart Corporation stock at $8 per share for cash.

Give the appropriate journal entries to record each of these transactions.

E9-3 Future Amounts—Simple Computations

Find the future amount of:

1. $5,000 to be invested for 5 years at 8 percent interest compounded semiannually.

2. $5,000 to be invested for 5 years at 8 percent compounded quarterly.

3. $7,500 to be invested for 10 years at 12 percent compounded quarterly.

4. $7,500 to be invested for 4 years and 9 months, at 12 percent compounded quarterly.

E9-4 Present Values—Simple Computations

Find the present value of:

1. $10,000 due in 10 years at 5 percent compounded annually.

2. $15,000 due in $8\frac{1}{2}$ years at 10 percent compounded semiannually.

3. $7,500 due in 4 years at 12 percent compounded quarterly.

4. $10,000 due in 20 years at 8 percent compounded semiannually.

E9-5 Future Amount of an Annuity—Simple Computations

For each of the following, determine the future amount of an annuity.

1. $5,000 a year for 10 years at 8 percent compounded annually.

2. $1,250 per quarter for 10 years at 8 percent compounded quarterly.

3. $7,500 every 6 months for 7 years at 6 percent compounded semiannually.

4. $5,000 per quarter for $3\frac{3}{4}$ years at 12 percent compounded quarterly.

E9-6 Present Value of an Annuity—Simple Computations

For each of the following, determine the present value of an annuity.

1. $1,000 per quarter for 5 years at 16 percent compounded quarterly.

2. $5,000 every 6 months for 15 years at 6 percent compounded semiannually.

3. $10,000 per year for 10 years at 5 percent compounded annually.

4. $2,000 every 6 months for $8\frac{1}{2}$ years at 10 percent compounded semiannually.

E9-7 Future Amounts of an Annuity

Abstract, Inc., recently borrowed $100,000 from the First National Bank for 5 years. The loan agreement specifies that Abstract, Inc., will establish a cash fund into which it will make equal annual installments at the end of each year during the next 5 years. At the end of the 5 years the fund is to have a balance of $100,000, just enough to repay the loan.

1. If the fund earns 8 percent compounded annually, how much must Abstract, Inc., contribute each year in order to have $100,000 at the end of 5 years?

2. Suppose the loan was for 10 years instead of 5. What would the required annual payment to the fund be if, again, it earned 8 percent compounded annually?

3. Suppose Abstract, Inc., desires to make equal quarterly payments over the 10-year period rather than annual installments. If interest is earned at 8 percent compounded quarterly, how much must be invested each quarter to have the required $100,000?

E9-8   Present Values of an Annuity

1. An investment opportunity costing $96,664 will earn a return of $20,000 per year for 10 years. What is the annual rate of return on this investment?

2. If a company can earn 10 percent per year by investing its capital elsewhere, should it make the investment described in part (1)?

3. Suppose the investment costs $147,202 and will earn $20,000 per year for 10 years. Should the company now make the investment? Why or why not?

E9-9   Future Amounts

1. In the year just ended, Best Lining Company had sales of $735,025. If Best's sales are increasing at a rate of 8 percent each year, how long will it be before sales reach $1,000,000?

2. How many years will it take for sales to double?

E9-10   Present Value of an Annuity

Electric Power Company accumulated $500,000 of excess cash during a recent profitable year. Management has determined that it needs to invest enough of the excess cash in marketable securities to provide a cash flow of $50,000 a year for the next 5 years. The remainder will then be spent on research and development activities. How much cash must Electric Power Company invest in marketable securities in order to provide the necessary cash flow if investment opportunities are available at 6 percent? At 10 percent?

E9-11   Bond Price Determination

Action Incorporated has decided to purchase bonds of Rain Company as a long-term investment. The 10-year bonds have a stated interest rate of 8 percent and interest payments are made semiannually. How much should Action be willing to pay for $30,000 of the bonds if:

1. A rate of return of 10 percent is deemed necessary to justify the investment?

2. A rate of return of only 6 percent is considered adequate for the investment?

E9-12   Long-Term Investments in Stock

On March 15, 1981, Jackson Inc. acquired 5,000 shares of Lexington Mills common stock as a long-term investment. Lexington has 50,000 shares of outstanding voting common stock. The Lexington Mills shares are the only holdings in Jackson's portfolio of long-term stocks. The following transactions occurred during the fiscal year ending December 31, 1981.

Mar. 15   Purchased 5,000 shares of Lexington Mills common stock at $45 per share.

Dec. 1   Received cash dividend of $2 per share from Lexington Mills.

31   Lexington announced earnings for the year of $150,000.

31   Closing market price of Lexington Mills common stock was $42 per share.

1. What accounting method should be used to account for this investment? Why?

2. Record the above transactions in General Journal form.

3. Prepare a partial Income Statement and Balance Sheet to show how the Investment and related accounts would be shown on the financial statements.

E9-13   Long-Term Investments in Stock

Assume the same facts as in E9-12, except that Jackson Inc. acquired 15,000 shares of Lexington Mill's common stock.

1. What accounting method should be used? Why?

2. Record the listed transactions in General Journal form.

E9-14   Long-Term Investments in Stock— Equity Method

During 1981, Jacob Company purchased 60,000 shares of $25 par value common stock of Suker Corporation. Suker had a total of 240,000 shares of common stock outstanding.

1. Record the following transactions.
   (a) February 1—Purchased 60,000 shares at $30 per share.
   (b) December 31—$175,000 of total net income reported by Suker Corporation.
   (c) December 31—$0.25 per share dividend declared and paid by Suker Corporation.

2. On December 31, the market price of Suker's stock was $27. Show how this investment would be reported on the Balance Sheet (assuming that this is the only stock owned by Jacob Company).

E9-15   Long-Term Investments in Bonds

On January 1, 1981, Company K purchased a $2,000, 5 percent bond at 97 as a long-term investment. The bond pays interest annually on each December 31, and matures on December 31, 1983. Assuming straight-line amortization, answer the following questions.

1. What will be the net amount of cash received from this investment over its life?

2. How much cash will be collected each year?

3. How much discount will be amortized each year?

4. By how much will the Long-Term Investment account increase each year?

5. How much investment revenue will be reported on the Income Statement each year?

E9–16   Long-Term Investments in Bonds

Baron Tools purchased twenty $1,000, 8 percent, 20-year bonds of Mr. Kleen Corporation on January 1, 1981, as a long-term investment. The bonds mature on January 1, 2001, and interest is payable every January 1 and July 1. Baron Tools' reporting year ends December 31 and the company uses the straight-line method of amortizing bond premiums and discounts.

Make all the necessary journal entries relating to the bonds for 1981, assuming that:

1. The purchase price is 105 percent of par.
2. The purchase price is 97 percent of par.

E9–17   Straight-Line Amortization of Bond Premiums

Phillips Company purchased on their issuance date twenty $1,000, 8 percent, 5-year bonds of Quigley Company as a long-term investment for $21,706. Interest payments and amortization entries are made semiannually. Prepare a schedule showing the amortization of the bond premium over the 5-year life of the bonds. Use the straight-line method of amortization.

E9–18   Effective-Interest Amortization of Bond Premiums

Assume the same facts as in E9–17. Prepare a schedule showing the amortization of the bond premium over the 5-year life of the bonds, using the effective-interest method of amortization. (Hint: First calculate the effective rate of interest earned on the bonds.)

PROBLEMS

P9–1   Short-Term Investments—Analysis

The following data pertain to the marketable securities of Reed Company during 1981, the company's first year of operations.

a. Purchased 200 shares of A Corporation stock at $40 per share, plus brokerage fees of $100.

b. Purchased $3,000 of B Corporation bonds at face value, plus accrued interest of $90.

c. Received a cash dividend of 50 cents per share on the A Corporation stock.

d. Sold 50 shares of A Corporation stock for $46 per share.

e. Received interest of $120 on the B Corporation bonds.

f. Purchased 50 shares of C Corporation stock for $3,500.

g. Received interest of $120 on the B Corporation bonds.

h. Sold 150 shares of A Corporation stock for $28 per share.

i. Received a cash dividend of $1.40 per share on the C Corporation stock.

j. Interest receivable at year-end on the B Corporation bonds amounts to $30.

Required:

Enter the foregoing transactions in T-accounts and determine the amount of each of the following for the year.

1. Dividend revenue.
2. Bond interest revenue.
3. Net gain or loss from selling securities.

P9–2   Short-Term Investments in Stocks

Wright Company often purchases common stocks of other companies as short-term investments. During the current year, the following stock transactions occurred.

July 1   Purchased the following common stocks.

Corporation	Number of Shares	Total Price per Share
A	200	$36
B	300	23
C	150	78
D	100	42

Sept. 30   Received a cash dividend of $1.25 per share on Corporation A stock.

Dec. 1   Sold the stock in Corporation D for $37 per share.

Dec. 31   Quoted market prices on this date were: Corporation A stock, $32; Corporation B stock, $24; Corporation C stock, $75.

Required:

1. Record the transactions in General Journal entry form.

2. Illustrate how these investments would be reported on the Balance Sheet at December 31.

3. What items and amounts would be reported on the Income Statement for the year?

4. **Interpretive Question**   Why are losses from the write-down of short-term investments in stock to the lower of cost or market included in the current year's income, whereas most similar losses for long-term investments in stock are not?

P9–3   Present Value

Required:

For each of the following cases, calculate the appropriate amount. Round your answer to the nearest penny.

1. Find the present value of $2,000 to be received 3 years from now if the prevailing interest rate is 8 percent compounded quarterly.

2. Find the present value of $300 to be received at the end of each year for the next 4 years if the interest rate is 6 percent compounded annually.

3. Find the present value of $150 to be received at the end of each 6 months for the next 4 years. The interest rate is 6 percent compounded semiannually.

4. Find the present value of $20 to be received at the end of each 6 months for the next 10 years plus a single sum of $1,000 to be received at the end of the tenth year if the interest rate is 4 percent compounded semiannually.

5. Find the present value of $30 to be received at the end of each 6 months for the next 20 years plus a single sum of $1,000 to be received at the end of the twentieth year if the interest rate is 6 percent compounded semiannually.

6. Find the present value of $50 to be received at the end of each year for 8 years, starting 2 years from now, if the rate of interest is 8 percent compounded annually.

P9–4   Long-Term Investments in Stock—Cost and Equity Methods

During January 1981, Needlecraft, Inc., acquired 37,500 shares of Corporation A common stock for $22 per share. In addition, it purchased 5,000 shares of Corporation B preferred (nonvoting) stock for $120 per share. Corporation A has 150,000 shares of common stock outstanding and Corporation B has 12,000 shares of nonvoting stock outstanding.

The following data were obtained from operations during 1981.

	1981
Net Income:	
Corporation A	$170,000
Corporation B	75,000
Dividends Paid (per Share):	
Corporation A	$ 0.50
Corporation B	2.50
Market Value per Share at Dec. 31:	
Corporation A	$ 24
Corporation B	118

Required:

1. **Interpretive Question**   What method should Needlecraft use in accounting for the investment of Corporation A stock? Why? What accounting method should be used in accounting for Corporation B nonvoting stock? Why?

2. Give the General Journal entries necessary to record the transactions for 1981.

P9–5   Long-Term Investments in Stock—Cost and Equity Methods

The following transactions relate to the activities of Martin Company during the years 1981 and 1982.

Feb. 15	Purchased 5,000 shares of Nelson Sporting Equipment stock for $35 per share.
Dec. 1	Received payment of $1.25 per share cash dividend from Nelson Sporting Equipment.
Dec. 31	Nelson Sporting Equipment announced earnings for the year of $60,000.
Dec. 31	Closing market price of Nelson Sporting Equipment common stock was $32 per share.
July 1	Sold 5,000 shares of Nelson Sporting Equipment stock for $37 per share.

Nelson Sporting Equipment had 25,000 shares of common stock outstanding on January 1, 1981.

Required:

1. Record the transactions in General Journal entry form, using (a) the cost method and (b) the equity method.

2. Show the amounts that would be reported on the financial statements of Martin Company at December 31, 1981, under each assumption.

3. **Interpretive Question**   What is the minimum number of shares of stock that Nelson could have outstanding in order for Martin to use the cost method?

P9–6   Long-Term Investments in Bonds

Clampett Corporation purchased $25,000 of Becker Construction Company's $6\frac{1}{2}$ percent bonds at $102\frac{1}{2}$ plus accrued interest on February 1, 1981. The bonds mature on April 1, 1988, and interest is payable on April 1 and October 1.

On June 1, 1983, Clampett Corporation sold the Becker Construction Company bonds at 97 plus accrued interest. Clampett Corporation uses the straight-line method of amortizing bond premiums and discounts and makes amortization adjustments at year-end.

Required:

1. Present all journal entries to account for this investment during the years 1981, 1982, and 1983, assuming that Clampett closes its books annually on December 31.

2. **Interpretive Question** At the time these bonds were purchased (February 1, 1981), was the market rate of interest above or below $6\frac{1}{2}$ percent?

P9–7 Long-Term Investments in Bonds

Desert Equipment Company made the following purchases of bonds during 1981. All are long-term investments and pay interest semiannually.

Purchase Date	Corp.	Face Amount	Cost	Interest Rate, %	Maturity Date	Last Interest Payment Date
10/15/81	A	$ 5,000	94	$7\frac{1}{2}$	1/1/88	7/1/81
12/1/81	B	10,000	$102\frac{1}{2}$	6	4/1/86	10/1/81
12/15/81	C	15,000	106	$8\frac{1}{4}$	6/1/87	12/1/81
12/31/81	D	12,000	$97\frac{3}{4}$	5	5/1/84	11/1/81

Required:

1. Record the purchases in General Journal entry form.

2. Show all adjusting entries relating to the bonds on December 31, 1981, assuming Desert Equipment closes its books on that date and uses the straight-line amortization method.

3. **Interpretive Question** Which of these four investments do you think has the highest rating—is the least risky—on the basis of these data?

P9–8 Determining the Price of a Bond and Effective-Interest Amortization

A total of $200,000 of 5-year, 8 percent bonds is being sold at a time when the market rate of interest for similar investments is 6 percent. These bonds pay semiannual interest.

Required:

1. Would these bonds be issued at a premium or discount?

2. Compute the total selling price of the bonds. (Hint: Determine the price that would result in an effective rate of interest of 6 percent.)

3. Ignore your solutions to (1) and (2), and assume that your calculations in (2) yielded a selling price of $220,000. Using this amount, compute the amount of bond premium to be amortized the first year using the effective-interest method. Assume that all bonds were sold on the first day of the year in which they were authorized.

P9–9 Determining the Purchase Price of Bonds and Effective-Interest Amortization

Glenn Corporation decided to purchase twenty $1,000, $7\frac{1}{2}$ percent, 10-year bonds of Shelton Aviation as a long-term investment on February 1, 1981. The bonds mature February 1, 1987, and interest payments are made semiannually on February 1 and August 1.

Required:

1. How much should Glenn Corporation be willing to pay for the bonds if the current interest rate on similar investments is 6 percent?

2. Prepare a schedule showing the amortization of the bond premium or discount over the remaining life of the bonds, assuming Glenn Corporation uses the effective-interest method of amortization.

3. How much interest would be earned each year if the straight-line method of amortization were used? Show how these amounts differ from the annual interest earned using the effective-interest method.

4. **Interpretive Question** Which of the two amortization methods is preferable? Why?

P9–10 Unifying Problem: Short-Term Investments in Stocks and Bonds

On January 1, Inland Aviation Company had surplus cash. The management decided to invest in marketable securities. The following transactions occurred during the year.

Jan. 1   Purchased twenty $1,000, 6 percent bonds of Swift Corporation at par, plus accrued interest. Semiannual interest payment dates are November 1 and May 1 each year.

Feb. 15   Purchased 400 shares of Canton Corporation stock at $35 per share, plus brokerage fees of $500.

May 1   Received a semiannual interest payment on the Swift Corporation bonds.

Sept. 30   Received an annual cash dividend of $1.50 per share on Canton stock.

Oct. 15   Sold 250 shares of the Canton Corporation stock at $42 per share.

Nov 1   Received a semiannual interest payment on the Swift Corporation bonds.

Dec. 31   Adjusted the accounts to accrue interest on the Swift Corporation bonds.

Required:

1. Record the transactions in General Journal entry form.

2. The market quote for Swift Corporation's bonds at closing on December 31 was 104. The Canton stock closed at $40 per share. Prepare a partial Balance Sheet showing all the necessary data for these securities. Assume that marketable securities are reported at cost and that market value is shown parenthetically.

P9–11 Unifying Problem: Present and Future Values

Required:

Your rich Aunt Jennifer is having a difficult time trying to decide how to invest $500,000. Because you are taking an accounting course, she has asked you to help her with each of the following decisions. Interest is compounded annually in each case.

1. She wants to invest in a $10,000 bond that has a stated interest rate of 6 percent and a term of 10 years. (The bond pays interest once a year.) She is unhappy with the 6 percent return and will only invest in the bonds if she can earn a return of 8 percent. Ignoring transaction costs, how much should she be willing to pay for the bond in order to earn her desired 8 percent return?

2. She wants to open a savings account for her grandchild who just turned 14 years old. She wants to make only one payment into the account (immediately) but would like the payment to be large enough so that the balance in the savings account will total $100,000 when the child becomes 21 years old. If the savings account pays 6 percent interest, compounded annually, how much does she need to invest today?

3. Your aunt has decided that she wants to put at least part of the money in a relatively riskless investment and so has decided to invest $10,000 a year in a savings account at the Palo Alto Savings and Loan Association. The savings account will pay 6 percent and she would like to know what the balance in this account will be when she reaches 65 (9 years from now).

4. Finally, your aunt wants your advice on one more decision. She is interested in buying part ownership in an oil well. She can buy a 10 percent ownership in the well in either one of two ways. The first alternative is to pay $14,000 a year for 10 years and the other is to pay $100,000 immediately. If money is worth 8 percent to your Aunt Jennifer, which alternative should she select to minimize her investment in the oil well?

5. As a reward for your excellent advice, she is going to give you your choice of two gifts. The first is $10,000 a year for the next 10 years and the second is two payments, $50,000 in 5 years and $64,000 in 10 years from now. If money is worth 6 percent, which alternative should you take to maximize your gift? (Ignore taxes.)

P9–12 Unifying Problem: Long-Term Investments in Stocks and Bonds

On January 1, 1981, Custom Disco purchased $25,000, 8 percent, 10-year bonds of Jefferson Trucking as a long-term investment at 96, plus accrued interest. The bonds mature on November 1, 1987, and interest is payable semiannually on May 1 and November 1. Custom Disco uses the straight-line method of amortizing bond premiums and discounts.

In addition, on January 2, 1981, Custom Disco purchased 30 percent of the 50,000 shares of outstanding common stock of Mayberry Company at $42 per share, plus brokers' fees of $450. On December 31, 1981, Mayberry announced that its net income for the year was $150,000, and paid an annual dividend of $2 per share. The closing market price of Mayberry common stock on that date was $38 per share.

Required:

1. Record these transactions in General Journal entry form.

2. Show how the long-term investments and the related revenues would be reported on the financial statements of Custom Disco at December 31, 1981.

Table I   Amount of $1 Due in n Periods
$FV = P(1 + i)^n$

n	2%	3%	4%	5%	6%	8%	10%	12%	16%	20%
1	1.0200	1.0300	1.0400	1.0500	1.0600	1.0800	1.1000	1.1200	1.1600	1.2000
2	1.0404	1.0609	1.0816	1.1025	1.1236	1.1664	1.2100	1.2544	1.3456	1.4400
3	1.0612	1.0927	1.1249	1.1576	1.1910	1.2597	1.3310	1.4049	1.5609	1.7280
4	1.0824	1.1255	1.1699	1.2155	1.2625	1.3605	1.4641	1.5735	1.8106	2.0736
5	1.1041	1.1593	1.2167	1.2763	1.3382	1.4693	1.6105	1.7623	2.1003	2.4883
6	1.1262	1.1941	1.2653	1.3401	1.4185	1.5869	1.7716	1.9738	2.4364	2.9860
7	1.1487	1.2299	1.3159	1.4071	1.5036	1.7138	1.9487	2.2107	2.8262	3.5832
8	1.1717	1.2668	1.3686	1.4775	1.5938	1.8509	2.1436	2.4760	3.2784	4.2998
9	1.1951	1.3048	1.4233	1.5513	1.6895	1.9990	2.3579	2.7731	3.8030	5.1598
10	1.2190	1.3439	1.4802	1.6289	1.7908	2.1589	2.5937	3.1058	4.4114	6.1917
11	1.2434	1.3842	1.5395	1.7103	1.8983	2.3316	2.8531	3.4785	5.1173	7.4301
12	1.2682	1.4258	1.6010	1.7959	2.0122	2.5182	3.1384	3.8960	5.9360	8.9161
13	1.2936	1.4685	1.6651	1.8856	2.1329	2.7196	3.4523	4.3635	6.8858	10.6993
14	1.3195	1.5126	1.7317	1.9799	2.2609	2.9372	3.7975	4.8871	7.9875	12.8392
15	1.3459	1.5580	1.8009	2.0789	2.3966	3.1722	4.1772	5.4736	9.2655	15.4070
16	1.3728	1.6047	1.8730	2.1829	2.5404	3.4259	4.5950	6.1304	10.7480	18.4884
17	1.4002	1.6528	1.9479	2.2920	2.6928	3.7000	5.0545	6.8660	12.4677	22.1861
18	1.4282	1.7024	2.0258	2.4066	2.8543	3.9960	5.5599	7.6900	14.4625	26.6233
19	1.4568	1.7535	2.1068	2.5270	3.0256	4.3157	6.1159	8.6128	16.7765	31.9480
20	1.4859	1.8061	2.1911	2.6533	3.2071	4.6610	6.7275	9.6463	19.4608	38.3376
25	1.6406	2.0938	2.6658	3.3864	4.2919	6.8485	10.8347	17.0001	40.8742	95.3962
30	1.8114	2.4273	3.2434	4.3219	5.7435	10.0627	17.4494	29.9599	85.8499	237.3763
40	2.2080	3.2620	4.8010	7.0400	10.2857	21.7245	45.2593	93.0510	378.7212	1469.7716
50	2.6916	4.3839	7.1067	11.4674	18.4202	46.9016	117.3909	289.0022	1670.7038	9100.4383

Table II   Present Value of $1 Due in n Periods

$$PV = F \left[\frac{1}{(1 + i)^n} \right]$$

n	2%	3%	4%	5%	6%	8%	10%	12%	16%	20%
1	0.9804	0.9709	0.9615	0.9524	0.9434	0.9259	0.9091	0.8929	0.8621	0.8333
2	0.9612	0.9426	0.9246	0.9070	0.8900	0.8573	0.8264	0.7972	0.7432	0.6944
3	0.9423	0.9151	0.8890	0.8638	0.8396	0.7938	0.7513	0.7118	0.6407	0.5787
4	0.9238	0.8885	0.8548	0.8227	0.7921	0.7350	0.6830	0.6355	0.5523	0.4823
5	0.9057	0.8626	0.8219	0.7835	0.7473	0.6806	0.6209	0.5674	0.4761	0.4019
6	0.8880	0.8375	0.7903	0.7462	0.7050	0.6302	0.5645	0.5066	0.4104	0.3349
7	0.8706	0.8131	0.7599	0.7107	0.6651	0.5835	0.5132	0.4523	0.3538	0.2791
8	0.8535	0.7894	0.7307	0.6768	0.6274	0.5403	0.4665	0.4039	0.3050	0.2326
9	0.8368	0.7664	0.7026	0.6446	0.5919	0.5002	0.4241	0.3606	0.2630	0.1938
10	0.8203	0.7441	0.6756	0.6139	0.5584	0.4632	0.3855	0.3220	0.2267	0.1615
11	0.8043	0.7224	0.6496	0.5847	0.5268	0.4289	0.3505	0.2875	0.1954	0.1346
12	0.7885	0.7014	0.6246	0.5568	0.4970	0.3971	0.3186	0.2567	0.1685	0.1122
13	0.7730	0.6810	0.6006	0.5303	0.4688	0.3677	0.2897	0.2292	0.1452	0.0935
14	0.7579	0.6611	0.5775	0.5051	0.4423	0.3405	0.2633	0.2046	0.1252	0.0779
15	0.7430	0.6419	0.5553	0.4810	0.4173	0.3152	0.2394	0.1827	0.1079	0.0649
16	0.7284	0.6232	0.5339	0.4581	0.3936	0.2919	0.2176	0.1631	0.0930	0.0541
17	0.7142	0.6050	0.5134	0.4363	0.3714	0.2703	0.1978	0.1456	0.0802	0.0451
18	0.7002	0.5874	0.4936	0.4155	0.3503	0.2502	0.1799	0.1300	0.0691	0.0376
19	0.6864	0.5703	0.4746	0.3957	0.3305	0.2317	0.1635	0.1161	0.0596	0.0313
20	0.6730	0.5537	0.4564	0.3769	0.3118	0.2145	0.1486	0.1037	0.0514	0.0261
25	0.6095	0.4776	0.3751	0.2953	0.2330	0.1460	0.0923	0.0588	0.0245	0.0105
30	0.5521	0.4120	0.3083	0.2314	0.1741	0.0994	0.0573	0.0334	0.0116	0.0042
40	0.4529	0.3066	0.2083	0.1420	0.0972	0.0460	0.0221	0.0107	0.0026	0.0007
50	0.3715	0.2281	0.1407	0.0872	0.0543	0.0213	0.0085	0.0035	0.0006	0.0001

Table III   Amount of an Annuity of $1 per Period

$$FV_n = R\left[\frac{(1 + i)^n - 1}{i}\right]$$

n	2%	3%	4%	5%	6%	8%	10%	12%	16%	20%
1	1.0000	1.0000	1.0000	1.0000	1.0000	1.0000	1.0000	1.0000	1.0000	1.0000
2	2.0200	2.0300	2.0400	2.0500	2.0600	2.0800	2.1000	2.1200	2.1600	2.2000
3	3.0604	3.0909	3.1216	3.1525	3.1836	3.2464	3.3100	3.3744	3.5056	3.6400
4	4.1216	4.1836	4.2465	4.3101	4.3746	4.5061	4.6410	4.7793	5.0665	5.3680
5	5.2040	5.3091	5.4163	5.5256	5.6371	5.8666	6.1051	6.3528	6.8771	7.4416
6	6.3081	6.4684	6.6330	6.8019	6.9753	7.3359	7.7156	8.1152	8.9775	9.9299
7	7.4343	7.6625	7.8983	8.1420	8.3938	8.9228	9.4872	10.0890	11.4139	12.9159
8	8.5830	8.8923	9.2142	9.5491	9.8975	10.6366	11.4359	12.2997	14.2401	16.4991
9	9.7546	10.1591	10.5828	11.0266	11.4913	12.4876	13.5795	14.7757	17.5185	20.7989
10	10.9497	11.4639	12.0061	12.5779	13.1808	14.4866	15.9374	17.5487	21.3215	25.9587
11	12.1687	12.8078	13.4864	14.2068	14.9716	16.6455	18.5312	20.6546	25.7329	32.1504
12	13.4121	14.1920	15.0258	15.9171	16.8699	18.9771	21.3843	24.1331	30.8502	39.5805
13	14.6803	15.6178	16.6268	17.7130	18.8821	21.4953	24.5227	28.0291	36.7862	48.4966
14	15.9739	17.0863	18.2919	19.5986	21.0151	24.2149	27.9750	32.3926	43.6720	59.1959
15	17.2934	18.5989	20.0236	21.5786	23.2760	27.1521	31.7725	37.2797	51.6595	72.0351
16	18.6393	20.1569	21.8245	23.6575	25.6725	30.3243	35.9497	42.7533	60.9250	87.4421
17	20.0121	21.7616	23.6975	25.8404	28.2129	33.7502	40.5447	48.8837	71.6730	105.9306
18	21.4123	23.4144	25.6454	28.1324	30.9057	37.4502	45.5992	55.7497	84.1407	128.1167
19	22.8406	25.1169	27.6712	30.5390	33.7600	41.4463	51.1591	63.4397	98.6032	154.7400
20	24.2974	26.8704	29.7781	33.0660	36.7856	45.7620	57.2750	72.0524	115.3797	186.6880
25	32.0303	36.4593	41.6459	47.7271	54.8645	73.1059	98.3471	133.3339	249.2140	471.9811
30	40.5681	47.5754	56.0849	66.4388	79.0582	113.2832	164.4940	241.3327	530.3117	1181.8816
40	60.4020	75.4013	95.0255	120.7998	154.7620	259.0565	442.5926	767.0914	2360.7573	7343.8579
50	84.5794	112.7969	152.6671	209.3480	290.3359	573.7702	1163.9085	2400.0182	10435.6489	45497.1914

Table IV   Present Value of an Annuity of $1 per Period

$$PV_n = R \left[\frac{1 - \dfrac{1}{(1 + i)^n}}{i} \right]$$

n	2%	3%	4%	5%	6%	8%	10%	12%	16%	20%
1	0.9804	0.9709	0.9615	0.9524	0.9434	0.9259	0.9091	0.8929	0.8621	0.8333
2	1.9416	1.9135	1.8861	1.8594	1.8334	1.7833	1.7355	1.6901	1.6052	1.5278
3	2.8839	2.8286	2.7751	2.7232	2.6730	2.5771	2.4869	2.4018	2.2459	2.1065
4	3.8077	3.7171	3.6299	3.5460	3.4651	3.3121	3.1699	3.0373	2.7982	2.5887
5	4.7135	4.5797	4.4518	4.3295	4.2124	3.9927	3.7908	3.6048	3.2743	2.9906
6	5.6014	5.4172	5.2421	5.0757	4.9173	4.6229	4.3553	4.1114	3.6847	3.3255
7	6.4720	6.2303	6.0021	5.7864	5.5824	5.2064	4.8684	4.5638	4.0386	3.6046
8	7.3255	7.0197	6.7327	6.4632	6.2098	5.7466	5.3349	4.9676	4.3436	3.8372
9	8.1622	7.7861	7.4353	7.1078	6.8017	6.2469	5.7590	5.3282	4.6065	4.0310
10	8.9826	8.5302	8.1109	7.7217	7.3601	6.7101	6.1446	5.6502	4.8332	4.1925
11	9.7868	9.2526	8.7605	8.3064	7.8869	7.1390	6.4951	5.9377	5.0286	4.3271
12	10.5753	9.9540	9.3851	8.8633	8.3838	7.5361	6.8137	6.1944	5.1971	4.4392
13	11.3484	10.6350	9.9856	9.3936	8.8527	7.9038	7.1034	6.4235	5.3423	4.5327
14	12.1062	11.2961	10.5631	9.8986	9.2950	8.2442	7.3667	6.6282	5.4675	4.6106
15	12.8493	11.9379	11.1184	10.3797	9.7122	8.5595	7.6061	6.8109	5.5755	4.6755
16	13.5777	12.5611	11.6523	10.8378	10.1059	8.8514	7.8237	6.9740	5.6685	4.7296
17	14.2919	13.1661	12.1657	11.2741	10.4773	9.1216	8.0216	7.1196	5.7487	4.7746
18	14.9920	13.7535	12.6593	11.6896	10.8276	9.3719	8.2014	7.2497	5.8178	4.8122
19	15.6785	14.3238	13.1339	12.0853	11.1581	9.6036	8.3649	7.3658	5.8775	4.8435
20	16.3514	14.8775	13.5903	12.4622	11.4699	9.8181	8.5136	7.4694	5.9288	4.8696
25	19.5235	17.4131	15.6221	14.0939	12.7834	10.6748	9.0770	7.8431	6.0971	4.9476
30	22.3965	19.6004	17.2920	15.3725	13.7648	11.2578	9.4269	8.0552	6.1772	4.9789
40	27.3555	23.1148	19.7928	17.1591	15.0463	11.9246	9.7791	8.2438	6.2335	4.9966
50	31.4236	25.7298	21.4822	18.2559	15.7619	12.2335	9.9148	8.3045	6.2463	4.9995

CHAPTER 10

Property, Plant, and Equipment; Natural Resources; and Intangible Assets

---

In Chapter 9, we discussed one category of noncurrent assets—investments. Here we describe noncurrent assets that are used in operations. These include: (1) property, plant, and equipment; (2) natural resources, such as minerals, ores, and timber; and (3) intangible assets, such as patents, franchises, and goodwill. Because the useful lives of these assets usually extend over a number of years, the method used in accounting for them can dramatically affect reported income throughout several accounting periods.

long-term operational assets *long-lived assets acquired for use in the business rather than for resale; includes property, plant, and equipment; natural resources; and intangible assets*

The theory underlying the accounting for these assets (which we shall refer to collectively as long-term operational assets) is basically the same as that for prepaid expenses (see Chapter 5). That is, when an operational asset is purchased, its cost is recorded as an asset; then, as the benefits expire (or as the asset is used up), the cost is transferred from an asset to an expense account.

The major elements in accounting for equipment, a typical long-term operational asset, are

1. Accounting for its purchase.

2. Accounting for the allocation of its cost over its useful life.

3. Accounting for its sale or disposal.

4. Accounting for expenditures that either increase its value or extend its life (for example, overhauling the engine of a truck).

Types of Long-Term Operational Assets

Long-term operational assets are generally identified as belonging to one of three major categories—property, plant, and equipment; natural resources; and intangible assets.

Property, plant, and equipment refers to long-term, tangible assets acquired for use in the operation of a business and not intended for resale. This category includes land, buildings, equipment, and furniture. The process of allocating the costs of these assets over their estimated useful lives is called depreciation. All of these assets, except land, are depreciated.

Natural resources, such as mineral deposits, oil wells, gravel deposits, and timber tracts, are assets that are physically consumed or that waste away. The process of allocating the costs of natural resources over their estimated useful lives is called depletion. All natural resources are depleted.

Intangible assets are long-lived assets that are used in the operation of a business but do not have tangible substance. In most cases, they provide their owners with competitive advantages over other firms. Typical intangible assets are patents, licenses, franchises, and goodwill. The process of allocating the costs of intangible assets over their estimated useful lives is called amortization. All intangible assets are eventually fully amortized, that is, written down to zero.

Accounting for the Initial Cost of Property, Plant, and Equipment

property, plant, and equipment *tangible, long-lived assets acquired for use in the business rather than for resale*

Like all other assets, property, plant, and equipment are initially recorded at cost. This includes the purchase price, shipping, installation, sales taxes, and any other costs incurred to get the asset installed and in operating condition. A company can purchase these operational assets by paying cash, incurring a liability, trading in another asset, or a combination of these.

If a single asset is purchased for cash, the accounting is simple. To illustrate, we assume that Marianna Hotel Corporation paid $10,000 cash for a new delivery truck. The entry to record this purchase would be

Delivery Truck	10,000	
Cash		10,000

Purchased a delivery truck.

In this instance, cash was paid for a single asset, the truck. An alternative would have been to borrow part of the purchase price. If the company had borrowed $8,000 of the $10,000 from a bank or other lending institution, the entry would have been as shown on the next page.

Delivery Truck   10,000
    Cash   2,000
    Note Payable   8,000

Purchased a delivery truck; borrowed $8,000 from Banker's Trust.

The $8,000 represents the principal of the note; it does not include any interest charged by the lending institution. (The interest is recognized later as an interest expense.)

Another type of transaction, a basket purchase, involves two or more assets. A common basket purchase is land and the building on it. Since a single price is usually assigned to the purchase, it may be difficult to know how much of the total cost should be allocated to the individual assets.

To illustrate, we will assume that Marianna Hotel Corporation purchased a 40,000-square-foot building on 2.6 acres of land for $360,000. How much of the total cost should be assigned to the land and how much to the building? Their respective costs can be determined by using the relative fair-market-value method. If the fair market values of the land and the building are $100,000 and $300,000, respectively, the resulting individual costs would be $90,000 and $270,000, as calculated here.

Asset	Fair Market Value	Percentage of Total Value	Apportionment of Lump-Sum Cost
Land	$100,000	25	0.25 × $360,000 = $ 90,000
Building	300,000	75	0.75 × 360,000 = 270,000
Total	$400,000	100	$360,000

The fair market values would probably have been determined by a real estate appraisal. The journal entry to record this basket purchase would be

Land   90,000
Building   270,000
    Cash   360,000

Purchased 2.6 acres of land and a 40,000-square-foot building.

Again, if part of the purchase price were financed by a bank, an additional credit to Notes Payable would have been included in the entry.

An asset can also be purchased by trading a used asset for a new asset. This type of transaction is discussed on pages 340–343. In brief, newly acquired assets should be recorded at the fair market value of the assets given up to obtain them. If both cash and a used asset are given to acquire a new asset, the cost of the new asset is the sum of the cash paid and the fair market value of the asset traded.

TO SUMMARIZE   There are three types of long-term operational assets: property, plant, and equipment; natural resources; and intangible assets. All are originally recorded at cost (which includes all associated costs, such as installation, sales tax, and shipping). The cost is then allocated over the estimated useful life of the asset. When two or more assets are purchased together (a basket purchase), the relative fair-market-value method is used to determine their respective costs. When one asset is traded for another, the recorded cost of the new asset is usually the fair market value of the asset given up.

Allocating the Cost of Plant and Equipment to Expense

The second element in accounting for plant and equipment is the allocation of the assets' costs over their useful lives. The matching principle requires that these costs be allocated to expense in all periods benefited.

To illustrate, we assume that Marianna Hotel purchased a delivery truck with an estimated useful life of 5 years. In following the matching principle, Marianna charges the cost of the delivery truck as an expense over the 5 years benefited.

The process of allocating the cost of the truck over its useful life is called depreciation. To calculate depreciation expense on plant and equipment, you need to know the following about the asset: (1) original cost, (2) estimated useful life (number of periods benefited), and (3) estimated salvage, or residual, value (the net portion of the asset's cost that will be recovered when it is sold or disposed of). Of course, when an asset is purchased, a company does not know the asset's actual useful life or salvage value. These amounts must be estimated, usually on the basis of experience with similar assets.

There are several common methods of depreciating the costs of assets, and each is based on a different assumed pattern of benefits. For example, if the truck is expected to benefit all five periods equally, a straight-line method of depreciation should probably be used. If, on the other hand, most of the benefits will be realized in the earlier periods of the truck's life, an accelerated method, such as sum-of-the-years'-digits or double-declining-balance method, should be used.

If the truck's benefits are thought to decline on the basis of the number of miles or hours driven, the units-of-production depreciation method would be appropriate. Exhibit 10–1 compares the first three depreciation methods.

depreciation   *the process of cost allocation that assigns the original cost of plant and equipment to the periods benefited*

salvage value   *estimated value or actual price of an asset at the conclusion of its useful life, net of disposal costs*

EXHIBIT 10–1   **Comparison of Depreciation Methods**

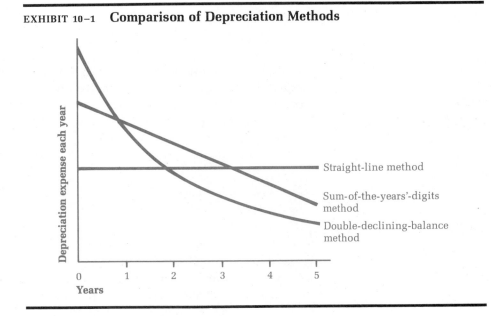

Obviously, the units-of-production method cannot be illustrated without knowing the number of miles the truck was driven during each of the 5 years of its useful life.

Because some operational assets benefit all periods equally, while others do not, companies are allowed to use any one of these methods. In reality, however, a method will generally be chosen with as much consideration given to its tax and earnings implications as to its theoretical appropriateness.

To illustrate the four depreciation methods, we assume that Marianna purchased a dishwasher for use in one of its hotels. The following facts apply.

Acquisition cost	$24,000
Estimated salvage value	$ 4,000
Estimated service life:	
In years	4 years
In dishes washed	40,000 loads of dishes

STRAIGHT-LINE METHOD OF DEPRECIATION

straight-line depreciation method   *the depreciation method in which the cost of an asset is allocated equally over the periods of the asset's estimated useful life*

The straight-line depreciation method is the simplest and one of the most commonly used depreciation methods. It assumes that an asset's cost should be assigned equally to all periods benefited. The formula for calculating annual straight-line depreciation is

$$\frac{\text{cost} - \text{salvage value}}{\text{estimated useful life (years)}} = \text{annual depreciation expense}$$

With this formula, the annual depreciation expense for the dishwasher would be calculated as follows:

$$\frac{\$24,000 - \$4,000}{4 \text{ years}} = \$5,000 \text{ depreciation expense per year}$$

accumulated depreciation   *the total depreciation charged on an asset since acquisition; a contra account deducted from the original cost of an asset on the Balance Sheet*

book value   *the net amount shown in the accounts for an asset, liability, or owners' equity item*

When the depreciation expense for an asset has been calculated, a schedule showing the annual depreciation expense, the total accumulated depreciation, and the asset's book value (undepreciated cost) for each year can be prepared. The depreciation schedule for the dishwasher is shown in Exhibit 10–2.

The entry to record straight-line depreciation would be

Depreciation Expense	5,000	
Accumulated Depreciation—Dishwasher.		5,000
To record the annual depreciation expense for the dishwasher.		

The debit entry, Depreciation Expense, is an expense and appears on the Income Statement. The credit entry, Accumulated Depreciation—Dishwasher, is a contra-asset account that is offset against the cost of the

EXHIBIT 10–2   **Depreciation Schedule with Straight-Line Depreciation**

Year	Depreciation Expense	Total Accumulated Depreciation	Book Value at End of Year
Acquisition date	—	—	$24,000
1	$5,000	$ 5,000	19,000
2	5,000	10,000	14,000
3	5,000	15,000	9,000
4	5,000	20,000	4,000

dishwasher on the Balance Sheet. At the end of the first year, the acquisition cost, accumulated depreciation, and book value of the machine would be presented on the Balance Sheet as follows:

Property, Plant, and Equipment:
Dishwasher $24,000
Less Accumulated Depreciation 5,000 $19,000

UNITS-OF-PRODUCTION METHOD OF DEPRECIATION

units-of-production depreciation method   *the depreciation method in which the cost of an asset is allocated to each period on the basis of the productive output of that asset during the period*

The units-of-production depreciation method is based on the assumption that an asset's decline in value is a function of use rather than time. Assets for which this method of depreciation may be appropriate are airplanes, where life is estimated in terms of number of hours flown; trucks, where life is estimated in terms of number of miles driven; and certain machines, where life is estimated in terms of number of units produced or processed. The formula for calculating units-of-production depreciation is

$$\frac{\text{number of units produced or processed during the current year}}{\text{total estimated life in units}} \times (\text{cost} - \text{salvage value}) = \text{depreciation expense}$$

To illustrate, we again consider Marianna's dishwasher, which has an expected life of 40,000 loads of dishes: 8,000 loads the first year, 10,000 the second year, 12,000 the third year, and 10,000 the fourth year. With the units-of-production method, the first year's depreciation expense would be calculated as follows:

$$\frac{8,000}{40,000} \times (\$24,000 - \$4,000) = \$4,000 \text{ depreciation expense for the first year}$$

The depreciation schedule for the 4 years is shown in Exhibit 10–3. The entry to record units-of-production depreciation during the first year of the

---

EXHIBIT 10–3   **Depreciation Schedule with Units-of-Production Depreciation**

Year	Depreciation Expense	Accumulated Depreciation	Book Value at End of Year
Acquisition date	—	—	$24,000
1	$4,000	$ 4,000	20,000
2	5,000	9,000	15,000
3	6,000	15,000	9,000
4	5,000	20,000	4,000

---

machine's life would be

Depreciation Expense   4,000
    Accumulated Depreciation—Dishwasher.................   4,000
To record depreciation for the first year of the dishwasher's life.

SUM-OF-THE-YEARS'-DIGITS METHOD OF DEPRECIATION

sum-of-the-years'-digits depreciation method (SYD) *the accelerated depreciation method in which a declining depreciation rate is multiplied by a constant balance (cost minus salvage value)*

The sum-of-the-years'-digits method (SYD) provides for a proportionately higher depreciation expense in the early years of an asset's life. It is therefore appropriate for assets that provide greater benefits in their earlier years as opposed to assets that benefit all years equally. The formula for calculating SYD is

$$\frac{\text{number of years of life remaining at beginning of year}}{\text{sum of the years' digits}} \times (\text{cost} - \text{salvage value})$$

$$= \text{depreciation expense}$$

The numerator is the number of years of estimated life remaining at the beginning of the current year. Therefore, an asset with a 10-year life would have 10 years remaining in the first year, 9 in the second, and so on.

The dishwasher, for example, would have 4 years of life remaining during the first year, 3 years during the second year, 2 years during the third year, and 1 year during the fourth year. The sum of the years' digits is 10, or (4 + 3 + 2 + 1). The depreciation on the machine for the first 2 years would be

First year: $\dfrac{4}{10} \times (\$24,000 - \$4,000) = \$8,000$

Second year: $\dfrac{3}{10} \times (\$24,000 - \$4,000) = \$6,000$

The depreciation schedule for 4 years is shown in Exhibit 10–4.

**EXHIBIT 10–4   Depreciation Schedule with
Sum-of-the-Years'-Digits Depreciation**

Year	Depreciation Expense	Total Accumulated Depreciation	Book Value at End of Year
Acquisition date	—	—	$24,000
1	$8,000	$ 8,000	16,000
2	6,000	14,000	10,000
3	4,000	18,000	6,000
4	2,000	20,000	4,000

When an asset has a long life, the computation of the denominator (sum of the years' digits) can become quite involved. There is, however, a simple formula to determine the denominator.

$$\frac{n(n+1)}{2}, \text{ where } n \text{ is the life of the asset}$$

Given that the dishwasher has a useful life of 4 years, the formula would work as follows:

$$\frac{4(5)}{2} = 10$$

As you can see, the answer is the same as if you had added the years' digits $(4 + 3 + 2 + 1)$. If an asset has a 10-year life, the sum of the years' digits is

$$\frac{10(11)}{2} = 55$$

DOUBLE-DECLINING-BALANCE METHOD OF DEPRECIATION

double-declining-balance depreciation method (DDB) *the accelerated depreciation method in which book value is multiplied by a constant depreciation rate (double the straight-line percentage)*

The double-declining-balance method (DDB) is similar to sum-of-the-years'-digits depreciation in that it provides for higher depreciation charges in the early years of an asset's life. In fact, double-declining-balance is the most accelerated depreciation method permitted by the IRS for tax purposes. Thus, DDB is quite widely used.[1]

Double-declining-balance depreciation is different from the other three methods discussed in two respects: (1) its initial computation ignores the asset's salvage value, and (2) it involves multiplying a constant depreciation

---

[1] The IRS only allows double-declining-balance depreciation on certain kinds of assets. On others, a maximum rate of 150 percent declining balance can be used, in which case 1.5 is substituted for 2 in the depreciation expense calculation.

EXHIBIT 10–5   **Depreciation Schedule with Double-Declining-Balance Depreciation**

Year	Computation	Depreciation Expense	Total Accumulated Depreciation	Book Value at End of Year
Acquisition date		—	—	$24,000
1	$24,000 × 0.50	$12,000	$12,000	12,000
2	12,000 × 0.50	6,000	18,000	6,000
3	6,000 × 0.50	2,000*	20,000	4,000
4			20,000	4,000

* Although the depreciation for the year was calculated to be $3,000 (6,000 × 0.50), only $2,000 can be depreciated because you cannot depreciate below the salvage value of $4,000. Note that the 50 percent is multiplied by book value at the beginning of the year, rather than by the last year's depreciation expense (which happens to produce identical results for a 4-year useful life).

---

rate by a decreasing undepreciated cost. The formula is

$$\left(\frac{1}{\text{estimated life (years)}} \times 2\right) \times \left(\text{cost} - \frac{\text{accumulated}}{\text{depreciation}}\right) = \frac{\text{depreciation}}{\text{expense}}$$

In the first part of this formula, the straight-line rate is converted to a percentage [1/estimated life (years)], which is doubled. The resulting percentage is then multiplied by the undepreciated cost (book value) to arrive at the amount of annual depreciation expense. For example, the depreciation calculation for the dishwasher would be

Straight-line rate   4 years = 1 ÷ 4 = 25 percent
Double the straight-line rate   25 percent × 2 = 50 percent
Annual depreciation expense   50 percent × undepreciated cost

The double-declining-balance depreciation for the 4 years is shown in Exhibit 10–5.

It is important to emphasize that although the calculation for double-declining-balance depreciation ignores the salvage value of an asset, this method never allows an asset to be depreciated below that salvage value.

COMPARISON OF DEPRECIATION METHODS

The amount of depreciation expense will vary according to the depreciation method used by a company. Exhibit 10–6 compares the annual depreciation expense on the dishwasher under each of the four methods.

This schedule makes it clear that the double-declining-balance method provides the highest amounts of depreciation in the early years of an asset's life. Because a higher depreciation expense results in a lower net income and hence lower income taxes, businesses like to use it or some other accelerated method when computing taxable income. On the other hand, since the straight-line method usually results in the lowest amount of

EXHIBIT 10-6   **Comparison of Depreciation Expense Using Different Depreciation Methods**

Year	Straight-Line Depreciation	Units-of-Production Depreciation	SYD Depreciation	DDB Depreciation
1	$5,000	$4,000	$8,000	$12,000
2	5,000	5,000	6,000	6,000
3	5,000	6,000	4,000	2,000
4	5,000	5,000	2,000	0

depreciation expense in the early years and hence the highest net income, businesses like to use it for financial reporting purposes. Unlike inventories, where businesses that use LIFO for tax purposes are required to use it for financial reporting, long-term operational assets can be depreciated differently for taxes and financial reports. Accordingly, many businesses use a dual set of depreciation methods: an accelerated method for computing taxable income, and a straight-line or other nonaccelerated method for financial reporting purposes. The result is that stockholders sometimes see the highest possible net income and the IRS sees the lowest possible net income. Thus, while a firm's method of depreciation is theoretically justified by the pattern of its assets' benefits, the choice is usually dictated by tax and financial reporting considerations.

The difference between any two methods is clearly one of timing. The tax reduction in the early years of an asset's life can be viewed as an interest-free loan from the government. Although this means that in the later years of an asset's life more taxes must be paid, inflation and the time value of money make deferring taxes a sound business decision.

Note that depreciation is not a process of valuation. A company never claims that an asset's recorded book value is equal to its market value. In fact, market values of assets often increase at the same time that depreciation expense is being recorded. Depreciation expense is an allocation of cost, not a process of reflecting market value changes.

PARTIAL-YEAR DEPRECIATION CALCULATIONS

Thus far, depreciation expense has been calculated on the basis of a full year. However, businesses purchase assets at all times during the year and so partial-year depreciation calculations are often required. To compute depreciation expense for less than a full year with any of the methods discussed, first calculate the depreciation expense for the year and then prorate it over the number of months the asset is held during the year. This is equivalent to saying that any one of the four methods can be used to calculate depreciation expense for full years, but a straight-line proportion (based on the number of months the expense applies out of the 12 months in a year) is always used when computing depreciation expense within a year.

EXHIBIT 10–7 **Partial-Year Depreciation**

Method	Full-Year Depreciation	Depreciation 1st Year (6 Months)	Depreciation 2nd Year (12 Months)	
Straight-line	$ 5,000	$2,500 (5,000 × $\frac{1}{2}$)	$5,000	
Sum-of-the-years'-digits	8,000	4,000 (8,000 × $\frac{1}{2}$)	7,000	$\begin{cases} 8,000 \times \frac{1}{2} \\ \text{plus} \\ 6,000 \times \frac{1}{2} \end{cases}$
Double-declining-balance	12,000	6,000 (12,000 × $\frac{1}{2}$)	9,000	$\begin{cases} 12,000 \times \frac{1}{2} \\ \text{plus} \\ 6,000 \times \frac{1}{2} \end{cases}$

To illustrate, we will assume that Marianna purchased its $24,000 dishwasher on July 1 instead of January 1. The depreciation calculations for the first $1\frac{1}{2}$ years would be as shown in Exhibit 10–7. In analyzing the amounts in Exhibit 10–7, you may find it helpful to refer to Exhibit 10–6, which shows the full-year calculations. The units-of-production method has been omitted from the exhibit. Midyear purchases do not complicate the calculations with this method, since it involves numbers of miles driven, hours flown, and so on, rather than time periods.

CHANGES IN DEPRECIATION ESTIMATES

As mentioned earlier, useful lives and salvage values are only estimates. Marianna's dishwasher, for example, was assumed to have a useful life of 4 years and a salvage value of $4,000. But, in reality, the machine's life and salvage value may be different. Thus, if after 3 years Marianna realizes that the machine will last another 3 years and that the salvage value will be $3,000 instead of $4,000, the accountant would need to calculate a new depreciation expense for the remaining 3 years. Using straight-line depreciation, the calculations would be

	Formula		Calculation		Total Depreciation
Annual depreciation for the first 3 years	$\dfrac{\text{cost} - \text{salvage value}}{\text{estimated useful life}}$	$=$ depreciation expense	$\dfrac{\$24,000 - \$4,000}{4 \text{ years}}$	$= \$5,000$	$15,000
Book value after 3 years	cost − depreciation to date	= book value	$24,000 − $15,000	= $9,000	
Annual depreciation for the last 3 years (new life of 6 years and new salvage value of $3,000)	$\dfrac{\text{book value} - \text{salvage value}}{\text{remaining useful life}}$	$=$ depreciation expense	$\dfrac{\$9,000 - \$3,000}{3 \text{ years}}$	$= \$2,000$	$ 6,000
Total depreciation					$21,000

EXHIBIT 10–8   Depreciation Schedule When There Is a Change in Estimate

Year	Depreciation Expense	Total Accumulated Depreciation	Book Value at End of Year
Acquisition Date	—	—	$24,000
1	$5,000	$ 5,000	19,000
2	5,000	10,000	14,000
3	5,000	15,000	9,000
Change			
4	2,000	17,000	7,000
5	2,000	19,000	5,000
6	2,000	21,000	3,000

This example shows that a change in estimate of useful life or salvage value does not require a modification of the depreciation expense already taken. New information only affects depreciation in future years. Exhibit 10–8 shows the revised depreciation expense.

TO SUMMARIZE   There are four common depreciation methods. Sum-of-the-years'-digits (SYD) and double-declining-balance (DDB) are accelerated methods. They provide for higher depreciation expense in the early years of an asset's life. The straight-line and units-of-production methods allocate cost proportionately over an asset's life on the basis of time and use, respectively. Regardless of which method is used, depreciation is only an estimate and it may require modification as new information becomes available.

Improving and Repairing Plant and Equipment

Sometime during its useful life, an asset will probably need to be repaired or improved. Two types of expenditures can be made on existing assets. The first is ordinary expenditures for repairs and other minor improvements. For example, a delivery truck requires oil changes and periodic maintenance. Since these types of expenditures typically benefit only the period in which they are made, they are expenses of the current period.

The second type is capital expenditures that either lengthen an asset's useful life or increase its capacity. These expenditures are capitalized; that is, they are added to the asset's cost instead of being expensed in the current period. For example, overhauling the engine of a delivery truck would involve a major expenditure. In order to qualify for capitalization, an expenditure should meet three criteria: (1) it must be significant in amount; (2) it should benefit the company over several periods, not just the current one; and (3) it should increase the productive life or capacity of the asset.

To illustrate the differences in accounting for capital and ordinary expenditures, we will assume that Marianna Hotel also purchased a larger delivery truck for $42,000. This truck had an estimated useful life of 8 years and a salvage value of $2,000. The straight-line depreciation on this delivery truck would be $5,000 per year [($42,000 − $2,000)/8 years]. Now, if the

capitalization   *the recording of an expenditure expected to benefit more than the current period as an asset*

company spent $1,500 each year for new tires and other normal maintenance, it would record these expenditures as

Repairs and Maintenance Expense	1,500	
Cash		1,500

Spent $1,500 for maintenance on $42,000 delivery truck.

This entry has no effect on either the recorded cost or the depreciation expense of the truck. On the other hand, if at the end of the sixth year of the truck's useful life, Marianna spent $8,000 to overhaul the engine (an expenditure that increases the truck's remaining life from 2 to 4 years), the depreciation for the last 4 years would be $4,500 per year, calculated as follows:

Annual depreciation for first 6 years	$\dfrac{\$42,000 - \$2,000}{8 \text{ years}} = \dfrac{\$5,000}{\text{per year}}$
Total depreciation for first 6 years	$30,000
Book value at end of 6 years	$12,000 ($42,000 − $30,000)
Capital expenditures	$8,000
New balance to be depreciated	$20,000 ($12,000 + $8,000)
Less salvage value	2,000
New depreciable amount	$18,000
Remaining life	4 years
Annual depreciation for last 4 years	$\dfrac{\$18,000}{4 \text{ years}} = \$4,500 \text{ per year}$

The journal entry to record the $8,000 capitalized expenditure would be

Delivery Truck[2]	8,000	
Cash		8,000

Spent $8,000 to overhaul the engine of the $42,000 delivery truck.

It is often difficult to determine whether a given expenditure should be capitalized or expensed. However, because the two procedures produce a different net income, every expenditure should be properly classified. In practice, if there is any doubt, a firm usually expenses rather than capitalizes, primarily because this results in the paying of lower taxes in the immediate year.

TO SUMMARIZE There are two types of expenditures for existing long-term operational assets: ordinary and capital. In general, for an expenditure to be capitalized, it must (1) be significant in amount, (2) provide benefits for more than one period, and (3) increase the productive life or capacity of an asset. Normal expenditures merely maintain an asset's productive capacity at the level originally projected. Capital expenditures are added to the cost of an asset, whereas ordinary expenditures are expenses of the current period.

---

[2] An alternative treatment would be to debit Accumulated Depreciation instead of Delivery Truck and recalculate net book value on the remaining life of the truck. The effect would be the same in that the book value would remain at $18,000 and the depreciation expense would still be $4,500 in each of the last 4 years.

Disposal of Property, Plant, and Equipment

Plant and equipment eventually become worthless or are sold. When a company removes one of these assets from service, it has to eliminate the asset's cost and accumulated depreciation from the accounting records. There are basically three ways to dispose of an asset: (1) discard or scrap it, (2) sell it, or (3) trade it in for a new one.

DISCARDING PROPERTY, PLANT, AND EQUIPMENT

When an asset becomes worthless and must be scrapped, its cost and its accumulated depreciation balance should be removed from the accounting records. If the asset's total cost has been depreciated, there is no loss on the disposal. If, on the other hand, the cost is not completely depreciated, the undepreciated cost represents a loss on disposal.

To illustrate, we assume that Marianna Hotel purchased a transport bus for $10,000. The bus had a 5-year life, no estimated salvage value, and was depreciated on a straight-line basis. If the bus were scrapped after 5 full years, the entry to record the disposal would be

Accumulated Depreciation—Transport Bus	10,000	
Transport Bus		10,000
Scrapped $10,000 transport bus.		

If it cost Marianna $300 to have the old bus towed away, the entry to record the disposal would be

Accumulated Depreciation—Transport Bus	10,000	
Loss on Disposal of Transport Bus	300	
Transport Bus		10,000
Cash		300
Scrapped $10,000 transport bus and paid disposal costs of $300.		

If the transport bus had been scrapped after only 4 years of service (and after $8,000 of the original cost had been depreciated), there would have been a loss on disposal of $2,000, and the entry to record the disposal would have been

Accumulated Depreciation—Transport Bus	8,000	
Loss on Disposal of Transport Bus	2,000	
Transport Bus		10,000
Scrapped $10,000 transport bus and recognized loss of $2,000.		

SELLING PROPERTY, PLANT, AND EQUIPMENT

A second way of disposing of property, plant, or equipment is to sell it. If the net sales price of the asset exceeds its book value, or undepreciated cost, there is a gain on the sale. Conversely, if the sales price is less than the book value, there is a loss.

To illustrate, we refer again to Marianna Hotel's $10,000 transport bus. If the bus were sold for $600 after 5 full years of service, the entry to record the sale would be

Cash	600	
Accumulated Depreciation—Transport Bus	10,000	
Transport Bus		10,000
Gain on Sale of Transport Bus		600

Sold $10,000 transport bus at a gain of $600.

Since the truck was fully depreciated, its book value was zero and the $600 was a gain. If the transport bus had been sold for $600 after only 4 years of service, there would have been a loss of $1,400 on the sale, and the entry to record the sale would have been

Cash	600	
Accumulated Depreciation—Transport Bus	8,000	
Loss on Sale of Transport Bus	1,400	
Transport Bus		10,000

Sold $10,000 transport bus at a loss of $1,400.

The $1,400 loss is the difference between the sales price of $600 and the book value of $2,000 ($10,000 − $8,000). The amount of a gain or loss is thus a function of two factors: (1) the amount of cash received from the sale; and (2) the book value of the asset at the date of sale.

EXCHANGING PROPERTY, PLANT, AND EQUIPMENT

A third way of disposing of property, plant, or equipment is to trade for another asset. Such exchanges occur regularly with cars, trucks, machines, and other types of large equipment.

Exchanging Similar Assets

How exchanges of assets are accounted for depends on whether the assets are similar or dissimilar. The entry to record a trade of similar assets depends on whether there is a gain or a loss. Normally, when the trade-in allowance is larger than the book value of the old asset, a gain is said to have occurred. However, two factors argue against recognizing the gain on such transactions: (1) the list price of the new asset may have been purposely set high to permit the seller to offer an inflated trade-in allowance, and (2) because the assets are similar, the exchange may be thought of as a continuation of a past transaction rather than as a new one. Instead of writing off the old asset and recording the new asset at its fair market value, it seems more appropriate, when the assets are similar and there is a gain, to extend the recognition of that gain over the life of the asset.

For these reasons, accountants generally do not recognize a gain on an exchange of similar assets.[3] Instead, accounting practice dictates that the

---

[3] A gain may be partially recognized in some situations where cash is received.

recorded cost of a new asset is the book value of the old asset plus the cash paid in acquiring the new asset.

To illustrate, we will assume that Marianna is exchanging an old delivery truck for a new one. If the old truck cost $10,000, accumulated depreciation is $8,000, and the price of the new truck is $14,000 ($11,000 in cash and a trade-in allowance of $3,000), the entry to record the exchange would be

Truck (New)	13,000	
Accumulated Depreciation (Old Truck).........	8,000	
Truck (Old)		10,000
Cash....................................		11,000

Exchanged used $10,000 delivery truck plus $11,000 for new delivery truck.

In this case, the cost of the new asset is equal to the book value of the old asset ($2,000) plus the cash paid. The computations for determining cost are as follows:

Old Truck		New Truck	
Cost	$10,000	Cash Paid....................	$11,000
Accumulated		Book Value of	
Depreciation	8,000	Old Truck	2,000
Book Value	$ 2,000	Cost of New Truck	$13,000

Because the new asset is recorded at $13,000 instead of $14,000, the total depreciation charges made over its useful life will be $1,000 less than they would have been otherwise. The result is that reported net income over those years will be $1,000 higher in total and so, in effect, the gain will be recognized but on a deferred basis.

While gains on exchanges of similar assets are usually not recognized at the time of the exchange, financial accounting rules require that material losses must be. This discrepancy between the handling of gains and losses is justified because not recognizing a loss may cause the new asset to be recorded at an amount greater than its future benefits.

To illustrate the accounting for a material loss, we will assume that Marianna trades a swimming-pool cleaner, which originally cost $20,000 and has a book value of $12,000, for a new one. If the price of the new cleaner is $30,000 and Marianna pays $25,000 plus the old cleaner, there will be a $7,000 loss on the transaction.

Old Cleaner		New Cleaner	
Cost	$20,000	Cash Paid	$25,000
Accumulated		Book Value of Old	
Depreciation	8,000	Cleaner....................	12,000
Book Value	$12,000	Total Paid	$37,000
		Price of New Cleaner	30,000
		Loss on Exchange	$ 7,000

The entry to record this exchange would be

Cleaner (New).............................	30,000	
Accumulated Depreciation (Old Cleaner)	8,000	
Loss on Exchange	7,000	
Cleaner (Old)...		20,000
Cash..		25,000

Exchanged used $20,000 swimming-pool cleaner plus $25,000 for new $30,000 cleaner (loss of $7,000).

Exchanging Dissimilar Assets

If dissimilar assets are traded, such as land for a truck or machinery for a building, both gains and losses are immediately recognized.

To illustrate, we assume that Marianna trades a delivery truck plus cash for a piece of land. The following data pertain to the trade.

Cost of Delivery Truck	$10,000
Accumulated Depreciation on Truck	4,000
Fair Market Value of Land	20,000

If Marianna gives the truck and $15,000 for the land, the entry will be

Land	20,000	
Accumulated Depreciation—Truck	4,000	
Loss on Trade-In	1,000	
Cash...		15,000
Truck		10,000

Exchanged used $10,000 truck plus $15,000 for land worth $20,000 (loss of $1,000: $6,000 book value of truck plus $15,000 cash equals $21,000 minus $20,000 land).

On the other hand, if Marianna pays only $12,000 plus the truck, the entry will be

Land	20,000	
Accumulated Depreciation—Truck	4,000	
Cash...		12,000
Truck		10,000
Gain on Trade-In		2,000

Exchanged used $10,000 truck plus $12,000 for land worth $20,000 (gain of $2,000: $20,000 land minus $6,000 book value of truck and $12,000 cash).

With dissimilar assets, gains and losses are recognized immediately. The exchange is considered a new transaction, requiring the old asset (in this case, the truck) to be written off and the future benefits of the new asset (land) to be recorded at its fair market value (in this case, $20,000). Accounting for exchanges of either similar or dissimilar assets is more complicated when the transaction includes a receipt of cash.

TO SUMMARIZE   There are three ways of disposing of assets: (1) scrapping, (2) selling, and (3) exchanging. If a scrapped asset has not been fully depreciated, a loss equal to the undepreciated cost or book value is recognized. When an asset is sold, there is a gain if the sales price exceeds the book value and a loss if the sales price is less than the book value. When assets are exchanged, the accounting depends on three factors: (1) whether the assets are similar or dissimilar, (2) whether there is a gain or loss on the exchange, and (3) whether cash is paid or received in the exchange. The following chart summarizes the required accounting for the different exchanges where cash is not received.

	Book value of exchanged assets plus cash exceeds fair market value of acquired assets:	Book value of exchanged assets plus cash is less than fair market value of acquired assets:
Similar assets are traded.	Loss is recognized—basis of new asset is its fair market value.	Gain is not recognized—basis of new asset is book value of old asset plus cash paid.
Dissimilar assets are traded.	Loss is recognized—basis of new asset is its fair market value.	Gain is recognized—basis of new asset is its fair market value.

Accounting for Natural Resources

natural resources *assets, such as minerals, oil, timber, or gravel, that are extracted or otherwise depleted*

depletion *the process of cost allocation that assigns the original cost of a natural resource to the periods benefited*

As noted at the beginning of this chapter, natural resources include such things as oil, timber, coal, and gravel. Like all other assets, newly purchased or developed natural resources are recorded at cost. This cost must be written off as the assets are extracted or otherwise depleted. The process of writing off the cost of natural resources is called depletion and involves the calculation of a depletion rate for each unit of the natural resource.

To illustrate, we will assume that Marathon Company, which manufactures heavy tractor equipment, decides to diversify (invest in another type of business) and purchases a coal mine for $1,200,000. The entry to record the purchase would be

Coal Mine	1,200,000	
Cash.		1,200,000

Purchased a coal mine.

If the mine has an estimated 200,000 tons of coal deposits, the depletion expense for each ton of coal extracted will be $6 ($1,200,000/200,000 tons). Now, if 12,000 tons of coal were mined in the current year, the depletion entry would be

Depletion Expense	72,000	
Coal Mine		72,000

To record depletion for the year: 12,000 tons at $6.00 per ton.

A contra-asset account, such as Accumulated Depletion, is not used in this example. Instead, the asset account, Coal Mine, is credited directly. Actually, either approach would be appropriate. We have used the direct approach because it is more common in practice in accounting for natural resources.

After the first year's depletion expense has been recorded, the coal mine will be shown on the Balance Sheet as follows:

Natural Resources:
Coal Mine (cost $1,200,000) $1,128,000

But how do you determine the number of tons of coal in a mine? Since most natural resources cannot be counted, the amount of the resource owned is an estimate. The depletion calculation is therefore likely to be revised as new information becomes available. When an estimate is changed, a new depletion rate per unit is calculated and used to compute depletion during the remaining life of the natural resource, or until another new estimate is made.

Accounting for Intangible Assets

intangible assets *long-lived assets that do not have physical substance and are not held for resale*

Intangible assets are those assets that are long-lived, are not held for resale, have no physical substance, and usually provide their owner with competitive advantages over other firms. Familiar examples are patents, franchises, licenses, and goodwill. Although intangible assets have no physical substance, they are accounted for in the same way as other long-term operational assets. That is, they are originally recorded at cost and the cost is written off over the useful or legal life, whichever is shorter. The periodic charge made to write off an intangible asset's cost is called amortization. Straight-line amortization is generally used for intangible assets.

amortization *the process of cost allocation that assigns the original cost of an intangible asset to the periods benefited*

PATENTS

patent *an exclusive right granted for 17 years by the federal government to manufacture and sell an invention*

A patent is an exclusive right to produce and sell a commodity that has one or more unique features. Issued to inventors by the federal government, patents have a legal life of 17 years. They may be obtained on new products developed in a company's own research laboratories or they may be purchased from others. If a patent is purchased from others, its cost is simply the purchase price. The cost of a patent for a product developed within a firm, however, is difficult to determine. Should it include research and development costs as well as the legal fees to obtain the patent? Should other company expenses be included? Prior to 1974, there were no real accounting guidelines specifying which expenditures should be capitalized as part of the cost of a patent. In 1974, however, the FASB determined that, because of the high degree of uncertainty about their future benefits, research and development costs must be expensed in the period in which they are incurred. Therefore, the costs of most internally developed patents are expensed.

To illustrate the accounting for patents, we assume that Marathon Company acquires, for $200,000, a patent granted 7 years earlier to another firm. The entry to record the purchase of the patent would be

Patent	200,000	
Cash		200,000

Purchased patent.

Because 7 years of its 17-year legal life have already elapsed, the patent now has a legal life of only 10 years. If its useful life is at least 10 years, one-tenth of the $200,000 cost should be amortized each year for the next 10 years. The entry each year to record the patent amortization expense would be

Amortization Expense—Patent	20,000	
Patent		20,000

To amortize one-tenth of the cost of the patent.

As was the case with natural resources, a contra-asset account, such as Accumulated Amortization, was not used in this example. While crediting such an account would have been appropriate, the direct approach is again more common in practice.

FRANCHISES AND LICENSES

franchise *an exclusive right to sell a product or offer a service in a certain geographical area*

Issued either by companies or government agencies, franchises and licenses are exclusive rights to perform services in certain geographical areas. For example, McDonald's Corporation sells franchises to individuals to operate its hamburger outlets in specific locations. Similarly, the Interstate Commerce Commission issues licenses to trucking firms, allowing them to transport certain types of goods in specific geographical areas. The cost of a franchise or license is amortized over its useful or legal life, whichever is shorter.

GOODWILL

goodwill *an intangible asset showing that a business is worth more than the value of its net assets because of strategic location, reputation, good customer relations, or similar factors; equal to the excess of cost over the fair market value of the net assets purchased*

When businesses are purchased, the negotiated price often exceeds the total value of the specific assets minus outstanding liabilities. This excess in purchase price that cannot be allocated to specific assets is called goodwill and is an intangible asset. Goodwill reflects such favorable characteristics as a good reputation, a strategic location, product superiority, or management skill.

Goodwill should be recorded only if its value can be objectively determined by an event or transaction. Therefore, even though two businesses may enjoy the same favorable factors, goodwill will be recognized only in the accounts of the buyer of a firm. This disparity in accounting exists because the action of a buyer in paying a premium for a firm is objective evidence that goodwill exists and has a specific value.

Unlike other intangible assets that decrease in value with time, goodwill often increases in value. Nevertheless, in order to ensure that different firms account for goodwill in similar ways, accounting practice dictates that goodwill must be amortized over a period not exceeding 40 years.

To illustrate the accounting for goodwill, we assume that Marathon Company purchased Ideal Drug Store for $400,000. At the time of purchase, the recorded assets and liabilities of Ideal Drug had the following fair market values. Note that fair market values (the current prices of items) will generally differ from book values (the historical costs paid for items less any depreciation, amortization, or depletion). The amount paid in excess of current market value is recorded as goodwill.

Inventory	$220,000
Long-Term Operational Assets	110,000
Other Assets (Prepaid Expenses, etc.)	10,000
Liabilities	(20,000)
Total Net Assets	$320,000

Because Marathon was willing to pay $400,000 for Ideal Drug, there must have been other favorable, intangible factors worth approximately $80,000. These factors are called goodwill and the entry to record the purchase of the drug store would be

Inventory	220,000	
Long-Term Operational Assets	110,000	
Other Assets	10,000	
Goodwill	80,000	
Liabilities		20,000
Cash		400,000

Purchased Ideal Drug Store for $400,000.

If Marathon decides to use 40 years as the useful life of the goodwill, each year the amortization entry will be

Amortization Expense—Goodwill	2,000	
Goodwill		2,000

To record annual straight-line amortization of goodwill ($80,000 ÷ 40 years).

TO SUMMARIZE Natural resources are assets, such as gravel or coal, that are consumed or wasted away. Intangible assets are long-term assets that have no physical substance but that provide competitive advantages to owners. Common intangible assets are patents, franchises, licenses, and goodwill. The costs of natural resources are depleted, whereas the costs of intangible assets are amortized.

CHAPTER REVIEW

There are three major types of long-term operational assets: (1) property, plant, and equipment; (2) natural resources; and (3) intangible assets. The four elements in accounting for these assets are (1) acquisition, (2) allocation of cost to expense over the life of the asset, (3) repairs and improvements, and (4) disposal. Long-term operational assets are always recorded at cost, which includes shipping, sales taxes, and other incidental expenses.

In the case of basket purchases, costs are usually determined by using the relative fair-market-value method.

Allocating costs over the lives of plant and equipment is called depreciation. There are four common techniques for depreciating the costs of these assets: straight-line, units-of-production, sum-of-the-years'-digits (SYD), and double-declining-balance (DDB). Two of these, SYD and DDB, are accelerated depreciation methods, and the other two assign cost proportionately over an asset's life, either as a function of time (straight-line) or of use (units-of-production). Changes in depreciation estimates affect depreciation amounts in current and subsequent years.

Repairs, maintenance, and improvement expenditures are either expensed or capitalized. Expenditures that provide benefits only in the current accounting period and do not increase productive capacity or useful life are charged against current income as expenses. Expenditures that are material in amount, provide benefits that extend beyond the current accounting period, and increase productive capacity or useful life are capitalized.

Assets can be disposed of in three ways: (1) scrapped, (2) sold, or (3) exchanged for new assets. There is usually no gain involved in scrapping an asset. Any loss to be recognized is equal to an asset's undepreciated cost or book value. If the proceeds received from the sale of an asset exceed its book value, there is a gain on the sale. If the proceeds are less than book value, a loss is experienced. Gains and losses are also recognized in exchanges of dissimilar assets. For exchanges of similar assets, losses are recognized but the recognition of gains depends on whether cash is paid or received. In the usual situation, where additional cash is paid, a gain is not recognized and the recorded cost of the new asset is the book value of the old asset plus the cash or other consideration paid in the exchange.

Accounting for natural resources is similar to that for property, plant, and equipment. Thus, natural resources are originally recorded at cost and the cost is subsequently depleted over an asset's useful life. Intangible assets are long-term operational assets that do not have physical substance and that usually provide owners with advantages over competitors. Common examples are patents, franchises, licenses, and goodwill. The process of writing off the costs of intangible assets over their useful lives is called amortization.

KEY TERMS AND CONCEPTS

accumulated
   depreciation (330)
amortization (344)
book value (330)
capitalization (337)
depletion (343)
depreciation (329)
double-declining-
   balance depreciation
   method (DDB) (333)

franchise (345)
goodwill (345)
intangible asset (344)
long-term operational
   assets (326)
natural resources (343)
patent (344)
property, plant, and
   equipment (327)
salvage value (329)

straight-line
   depreciation method
   (330)
sum-of-the-years'-digits
   depreciation method
   (SYD) (332)
units-of-production
   depreciation method
   (331)

DISCUSSION QUESTIONS

1. What is the difference between an asset and an expense?

2. What expenditures, other than the net purchase price, can be included in the cost of an asset?

3. When is it necessary to use the relative fair-market-value method to determine the cost of long-term operational assets?

4. Is depreciation a method of allocating the cost of an asset over its useful life or is it a way of reflecting the annual reduction in market value as the asset ages? Discuss.

5. Which of the depreciation methods discussed in this chapter will usually result in the highest net income in the early years of an asset's life?

6. Which of the depreciation methods discussed in this chapter will usually allow a firm to pay the least amount of taxes in the early years of an asset's life?

7. In which of the four methods of depreciation is the estimated salvage value ignored in the calculation?

8. What type of an account is Accumulated Depreciation? Where does it appear on the financial staments?

9. It is said that no matter which depreciation method is being used to allocate costs between years, a straight-line method apportionment is always made within a year. What does this statement mean?

10. When changing the estimate of the useful life of an asset, should depreciation expense for all of the previous years be recalculated? If not, how do you account for a change in the estimate of the useful life of an asset?

11. What is the difference between an ordinary and a capital expenditure?

12. If it is uncertain whether an expenditure will benefit one or more than one accounting period, or whether it will increase the capacity or useful life of an operational asset, most firms will expense rather than capitalize the expenditure. Why?

13. Why is it common to have a gain or loss on the disposal of a long-term operational asset? Is it true that if the useful life and salvage value of an asset are known with certainty and are realized, there would never be such a gain or loss?

14. When recording the disposal of a long-term operational asset, why is it necessary to debit the accumulated depreciation of the old asset?

15. Why is the list price of a new asset often ignored when accounting for the purchase of long-term operational assets?

16. Why is it often necessary to recalculate the depletion rate for natural resources?

17. Is raw land depleted like other natural resources? If not, why not?

18. Why are intangible assets considered assets if they have no physical substance?

19. Why does accounting practice require that research and development costs be expensed as incurred?

20. When should goodwill be recorded? Why?

21. Goodwill can only be recorded when a business is purchased. Does this result in similar businesses having incomparable financial statements?

22. Why does the accounting profession require goodwill to be amortized over a period not to exceed 40 years?

EXERCISES

E10–1 Accounting for the Acquisition of Assets

Straw Furniture Company decided to purchase a new furniture-polishing machine for its store in New York City. After a long search, it found the appropriate polisher in Chicago. The machine cost $25,000, and had an estimated 10-year life and no salvage value. Straw Company had the following additional expenditures with respect to this purchase.

Sales tax	$1,250
Delivery costs (FOB shipping point)	1,500
Installation costs	600
Painting of machine to match the decor	1,000

1. What is the cost of the machine to Straw Furniture Company?

2. What is the amount of the first year's depreciation if Straw Company uses the straight-line depreciation method?

E10–2 Accounting for the Acquisition of Assets (Basket Purchase)

XYZ Corporation purchased land and a building for a total cost of $200,000. After the purchase, the property was appraised. Fair market values were determined to be $60,000 for the land and $120,000 for the building. Given these appraisals, record the purchase of the property by XYZ Corporation.

E10-3   The Acquisition and Depreciation of Assets

Big Oil Company purchased new drilling equipment on July 1, 1981, using checks #1015 and #1016 to do so. The check totals are shown below, along with a breakdown of the charges.

1015 (Payee—Oil Equipment, Inc.):

Cost of drilling equipment	$ 75,000
Cost of cement platform	25,000
Installation charges	13,000
Total.................................	$113,000

1016 (Payee—Red Ball Freight):

Freight-In on drilling equipment	$ 2,000

Assuming that the estimated life of the drilling equipment is 10 years and its salvage value is $5,000:

1. Record the disbursements on July 1, 1981, assuming that no previous entry had been recorded for the drilling equipment.

2. Disregarding the information given about the two checks, assume that the drilling equipment was capitalized at a total cost of $95,000. Calculate the amount of depreciation expense for 1981 using the following methods.
   (a) Sum-of-the-years'-digits.
   (b) Double-declining-balance.
   (c) Straight-line.

3. Prepare the journal entry to record the depreciation for 1981 in accordance with part 2(a).

E10-4   The Acquisition, Depreciation, and Disposal of Assets

On January 1, 1981, Hybird Company purchased a building and land for $300,000. The most recent appraisals of the building and the land were $100,000 and $50,000, respectively. The building has an estimated useful life of 20 years and salvage value of $10,000. (Assume cash transactions and straight-line depreciation.)

1. Prepare journal entries to record: (a) purchase of the building and land on January 1, 1981, and (b) depreciation expense on December 31, 1981.

2. Assume that after 3 years the property (land and building) was sold for $225,000. Prepare the journal entry to record the sale.

E10-5   The Acquisition and Trade-In of Assets

Prepare entries in the books of Acquisitions Unlimited to reflect the following (assume cash transactions).

1. Purchased a machine to be used by the firm in its production process.

Invoice price	$10,000
Cash discount taken	100
Installation costs	600
Sales tax on the machine...................	50

2. Added a waste-reducing gauge, which cost $500, to the machine. This gauge is expected to increase the resale value of the machine.

3. Performed normal periodic maintenance on the machine at a cost of $300.

4. Added governor costing $400, which is expected to increase the machine's life but will not increase its resale value.

5. On January 1, traded a $5,000 cleaning machine for a new $6,000 cleaning machine. At the time of the trade, the old machine had an accumulated depreciation balance of $3,000. The company received a trade-in allowance of $2,100 and paid $3,900 in cash.

E10-6   Depreciation Calculations

Davidson Company purchased a new car on July 1, 1980, for $6,000. The estimated life of the car was 4 years or 108,000 miles and its salvage value was estimated to be $600. The car was driven 8,000 miles in 1980 and 10,000 miles in 1981.

Compute the amount of depreciation expense for both 1980 and 1981, using the following methods.

1. Straight-line.
2. Sum-of-the-years'-digits.
3. Double-declining-balance.
4. Units-of-production.

E10-7   Depreciation Calculations

On January 1, 1981, a machine was purchased for $70,000. Installation cost was $2,000. It was determined that the salvage value of the machine would be $7,000. The machine has a useful life of 5 years.

Compute the depreciation expense for 1980 and 1981, using the following methods.

1. Straight-line.
2. Double-declining-balance.
3. Sum-of-the-years'-digits.

E10-8   Depreciation Calculations

On October 1, 1980, Aaron, Inc., bought a pitching machine to be used in its newly established "Sports World Complex." The machine cost $10,000 and is estimated to have a useful life of 5 years or 450,000 pitches, after which it can be sold for $1,000.

Assuming that Aaron, Inc., is a calendar year business, compute the amount of depreciation using the

1. Straight-line method for 1980.
2. Sum-of-the-years'-digits method for 1981.
3. Double-declining-balance method for 1980.
4. Units-of-production method for 1980, assuming there were 50,000 pitches.
5. Double-declining-balance method for 1981.

E10–9   Depreciation Calculations

Harker Hardware Company has a giant paint mixer that cost $42,500 plus $200 to install. The estimated salvage value of the paint mixer at the end of its useful life in 15 years is estimated to be $900. Harker estimates that the machine can mix 850,000 cans of paint during its lifetime.

Compute the second full year's depreciation expense, using the following methods.

1. Straight-line.
2. Double-declining-balance.
3. Sum-of-the-years'-digits.
4. Units-of-production, assuming that the machine mixes 56,000 cans of paint during the second year.

E10–10   Depreciation Calculations

On January 1, AT Company purchased a $19,000 machine. The estimated life of the machine is 5 years and the estimated salvage value is $4,000. The machine has an estimated useful life in productive output of 75,000 units. Actual output was: year 1, 20,000 units; year 2, 15,000 units.

1. Compute the amount of depreciation expense for year 1, using each of the following methods.
   (a) Straight-line.
   (b) Units-of-production.
   (c) Sum-of-the-years'-digits.
   (d) Double-declining-balance.
2. What would be the book value of the machine at the end of the first year, assuming that straight-line depreciation was used?
3. If the machine was sold at the end of the fourth year for $14,000, how much would the company report as a gain or loss (assume straight-line depreciation)?

E10–11   Change in Depreciation Estimates

Mildew Brewing Company purchased a $400,000 vat for its brewery on January 1, 1981. The vat's estimated useful life is 20 years with no salvage value. Mildew uses straight-line depreciation on all its brewery equipment.

1. Compute the depreciation expense for year 1.
2. What will the book value of the vat be on December 31, 1992?
3. If, on January 1, 1993, Miller determines the vat will last another 16 years instead of 8 years, what will the depreciation expense be for 1993?
4. Given the information in (3), what will the book value of the vat be on December 31, 1995?

E10–12   Disposal of Long-Term Operational Assets

ZZZ Mattress Company purchased a delivery truck 5 years ago for $15,000. Presently, accumulated depreciation on the truck is $9,000. The current fair market value of the truck is $5,000.

Prepare journal entries to record the sale or exchange of the truck, assuming that

1. The truck is sold for $7,000 cash.
2. The truck is exchanged for $4,000 of supplies.
3. The truck is exchanged for a new truck with a fair market value of $10,000. In addition to the old truck, $3,000 cash was paid in the exchange.
4. The truck was exchanged for a $5,000 note.
5. The truck, plus a cash payment of $2,000, was exchanged for a new truck having a fair market value of $7,000.

E10–13   Accounting for the Exchange of Assets

On June 30, 1981, Newgood Corporation exchanged a used $40,000 machine for a new one with a list price of $60,000. The old machine was originally purchased on January 1, 1978, and had a 4-year life expectancy with no estimated salvage value. In trading for the new machine, the company received an allowance of $5,000 for the old machine. Newgood Corporation uses SYD depreciation.

Assuming that Newgood is a calendar year corporation, complete the following.

1. Update the depreciation on the old machine to the date of trade.
2. Compute the book value of the old machine at the date of trade.
3. Record the exchange in General Journal form.

E10–14   Exchanges and Depreciation of Assets

Equipment belonging to Johnson Manufacturing Company had a market value of $95,000 on March 31, 1981, when it was traded for new similar equipment that was priced at $120,000. A trade-in allowance of $90,000 was given and the balance was paid in cash. Accounts relating to the old equipment had the following balances on December 31, 1980.

	Debit	Credit
Equipment......................	100,000	
Accumulated Depreciation—		
Equipment		4,950

Depreciation expense is calculated using the units-of-production method, with the machine's estimated useful life being 100,000 units. Salvage value is expected to be $1,000. Two thousand units were produced in the first quarter of 1981.

1. Provide the journal entries necessary on March 31, 1981, to update the depreciation expense and record the exchange.

2. Calculate the implicit gain or loss in this transaction.

3. Now assume that the March 31, 1981, exchange did not take place. If the cost of the old machine is still $100,000, record its depreciation expense for 1981 if a salvage value of $5,000 is now expected. Useful life is estimated to be 23,750 units, and 3,500 units were produced in the first quarter of 1981.

E10–15   Accounting for the Exchange of Assets

Dixon Company decided to purchase a new vehicle that had a list price of $4,500 and a cash price without trade-in of $4,200. The dealer required a cash payment of $3,300 in addition to the trade-in of an old vehicle that had a $700 book value. (The cost of the old vehicle was $4,000.)

1. Give the entry to record the exchange.

2. Record the exchange, assuming that $3,800 cash plus the old vehicle were given for the new one.

E10–16   Accounting for the Disposal of Assets

Gale Cement Company has a truck it would like either to sell or trade. The truck had an original cost of $60,000, was purchased 3 years ago, and was expected to have a useful life of 5 years with no salvage value. (Assume straight-line depreciation.)

Assuming that depreciation expense to the date of sale has been properly recorded, prepare journal entries to record the disposal of the truck under each of the following conditions.

1. Gale Company sells the truck for $25,000 cash.

2. Gale Company sells the truck for $20,000 cash.

3. Gale Company trades the truck for a new one with a list price of $80,000 and is given a trade-in allowance on the old truck of $30,000.

4. Gale Company trades the truck for a piece of land that is valued at $60,000, and pays $32,000 in addition to the old truck.

5. The old truck is wrecked and Gale Company hauls it to the junkyard.

E10–17   Accounting for Natural Resources

On January 1, 1981, McDonald Investment Corporation purchased for cash a coal mine, having taken into consideration the favorable tax consequences and the inevitable energy crunch in the future. McDonald paid $800,000 for the mine. Shortly after the purchase, an engineer estimated that there were 80,000 tons of coal in the mine.

1. Record the purchase of the mine on January 1, 1981.

2. Record the depletion expense for 1981, assuming that 20,000 tons of coal were mined during the year.

3. Assume that on January 1, 1982, the company received a new estimate that the mine contained 120,000 tons of coal. Record the entry (if any) to show the change in estimate.

4. Record the depletion expense for 1982, assuming that another 20,000 tons of coal were mined.

E10–18   Accounting for Natural Resources

On April 31, 1981, Super Oil Company purchased for cash an oil well, with reserves of an estimated 100,000 barrels of oil, for $500,000.

Prepare journal entries to record the following.

1. The purchase of the oil well.

2. During 1981, 7,000 barrels of oil were extracted from the well.

3. During 1982, 15,000 barrels of oil were extracted from the well.

4. At the beginning of 1983, it was determined that only 60,000 barrels of oil remained in the well. During 1983, 20,000 barrels of oil were extracted from the well. Record the appropriate depletion expense.

E10–19   Accounting for Intangible Assets

During 1981, Temple Research Institution had the following intangible assets.

Asset	Cost	Date Purchased	Expected Useful or Legal Life
Goodwill	$ 8,000	January 1, 1976	40 years
Patent	68,000	January 1, 1978	17 years
Franchise	90,000	January 1, 1979	10 years

1. Record the amortization expense for each of these intangible assets for 1981.

2. Prepare an intangible asset section of the Balance Sheet for Temple Research Institution as of December 31, 1981.

E10–20 Accounting for Intangible Assets (Goodwill)

On January 1, 1981, Leech Company purchased the following assets and liabilities of Brooke Company for $250,000.

	Book Value	Fair Market Value
Inventory	$40,000	$ 50,000
Building	80,000	100,000
Land	50,000	60,000
Accounts receivable	20,000	20,000
Accounts payable	(10,000)	(10,000)

1. Prepare a journal entry to record the purchase of Brooke by Leech Company.

2. Record any amortization of goodwill as of December 31, 1981. (Assume a 40-year amortization period for the goodwill.)

PROBLEMS

P10–1 The Acquisition, Depreciation, and Sale of an Asset

On July 1, 1981, George Meyer bought a used pickup truck at a cost of $1,150 for use in his business. On the same day, Mr. Meyer had the truck painted blue and white (his company's colors) at a cost of $165. Mr. Meyer estimates the life of the truck to be 3 years or 40,000 miles. He further estimates that the truck will have a $200 scrap value at the end of its life, but that it will also cost him $25 to transfer the truck to the junkyard.

Required:

1. Record the following in General Journal form.
   - (a) July 8, 1981   Paid all bills pertaining to the truck. (No previous entries had been recorded concerning these bills.)
   - (b) Dec. 31, 1981   The depreciation expense for the year, using the straight-line method.
   - (c) Dec. 31, 1982   The depreciation expense for 1982, again using the straight-line method.
   - (d) Jan. 2, 1983   Sold the truck for $1,000 cash.

2. What would have been the depreciation expense for 1981 if the truck had been driven 8,000 miles and the units-of-production method of depreciation had been used?

3. **Interpretive Question**   In 1(d), there is a gain of $255. Why did this gain occur?

P10–2 Acquisition, Depreciation, and Sale of an Asset

On January 2, 1981, Far Eastern Oil Company purchased a new airplane. The following costs are related to the purchase.

Airplane—base price	$62,000
Cash discount (if paid prior to 1/31/81)	2,000
Sales tax	4,000
Delivery charges	3,000

Required:

1. In General Journal form, record the payment of these items on January 2, 1981.

2. Ignore your answer to (1) and assume that the airplane cost $50,000 and has an expected useful life of 5 years or 1,500 hours. The estimated salvage value is $5,000. Using each of the following methods, calculate the amount of depreciation expense to be recorded for the second year.
   - (a) Units-of-production (assume that 300 hours were flown in 1982).
   - (b) Sum-of-the-years'-digits.
   - (c) Double-declining-balance.

3. Ignore the information in (1) and (2) and assume that the airplane costs $50,000, its expected useful life is 5 years, and its estimated salvage value is $5,000. The company now uses the straight-line depreciation method and on July 1, 1984, the following balances appeared in the related accounts.

Airplane	$50,000
Accumulated Depreciation—Airplane	27,000

Prepare the necessary journal entries to record the trade-in of this airplane on July 1, 1984, for a smaller airplane with a list price of $35,000. No additional cash was paid for the new airplane.

4. **Interpretive Question**   In (3), why is the new airplane not recorded at $35,000? What effect does the recording of the new airplane at a cost of less than $35,000 have on depreciation charges in subsequent years?

P10–3 Depreciation Calculations

Bigfoot, Inc., a firm that makes oversized boots, purchased a machine for its factory. The following data relate to the machine.

Price	$12,000
Delivery charges	100
Installation charges	500
Date purchased	May 1, 1981
Estimated useful life:	
In years	8 years
In hours of production	14,000 hours of operating time
Residual (scrap) value	$1,800

During 1981, the machine was used 1,400 hours. During 1982, the machine was used 2,100 hours.

Required:

Determine the depreciation expense and the year-end book values for the machine for the years 1981 and 1982, assuming:

1. The straight-line method is used.
2. The double-declining-balance method is used.
3. The units-of-production method is used.
4. The sum-of-the-years'-digits method is used.
5. Which method would you use in order to pay the lowest taxes in 1981 and 1982?
6. **Interpretive Question** Why would a company want to delay the payment of taxes?

P10–4 Depreciation Calculations

On April 1, 1981, Jesse James Bank purchased a new computer at a price of $70,000. Additional costs of $10,000 were incurred for installation. The computer has an estimated useful life of 10 years and a salvage value of $5,000. (The bank operates on a calendar year basis.)

Required:

1. Determine depreciation expense for the first 3 years, using the following methods.
   (a) Straight-line.
   (b) Sum-of-the-years'-digits.
   (c) Double-declining-balance.
2. **Interpretive Question** Which method would be most favorable for tax purposes? Why?

P10–5 The Depreciation and Disposal of an Asset

A truck with an estimated life of 5 years was acquired on January 1, 1981, for $10,800. The estimated salvage value is $1,000 and the service life is estimated to be 140,000 miles. The accounting year ends December 31.

Required:

1. Compute the depreciation expense for 1981 and 1982, using the following four methods.
   (a) Straight-line.
   (b) Sum-of-the-years'-digits.
   (c) Double-declining-balance.
   (d) Units-of-production, given 20,000 miles in 1981 and 30,000 miles in 1982.
2. A machine that cost $54,000 has an estimated useful life of 7 years and a salvage value of $5,000. Journalize the disposal of the machine under each of the following conditions (assume straight-line depreciation).
   (a) Sold the machine for $42,000 cash after 2 years.
   (b) Sold the machine for $18,000 cash after 5 years.
   (c) After 3 years traded the old machine for a similar new one that had a list price of $57,000. A trade-in allowance of $20,000 was received.
3. **Interpretive Question** Why is the loss on the trade-in in question 2(c) recognized? If only $5,000 cash had been paid, would a gain have been recognized?

P10–6 Comparison of Depreciation Methods—Effect on Net Income and Taxes

On January 1, 1981, Johnson Ski Company purchased a new factory in which skis could be made twice as rapidly as in the past. The new factory cost $400,000 and was the largest investment ever made by Johnson. The president has asked you, as the accountant for the company, how much the annual depreciation expense on the new factory will reduce net income. You reply that the factory can be depreciated in several ways, some of which would reduce net income more than others during the first years of the factory's useful life. The president feels that the same depreciation method should be used for both income tax and financial reporting purposes and asks you to estimate how much difference there would be during the first 4 years in both net income and income taxes if different depreciation methods were used. You estimate that the factory will have a 10-year life, after which time it will be obsolete and have no salvage value. If you estimate that net income for the next 4 years (before taxes and depreciation on the factory) will be $100,000, $90,000, $80,000, and $70,000, respectively, what would be the amounts of Johnson's net income and income taxes in each of these 4 years if you use: (1) straight-line depreciation, (2) SYD depreciation, and (3) DDB depreciation? Assume that Johnson Ski Company pays taxes at the rate of 30 percent of net income.

P10-7   Changes in Depreciation Estimates

On January 1, 1975, Woodfield Trucking Company purchased two new trucks at a total cost of $225,000. It was estimated that the trucks would have a useful life of 8 years and a salvage value of $4,500 each. Woodfield uses the SYD method of depreciation for all of its equipment.

Required:

1. Record the purchase of the trucks on January 1, 1975.

2. Record the depreciation expense on the trucks for 1980.

3. Assume that during 1981 the company realized the trucks would last 4 more years instead of 2 but would still have the same salvage value. Record the revised depreciation expense on the trucks for 1981.

4. Make the necessary entry to record the sale of one of the trucks on December 31, 1981. The truck was sold for $10,000. (Assume that the two trucks had an equal cost.)

5. **Interpretive Question**   How much depreciation expense would be recorded on the second truck during 1987 if it were still being used and if its estimated salvage value was still $4,500? Why?

P10-8   Unifying Problem: Property, Plant, and Equipment

Sherwood Corporation owns and operates three sawmills that make lumber for building homes. The operations consist of cutting logs in the forest, hauling them to the various sawmills, sawing the lumber, and shipping it to building supply warehouses throughout the western part of the United States. To haul the logs, Sherwood has several trucks. Relevant data pertaining to one truck are

a. Date of purchase: July 1, 1979

b. Cost: Truck | $60,000
      Trailer | 20,000
      Paint job
      (to match company colors) | 1,500
      Sales tax | 3,500

c. Estimated useful life of the truck: 150,000 miles

d. Estimated salvage value: Zero

e. 1980 expenditures on truck:

   (1) Spent $5,000 on tires, oil changes, greasing, and other miscellaneous items.

   (2) Spent $22,000 to overhaul the engine, replace the brakes, and replace the gears on January 1, 1980. This expenditure increased the life of the truck by 100,000 miles.

f. Exchanged the truck on April 1, 1981, for a new truck with a list price of $90,000. The old truck was driven 30,000 miles in 1981. A payment of $50,000 was made on the exchange.

Required:

Record journal entries to account for:

1. The purchase of the truck.

2. The 1979 depreciation expense using units-of-production depreciation and assuming the truck was driven 90,000 miles.

3. The expenditures relating to the truck during 1980.

4. The 1980 depreciation expense using the units-of-production method and assuming the truck was driven 60,000 miles.

5. The exchange of the truck on April 1, 1981.

P10-9   Unifying Problem: Accounting for Natural Resources

Wilderness Associates believes that buying and developing natural resources represent excellent profitable ventures. Since 1979, it has had the following activities.

1/1/80   Purchased for $800,000 a tract of timber estimated to contain 1,600,000 board feet of lumber.

1/1/81   Purchased for $600,000 a silver mine estimated to contain 30,000 tons of silver.

7/1/81   Purchased for $60,000 a uranium mine estimated to contain 5,000 tons of uranium.

1/1/82   Purchased for $500,000 an oil well estimated to contain 100,000 barrels of oil.

Required:

1. Provide the necessary journal entries to account for the following.

   (a) The purchase of these assets.

   (b) The depletion expense for 1982 on all four assets, assuming that the following were extracted.

   (1) 200,000 board feet of lumber

   (2) 5,000 tons of silver

   (3) 1,000 tons of uranium

   (4) 10,000 barrels of oil

2. Assume that on January 1, 1983, after 20,000 tons of silver had been mined, engineers' estimates revealed that only 4,000 tons of silver remain. Record the depletion expense for 1983 assuming 2,000 tons were mined.

3. Compute the book values of all four assets as of December 31, 1983, assuming that the total extracted to date is

   (a) Timber tract—800,000 board feet.

   (b) Silver mine—22,000 tons (only 2,000 tons left per part 2).

   (c) Uranium mine—3,000 tons.

   (d) Oil well—80,000 barrels.

P10–10   Unifying Problem: Accounting for Intangible Assets

R&D Nightclub owns several intangible assets:

a. A patent on a cash register that shows various mixed drinks instead of dollar amounts on its keys. When the key for a certain drink is pushed, that drink is automatically mixed and an amount equal to the cost of the drink must be deposited in the cash register. This patent, which cost $90,000 on July 1, 1980, is valuable because it makes it almost impossible for bartenders to steal. The patent had a remaining life of 15 years when purchased.

b. A franchise that provides R&D with the exclusive right to sell Highlight Beer in the eastern part of the United States. This franchise cost $10,000 on January 1, 1979, at which time it had a life of 10 years.

c. Goodwill was purchased with the nightclub on December 30, 1960, for $40,000 and is being amortized over 40 years.

d. A license to sell liquor, which originally cost $6,500 on January 1, 1979 and had a 13-year life.

Required:

1. Make the journal entries to record the acquisition of these four intangible assets. (Assume the goodwill was paid for separately at the time the company was purchased.)

2. Record the amortization expense on the four intangible assets for 1981.

3. Compute the book values of the four intangibles at December 31, 1981.

CHAPTER 11

Long-Term Liabilities

---

equity financing *raising money, or capital, by issuing stock*

debt financing *raising money, or capital, by borrowing*

Financing a business often requires resources beyond those available from current earnings. Two common ways of generating additional financial resources are (1) by issuing stock (equity financing), and (2) by borrowing money (debt financing). Because both types of financing have their advantages and disadvantages, firms usually try to reach an appropriate balance between the two.

Equity financing, which is covered in Chapter 12, essentially has two major advantages: The proceeds from the issuance of stock are interest-free (although dividends are usually paid to stockholders), and the proceeds do not have to be repaid. The major disadvantage of equity financing is ownership dilution. When new stock is issued, current owners possess a smaller interest in the company. For example, if you own 50 of 100 shares issued, you have a 50 percent ownership. If another 50 shares are issued to someone else, your ownership interest drops to $33\frac{1}{3}$ percent (50/150).

The major advantages and disadvantages of obtaining additional financial resources through borrowing are outlined in Exhibit 11–1. While most of these advantages and disadvantages are self-explanatory, two may need some clarification. As mentioned in the second advantage, interest paid on debts is deductible for income tax purposes. This means that, for a profitable company, the real cost of borrowing is reduced. For example, if a company that is taxed at 40 percent of income can borrow money at

---

EXHIBIT 11-1 **Debt Financing**

Advantages	Disadvantages
Borrowing does not dilute the ownership of a firm, as does the selling of stock.	Borrowed money must be repaid at some specified future date.
Interest paid on borrowed money is tax deductible, whereas dividends paid to stockholders are not.	Interest on borrowed money must be paid, usually each year throughout the life of the debt.
Since the number of shares of stock is not increased through borrowing, earnings per share usually will be higher than if stock were sold.	Interest payments generally reduce the absolute amount of net income.
If a firm can borrow at a net interest rate that is less than its rate of earnings, profits can be increased. This is called leveraging.	In the case of liquidation or bankruptcy of a firm, debtholders rank ahead of stockholders in receiving the firm's assets. Thus, stockholders may lose some or all of their investment.

---

10 percent, its real cost of borrowing is only 6 percent. Or, put another way, every dollar of interest paid reduces the amount of taxes owed by 40 cents. Thus, when this 40-cent reduction in taxes is combined with the $1 interest cost, the net cost of borrowing is only 60 cents, or in this case [(60/100) × 10 percent interest] 6 percent.[1]

leveraging the advantage (or disadvantage) obtained from using borrowed money to finance a business when the net interest rate of the borrowed funds is less (more) than the company's earnings rate

A second advantage of borrowing that may need explanation is lever-aging. If a company's annual profits are regularly 20 percent of total assets, it can increase its earnings significantly by borrowing (to purchase additional assets) at 10 percent. In this case, total earnings would be the original 20 percent plus a 10 percent net return on borrowed resources (or even more, if we take into account the tax deductibility of the interest on the loan). This use of outside money is a real advantage for a company with a good earnings rate. Leveraging becomes a disadvantage, however, if the earnings rate drops below the interest rate. And if a company has losses, not only are those losses greater than they would be if there were no borrowing, but also, since there are no income taxes on a loss, the real cost of borrowing is not reduced by the fact that interest is tax deductible.

Measuring Long-Term Liabilities

Money borrowed for a long period of time is classified on the Balance Sheet as a long-term liability. There are many different types of long-term liabilities; the most common are notes payable, mortgages payable, deferred

---

[1] This principle also holds true for individuals who borrow money to purchase a house or other asset. Since interest paid on home mortgages is tax deductible (if deductions are itemized), the net interest cost of a home loan is less than the stated amount of interest.

income taxes payable, lease obligations, and bonds payable. Before discussing these individual liabilities, we should mention some factors that affect the measurement of all long-term liabilities.

Conceptually, the amount of a liability, at any particular time, is the present value of all future outflows of assets required to pay the liability in full. Obviously, if a liability is short-term, the present value of outflows needed to pay it is approximately equal to the stated amount of the liability. (Recall from Chapter 9 that the difference between stated amounts and present values increases as the number of discount periods increases.) Thus, the value of short-term liabilities is easily measured. In the case of long-term liabilities, however, the present value of future outflows of assets needed to settle an obligation is often significantly different from the stated amount of that liability.

To illustrate, we will assume that Jacobs Automobile Company buys a car-washing machine. Jacobs purchased the machine by issuing a $100,000 5-year non-interest-bearing note. This means that $100,000 is due in one lump sum five years from now. Is the liability really $100,000? Certainly, in an economy where money has value over time, a loan with such favorable terms would never be extended. (That is, the manufacturer would never extend to Jacobs a 5-year interest-free loan, which is what the transaction would amount to if the current price of the machine actually were $100,000.) Therefore, the $100,000 must include a finance charge and the real liability (the cash price for which the car-washing machine could have been purchased today) must be less than $100,000. If the market rate of interest is 8 percent, then the $100,000 should be discounted to a present value of $68,060 (see Table II, page 323). Given a cash-equivalent price of $68,060, the purchase would be recorded as follows:

Car-Washing Machine......................	68,060	
Discount on Note Payable....................	31,940	
Note Payable		100,000

Purchased car-washing machine by issuing a 5-year non-interest-bearing $100,000 note.

The discount represents the implicit finance charge and is a contra-liability account. As such, it must be subtracted from Note Payable on the Balance Sheet and amortized, or written off, as interest expense over the life of the loan. Thus, in the car-washing machine example, the annual journal entry to recognize the interest expense and discount amortization would be[2]

Interest Expense	5,445	
Discount on Note Payable		5,445

To recognize the annual implicit interest expense on a note ($68,060 × 0.08 = $5,445).

present value   *the value today of an amount to be received or paid in the future; the future amount must be discounted at a specified rate of interest*

[2] According to APB 21, accounting practice requires that the effective-interest method be used to amortize discounts of this nature unless the difference between effective-interest and straight-line amortization is immaterial. Because there is often little difference between the two methods, the straight-line method is sometimes used in practice.

EXHIBIT 11–2   Measurement of Liabilities

Type of Liability	Amount of Liability (as recorded in the accounting records)	Reason
Short-term	The stated amount of the liability, which is approximately equal to its present value	The time period involved is usually so short that the difference between the present value and the stated amount of the liability is immaterial.
Long-term, non-interest-bearing	The present value of the liability, which is less than its stated amount	Part of the stated amount of the liability is really implicit interest being charged to the borrower.
Long-term interest-bearing— interest rate is lower than the market rate of interest	The present value of the liability, which is less than its stated amount	Part of the stated amount of the liability is really implicit interest (less than in the case of a non-interest-bearing note, but still an amount significant enough to warrant discounting).
Long-term interest-bearing— interest rate is equivalent to the market rate of interest	The stated amount of the liability, which is equivalent to its present value	The present value of the sum of the principal and interest payments is approximately equal to the stated amount of the liability.

Thus, while this type of note is sometimes referred to as non-interest-bearing, it is really an interest-bearing note because the present value is less than the face value.

What about an interest-bearing, long-term note? Is its present value equal to its stated amount? If the stated rate of interest on a long-term liability is less than the market rate of interest, the present value is again less than the stated amount of the liability. On the other hand, if the stated rate of interest is approximately equal to the market rate of interest, the stated amount and its present value are equal and no discounting is necessary. These measurement issues are summarized in Exhibit 11–2.

Notes Payable

note payable   *a debt owed to a creditor, evidenced by an unconditional written promise to pay a sum of money on or before a specified future date*

A note payable is an unconditional written promise to pay a stated sum of money on or before some specified future date. Long-term notes payable are accounted for in the same way as short-term notes payable (see Chapter 8, page 269), except that they must be discounted to their present value when they bear no stated interest or have an interest rate that is significantly different from the market rate of interest. When long-term notes payable are discounted, the difference between the present value and the stated amount of the note is implicit interest, which should be amortized over the life of the note. Exhibit 11–3 illustrates the accounting for long-term notes payable.

EXHIBIT 11-3 Accounting for Long-Term Notes

Type of note	Interest-bearing note with stated rate of interest equal to market rate of interest	Interest-bearing note with stated rate of interest less than market rate of interest	Non-interest-bearing note
Situation	On January 1, 1981, XYZ Company borrowed $10,000 from City Bank for 3 years at 10%. Interest is payable annually on December 31. The market rate of interest is 10%.	On January 1, 1981, XYZ Company purchased a machine from ABC Company. There was no down payment and $10,000 is to be paid in 3 years. Interest of 6% must be paid annually every December 31. The market rate of interest is 10%.	On January 1, 1981, XYZ Company purchased a machine from Alvin Company. There was no down payment and $10,000 is to be paid in 3 years. There is no interest to be paid and the market rate of interest is 10%.

Entry to record the note, rounded to the nearest dollar	Cash 10,000
	    Note Payable 10,000
		Machine 9,005
		Discount on Note
		Payable 995
		    Note Payable 10,000
		(The $600 annuity and the $10,000 are discounted at 10% for 3 years, rounded to the nearest dollar.)
			Machine 7,513
			Discount on Note
			Payable 2,487
			    Note Payable 10,000
			(Discounted at 10% for 3 years.)

Entry on December 31, 1981	Interest Expense 1,000
	    Cash 1,000
	($10,000 × 0.10)
		Interest Expense 901
		    Discount on Note
		    Payable 301
		    Cash 600
		(See amortization schedule A.)
			Interest Expense 751
			    Discount on Note
			    Payable 751
			(See amortization schedule B.)

Entry on December 31, 1982	Interest Expense 1,000
	    Cash 1,000
	($10,000 × 0.10)
		Interest Expense 931
		    Discount on Note
		    Payable 331
		    Cash 600
		(See amortization schedule A.)
			Interest Expense 826
			    Discount on Note
			    Payable 826
			(See amortization schedule B.)

Entries on December 31, 1983	Interest Expense 1,000
	    Cash 1,000
	($10,000 × 0.10)
	Note Payable 10,000
	    Cash 10,000
		Interest Expense 964
		    Discount on Note
		    Payable 364
		    Cash 600
		(See amortization schedule A.)
		Note Payable 10,000
		    Cash 10,000
			Interest Expense 909
			    Discount on Note
			    Payable 909
			(See amortization schedule B.)
			Note Payable 10,000
			    Cash 10,000

Amortization Schedule A

Date	Interest Expense	Cash Payment ($10,000 × 0.06)	Discount Amortization (1)−(2)	Loan Balance
Beginning Balance				$ 9,005
December 31, 1981	($9.005 × 0.10) = $901	$600	$301	9,306
December 31, 1982	($9,306 × 0.10) = 931	600	331	9,637
December 31, 1983	($9,637 × 0.10) = 964	600	364	10,000 (rounded)

Amortization Schedule B

Date	Interest Expense and Discount Amortization	Loan Balance
Beginning Balance		$ 7,513
December 31, 1981	($7,513 × 0.10) = $751	8,264
December 31, 1982	($8,264 × 0.10) = 826	9,090
December 31, 1983	($9,090 × 0.10) = 909	10,000 (rounded)

Mortgages Payable

A mortgage payable is similar to a note payable in that it is a written promise to pay a stated sum of money at one or more specified future dates. It is different from a note in the way it is applied: Whereas money borrowed with a note can often be used for *any* business purpose, mortgage money is usually related to a specific asset. Assets purchased with a mortgage are usually pledged as security or collateral on the loan, and the liability involves a separate mortgage document, which is appended to the loan agreement. Among individuals, home mortgages are common, and among companies, plant mortgages are frequent. In either case, mortgages typically require periodic (usually monthly) payments on the principal.

To illustrate the accounting for a mortgage, we will assume that Jacobs Automobile Company borrows $600,000 to purchase a new showroom and signs a mortgage agreement pledging the showroom as collateral on the loan. If the mortgage is at 9 percent for 30 years, and the monthly payment is $4,828, the entries to record the acquisition of the mortgage and the first monthly payment will be

Cash	600,000	
Mortgage Payable		600,000

Borrowed $600,000 to purchase the automobile showroom.

Mortgage Payable	328	
Interest Expense	4,500	
Cash		4,828

Made first month's mortgage payment.

As this entry shows, only $328 of the $4,828 payment is applied to reducing the mortgage; the remainder is interest ($600,000 $\times$ 0.09 $\times \frac{1}{12} =$ $4,500). In each successive month, the amount applied to reducing the mortgage will increase slightly until, toward the end of the 30-year mortgage, almost all of the payment will be for principal. A mortgage amortization schedule identifies how much of each mortgage payment is interest and how much is principal reduction.

At the end of each year, a mortgage is reported on the Balance Sheet in two places: (1) the principal to be paid during the next year is shown as a current liability, and (2) the balance of the mortgage payable is shown as a long-term liability. Also, any interest owed on the mortgage is reported as a current liability and the interest expense for the year is included with other expenses on the Income Statement. Note that since the 9 percent interest rate charged on this mortgage is assumed to be approximately equal to the market rate of interest, the stated value of $600,000 is not discounted.

Deferred Income Taxes Payable

Often, the income taxes a company pays to federal and local governments differ considerably from the income tax expense shown on the Income

Statement. This happens because different bases are used for calculating these amounts. While income tax expense is obtained by accounting for income on the basis of generally accepted accounting principles, income taxes payable to governments are calculated on the basis of taxable income as defined by IRS and state government codes. A discussion of the many differences between generally accepted accounting principles and the IRS and other tax codes is beyond the scope of this book. However, it is important to mention that there are two types of differences: (1) permanent differences, which are never reversed; and (2) timing differences, which reverse in the future. Because timing differences often create long-term liabilities, we will describe how they work with a common business element—depreciation.

Assume that Jacobs Automobile Company has been in business for four years and that abbreviated Income Statements for those years are as shown in the table below. On the first day of year 1, Jacobs purchased a $10,000 tune-up machine with a 4-year life and no salvage value.

Jacobs Automobile Company
Condensed Income Statements for Financial Reporting (Years 1–4)

	Year 1	Year 2	Year 3	Year 4	Total
Revenues	$10,000	$10,000	$10,000	$10,000	$40,000
Expenses (Excluding Depreciation on Tune-Up Machine)	4,000	4,000	4,000	4,000	16,000
Income Before Depreciation and Taxes	$ 6,000	$ 6,000	$ 6,000	$ 6,000	$24,000
Depreciation Expense on Tune-Up Machine—Straight-Line Basis	2,500	2,500	2,500	2,500	10,000
Income Before Taxes	$ 3,500	$ 3,500	$ 3,500	$ 3,500	$14,000
Income Tax Expense (40% × $3,500)	1,400	1,400	1,400	1,400	5,600
Net Income	$ 2,100	$ 2,100	$ 2,100	$ 2,100	$ 8,400

As the statements show, net income and income tax expense are $2,100 and $1,400, respectively, in each of the four years. Because Jacobs chose to use the straight-line method, the depreciation expense on the tune-up machine is the same in each of the four years. As indicated in Chapter 9, however, because money has a time value, companies usually prefer to delay the payment of taxes as long as possible. Delaying the payment of taxes is essentially equal to receiving an interest-free loan from the government.

One way Jacobs could delay a portion of its tax payments would be to use an accelerated depreciation method, such as the sum-of-the-years'-digits or the double-declining-balance method, for tax purposes. This would be a sound business decision because, unless tax rates increase, the present value of tax payments made in early years is greater than the present value of payments made in later years. If, for tax purposes, Jacobs had used the sum-of-the-years'-digits method of depreciation on the tune-up machine, the company's income tax payable and net income for its tax return in each of the four years would be

Jacobs Automobile Company
Condensed Income Statements for Tax Return (Years 1–4)

	Year 1	Year 2	Year 3	Year 4	Total
Revenues	$10,000	$10,000	$10,000	$10,000	$40,000
Expenses (Excluding Depreciation on Tune-Up Machine)	4,000	4,000	4,000	4,000	16,000
Income Before Depreciation and Taxes	$ 6,000	$ 6,000	$ 6,000	$ 6,000	$24,000
Depreciation Expense on Tune-Up Machine—SYD	4,000	3,000	2,000	1,000	10,000
Income Before Taxes..............	$ 2,000	$ 3,000	$ 4,000	$ 5,000	$14,000
Income Tax Payable (40%)	800	1,200	1,600	2,000	5,600
Net Income......................	$ 1,200	$ 1,800	$ 2,400	$ 3,000	$ 8,400

Although both depreciation methods result in the same total amount of income taxes over the four years, the timing of the payments is different, as shown in the following.

	Year 1	Year 2	Year 3	Year 4	Total
Using Straight-Line Depreciation (Books)	$1,400	$1,400	$1,400	$1,400	$5,600
Using SYD Depreciation (Tax Return)...................	800	1,200	1,600	2,000	5,600
Difference in Taxes	$ 600	$ 200	$ (200)	$ (600)	0

With SYD depreciation, Jacobs has the use of an extra $600 in year 1 and $200 in year 2. Although income taxes must eventually be paid, in the meantime the money can be invested to earn a return for the company. The differences between income tax expense per the books and income taxes payable per the tax return are called deferred income taxes. Because deferred income taxes usually are not paid for several periods, they may be classified as long-term liabilities on the Balance Sheet.

deferred income taxes *the difference between income tax expense, calculated as a function of accounting income based on generally accepted accounting principles, and current taxes payable, calculated as a function of taxable income based on the Internal Revenue and other tax codes*

As explained in Chapter 10, federal and state governments allow the simultaneous use of different depreciation methods. Therefore, firms often use an accelerated method for tax purposes because it tends to delay tax payments, and use the straight-line or some other appropriate method for financial reporting purposes.

The entries to record income taxes in this example (where both the SYD and straight-line methods were used) would be

	Year 1		Year 2		Year 3		Year 4	
	DR	CR	DR	CR	DR	CR	DR	CR
Income Tax Expense.........................	1,400		1,400		1,400		1,400	
Deferred Income Taxes Payable		600		200	200			600
Income Taxes Payable—Current		800		1,200		1,600		2,000

In practice, deferred income tax liabilities seldom decrease. This is because as a business expands, it continues to buy new depreciable assets that are often more expensive than the old ones (as a result of inflation).

The accelerated depreciation benefits derived from these new assets are usually large enough to offset the declining benefits of the old assets. Therefore, deferred income tax liabilities only diminish when a firm is not expanding or when there is no inflation. However, firms often stop expanding only when they are losing money, and since there is no tax when there is no income, the deferred taxes may never be paid. As a result, many accountants argue that these taxes should not be considered a liability. Others argue that even if deferred income taxes are paid, the present value of the payments is so small that these taxes should not be reported with the other liabilities. So far, neither of these arguments has persuaded rule-makers to change the accounting for deferred income taxes.

TO SUMMARIZE   The amount of income taxes a business actually pays is often different from the income tax expense reported on the Income Statement. This occurs because of permanent and timing differences between generally accepted accounting principles and the IRS and other tax codes. Timing differences often give rise to a long-term liability called deferred income taxes payable.

Accounting for Leases

lease   *a contract whereby the lessee (user) agrees to pay the lessor (owner) for the use of an asset*

Most assets are either purchased or leased (a few are donated). Leasing an asset is like renting an apartment: Instead of one large initial payment and the transfer of title, smaller periodic payments are involved with no initial transfer of ownership. Because leasing can be an attractive way of financing the use of assets, it has grown in popularity. With a lease, the entity acquiring the use of the asset and making the payments is known as the lessee and the owner or renter is called the lessor.

lessee   *an entity that agrees to pay periodic rents for the use of leased property*

lessor   *renter or owner of leased property*

lease obligations   *net present value of all future lease payments discounted at an appropriate rate of interest*

Until recently, most periodic lease payments were considered expenses of the period in which they were payable, and future lease liabilities (lease obligations) and leased assets were not shown on the financial statements. However, because some companies leased rather than purchased assets solely because of the favorable effects on the Balance Sheet (no long-term debt was reported), and because many leases are in fact equivalent to acquiring an asset, accounting practice now requires the capitalization of leases in many instances—that is, recording of asset and liability balances. Under current accounting guidelines, a lease containing at least one of the following features must be treated as a purchase and shown on the Balance Sheet as both an asset and a liability.

1. Ownership is to be transferred to the lessee at the end of the lease.

2. The lease contains a bargain (less than fair market value) purchase option. That is, at the end of the lease the asset can be purchased for a sum significantly lower than its fair market value.

3. The lease term is 75 percent or more of the leased property's estimated economic life.

4. The present value of the lease payments is 90 percent or more of the fair market value of the property.

If a lease meets any of these criteria, it must be capitalized for an amount equal to the present value of the lease payments discounted at the market interest rate. If a lease does not meet any of these criteria, it is expensed—that is, the periodic payments are recorded as lease expenses and no asset or liability accounts are established. If a lease requires capitalization under criterion 1 or 2, the leased asset is depreciated over its useful life because the lessee will receive the asset at the termination of the lease. If criterion 3 or 4 is applicable, the leased asset is amortized over the life of the lease.

To illustrate the accounting for a capitalized lease, we will assume that Jacobs Automobile Company leased a computer from the Macro Data Corporation for $10,000 a year for 10 years. The computer has an estimated useful life of 12 years, its fair market value is $70,000, and the current rate of interest is 8 percent. Because the life of the lease is at least 75 percent of the computer's life (10 ÷ 12 = 83 percent), or because the present value of the lease payments ($67,101) is more than 90 percent of the fair market value of the computer, the lease must be capitalized. (See Table IV, page 325,[3] for the present value of an annuity of 10 payments of $10,000 discounted at 8 percent.) The entry to record the lease in Jacobs' books would be

Leased Asset—Computer	67,101	
Lease Obligation		67,101

Leased a Macro Data computer for $10,000 a year for 10 years at 8% interest.

At the end of the first year, the Balance Sheet would include the long-term accounts Leased Asset—Computer and Lease Obligation.

Although at first the asset and liability accounts have equal balances, they seldom remain the same during the lease period. The asset should be amortized over the life of the lease and the lease liability should be reduced in a way that produces a constant interest rate each period. In this case, the asset is amortized over 10 years using the straight-line method and the interest expense each period is 8 percent of the lease balance. If we assume that the lease payments are due at the end of each year, the interest for each year would be as shown in Exhibit 11–4.

The entries to account for the lease during the first year would be

Lease Obligation	4,632	
Interest Expense	5,368	
Cash		10,000

Paid first-year lease obligation for computer ($67,101 × 0.08 = $5,368).

Amortization Expense—Leased Computer	6,710	
Accumulated Amortization—Leased Computer		6,710

Amortized the leased computer for the first year ($67,101 ÷ 10 years).

Similar entries would be made in each of the 10 years of the lease, except that the principal payment (Lease Obligation) would increase while the interest payment (Interest Expense) would decrease.

---

[3] While most leases require payments at the beginning of each year, end-of-year payments are assumed here in order to simplify the calculations.

EXHIBIT 11–4 **Payments on Computer Lease**

	Interest Expense	Lease Payment			
Year	(0.08 × Lease Obligation)	Total Amount	Interest	Principal	Lease Obligation
					$67,101
1	$(67,101 × 0.08) = $5,368	$10,000	$5,368	$4,632	62,469
2	(62,469 × 0.08) = 4,997	10,000	4,997	5,003	57,466
3	(57,466 × 0.08) = 4,597	10,000	4,597	5,403	52,063
4	(52,063 × 0.08) = 4,165	10,000	4,165	5,835	46,228
5	(46,228 × 0.08) = 3,698	10,000	3,698	6,302	39,926
6	(39,926 × 0.08) = 3,194	10,000	3,194	6,806	33,120
7	(33,120 × 0.08) = 2,650	10,000	2,650	7,350	25,770
8	(25,770 × 0.08) = 2,062	10,000	2,062	7,938	17,832
9	(17,832 × 0.08) = 1,427	10,000	1,427	8,573	9,259
10	(9,259 × 0.08) = 741	10,000	741	9,259	0

TO SUMMARIZE If a lease meets any one of four conditions, it must be recorded both as an asset and as a liability. The amount recorded is the lesser of the present value of the total lease payments or the fair market value. The resulting asset is amortized and interest expense must be recorded with each lease payment.

Bonds Payable

There are many different types of bonds and the accounting for each depends on its specific characteristics. Because of this, accounting for bonds is a complex subject.

CHARACTERISTICS OF BONDS

bond *long-term borrowing by a company or government agency*

In Chapter 9, bonds were introduced from the viewpoint of the investor. Here, bonds and their accounting are discussed from the borrower's standpoint. As you recall, bonds are long-term interest-bearing liabilities that are commonly used by businesses and other organizations, such as communities, school districts, and public utilities, to raise capital. When an organization issues bonds, it usually sells them to underwriters (bond-brokers and investment bankers), who in turn sell them to various institutions and to the public. At the time of the original sale, the company issuing bonds chooses a trustee to represent the bondholders. In most cases, the trustee is a large bank or trust company to which the company issuing bonds delivers a contract that provides security for the bonds. This contract, which is called a deed of trust, bond indenture, or trust indenture, specifies that in return for an investment of cash by investors, the company promises to pay a specific amount of interest each period that the bonds are outstanding and to repay the principal amount of the bonds at a specific future date. It is the duty of the trustee to protect investors and to make sure that the bond issuer fulfills its responsibilities.

bond indenture *a contract between a bond issuer and a bond purchaser that specifies the terms of a bond*

principal *amount that will be paid on a bond on the maturity date*

The total value of the bonds issued by an organization often exceeds several million dollars. These "bond issues" are generally divided into a number of individual bonds, which may be of varying denominations. Usually, the principal (also called face value) of each bond is $1,000, or a multiple thereof. By issuing bonds in small denominations, a company increases the chances that a broad range of investors is able to compete for the purchase of the bonds.

When a bond is sold, the investor receives a bond certificate, like the one shown in Chapter 9. This certificate is evidence of bond ownership and can be sold to another investor. In fact, there are ready financial markets (such as the New York and American Exchanges) where most bonds can be sold at any time.

Although most bonds have a face value of $1,000, they often sell for more or less than that amount. As you will remember from Chapter 9, two major factors affect the selling price of bonds: (1) their riskiness, based on the financial stability of the organization issuing the bonds (its ability to repay on a timely basis), and (2) their stated interest rate. In general, organizations with greater financial strength can sell bonds at lower interest rates or at higher prices than less stable organizations can. Several agencies, such as Moody's and Standard and Poor's, provide risk ratings on bonds.

market rate of interest *the prevailing interest rate in the marketplace for individual categories and grades of securities*

Ordinarily, when the stated rate of interest on a bond is less than the market rate of interest for bonds issued by similar-risk companies, the bonds will sell at a price below their face value, that is, at a discount. When the stated rate of interest is above the market rate of interest, the bonds will sell at a price above face value, that is, at a premium. It is the market, or effective interest, rate demanded by investors in relation to the stated interest rate that determines the amount they are willing to pay for bonds.

TYPES OF BONDS

Bonds can be categorized on the basis of certain characteristics. A three-way classification system is

1. On the basis of whether the bonds are secured:

   debentures *bonds on which no collateral has been pledged*

   (a) *Debentures or unsecured bonds*. Bonds that have no underlying security, such as a mortgage or pledge of assets, as a guarantee of their repayment.

   secured bonds *bonds for which there are pledged assets to guarantee repayment*

   (b) *Secured bonds*. Bonds that have a pledge of assets as a guarantee of their repayment.

2. On the basis of how the bond interest is paid:

   registered bonds *bonds for which the names and addresses of the bondholders are kept on file by the issuing company*

   (a) *Registered bonds*. Bonds for which the issuing company keeps a file of the names and addresses of all bondholders and pays interest only to those individuals whose names are on file.

   coupon bonds *bonds for which owners receive periodic interest payments by clipping a coupon from the bond and sending it to the issuer as evidence of bond ownership*

   (b) *Coupon bonds*. Bonds for which the issuer has no record of current bondholders but instead pays interest to anyone who can show evidence of ownership. Usually, these bonds contain a printed coupon for each interest payment. When a payment is due, the bondholder "clips" the coupon from the certificate, and sends it to the issuer as evidence of bond ownership. The issuer then sends an interest payment to the bondholder.

term bonds *bonds that mature in one lump sum at a specified future date*

serial bonds *bonds that mature in a series of installments at specified future dates*

callable bonds *bonds for which the issuer reserves the right to pay the obligation before its maturity date*

convertible bonds *bonds that can be traded for or converted to capital stock after a specified period of time*

3. On the basis of how the bonds mature:
(a) *Term bonds.* Bonds that mature in one lump sum on a specified future date.
(b) *Serial bonds.* Bonds that mature in a series of installments.
(c) *Callable bonds.* Term or serial bonds that the issuer can redeem at any time at a specified price.
(d) *Convertible bonds.* Term or serial bonds that can be converted to other securities, such as stocks, after a specified period, at the option of the bondholder.

ACCOUNTING FOR BONDS PAYABLE

The accounting for the issuance of bonds is influenced by two factors: (1) the initial price of the bonds, and (2) the date on which the bonds were issued. If bonds are sold at their face value on an interest payment date, the accounting is relatively simple. However, if they are issued at a price above or below face value or between interest dates, the accounting can be quite complicated. In this section, we explain the accounting for bonds under each of these different circumstances, using the following basic data to illustrate our points.

On January 1, 1981, Jacobs Automobile Company issued 10-year bonds with a face value of $100,000, a stated interest rate of 8 percent, and interest payable semiannually on January 1 and July 1. As you will recall from Chapter 9, investors determine how much they are willing to pay for bonds by computing the sum of the present values of the interest payments and the principal.

Bonds Sold at Face Value

If we assume that Jacobs Company is no more or less risky than other firms in its industry and that 8 percent is the market rate of interest for similar bonds, we can also assume that investors will be willing to pay approximately the face amount for the bonds. In such cases, the bonds are said to sell at par and the journal entry to record their sale on January 1, 1981, would be

par *the nominal amount printed on the face of a bond or share of stock*

```
Cash ........................................    100,000
    Bonds Payable.........................................        100,000
Sold $100,000, 8%, 10-year bonds at par.
```

The entry to record the first payment of interest on July 1, 1981, would be

```
Bond Interest Expense ......................    4,000
    Cash .............................................        4,000
Paid semiannual interest on the $100,000, 8%, 10-year bonds ($100,000 × 0.08 ×
½ year).
```

If Jacobs Automobile Company operates on a calendar year basis, it would need to make the following adjusting entry on December 31, 1981, to account for the interest expense between July 1 and December 31, 1981.

```
Bond Interest Expense .....................      4,000
    Accrued Bond Interest Payable........................            4,000
```
To recognize interest expense for the 6 months July 1 to December 31, 1981 ($100,000 × 0.08 × ½ year).

Then, on January 1, 1982, when semiannual interest is paid, the accrued Bond Interest Payable account is eliminated. The January 1 entry would be

```
Accrued Bond Interest Payable ..............      4,000
    Cash ...............................................            4,000
```
Made semiannual interest payment.

At the end of the accounting period (December 31, 1981), the financial statements would report the following.

Income Statement

```
Bond Interest Expense ...........................................    $8,000
```

Balance Sheet

Current Liabilities:
```
Accrued Bond Interest Payable ...................................    $  4,000
```

Long-Term Liabilities:
```
Bonds Payable (8%, due January 1, 1991) .........................     100,000
```

The entries to record the interest expense payments during the remaining nine years would be the same as those made during 1981 and on January 1, 1982. The only other entry required in accounting for these bonds is the recording of their retirement on January 1, 1991. That entry, assuming all interest has been accounted for, would be

```
Bonds Payable ............................     100,000
    Cash ...............................................          100,000
```
Retired the $100,000, 10-year, 8% bonds.

Bonds Sold at a Discount

Investors are often unwilling to pay the face amount of a bond, either because its stated interest rate is lower than the market rate or because the issuing firm is riskier (less stable) than other firms issuing bonds with the same interest rate. When bonds sell at a price below their face value, they are said to have been sold at a discount.

bond discount   *the difference between the face value and the issuance or sales price when bonds are sold below their face value*

To illustrate the accounting for bonds sold at a discount, we will assume that the $100,000, 10-year, 8 percent bonds issued by Jacobs Automobile on January 1, 1981, were sold for $98,000. Since bonds are usually sold in relatively small denominations (such as $1,000), it is said that the bonds were issued at 98 (which means 98 percent of their face value). The entry to record the issuance of the bonds on January 1, 1981, would be

```
Cash .........................................     98,000
Discount on Bonds..........................      2,000
    Bonds Payable...................................          100,000
```
Sold $100,000, 8%, 10-year bonds at 98.

Discount on Bonds is a contra account that is deducted from Bonds Payable on the Balance Sheet. Bonds Payable is recorded at the full $100,000 because, although the bonds were issued for only $98,000, $100,000 is the amount the company will have to repay investors in 10 years.

The $2,000 discount is not an immediate loss or expense to Jacobs Automobile; it represents an adjustment to the interest expense over the life of the bonds. This can be illustrated by comparing the proceeds received by Jacobs ($98,000) with the amounts it must pay its bondholders ($180,000 over the life of the bonds: $100,000 face value plus 20 interest payments of $4,000 each). Thus, the comparison shows the following.

Amounts To Be Paid to Bondholders	$180,000
Proceeds Received from Sale of Bonds	98,000
Total Interest To Be Paid	$ 82,000
Average Expense Each Year ($82,000/10 years)	$ 8,200

Although Jacobs pays only $8,000 in interest each year, its actual interest expense is $8,200 (assuming straight-line amortization of the discount). To show this larger interest expense, the discount on bonds must be amortized so that each year $200 is transferred from the contra account, Bond Discount, to Interest Expense.

straight-line interest amortization   *a method of systematically writing off a bond premium or discount, resulting in equal amounts being amortized each period*

effective-interest amortization   *a method of systematically writing off a bond premium or discount that takes into consideration the time value of money; results in an equal rate of amortization for each period*

As we explained in Chapter 9, there are two ways of accounting for amortization of bond discounts: (1) straight-line interest and (2) effective interest. Because of its simplicity, the straight-line method is used for this example; the effective-interest amortization method is illustrated later in the chapter.

With the straight-line amortization method, an equal amount of the discount is amortized each year of the bond's 10-year life. Thus, Jacobs would amortize $200 ($2,000/10 years) each year. The semiannual entry to record amortization of the bond discount would be made at the same time as the interest expense, so the July 1, 1981 entry would be

Bond Interest Expense	4,100	
Discount on Bonds		100
Cash		4,000

Paid semiannual interest on the $100,000, 8%, 10-year bonds ($100,000 × 0.08 × $\frac{1}{2}$ year) and amortized the bond discount ($2,000 ÷ 10 years × $\frac{1}{2}$ year).

effective interest rate   *the actual rate of return earned or paid on a bond*

As illustrated, amortization of a discount increases a bond's interest expense. In this case, the interest expense is $4,100, or the sum of the semiannual interest payments and the semiannual amortization of the bond discount. Over the 10-year life of the bonds, the interest expense will be increased by $2,000, the amount of the discount, and thus will be higher than the 8 percent stated rate. Thus, these bonds pay an effective interest rate of approximately 8.37 percent[4] per year ($8,200 interest/$98,000 received on the bonds).

---

[4] Because straight-line amortization was used, this effective rate of 8.37 percent is only an approximation that will change slightly each period. An accurate effective rate can only be calculated if the effective-interest method of amortization is used.

The adjusting entry to record the accrual of the interest expense on December 31, 1981, would be

```
Bond Interest Expense .....................      4,100
    Discount on Bonds .....................              100
    Accrued Bond Interest Payable ..........            4,000
```
To recognize interest expense for the 6 months July 1 to December 31, 1981.

At the end of the accounting period (December 31, 1981), the financial statements would report the following.

Income Statement

```
Bond Interest Expense ($4,100 × 2) ...............                 $ 8,200
```

Balance Sheet

```
Current Liabilities:
Accrued Bond Interest Payable ...................                  $ 4,000

Long-Term Liabilities:
Bonds Payable (8%, due January 1, 1991) ..........    $100,000
Less Unamortized Discount .......................        1,800       98,200
```

The entries to account for the interest expense and bond discount amortization during the remaining nine years would be the same as those made in 1981. And, since the bond discount would be completely amortized at the end of the 10 years, the entry to record the retirement of the bonds would be the same as that for bonds issued at face value. As previously shown, that entry would be

```
Bonds Payable ..........................      100,000
    Cash ...............................              100,000
```
Retired the $100,000, 8%, 10-year bonds.

Note that although amortization entries were made as part of each interest entry (semiannually in this example), one amortization entry for $200 at year-end would have been sufficient. The critical factor is that the discount be properly amortized for the year-end financial statements.

Bonds Sold at a Premium

Just as bonds may be sold at a discount when the interest rates or risk factors are less favorable than those of competing bonds, bonds may sell at amounts above their face value when one or both of these factors are more favorable than those of similar bonds. Bonds that sell at amounts above face value are said to sell at a premium. Like discounts, premiums must be amortized over the life of the bonds.

bond premium   the difference between the face value and the issuance or sales price when bonds are sold above their face value

To illustrate the accounting for bonds sold at a premium, we will assume that Jacobs Automobile Company was able to sell its $100,000, 8 percent, 10-year bonds at 103 (that is, at 103 percent of par). The entry to record the issuance of these bonds on January 1, 1981, would be

```
Cash ...................................      103,000
    Premium on Bonds ...................                3,000
    Bonds Payable ......................              100,000
```
Sold $100,000, 8%, 10-year bonds at 103.

Premium on Bonds is added to Bonds Payable on the Balance Sheet and, like Discount on Bonds, is amortized using either the straight-line or effective-interest method. Thus, if Jacobs were to use the straight-line method, the annual amortization of the premium would be $300 ($3,000/10 years), or $150 every six months. The entry to record the first semiannual interest payment and the premium amortization on July 1, 1981, would be

Bond Interest Expense 3,850
Premium on Bonds.......................... 150
   Cash 4,000

Paid semiannual interest on the $100,000, 8%, 10-year bonds ($100,000 × 0.08 × ½ year) and amortized the bond premium ($3,000 ÷ 10 years × ½).

The amortization of a premium on bonds has the opposite effect of the amortization of a discount in that it reduces the actual interest expense on the bonds. In this case, with each semiannual interest payment of $4,000 the company is repaying one-twentieth (1/20) of the bond premium. Thus, the actual interest expense is not the stated rate of 8 percent, but an effective rate of approximately 7.48 percent ($7,700/$103,000).

The adjusting entry to record the accrual of the interest expense on December 31, 1981, would be

Bond Interest Expense 3,850
Premium on Bonds.......................... 150
   Accrued Bond Interest Payable 4,000

To recognize interest expense on the bonds for the 6 months July 1 to December 31, 1981.

At the end of the accounting period (December 31, 1981), the financial statements would report the following.

Income Statement

Bond Interest Expense ($3,850 × 2) .... $ 7,700

Balance Sheet

Current Liabilities:
Accrued Bond Interest Payable .... $ 4,000

Long-Term Liabilities:
Bonds Payable (8%, due January 1, 1991) $100,000
Plus Unamortized Premium ($3,000 − 300) 2,700   102,700

Like discounts, premiums can be amortized once at year-end, instead of when the interest payments are made.

Bonds Sold Between Interest Dates

As noted in Chapter 9, when bonds are sold between interest dates, the accounting for interest payments and the amortization of the premium or discount becomes somewhat more complicated. With regard to the interest payments, the complication arises because interest is usually paid for a full period regardless of how long the bonds have been issued. Therefore, if interest is to be paid semiannually and the bonds are sold between interest

EXHIBIT 11–5   **Interest for Bonds Issued Between Periods**

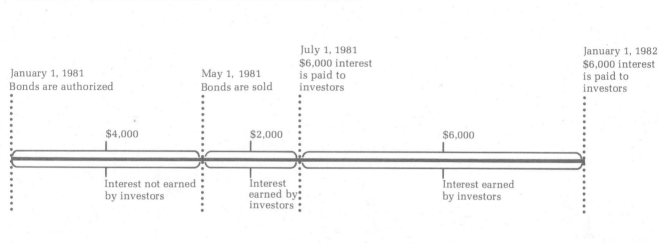

dates, it is customary for the bond investor to pay the seller (previous owner or original issuer) for that portion of the six months' interest that will be received but not earned.

To illustrate, we will assume that on January 1, 1981, ReMae Corporation received authorization to issue $200,000 of 6 percent, 7-year bonds with interest payments to be made on January 1 and July 1 of each year. Since the bonds mature in 7 years they should have a life of 84 months and pay interest of $6,000 ($200,000 × 6 percent × $\frac{1}{2}$ year) every January 1 and July 1. However, if ReMae Corporation did not actually sell the bonds until May 1, 1981, then on July 1 the investors would have held the bonds for only two months and would have earned only $2,000 in interest ($200,000 × 6 percent × $\frac{1}{6}$ year). Since the investors would receive $6,000 on July 1, ReMae Corporation would add the $4,000 in unearned interest to the selling price of the bonds. This interest complication can be diagrammed as shown in Exhibit 11–5.

If the bonds were sold on May 1, 1981, for 104 (at a premium), the entry to account for the sale of the bonds and the payment of $4,000 interest by investors would be

Cash	212,000	
Bonds Payable......................................		200,000
Premium on Bonds Payable		8,000
Bond Interest Expense		4,000

Sold $200,000, 6%, 7-year bonds at 104 plus accrued interest.

The $4,000 interest is credited to Bond Interest Expense so that on July 1, 1981, when the full $6,000 of interest paid is debited to that account, there is a net interest expense of $2,000 for the two months. This is shown on the next page.

Bond Interest Expense

July 1, 1981..........6,000	4,000 ....May 1, 1981
2,000	

Alternatively, the $4,000 could have been credited to Bond Interest Payable instead of Bond Interest Expense. With this approach, the entry on the interest payment date would include two debits: $2,000 to Bond Interest Expense and $4,000 to Bond Interest Payable.

At this point you are probably wondering why the issuer does not simply keep track of bonds as they are sold, and pay only the net amount of interest due on that date instead of the full amount due for the period. Unfortunately, such a system would actually be more complicated than the one just outlined. There are two reasons for this: First, since many bonds are coupon bonds, each coupon is worth a certain amount of interest. Second, since bonds are traded daily, it would be an impossible task for bond issuers to keep track of which investors own how many bonds and on what dates the different bonds were purchased. In summary, issuers pay specified amounts of interest every period and require investors who buy between interest dates to pay, in advance, for any unearned interest.

With regard to premium and discount amortizations, the complication arises because the bond premium or discount must be amortized over the actual time the bonds are outstanding, not over their entire authorized life. In this case, since the bonds were authorized on January 1, 1981, but were not issued until May 1, 1981, the amortization period would be six years and 8 months (80 months), not the full seven years. The monthly amortization of the premium (assuming that the straight-line amortization method was used) would therefore be $100 per month ($8,000/80 months). On July 1, 1981, with the bonds outstanding for only two months, the entry to record the interest payment and premium amortization would be

Bond Interest Expense	5,800	
Premium on Bonds.........................	200	
Cash		6,000

Made semiannual interest payment on the $200,000, 6%, 7-year bonds ($200,000 × 0.06 × ½ year) and amortized the bond premium ($8,000 ÷ 80 months × 2).

Note that on all succeeding interest payment dates, the amount of the premium amortization would be $600 ($100 per month × six months).

Effective-Interest Amortization

Companies justify use of the straight-line method of amortizing bond premiums and discounts on grounds that its results are not significantly different from those of the theoretically more accurate effective-interest method. However, as noted in Chapter 9, the effective-interest method is also widely used because it considers the time value of money and is required by the FASB if its results differ significantly from those of the straight-line method.

To illustrate the effective-interest method, we assume that on January 1, 1981, Howe Baking Company sold $40,000 of 10 percent, 5-year bonds for $43,246. If the bonds pay interest semiannually on January 1 and July 1, their effective interest rate is approximately 8 percent a year, or 4 percent every six months. Since the actual interest expense for each period is equal to the effective rate of 8 percent multiplied by the bond balance, the amortization (rounded to the nearest $1) for the five years would be as follows:

Period	(1) Cash Paid for Interest	(2) Semiannual Interest Expense	(3) Premium Amortization	(4) Balance
Issuance date:				$43,246
Year 1, 1st six months	$2,000	(4% × $43,246) = $1,730	$270	42,976
Year 1, 2nd six months	2,000	(4% × $42,976) = $1,719	281	42,695
Year 2, 1st six months	2,000	(4% × $42,695) = $1,708	292	42,403
Year 2, 2nd six months	2,000	(4% × $42,403) = $1,696	304	42,099
Year 3, 1st six months	2,000	(4% × $42,099) = $1,684	316	41,783
Year 3, 2nd six months	2,000	(4% × $41,783) = $1,671	329	41,454
Year 4, 1st six months	2,000	(4% × $41,454) = $1,658	342	41,112
Year 4, 2nd six months	2,000	(4% × $41,112) = $1,644	356	40,756
Year 5, 1st six months	2,000	(4% × $40,756) = $1,630	370	40,386
Year 5, 2nd six months	2,000	(4% × $40,386) = $1,614	386	40,000

In this computation, the $2,000 in column (1) is the actual interest paid each six months; column (2) shows the interest expense for each six months, which is the amount that will be reported on the Income Statement; column (3), which is the difference between columns (1) and (2), represents amortization of the premium; and column (4) shows the bond balance, which is the amount that will be reported on the Balance Sheet each period. Using the effective-interest method, the bond balance is always equal to the present value of the bond obligation. Note that as the bond balance decreases, the amount of money borrowed decreases, and the interest expense also decreases. This provides for a constant interest rate of 8 percent.

Because the straight-line method shows a constant interest expense ($3,246 ÷ 10 = $324.60 per 6-month period) on a decreasing bond balance, the straight-line interest rate cannot be constant. Thus, unless the straight-line results do not differ significantly from the effective-interest results, FASB guidelines advise against its use. Because they are often quite similar, however, both methods continue to be used. One final note: The effective-interest method of amortizing a bond discount would be essentially the same as amortizing a bond premium. The main difference is that the bond balance increases instead of decreases.

BOND SINKING FUNDS

bond sinking fund *an interest-bearing investment account, usually managed by an independent trustee, in which periodic deposits are made and interest accrues to retire bonds at maturity*

A company issuing bonds must be sure that it will have enough money on hand to retire the bonds when they mature. There are several ways of accomplishing this. One of the most common, often required by investors or trustees, is a bond sinking fund. This is essentially an interest-bearing investment (usually a savings account) into which the issuer makes periodic cash deposits. These deposits, together with the interest they earn, should be sufficient to retire the bonds at maturity. Bond sinking funds are usually kept by an independent trustee (such as a bank).

To illustrate the accounting for a bond sinking fund, we will assume that Champaign Foundry issued 10-year bonds of $100,000 on July 1, 1981. Investors required Champaign to maintain a bond sinking fund, so that exactly $100,000 would be available to retire the bonds on July 1, 1991. If Champaign Foundry makes 10 equal payments (one at the end of each year) into a fund that earns 7 percent interest, the annual required payment would be approximately $7,238. This number is calculated by dividing the future amount of an annuity factor at 7 percent and 10 periods into $100,000 as follows (see Table III, page 324):

$$\frac{\$100,000}{13.8164} = \$7,238$$

Thus, if Champaign Foundry deposits $7,238 each year in a bond sinking fund that earns 7 percent, in 10 years the fund balance will be $100,000.

In accounting for a bond sinking fund, a company must record the annual deposits to the fund, the interest earned on the fund balance, and the withdrawal of funds at maturity to pay off the bonds. For Champaign, the entry to record the first annual deposit would be

Bond Sinking Fund	7,238	
Cash		7,238

Deposited $7,238 in the bond sinking fund.

At the end of the second year, interest of approximately $507 would be earned by the fund and recorded in the books. The entry would be

Bond Sinking Fund	507	
Bond Sinking Fund Revenue		507

To recognize sinking fund earnings ($7,238 × 0.07 = $507).

Similar entries would be made during each of the remaining eight years.

Finally, after all of the deposit and interest revenue entries have been made, the entry to record payment to bondholders would be

Bonds Payable	100,000	
Bond Sinking Fund		100,000

Retired bonds payable with sinking fund proceeds.

During its life, the bond sinking fund is classified as a long-term investment or other asset on the Balance Sheet and bond sinking fund revenue is included with Other Revenues on the Income Statement.

TO SUMMARIZE   Bonds are long-term interest-bearing liabilities of businesses and government agencies. They can be classified by their level of security (debentures versus secured bonds), by the way interest is paid (registered versus coupon bonds), and by the way they mature (term bonds, callable bonds, serial bonds, and convertible bonds). The accounting for bonds involves four steps: (1) accounting for their issuance, (2) accounting for the periodic interest payments over their lives, (3) accounting for the amortization of discounts and premiums, and (4) accounting for their maturity.

CHAPTER REVIEW

The two most common nonoperating sources of funds are (1) debt financing (borrowing money) and (2) equity financing (issuing stock). Although both have advantages and disadvantages, debt financing does not dilute the ownership of a firm, provides tax-deductible interest payments, usually allows for a higher earnings per share, and often helps increase profits through leveraging.

Long-term liabilities are measured in the accounting records at the present value of all future outflows of assets required to pay for them. If the interest rate of a long-term liability is approximately equal to the market rate of interest, the present value is approximately equal to the stated amount of the liability. On the other hand, if there is no interest or if the interest rate is below the market rate of interest, the long-term liability must be discounted to its present value.

The most common types of long-term liabilities are notes payable, mortgages payable, deferred income taxes payable, lease obligations, and bonds payable. A note is a written promise to pay a stated sum of money on or before some specified future date. It can be interest-bearing or non-interest-bearing. If the latter, the note must be discounted to its present value using the market rate of interest. A mortgage is similar to a note in that it is also a written promise to pay a stated sum of money in the future; however, a specific asset is pledged as collateral in the case of a mortgage. Most mortgage loans usually require monthly or other periodic payments over their lives.

Deferred income taxes arise when a firm is able to defer into the future a portion of the income taxes it would otherwise pay in the current year. Many items give rise to deferred taxes, but one of the most common is depreciation, whereby one method of depreciation is used for financial reporting purposes and another for tax purposes.

A firm can acquire new assets either by purchasing or leasing them. Leasing involves periodic payments over the life of the lease. A lease is treated as a purchase if it meets at least one of four characteristics and, as such, is recorded as both an asset and a long-term liability. Over the life of a lease, the asset is amortized and the liability is reduced as payments are made.

There are many types of bonds, each of which requires its own special accounting treatment. Bonds are essentially long-term interest-bearing notes issued by businesses and other organizations through underwriters to institutions and to the public. If sold at par on an interest date, accounting for them is relatively simple. However, if they are sold at either a discount or a premium or between interest dates, the accounting becomes more complicated. Premiums and discounts on bonds may be amortized using either the straight-line or the effective-interest method. Issuers sometimes maintain a bond sinking fund to ensure that they will have sufficient money on hand to retire bonds at maturity.

KEY TERMS AND CONCEPTS

bond (366)
bond discount (369)
bond indenture (366)
bond premium (371)
bond sinking fund
   (376)
callable bonds (368)
convertible bonds (368)
coupon bonds (367)
debentures (367)
debt financing (356)
deferred income taxes
   (363)

effective-interest
   amortization (370)
effective interest rate
   (370)
equity financing (356)
lease (364)
lease obligations (364)
lessee (364)
lessor (364)
leveraging (357)
market rate of interest
   (367)
mortgage amortization

schedule (361)
mortgage payable (361)
note payable (359)
par (368)
present value (358)
principal (367)
registered bonds (367)
secured bonds (367)
serial bonds (368)
straight-line interest
   amortization (370)
term bonds (368)

DISCUSSION QUESTIONS

1. What is the difference between debt and equity financing?

2. Why is the effective cost of borrowing to a profitable company usually lower than the stated interest rates on loans?

3. What are the advantages and disadvantages of debt financing?

4. When does the stated amount of a liability equal its present value?

5. What is the difference between a note and a mortgage payable?

6. Why is the real monthly cost of a home mortgage less than the monthly cash payment?

7. Why would a company defer the payment of taxes into the future?

8. On the basis of what you've read in the chapter, what do you think the term "off-Balance-Sheet financing" implies?

9. Under what conditions is it necessary to capitalize a lease?

10. To whom do companies usually sell bonds?

11. What two major factors affect the issuance price of bonds?

12. If a bond's stated interest rate is below the market interest rate, will the bond sell at a premium or a discount?

13. If you thought the market interest rate was going to drop in the near future, should you invest in bonds?

14. When do you think bonds would sell at or near face value?

15. What type of account is Discount on Bonds?

16. Why does the amortization of a bond discount increase the effective interest rate on bonds?

17. Why is the effective-interest amortization method more theoretically appropriate than the straight-line amortization method?

18. Why must investors pay for unearned interest when purchasing bonds between interest dates?

19. Why do investors often require bond issuers to maintain a bond sinking fund?

20. Why are bond sinking funds usually maintained by independent trustees?

EXERCISES

E11-1   Accounting for Interest-Bearing Notes

Company A borrowed $4,000 on a 9 percent, 2-year interest-bearing note dated October 1, 1981. The annual accounting period ends on December 31. Give entries on the following dates (assume that all interest is paid on the maturity date).

1. October 1, 1981
2. December 31, 1981
3. December 31, 1982
4. October 1, 1983

E11-2   Accounting for Interest-Bearing Notes

On July 1, 1981, XYZ Corporation borrowed $2,000 for two years from a bank at 8 percent interest. Give all necessary journal entries to account for this note, assuming that the company's accounting year ends on December 31 and that interest is paid annually on July 1.

E11-3   Accounting for Interest-Bearing Notes

Company A borrowed $6,000 on a 9 percent, 3-year interest-bearing note dated October 1, 1981. The annual accounting period ends on December 31. Give entries on the following dates (assume that all interest is paid at maturity and that interest is accrued each year on December 31).

1. October 1, 1981
2. December 31, 1981
3. December 31, 1983
4. October 1, 1984

E11-4   Accounting for a Non-Interest-Bearing Note

On January 1, 1981, John E. Appleseed, Inc., makers of quality applesauce, purchased two new delivery trucks by issuing a non-interest-bearing note for $30,000, payable in full at the end of five years. The current market rate of interest is 9 percent.

Prepare journal entries to account for the purchase of trucks on January 1, 1981, and related entries at December 31, 1981, and December 31, 1982, to account for the interest expense. You are not required to make any depreciation entries.

E11-5   Deferred Income Taxes

TNT Corporation had pretax income of $20,000, $50,000, $10,000, zero, and $30,000 during the years 1979–1983. TNT Corporation pays taxes at a rate of 40 percent. During those same five years, TNT determined that current taxes payable to the IRS were $5,000, $10,000, $8,000, $3,000, and $7,000, respectively.

1. Record the 1981 income tax expense and income taxes payable in General Journal format.
2. Calculate the balance of deferred income taxes for these five years as of December 31, 1983.

E11-6   Deferred Income Taxes

In 1981 RCB Corporation purchased a computer at a cost of $80,000. The computer had a 4-year life, is depreciated on a straight-line basis for financial reporting, and has no expected salvage value. Using straight-line depreciation, RCB Corporation had pretax financial income in the four years 1981–1984 of $20,000, $30,000, $40,000, and $30,000, respectively. Assuming that RCB Corporation's tax rate is 40 percent and that it depreciates the computer on the SYD basis for tax purposes, record the tax entries for each of the four years.

E11-7   Lease Accounting

Damond Corporation signed a noncancelable lease to use a machine for 10 years. The fair market value of the machine is $80,000, which is equal to the present value of the lease payments. The annual lease payment is $10,018, payable at the end of each year.

1. Record the lease, assuming that the lease should be capitalized.
2. For the initial year only, record the annual payment of the lease and interest expense (assuming 4 percent interest). Also record amortization expense using the straight-line method and assuming no salvage value.
3. Now record the annual payment of the lease, assuming that the lease is not capitalized.

E11-8   Lease Accounting

On July 1, 1981, Farmer John leased a grain harvester. The lease agreement called for payments of $5,000 a year (payable each July 1) for 10 years. The fair market value of the harvester is $37,500 and the market rate of interest is 7 percent. (Assume that Farmer John uses straight-line depreciation and amortization and his accounting year-end is December 31.)

1. Prepare journal entries for the following dates.
   (a) July 1, 1981, to record the capitalization of the lease.
   (b) December 31, 1981, to recognize interest and record amortization.
   (c) July 1, 1982, to show the first payment on the lease.

2. Now assume that the fair market value of the harvester is $40,000 when purchased. Prepare journal entries for the same dates as in part 1.

E11–9   Bond Definitions

Match the following terms with the appropriate definition.

(a) Debentures   (e) Callable bonds
(b) Secured bonds   (f) Convertible bonds
(c) Term bonds   (g) Registered bonds
(d) Serial bonds   (h) Coupon bonds

1. When the bond interest date approaches, the investor detaches a form from the bond, signs it, and mails it to the issuing company.

2. Bonds that can be exchanged for other securities of the issuer, at the option of the investor.

3. There is no pledge of assets, or mortgage, as a guarantee of payment of the bonds at maturity.

4. Bonds that may be called for early retirement, at the option of the issuer.

5. The payment of the principal is a single sum at a certain date.

6. Payment of bond interest is made only to the name currently on the records of the issuer.

7. Bonds that include a mortgage, or pledge of specific assets, as a guarantee of repayment at maturity.

8. Bonds that mature in installments rather than as a single payment.

E11–10   Accounting for Bonds Sold at a Discount

Y Corporation issued $200,000 of 5 percent, 10-year bonds at 98 on April 1, 1981. Interest is payable semi-annually on April 1 and October 1.

1. Record the necessary entries to account for these bonds on the following three dates. (Use the straight-line method to amortize the bond discount and record discount amortization with each interest entry.)
    (a) April 1, 1981
    (b) October 1, 1981
    (c) December 31, 1981

2. Show how the bonds would be reported on the Balance Sheet of Y Corporation on December 31, 1981.

E11–11   Accounting for Bonds Sold at a Premium

Mapleton Implement Corporation issued $500,000 of 6 percent, 10-year bonds at 102 on June 30, 1981. Interest is payable on June 30 and December 31. The corporation uses the straight-line method to amortize bond premiums and discounts. The corporation's fiscal year runs from February 1 through January 31.

Prepare all necessary entries to account for the bonds from the date of issuance through June 30, 1982. Also, record the retirement of the bonds on June 30, 1991, assuming that all interest has been paid and that the premium has been amortized. Note that the bond premium should be amortized with each interest entry.

E11–12   Accounting for Bonds Sold at a Premium

On April 1, 1981, Rice Corporation issued a $1,000, 6 percent, 5-year bond for $1,177 plus accrued interest. The bond was dated March 1, 1981, and interest is payable each March 1 and September 1. Provide entries at each of the following dates.

1. April 1, 1981   Issuance
2. September 1, 1981   Interest payment (assume straight-line amortization of bond premium)
3. December 31, 1981   Adjusting entry
4. December 31, 1981   Closing entry

E11–13   Analysis of Bonds

A $200,000, 6 percent bond was sold on March 1, 1981. The bonds pay interest each February 28 and August 31 and mature 10 years from March 1, 1981. Using these data, complete the table below (show computations and assume straight-line amortization).

Case A: The bonds sold at par.
Case B: The bonds sold at 79.
Case C: The bonds sold at 103.

	Case A	Case B	Case C
Cash inflow at issuance date	_____	_____	_____
Total cash outflow through maturity	_____	_____	_____

Income Statement for 1981

Bond Interest Expense	_____	_____	_____

Balance Sheet at December 31, 1981

Long-Term Liabilities:

Bonds Payable, 6%	_____	_____	_____
Unamortized Discount	_____	_____	_____
Unamortized Premium	_____	_____	_____
Net Liability	_____	_____	_____
Approximate Effective Interest Rate	_____	_____	_____

E11–14   Accounting for Bonds

ABC Corporation, a calendar year firm, is authorized to issue $500,000 of 6 percent, 10-year bonds dated April 1, 1981, with interest payable semiannually on April 1 and October 1.

Provide General Journal entries to record the following events, assuming that the bonds sold at 104 on April 1, 1981. Amortization of bond premiums or discounts is recorded only at year-end and the straight-line amortization method is used.

1. The bond issuance on April 1, 1981.
2. Payment of interest on October 1, 1981.
3. Adjusting entries at December 31, 1981.

E11–15   Effective-Interest Amortization of Bond Premium

Johnson Company issued a 6 percent, 4-year, $1,000 bond on January 1, 1981. The interest is payable each year on December 31. The bond was sold at an effective interest rate of 5 percent. With respect to these bonds, the following computations have been made.

Date	Cash	Interest	Principal	Balance
January 1, 1981				$1,036
End of year 1 . . .	$60	$52	$ 8	1,028
End of year 2 . . .	60	51	9	1,019
End of year 3 . . .	60	51	9	1,010
End of year 4 . . .	60	50	10	1,000

1. At what price was the bond issued?
2. Did the bond sell at a premium or a discount? How much?
3. How much interest expense would be shown on the Income Statement each year?
4. What long-term liability amount would be shown on the Balance Sheet at the end of year 3?

5. How were the following amounts calculated for year 3? (a) $60 (b) $51 (c) $9 (d) $1,010

E11–16   Effective-Interest Calculations

Determine the approximate effective rate of interest for $100,000, 7 percent, 5-year bonds, which are issued at 96 (assume straight-line amortization).

E11–17   Accounting for a Bond Sinking Fund

Bossal Wood Company maintains a bond sinking fund. Record in General Journal form the entries to account for the following transactions. (Note: Each part is independent of the others.)

1. Deposited $45,000 in the bond sinking fund.
2. Annual income of $5,000 on sinking fund securities reported to Bossal Wood Company.
3. Used $10,000 of the sinking fund to retire bonds on their maturity date. (Assume that entries for interest and amortization of any discount or premium on the bonds have already been made.)

E11–18   Accounting for a Bond Sinking Fund

On January 1, 1981, Slim Pickens Dating Service agreed to set up a special fund to pay off a $50,000 bond that matures on December 31, 1985. Five equal annual payments will be made to the fund on December 31 of each year.

1. If the fund earns 6 percent interest, what is the amount of the five equal payments?
2. Prepare journal entries for:
   (a) December 31, 1981, deposit to the fund.
   (b) December 31, 1982 and 1983, interest revenue on fund.
   (c) Retirement of bonds on December 31, 1985.

PROBLEMS

P11–1   Account for Interest- and Non-Interest-Bearing Notes

Lewis Lollypop Company needed cash for working capital purposes. On March 1, 1981, the company secured a $5,000 interest-bearing note at 8.5 percent due in two years from Peterson Bank (interest payable at maturity). It also received $2,500 from Laurence National Bank in return for a non-interest-bearing note of $4,000 due in three years.

Required:

1. Give the journal entries to record the receipt of cash on March 1, 1981.
2. Give the entries to record the interest expense on the two notes for 1981 (assume straight-line amortization of the Laurence National Bank discount).
3. Give the entries that would be required on the payment dates of the two notes, assuming that adjusting entries had been made each year on December 31.

4. Compute the effective rate of the Laurence National Bank note.

5. **Interpretive Question** What would have been the Laurance Bank note's rate of interest if the amount of interest had remained the same—$1,500—but it was a $4,000 interest-bearing note (instead of $2,500). Explain why it is higher or lower than the interest rate calculated in part 4.

P11–2 Deferred Income Taxes

On January 1, 1977, Big Horn Mountain Association purchased a road grader for $100,000. Big Horn depreciates the road grader on a straight-line basis for financial reporting purposes but on a SYD basis for tax purposes. The grader has an expected useful life of five years and no salvage value.

Required:

1. Given that the financial statements of Big Horn Mountain Association show income before taxes of $60,000, $50,000, $40,000, $60,000, and $70,000 in the years 1977–1981, prepare the journal entry in each of the five years to record the income tax expense. (Note: The Big Horn Mountain Association is taxed at 30 percent.)

2. **Interpretive Question** Why would a company want to defer income tax payments into the future?

P11–3 Lease Accounting

On January 1, 1981, Eimco Trucking Company leased a truck from Peterbuilt, Inc. The lease terms call for payments of $6,000 per year for 10 years. The truck is expected to have a 10-year useful life, after which time it will have no value to either Eimco or Peterbuilt.

Required:

Assuming that the payments are due at the end of each year, and the market rate of interest is 12 percent, complete the following.

1. What is the present value of the lease payments?

2. Record the lease in the accounting records at January 1, 1981.

3. Complete a lease amortization schedule (rounded to the nearest dollar).

4. **Interpretive Question** Why should this lease be capitalized?

P11–4 Accounting for Bonds

Required:

1. On July 1, 1981, Cox Corporation issued $90,000, 10-year, 6 percent bonds at 96. The bonds were dated July 1, 1981, and pay interest each June 30 and December 31.

(a) Give the entry to record the issuance of the bonds.

(b) Give the December 31, 1981, interest payment entry. Assume straight-line amortization of bond discount.

2. On May 1, 1981, Merrimae Corporation sold a $1,000, 6 percent, 5-year bond for $1,058 plus accrued interest. The bond was dated March 1, 1981, and interest is payable each March 1 and September 1. Record the issuance of the bond.

3. **Interpretive Question** Why must investors who buy bonds between interest dates pay for accrued interest?

P11–5 Accounting for Bonds

W. R. Sheldon and W. O. Rentz incorporated their training school in 1981. On January 1, 1982, $100,000 of callable bonds at 6 percent were authorized. The maturity date is January 1, 1989. Interest is payable on July 1 and January 1. The bonds were sold at 102 plus accrued interest on May 1, 1982. The company uses straight-line bond amortization and closes its books each year on December 31. (Note: Any bond premium or discount is amortized only on December 31, using the straight-line method.)

Required:

1. Make the appropriate General Journal entries on the following dates.

(a) May 1, 1982

(b) July 1, 1982

(c) December 31, 1982

2. Due to the cancellation of a previously planned school expansion and the lowering of market interest rates, the corporation reacquired all the bonds on the open market at 105, plus accrued interest, on April 1, 1983. Show these transactions in General Journal format.

P11–6 Accounting for Bonds

Jacobs Boat Company authorized and sold $75,000 of 8 percent, 15-year bonds on April 1, 1981. The bonds pay interest each April 1 and Jacobs' year-end is December 31.

Required:

1. Prepare journal entries to record the issuance of these bonds under each of the following three assumptions.

(a) Sold at 97.

(b) Sold at par.

(c) Sold at 105.

2. Prepare adjusting journal entries for the bonds under all three assumptions on December 31, 1981 (use the straight-line amortization method).

3. Show how the bond liabilities would appear on the December 31, 1981, Balance Sheet under each of the three assumptions.

4. **Interpretive Question** What situation would cause the bonds to sell at 97? At 105?

P11-7 Effective-Interest Amortization

Emco Trucking Company issued $100,000 of 6 percent bonds on January 1, 1981. The bonds pay interest on December 31 of each year and have a 4-year life.

Required:

Given that the bonds sold at a price that yielded an 8 percent return, complete the following.

1. At what price were the bonds issued?

2. Prepare a bond amortization schedule to amortize any premium or discount on the bonds using the effective-interest amortization method.

3. **Interpretive Question** When must this method of amortization be used? Why?

P11-8 Unifying Problem: Bonds

On January 1, 1981, the ABC Company decided to issue $1,000,000 of 8 percent, 10-year bonds with interest payable on January 1 and July 1 of each year. Due to several problems, ABC was not able to sell the bonds until September 1, 1981, at which time the bonds were issued at 104. (Assume straight-line amortization of any discount or premium and record the amortization with each interest expense entry.)

Required:

1. Prepare all necessary journal entries to account for the bonds through December 31, 1982.

2. Determine the effective rate of interest on the bonds.

3. Show how all the bond-related items would appear on the December 31, 1981, Balance Sheet.

4. **Interpretive Question** Why isn't the bond premium amortized over 120 months?

P11-9 Unifying Problem: Callable Bonds

Patterson Construction Company decided to issue $200,000 of 6 percent callable bonds on January 1, 1981. Maturity date of the bonds is January 1, 1992. Interest is payable on July 1 and January 1. The bonds

were sold at 96 plus accrued interest on August 1, 1981. The company uses the straight-line method of amortizing bond premiums and discounts and records such amortizations only at year-end, December 31.

Required:

1. Make the required journal entries for each of the following dates.
   (a) August 1, 1981
   (b) December 31, 1981
   (c) January 1, 1982
   (d) July 1, 1982

2. Because of economic considerations (the lowering of the market rate of interest), Patterson Company reacquired all of the bonds on the open market at face value (100). The bonds were reacquired on July 1, 1984. The following entry had just been made on that day.

Bond Interest Expense.   6,000
   Cash   6,000
Made semiannual interest payment on the bonds.

Record the entry to reacquire the bond. (Hint: Your entry must include an updating of the discount amortization.)

P11-10 Unifying Problem: Callable Bonds with Partial Retirement

Boulder Mountain Corporation was authorized to issue $2,000,000 of 6 percent, 15-year callable bonds, dated January 1, 1981. However, because of an unusually tight money market, it could not sell the bonds until November 1, 1981, at which time they were sold for $91\frac{1}{2}$ plus accrued interest. Interest is payable semiannually on January 1 and July 1. The

Required:

1. Record, in General Journal form, entries on:
   (a) November 1, 1981
   (b) December 31, 1981
   (c) January 1, 1982

2. On February 1, 1984, the corporation retired $400,000 of the 15-year bonds at 96. Record all necessary journal entries.

3. **Interpretive Question** Why would the company call the bonds at 96 and suffer a loss on the retirement?

CHAPTER 12

Owners' Equity

Assets and liabilities were discussed in Chapters 7–11. Here, the focus is on owners' equity, thus completing our coverage of the Balance Sheet. Although the same asset and liability accounts are generally used by all forms of business (corporation, partnership, or proprietorship), the owners' equity accounts are different for each and so are dealt with separately in this chapter.

There are certain basic characteristics common to all owners' equity accounts, no matter what the type of business. The first is that they represent the owners' interests in a firm, revealing how much the owners have contributed and how much of the firm's earnings have been retained for its owners. They can therefore be thought of as identifying sources of a firm's assets. Second, if all three types of businesses entered into the same transactions over their lifetimes, the total amounts in their owners' equity sections would be approximately the same.[1] These totals are determined by the types of transactions entered into and the amounts involved, not by the type of organization. In other words, while owners' equity accounts differ in ways that will be illustrated for the three types of businesses, their purpose and function are the same.

---

[1] There may be some differences due to differing tax treatments. If taxes are ignored, the totals would be equivalent.

The Corporation

corporation *a legal entity chartered by a state with ownership represented by transferable shares of stock*

Corporations are the dominant form of business enterprise in the United States. Established as separate legal entities, corporations are distinct from the persons responsible for their creation. Like people, they conduct business, sue, are sued, enter into contracts, and own property. Firms are incorporated by the state in which they are organized and are subject to its laws and requirements.

Suppose that you wanted to start a corporation. First, you would study your state's corporate laws (usually with the aid of an attorney). Then you would apply for a charter with the appropriate state official. In the application, you would give the intended name of your corporation, its purposes (that is, the type of activity it will engage in), the type and amount of stock you plan to have authorized for your corporation, and, in some cases, the names and addresses of the potential stockholders. Finally, if the state approves your application, you will be issued a charter (also called articles of incorporation), giving legal status to your corporation.

charter (articles of incorporation) *a document issued by a state that gives legal status to a corporation and details its specific rights, including the authority to issue a certain maximum number of shares of stock*

Characteristics of a Corporation

limited liability *the legal protection given stockholders whereby they are responsible for the debts and obligations of a corporation only to the extent of their capital contribution*

Corporations have several characteristics that distinguish them from other types of business entities. Probably the most significant is the limited liability of stockholders. This means that in the event of corporate bankruptcy the maximum financial loss any stockholder can sustain is his or her investment in the corporation (unless fraud can be proved). Since a corporation is a separate legal entity and is responsible for its own acts and obligations, creditors cannot usually look beyond its assets for satisfaction of their claims. This is not true of other forms of business. In a partnership, for example, the partners can usually be held liable for the debts of the partnership, even to the extent of their personal assets. This limited liability feature has probably been most responsible for the phenomenal growth of the corporate form of business.

stock certificate *a document issued by a corporation to shareholders evidencing ownership in the corporation*

stockholders *individuals or organizations that own a portion (shares of stock) of a corporation*

board of directors *individuals elected by the shareholders to govern a corporation*

A second characteristic of a corporation is the easy transferability of ownership interests. This means that shares of stock in a corporation can be bought, sold, passed from one generation to another, or otherwise transferred, without affecting the legal or economic status of the corporation. When you buy stock in a corporation, you become an owner and receive a stock certificate as evidence of ownership (see Exhibit 12–1). All of the owners are called stockholders and they govern the corporation through an elected board of directors. (In most corporations, the board of directors then chooses a management team to direct the daily affairs of the corporation.)

EXHIBIT 12–1   **Typical Stock Certificate**

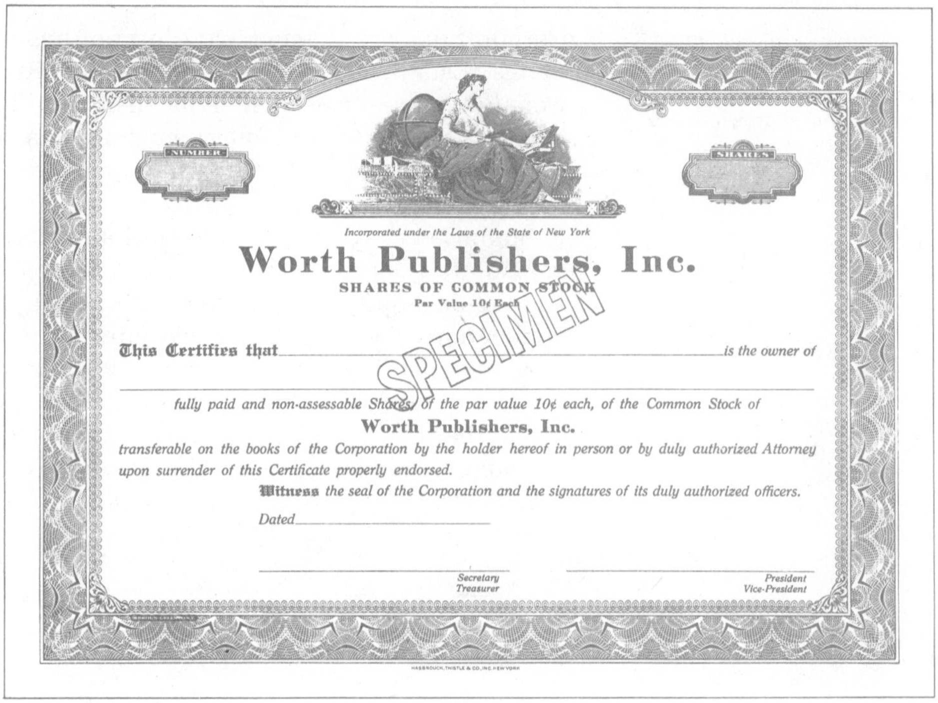

A third characteristic of corporations is their separate taxation. Because corporations are separate legal entities, they are taxed independently of their owners. This often results in a disadvantage, however, because the portion of corporate profits that is paid out in dividends is taxed twice. First, the profits are taxed to the corporation; second, assuming that dividends have been declared, the owners are taxed on their dividend income. (Small corporations can avoid this double taxation by forming a Subchapter S corporation.)

A fourth characteristic of very large corporations is that they are closely regulated by government. Because large corporations may have millions of shareholders, each with only small ownership interests, government has assumed the task of monitoring corporate activities. An example of government regulation is the requirement that all major corporations be audited and issue periodic financial statements. As a result, major corporations often enjoy less freedom than do partnerships or proprietorships.

TO SUMMARIZE   With the exception of the owners' equity section of the Balance Sheet, corporations, partnerships, and proprietorships have similar financial statements. A corporation is a business entity that has legal existence separate from that of its owners; it can conduct business, own property, and enter into contracts. The four major features of a corporation are (1) limited liability for stockholders, (2) easy transferability of ownership, (3) separate taxation, and (4) (for major corporations) close regulation by government.

Subchapter S corporation
a company legally organized as a corporation in which income or loss is passed through and taxed to individual shareholders

The Stock of a Corporation

contributed capital   *the portion of owners' equity contributed by investors (the owners) through the issuance of stock*

capital stock   *the general term applied to all shares of ownership in a corporation*

authorized stock   *the number of shares and type of stock that may be issued by a company as specified in its articles of incorporation*

issued stock   *authorized stock originally issued to stockholders, which may or may not still be outstanding*

outstanding stock   *issued stock that is still being held by investors*

treasury stock   *issued stock that has subsequently been reacquired and not retired by the corporation*

common stock   *the class of stock most frequently issued by corporations; it usually confers a voting right in the corporation; its dividend and liquidation rights are usually inferior to those of preferred stock*

preferred stock   *a class of stock issued by corporations, usually having dividend and liquidation preferences over common stock*

The owners' equity section of a corporation is usually divided into two parts: (1) contributed capital, which identifies capital contributed by the owners of a firm, and (2) retained earnings, which shows the undistributed earnings of a firm since incorporation. In this section, we focus on the contributed capital accounts.

When a corporation is given its charter by a state, it can sell shares of stock to raise capital. These shares, which are generally referred to as capital stock, may be sold publicly to many individuals, or privately to only a few individuals.

Corporate stock that has been approved for sale by a state is known as authorized stock. When the stock is sold, it becomes issued stock. If it is issued and not bought back by the corporation, it is said to be issued and outstanding, but if it has been reacquired by the corporation, it is known as treasury stock. These stages in the status of stock are diagrammed in Exhibit 12–2.

In addition, several types of stock can be authorized by the charter and issued by the corporation. The most familiar types are common stock and preferred stock, and the major difference between them concerns the degree to which their holders are allowed to participate in the rights of ownership of the corporation. The three basic rights inherent in the ownership of common stock are (1) the right to vote in corporate matters, (2) the right to share in distributed corporate earnings, and (3) the right to share in corporate assets upon liquidation. Usually, preferred stock has superior claims to rights (2) and (3), while common stock is often the only type of stock that provides voting rights. By issuing stocks with different rights and privileges, companies can appeal to a wider range of investors.

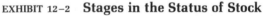

EXHIBIT 12–2   **Stages in the Status of Stock**

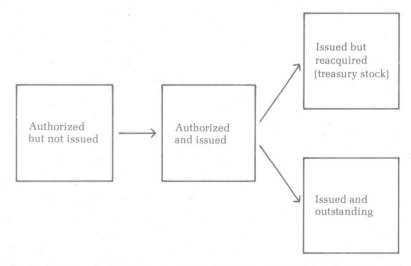

par-value stock stock that has a nominal value assigned to it in the corporation's charter and printed on the face of each share of stock

premium on stock the excess of the issuance (market) price of stock over its par or stated value

no-par stock stock that does not have a par value printed on the face of the stock certificate

stated value a nominal value assigned to no-par stock by the board of directors of a corporation

legal capital the amount of contributed capital not available for dividends, as restricted by state law for the protection of creditors; usually equal to the par or stated value of issued capital stock

When only one type of stock is issued by a corporation, it is common stock. There are several different types of common stock, the most popular of which is par-value stock. Basically, this stock has a par, or nominal, value provided for in the corporate charter and printed on the face of each stock certificate. When par-value stock sells for a price above par, it is said to sell at a premium; it generally cannot be issued for a price below par value. Historically, a par value was assigned the stock as a means of protecting a company's creditors. The par value multiplied by the total number of shares outstanding was supposed to represent the minimum amount of assets to be maintained by a corporation. Because the assignment of a par value to stock has proved to be an ineffective way of protecting creditors, most states now allow the sale of no-par stock. Many states require, however, that no-par stock have a stated value, which is a designated amount established by the board of directors of a corporation, thus having the same purpose as par value. According to individual states' laws, all corporations generally maintain some minimum contribution by stockholders as protection to the company's creditors. This minimum amount is called the legal capital of a corporation. If a stock has a par or stated value, the legal capital is usually equal to that amount times the number of shares issued. If there is no par or stated value, the legal capital is usually the total amount for which the stock was initially sold.

A final note about par value: Stock often sells for a much higher price than its par value. Indeed, the trend has been for companies to establish a very low par value, say $1 per share, and then sell the stock for a much higher amount, say $10 per share. This strategy usually eliminates the possibility of stock ever selling below par value. If stock were to be issued at a discount (below par), investors could be liable for legal capital in excess of their investment.

TO SUMMARIZE The owners' equity section of a corporation's Balance Sheet is divided into two parts: (1) contributed capital and (2) retained earnings. A corporation's stock can be authorized but unsold, issued and outstanding, or repurchased by the company and held as treasury stock. Common stock confers three rights upon its owners: (1) the right to vote in corporate matters, (2) the right to share in company earnings, and (3) the right to share in the assets upon liquidation of a corporation. Stock can be par value, no par with a stated value, or no par with no stated value. If par value, it usually sells above par (at a premium). The minimum amount of contributed capital a firm must maintain is called its legal capital.

ACCOUNTING FOR THE ISSUANCE OF PAR-VALUE STOCK AND NO-PAR STOCK WITH A STATED VALUE

When par-value stock is issued by a corporation, Cash is usually debited and the appropriate stockholders' equity accounts credited. For par-value common stock, the equity accounts credited are Common Stock, for an amount equal to the par value, and Paid-in Capital in Excess of Par—Common Stock, for the premium on common stock.

To illustrate, we will assume that the Minnesota Raiders Football Team (a corporation) issued 1,000 shares of $10 par common stock for $50 per share. (Note that no accounting entry is required at the time the stock is authorized, only when it is issued.) The entry to record the stock issuance would be

Cash (1,000 shares × $50) 50,000
    Common Stock (1,000 shares × $10 par value). 10,000
    Paid-in Capital in Excess of Par—
    Common Stock (1,000 shares × $40) 40,000
Issued 1,000 shares of $10 par-value stock at $50 per share.

If the par-value stock being issued is preferred stock, the entry would be

Cash (1,000 shares × $50) 50,000
    Preferred Stock (1,000 shares × $10 par value) 10,000
    Paid-in Capital in Excess of Par—
    Preferred Stock (1,000 shares × $40) 40,000
Issued 1,000 shares of $10 par-value preferred stock at $50 per share.

This illustration points out two important elements in accounting for the issuance of stock: (1) the equity accounts identify the type of stock being issued (common or preferred), and (2) the proceeds from the sale of the stock are divided into that portion attributable to its par value and that portion paid in excess of par value. These distinctions are important because the owners' equity section of the Balance Sheet should correctly identify the specific sources of capital, so that the respective rights of the various shareholders can be known.

If issued stock is no par with a stated value, the entries are virtually the same. To illustrate, we now assume that the Minnesota Raiders' authorized stock is no-par stock with a stated value of $1 per share and that 4,000 shares are issued for $5 per share. The entry would be

Cash (4,000 shares × $5) 20,000
    Common Stock (4,000 shares × $1 stated value) 4,000
    Paid-in Capital in Excess of Stated Value—
    Common Stock (4,000 shares × $4) 16,000
Issued 4,000 shares of no-par stock with a $1 stated value at $5 per share.

Again, if the stock being issued were preferred stock, the only change in this entry would be to identify the stock as preferred stock.

Although stock is usually issued for cash, other considerations may be involved. When a corporation is being organized, for example, attorneys and accountants may be paid with stock. The only difference between stock issued for noncash considerations and stock purchased for cash is in the debit entry.

To illustrate, we will assume that a prospective stockholder donated a piece of land (with fair market value of $25,000) to the Minnesota Raiders for 5,000 shares of the $1 per share stated value common stock. The entry would be as shown on the next page.

Land	25,000	
Common Stock (5,000 shares × $1)		5,000
Paid-in Capital in Excess of Stated Value—		
Common Stock		20,000

Issued 5,000 shares of no-par stock, $1 stated value, for land valued at $25,000.

ACCOUNTING FOR THE ISSUANCE OF NO-PAR STOCK WITHOUT A STATED VALUE

If the stock being issued is no par without a stated value, only one credit is recorded in the entry. To illustrate, we assume that Minnesota's stock does not have a par or stated value and that the Raiders issued 2,000 shares for $14 per share. The entry to record this issuance would be

Cash (2,000 shares × $14)	28,000	
Common Stock		28,000

Issued 2,000 shares of no-par stock at $14 per share.

Since most stock issued is either par-value stock or no-par stock with a stated value, only these two categories will be discussed in the remainder of this chapter.

ACCOUNTING FOR TREASURY STOCK

As noted earlier, a corporation may acquire some of its own outstanding stock. This reacquired stock is called treasury stock and is much like unissued stock in that it has no voting, dividend, or other rights. Because the acquisition of treasury stock effectively reduces the amount of stock outstanding and thereby allows a corporation to reduce its legal capital, most states restrict the amount of treasury stock a firm can have.

There are many reasons for a firm to buy back its own stock. Five of the most common are that management: (1) may need the stock for a profit-sharing, bonus, or stock-option plan; (2) may feel that the stock is selling for an unusually low price and is a good buy; (3) may want to stimulate trading in their stock; (4) may want the stock for a future merger or acquisition; and (5) may want to increase reported earnings per share by reducing the number of shares of stock outstanding.

When a firm purchases other companies' stock, the investment is included as an asset on the Balance Sheet. However, a corporation cannot own part of itself, so treasury stock is not considered an asset. Instead, it is a contra-equity account and is included on the Balance Sheet as a deduction from stockholders' equity.

Most commonly, treasury stock is accounted for on a cost basis (although other methods exist, they will not be shown here). That is, the stock is debited at its cost, not its par or stated value. To illustrate, we assume that 100 shares of the $10 par common stock was reacquired by the Minnesota Raiders Football Team for $60 per share. The entry to record the acquisition would be

Treasury Stock, Common (100 shares at $60).... 6,000
    Cash 6,000
Acquired 100 shares of treasury stock at $60 per share.

The effect of this entry on the Balance Sheet is to reduce both total assets (cash) and total stockholders' equity by $6,000.

When treasury stock is reissued, the entry depends on its issuance price. If the stock's price exceeds its cost, there is an increase in total stockholders' equity; if its price is below cost, there is an overall decrease in stockholders' equity.

To illustrate, we assume that 40 of the 100 shares of treasury stock are reissued at $80 per share. The entry to record this reissuance would be

Cash (40 shares × $80) 3,200
    Treasury Stock, Common (40 shares × $60 cost) 2,400
    Paid-in Capital—Treasury Stock 800
Reissued 40 shares of treasury stock at $80 per share.

As indicated, when price exceeds cost, the excess is entered in a special àccount: Paid-in Capital—Treasury Stock. The $800 is thus the difference between the purchase price and the sales price ($80 − $60 = $20) multiplied by the number of shares reissued. After this transaction, the company retains a balance of $3,600 in treasury stock (60 shares held at $60 per share).

If additional treasury stock is subsequently issued for less than the acquisition price, the entry depends on whether Paid-in Capital—Treasury Stock has a balance from previous transactions. If it has a balance, then it can be reduced to account for the difference between cost and selling price; if not, Retained Earnings is reduced to account for the difference. Alternatively, Retained Earnings can be reduced for the entire amount.

To illustrate, we assume that another 50 shares of treasury stock are reissued for $50 per share, $10 less than their cost. Since Paid-in Capital—Treasury Stock has a balance of $800, the entry to record this subsequent transaction may be

Cash (50 shares × $50) 2,500
Paid-in Capital—Treasury Stock 500
    Treasury Stock, Common (50 shares × $60 cost) 3,000
Issued 50 shares of treasury stock at $50 per share; original cost was $60 per share. (Note: Management has the option of reducing Retained Earnings even if Paid-in Capital—Treasury Stock exists. In this book, we will always assume that if Paid-in Capital—Treasury Stock exists, it will be reduced first, then any balance to Retained Earnings.)

If Paid-in Capital—Treasury Stock had not had a balance from previous transactions, the entry would have been

Cash (50 shares × $50) 2,500
Retained Earnings 500
    Treasury Stock, Common (50 shares × $60 cost) 3,000
Issued 50 shares of treasury stock at $50 per share; cost was $60 per share.

SUMMARIZING STOCKHOLDERS' EQUITY

Thus far, we have discussed the ways in which individual transactions affect owners' equity accounts. It is now appropriate to show how these accounts are summarized and presented on the Balance Sheet. The following data, which summarize the stockholders' equity transactions of the Minnesota Raiders Football Team, will be used to illustrate our points.

1. $10 par-value preferred stock: Issued 1,000 shares at $50 per share.

2. $10 par-value common stock: Issued 1,000 shares at $50 per share.

3. No-par common stock with a $1 stated value: Issued 4,000 shares at $5 per share.

4. No-par common stock with a $1 stated value: Issued 5,000 shares for land with a fair market value of $25,000.

5. No-par, no-stated-value common stock: Issued 2,000 shares at $14 per share.

6. Treasury stock, common: purchased 100 shares at $60; reissued 40 shares at $80; reissued 50 shares at $50.

With these data, the stockholders' equity section would be as follows:

Minnesota Raiders Football Team
Summarized Stockholders' Equity Section (Note: The number of shares authorized is deleted in this illustration.)

Preferred Stock ($10 par value, 1,000 shares issued). . . .	$10,000	
Common Stock ($10 par value, 1,000 shares issued)	10,000	
Common Stock (no par, $1 stated value, 9,000 shares issued)	9,000	
Common Stock (no par, no stated value, 2,000 shares issued)	28,000	
Paid-in Capital in Excess of Par—Preferred Stock	40,000	
Paid-in Capital in Excess of Par—Common Stock	40,000	
Paid-in Capital in Excess of Stated Value— Common Stock	36,000	
Paid-in Capital—Treasury Stock	300	
Total Contributed Capital		$173,300
Retained Earnings (discussed later)		0
		$173,300
Less Cost of Treasury Stock on Hand (10 shares at $60) .		600
Total Stockholders' Equity		$172,700

Although this stockholders' equity section is not realistic (companies rarely issue more than one type of common stock), it does summarize the information discussed thus far, and it illustrates that the various types of stock, as well as their par or stated values, must be separately identified in the stockholders' equity section.

TO SUMMARIZE When a company issues stock, it debits Cash or a noncash account (property, for example) and credits various stockholders' equity accounts. The credit entries depend on the type of stock issued (common or preferred), features (par value, no par with stated value, or no par without a stated value), and the per-share amounts the stock is issued for (above par and at par). A company's own stock that is reacquired in the marketplace is known as treasury stock and is included in the financial statements as a contra-stockholders' equity account. Treasury stock is usually accounted for on a cost basis. The stockholders' equity section of a Balance Sheet contains separate accounts for each type of stock issued, amounts paid in excess of par or stated values, treasury stock, and retained earnings.

Distributing the Earnings

pro rata   *a term for an allocation that is based on a proportionate distribution of the total*

dividends   *the periodic distribution of earnings in the form of cash, stock, or other property to the owners (stockholders) of a corporation*

If you had your own business and wanted to withdraw money for personal use, you would simply withdraw it from the company's checking account or cash register. In a corporation, a formal action by the board of directors is required before money can be distributed to the owners. In addition, such payments must be made on a pro rata basis (that is, each owner must receive a proportionate amount based on percentage of ownership). These pro rata distributions to owners are called dividends and are paid on a per-share basis. Thus, the amount of dividends a shareholder receives depends on the number of shares owned and the per-share amount of the dividend.

Note that a company does not have to pay dividends. Theoretically, a company that does not pay dividends should be able to reinvest its earnings in assets that will enable it to grow more rapidly than its dividend-paying competitors. This added growth will presumably be reflected in increases in the per-share price of the stock. In practice, most public companies pay regular cash dividends.

ACCOUNTING FOR DIVIDENDS

cash dividend   *a cash distribution of earnings to shareholders*

liquidating dividend   *the distribution of a firm's assets when a corporation is permanently reducing its operations or going out of business*

stock dividend   *a pro rata distribution of additional shares of stock by a corporation to its shareholders*

property dividend   *the distribution to shareholders of assets other than cash or stock*

declaration date   *the date on which a corporation's board of directors formally decides to distribute a dividend to shareholders*

Corporations can pay any one of several types of dividends. The most common is a cash dividend, which is a payment of cash out of corporate earnings. Another type is a liquidating dividend, which is a cash dividend paid from previous owner contributions. Liquidating dividends are usually paid only when a corporation is permanently reducing its operations or winding down its affairs. Third is a stock dividend, which is a distribution of stock to shareholders. Stock dividends will be discussed later in the chapter. Finally, there is a property dividend, which is a distribution of corporate assets (for example, the stock of another firm) to shareholders. Property dividends are quite rare.

Three important dates are associated with dividends. The first is when the board of directors formally declares its intent to pay a dividend. On this declaration date, the company becomes legally obligated to pay the dividends. This liability may be recorded as follows:

Dividends—Common Stock   8,000
   Dividends Payable   8,000
Declared a 50 cent per share dividend to stockholders of record on December 15, 1981.

At the end of the year, the account Dividends—Common Stock is closed to Retained Earnings by the following entry.

Retained Earnings   8,000
    Dividends—Common Stock   8,000
To close Dividends to Retained Earnings.

From this entry you can see that a declaration of dividends reduces Retained Earnings, and, eventually, the amount of cash on hand. Thus, while they are not considered to be expenses, dividends do reduce the amount a company could otherwise invest in productive assets.

An alternative way of recording the declaration of dividends involves debiting Retained Earnings directly. However, using the Dividend account instead of Retained Earnings allows a company to keep separate records of dividends paid to preferred and common shareholders. Whichever method is used, the result is the same: an eventual decrease in Retained Earnings.

The second important dividend date is the date of record. Falling somewhere between the declaration date and the payment date, this is the date selected by the board of directors on which dividend-receiving shareholders are identified. Since many corporate stocks are in flux—being bought and sold daily—it is important that the shareholders who will receive the dividends be identified. No accounting entry is required on the date of record.

As you might expect, the third important date is the dividend payment date. This is the date on which, by order of the board of directors, dividends will be paid. The entry to record the payment of a dividend would typically be

Dividends Payable   8,000
    Cash   8,000
Paid a 50 cent per share dividend.

Once a dividend-paying pattern has been established, the expectation of dividends is built into the per-share price of the stock. A break in the pattern usually produces a sharp drop in the price. Similarly, an increased dividend is a sign of growth and usually triggers a stock price increase. Dividend increases are usually considered to set a precedent, indicating that future dividends will be at this per-share amount or more. With this in mind, boards of directors are careful about raising dividends.

Cash Dividends and Dividend Preferences

The declaration and payment of a cash dividend requires: (1) a sufficient amount of uncommitted retained earnings, (2) cash to pay the dividend, and (3) a formal written action by the board of directors, which is referred to as a dividend declaration. Cash dividends are by far the most common types of dividends. They can be paid on any kind of stock, except, of course, treasury stock.

When cash dividends are declared, allocation of the dividends depends on the dividend preferences of the preferred stock, which are identified

date of record *the date selected by a corporation's board of directors on which dividend-receiving shareholders are identified*

payment date *the date on which dividends are paid by a corporation to its shareholders*

when the stock is approved by the state. The three most common are (1) current-dividend preference, (2) cumulative-dividend preference, and (3) participating-dividend preference. Preferred stockholders often have current- and cumulative-dividend preferences, but the participating feature is rare.

Current-Dividend Preference   Preferred stock has a dividend-paying percentage associated with it and is typically described as follows: "5 percent preferred, par $10 per share, 6,000 shares outstanding." The "5 percent" is a percentage of the par value of the outstanding preferred stock. This percentage is the amount that will be paid in dividends to preferred stockholders each year that dividends are declared. It is somewhat similar to interest paid to bondholders. The current-dividend preference requires that, when dividends are paid, this percentage of the preferred stock's par value will be paid to preferred shareholders before common shareholders receive anything.

To illustrate the payment of different types of dividends, the following data from the Minnesota Raiders Football Team will be used throughout this section. (The various combinations of dividend preferences illustrated on this and the following two pages are classified as Cases 1–6 and are summarized in Exhibit 12–3.) Assume that outstanding stock includes

Preferred Stock (5%, $10 par value, 6,000 shares issued)	$ 60,000
Common Stock ($5 par value, 8,000 shares issued)	40,000
Total	$100,000

To begin, assume that Raiders' 5 percent preferred stock has a current-dividend preference: Before any dividends can be paid to common shareholders, preferred shareholders must be paid a total of $3,000 ($60,000 × 0.05). Thus, if only $2,000 of dividends were declared (Case 1), preferred shareholders would receive the entire dividend payment. If $4,000 were declared (Case 2), preferred shareholders would receive $3,000 and common shareholders, $1,000.

Cumulative-Dividend Preference   The cumulative-dividend preference can be quite costly for common shareholders, because it requires that preferred shareholders be paid all unpaid dividends from past years before common shareholders receive anything. If dividends have been paid in all previous years, then only the current 5 percent must be paid to preferred stockholders. But, if dividends on preferred stock were not paid in full in prior years, the cumulative deficiency must be paid before common shareholders receive a penny.

With respect to the cumulative feature, it is important to repeat that companies are not required to pay dividends. Such past unpaid dividends are called dividends in arrears. Since their payment depends on the payment of dividends in the future, dividends in arrears do not represent actual liabilities. Instead, they are reported in the notes to the financial statements.

To illustrate the distribution of dividends for cumulative preferred stock, we will assume that the Minnesota Raiders Football Team has not paid

current-dividend preference *the right of preferred shareholders to receive current dividends before common shareholders receive dividends*

cumulative-dividend preference *the right of preferred shareholders to receive dividends for all past years in which no dividends were paid before common shareholders receive any dividends*

dividends in arrears *missed dividends for past years that preferred shareholders have a right to receive under their cumulative-dividend preference, when dividends are declared*

EXHIBIT 12–3   Dividend Preferences: Summary of Cases 1–6

Case	Preferred Dividend Feature	Years in Arrears	Total Dividend	Preferred Dividend	Common Dividend
1	5%, noncumulative, nonparticipating	Non-applicable	$ 2,000	$ 2,000	$ 0
2	5%, noncumulative, nonparticipating	Non-applicable	4,000	3,000	1,000
3	5%, cumulative, nonparticipating	Two	7,000	7,000	0
4	5%, cumulative, nonparticipating	Two	11,000	9,000	2,000
5	5%, noncumulative, participating	Non-applicable	20,000	12,000	8,000
6	5%, cumulative, participating	Two	20,000	14,400	5,600

any dividends for the last two years but has declared a dividend in the current year. The Raiders must pay $9,000 in dividends to preferred shareholders before they can give anything to the common shareholders. The calculation is as follows:

Dividends in Arrears—Two Years (0.05 × $60,000 × 2) $6,000
Current Dividend Preference (0.05 × $60,000)   3,000
    Total $9,000

However, if the Raiders paid only $7,000 in dividends (Case 3), preferred shareholders would receive all of the dividends, common shareholders would receive nothing, and there would still be dividends in arrears of $2,000 the next year. If $11,000 in dividends were paid (Case 4), preferred shareholders would receive $9,000 and common shareholders would receive $2,000.

Participating-Dividend Preference   A third dividend preference that can be accorded preferred shareholders is that of participation. Basically, this feature describes the distribution of dividends after the current and cumulative (if any) preferences have been met. Thus, if preferred stock is fully participating, then after these other preferences are fulfilled, common shareholders first receive a pro rata share of the dividends (in this case, 5 percent of the value of the common stock), and preferred shareholders participate in the remaining dividends on an equal percentage basis with common shareholders. If preferred stock is nonparticipating, after preferred shareholders have received their rightful dividends (on the basis of current and cumulative preferences), common shareholders receive all remaining dividends.

participating-dividend preference   *the right of preferred shareholders to receive equal distributions of dividends on a proportionate basis with common shareholders*

To illustrate the accounting for this preference, we will assume that the preferred stock of the Minnesota Raiders Football Team is fully participating and that the company pays $20,000 in dividends (Case 5). If the preferred stock were noncumulative or cumulative with no dividends in arrears, the dividend allocation would be

	Preferred	Common	Total Dividend
Current-dividend preference ($60,000 × 0.05).......	$ 3,000		$ 3,000
Common's pro rata share ($40,000 × 0.05)		$2,000	2,000
Allocation of remainder (3/5, 2/5 basis)*	9,000	6,000	15,000
	$12,000	$8,000	$20,000

* Preferred $60,000/$100,000 = 3/5; common $40,000/$100,000 = 2/5.

If the preferred stock were cumulative and if there were two years of dividends in arrears (Case 6), the dividend allocation would be

	Preferred	Common	Total Dividend
Cumulative-dividend preference ($60,000 × 0.05 × 2)	$ 6,000		$ 6,000
Current-dividend preference ($60,000 × 0.05).......	3,000		3,000
Common's pro rata share ($40,000 × 0.05)		$2,000	2,000
Allocation of remainder (3/5, 2/5 basis),			
Preferred ($60,000/$100,000 × $9,000)	5,400		5,400
Common ($40,000/$100,000 × $9,000)...........		3,600	3,600
	$14,400	$5,600	$20,000

The entries to account for the transactions in Case 6 would be

Date of Declaration

Dividends—Preferred (or Retained Earnings) ...	14,400	
Dividends—Common (or Retained Earnings)....	5,600	
Dividends Payable		20,000

Declared dividends on preferred and common stock.

Date of Payment

Dividends Payable	20,000	
Cash		20,000

Paid dividends on preferred and common stock.

Stock Dividends

Corporations sometimes issue a stock dividend instead of paying a cash dividend. Basically, a stock dividend is a distribution of additional stock to each owner in proportion to the number of shares held. For example, if a company issued a 10 percent stock dividend, each shareholder would receive one additional share for every 10 shares owned.

There is considerable disagreement as to whether stockholders receive anything of value from a stock dividend. Certainly, they do not receive cash or any other corporate asset, as with a cash or property dividend. In addition, since each shareholder receives a pro rata share of the stock issued, no single stockholder owns a larger percentage of the corporation after the stock dividend than before. Those who argue that stock dividends have value to stockholders give two reasons for their view.

1. If a company maintains the same level of cash dividends per share after the stock dividend as before, then an investor's long-run cash dividends will be increased by a stock dividend. Clearly, the issuance of a stock dividend in such a case represents a firm's decision to increase the amount of cash dividends it will pay in the future.

2. If the stock dividend is small, say 10 percent, it is commonly believed that the market will probably not discount the company's stock to a price that reflects the new total of shares outstanding. In other words, the stock's market price will probably not drop by a percentage equivalent to that of the stock dividend. The investor now has more shares which would, if this view is correct, have an increased value.

Stock dividends play an important role for the corporation issuing them. That role is to maintain dividend consistency. Corporations that issue dividends each year do not want to miss a year, so for them a stock dividend can be a useful substitute for cash. Because of the expectation of increased future dividends, most investors are satisfied with stock dividends.

To illustrate the accounting for a stock dividend, we will assume that stockholders' equity of the Minnesota Raiders Football Team was

Common Stock ($10 par value, 1,000 shares issued)	$10,000
Paid-in Capital in Excess of Par—Common Stock	40,000
Retained Earnings	50,000
Total Stockholders' Equity	$100,000

If a 10 percent stock dividend is issued when the current market price of the company's stock is $70, the entry to record the stock dividend would be

Retained Earnings (100 shares × $70)	7,000	
Common Stock (100 shares × $10 par)		1,000
Paid-in Capital—Stock Dividend		6,000

Declared and issued a 10% stock dividend.

Since the dividend was 10 percent, and since there were previously 1,000 shares outstanding, 100 additional shares were issued for the dividend. The market value of the stock ($70) was used as the basis for converting retained earnings to contributed capital because this was a relatively small stock dividend and presumably would not have a significant effect on the existing market price of the stock. The alternative would have been to debit the Retained Earnings account only for the par value of $10, but that would not have been realistic since the market value of the stock was much greater than $10.

If the stock dividend had been relatively large, the market price of the outstanding stock would have been severely affected and so would no longer be relevant. Thus, the accounting profession has required that par value be used for reporting large stock dividends.

Where does one draw the line between a large and a small stock dividend? Although somewhat arbitrary, the range of 20 to 25 percent of total outstanding stock has been selected by accounting rule-makers. Thus, for a stock dividend of 20 percent or larger, retained earnings are generally debited at par value; for stock dividends smaller than 20 percent, the market value is normally used.

To illustrate the accounting for a large stock dividend, we assume the same stockholders' equity for the Minnesota Raiders Football Team, except that the stock dividend is now 30 percent. The entry would be

Retained Earnings   3,000
    Common Stock (300 shares × $10 par)   3,000
Declared and issued a 30% stock dividend.

ACCOUNTING FOR STOCK SPLITS

stock split *an action by a corporation's management that reduces the par or stated value of its stock and proportionately increases the number of shares outstanding*

A stock split is a more dramatic way than a stock dividend of increasing the amount of outstanding stock. With a stock split, a company reduces the par or stated value of its stock by a certain amount, say half, and at the same time increases the number of shares outstanding by the reciprocal amount, in this case doubling it. Thus, the total par or stated value of stock outstanding is unchanged. For example, a firm with 20,000 shares of $10 par-value stock outstanding may reduce the par value to $5 and increase the number of shares outstanding to 40,000. In this case—involving a two-for-one stock split—an investor who had one share of stock will instead own two shares of the new $5 par-value stock. (Three for one, four for one, and other ratio splits are also common.)

A company generally authorizes a stock split in order to reduce the market price of its stock. Presumably, more investors will be encouraged to enter the market for a given stock if its trading price is lowered.

In contrast to a stock dividend, a stock split does not require an accounting entry or involve a transfer of retained earnings to contributed capital. Rather, the company simply notes in the records that both the par value and the number of shares of stock outstanding have changed.

TO SUMMARIZE The four types of dividends are cash dividends, liquidating dividends, stock dividends, and property dividends. The important dividend dates are the date of declaration, the date of record, and the payment date. Preferred stockholders can be granted a current preference, a cumulative preference, and a participating preference. Stock dividends are distributions of additional stock to shareholders. Although a stock dividend does not increase percentage ownership in a corporation, the additional stock provides the expectation of increased future cash dividends. With small stock dividends, Retained Earnings is debited at the stock's market value; with large stock dividends (20 percent or more), Retained Earnings is debited at the stock's par value.

A stock split is an increase in the number of shares outstanding corresponding to a reduction of the par or stated value of the stock. Generally, stock splits are authorized so that companies can lower their stock's market price per share.

ACCOUNTING FOR RETAINED EARNINGS

Retained Earnings is the account into which all of a company's earnings are closed. As such, it is increased each year by net income and decreased by losses and dividends declared. Thus, the Retained Earnings account balance represents the cumulative undistributed earnings of a business.

As we pointed out in Chapter 7, retained earnings is not the same as cash. In fact, a company can have a large retained earnings balance and be without cash, or it can have a lot of cash and very little retained earnings. Although both cash and retained earnings are usually increased when a company has earnings, the amounts by which they are increased are usually different. This occurs for two reasons: (1) the company's net income, which increases retained earnings, is accrual based, not cash based; and (2) cash from earnings may be invested in productive assets, such as inventories, or used to pay off loans or for any number of purposes, many of which do not affect net income or retained earnings.

Prior-Period Adjustments

prior-period adjustments
adjustments made directly to Retained Earnings, which are required to correct errors in the financial statements of prior periods

Besides profits and losses, dividends, and certain treasury stock transactions, there is one other type of event that affects retained earnings directly. This category includes adjustments to correctly restate the net income of prior periods; these are called, as you would expect, prior-period adjustments. Prior-period adjustments are rare. In addition to some technical prior-period adjustments involving taxes and bonds, which are beyond the scope of this book, the main event that qualifies as a prior-period adjustment is the correction of a material error in the financial statements of a prior period. A common type of prior-period adjustment is a correction of errors in accounting for the inventory of prior periods.

In accounting for prior-period adjustments, retained earnings is increased or decreased because the net income for the years affected by the adjustments has already been closed to the Retained Earnings account.

Statement of Retained Earnings

Statement of Retained Earnings   *a report that shows the changes in the Retained Earnings account during a period of time*

Prior-period adjustments and dividends are usually disclosed in a Statement of Retained Earnings. While it is not required, such a statement is usually provided by corporations. Exhibit 12–4 shows how the Minnesota Raiders Football Team might present such a statement, using arbitrary numbers.

Retained Earnings Restrictions

Corporations frequently place restrictions on part of retained earnings. This means that the earnings are earmarked for special purposes, such as plant expansion or the purchase of treasury stock, and hence are removed from dividend-availability status.

While restrictions on retained earnings do not actually create cash funds, they do serve to alert stockholders and others of management's intents and requirements. Such restrictions are usually disclosed in the financial statements.

EXHIBIT 12–4   **Minnesota Raiders Football Team**
Statement of Retained Earnings for the Year Ended December 31, 1981

Retained Earnings Balance, January 1, 1981		$300,000
Prior-Period Adjustment:		
Deduct Adjustment for 1980 Inventory Correction		25,000
Balance as Restated		$275,000
Net Income for 1981		50,000
Total		$325,000
Less Dividends Declared in 1981:		
On Preferred Stock	$10,000	
On Common Stock	12,000	22,000
Retained Earnings Balance, December 31, 1981		$303,000

To illustrate, we will assume that Timpview Corporation has a $160,000 balance in Retained Earnings. If $40,000 of that amount had been appropriated to retire preferred stock, the entry would be

Retained Earnings	40,000	
Retained Earnings Appropriated for Retirement of Preferred Stock		40,000

Appropriated $40,000 of retained earnings for the retirement of preferred stock.

Exhibit 12–5 is the owners' equity section of Timpview's Balance Sheet. (Note that the entries under Contributed Capital are arbitrary.) In the absence of any restrictions, the balance in Retained Earnings usually represents the maximum amount of dividends that can be declared and paid.

EXHIBIT 12–5   **Timpview Corporation**
Owners' Equity Section of Balance Sheet as of December 31, 1981

Contributed Capital:		
Common Stock ($10 par, 10,000 shares authorized, 5,000 shares issued and outstanding)	$ 50,000	
Preferred Stock (10%, $30 par, 4,000 shares authorized, 2,000 shares issued and outstanding)	60,000	
Paid-in Capital in Excess of Par—Common Stock	20,000	
Paid-in Capital in Excess of Par—Preferred Stock	10,000	
Total Contributed Capital		$140,000
Retained Earnings:		
Retained Earnings Appropriated for the Retirement of Preferred Stock	$ 40,000	
Unappropriated Retained Earnings	120,000	
Total Retained Earnings		160,000
Total Owners' Equity		$300,000

TO SUMMARIZE The Retained Earnings account reflects the total undistributed earnings of a business since incorporation. It is increased by net income and decreased by dividends, losses, some treasury stock transactions, and certain prior-period adjustments. Prior-period adjustments usually involve corrections of errors in prior years' financial statements. Retained earnings can be appropriated or restricted for special purposes, such as the retirement of preferred stock or debt. Such appropriations do not provide cash, but they do remove these retained earnings from dividend-availability status and alert financial statement users to management's plans.

The Proprietorship

proprietorship *an unincorporated business owned by one person*

Although corporations dominate business activity in the United States, by far the most common type of business is the proprietorship. A proprietorship is owned by one person and is usually a rather small company.

Unlike corporations, proprietorships are not chartered by a state. When a person decides to establish a proprietorship, he or she merely acquires the necessary inventory, tools, or other equipment, and begins working. Because proprietorships are so informal, they are not taxed separately from their owners, nor can they separately own property, incur debts, or enjoy many of the privileges of corporations. Instead, all liabilities and rights of ownership are borne by the proprietor.

The main difference between accounting for a proprietorship and a corporation is in the owners' equity accounts. In a corporation, owners' equity is divided into contributed capital and retained earnings, with each of these categories made up of several different accounts. In a proprietorship, all owner's equity transactions are handled by only two accounts: a capital account and a Drawings account.

Drawings *a temporary account for recording withdrawals of cash or other assets from a partnership or proprietorship by the owner(s)*

To illustrate the accounting for the owner's equity section of a proprietorship, we will assume that Julie Shaw decides to become a real estate broker. On January 1, 1981, she puts $10,000 into a bank account to finance the business. The entry to record the $10,000 deposit would be

Cash 10,000
  Julie Shaw, Capital 10,000
Invested $10,000 to start real estate business.

Once the business is established, the entries to account for the purchase of assets, the payment of business expenses, and the receipt of revenues are similar to those of a corporation. If Mrs. Shaw decided to withdraw cash for personal use or as salary, the entry would be.

Julie Shaw, Drawings 650
  Cash 650
Withdrew $650 for personal use.

As this entry shows, a proprietor's withdrawals (for salary or otherwise) are not expenses of the business. Instead, they are accounted for in a drawings account. Julie Shaw, Drawings is similar to a dividends account in a corporation, and so would be closed to Julie Shaw, Capital at year-end.

If we assume that there is a $14,000 credit balance (profit) in the Income Summary account at year-end, Julie Shaw's closing entry for income would be

Income Summary	14,000	
Julie Shaw, Capital		14,000

To close net income to the owner's capital account.

The closing entry to eliminate the balance in the drawings account would be

Julie Shaw, Capital	650	
Julie Shaw, Drawings		650

To close the drawings account for the year.

As we noted earlier, with the exception of the owners' equity portion of the Balance Sheet, the financial statements of a proprietorship are basically the same as those of a corporation. The owner's equity section of Julie Shaw's Balance Sheet might appear as follows:

Owner's Equity

Julie Shaw, Capital, January 1, 1981	$10,000
Add Net Income	14,000
Total	$24,000
Less Withdrawals..	650
Julie Shaw, Capital, December 31, 1981	$23,350

The Partnership

partnership *an unincorporated business owned by two or more persons or entities*

A partnership is an unincorporated business owned by two or more persons. Used by many owners of small businesses and by professional people, such as doctors, lawyers, dentists, and accountants, a partnership is easy to establish. It requires only that two or more people voluntarily decide to set up a business. The owners do not need the state's approval, nor are their profits subject to separate taxation. Instead, the profits of a partnership are taxed as part of the individual partners' personal incomes.

partnership agreement *an agreement between partners that usually specifies the capital contributions required by each partner, the ratios in which partnership earnings will be distributed, the management responsibilities of the partners, and the partners' rights to transfer or sell their individual interests*

Because a partnership is a voluntary association of two or more people, distribution of capital or profits is not legally fixed. It is up to the partners to decide who contributes how much and how the profits will be shared. Those decisions are usually written into a partnership agreement, which also specifies the managerial responsibilities of the individual partners; the restrictions on the sale or transfer of individual partnership interests; the method by which assets will be distributed in case of liquidation; and the steps to be taken if a partner dies, since a partnership can be dissolved with the death of a partner.

While partnerships are extremely easy to form, are free from separate taxation, and can be easily terminated, they have one major disadvantage: Each partner has unlimited liability. Since a partnership is not legally separate from its owners, the partners are legally responsible for its debts and obligations, even to the extent of their personal assets.

Like a proprietorship, a partnership has only two types of owners' equity accounts: capital and drawings. The accounting for both forms of business is therefore the same, except that the partnership involves two or more capital and drawings accounts.

To illustrate the accounting for a partnership, we assume that Dr. Adams and Dr. Baker decide to form a partnership on January 1, 1981. Their partnership agreement specifies that they are to contribute $6,000 and $4,000, respectively, for the purchase of medical and office equipment. The entry to record the capital contributions of the two partners would be

```
Cash ...................................   10,000
    Adams, Capital ....................              6,000
    Baker, Capital ....................              4,000
Contributed capital to the partnership.
```

The partnership agreement specifies a monthly salary of $2,000 for each partner and so the entry to record their salaries is

```
Adams, Drawings .......................    2,000
Baker, Drawings .......................    2,000
    Cash ..............................              4,000
Withdrew monthly salaries.
```

As shown in this entry, salaries are not expenses of a partnership, but rather are withdrawals agreed upon in advance and based upon expected earnings.

During the year there will be numerous entries to record revenues, expenses, the purchase of assets, and the payment of debts, all handled just as they are for a corporation.

If there was a $70,000 credit balance (profit) in the Income Summary account at year-end and if each partner is to be credited with 50 percent of the profits, the entry to close earnings would be

```
Income Summary ........................   70,000
    Adams, Capital ....................             35,000
    Baker, Capital ....................             35,000
To close the year's profits to the partners' capital accounts.
```

If a full 12 months' salary was withdrawn by each partner, the entry to close their drawings accounts for the year would be

```
Adams, Capital ........................   24,000
Baker, Capital ........................   24,000
    Adams, Drawings ...................             24,000
    Baker, Drawings ...................             24,000
To close partners' drawings accounts for the year.
```

EXHIBIT 12–6   Adams–Baker Partnership
Statement of Partners' Capital for the Year Ended December 31, 1981

	M. Adams	J. Baker	Total
Investment, January 1, 1981	$ 6,000	$ 4,000	$10,000
Add: Investments During the Year ...	0	0	0
Net Income for the Year	$35,000	$35,000	$70,000
Total	$41,000	$39,000	$80,000
Less Drawings During the Year	24,000	24,000	48,000
Partners' Capital, December 31, 1981..	$17,000	$15,000	$32,000

Statement of Partners' Capital *a partnership report that reconciles the balances in the partners' equity accounts from year to year*

The financial statements of a partnership are basically the same as those of a corporation. However, they differ in two ways: The owners' equity section of the Balance Sheet includes only capital accounts; and, instead of a Statement of Retained Earnings, there is a Statement of Partners' Capital, which reconciles the partners' capital accounts from one year to the next. In the case of the Adams–Baker partnership, the Statement of Partners' Capital would be as shown in Exhibit 12–6.

CHAPTER REVIEW

The accounting for all three types of business entities—corporations, proprietorships, and partnerships—is identical except for owners' equity.

A corporation is a business entity, legally separate from its owners, which is chartered by a state. It is separately taxed, and it can incur debts, conduct business, own property, and enter into contracts. The owners' equity section of a corporation's Balance Sheet is generally divided into two sections: contributed capital and retained earnings. Contributed capital identifies the resources contributed by owners and the stock that has been issued by the corporation.

The two major types of stock are common and preferred. Common stock is usually voting stock. Preferred stock may have current-, cumulative-, and participating-dividend privileges, and is usually nonvoting. Stock can be authorized but not yet issued; authorized, issued, and outstanding; or authorized, issued, and reacquired by the corporation. Reacquired stock is called treasury stock. Stock can have a par value, no par with a stated value, or it can be no-par stock with no stated value. The accounting is different for each. When treasury stock is purchased by a corporation, it is usually accounted for at cost and is deducted from total stockholders' equity as a contra-equity account.

Corporations usually pay dividends to their owners. These distributions to owners can be in the form of cash, property, or additional stock. The three important dates in accounting for dividends are the declaration date, the date of record, and the payment date. Dividends are not a liability until declared. If a company has common and preferred stock, the allocation of dividends between the two types depends on the dividend preferences of the preferred stock.

A company can also have a stock split, such as a two-for-one split, which increases the number of shares outstanding and decreases proportionately the par or stated value of the stock.

Owners' equity also includes retained earnings, which shows the cumulative undistributed earnings of a company since incorporation. Retained earnings is decreased by: (1) the declaration of dividends, (2) operating losses, (3) some treasury stock transactions, and (4) certain prior-period adjustments. Retained earnings may be restricted or appropriated for specific uses.

A proprietorship is an unincorporated business owned by one person. Proprietorships are not legal entities separate from their owners and thus cannot incur debts, own property, or enjoy other rights associated with corporations. The owner's equity section of a proprietorship includes only two accounts: capital and drawings. The drawings account is closed to the capital account at year-end.

A partnership is an unincorporated business owned by two or more persons. Like a proprietorship, it is not a legal entity separate from its owners and therefore does not enjoy rights associated with corporations. Advantages of a partnership are ease of formation, freedom from separate taxation, and ease of termination. The major disadvantage is the unlimited liability of the partners. Like a proprietorship, only two types of accounts (capital and drawings) are included in a partnership's owners' equity section. There is a set of these accounts for each partner. A Statement of Partners' Capital reconciles the partners' capital accounts from one year to the next.

KEY TERMS AND CONCEPTS

authorized stock (387)
board of directors (385)
capital stock (387)
cash dividend (393)
charter (articles of
    incorporation) (385)
common stock (387)
contributed capital
    (387)
corporation (385)
cumulative-dividend
    preference (396)
current-dividend
    preference (395)
date of record (394)
declaration date (393)
dividends (393)

dividends in arrears
    (396)
Drawings (402)
issued stock (387)
legal capital (388)
limited liability (385)
liquidating dividend
    (393)
no-par stock (388)
outstanding stock (387)
participating-dividend
    preference (396)
partnership (403)
partnership agreement
    (403)
par-value stock (388)
payment date (394)
preferred stock (387)

premium on stock (388)
prior-period
    adjustments (400)
property dividend (393)
proprietorship (402)
pro rata (393)
stated value (388)
Statement of Partners'
    Capital (405)
Statement of Retained
    Earnings (400)
stock certificate (385)
stock dividend (393)
stockholders (385)
stock split (399)
Subchapter S
    corporation (386)
treasury stock (387)

DISCUSSION QUESTIONS

1. In what way is the Balance Sheet of a corporation different from that of a partnership or proprietorship?

2. In what way does the owners' equity section of a Balance Sheet identify the sources of the assets?

3. In which type of business entity do owners have limited liability?

4. What is meant by the term "transferability of ownership"? Do partnerships have this attribute?

5. In what way is there a double taxation of corporate profits?

6. How are common and preferred stock different from each other?

7. How is treasury stock different from unissued stock?

8. Is treasury stock an asset? If not, why not?

9. What is the purpose of having a par or stated value on stocks?

10. Does treasury stock possess the same voting, dividend, and other rights that outstanding stock does?

11. How is treasury stock usually accounted for?

12. When does a corporation have a legal obligation to pay dividends to its shareholders?

13. What do you suppose is the difference between a "growth company" and a "dividend company"?

14. Why should a potential common stockholder carefully examine the dividend preferences of a company's preferred stock?

15. Are dividends in arrears a liability? If not, why not?

16. Does a stock dividend have value to stockholders? Explain.

17. What is the difference between a stock dividend and a stock split? Why would a company split its stock?

18. Is it possible for a firm to have a large Retained Earnings balance and no cash? Explain.

19. Why are prior-period adjustments entered directly into Retained Earnings instead of reflected on the Income Statement?

20. Are there ever Income Tax Payable or Income Tax Expense accounts on the books of a proprietorship or partnership? If not, why not?

21. What are the major disadvantages of a partnership?

EXERCISES

E12–1 Issuance of Stock

Davis Corporation was organized on July 15, 1981. Record the journal entries to account for the following.

1. The state authorized 25,000 shares of 6 percent preferred stock ($20 par) and 100,000 shares of no-par common stock.

2. Davis gave 2,000 shares of common stock to his attorney in return for her help in incorporating the business. Fees for this type of work are normally about $6,000.

3. Davis gave 15,000 shares of common stock to a friend who contributed a building worth $30,000 to the business.

4. Davis paid $50,000 cash for 40,000 shares of common stock.

5. Another friend donated a $10,000 machine and received 3,000 shares of common stock.

6. The attorney sold all her shares to her brother-in-law for $7,000.

E12–2 No-Par Stock Transactions

Miller Maintenance Corporation was organized in early 1981 with 20,000 shares of no-par common stock

authorized. During 1981, the following additional transactions occurred.

a. Issued 8,500 shares of stock at $36 per share.

b. Issued another 1,200 shares at $38 per share.

c. Issued 1,000 shares for a building appraised at $40,000.

d. Declared dividends of $1 per share.

e. Earned $49,500 during the year.

Given the above information:

1. Journalize the transactions.

2. Present the stockholders' equity section of the Balance Sheet as it would appear on December 31, 1981.

E12–3 Stock Transactions

On January 1, 1981, Springfield Corporation was granted a charter authorizing the following capital stock: common stock $20 par, 50,000 shares; preferred stock, $10 par, 6 percent, 15,000 shares.

Record the following 1981 transactions.

1. Issued 40,000 shares of common stock at $35 per share.

2. Issued 7,000 shares of preferred stock at $12 per share.

3. Bought back 5,000 shares of common stock at $40 per share.

4. Reissued 500 shares of treasury stock at $25 per share.

5. Paid dividends of $9,525. How much is the dividend per share on common stock? (Preferred stock is non-cumulative and nonparticipating.)

E12–4   Stockholders' Equity Transactions

On January 1, 1981, Rose Corporation was authorized to issue 100,000 shares of common stock, par value $10 per share, and 20,000 shares of 6 percent preferred stock, par value $50 per share.

Journalize the following transactions.

1. Issued 30,000 shares of common stock at $12 per share.

2. Issued 6,000 shares of preferred stock at $56 per share.

3. Reacquired 500 shares of common stock for the treasury at $14 per share.

4. Reissued 100 of the treasury shares for $1,300.

5. Declared a cash dividend sufficient to meet the current-dividend preference on preferred stock and pay common stockholders $1 per share.

E12–5   Trading Stock for Other Assets

If 200 shares of common stock with a par value of $5 and a market price of $16 are traded for a machine with a fair market value of $3,200, complete the following.

1. Provide the journal entry to record the transaction.

2. If the machine's appraised fair market value was $3,100, what would be the correct journal entry to record the transaction?

3. Make the necessary journal entry, assuming the same facts as in 2, except that the stock is not actively traded and therefore its market price is unknown.

4. Record the necessary journal entry, assuming the stock's par is $10 and its market price is $15 per share.

E12–6   Treasury Stock Transactions

Provide the necessary journal entries to record the following:

1. Worth Corporation was granted a charter authorizing the issuance of 50,000 shares of no-par common stock. Management established a stated value of $8 per share.

2. The company issued 20,000 shares of common stock at $10 per share.

3. The company reacquired 1,000 shares of its own stock at $11 per share to be held in treasury.

4. Another 1,000 shares of stock were reacquired at $12 per share.

5. Four hundred of the shares reacquired in part 3 were reissued for $13 per share.

6. Seven hundred of the shares reacquired in part 4 were reissued for $9 per share.

7. Given the preceding transactions, what is the balance in the Treasury Stock account?

E12–7   Preparing a Stockholders' Equity Section

The following account balances appear on the books of Allred Corporation as of December 31, 1981.

Common Stock (par value $3, 200,000 shares authorized, 150,000 shares outstanding)	$ 450,000
Preferred Stock ($40 par value, 7%, 30,000 shares authorized, 25,000 shares outstanding)	1,000,000
Paid-in Capital in Excess of Par:	
Common Stock	245,000
Preferred Stock	155,000
Net Income for 1981	65,000
Dividends Paid During 1981	35,000
Retained Earnings, January 1, 1981	680,000

1. If the preferred stock is selling at $45 per share, what is the maximum cash that Allred Corporation can obtain by issuing preferred stock?

2. If common stock is selling for $12 per share, what is the maximum cash that can be obtained by issuing common stock?

3. Given the above data, and ignoring parts 1 and 2, prepare the stockholders' equity section of the Balance Sheet.

E12–8   Analysis of Stockholders' Equity

The stockholders' equity section of Packer Corporation at the end of the current year showed:

Preferred Stock (6%, $40 par value, 10,000 shares authorized, 6,000 shares outstanding) .	?
Common Stock ($6 par value, 80,000 shares authorized, 53,000 issued—including 350 shares of treasury stock)	318,000
Paid-in Capital in Excess of Par— Preferred Stock.	?
Paid-in Capital in Excess of Par— Common Stock	129,000
Retained Earnings	86,000
Less Treasury Stock.	(2,000)
Total Stockholders' Equity	?

1. What is the dollar amount to be entered under Preferred Stock?

2. What is the average price for which common stock was issued?

3. If preferred stock was issued at an average price of $43 per share, what amount should appear in the Paid-in Capital in Excess of Par—Preferred Stock account?

4. What is the average cost per share of treasury stock?

5. Assuming that the preferred stock was issued for an average price of $43 per share, what is total stockholders' equity?

6. If net income for the year were $67,000 and if only preferred dividends were paid, by how much would retained earnings increase?

E12–9 Analysis of Stockholders' Equity

The stockholders' equity section of the Balance Sheet of Ready Corporation as of December 31, 1982, is as follows:

Stockholders' Equity

Contributed Capital:

Preferred Stock (6%, $10 par value, cumulative and nonparticipating, 100,000 shares authorized)		$ 500,000
Common Stock (no par, $10 stated value, 100,000 shares authorized) .		900,000
Paid-in Capital in Excess of Stated Value—Common Stock		450,000
Total		$1,850,000

Retained Earnings:

Retained Earnings—Unrestricted .	$600,000	
Retained Earnings—Appropriated .	200,000	800,000
Total		$2,650,000
Less Treasury Stock (Common) (5,000 shares at $15 per share) . . .		75,000
Total Stockholders' Equity		$2,575,000

1. How many shares of preferred stock have been issued?

2. How many shares of common stock have been issued?

3. How many shares of preferred stock are outstanding?

4. How many shares of common stock are outstanding?

5. What is the total amount of legal capital?

E12–10 Retained Earnings Statement and Stockholders' Equity

The following balances appear on the accounts of Kelling Corporation as of December 31, 1981.

Retained Earnings, January 1, 1981	$64,000
Prior-Period Adjustment (tax adjustment for 1979)	(28,500)
Net Income for 1981	19,000
Common Stock ($5 par, 8,000 shares issued, of which 200 shares are in the treasury)	40,000
Paid-in Capital in Excess of Par— Common Stock	21,400
Preferred Stock ($12 par, 7%, 2,500 shares issued and outstanding)	30,000
Paid-in Capital in Excess of Par— Preferred Stock	6,700
Treasury Stock	1,800
Cash Dividends Paid During 1981	5,000

1. Prepare the Retained Earnings Statement for Kelling Corporation as of December 31, 1981.

2. Prepare the stockholders' equity section of Kelling Corporation's Balance Sheet as of December 31, 1981.

E12–11 Dividend Calculations

On January 1, 1981, Blue Corporation had 65,000 shares of common stock issued and outstanding (market price = $8/share). During 1981, the following transactions occurred (in chronological order).

a. 5,000 new shares of common stock were issued.

b. 1,000 shares of stock were reacquired for use in the company's stock option plan.

c. At the end of the option period, 600 shares had been purchased by corporate officials through the option plan.

Given this information, compute the following.

1. After the foregoing three transactions occur, what amount of dividends must Blue Corporation declare in order to pay $2 per share? To pay $3 per share?

2. What is the dividend per share if $200,000 is paid?

3. If all 1,000 treasury shares had been purchased by corporate officials through the stock-option plan, what would the dividends per share have been, again assuming $200,000 in dividends were paid?

E12–12 Dividend Calculations

Miller's stockholders' equity section shows:

Common Stock ($20 par, 20,000 shares outstanding)	$400,000
Preferred Stock ($50 par, 6%, 4,000 shares outstanding)	200,000
Retained Earnings	250,000

The board of directors is considering the declaration of dividends. No dividends were declared last year. For each of the following situations, compute the amount of dividends that would be declared and paid to common and preferred stockholders and make the journal entries that are necessary to record the declaration.

1. The preferred stock is noncumulative and non-participating and dividends of $45,000 are declared.
2. The preferred stock is noncumulative and participating and dividends of $54,000 are declared.
3. The preferred stock is cumulative and nonparticipating and dividends of $35,000 are declared.
4. The preferred stock is cumulative and participating and dividends of $60,000 are declared.

E12–13 Dividend Calculations

Farnsworth Corporation has the following stock outstanding.

Preferred Stock (5%, $20 par, 5,000 shares) $100,000
Common Stock ($5 par, 40,000 shares) 200,000

For each of the three cases below, compute the amount of dividends that would be paid to preferred and common shareholders. Assume that total dividends paid are $28,000. No dividends have been paid for the past two years.

Case A—Preferred is noncumulative and nonparticipating.
Case B—Preferred is cumulative and nonparticipating.
Case C—Preferred is cumulative and fully participating.

E12–14 Cash Dividends and Treasury Stock Transactions

During 1981, Siesta Corporation had the following transactions and related events.

Jan. 15 Issued 6,500 shares of common stock at par ($16 per share), bringing the total number of shares outstanding to 121,300.
Feb. 6 Declared a 50 cent per share dividend on common stock for shareholders of record on March 6.
Mar. 6 Date of record.
Mar. 8 John Jones, a prominent banker, purchased 20,000 shares of Siesta Corporation stock from the company for $346,000.
Apr. 6 Paid dividends declared on February 6.
Jun. 19 Reacquired 800 shares of common stock as treasury stock at a total cost of $9,350.
Sept. 6 Declared dividends of 55 cents per share to be paid to shareholders of record on October 15, 1981.

Oct. 6 The Dow Jones Industrial average plummeted 24 points and Siesta's stock price fell $3 per share.
Oct. 15 Date of record.
Nov. 6 Paid dividends that were declared on September 6.
Dec. 15 Declared and paid a 6 percent dividend on 18,000 outstanding shares of preferred stock (par value $32).

Given this information:

1. Prepare the journal entries for these transactions.
2. What is the total amount of dividends paid to common and preferred shareholders during 1981?

E12–15 Accounting for Stock Dividends and Stock Splits

Wynder Meat Packing Corporation would like to pay a cash dividend to its stockholders but has a very low cash balance. In an attempt to satisfy stockholders, the company decides to pay a stock dividend.

You are required to record the following transactions.

1. Wynder issues 4,000 shares of common stock at a price equal to the par value of $17 per share. This brings the number of common shares outstanding to 76,000.
2. A 30 percent stock dividend is declared and paid. Market price of the stock at the time of the dividend is $20 per share.
3. An additional 5,000 shares of common stock are issued at $21 per share.
4. A stock dividend of 10 percent is declared and paid. The market price of the stock is now $19 per share.
5. A three-for-one stock split is declared. How would it affect the stockholders' equity accounts?

E12–16 Accounting for Stock Dividends and Stock Splits

The Johnson Company's stockholders' equity section is shown below.

Common Stock ($20 par, 20,000 shares
  outstanding) $400,000
Preferred Stock ($50 par, 6%, 4,000 shares
  outstanding) 200,000
Retained Earnings 250,000

Given these data, complete the following four independent requirements.

1. Make the necessary journal entry to record a 10 percent common stock dividend. (The market value of the common stock at the time of the dividend is $30 per share.)

2. Make the necessary journal entry to record a 5 percent common stock dividend. (The market value of the common stock at the time of the dividend is $35 per share.)

3. Make the necessary journal entry to record a 50 percent common stock dividend. (The market value of the common stock at the time of the dividend is $40 per share.)

4. What entry would be made to record a four-for-one split of common stock? What difference would a four-for-one stock split make in the equity section of the Balance Sheet?

E12–17   Accounting for Stock Dividends

Using the data given in E12–10, make the necessary journal entries to record the following independent transactions.

1. A 2 percent stock dividend on common stock is declared. (Market price of common stock at the time of the dividend is $5.50 per share.)

2. A 5 percent stock dividend on common stock is declared. (Market price of common stock at the time of the dividend is $5.50 per share.)

3. A 50 percent stock dividend on common stock is declared. (Market price of common stock at the time of the dividend is $6.50 per share.)

4. A stock split (two for one) is declared.

E12–18   Accounting for a Proprietorship

Myrtle Johnson decided to go into the business of making and selling sweaters and socks. During the year, she had the following transactions.

1. Invested $12,000 in a company and immediately spent the entire amount to purchase needles and yarn.
2. Invested another $6,000 in the business.
3. Sold 50 sweaters at $60 each for cash.
4. Sold 100 pairs of socks and 60 more sweaters. The socks sold for $4 a pair and the sweaters sold for $60 each.
5. Paid expenses for the year of $4,250 (includes cost of needles and yarn that were sold).
6. Withdrew $2,500 for personal use.

Journalize these transactions and prepare a Statement of Owner's Equity for Myrtle Johnson's proprietorship at year-end.

E12–19   Accounting for a Proprietorship

Juan Garcia, sole proprietor, opened a grocery store on June 1, 1981. During the year, the following transactions took place.

a. Garcia contributed a building worth $50,000, furniture worth $20,000, and $10,000 cash to establish the business.

b. From the interim earnings of the proprietorship, he withdrew $6,000 for personal use.

c. He contributed a new set of shelves to the business. The cost of the shelves was $4,500.

d. He contributed another $3,000 in cash to the business.

e. During 1981, Garcia's income from the business was $14,300.

f. He withdrew all remaining earnings except $2,000, which he left in the business.

Given this information:

1. Prepare the journal entries (including closing entries) for the above transactions.

2. Prepare the equity section of the Balance Sheet for Garcia's Corner Grocery Store as of December 31, 1981.

E12–20   Partnership Accounting

On August 1, 1982, Mr. Garcia (see E12–19) accepted Albert Paolini as a partner. At that time, Garcia's capital account showed a $135,000 balance. Paolini contributed $90,000 cash and agreed to a 40/60 split of earnings, with Paolini receiving 40 percent and Garcia 60 percent. During the rest of 1982, the following transactions took place.

a. Garcia withdrew $12,000 in cash and Paolini withdrew $3,000 in cash and $1,000 in groceries.

b. Garcia invested another $4,500 cash and Paolini invested a delivery truck worth $6,000.

c. Net earnings for 1982 were $26,700.

Given this information:

1. Record these transactions.

2. Prepare a Statement of Partners' Capital as of December 31, 1982, for the Garcia–Paolini partnership.

E12–21   Stockholders' and Partners' Equity Sections

On January 1, 1981, Little, Madsen and Norris (LMN) formed a company by contributing $90,000, $60,000, and $50,000, respectively. In 1981, profits (ignore taxes) amounted to $40,000, which were shared by the three partners in proportion to their initial investments. Each partner withdrew half of his share of the income.

Prepare the equity section of the Balance Sheet as of December 31, 1981, if the LMN Company is

1. A corporation (the only stock issued is common with a $10 par value; each of the owners paid $25 per share for stock; the profits returned were in the form of dividends).

2. A partnership.

PROBLEMS

P12–1   Stock Transactions and Analysis

The following selected accounts and amounts were taken from the Balance Sheet of Gulf Shipping Company as of December 31, 1980.

Cash...................................	$ 93,000
Property, Plant, and Equipment	850,000
Accumulated Depreciation	150,000
Liabilities	50,000
Preferred Stock ($100 par, 7% noncumulative, nonparticipating, 10,000 shares authorized, 5,000 shares outstanding).................	500,000
Common Stock ($10 par, 100,000 authorized) . . .	800,000
Paid-in Capital in Excess of Par— Preferred Stock.........................	1,000
Paid-in Capital in Excess of Par— Common Stock.........................	125,000
Paid-in Capital—Treasury Stock	1,000
Retained Earnings:	
Appropriated for Plant Expansion............	84,000
Unappropriated	226,000

Required:

For each part (1–7), (a) prepare the necessary journal entry (or entries) to record each transaction; and (b) calculate the amount that will appear on the December 31, 1981, Balance Sheet as a consequence of this transaction only. (Note: In your answer to each part of this problem, consider this to be the *only* transaction that took place during 1981.)

1. One hundred shares of Common Stock are issued in exchange for a cash payment of $2,000.
   (a) Entry
   (b) Paid-in Capital in Excess of Par—Common Stock $ _____

2. One hundred shares of preferred stock are issued at a price of $102 per share.
   (a) Entry
   (b) Paid-in Capital in Excess of Par—Preferred Stock $ _____

3. Five hundred shares of common stock are issued in exchange for a building. The common stock is not actively traded, but the building was recently appraised at $11,000.
   (a) Entry
   (b) Property, Plant, and Equipment $ _____

4. One thousand shares of common stock were reacquired from a stockholder for $23,000 and subsequently reissued for $21,500 to a different investor. (Note: Make two entries.)
   (a) Entries
   (b) Paid-in Capital—Treasury Stock $ _____

5. The board of directors *declared* (not paid) dividends of $75,000.
   (a) Entry
   (b) Retained Earnings—Unappropriated
                                            $ _____

6. The board of directors declared and the stockholders approved a five-for-four stock split.
   (a) Entry
   (b) Retained Earnings—Unappropriated
                                            $ _____

7. The planned plant expansion is now expected to cost $100,000, and the additional appropriation has been authorized.
   (a) Entry
   (b) Total Retained Earnings $ _____

P12–2   Stock Transactions and Preparation of Stockholders' Equity Section

The Balance Sheet for Dyer Corporation as of December 31, 1980, is as follows:

Assets........................		$750,000
Liabilities		$410,000
Stockholders' Equity:		
Convertible Preferred Stock (5%, $20 par).................	$ 50,000	
Common Stock ($10 par)	150,000	
Paid-in Capital in Excess of Par— Common Stock	30,000	
Retained Earnings	116,000	
	$346,000	
Less Treasury Stock, Common (500 shares at cost).............	6,000	340,000
Total Liabilities and Stockholders' Equity.........		$750,000

During 1981, the following transactions were completed in the order given.

a. 750 shares of outstanding common stock were reacquired by the company at $7 per share. (Treasury stock is recorded at cost.)

b. 150 shares of common stock were reacquired in settlement of an account receivable of $1,500.

c. Semiannual cash dividends of 75 cents per share on common stock and 50 cents per share on preferred stock were declared and paid.

d. Each share of preferred stock is convertible into four shares of common stock. Five hundred shares of preferred stock were traded for common stock. Accrued dividends totaling $100 were paid to preferred stockholders exchanging their holdings. (Hint: Shares are traded at par value and any excess must come from Retained Earnings.)

e. The 900 shares of common treasury stock acquired during 1981 were sold at $13. The remaining treasury shares were exchanged for machinery with a fair market value of $6,300.

f. 3,000 shares of common stock were issued in exchange for land appraised at $39,000.

g. Semiannual cash dividends of 75 cents on common stock and 50 cents on preferred stock were declared and paid.

h. Net income was $35,000.

Required:

1. Give the necessary journal entries to record the transactions listed.

2. Prepare the stockholders' equity section of the Balance Sheet as of December 31, 1981.

P12–3   Dividend Calculations

Good and Plenty Company has authorization for 10,000 shares of 6 percent preferred stock, par value $10 per share, and 4,000 shares of common stock, par value $100 per share, all of which are issued and outstanding. During the years beginning in 1980, Good and Plenty maintained a policy of paying out 50 percent of net income in cash dividends. Net income for the three years beginning in 1980 was $8,000, $80,000, and $64,000.

Required:

Compute the amount of dividends paid to each class of stock for each year under the following separate cases.

1. Preferred stock is noncumulative and nonparticipating.

2. Preferred stock is cumulative and nonparticipating.

3. Preferred stock is noncumulative and fully participating.

4. Preferred stock is cumulative and fully participating.

5. **Interpretive Question**   Why is it important that a common shareholder know about the dividend privileges of the preferred stock?

P12–4   Dividend Transactions and Calculations

Bowman Company currently has 200,000 shares of $10 par-value common stock authorized, with 100,000 of these shares issued and outstanding.

Required:

1. Prepare journal entries to record the following 1981 transactions.

(a) January 1. Received authorization for 100,000 shares of 7 percent fully participating, cumulative preferred stock with a par value of $10.

(b) January 2. Issued 10,000 shares of the preferred stock at $15 per share.

(c) February 1. Declared a two-for-one common stock split to be effective on February 15.

(d) February 15. Common stock is split as announced at the beginning of the month.

(e) June 1. Reacquired 20 percent of the common stock outstanding for $18 per share.

(f) June 2. Declared a cash dividend of $10,000. The date of record is June 15.

(g) June 30. Paid the previously declared cash dividend of $10,000.

(h) October 10. A 40 percent common stock dividend was declared and issued to common shareholders. (Market price of common stock is $16 per share.)

2. Determine the proper allocation to preferred and common shareholders of a $100,000 cash dividend declared on December 31, 1981. (This dividend is in addition to the June 2 dividend.)

3. **Interpretive Question**   Why didn't the preferred shareholders receive their current-dividend preference of $7,000 in part 2?

P12–5   Treasury Stock and Dividend Transactions

The following is Christensen Company's stockholders' equity section as of December 31, 1981.

Common Stock (60,000 shares authorized, $10 par—40,000 shares issued and outstanding)	$400,000
Paid-in Capital in Excess of Par—Common Stock	126,000
Preferred Stock (8,000 shares authorized, 4,000 shares issued and outstanding, 7%, $60 par, noncumulative, nonparticipating)	240,000
Paid-in Capital in Excess of Par— Preferred Stock	65,000
Retained Earnings	165,000

Required:

1. Journalize the following 1982 transactions.

(a) Issued 1,000 preferred shares at $70 per share.

(b) Reacquired 500 of the common shares for the treasury at $13 per share.

(c) Declared and paid a $2 per share dividend on common stock and paid it in addition to paying the required preferred dividends.

(d) Reissued 300 of the treasury shares at $14 per share.

(e) Reissued the remaining treasury shares at $12 per share.

(f) Earnings for the year were $46,000.

2. Prepare a stockholders' equity section for the company at December 31, 1982.

P12–6 Statement of Retained Earnings

Davidson Brothers Corporation records show the following at December 31, 1981.

a. Extraordinary loss (net of tax) . . . . $ (25,000)

b. Current year retained earnings appropriation to bond sinking fund 10,000

c. January 1, 1981, retained earnings appropriation balance for sinking fund . . . 90,000

d. Cash dividends paid during 1981 15,000

e. Stock dividends issued during 1981 . . . 7,000

f. January 1, 1981, unappropriated retained earnings balance 255,000

g. Prior-period adjustment (net of tax) . . . (12,000)

h. Net income before extraordinary items and taxes (assume a 40 percent tax rate) . 80,000

Required:

1. Prepare a 1981 Statement of Retained Earnings.

2. **Interpretive Question** Why would a firm appropriate retained earnings if such action does not provide any cash?

P12–7 Accounting for a Proprietorship

In 1981, Joe Young decided to give business a try. In order to fund his Fantastic Pizza Shop, Joe deposited $10,000 of his own money in a company bank account and obtained a $7,500 loan from a local bank. During its first year of operations, the shop had earnings of $21,000. During the year, Joe withdrew $9,000 from the business for personal living expenses.

Required:

1. Prepare journal entries to record:
    (a) Joe's original contribution to the firm.
    (b) The bank loan.
    (c) Joe's withdrawal for his living expenses.
    (d) Any closing entries required at year-end.

2. Prepare an owner's equity section for Joe for 1981.

3. **Interpretive Question** How would the accounting for the four journal entries in part 1 be different if Joe's business were a corporation?

P12–8 Partnership Accounting

Delta and Epsilon have established a partnership to sell Olympic wreaths.

a. Delta invested $42,000 in cash and Epsilon invested $20,000 cash and a building worth $25,000 in the partnership.

b. Delta invested another $6,000 in cash. Epsilon donated a truck worth $7,000.

c. Net income from operations for the year was $19,000. (Note: The partners share profits equally.)

d. Delta withdrew $11,000 in cash and Epsilon withdrew $6,300 in inventory.

e. A fire destroyed one-half of the building donated by Epsilon. There was no insurance on the building.

f. Delta and Epsilon agree to admit a third partner on March 1 of the next year. This partner, Gamma, promises to invest $50,000 cash.

Required:

1. Journalize each of the above transactions.

2. Journalize the closing entries.

3. Compute each of the partners' capital balances.

4. **Interpretive Question** What is the relationship between the amount of capital contributed by each owner and the way profits are to be allocated?

P12–9 Unifying Problem: Stock Transactions and Preparation of Stockholders' Equity Section

Edwards Corporation was founded on January 1, 1981, and is heavily involved in raising capital through the issuance of stock.

a. Received authorization for 100,000 shares of $20 par-value common stock, 50,000 shares of 6 percent preferred stock with a stated value of $5, and 50,000 shares of no-par common stock.

b. Issued 25,000 shares of the $20 par-value common stock at $24 per share.

c. Issued 10,000 shares of the preferred stock at $8 per share.

d. Issued 5,000 shares of the no-par common stock at $22 per share.

e. Reacquired 1,000 shares of the $20 par-value stock at $25 per share.

f. Reacquired 500 shares of no-par common stock at $20 per share.

g. Reissued 250 of the 1,000 reacquired shares of $20 par-value common stock at $23 per share.

h. Reissued all of the 500 reacquired shares of no-par stock at $23 per share.

i. Income for the year was $10,500.

Required:

1. Prepare journal entries to record the above 1981 transactions in Edwards Corporation books.

2. Prepare the stockholders' equity section of Edwards Corporation's Balance Sheet at December 31, 1981. Assume that the above transactions represent all of the events involving equity accounts during 1981.

P12–10 Unifying Problem: Owners' Equity

Tyler Corporation was organized during 1978. At the end of 1980 the equity section of its Balance Sheet appeared as follows:

Contributed Capital:

Common Stock ($10 par, 50,000 shares authorized, 11,000 shares issued, 1,000 held as treasury stock)	$110,000	
Preferred Stock (6%, $20 par, 10,000 shares authorized, 5,000 shares issued)	100,000	
Paid-in Capital in Excess of Par— Preferred Stock	20,000	
Total Contributed Capital		$230,000
Retained Earnings		100,000
Total		$330,000
Less Treasury Stock		12,000
Total Owners' Equity		$318,000

During 1981, the following stockholders' equity transactions occurred (in chronological sequence).

a. Issued 500 shares of common stock at $13 per share.

b. Reissued 500 shares of treasury stock at $13 per share.

c. Issued 1,000 shares of preferred stock at $25 per share.

d. Reissued 500 shares of treasury stock at $10 per share.

e. Declared a dividend large enough to meet the current-dividend preference of the preferred stock and to pay the common shareholders $2 per share.

f. Appropriated $15,000 of retained earnings for the retirement of debt.

g. Declared a two-for-one stock split.

h. Net income is $65,000.

Required:

1. Journalize the transactions.

2. Prepare the stockholders' equity section at December 31, 1981.

3. **Interpretive Question** Does the appropriated retained earnings mean that $15,000 cash is available to retire the debt? If not, what is the purpose of such an account?

SECTION 4

Other Dimensions of Financial Reporting

This woodcut, made in 1877, shows one of the first calculators. The wheel on the right side had to be rotated until the numbers to be added or subtracted appeared at the front of the cylinder. (The Bettmann Archive)

CHAPTER 13

Statement of Changes in Financial Position

The objectives of a Funds Statement.

Various ways of defining funds, highlighting the all-financial-resources concept.

How to prepare a Funds Statement on a working capital basis.

How to prepare a Funds Statement on a cash basis.

Annual reports to stockholders include three primary financial statements: the Income Statement, the Balance Sheet, and the Statement of Changes in Financial Position (frequently called the Funds Statement). In earlier chapters the Income Statement and Balance Sheet were discussed in some detail. In this chapter we present the Statement of Changes in Financial Position.

Purpose and Significance of the Statement of Changes in Financial Position

Statement of Changes in Financial Position (Funds Statement) *the primary financial report that shows an entity's major sources and uses of financial resources (funds) during a period of time*

Like the Income Statement, the Statement of Changes in Financial Position is a connecting link between two Balance Sheets. It makes the connection in a somewhat different manner, however. The Income Statement ties two Balance Sheets together by measuring a company's earnings, which, along with dividends, usually make up the difference between the beginning and ending balances in the Retained Earnings account. In contrast, the Statement of Changes in Financial Position lists changes in the balances of all asset, liability, and owners' equity accounts. This shows what financial resources have flowed into the business during the accounting period and how those resources have been used.

Companies obtain resources from three main sources: earnings, issuing stock (equity financing), and borrowing money (debt financing). While the Income Statement reports the major internal source of funds—earnings, the Funds Statement identifies both internal and external sources. It also highlights the major uses of funds: to pay dividends, retire debt, reacquire stock, replace assets, and/or acquire additional assets in order to maintain and expand operations.

Knowledge of the primary sources and uses of a company's funds will help investors, creditors, and others compare the firm's financial policies with those of competing firms in light of the current economic environment (see Exhibit 13–1). Indeed, it enables them to determine whether a firm is (1) retrenching or expanding; (2) increasing or decreasing debt; (3) increasing or decreasing its reliance on earnings, equity capital, or borrowing; and (4) following financial policies that are in keeping with or in contrast to those of previous years and those of other firms in the industry.

While the data for preparing a Funds Statement are derived from comparative Balance Sheets and an Income Statement, the Funds Statement should not be considered a duplication of these other statements. It highlights particular relationships that are not readily apparent from a review

EXHIBIT 13–1   Flow of Funds

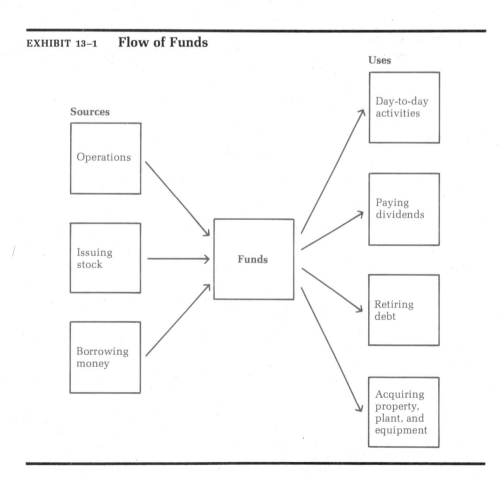

of an Income Statement or a Balance Sheet. For example, the Funds Statement helps to answer such specific questions as: How is a company able to pay dividends when it has a net loss? Why might a company be short on cash despite increased earnings? How was a new office building financed? Why were larger dividends not paid, given the amount of net income reported? In answer to the first question, for example, the Funds Statement may suggest that external borrowing or the issuance of capital stock provided the funds from which the normal dividend was paid.

Various Ways of Defining Funds

cash concept of funds *a concept used in preparing a Funds Statement that reflects transactions in which cash is either received or paid*

working capital concept of funds *a concept used in preparing a Funds Statement that reflects transactions which increase or decrease current assets or current liabilities*

all-financial-resources concept *a concept used in preparing a Funds Statement that reflects all financing and investing activities for a period as sources and uses of funds, whether or not they increase or decrease cash or working capital*

funds *measures of the flow of financial resources, usually defined as working capital or cash*

Funds may be defined in a number of ways, but most firms use either a cash or a working capital definition, as modified by the "all-financial-resources concept." The cash concept of funds measures the inflow and outflow of cash that results from transactions in which cash is either received or paid. The working capital concept of funds measures the change in working capital that occurs from transactions that increase or decrease working capital. The all-financial-resources concept measures all financing and investing activities, even those that do not actually result in an increase or decrease in cash or working capital. It may be applied on either a cash or a working capital basis and its use is required by generally accepted accounting principles.

Whichever concept is used, the term funds always refers to a measure of the financial resources flowing into and out of a company. In this chapter we will begin with the working capital concept of funds, modified to incorporate the all-financial-resources concept.

THE WORKING CAPITAL CONCEPT OF FUNDS

When the Funds Statement is based on the working capital concept, attention is focused on the sources and uses of working capital. As you will recall, *working capital* is a general measure of a firm's liquidity—that is, its ability to pay short-term liabilities (current liabilities) with short-term assets (current assets). The major sources and uses of working capital are listed below.

Sources (Increases) of Working Capital	Uses (Decreases) of Working Capital
Earnings	Losses
Sale of long-term investments	Declaration of cash dividends
Sale of property, plant, and equipment	Purchase of long-term investments
Sale of other assets	Purchase of property, plant, and equipment
Long-term borrowing	Purchase of other assets
Issuance of capital stock	Payment of long-term liabilities
	Reacquisition of capital stock (treasury stock)

Each of these transactions results in an increase or decrease in working capital. Note that each transaction affects both a working capital account and a <u>noncurrent (non-working-capital) account</u>. Transactions that affect only one type of account—that is, two current accounts or two noncurrent accounts—do not produce a change in working capital. For example, if an account receivable is collected, or if an account payable is paid, the amount of working capital does not change. When the working capital concept of funds is strictly applied, the Funds Statement includes only the types of transactions listed here, because these are the types of transactions that reflect sources and uses of working capital.

noncurrent accounts *all operational asset, long-term investment, long-term liability, and owners' equity accounts; all accounts except for working capital accounts*

THE ALL-FINANCIAL-RESOURCES CONCEPT

The pure working capital concept of funds does not provide a full picture of changes in financial position, because many firms engage in transactions that directly and significantly affect their financial position but do not affect their working capital. Thus, the working capital concept should be modified to include not only transactions reflecting direct changes in working capital, but also the following types of transactions.

1. Acquisition of property, plant, and equipment in exchange for capital stock or long-term liabilities.

2. Conversion of a long-term liability into stockholders' equity—that is, conversion of a bond into preferred or common stock.

3. Conversion of preferred stock into common stock.

These transactions represent investing or financing activities, or changes in internal debt–equity relationships, and should be called to the attention of financial statement readers. Notice that none of these transactions affects working capital. However, since each represents a significant investing and financing activity, they all should be presented in the Funds Statement just as if they did affect working capital.

Several typical transactions that involve investing and financing activities, but do not affect working capital, are reported as if working capital were simultaneously increased and decreased. When property, plant, and equipment is purchased by issuing a long-term liability, such as a bond, working capital is shown as increased by the creation of the debt and decreased by the purchase of the operational assets. When long-term bonds or preferred stock are converted to common stock, working capital is shown as being increased by the issuance of the stock and decreased by the retirement of the bonds or preferred stock. As shown below, each transaction represents both a source and a use of funds.

Source of Funds	Use of Funds
Sale of a long-term bond	Purchase of property, plant, and equipment
Issuance of common stock	Retirement of long-term bonds
Issuance of common stock	Retirement of preferred stock

By using the all-financial-resources concept, a company can include all relevant transactions in the Funds Statement, whether the statement is prepared on a working capital or a cash basis.

Preparing a Statement of Changes in Financial Position (Working Capital Basis)

A number of techniques can be used in preparing a Funds Statement. One of these involves a columnar worksheet, which is illustrated in the Supplement to this chapter. In the text we use the T-account method. It is easily understood by students because transactions are recorded in a manner similar to their initial recording in the General Ledger.

In preparing a Funds Statement under the T-account approach, a five-step procedure may be used. We will assume that Star Manufacturing Company had the Income Statement, Statement of Retained Earnings, and Balance Sheets shown in Exhibits 13-2 and 13-3. The data in these statements will be employed in explaining the preparation of a working capital basis Funds Statement.

EXHIBIT 13-2   Star Manufacturing Company
Income Statement for the Year Ended December 31, 1981

Revenues:

Net Sales	$859,400
Other Revenues (Note 1)	7,800
Total Revenues	$867,200

Expenses:

Cost of Goods Sold	$610,100
Selling and Administrative Expenses	147,000
Depreciation Expense	32,100
Interest Expense	14,200
Total Expenses	$803,400
Income Before Taxes	$ 63,800
Income Taxes	27,200
Net Income	$ 36,600

Note 1   Gain on the sale of equipment.

Star Manufacturing Company
Statement of Retained Earnings for the Year Ended December 31, 1981

Retained Earnings, January 1, 1981	$368,400
Add Net Income	36,600
	$405,000
Dividends Declared and Paid	21,800
Retained Earnings, December 31, 1981	$383,200

EXHIBIT 13–3   Star Manufacturing Company
Balance Sheets as of December 31, 1981 and 1980

Assets	1981	1980
Current Assets:		
Cash	$ 7,600	$ 7,900
Short-Term Securities	30,000	
Accounts and Notes Receivable (Net of Allowance for		
Doubtful Accounts)	106,700	104,900
Inventory	167,300	197,500
Prepaid Expenses	7,000	9,200
Total Current Assets	$318,600	$319,500
Property, Plant, and Equipment:		
Land (Note 2)	$110,000	$ 10,000
Plant and Equipment (at Cost).....................	603,200	577,200
Less Accumulated Depreciation....................	(243,900)	(223,600)
Total Property, Plant, and Equipment	$469,300	$363,600
Other Noncurrent Assets: Notes Receivable	$ 42,800	$ 50,900
Total Assets	$830,700	$734,000

Liabilities and Stockholders' Equity

	1981	1980
Current Liabilities:		
Notes Payable—Bank............................	$ 6,800	$ 38,000
Accounts Payable	72,200	61,700
Income Taxes Payable............................	7,000	1,500
Total Current Liabilities	$ 86,000	$101,200
Long-Term Liabilities:		
Note Payable (Note 2)	$100,000	
Bonds Payable (Note 3)...........................		$ 80,000
Other Long-Term Debt	92,100	95,000
Total Long-Term Liabilities......................	$192,100	$175,000
Stockholders' Equity:		
Common Stock, $1 Par Value (Note 3)	$ 82,500	$ 42,500
Additional Contributed Capital (Note 3)..............	86,900	46,900
Retained Earnings...............................	383,200	368,400
Total Stockholders' Equity	$552,600	$457,800
Total Liabilities and Stockholders' Equity	$830,700	$734,000

Note 2   Land with a fair market value of $100,000 was acquired through the issuance of a long-term note.

Note 3   The bonds were retired by conversion into 40,000 shares of common stock. At the time of conversion the bonds were selling at par and the common stock was selling at $2 per share.

STEP 1

Set up two basic T-accounts for the period: (1) a summary account, Sources and Uses of Working Capital, and (2) a subsidiary account, Sources of Working Capital from Operations. Then, compute the net change in working capital for the period, record it in the summary account, and, as supporting information, prepare a schedule of changes in individual working capital accounts.

Sources and Uses of Working Capital *a summary account used in preparing a Funds Statement based on the working capital concept of funds*

All sources and uses of working capital, as modified by the all-financial-resources concept, will be set forth in the summary account, Sources and Uses of Working Capital, and the difference in amount between total sources and total uses will equal the net change in working capital. Thus, the T-account for Sources and Uses of Working Capital will have two sections, as shown here.

Sources and Uses of Working Capital

increases in working capital	*decreases in working capital*
transactions that constitute a *source of* working capital	transactions that constitute a *use of* working capital

The section above the line is for recording the net change in working capital for the period. The section below the line is for recording the transactions that explain why working capital increased or decreased.

Sources of Working Capital from Operations *a subsidiary account used in preparing a Funds Statement based on the working capital concept of funds*

The subsidiary account, Sources of Working Capital from Operations, is used to determine the amount of working capital that flowed into the business from regular operations. Working capital provided by operations is usually different from net income because certain Income Statement increases and decreases are bookkeeping items that do not reflect inflows or outflows of working capital. For example, depreciation is an expense that reduces income but is not a transaction resulting in an outflow of working capital. The debits to this subsidiary account reflect increases in working capital from operations and credits represent decreases. As shown below, the subsidiary account has only one section.

Sources of Working Capital from Operations

increases in working capital from regular operations	*decreases* in working capital from regular operations

The balance of Sources of Working Capital from Operations is eventually transferred to Sources and Uses of Working Capital, since working capital from operations is one of the main sources (or uses) of funds.

Having set up the summary and subsidiary T-accounts, we are ready to begin the calculations. The first figure to be included in the summary account is the net change in working capital from 1980 to 1981, computed as follows:

	12/31/81	12/31/80	Net Change
Current Assets	$318,600	$319,500	$ (900)
Less Current Liabilities	86,000	101,200	15,200
Working Capital	$232,600 −	$218,300 =	$14,300

The $14,300 *increase* in working capital is then debited to the summary account.

Sources and Uses of Working Capital

14,300	

Generally, a supporting schedule of changes in the individual working capital accounts accompanies the Statement of Changes in Financial Position (see Exhibit 13–4). An analysis of this schedule will indicate the specific changes in the working capital accounts that result in a $14,300 net increase in working capital.

EXHIBIT 13-4   **Star Manufacturing Company**
Schedule of Changes in Working Capital for the Year Ended December 31, 1981

Current Assets	12/31/81	12/31/80	Net Change
Cash..............................	$ 7,600	$ 7,900	$ (300)
Short-Term Securities	30,000		30,000
Accounts and Notes Receivable	106,700	104,900	1,800
Inventory	167,300	197,500	(30,200)
Prepaid Expenses	7,000	9,200	(2,200)
Decrease in Current Assets	$318,600	$319,500	$ (900)
Current Liabilities			
Notes Payable—Bank	$ 6,800	$ 38,000	$31,200
Accounts Payable	72,200	61,700	(10,500)
Income Taxes Payable	7,000	1,500	(5,500)
Decrease in Current Liabilities	$ 86,000	$101,200	$15,200
Increase in Working Capital			$14,300

STEP 2

Set up a T-account for each noncurrent account on the Balance Sheet that changed during the year and record above the line in each account the change in the balance since the previous year. Then check to be certain that, when all of these T-accounts are added together, including the net change in working capital from the summary account, the debits equal the credits.

As we noted earlier, the process of identifying the sources and uses of working capital involves an analysis of the transactions that caused the accounts either to increase or to decrease. In some cases a net change in one noncurrent account produces a change in another noncurrent account; in others, a net change in a noncurrent account results in a change in working capital. Therefore, we need to analyze the changes in all noncurrent accounts in order to isolate those changes that resulted in inflows and outflows of working capital.

The changes in the noncurrent accounts of Star Manufacturing Company's Balance Sheets and the summary account would be set up in T-accounts as follows:[1]

Sources and Uses of Working Capital		Land		Plant and Equipment		Accumulated Depreciation— Plant and Equipment	
14,300		100,000		26,000			20,300

Other Noncurrent Assets		Note Payable		Bonds Payable		Other Long-Term Debt	
	8,100		100,000	80,000		2,900	

Common Stock		Additional Contributed Capital		Retained Earnings	
	40,000		40,000		14,800

In general, T-accounts are set up only for accounts with balances that have changed. In the rare case where the increases and decreases exactly offset each other, a T-account should still be prepared as a record of both types of transactions.

The changes in the summary and noncurrent accounts of Star Manufacturing Company are in balance, as shown on the next page.

---

[1] Sources of Working Capital from Operations is not included because no numbers have changed.

	Debits	Credits
Working Capital	$ 14,300	
Land	100,000	
Plant and Equipment	26,000	
Accumulated Depreciation		$ 20,300
Other Noncurrent Assets		8,100
Note Payable		100,000
Bonds Payable	80,000	
Other Long-Term Debt	2,900	
Common Stock.................................		40,000
Additional Contributed Capital		40,000
Retained Earnings		14,800
Totals....................................	$223,200	$223,200

If total debits do not equal total credits, each account should be analyzed until the error is discovered and corrected. When the debits and credits representing the account changes for the year are not equal, the causes of all of the changes in the noncurrent accounts cannot be fully explained and the Funds Statement will be out of balance.

STEP 3

Analyze each of the noncurrent accounts by recording below the line the transactions that explain the change in the balance above the line.

In explaining the impact of a transaction on a noncurrent account, the offsetting debit or credit may be made to another noncurrent account, to the Sources and Uses of Working Capital account, or to the Sources of Working Capital from Operations account.

To illustrate this step, we will analyze each of Star Manufacturing Company's noncurrent accounts that have changed. It is usually helpful to analyze changes in the Retained Earnings account first.

Retained Earnings
Transaction 1: Income earned.
Transaction 2: Declaration of cash dividends.

Retained Earnings	
	14,800
2 21,800	36,600 .... **1**

Sources and Uses of Working Capital	
14,300	
	21,800 ....Dividends **2**

Sources of Working Capital from Operations	
1 Net Income 36,600	

Transaction 1 is the net income earned for the period as taken from the Income Statement. Since net income increases Retained Earnings and represents a source of working capital from operations, it is credited to the Retained Earnings account and debited to Sources of Working Capital from Operations.

Transaction 2 is a declaration of cash dividends. Since dividends result in a reduction of Retained Earnings and constitute a use of working capital, the transaction is recorded as a debit to Retained Earnings and as a credit to Sources and Uses of Working Capital.

Note that the amounts included in Sources and Uses of Working Capital below the line and in Sources of Working Capital from Operations are labeled. These labels facilitate preparation of the formal statement after all transactions have been accounted for.

Land

Transaction 3: Acquisition of 50 acres of land as a future plant site. A note was issued for $100,000 in payment; the note is due in three years.

Land		Note Payable		Sources and Uses of Working Capital	
100,000			100,000	14,300	
3 .. 100,000			100,000 .. **3**	**3** Note Payable ..100,000	21,800......Dividends **2**
					100,000......... Land **3**

The entry to record the land acquisition would be

| Land .... | 100,000 | |
| Note Payable .... | | 100,000 |
Purchased 50 acres of land for $100,000.

Transaction 3 would be recorded in the summary T-account as a *source* of funds for the issuance of a note and as a *use* of funds for the acquisition of the land. Note that recording this transaction as both a source and a use of funds is an application of the all-financial-resources modification of the working capital concept of funds. As the example makes clear, this approach includes all significant financing and investing activities, whether or not working capital is directly involved. The issuance of the note represents the financing activity and the purchase of the land represents the investing activity.

Plant and Equipment and Accumulated Depreciation

Transaction 4: Sale of equipment at a gain. Equipment purchased for $12,300, with accumulated depreciation of $11,800, is sold for $8,300 in cash.

Transaction 5: Purchase of plant and equipment costing $38,300.

Transaction 6: Depreciation for the year on plant and equipment amounting to $32,100.

Plant and Equipment	
26,000	
5 38,300	12,300 .... **4**

Accumulated Depreciation—Plant and Equipment	
	20,300
4 11,800	32,100 .... **6**

Sources and Uses of Working Capital	
14,300	
3 Note Payable 100,000	21,800...... Dividends **2**
4 Plant and	100,000...... Land **3**
Equipment 8,300	38,300...... Plant and
	Equipment **5**

Sources of Working Capital from Operations	
1 Net Income.......36,600	7,800.... Gain on Plant
6 Depreciation......32,100	and Equipment **4**

The journal entry to record transaction 4 would be

Cash	8,300	
Accumulated Depreciation	11,800	
Plant and Equipment		12,300
Gain on Sale		7,800

Sold used equipment for $8,300.

This transaction is different from those explained so far. The $12,300 credit to Plant and Equipment and the $11,800 debit to Accumulated Depreciation are required to close those accounts upon the sale of the asset. However, these amounts relate back to earlier accounting periods, dating from the time the equipment was first purchased. They are not sources or uses of working capital in the current period. It is the proceeds from the sale ($8,300) that provide funds during the current period, and so this is the amount we enter as a source of working capital.

On the other hand, the gain from the sale ($7,800) must be subtracted from sources of working capital from operations. The reason is that this amount has now been included twice: in the $36,600 of net income and in the $8,300 proceeds from the sale. If the $8,300 proceeds are to be shown in full as a separate source of working capital, then the $7,800 gain must be subtracted from sources of working capital from operations to avoid a double counting. The net result is that the total proceeds from the sale of plant and equipment ($8,300), are shown as a separate source of working capital, along with the funds provided from operations ($36,600 − $7,800).

Transaction 5 is a use of working capital to acquire plant and equipment. Hence, it is a debit to the Plant and Equipment account and a credit to Sources and Uses of Working Capital.

Transaction 6 is a bookkeeping entry that records the depreciation expense for the year. As the expense account is debited for $32,100, the Accumulated Depreciation account is credited. Although net income has been reduced by the amount of the depreciation expense, no working capital has actually flowed out of the company. Since there is no outflow of funds, the depreciation expense must be added back to net income to correctly measure working capital generated from operations. To accomplish this, $32,100 is debited to Sources of Working Capital from Operations to arrive at net income before depreciation. The resulting debit balance in Sources of Working Capital from Operations should reflect the actual inflow of working capital from operations, assuming that there are no other bookkeeping additions to or deductions from net income.

Other Noncurrent Assets

Transaction 7: Receipt of partial payment of a long-term note owed to Star Manufacturing Company by a subsidiary.

Other Noncurrent Assets		Sources and Uses of Working Capital	
8,100		14,300	
8,100 ..... **7**	**3** Note Payable 100,000	21,800 .... Dividends **2**	
	4 Plant and Equipment.......... 8,300	100,000 .... Land **3**	
	7 Notes Receivable 8,100	38,300 .... Plant and Equipment **5**	

A subsidiary of Star Manufacturing Company makes a partial payment on a long-term note for money advanced by Star in prior years. The cash received by Star constitutes a source of funds. This transaction is recorded as a credit to Other Noncurrent Assets and as a debit to Sources and Uses of Working Capital, thus reflecting the increase in working capital. Note that the increase in working capital relates only to the payment on the principal of the note. Any interest received was included in net income and is shown as part of the increase in working capital from operations.

Long-Term Debt: Bonds Payable

Transaction 8: Conversion by bondholders of $80,000 face value of bonds payable into 40,000 shares of $1 par common stock. The common stock was selling at $2 per share and the bonds were selling at par at the time of conversion.

Bonds Payable		Common Stock		Additional Contributed Capital	
80,000		40,000		40,000	
8 .. 80,000		40,000 .. **8**		40,000 .. **8**	

Sources and Uses of Working Capital

	14,300		

3	Note Payable 100,000	21,800..................Dividends	2
4	Plant and Equipment.......... 8,300	100,000....................... Land	3
7	Notes Receivable 8,100	38,300..........Plant and Equipment	5
8	Common Stock* 80,000	80,000......................Bonds	8

* The $80,000 is explained by two entries: $40,000 to Common Stock and $40,000 to Additional Contributed Capital (also called Paid-in Capital in Excess of Par).

Transaction 8 represents a significant financing activity that does not directly affect working capital since it reduces the company's outstanding noncurrent debt and increases by the same amount its owners' equity. This transaction would be recorded in the summary account as a *source* of funds for issuance of the stock and as a *use* of funds for retirement of the long-term debt. The inclusion of this transaction as both a source and a use of funds is another example of the application of the all-financial-resources concept. In other words, it involves the disclosure of financing activities that do not directly affect working capital.

Other Long-Term Debt

Transaction 9: Payment of other long-term debt.

Other Long-Term Debt

	2,900	
9	 2,900	

Sources and Uses of Working Capital

	14,300		

3	Note Payable 100,000	21,800.................... Dividends	2
4	Plant and Equipment.......... 8,300	100,000....................... Land	3
7	Notes Receivable 8,100	38,300..........Plant and Equipment	5
8	Common Stock 80,000	80,000..................... Bonds	8
		2,900............. Long-Term Debt	9

Star Manufacturing Company reduced its other long-term debt during the year, primarily by paying off liabilities to foreign banks. Since the reduction in this long-term debt is a use of working capital, Other Long-Term Debt is debited for $2,900 and Sources and Uses of Working Capital is credited for $2,900. Any interest paid on the debt during the year or when it is retired is recorded as an expense in computing net income and thus reduces working capital from operations. The $2,900 decrease in working capital relates only to a reduction in the principal of the debt.

At this point all of the noncurrent accounts have been explained. The net change in each account balance, recorded above the line, has been accounted for by equal amounts recorded below the line, as shown on the next page. The only accounts needing further explanation at the completion of step 3 are Sources and Uses of Working Capital and Sources of Working Capital from Operations.

	Retained Earnings	
	14,800	
2 ...21,800	36,600... **1**	

	Land	
100,000		
3 ..100,000		

	Note Payable	
	100,000	
	100,000.. **3**	

	Plant and Equipment	
26,000		
5 ...38,300	12,300... **4**	

	Accumulated Depreciation— Plant and Equipment	
	20,300	
4 ...11,800	32,100... **6**	

	Other Noncurrent Assets	
8,100		
	8,100.... **7**	

	Bonds Payable	
80,000		
8 ...80,000		

	Common Stock	
	40,000	
	40,000... **8**	

	Additional Contributed Capital	
	40,000	
	40,000... **8**	

	Other Long-Term Debt	
	2,900	
9 2,900		

Sources and Uses of Working Capital

	14,300	
3 Note Payable 100,000	21,800...... Dividends **2**	
4 Plant and Equipment 8,300	100,000.......... Land **3**	
7 Notes Receivable . 8,100	38,300...... Plant and Equipment **5**	
8 Common Stock... 80,000	80,000.......... Bonds **8**	
	2,900..Long-Term Debt **9**	

Sources of Working Capital from Operations

1 Net Income 36,600	7,800.... Gain on Plant
6 Depreciation 32,100	and Equipment **4**

STEP 4

Transfer the balance in Sources of Working Capital from Operations to the summary account, Sources and Uses of Working Capital. Then check the summary account to be certain that the difference between total sources and total uses is equal to the change in working capital shown above the line in the summary account.

Changes in the noncurrent accounts have now been fully accounted for through offsetting debits or credits to other noncurrent accounts, to Sources and Uses of Working Capital, or to Sources of Working Capital from Operations. Now the subsidiary account can be transferred to the summary account. The amount being transferred, in this case $60,900, represents the amount of working capital that flowed into the company from normal operations. It is the equivalent of net income for the year plus non-working-capital deductions (the depreciation expense) and minus non-working-capital additions (the gain on the sale of plant and equipment). (Non-working-capital additions and deductions simply mean bookkeeping items that do not reflect actual inflows and outflows of working capital.) If these non-working-capital effects were removed from the Income Statement, the total would be the same $60,900, as shown here.

Net Sales	$859,400
Expenses:	
Cost of Goods Sold	$610,100
Selling and Administrative Expenses	147,000
Interest Expense	14,200
Total Expenses	$771,300
Working Capital from Operations Before Income Taxes	$ 88,100
Less Income Taxes	27,200
Net Working Capital from Operations	$ 60,900

By comparing this modified version of the Income Statement with Exhibit 13–2, you will be able to note the differences. The modified statement excludes the gain on the sale of equipment and the depreciation expense. Neither item represents a flow of working capital from operations during the year.

Note also that the working capital generated from operations is frequently referred to as "cash flow" by the financial community. Although cash flow is a misnomer (it is working capital flow), this term is commonly used to describe the amount of liquid funds generated during a period.

The transfer of working capital from operations to the summary account results in all of the inflows and outflows of working capital being accumulated in that account.

Sources of Working Capital from Operations		Sources and Uses of Working Capital	
Net Income 36,600	7,800 . . . . Gain on Plant	14,300	
Depreciation 32,100	and Equipment		
	60,900 . . Balance Transferred		
	to Summary	Note Payable 100,000	21,800 . . . . Dividends
	account	Plant and Equipment 8,300	100,000 . . . . Land
		Notes Receivable . . . 8,100	38,300 . . . . Plant and
		Common Stock 80,000	Equipment
		Operations 60,900	80,000 . . . . Bonds
		257,300	2,900 . . . . Long-Term Debt
			243,000

After working capital from operations has been transferred to the summary account, the total sources should be greater than the uses by the amount of the increase in working capital, which they are: $257,300 − $243,000 = $14,300. Conversely, a decrease in working capital would mean that total uses exceeded total sources by the amount of the decrease.

STEP 5

Prepare a formal Statement of Changes in Financial Position.

With the information in the summary and subsidiary accounts, an accountant can prepare a formal Statement of Changes in Financial Position. Exhibit 13–5 shows the format of this statement, although in most cases it is presented on a comparative basis with the previous year.

The statement in Exhibit 13–5 is balanced. In some cases, however, the change in working capital is not shown as a use (when it increases) or as a source (when it decreases). Instead, total uses of funds are subtracted from total sources (both exclusive of a change in working capital), producing a residual figure labeled Increase (Decrease) in Working Capital. We prefer the balanced form because the change in working capital is not necessarily the most important financing, investing, or operating activity and should therefore not be given the prominence of a residual figure.

EXHIBIT 13-5   **Star Manufacturing Company**

Statement of Changes in Financial Position (Working Capital Basis) for the Year Ended December 31, 1981

Sources of Working Capital

Operations:		
Net Income	$36,600	
Add Items Not Requiring Working Capital:		
Depreciation	32,100	
Total	$68,700	
Less Items Not Generating Working Capital:		
Gain on Sale of Equipment	7,800	
Total Working Capital from Operations		$ 60,900
Issuance of Note To Acquire Land		100,000
Proceeds from Long-Term Notes		8,100
Proceeds from Sale of Equipment		8,300
Issuance of Common Stock To Retire Debt		80,000
Total Sources of Working Capital		$257,300

Uses of Working Capital

Declaration of Dividends	$ 21,800
Acquisition of Land by Issuance of Note	100,000
Purchases of Plant and Equipment	38,300
Retirement of Bonds by Issuance of Common Stock	80,000
Reduction in Other Long-Term Debt	2,900
Increase in Working Capital	14,300
Total Uses of Working Capital	$257,300

As noted earlier, a Funds Statement is usually supported by a schedule of changes in working capital. This schedule might be presented in a number of ways. Exhibit 13–4 on page 425 is one. Another approach would be to present only the increase or decrease in each account. However, such a schedule must be read with particular care since decreases in current liabilities are increases in working capital, and vice versa.

Preparing a Statement of Changes in Financial Position (Cash Basis)

Sources and Uses of Cash *a summary account used in preparing a Funds Statement based on the cash concept of funds*

Sources of Cash from Operations *a subsidiary account used in preparing a Funds Statement based on the cash concept of funds*

Thus far, we have used the all-financial-resources concept only as it applies to the working capital basis in preparing a Statement of Changes in Financial Position. In this section we illustrate how the all-financial-resources concept is applied on a cash basis.

As a starting point, the two key accounts, Sources and Uses of Cash and Sources of Cash from Operations, are established. Then, the change in the Cash account for the period is entered above the line in the summary account, Sources and Uses of Cash. As Exhibit 13–3 (page 423) shows, Star had a $300 decrease ($7,900 – $7,600) in its Cash account during 1981. The entries below the line are the same as those that appeared below the line in the Sources and Uses of Working Capital account presented earlier, *except* for $60,900, which is the working capital from operations. With this change the summary account, Sources and Uses of Cash, would appear as follows:

Sources and Uses of Cash

		300	
Note Payable	100,000	21,800 .... Dividends
Plant and Equipment	8,300	100,000 .... Land
Notes Receivable	8,100	38,300 .... Plant and Equipment
Common Stock	80,000	80,000 .... Bonds
		2,900 .... Long-Term Debt

Information missing from this account includes the cash generated by operations, which will come from the subsidiary account, Sources of Cash from Operations. So far, the subsidiary account contains the same entries as the Sources of Working Capital from Operations account.

Sources of Cash from Operations

Net Income	36,600	7,800 .... Gain on Plant and Equipment
Depreciation	32,100	

The two key accounts now contain all the information on Star's Balance Sheet, except changes in the current asset and current liability accounts other than cash. These accounts must therefore be set up and their changes explained. The accounts would be set up in the following manner.

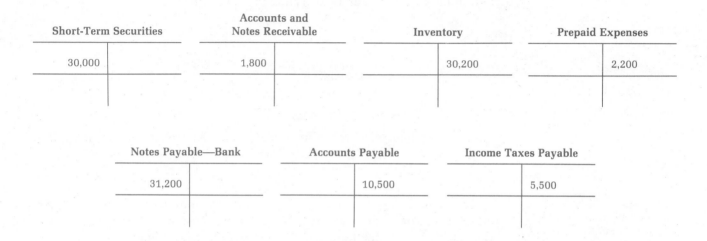

Short-Term Securities	Accounts and Notes Receivable	Inventory	Prepaid Expenses
30,000	1,800	30,200	2,200

Notes Payable—Bank	Accounts Payable	Income Taxes Payable
31,200	10,500	5,500

The current asset and current liability accounts would then be related to the two key accounts on the following basis.

1. The change in a current account is entered into Sources of Cash from Operations if it has a bearing on the conversion of net income from an accrual basis to a cash basis.[2] Since the net income figure is on an accrual basis, it must be converted to a cash basis in order to determine cash generated by operations. Accounts and Notes Receivable, Inventory, Prepaid Expenses, Accounts Payable, Accrued Expenses, and Income Taxes Payable all affect net income and are entered into the subsidiary account, thereby converting net income to a cash basis from an accrual basis.

2. A current account is entered directly into Sources and Uses of Cash if the change in the account had no effect on the measurement of income on an accrual basis. The changes in Short-Term Securities and Notes Payable—Bank did not affect the measurement of income since they represent direct sources and uses of cash and did not involve cash from operations.

Thus, when cash is used as the concept of funds, current asset and current liability accounts other than cash become "noncurrent" in the same sense as noncurrent accounts are used under the working capital concept. The current asset and current liability accounts would be entered into the summary and subsidiary accounts in the following manner.

---

[2] An accrual-basis Income Statement reports revenues when earned and expenses when incurred. A cash-basis Income Statement reflects revenues when cash is received and expenses when cash is paid. Revenues are converted from an accrual to a cash basis by adjusting for the change in accounts and notes receivable. Expenses are converted from an accrual to a cash basis by adjusting for changes in inventories, prepaid expenses, accounts payable, accrued expenses, and income taxes payable.

Short-Term Securities		Accounts and Notes Receivable		Inventory		Prepaid Expenses	
30,000		1,800		30,200		2,200	
1 ... 30,000		2... 1,800		30,200.. **3**		2,200... **4**	

Notes Payable—Bank		Accounts Payable		Income Taxes Payable	
	31,200		10,500		5,500
5... 31,200		10,500.. **6**		5,500... **7**	

Sources and Uses of Cash

	300
Note Payable 100,000	21,800......Dividends
Plant and Equipment ..8,300	100,000..........Land
Notes Receivable.....8,100	38,300.......Plant and Equipment
Common Stock 80,000	80,000..........Bonds
_303,900_	2,900......Long-Term Debt
	30,000......Short-Term Securities **1**
	31,200..........Notes Payable—Bank **5**
	_303,900_

Sources of Cash from Operations

	Net Income 36,600	7,800 ... Gain on Plant and Equipment
	Depreciation 32,100	1,800 ... Accounts and Notes Receivable **2**
3	Inventory 30,200	
4	Prepaid Expenses.2,200	
6	Accounts Payable 10,500	
7	Income Taxes Payable 5,500	

A careful analysis of these T-accounts will help explain why certain current accounts are transferred to Sources of Cash from Operations. For example, inventory decreased during the year. Instead of using cash to purchase new inventory, the company allowed inventory to decline. The cash-basis income, therefore, should be greater than the accrual-basis income and the inventory decrease should be treated as an addition to accrual-basis net income. Similar reasoning can be used to explain the other debits to Sources of Cash from Operations. On the other hand, Accounts and Notes Receivable increased during the year. This produces an increase in accrual-basis income, but not in cash-basis income, since the inclusion of receivables in income on an accrual basis overstates the income on a cash basis. The $1,800 increase in receivables should thus be treated as a reduction in accrual-basis net income.

After the current asset and current liability accounts other than Cash have been explained, only the two key accounts, Sources and Uses of Cash and Sources of Cash from Operations, remain open. The $107,500 balance in Sources of Cash from Operations is then transferred into Sources and Uses of Cash.

Sources and Uses of Cash

		300	
Notes Payable	100,000	21,800 .... Dividends
Plant and		100,000 .... Land
Equipment	8,300	38,300 .... Plant and
Notes Receivable...	8,100		Equipment
Common Stock	80,000	80,000 .... Bonds
Operations	107,500	2,900 .... Long-Term Debt
		30,000 .... Short-Term
			Securities
		31,200 .... Notes
			Payable—Bank

Sources of Cash from Operations

Net Income........	36,600	7,800 ...... Gain on Plant
Depreciation	32,100		and Equipment
Inventory	30,200	1,800 ...... Accounts and
Prepaid Expenses ..	2,200		Notes Receivable
Accounts Payable ..	10,500	107,500 .... Balance
Income Taxes			Transferred to
Payable	5,500		Summary
			Account

The $107,500 transferred from Sources of Cash from Operations to Sources and Uses of Cash represents the cash that flowed into the company from normal operations during the period. This amount could have been computed by converting individual elements on the Income Statement to a cash basis from an accrual basis, as shown in Exhibit 13–6.

Cash from operations can also be reconciled with working capital from operations by adjusting for the changes in working capital accounts other than cash, as shown on the next page.

EXHIBIT 13–6 **Star Manufacturing Company**
Income Statement for the Year Ended December 31, 1981

	Accrual Basis	Adjustments DR	Adjustments CR	Cash Basis
Revenues:				
Net Sales	$859,400	1 $1,800		$857,600
Other Revenues	7,800	2 7,800		
Total Revenues	$867,200			$857,600
Expenses:				
Cost of Goods Sold	$610,100		3 $30,200	$569,400
Selling and Administrative Expenses	147,000		4 10,500	144,800
Depreciation Expense	32,100		5 2,200	
Interest Expense......................	14,200			14,200
Total Expenses	$803,400			$728,400
Income Before Taxes	$ 63,800			$129,200
Income Taxes	27,200		6 $ 5,500	21,700
Net Income	$ 36,600			$107,500

1. Increase in Accounts and Notes Receivable
2. Gain on Sale of Equipment
3. Decrease in Inventory
4. Increase in Accounts Payable
5. Decrease in Prepaid Expenses
6. Increase in Income Taxes Payable

Working Capital from Operations...................		$ 60,900
Add Decrease in Inventory.........................	$30,200	
Increase in Accounts Payable	10,500	
Decrease in Prepaid Expenses.....................	2,200	
Increase in Income Taxes Payable	5,500	48,400
Total		$109,300
Less Increase in Accounts and Notes Receivable		1,800
Cash from Operations..............................		$107,500

If you refer to the summary account on the preceding page, you will note that the credits below the line exceed the debits by the $300 decrease in cash. These debits and credits below the line reflect the key transactions that account for the $300 decrease in cash. As shown in Exhibit 13–7, the information in this summary account, supplemented by the detailed information in the Sources of Cash from Operations, can now be used to

EXHIBIT 13–7   Star Manufacturing Company
Statement of Changes in Financial Position (Cash Basis) for the Year Ended December 31, 1981

Sources of Cash

Operations:		
Net Income		$ 36,600
Add Items Not Requiring Cash:		
Depreciation....................................	$32,100	
Decrease in Inventory	30,200	
Decrease in Prepaid Expenses	2,200	
Increase in Accounts Payable	10,500	
Increase in Income Taxes Payable	5,500	80,500
		$117,100
Less Items Not Generating Cash:		
Gain on Sale of Equipment	$7,800	
Increase in Accounts and Notes Receivable	1,800	9,600
Total Cash Generated by Operations		$107,500
Issuance of Note To Acquire Land		100,000
Proceeds from Long-Term Note Receivable		8,100
Proceeds from Sale of Equipment		8,300
Issuance of Common Stock To Retire Debt		80,000
Decrease in Cash		300
Total Sources of Cash		$304,200

Uses of Cash

Payment of Dividends	$ 21,800
Acquisition of Land by Issuance of Note	100,000
Purchase of Plant and Equipment	38,300
Payment of Notes.................................	31,200
Retirement of Bonds by Issuance of Common Stock	80,000
Purchase of Short-Term Securities	30,000
Reduction in Other Long-Term Debt	2,900
Total Uses of Cash.............................	$304,200

prepare a Statement of Changes in Financial Position under the cash concept of funds.

Like the working capital basis of funds, the cash basis meets the conditions of the all-financial-resources concept by including the acquisition of land through the issuance of a note and the retirement of bonds through the issuance of common stock in the Statement of Changes in Financial Position.

When preparing a Funds Statement, how does management decide whether to use a cash or a working capital basis? If the primary emphasis is on immediate liquidity and cash flows, then a cash basis is likely to be more appropriate. If a broader definition of the economic resources available for debt retirement, dividends, and so on, is more suitable, then the working capital basis is probably used. In practice, most firms use the working capital basis.

CHAPTER REVIEW

Together with the Balance Sheet and Income Statement, the Statement of Changes in Financial Position (Funds Statement) is one of the three primary financial statements. A careful analysis of the Funds Statement will indicate shifts in the operating, investing, and financing policies of a company. The Funds Statement explains changes in Balance Sheet accounts, emphasizing the major sources and uses of funds during a period.

The most common definitions of funds are working capital and cash. However, neither of these concepts is to be used in its pure form. Rather, both should be modified to include the all-financial-resources concept. Under this concept, the Statement of Changes in Financial Position includes all transactions that reflect significant financing and investing activities, whether or not working capital or cash is directly affected.

With a T-account approach, five steps may be used in preparing a Statement of Changes in Financial Position on a working capital, all-financial-resources basis.

1. Set up two basic T-accounts: a summary account, Sources and Uses of Working Capital, and a subsidiary account, Sources of Working Capital from Operations. Compute the net change in working capital for the period to be covered by the Funds Statement and record the change in Sources and Uses of Working Capital. Prepare a supporting schedule of changes in individual working capital accounts.

2. Set up a T-account for each noncurrent account and record the change for the period "above the line." Then check to be certain that the total noncurrent account changes recorded as debits minus the total changes recorded as credits are equal to the net change in working capital.

3. Analyze each of the noncurrent accounts by recording appropriate transactions until the change in the balance of each account for the period has been explained.

4. Transfer the balance in Sources of Working Capital from Operations to Sources and Uses of Working Capital. Check the summary account to be certain that the difference between total sources and total uses is equal to the change in working capital computed in step 1.

5. Prepare a formal Statement of Changes in Financial Position using the information in the summary account, Sources and Uses of Working Capital, and its subsidiary account, Sources of Working Capital from Operations.

The steps required to prepare a Funds Statement using the cash basis are similar to those for a statement based on working capital, except, of course, that the focus is on cash instead of working capital.

When the working capital basis of funds is used in preparing a Funds Statement, a schedule similar to Exhibit 13–4 should be attached, showing the changes in the individual working capital accounts. When the cash basis of funds is used, significant changes in the individual working capital accounts are reflected in the body of the statement, so no such schedule is necessary.

KEY TERMS AND CONCEPTS

all-financial-resources concept (420)

cash concept of funds (420)

funds (420)

noncurrent accounts (421)

Sources and Uses of Cash (435)

Sources and Uses of Working Capital (424)

Sources of Cash from Operations (435)

Sources of Working Capital from Operations (424)

Statement of Changes in Financial Position (Funds Statement) (418)

working capital concept of funds (420)

DISCUSSION QUESTIONS

1. What is the purpose of a Statement of Changes in Financial Position?

2. The accounting profession has made the Statement of Changes in Financial Position one of the primary statements, along with the Balance Sheet and Income Statement. Why?

3. What is the relationship between the Statement of Changes in Financial Position and the Balance Sheet? Between the Funds Statement and the Income Statement?

4. What are the major sources and uses of funds under (a) the working capital concept of funds and (b) the cash concept of funds?

5. Explain the meaning of the account title "Sources of Working Capital from Operations."

6. Why are certain amounts added back to or subtracted from net income in computing the amount of funds from operations?

7. (a) What amounts are added back to or subtracted from net income in computing working capital from operations?

(b) What amounts are added back to or subtracted from net income in computing cash from operations?

8. How would a company's decision to shift from the straight-line method of depreciation to an accelerated method of depreciation affect the amount of working capital from operations?

9. Depreciation is added back to net income in the process of determining funds from operations. Does this mean that depreciation is a source of funds? Explain.

10. If working capital is selected as the concept of funds in preparing a Statement of Changes in Financial Position, explain what effect (source of funds, use of funds, or no effect) each of the following transactions or events has on working capital.

(a) Purchase of inventory for cash.

(b) Collection of an account receivable.

(c) Writing off the undepreciated cost of equipment when it is scrapped.

(d) Sale of an operational asset at a gain.

(e) Declaration of a cash dividend.

(f) Payment of a cash dividend.

(g) Acquisition of land by issuing a long-term note.

(h) Purchase of inventory on account.

(i) Payment of an account payable.

(j) Sale of an operational asset at a loss.

11. What does it mean to use the all-financial-resources concept of funds in preparing the Statement of Changes in Financial Position?

12. Describe the differences between a Statement of Changes in Financial Position prepared under the working capital concept of funds and one prepared under the cash concept of funds.

13. What does the financial community mean by the term "cash flow"?

14. Does cash flow provide a better indication of the results of a company's operations than net income does, as is sometimes contended? Explain.

15. Is it possible for a company to report a positive amount of working capital provided by operations even though a net loss is reported for the year? Explain.

16. Briefly, explain why a company's cash balance may have decreased during the year, even though the company reported a substantial net income.

17. In advising a company with respect to the preparation of a Statement of Changes in Financial Position, what factors would you consider in choosing between the working capital and cash concepts of funds?

EXERCISES

E13–1 Account Balance Changes

The treasurer of Adams Company provides you with the following information.

Adams Company
Partial Balance Sheets as of December 31, 1981 and 1980

	1981	1980
Current Assets:		
Cash	$ 25,000	$ 30,000
Accounts Receivable	48,000	42,000
Inventory	98,000	80,000
Prepaid Insurance	4,000	5,000
Total Current Assets	$175,000	$157,000
Current Liabilities:		
Accounts Payable	$ 50,000	$ 72,000
Short-Term Notes Payable	27,000	22,000
Accrued Salaries Payable	1,700	1,500
Total Current Liabilities	$ 78,700	$ 95,500

Determine the change in each of the following accounts from 1980 to 1981. Indicate whether the change is an increase or a decrease.

1. Current Assets.

2. Accounts Receivable.

3. Prepaid Insurance.

4. Short-Term Notes Payable.

5. Current Liabilities.

E13–2 Working Capital Changes

On the basis of the data in E13–1, answer the following questions:

1. What was the amount of working capital on December 31, 1981?

2. What was the amount of working capital on December 31, 1980?

3. What was the change in working capital from 1980 to 1981?

E13–3 Working Capital Changes

Excon Company, a manufacturer of burglar alarms, has provided you with the following information.

	1981	1980
Current Assets:		
Cash	$ 22,000	$ 19,000
Accounts Receivable	21,000	24,000
Marketable Securities	44,000	38,000
Inventory	67,000	73,000
Prepaid Insurance	4,000	3,000
Total Current Assets	$158,000	$157,000
Current Liabilities:		
Accounts Payable	$ 40,000	$ 46,000
Interest Payable	8,000	7,000
Dividends Payable	9,000	2,000
Notes Payable	71,000	85,000
Total Current Liabilities	$128,000	$140,000

Determine the change in working capital from 1980 to 1981.

E13-4   Working Capital Provided by Operations

The following five transactions were the only transactions during the year for Abda Company.

a. Sold merchandise costing $6,000 for $10,000 on account. The company uses the perpetual inventory method.

b. Paid $100 rent for office space.

c. Paid $500 in wages.

d. Received a bill of $60 for insurance for the year.

e. Depreciation on equipment used by the company was $2,000.

Complete the following:

1. Prepare the journal entry for each of these transactions.

2. Indicate whether each transaction provided working capital, used working capital, or had no effect on working capital.

3. Determine the net amount of working capital provided or used by these five transactions.

4. Prepare an Income Statement for Abda Company.

5. Compare Abda Company's net income from operations with the net working capital provided by operations, as calculated in 3.

E13-5   Cash Provided by Operations

In addition to the five transactions listed in E13-4, assume that $3,000 of accounts receivable were collected by Abda Company.

1. Prepare the journal entry for this additional transaction.

2. What was the net cash provided or used during the year?

3. Compare Abda Company's net income from operating the business with the net amount of cash provided by these transactions.

E13-6   Working Capital Provided by Operations

Consider the following information.

Net Income..............................	$20,000
Depreciation:	
Machinery.............................	2,000
Equipment.............................	1,200
Gain on Sale of Investments..................	1,000
Loss on Sale of Plant	3,500

Prepare the Working Capital Provided by Operations portion of the Statement of Changes in Financial Position.

E13-7   Transaction Analysis

Following are transactions of Trove Crane Company.

a. Sold equipment for $1,000. The original cost was $15,700 with accumulated depreciation of $14,000.

b. Purchased plant and equipment costing $710,000 by issuing a 20-year note.

c. Received $5,000 of principal and $100 of interest on a long-term note.

d. Bondholders converted bonds with a $100,000 face value into 50,000 shares of $1 par common stock. The common stock was selling at $2 per share and the bonds were selling at par at the time of the conversion.

1. Prepare journal entries for each of these transactions.

2. Indicate the amount of working capital provided or used by each transaction.

E13-8   Uses of Working Capital

You are given the following information.

Dividends Declared and Paid..................	$10,000
Payment on Mortgage Payable	6,000
Acquisitions:	
Plant.....................................	20,000
Machinery	17,000
Investments	12,000

Prepare the Uses of Working Capital portion of a Statement of Changes in Financial Position.

E13-9   Working Capital from Operations

For the year ended December 31, 1981, Hosler Company reported net income of $300,000. Additional information is as follows:

Depreciation Expense—Plant and Equipment ...	$330,000
Allowance for Doubtful Accounts..............	90,000
Interest Expense on Short-Term Borrowings.....	20,000
Interest Expense on Long-Term Borrowings	110,000

On the basis of this information, compute the working capital from operations for a 1981 Statement of Changes in Financial Position.

E13-10   Change in Working Capital

The following information was taken from the 1981 accounting records of Martin Corporation.

Purchase of Plant and Equipment..............	$280,000
Collection of Accounts Receivable	400,000
Payment of Accounts Payable	300,000
Proceeds from Long-Term Borrowings	150,000

Dividends Declared on Common Stock..........	$ 90,000
Purchase of Treasury Stock...................	20,000
Payment on Long-Term Borrowings	50,000
Working Capital Provided from Operations	200,000
Working Capital at December 31, 1980	900,000

If funds are defined as working capital, what should be the change in working capital shown on the December 31, 1981, Statement of Changes in Financial Position for Martin Corporation?

E13–11 Analyzing Accounts

Comparative Balance Sheets for Berry Corporation for the years ending December 31, 1981 and 1980, are as follows:

	December 31	
	1981	1980
Current Assets	$23,700	$16,000
Equipment........................	61,500	60,000
Accumulated Depreciation	(21,800)	(21,000)
Goodwill	24,000	25,000
Total.........................	$87,400	$80,000
Current Liabilities	$18,000	$ 8,000
Bonds Payable	20,000	30,000
Common Stock	55,000	55,000
Retained Earnings	(5,600)	(13,000)
Total.........................	$87,400	$80,000

Additional information:

a. During 1981 the corporation sold old equipment at its book value (no gain or loss) of $3,800 and purchased new equipment costing $7,500.

b. During 1981 bonds payable with a face value of $10,000 were retired.

c. Retained earnings was affected only by the 1981 net income or loss. There were no dividends paid during the year.

On the basis of the above:

1. What was the amount of net income or net loss for 1981?

2. How much working capital was provided by operations in 1981?

E13–12 Change in Working Capital

The following information was taken from Rio Hondo Company's financial statements for 1981.

Proceeds from Short-Term Borrowings	$ 60,000
Proceeds from Long-Term Borrowings	200,000
Purchase of Operational Assets	160,000
Purchase of Inventory	400,000
Proceeds from the Sale of Rio Hondo Company Stock	100,000

If funds are defined as working capital, what is the increase or decrease in working capital for 1981 as a result of the foregoing information?

E13–13 Determining Total Sources and Uses

The following information was taken from the financial statements of Chris Corporation for the year ended December 31, 1981.

Proceeds from the Issuance of Preferred Stock ...	$200,000
Proceeds from the Issuance of Common Stock ...	800,000
Dividends on Preferred Stock	40,000
Dividends on Common Stock..................	100,000
Purchases of Treasury Stock—Common	50,000

If funds are defined as working capital, what is the amount of total sources of working capital and the amount of total uses of working capital for Chris Corporation for 1981?

E13–14 Change in Working Capital

During 1981, Roberts Company wrote off uncollectable accounts receivable of $35,000 using the allowance method (see page 172). The charge to bad-debt expense for the year amounted to $52,000. By how much would working capital be decreased by these entries?

E13–15 Working Capital Provided by Operations

Davidson Corporation had net income of $300,000 for 1981. The following additional information was taken from the 1981 financial statements.

Provision for Uncollectable Accounts Receivable .	$ 91,000
Interest Expense on Long-Term Debt	273,000
Depreciation Expense on Plant and Equipment ..	320,000
Amortization of Goodwill	8,000

If funds are defined as working capital, what is the amount of working capital provided by operations for 1981?

PROBLEMS

P13–1   Funds Statement: Working Capital Concept

The 1981 and 1980 Balance Sheets of Specific Electric Company are as follows:

Specific Electric Company
Balance Sheets as of December 31, 1981 and 1980

Assets	1981	1980
Cash	$ 9,000	$ 4,000
Accounts Receivable	14,000	6,000
Inventory	10,000	11,000
Plant and Equipment	47,000	34,000
Less Accumulated Depreciation	(17,000)	(12,000)
Goodwill	8,000	9,000
Total Assets	$71,000	$52,000

Liabilities and Stockholders' Equity		
Accounts Payable	$11,000	$ 9,000
Accrued Wages Payable	2,000	3,000
Bond Payable	8,000	0
Common Stock	29,000	26,000
Retained Earnings	21,000	14,000
Total Liabilities and Stockholders' Equity	$71,000	$52,000

Specific Electric Company's net income for 1981 was $11,000. The company paid dividends of $4,000 to shareholders in 1981. No equipment was sold during 1981.

Required:

1. Determine the change in working capital for Specific Electric from 1980 to 1981.

2. Prepare a working capital basis Statement of Changes in Financial Position for Specific Electric for 1981.

P13–2   Reconstruction of a Balance Sheet

A flood recently destroyed the records of Kingline Manufacturing Company. Luckily, however, the president had taken home the 1980 Balance Sheet and the Statement of Changes in Financial Position for the year just past, 1981. Correspondence from creditors indicates that the current liabilities of Kingline at December 31, 1981, were $20,000.

Kingline Manufacturing Company
Balance Sheet as of December 31, 1980

Current Assets	$ 40,000
Property, Plant, and Equipment	120,000
Less Accumulated Depreciation	(24,000)
Goodwill	9,000
	$145,000

Current Liabilities	$ 24,000
Bonds Payable	60,000
Capital Stock	40,000
Retained Earnings	21,000
	$145,000

Kingline Manufacturing Company
Statement of Changes in Financial Position for the Year Ended December 31, 1981

Sources of Funds

Operations:		
Net Income		$18,000
Add Items Not Requiring Working Capital:		
Depreciation	6,000	
Amortization of Goodwill	1,000	7,000
Total Sources Provided by Operations		$25,000
Issuance of Common Stock		22,000
Sale of Equipment (Original Cost $10,000)		6,000
Total Sources of Funds		$53,000

Uses of Funds

Payment of Dividends		$ 4,000
Retirement of Bonds		25,000
Acquisition of a Patent		5,000
Total Uses of Funds		$34,000
Increase in Working Capital		$19,000

Required:

The president of Kingline has hired you as a consultant to reconstruct the destroyed 1981 Balance Sheet.

P13–3   Funds Statement: Cash Concept

The treasurer of Rocky Mountain Trucking Company has received a request from a creditor for a cash basis Statement of Changes in Financial Position. The treasurer has hired you to prepare the statement and has provided you with a working capital basis Statement of Changes in Financial Position and partial Balance Sheets for 1980 and 1981.

Rocky Mountain Trucking Company
(Partial) Balance Sheets as of December 31, 1981 and 1980

	1981	1980
Current Assets:		
Cash	$15,000	$12,000
Accounts Receivable	4,000	6,000
Inventory	8,000	7,000
Prepaid Expenses	3,000	1,000
Total Current Assets	$30,000	$26,000

	1981	1980
Current Liabilities:		
Accounts Payable..................	$ 8,000	$ 6,000
Accrued Wages	2,000	3,000
Income Taxes Payable	7,000	3,000
Total Current Liabilities	$17,000	$12,000

Rocky Mountain Trucking Company
Statement of Changes in Financial Position for the Year Ended December 31, 1981

Sources of Funds

Operations:	
Net Income	$36,000
Add Items Not Requiring Working Capital:	
Depreciation	4,000
Total Sources Provided by Operations....................	$40,000
Issuance of Long-Term Note	3,000
Total Sources of Funds	$43,000

Uses of Funds

Purchase of Equipment	$30,000
Payment of Dividends...............	9,000
Payment of Long-Term Debt	5,000
Total Uses of Funds	$44,000
Decrease in Working Capital.........	$ 1,000

Required:
Prepare a Statement of Changes in Financial Position based on the cash concept of funds.

P13–4   Funds Statement: Working Capital Concept

The following information was provided by the treasurer of R. U. Forit, Inc., a manufacturer of voting machine equipment, for the year 1981.

a. Net income for the year was $134,000.

b. Depreciation of equipment for the year was $27,000.

c. Bad-debt expense was $9,000.

d. Amortization of goodwill was $2,000.

e. Amortization of bond premium was $7,000.

f. Write off of bad debts was $11,000.

g. Collection of accounts receivable was $38,000.

h. Payments on accounts payable was $39,000.

i. Rent expense was $11,000.

j. The company issued 20,000 shares of $10 par stock for $12 per share.

k. Land was acquired by issuing a $100,000 bond that would have sold on the market at 102.

l. Equipment was purchased at a cost of $84,000.

m. The company declared dividends of $6,000.

n. The company paid $5,000 of dividends, which had been declared the previous year.

o. The company declared a two-for-one stock split at a time when 80,000 shares were issued and outstanding.

p. A machine used on the manufacturing assembly line was sold for $8,000. The machine had a book value of $7,000.

q. Another machine with a book value of $1,000 was scrapped and was reported as an ordinary loss.

r. The company purchased 2,000 shares of its own stock at a cost of $14 per share. The cost method is used in accounting for treasury stock.

Required:
Prepare a Statement of Changes in Financial Position for R. U. Forit, Inc., for the year ending December 31, 1981, using the working capital concept of funds.

P13–5   Funds Statement: Working Capital Concept

Balance Sheets and additional information for Mutual Company for 1980 and 1981 are presented here.

Mutual Company
Balance Sheets as of December 31, 1981 and 1980

Assets	1981	1980
Cash.............................	$ 59	$1,638
Inventory	2,349	1,434
Equipment........................	8,600	7,000
Less Accumulated Depreciation	(405)	(293)
Total Assets....................	$10,603	$9,779

Liabilities and Stockholders' Equity		
Accounts Payable..................	$ 853	$ 781
Bonds Payable	3,500	4,000
Common Stock	3,800	3,000
Retained Earnings	2,450	1,998
Total Liabilities and Stockholders' Equity	$10,603	$9,779

Additional information:

a. Net income for 1981 was $677.

b. A dividend of $225 was declared to shareholders of record on March 31, 1981.

c. Equipment was purchased for $1,600 during 1981. No equipment was disposed of during 1981.

d. Mutual issued stock at par to help finance the purchase of equipment.

e. Bonds were retired during 1981 at face value.

Required:
1. Using the working capital concept, prepare a Statement of Changes in Financial Position including a Schedule of Changes in Working Capital accounts.

2. **Interpretive Question** How was Mutual able to finance its equipment purchases in 1981?

P13-6 Unifying Problem: Working Capital and Cash Concepts of Funds

Balance Sheets and additional information for Continental Fashions, Inc., for the years 1981 and 1982 are presented below. (All numbers are shown rounded to the nearest thousand, with the final three zeros omitted.)

Continental Fashions, Inc.
Balance Sheets as of December 31, 1982 and 1981

Assets	1982	1981
Cash	$ 549	$ 633
Accounts Receivable	354	211
Advances to Suppliers	245	105
Inventory	614	562
Long-Term Investments	620	807
Machinery and Equipment	812	344
Accumulated Depreciation	(441)	(224)
Land	344	400
Total Assets	$3,097	$2,838

Liabilities and Stockholders' Equity		
Accounts Payable	$ 583	$ 488
Short-Term Note Payable		200
Payroll Taxes Payable	147	233
Noncurrent Liabilities	657	767
Common Stock, Par $5	1,250	800
Paid-in Capital in Excess of Par	155	75
Retained Earnings	305	275
Total Liabilities and Stockholders' Equity	$3,097	$2,838

Additional information:

a. Net income during 1982 was $108 and dividends of $78 were declared.

b. Machinery with a book value of $85 (cost, $120; accumulated depreciation, $35) was sold for $92.

c. Investments purchased for $187 were sold for $246.

d. A petition for a zoning change was unsuccessful and land was disposed of at a loss of $32.

e. Common stock was sold for $530.

f. Noncurrent liabilities were retired at face value.

Required:

1. Prepare T-accounts or a worksheet for a Statement of Changes in Financial Position for 1982 using the working capital concept of funds.

2. Prepare T-accounts or a worksheet for a Statement of Changes in Financial Position for 1982 using the cash concept of funds.

P13-7 Statement of Changes in Financial Position: Working Capital Concept

The president of Fast Food Company has received letters from stockholders inquiring about some financial aspects of the company's operations for the year 1981. One of the stockholders cannot understand how the firm could retire more debt than it earned in after-tax ,income. Another stockholder said that the firm made more money from depreciation than from selling food. (All numbers are rounded to the nearest thousand, with the final three zeros omitted.)

Required:

1. Using the following information, prepare a Statement of Changes in Financial Position.

2. **Interpretive Question** Write a one-paragraph response to each of the stockholders.

Fast Food Corporation
1981 Income Statement

Revenues	$740
Cost of Goods Sold	351
Gross Margin	$389
Advertising Expense	$ 86
Depreciation	126
Rent	68
Interest Expense	29
Utilities	17
Loss on Sale of Equipment	3
General Administration	15
Total Expenses	$344
Income Before Taxes	$ 45
Income Taxes	21
Net Income	$ 24
Dividends	5
Increase in Retained Earnings	$ 19

Fast Food Corporation
Comparative Balance Sheets

	1981	1980
Current Assets	$ 47	$ 30
Property, Plant, and Equipment	379	352
Accumulated Depreciation	(139)	(39)
Total Assets	$287	$343
Current Liabilities	$ 38	$ 29
Long-Term Debt	21	131
Total Liabilities	$ 59	$160
Common Stock	$204	$178
Retained Earnings	24	5
Total Stockholders' Equity	$228	$183
Total Liabilities and Stockholders' Equity	$287	$343

Additional information:

a. Equipment with a book value of $9 was sold for $6 (cost, $35; accumulated depreciation, $26).

b. Other property, plant, and equipment was purchased and long-term debt was retired.

c. Common stock was sold at par.

P13–8   Funds Statement: Working Capital Concept

Comparative Balance Sheets for Crystal Lake Corporation as of December 31, 1982 and 1981 are presented here.

Crystal Lake Corporation

Balance Sheets as of December 31, 1982 and 1981

Assets	1982	1981
Cash	$ 105,000	$ 115,000
Accounts Receivable (Net)	267,000	273,000
Merchandise Inventory	685,000	642,000
Prepaid Expenses	13,000	8,000
Office Equipment	60,000	61,700
Accumulated Depreciation—Office Equipment	(20,000)	(19,000)
Store Equipment	400,000	375,000
Accumulated Depreciation—Store Equipment	(110,000)	(75,000)
Total Assets	$1,400,000	$1,380,700

Liabilities and Stockholders' Equity

Notes Payable	$ 20,000	$ 25,000
Accounts Payable	173,000	176,000
Common Stock ($5 Par)	805,000	800,000
Paid-in Capital in Excess of Par— Common Stock	55,000	53,500
Retained Earnings	347,000	326,200
Total Liabilities and Stockholders' Equity	$1,400,000	$1,380,700

Additional information:

a. Net income for 1982 was $47,300.

b. Depreciation on office equipment was $3,000; depreciation on store equipment was $35,000.

c. Office equipment costing $300 was purchased during the year. Fully depreciated office equipment costing $2,000 was discarded and its cost and accumulated depreciation were removed from the accounts.

d. A stock dividend was declared and distributed during the year. The shares were selling for $6.50 per share when the dividend was declared. The total distribution amounted to 1,000 shares.

e. Cash dividends of $20,000 were paid during the year.

f. The only change in the Store Equipment account came from the purchase of additional equipment during 1982.

Required:

Assuming that funds are defined as working capital, prepare a Statement of Changes in Financial Position.

P13–9   Unifying Problem: Funds Statement, Preparation and Analysis

The financial statements of Consolidated Department Stores and Amalgamated Retail Corporation are presented on the following pages. Consolidated Stores and Amalgamated Corporation are competing firms within their marketing region. As an investment adviser, you have been asked to identify the financial policies of the two firms and explain the similarities and differences between them. (All numbers are shown rounded to the nearest thousand, with the final three zeros omitted.)

Consolidated Department Stores, Inc.

Income Statement for the Year Ended December 31, 1981

Sales Revenue	$1,290
Cost of Goods Sold	978
Gross Margin	$ 312
Operating Expenses:	
Depreciation Expense	14
Sales and Administration Expenses	105
Other Expenses	87
Total Operating Expenses	$ 206
Income Before Taxes	$ 106
Income Taxes	51
Net Income	$ 55
Dividends Paid	10
Increase in Retained Earnings	$ 45

Consolidated Department Stores, Inc.

Balance Sheets as of December 31, 1981 and 1980

Assets	1981	1980
Cash	$ 852	$ 725
Accounts Receivable	461	448
Appliances Inventory	38	225
Housewares Inventory	101	301
Clothing Inventory	87	427
Land	1,240	1,240
Store Fixtures	369	369
Less Accumulated Depreciation— Store Fixtures	(51)	(37)
Total Assets	$3,097	$3,698

Liabilities and Stockholders' Equity	1981	1980
Liabilities:		
Accounts Payable..................	$ 175	$ 378
Short-Term Notes Payable..........	525	768
Long-Term Debt	804	1,004
Total Liabilities	$1,504	$2,150
Stockholders' Equity:		
Common Stock	$ 448	$ 448
Paid-in Capital in Excess of Par......	500	500
Retained Earnings	645	600
Total Stockholders' Equity	$1,593	$1,548
Total Liabilities and Stockholders' Equity..............	$3,097	$3,698

Liabilities and Stockholders' Equity	1981	1980
Liabilities:		
Accounts Payable..................	$ 270	$ 300
Short-Term Notes Payable..........	601	491
Long-Term Debt	709	1,102
Total Liabilities	$1,580	$1,893
Stockholders' Equity:		
Common Stock ($1 Par)	$ 750	$ 500
Paid-in Capital in Excess of Par......	840	435
Retained Earnings	772	665
Total Stockholders' Equity	$2,362	$1,600
Total Liabilities and Stockholders' Equity	$3,942	$3,493

Amalgamated Retail Corporation

Income Statement for the Year Ended December 31, 1981

Sales Revenue.............................	$1,233
Cost of Goods Sold	1,018
Gross Margin..............................	$ 215
Operating Expenses:	
Depreciation Expense......................	$ 6
Sales and Administration Expenses	110
Other Expenses...........................	41
Total Operating Expenses	$ 157
Income from Operations.....................	$ 58
Gain on Sale of Real Estate	110
Income Before Taxes	$ 168
Less Income Taxes	61
Net Income................................	$ 107
Dividends Paid	0
Increase in Retained Earnings.................	$ 107

Amalgamated Retail Corporation

Balance Sheets as of December 31, 1981 and 1980

Assets	1981	1980
Cash............................	$ 149	$ 761
Accounts Receivable	163	151
Appliances Inventory..............	796	142
Housewares Inventory.............	618	253
Clothing Inventory	807	317
Land............................	1,159	1,639
Store Fixtures	281	255
Less Accumulated Depreciation—Store Fixtures....................	(31)	(25)
Total Assets	$3,942	$3,493

Required:

1. Prepare a Statement of Changes in Financial Position for Consolidated Department Stores using the working capital concept of funds.

2. **Interpretive Question**   Does the working capital concept reveal what changes are taking place in the firm's assets?

3. Prepare a Statement of Changes in Financial Position for Amalgamated Retail Corporation using the working capital concept of funds.

4. **Interpretive Question**   How has management changed Amalgamated's commercial strategy for 1981 in contrast to 1980?

5. **Interpretive Question**   Contrast the postures of the two firms. Which firm would benefit most from increased consumer spending during 1982? Which firm would be more seriously affected if 1982 were a recession year?

P13–10   Unifying Problem: Working Capital and Cash Concepts of Funds

A stockholder of Aurora Mining and Smelting Corporation has written to the president inquiring how the company was able to operate in 1981 and 1982 despite the fact that each year the Income Statement showed a substantial net loss. The president sent the stockholder's letter to the controller who has asked you to make an analysis that can be used as the basis for a response. The controller asks you to prepare a Statement of Changes in Financial Position for both 1981 and 1982. In order to assess the relative merits of the cash concept and the working capital concept of funds, the controller asks you to prepare the statement for 1981 using the cash concept and for 1982 using the working capital concept. Following are Comparative Balance Sheets and Income Statements for 1981 and 1982 for Aurora Mining. (All numbers are shown rounded to the nearest thousand, with the final three zeros omitted.)

Aurora Mining and Smelting Corporation
Balance Sheets as of December 31, 1982, 1981, and 1980

Assets	1982	1981	1980
Cash	$ 800	$ 987	$ 1,132
Accounts Receivable	422	271	328
Ore Stockpile—Bauxite	548	516	493
Galena	222	307	358
Metal Ingots—Aluminum	512	882	543
Lead	151	490	857
Tin	788	774	745
Land and Buildings	6,390	6,974	5,491
Machinery and Equipment	4,635	3,839	3,564
Accumulated Depreciation	(1,500)	(1,391)	(1,132)
Total Assets	$12,968	$13,649	$12,379

Liabilities and Stockholders' Equity

Liabilities:			
Accounts Payable	$ 1,724	$ 1,681	$ 1,951
Short-Term Notes Payable— Banks	578	373	352
Total Liabilities	$ 2,302	$ 2,054	$ 2,303
Stockholders' Equity:			
Common Stock	$ 7,000	$ 7,000	$ 5,000
Paid-in Capital in Excess of Par—Common Stock	2,000	2,000	1,000
Retained Earnings	1,666	2,595	4,076
Total Stockholders' Equity	$10,666	$11,595	$10,076
Total Liabilities and Stockholders' Equity	$12,968	$13,649	$12,379

Aurora Mining and Smelting Corporation
Income Statements for the Years Ended December 31, 1982 and 1981

	1982	1981
Revenues	$6,303	$7,408
Operating Expenses:		
Wages and Salaries	$5,973	$6,421
Supplies	934	1,637
Depreciation	256	259
Interest	58	37
Other Expenses	11	235
Total Operating Expenses	$7,232	$8,589
Net Loss	$ (929)	$(1,181)
Dividends Paid	—	300
Decrease in Retained Earnings	$ (929)	$(1,481)

Additional information:

a. Revenues included gain on sale of equipment of $23 during 1982 (cost, $240; accumulated depreciation, $147).

b. Sold land at book value.

Required:

Using the foregoing financial statement information for 1981 and 1982, prepare the following.

1. A Statement of Changes in Financial Position for 1981, using the cash concept.

2. A Statement of Changes in Financial Position for 1982, using the working capital concept.

3. **Interpretive Question** Comment on how the operating losses are being financed in this case.

Using a Worksheet to Prepare a Statement of Changes in Financial Position

The worksheet approach to preparing a Statement of Changes in Financial Position produces the same results as the T-account method. To give you a sense of how these methods compare, we will again use the data for Star Manufacturing Company to prepare this Statement on a working capital basis. For convenience, Exhibits 13–8 and 13–9 reproduce the Income Statement, Statement of Retained Earnings, and Balance Sheets for 1980 and 1981.

The Worksheet Method

Like the T-account approach, the worksheet method involves several sequential steps. As you read about these steps, refer to the worksheet in Exhibit 13–10 on page 454.

Step 1
Set up a four-column worksheet.
(a) Column 1: Balance Sheet account balances at the end of the preceding year.
(b) Columns 2 and 3: Analysis of entries.
(c) Column 4: Balance Sheet account balances at the end of the current year.

Step 2
Determine the amount of working capital (current assets minus current liabilities) at the beginning and end of the year and record these amounts on the first line of columns 1 and 4. It is not necessary to list all current account balances since we are only trying to explain the total working capital difference.

Step 3
Record the beginning and end-of-year non-working-capital Balance Sheet account balances in columns 1 and 4.

EXHIBIT 13–2 **Star Manufacturing Company**
Income Statement for the Year Ended December 31, 1981

Revenues:

Net Sales	$859,400
Other Revenues (Note 1)	7,800
Total Revenues	$867,200

Expenses:

Cost of Goods Sold	$610,100
Selling and Administrative Expenses.................	147,000
Depreciation and Amortization Expenses	32,100
Interest Expense	14,200
Total Expenses	$803,400
Income Before Taxes	$ 63,800
Income Taxes	27,200
Net Income..	$ 36,600

Note 1   Gain on the sale of equipment.

Star Manufacturing Company
Statement of Retained Earnings for the Year Ended
December 31, 1981

Retained Earnings, January 1, 1981	$368,400
Add Net Income	36,600
	$405,000
Dividends Declared and Paid....................................	21,800
Retained Earnings, December 31, 1981............................	$383,200

Step 4

Record the transactions and bookkeeping entries in columns 2 and 3 to explain the change in working capital and in each non-working-capital Balance Sheet account from the beginning to the end of the year. Each analysis entry should be keyed as a source or a use of working capital, or as having no effect on working capital. Those entries that do not affect working capital are included because they explain changes in other non-working-capital Balance Sheet accounts. The total debits in column 2 should equal total credits in column 3. Also, after all entries have been keyed, the total *uses* should be in balance with the total *sources*.

Step 5

Use the information in the worksheet to prepare a formal Statement of Changes in Financial Position, with an accompanying schedule of changes in working capital accounts (see Exhibit 13–4 on page 425). (We have not shown the formal statement here because it is the same as the one in Exhibit 13–5 on page 434.) The worksheet approach can also be used to prepare a Statement of Changes in Financial Position on a cash basis. A formal cash-basis Funds Statement prepared using a worksheet would be identical to Exhibit 13–7 on page 439.

EXHIBIT 13-9   **Star Manufacturing Company**
Balance Sheets as of December 31, 1981 and 1980

Assets	1981	1980
Current Assets:		
Cash	$ 7,600	$ 7,900
Short-Term Securities	30,000	
Accounts and Notes Receivable (Net of Allowance for		
Doubtful Accounts)	106,700	104,900
Inventory	167,300	197,500
Prepaid Expenses	7,000	9,200
Total Current Assets	$318,600	$319,500
Property, Plant, and Equipment:		
Land (Note 2)	$110,000	$ 10,000
Plant and Equipment (at Cost)	603,200	577,200
Less Accumulated Depreciation	(243,900)	(223,600)
Total Property, Plant, and Equipment	$469,300	$363,600
Other Noncurrent Assets: Notes Receivable	$ 42,800	$ 50,900
Total Assets	$830,700	$734,000

Liabilities and Stockholders' Equity

	1981	1980
Current Liabilities:		
Note Payable	$ 6,800	$ 38,000
Accounts Payable	72,200	61,700
Income Taxes Payable	7,000	1,500
Total Current Liabilities	$ 86,000	$101,200
Long-Term Liabilities:		
Notes Payable—Bank (Note 2)	$100,000	
Bonds Payable (Note 3)		$ 80,000
Other Long-Term Debt	92,100	95,000
Total Long-Term Liabilities	$192,100	$175,000
Stockholders' Equity:		
Common Stock, $1 Par Value (Note 3)	$ 82,500	$ 42,500
Additional Contributed Capital (Note 3)	86,900	46,900
Retained Earnings	383,200	368,400
Total Stockholders' Equity	$552,600	$457,800
Total Liabilities and Stockholders' Equity	$830,700	$734,000

Note 2   Land with a fair market value of $100,000 was acquired through the issuance of a long-term note.
Note 3   The bonds payable were retired by conversion into 40,000 shares of common stock. At the time of conversion the bonds were selling at par and the common stock was selling at $2 per share.

EXHIBIT 13–10   **Star Manufacturing Company**

Worksheet for Statement of Changes in Financial Position (Working Capital Basis)
for the Year Ended December 31, 1981

	Column 1 Beginning Balances 12-31-80	Column 2 Analysis of Entries Debit	Column 3 Analysis of Entries Credit	Column 4 Ending Balances 12-31-81
Debits				
Working Capital	218300	(10) 14300		232600
Land	10000	(4) 100000		110000
Plant and Equipment	577200	(6) 38300	(3) 12300	603200
Notes Receivable	50900		(7) 8100	42800
Total Debits	856400			988600
Credits				
Accumulated Depreciation	223600	(3) 11800	(2) 32100	243900
Notes Payable			(4) 100000	100000
Bonds Payable	80000	(8) 80000		
Other Long-Term Debt	95000	(9) 2900		92100
Common Stock	42500		(8) 40000	82500
Additional Contributed Capital	46900		(8) 40000	86900
Retained Earnings	368400	(5) 21800	(1) 36600	383200
Total Credits	856400			988600
Sources of Working Capital:				
Operations:				
Net Income		(1) 36600		
Depreciation		(2) 32100		
Gain on Sale of Equipment			(3) 7800	
Increase in Long-Term Note		(4) 100000		
Collection of Long-Term Note		(7) 8100		
Proceeds from Sale of Equipment		(3) 8300		
Issuance of Common Stock		(8) 80000		
Uses of Working Capital:				
Payment of Dividends			(5) 21800	
Acquisition of Land			(4) 100000	
Purchase of Plant and Equipment			(6) 38300	
Retirement of Bonds			(8) 80000	
Reduction in Other Long-Term Debt			(9) 2900	
Increase in Working Capital			(10) 14300	
		534200	534200	

EXPLANATION OF WORKSHEET ENTRIES

1. Net income for the period.

2. Depreciation expense is a non-working-capital deduction added back to net income in computing working capital from operations.

3. Sale of plant and equipment at a gain. The sale is a non-working-capital addition to net income that is subtracted in computing working capital from operations. Note that the original entry showed a gain on sale of equipment as follows:

Actual Proceeds from Sale		$8,300
Less Book Value:		
Asset Amount	$12,300	
Less Accumulated Depreciation.	11,800	500
Gain on Sale		$7,800

4. Issuance of a long-term note to acquire land. Under the all-financial-resources concept, the issuance of a note is a source of working capital and the acquisition of land is a use of working capital.

5. Payment of dividends is a use of working capital.

6. Purchase of plant and equipment is a use of working capital.

7. Collection of a long-term note is a source of working capital.

8. Issuance of common stock to retire bonds. Under the all-financial-resources concept, the issuance of stock is a source of funds and the retirement of bonds is a use of funds.

9. Reduction in other long-term debt is a use of working capital.

10. Increase in working capital for the period.

CHAPTER 14

Financial Statement Analysis

The reasons for financial statement analysis.

The basic techniques of financial statement analysis.

Analysis of operating performance, asset turnover, debt–equity management, and return on assets and equity.

Some limitations of financial statement analysis.

We have dealt thus far with the way a firm collects and uses financial data in the preparation of the Income Statement, the Balance Sheet, and the Statement of Changes in Financial Position. These statements conveniently and succinctly summarize a firm's performance and its financial status at the end of each accounting period. Although they are historical in nature, they usually provide a good indication of what a firm's performance is likely to be during subsequent accounting periods. These clues may not be immediately evident, however. Interested users must analyze the statements carefully in order to obtain the particular information that suits their purposes.

Reasons for Financial Statement Analysis

There are several reasons why careful analysis of financial statements is necessary.

1. Financial statements are general-purpose statements. They are prepared for use by a variety of interested parties: stockholders, short- and long-term creditors, potential investors, government agencies, and management. These different users are involved in making different types of decisions, ranging from whether to make an investment (potential owner), or whether opportunities exist for improving performance (manager), to

whether the firm's activities require regulation (government agency). Each type of decision involves the need for different information, and therefore a different analysis.

2. The relationship between key figures on the Income Statement, the Balance Sheet, or on both, and the relationship between amounts on successive financial statements, are not obvious without analysis. Accordingly, knowledgeable users will want to develop ratios and percentages that reflect meaningful relationships and that show trends from previous years.

3. Sophisticated users of financial statements may be interested in seeing how well a company is doing in comparison to predetermined objective standards, other companies in the industry, or alternative opportunities for investment. Consideration of the broader economic and social environment is also a relevant factor in many business decisions.

To a large extent, then, the amount of information one is able to draw from financial statements depends on the care and experience with which they are analyzed.

THE TYPE OF INFORMATION TO BE GAINED FROM FINANCIAL STATEMENT ANALYSIS

Most people who analyze financial statements are interested in making investment, managerial, or regulatory decisions. What type of financial information do these users need?

Investment and Credit Decisions

Owners, creditors, or potential owners or creditors of a company want to know what their return on investment is likely to be and what the chances (probabilities) are of achieving that return. The probability of achieving a certain return on an investment is referred to as the degree of risk, or uncertainty, involved. The amount of return to be expected and the degree of uncertainty are likely to be different for each type of investor: stockholder, short-term creditor, or long-term creditor.

profitability *a company's ability to generate revenues in excess of costs incurred in producing those revenues*

Stockholders can gain a return on investment both from dividends and from proceeds on the sale of stock at an increased price. They want to be able to predict a firm's future profits because profitability is the best indicator of the ability to pay dividends and of the value the market is likely to place on the stock.

liquidity *a company's ability to meet current obligations with cash or other assets that can be quickly converted to cash*

Short-term creditors, such as banks, are clearly going to be interested in a firm's ability to repay a loan promptly. Hence, the short-term cash-generating ability of a firm, its degree of liquidity, is important to these creditors.

solvency *a company's long-run ability to meet all financial obligations*

Long-term creditors, such as bondholders, would like to be able to predict a firm's ability to pay the interest obligation regularly and to repay the principal at maturity. Such payments are made over periods of years, and so these creditors are interested in judging a firm's long-run solvency.

Managerial Decisions

The managers of a company have a responsibility to all other users of the financial statements (creditors, owners, government agencies, customers, suppliers, workers, and society in general). They must constantly monitor the firm's financial position and performance and take corrective action where necessary. Before they can take action, however, they must understand the company's major strengths and weaknesses. Financial statement analysis can help management identify problems having to do with operating efficiency and debt–equity management—problems that must be solved if a firm is to meet its short- and long-run profitability, liquidity, and solvency goals.

Regulatory Decisions

All firms are subject to some degree of government regulation. In discharging their oversight responsibilities, government agencies need to assess the operating results and financial status of companies under their jurisdiction. The Internal Revenue Service, for example, might want to determine whether related companies are avoiding income taxes by illegally shifting income. Or the IRS may make use of financial statement analysis to justify an assessment of taxes on the accumulated earnings of closely held corporations that forgo dividends in order to save income taxes for their high-tax-bracket owners. Similarly, the Federal Trade Commission and the Justice Department may use statement analysis to determine whether too much economic power is concentrated in too few companies in an industry. The Securities and Exchange Commission, in executing its enforcement powers with respect to new stock offerings and annual reporting, may use financial statement analysis to judge whether a company is misleading potential investors by not disclosing all relevant data in its financial statements.

TO SUMMARIZE   Current and potential investors and creditors use financial statement analysis to help them judge the degree of profitability, liquidity, or solvency of a firm. Managers use statement analysis to identify problems having to do with operating efficiency and debt–equity management. Government agencies use financial statement analysis in assessing the operating results and financial status of companies under their jurisdiction.

Overview of Financial Statement Analysis

Financial statement analysis clearly has many applications for a variety of users. In the remainder of this chapter, we will describe some of the most useful techniques of analysis. The experienced user will begin an analysis by identifying an objective (assessing profitability, liquidity, or solvency) and will then choose the techniques that will accomplish the objective. Such a careful approach will usually provide valuable information, but it will not answer all questions. Financial statement analysis has limitations that must be kept in mind, as will be explained later.

SOME BASIC TECHNIQUES

Four techniques are widely used in analyzing the financial statements of profit-oriented companies. They are

1. Ratio analysis: the appraisal of certain key relationships.
2. Vertical analysis: measuring relationships between items on a single year's Income Statement or Balance Sheet.
3. Horizontal analysis: measuring changes in the same items on comparative statements over two or more years.
4. Common-size statements: measuring relationships between items that are expressed as percentages on a single year's Income Statement or Balance Sheet.

These techniques are sometimes presented as alternative ways of assessing a company's status, unrelated to the particular objectives of the user. A more logical approach is to consider each technique as an important part of a single, comprehensive analysis. This is the way financial statement analysis will be presented here.

To illustrate, we will use hypothetical data from Marvel Company's financial statements for the calendar years ending December 31, 1981 and 1980, shown in Exhibits 14–1 and 14–2.

KEY RELATIONSHIPS

Four key relationships (ratios) serve as a basis for the assessment of a firm's profitability, liquidity, and solvency.

$$1. \ \frac{\text{net income (earnings)}}{\text{net sales}} \qquad \text{a measure of operating performance for a period}$$

$$2. \ \frac{\text{net sales}}{\text{average total assets}} \qquad \text{a measure of asset utilization}$$

$$3. \ \frac{\text{average total assets}}{\text{average stockholders' equity}} \qquad \text{a measure of the management of debt and equity}$$

$$4. \ \frac{\text{net income (earnings)}}{\text{average stockholders' equity}} \qquad \text{a measure of performance from a stockholder's viewpoint}$$

The first ratio relates two Income Statement items, net income and net sales. It provides a measure of operating performance for a period by showing the amount of earnings generated by each sales dollar, which is one way of measuring profitability.

The second ratio relates an Income Statement amount (net sales) to a Balance Sheet amount (total assets). However, since the Income Statement covers a period of time and the Balance Sheet presents the financial position at a given moment in time, the relationship will not be entirely valid unless the Balance Sheet amount is revised to cover a period of time. This can be accomplished by using the monthly, quarterly, or annual average of the

EXHIBIT 14–1 **Marvel Company**
Income Statements for the Years Ended December 31, 1981 and 1980

	1981	1980
Net Sales*	$1,086,944	$988,417
Costs and Expenses:		
Cost of Goods Sold	$ 786,523	$700,263
Selling and Administrative Expenses	190,090	172,661
Interest Expense	14,995	13,046
Total Costs and Expenses	$ 991,608	$885,970
Income from Operations Before Taxes	$ 95,336	$102,447
Income Taxes	54,961	50,197
Net Income from Operations	$ 40,375	$ 52,250
Extraordinary Gain (Net of Tax)		12,400
Net Income (Earnings)	$ 40,375	$ 64,650

* All sales were made on credit.

EXHIBIT 14–2 **Marvel Company**
Balance Sheets as of December 31, 1981 and 1980

Assets	1981	1980
Current Assets:		
Cash	$ 16,982	$ 9,020
Short-Term Securities	37,683	39,712
Accounts and Notes Receivable (Net)	127,544	121,614
Inventory	195,512	173,999
Other Current Assets	9,499	7,634
Total Current Assets	$387,220	$351,979
Property, Plant, and Equipment (Net)	406,599	395,098
Other Noncurrent Assets	28,571	40,801
Total Assets	$822,390	$787,878

Liabilities and Stockholders' Equity	1981	1980
Current Liabilities:		
Notes Payable—Bank	$ 24,658	$ 22,576
Current Installments of Long-Term Debt	1,919	3,320
Accounts Payable and Notes Payable	78,967	69,475
Income Taxes Payable	15,090	14,656
Total Current Liabilities	$120,634	$110,027
Long-Term Debt	155,881	148,400
Deferred Income Taxes	31,361	29,210
Stockholders' Equity (Including Capital Stock and Retained Earnings)	514,514	500,241
Total Liabilities and Stockholders' Equity	$822,390	$787,878

total assets for the period selected. (For example, take total assets at the beginning and end of each year, add them, and divide by two.) This second key ratio indicates how efficiently assets are being utilized and is often called the asset turnover ratio. The more efficiently assets are used, the more profitable a firm will be and the more likely it is to be able to pay its obligations on a timely basis.

The third ratio relates two Balance Sheet amounts, and shows the degree to which debt and equity are used in financing the operations of a company. Average total assets divided by average stockholders' equity measures the assets per dollar of stockholders' equity used by a firm. That is, it shows the degree to which a firm is financing its total assets through the issuance of stock together with the accumulation of past earnings. Since total assets minus total stockholders' equity is equal to total liabilities or debt, this ratio also may be used to analyze the amount of debt used during a period to maintain assets. The amount of debt a firm has obviously relates directly to the amount of liquid resources it needs to remain solvent. The debt–equity relationship also bears on profitability through the use of leveraging, the ability to earn for stockholders a rate of return higher than the cost of borrowed money. This concept was introduced in Chapter 11 and is also discussed later in this chapter.

The fourth ratio relates an Income Statement amount (net income) to an average of Balance Sheet amounts (average stockholders' equity). It is a measure of a company's current earnings productivity in relation to stockholders' investments plus accumulated earnings. That is, it shows how much income was earned in the period per dollar of investment and accumulated earnings. The greater the return on stockholders' equity, the more profitable a firm is and the more likely it is to remain solvent.

If you think carefully about each of these ratios in terms of their components and their significance as indicators of profitability, liquidity, and solvency, you will notice that the first three can be chained together as a basis for explaining the fourth.

Operating Performance		Asset Turnover		Debt–Equity Management		Overall Performance
$\dfrac{\text{net income}}{\text{net sales}}$	$\times$	$\dfrac{\text{net sales}}{\text{average total assets}}$	$\times$	$\dfrac{\text{average total assets}}{\text{average stockholders' equity}}$	$=$	$\dfrac{\text{net income}}{\text{average stockholders' equity}}$

The overall performance ratio (net income/average stockholders' equity) can be computed directly from the Income Statement and comparative Balance Sheets. However, an explanation of the factors that contributed to overall performance is to be found in an analysis of the three areas of activity that influence it: operations, asset utilization, and management of debt and equity in financing operations.

To illustrate the relationships between these key ratios, Marvel Company's financial statements for 1980 and 1981 (Exhibits 14–1 and 14–2) were used in computing the following.

Operating Performance		Asset Turnover		Debt–Equity Management		Overall Performance
$\dfrac{\text{net income}}{\text{net sales}}$	×	$\dfrac{\text{net sales}}{\text{average total assets}}$	×	$\dfrac{\text{average total assets}}{\text{average stockholders' equity}}$	=	$\dfrac{\text{net income}}{\text{average stockholders' equity}}$
1980:						
$\dfrac{\$64,650}{\$988,417}$	×	$\dfrac{\$988,417}{\$764,306^*}$	×	$\dfrac{\$764,306}{\$477,210^*}$	=	$\dfrac{\$64,650}{\$477,210^*}$
6.54%	×	1.29 times	×	1.60 times	=	13.55%†
1981:						
$\dfrac{\$40,375}{\$1,086,944}$	×	$\dfrac{\$1,086,944}{\$805,134^*}$	×	$\dfrac{\$805,134}{\$507,378^*}$	=	$\dfrac{\$40,375}{\$507,378^*}$
3.71%	×	1.35 times	×	1.59 times	=	7.96%

* These numbers are averages of beginning- and end-of-year balances.
† Percentages and factors may not multiply to products due to rounding.

Analysis of Operating Performance

operating performance ratio *an overall measure of the efficiency of operations during a period; computed by dividing net income by net sales*

The ratio of net income to net sales is a measure of a firm's operating performance, or its profitability. Marvel Company, for example, in 1981 earned for its stockholders approximately 3.71 cents on each net sales dollar. In 1980 the company had earned 6.54 cents per sales dollar on a smaller sales volume. In order to judge whether a particular ratio is satisfactory, an analyst must not only compare the current figure against the previous years' ratio, but also, if possible, against the company's expected operating performance ratio and against the operating performance of other companies in the same industry.

There are two ways of increasing the operating performance of a company.

1. Increase net income and maintain the same level of sales revenue; that is, reduce costs without reducing sales revenue.
2. Maintain net income and reduce revenue by eliminating the least profitable sales or products, in other words, by increasing the profit margin on each dollar of sales.

Two techniques used in assessing the likelihood of improving this ratio are vertical analysis of each year's Income Statement and horizontal analysis of the Income Statements of two or more periods.

INCOME STATEMENT VERTICAL ANALYSIS

vertical analysis *a technique for analyzing the relationships among items on a particular year's Income Statement or Balance Sheet by expressing all items as percentages*

The vertical analysis of an Income Statement examines the relationship of each item to sales. Generally, net sales is assigned 100 percent. This analysis reveals whether any particular revenue or expense item is out of line in its relationship to net sales. It also provides the analyst with clues

EXHIBIT 14–3   Marvel Company

Vertical Analysis of Income Statements for the Years Ended December 31, 1981 and 1980

	1981		1980	
Net Sales	$1,086,944	100.0%	$988,417	100.0%
Expenses:				
Cost of Goods Sold	$ 786,523	72.4%	$700,263	70.8%
Selling and Administrative Expenses	190,090	17.5	172,661	17.5
Interest Expense..................................	14,995	1.4	13,046	1.3
Total Expenses	$ 991,608	91.2%*	$885,970	89.6%
Income from Operations Before Taxes	$ 95,336	8.8%	$102,447	10.4%
Income Taxes	54,961	5.1	50,197	5.1
Net Income from Operations.......................	$ 40,375	3.7%*	$ 52,250	5.3%
Extraordinary Gain (Net of Tax)		0	12,400	1.3
Net Income	$ 40,375	3.7%	$ 64,650	6.5%*

* Percentages may not add to totals due to rounding.

as to the company's potential strengths and weaknesses in controlling costs and in achieving its profitability objectives. Exhibit 14–3 is a vertical analysis of the 1980 and 1981 Income Statements of Marvel Company.

This vertical analysis reveals that Marvel's expenses were higher as a percentage of sales in 1981 than in 1980 (91.2 percent versus 89.6 percent). The combination of this and the lack of an extraordinary gain in 1981 resulted in a significant drop in net income from 6.5 percent of sales to 3.7 percent of sales.

INCOME STATEMENT HORIZONTAL ANALYSIS

horizontal analysis *a technique for analyzing the percentage change in individual Income Statement or Balance Sheet items from one year to the next*

In contrast to vertical analysis, which compares each Income Statement item with net sales for each year, horizontal analysis computes the amount of change in Income Statement items from one year to the next. This analysis enables the user to determine whether any particular item has changed in an unusual way in relation to the change in net sales from one period to the next. Exhibit 14–4 is a horizontal analysis of Marvel Company's 1980 and 1981 Income Statements. Note that the change for each item between 1980 and 1981 is shown on a dollar basis in column (3) and on a percentage basis in column (4).

This horizontal analysis reveals that from 1980 to 1981 cost of goods sold increased by 12.3 percent and total expenses increased by 11.9 percent, whereas net sales increased by only 10.0 percent. These changes resulted in a 6.9 percent decrease in income from operations before taxes. Despite lower earnings, taxes on income were higher in 1981, probably because of the timing of reporting certain revenue and expense items. In addition, there were no extraordinary gains in 1981. The overall effect of these changes was that net income in 1981 was 37.5 percent less than in 1980,

EXHIBIT 14-4 **Marvel Company**

Horizontal Analysis of Income Statements for the Years Ended December 31, 1981 and 1980

	(1) 1981	(2) 1980	(3) Dollar Change	(4) Percentage Change
Net Sales	$1,086,944	$988,417	+$ 98,527	+10.0
Expenses:				
Cost of Goods Sold	$ 786,523	$700,263	+$ 86,260	+12.3
Selling and Administrative Expenses	190,090	172,661	+ 17,429	+10.1
Interest Expense.	14,995	13,046	+ 1,949	+14.9
Total Expenses	$ 991,608	$885,970	+$105,638	+11.9
Income from Operations Before Taxes.	$ 95,336	$102,447	−$ 7,111	− 6.9
Income Taxes	54,961	50,197	+ 4,764	+ 9.5
Net Income from Operations.	$ 40,375	$ 52,250	−$ 11,875	−22.7
Extraordinary Gain (Net of Tax)		12,400	− 12,400	
Net Income	$ 40,375	$ 64,650	−$ 24,275	−37.5

and that gross margin declined by 1.6 percent of net sales, as the following vertical analysis reveals.

	1981	1980
Net Sales.	100.0%	100.0%
Cost of Goods Sold	72.4	70.8
Gross Margin	27.6%	29.2%

This vertical analysis of the relationship of cost of goods sold and gross margin to net sales is an excellent means of revealing significant changes. It shows that a major factor in the decline in Marvel Company's net income in 1981 was the disproportionate increase in cost of goods sold.

COMMON-SIZE STATEMENTS

common-size statement *an Income Statement or Balance Sheet providing percentage relationships or ratios of individual items to the total*

When relationships between or among all accounts on a statement are expressed in percentages, a common-size statement has been prepared. This approach helps the reader understand the proportionate relationship of one item in a statement to the total of all like items. For example, it shows the ratio of cash to total assets and the ratio of long-term debt to total liabilities and stockholders' equity. A common-size Balance Sheet focuses the reader's attention on: (1) the distribution of liabilities and equities among current liabilities, long-term liabilities, and stockholders' equity and (2) the distribution of assets among current assets, property, plant, and equipment, and other assets. A common-size Income Statement focuses attention on the proportionate relationship of each item to net sales; it is, in effect, vertical analysis without the dollar amounts.

EXHIBIT 14-5 Marvel Company
Common-Size Income Statements for the Years
Ended December 31, 1981 and 1980

	1981	1980
Net Sales	100.0%	100.0%
Cost of Goods Sold	72.4	70.8
Gross Margin	27.6%	29.2%
Selling and Administrative Expenses	17.5%	17.5%
Interest Expense	1.4	1.3
Total Expenses	18.9%	18.8%
Income from Operations Before Taxes	8.8%	10.4%
Income Taxes	5.1	5.1
Net Income from Operations	3.7%*	5.3%
Extraordinary Gain (Net of Tax)		1.3
Net Income	3.7%	6.5%*

* Percentages may not add to totals due to rounding.

Common-size statements can be used to compare several years of a firm's operations, thus revealing the changing proportions of assets, liabilities, equity, costs, expenses, and income. They are also well suited to comparisons between and among firms regardless of their relative size. Comparisons among companies in the same industry can draw attention to, and thus encourage investigation of, the variations in accounting practices and financial policies.

A common-size Income Statement for Marvel Company is presented in Exhibit 14-5. This statement is a comparison of operating performance in 1980 and 1981. Common-size Income Statements comparing Marvel with other companies in the industry or with industry averages could also be prepared.

Operating performance can be analyzed in a variety of other ways. For example, the current year's operating results (as reflected in the Income Statement) could be compared with the budgeted Income Statement for the period. Using several methods of analyzing operating performance will help management and others understand the company's operating strengths and weaknesses.

Analysis of Asset Turnover

asset turnover ratio *an overall measure of how effectively assets are used during a period; computed by dividing net sales by average total assets*

A measure of a company's efficiency in utilizing its resources is the asset turnover ratio; it is net sales divided by average total assets. This ratio shows the rate at which assets are "turned over." Stated in another way, it is a measure of the amount of sales revenue generated with each dollar of assets owned by the company. Marvel Company increased its asset turnover from 1.29 times in 1980 to 1.35 times in 1981.

$$1980 \quad \frac{\$988,417}{\$764,306} = 1.29$$

$$1981 \quad \frac{\$1,086,944}{\$805,134} = 1.35$$

As we noted earlier, in this ratio the numerator (sales) is an Income Statement amount that covers a period of time, whereas the denominator relates to a particular date. To develop a reliable ratio, the analyst must convert the denominator into a figure that reflects a period of time. This is accomplished by averaging total assets for the period. Thus, for Marvel Company, the beginning- and end-of-year balances for total assets would be added and divided by two ($822,390 + $787,878)/2 = $805,134. If more precise results are desired, quarterly or monthly totals can be used in computing the average.

The asset turnover ratios for two years can be compared to indicate how well a company performed in the current year compared with the previous year. Similarly, the ratio for the current year can be compared with the projected turnover, or with competitors' turnovers.

In order to improve its asset turnover, a company must analyze how well each of its major types of assets is being utilized. To do so, management would use vertical, horizontal, and ratio analysis.

BALANCE SHEET VERTICAL ANALYSIS

Vertical analysis of a Balance Sheet relates each account to total assets or to total liabilities and stockholders' equity, with each account being expressed as a percentage of one of these larger categories. For example, cash would be expressed as a percentage of total assets, and accounts payable as a percentage of total liabilities and stockholders' equity. Exhibit 14–6 is a vertical analysis of the 1980 and 1981 Balance Sheets of Marvel Company.

As you can see, there has been only a small increase in the percentage of current assets in relation to total assets, with a corresponding decrease in property, plant, and equipment and other assets. Thus, this vertical analysis does not reveal any significant shifts in the turnover of assets between the two years.

BALANCE SHEET HORIZONTAL ANALYSIS

Horizontal analysis of two or more Balance Sheets indicates the dollar and percentage changes from year to year for individual accounts. Exhibit 14–7 on page 468 is a horizontal analysis of Marvel Company's 1980 and 1981 Balance Sheets.

The four accounts that had the most significant dollar changes were Inventory; Property, Plant, and Equipment; Other Noncurrent Assets; and Stockholders' Equity. Major percentage changes also occurred in Balance Sheet items that were small in size, such as Cash and Current Installments of Long-Term Debt.

EXHIBIT 14-6   Marvel Company

Vertical Analysis of the Balance Sheets as of December 31, 1981 and 1980

Assets	1981		1980	
Current Assets:				
Cash...............................	$ 16,982	2.1%	$ 9,020	1.1%
Short-Term Securities	37,683	4.6	39,712	5.0
Accounts and Notes Receivable (Net)	127,544	15.5	121,614	15.4
Inventory	195,512	23.8	173,999	22.1
Other Current Assets.............................	9,499	1.2	7,634	1.0
Total Current Assets	$387,220	47.1%*	$351,979	44.7%*
Property, Plant, and Equipment (Net)	406,599	49.4	395,098	50.1
Other Noncurrent Assets	28,571	3.5	40,801	5.2
Total Assets.................................	$822,390	100.0%	$787,878	100.0%
Liabilities and Stockholders' Equity				
Current Liabilities:				
Notes Payable—Bank	$ 24,658	3.0%	$ 22,576	2.9%
Current Installments of Long-Term Debt..............	1,919	.2	3,320	.4
Accounts Payable and Notes Payable	78,967	9.6	69,475	8.8
Income Taxes Payable	15,090	1.8	14,656	1.9
Total Current Liabilities.........................	$120,634	14.7%*	$110,027	14.0%
Long-Term Debt	155,881	19.0	148,400	18.8
Deferred Income Taxes	31,361	3.8	29,210	3.7
Stockholders' Equity	514,514	62.6	500,241	63.5
Total Liabilities and Stockholders' Equity...........	$822,390	100.0%*	$787,878	100.0%

* Percentages may not add to totals due to rounding.

With horizontal analysis, it is important to recognize that a large percentage change in an item with a small absolute dollar amount (such as Current Installments of Long-Term Debt) is probably not a very significant change, not only because the dollar amount is small, but also because management may not have any immediate control over the item.

BALANCE SHEET RATIO ANALYSIS

A number of ratios indicate how efficiently individual assets were utilized during a period. These ratios are discussed separately and then related to asset turnover.

Current Ratio

Working capital is the excess of total current assets over total current liabilities. The amount of the excess is a measure of liquidity and represents a margin of safety for meeting current liabilities. The relative margin of

EXHIBIT 14–7 **Marvel Company**
Horizontal Analysis of the Balance Sheets as of December 31, 1981 and 1980

Assets	1981	1980	Dollar Change	Percentage Change
Current Assets:				
Cash..	$ 16,982	$ 9,020	$ 7,962	88.3
Short-Term Securities	37,683	39,712	(2,029)	(5.1)
Accounts and Notes Receivable (Net)	127,544	121,614	5,930	4.9
Inventory	195,512	173,999	21,513	12.4
Other Current Assets.............................	9,499	7,634	1,865	24.4
Total Current Assets	$387,220	$351,979	$35,241	10.0
Property, Plant, and Equipment (Net)	406,599	395,098	11,501	2.9
Other Noncurrent Assets	28,571	40,801	(12,230)	(30.0)
Total Assets..................................	$822,390	$787,878	$34,512	4.4
Liabilities and Stockholders' Equity				
Current Liabilities:				
Payable to Banks	$ 24,658	$ 22,576	$ 2,082	9.2
Current Installments of Long-Term Debt..............	1,919	3,320	(1,401)	(42.2)
Accounts Payable and Notes Payable	78,967	69,475	9,492	13.7
Income Taxes Payable	15,090	14,656	434	3.0
Total Current Liabilities........................	$120,634	$110,027	$10,607	9.6
Long-Term Debt	155,881	148,400	7,481	5.0
Deferred Income Taxes	31,361	29,210	2,151	7.4
Stockholders' Equity	514,514	500,241	14,273	2.9
Total Liabilities and Stockholders' Equity...........	$822,390	$787,878	$34,512	4.4

current (working capital) ratio
a measure of liquidity that represents a margin of safety for meeting current liabilities; computed by dividing current assets by current liabilities

safety is usually expressed as a ratio of current assets to current liabilities, which is called the current ratio, or the working capital ratio.

The working capital totals and current ratios for Marvel Company for 1980 and 1981 are

	1981	1980
Current Assets.............................	$387,220	$351,979
Current Liabilities	120,634	110,027
Working Capital	$266,586	$241,952
Current (Working Capital) Ratio...............	$\frac{\$387,220}{\$120,634} = 3.21$	$\frac{\$351,979}{\$110,027} = 3.20$

Working capital increased by $24,634 ($266,586 − $241,952) from 1980 to 1981, which represents a 0.01 change in the current ratio. At the end of

1981, the firm had $3.21 of current assets for every $1.00 of current liabilities. A particular current ratio is considered high or low depending on the nature of the business and the industry involved. Many financial statement readers use two to one as an acceptable ratio of current assets to current liabilities. However, companies have different liquidity needs, which means that a two-to-one ratio may not be good for every type of business. Rule-of-thumb guidelines for any ratio are arbitrary and cannot be appropriate for all companies in all industries. The important thing is for the current ratio to be at the right level to meet the particular company's needs. If the ratio is too low, the company may not be sufficiently liquid to pay current liabilities or to take advantage of discounts for prompt payment. If it is too high, the company probably has too many assets tied up in working capital for its current level of activity and the excess assets are not earning an appropriate return.

Acid-Test Ratio

acid-test (quick) ratio   *a more precise measure of a firm's ability to meet current liabilities: computed by dividing net quick assets (all current assets, except inventories and prepaid expenses) by current liabilities*

The acid-test ratio (sometimes called the quick ratio) is calculated because the current ratio does not reflect the fact that a large portion of current assets may not be very liquid and therefore not readily available for paying current liabilities. Inventory and prepaid expenses are examples of such current assets.

The acid-test ratio is computed by dividing cash, marketable securities, and notes and accounts receivable by current liabilities. To illustrate, the acid-test ratios for Marvel Company for 1980 and 1981 are

	1981	**1980**
$\dfrac{\text{cash, short-term securities,}\\ \text{notes and accounts receivable}}{\text{current liabilities}}$	$\dfrac{\$182,209}{\$120,634} = 1.51$	$\dfrac{\$170,346}{\$110,027} = 1.55$

These figures show a slight drop in the acid-test ratio. For both years, liquid current assets are approximately one and one-half times as large as current liabilities.

Accounts Receivable Turnover

accounts receivable turnover   *a measure of a company's average collection period for receivables; computed by dividing net sales (or net credit sales) by average accounts receivable*

number of days sales in receivables   *a measure of the average number of days it takes to collect a credit sale; computed by dividing 365 days by the accounts receivable turnover*

Accounts receivable turnover reflects a company's collection record. A trend toward a lower turnover could indicate a laxness in collection activity or a change in credit policy.

This ratio is computed by dividing net credit sales by average accounts receivable for a period. If net credit sales cannot be determined easily from the financial statements, then total sales are used as a substitute.

Accounts receivable turnover is often more useful if dollar amounts are converted into the number of days of uncollected sales, which reflects the average time taken to collect a credit sale. The easiest way to compute the number of days sales in receivables is to divide the number of days in the period by the accounts receivable turnover.

To illustrate the calculation of accounts receivable turnover and the number of days sales in receivables, we will use the following data for Marvel Company.

	1981	1980
Net Credit Sales	$1,086,944	$988,417
Accounts Receivable (net):		
January 1	$ 121,614	$106,675
December 31	127,544	121,614
Total	$ 249,158	$228,289
Average ($\div$ 2)	$ 124,579	$114,145

$$\text{Accounts receivable turnover} = \frac{\text{net credit sales}}{\text{average accounts receivable}}$$

1980 $\dfrac{\$988,417}{\$114,145} = 8.66$

1981 $\dfrac{\$1,086,944}{\$124,579} = 8.72$

$$\text{Number of days sales in receivables} = \frac{\text{number of days in a period}}{\text{accounts receivable turnover}}$$

1980 $\dfrac{365^*}{8.66} = 42.1 \text{ days}$

1981 $\dfrac{365}{8.72} = 41.9 \text{ days}$

Marvel Company increased its accounts receivable turnover from 8.66 times to 8.72 times between 1980 and 1981. This very small improvement in turnover reduced the number of days sales in receivables from 42.1 to 41.9. An improvement in accounts receivable turnover and in the collection period means that less money is tied up in receivables, which, in turn, contributes to a higher asset turnover ratio. And as we have seen, Marvel's asset turnover increased from 1.29 times in 1980 to 1.35 times in 1981, showing more efficient utilization of assets.

Inventory Turnover

inventory turnover   *a measure of the efficiency with which inventory is managed; computed by dividing cost of goods sold by average inventory for a period*

Another influence on the asset turnover ratio is inventory turnover. This ratio, which is computed by dividing cost of goods sold for a period by the average inventory for the period, is useful in indicating whether a company

---

* In this chapter we assume 365 days in a year.

is managing its inventory efficiently. If the turnover is low, it means that the company is either overstocking or building up a stock of obsolete merchandise. Whichever the case, too high an inventory reflects excess resources tied up in working capital that are not earning a return for the company. If the turnover is too high, the company may lose sales because the goods are not in inventory when customers want them.

Inventory turnover is often more meaningful if dollar amounts are converted into <u>number of days sales in inventory</u>. This ratio indicates the average time it takes to dispose of inventory. It is computed by dividing the number of days in a period by the inventory turnover.

To illustrate the calculation of inventory turnover and the number of days of sales in inventory, we will use the following data from Marvel Company.

number of days sales in inventory   *an alternative measure of how well inventory is being managed; computed by dividing 365 days by the inventory turnover ratio*

	1981	1980
Cost of Goods Sold	$786,523	$700,263
Inventories:		
January 1	$173,999	$167,286
December 31	195,512	173,999
Total	$369,511	$341,285
Average Inventory ($\div 2$)	$184,756	$170,643

$$\text{Inventory turnover} = \frac{\text{cost of goods sold}}{\text{average inventory}}$$

$$1980 \quad \frac{\$700,263}{\$170,643} = 4.10$$

$$1981 \quad \frac{\$786,523}{\$184,756} = 4.26$$

$$\text{Number of days sales in inventory} = \frac{\text{number of days in a period}}{\text{inventory turnover}}$$

$$1980 \quad \frac{365}{4.10} = 89.0 \text{ days}$$

$$1981 \quad \frac{365}{4.26} = 85.7 \text{ days}$$

Marvel Company increased its inventory turnover from 4.10 in 1980 to 4.26 in 1981. This had the effect of reducing the number of days sales in inventory from 89.0 in 1980 to 85.7 in 1981. The improvement in inventory turnover, like the improvement in accounts receivable turnover, contributed to the improvement in Marvel's asset turnover ratio from 1980 to 1981.

Working Capital Turnover

A more general ratio, which includes both accounts receivable turnover and inventory turnover, is working capital turnover. It is computed by dividing net sales by average working capital for a period, and it indicates the amount of working capital used in sustaining the sales of that period.

Like the other ratios we have discussed, this ratio may be more useful if dollar amounts are converted to days sales invested in working capital. A decrease in number of days sales invested in working capital would suggest an improvement in the utilization of current assets, which, in turn, would contribute to an improvement in the key ratio, the asset turnover ratio.

To illustrate the method of calculating working capital turnover and the number of days sales invested in working capital, we will use the following data for Marvel Company.

working capital turnover *a measure of the amount of working capital used in sustaining the sales of a period; computed by dividing net sales by average working capital*

days sales invested in working capital *an alternative measure of the amount of working capital used in sustaining the sales of a period; computed by dividing 365 days by the working capital turnover*

	1981	1980
Net Sales	$1,086,944	$988,417
Working Capital:		
January 1	$ 241,952	$217,848
December 31	266,586	241,952
Total	$ 508,538	$459,800
Average ($\div 2$)	$ 254,269	$229,900

$$\text{Working capital turnover} = \frac{\text{net sales}}{\text{average working capital}}$$

1980 $\dfrac{\$988,417}{\$229,900} = 4.30$

1981 $\dfrac{\$1,086,944}{\$254,269} = 4.27$

$$\text{Days sales invested in working capital} = \frac{\text{number of days in a period}}{\text{working capital turnover}}$$

1980 $\dfrac{365}{4.30} = 84.9 \text{ days}$

1981 $\dfrac{365}{4.27} = 85.5 \text{ days}$

The working capital turnover for Marvel Company decreased very slightly from 1980 to 1981. This suggests that the small improvements in the accounts receivable and inventory turnovers were offset by larger investments in other current assets in relation to current liabilities. Marvel's overall improvement in asset turnover must therefore have been generated by an improvement in the turnover of property, plant, and equipment.

Property, Plant, and Equipment Turnover

The property, plant, and equipment turnover is computed by dividing net sales by property, plant, and equipment.[1] This ratio indicates how efficiently these assets are being utilized in generating sales volume.

To illustrate, we will calculate Marvel's property, plant, and equipment turnover for 1980 and 1981.

$$1980 \quad \frac{\$988{,}417}{\$395{,}098^1} = 2.50$$

$$1981 \quad \frac{\$1{,}086{,}944}{\$406{,}599^1} = 2.67$$

The increase in property, plant, and equipment turnover from 2.50 times in 1980 to 2.67 times in 1981 was a primary contributor to the increase in the asset turnover ratio from 1.29 times in 1980 to 1.35 times in 1981.

TO SUMMARIZE   The asset turnover ratio is an important overall indicator of a company's efficiency in utilizing its assets. A number of ratios represent components of the asset turnover ratio: the current ratio, the acid-test ratio, accounts receivable turnover, inventory turnover, working capital turnover, and property, plant, and equipment turnover. Proper interpretation of these ratios not only helps managers determine how to improve asset turnover, but also enables investors and creditors to assess the profitability and liquidity of a company.

Analysis of Debt–Equity Management

The third key ratio, debt–equity management, indicates the extent to which debt and equity are used in financing a company's operations. It is computed by dividing average total assets by average stockholders' equity. The excess of average total assets over average stockholders' equity represents the average amount of debt outstanding during the year (A − SE = L).

The debt–equity management relationship is used in determining the margin of safety for creditors by identifying the extent to which a company is leveraging, or trading on, equity. Leveraging, as you recall, refers to the use of stockholders' equity as a base for borrowing money. If a company can use borrowed funds to earn more than the funds cost, the excess return accrues to the stockholders. Thus, leveraging benefits both the company, by increasing its assets, and stockholders, by increasing earnings.

The amount of leveraging a company can employ is limited, however. Banks and other lending institutions will expect a company, especially a young company without much of a borrowing history, to have a satisfactory equity-to-debt ratio in order to be eligible for a loan. Also, interest on borrowed funds has to be paid before any dividends may be paid to stockholders. If net income before the interest deduction is not large enough to cover the interest charge, then the stockholders will be deprived of dividends.

[1] The ending amounts of property, plant, and equipment were used to calculate this ratio. An average amount for the year is preferable unless there has been little change in the account during the year.

A prudent management tries to keep the amount of borrowed funds at such a level that the interest charges will be considerably less than net income before the interest deduction. The more stable a company's earnings, the greater the confidence with which management can determine the level of borrowed funds it can maintain without taking undue risks. A public utility, for example, can maintain a relatively large amount of debt because, as a quasi-monopoly, its earnings are relatively stable. An automobile manufacturing company, on the other hand, has large fluctuations in its earnings and so has to keep its debt small in relation to stockholders' equity. Otherwise, in a bad year the fixed interest charges may exceed earnings and cause a liquidity problem.

While the ratio of average total assets to average stockholders' equity is the key measure of debt–equity management used in this chapter, analysts also use other ratios to complement and supplement this one. Some of these ratios are

1. Long-term debt to total assets $= \dfrac{\text{long-term debt}}{\text{total assets}}$

This ratio provides an indication of how much loss a corporation can suffer without any loss to creditors.

2. Times interest earned $= \dfrac{\text{income before interest and income taxes}}{\text{interest charges}}$

This ratio indicates the company's margin above the fixed interest charges to be paid to creditors.

3. Long-term debt to stockholders' equity $= \dfrac{\text{long-term debt}}{\text{stockholders' equity}}$

This ratio indicates the amount of funds supplied to a company by creditors as opposed to stockholders plus accumulated earnings. Industry experience would dictate the maximum percentage of debt that would be reasonable.

These debt–equity management ratios are primarily measures of a firm's long-term solvency. Thus, they indicate the degree of protection available to mortgage lenders and bondholders, as well as the risk to common stockholders whose return becomes less certain as the proportion of debt increases.

To illustrate the calculations for these debt–equity management ratios, we will use data from Marvel's 1980 and 1981 financial statements.

	1981	1980
1. Long-term debt to total assets	$\dfrac{\$155,881}{\$822,390} = 18.95\%$	$\dfrac{\$148,400}{\$787,878} = 18.84\%$
2. Times interest earned	$\dfrac{\$110,331}{\$14,995} = 7.36$ times	$\dfrac{\$115,493}{\$13,046} = 8.85$ times
3. Long-term debt to stockholders' equity	$\dfrac{\$155,881}{\$514,514} = 30.30\%$	$\dfrac{\$148,400}{\$500,241} = 29.67\%$

As we have shown on page 462, Marvel's ratio of average total assets to average stockholders' equity decreased from 1.60 times in 1980 to 1.59 times in 1981. This decrease, although slight, reflects a shift toward a greater use of leveraging and is confirmed by the trend in the debt–equity management ratios computed above. Note that the percentage of debt in Marvel Company's financial structure is not large. The margin of safety of earnings is comfortable (7.36 times) and will cover any fixed interest charges in 1981, despite the fact that 1981 was not a good earnings year. Finally, note that the relationship of long-term debt to stockholders' equity is relatively unchanged.

TO SUMMARIZE   The various debt–equity management ratios are generally consistent with each other and provide a picture of the amount of debt in relation to total assets and stockholders' equity, and the extent of fixed interest charges relative to the earnings available to cover those charges.

Return on Assets and Stockholders' Equity

overall performance ratio   *a measure of overall performance, including management of operations, use of assets, and management of debt and equity; computed by dividing net income by average stockholders' equity*

Each of the three key ratios—operating performance, asset turnover, and debt–equity management—gives an analyst important information about a company. However, as explained earlier, only when the ratios are brought together is a view of a company's overall performance provided. Thus, if the ratios for operating performance and asset turnover are chained together, the analyst can determine return on total assets (investment by creditors and stockholders). And if all of the key ratios are chained together, return on stockholders' equity can be computed.

RETURN ON TOTAL ASSETS

return on total assets ratio   *a measure of operating performance and efficiency in utilizing assets; computed in its simplest form by dividing net income by average total assets*

The return on total assets ratio may be computed directly by dividing net income by average total assets. It may also be computed by chaining together the operating performance and asset turnover ratios.

Operating Performance	× Asset Turnover	= Return on Total Assets
$\dfrac{\text{net income}}{\text{net sales}}$	$\times \dfrac{\text{net sales}}{\text{average total assets}}$	$= \dfrac{\text{net income}}{\text{average total assets}}$

To illustrate, we will calculate return on total assets for Marvel Company for 1980 and 1981.

1980 $\dfrac{\$64,650}{\$988,417} \times \dfrac{\$988,417}{\$764,306} = \dfrac{\$64,650}{\$764,306}$

6.54% × 1.29 times = 8.46%

1981 $\dfrac{\$40,375}{\$1,086,944} \times \dfrac{\$1,086,944}{\$805,134} = \dfrac{\$40,375}{\$805,134}$

3.71% × 1.35 times = 5.01%

In computing return on total assets by chaining the operating performance and asset turnover ratios, an analyst is reminded that the total return is a function of both efficient expense control and efficient utilization of assets. To judge how satisfactory a return is, the analyst must compare it with the industry average and with the average cost of capital to the company. Return on assets is thus a measure of a company's overall performance in meeting its responsibilities to its creditors and owners.

RETURN ON STOCKHOLDERS' EQUITY

return on stockholders' equity
a measure of performance from a stockholder's viewpoint

Return on stockholders' equity is computed by chaining together the three key ratios: operating performance, asset turnover, and debt–equity management. To illustrate, we again present the calculation for Marvel Company in 1980 and 1981. You will see that return on stockholders' equity is the same ratio that we called overall performance at the start of this discussion.

Operating Performance		Asset Turnover		Debt–Equity Management		Return on Stockholders' Equity
$\dfrac{\text{net income}}{\text{net sales}}$	×	$\dfrac{\text{net sales}}{\text{average total assets}}$	×	$\dfrac{\text{average total assets}}{\text{average stockholders' equity}}$	=	$\dfrac{\text{net income}}{\text{average stockholders' equity}}$
1980:						
$\dfrac{\$64,650}{\$988,417}$	×	$\dfrac{\$988,417}{\$764,306}$	×	$\dfrac{\$764,306}{\$477,210}$	=	$\dfrac{\$64,650}{\$477,210}$
6.54%	×	1.29 times	×	1.60 times	=	13.55%*
1981:						
$\dfrac{\$40,375}{\$1,086,944}$	×	$\dfrac{\$1,086,944}{\$805,134}$	×	$\dfrac{\$805,134}{\$507,378}$	=	$\dfrac{\$40,375}{\$507,378}$
3.71%	×	1.35 times	×	1.59 times	=	7.96%

* Percentages and factors may not multiply to product due to rounding.

Marvel's return on equity was lower in 1981 than in 1980, primarily because 1981 net income was only 3.71 percent of net sales, as compared with 6.54 percent in 1980.

Chaining the three key ratios is only one way of measuring the return to stockholders. Several others are useful. In this section, we will discuss the four most commonly used methods: earnings per share, price–earnings ratio, dividend payout ratio, and book value per share.

Earnings per Share

earnings per share   *the amount of net income (earnings) related to each share of stock; computed by dividing net income by the weighted-average number of shares of stock outstanding during the period*

Earnings per share is used to measure earnings growth and earnings potential. If a company has a simple capital structure, with only common stock outstanding, earnings per share is computed by dividing net income by the weighted-average number of shares of common stock outstanding during the year. If the capital structure includes both preferred and common stock, the preferred dividend requirement must be subtracted from net income before computing earnings per share.

For example, if total net income for the year is $130,000, and preferred stock is entitled to a current-dividend preference of $20,000, then earnings per share for common stock (assuming a weighted average of 26,000 common shares outstanding for the entire year) would be computed by dividing $110,000 of net income ($130,000 − $20,000) by 26,000 common shares to obtain earnings per common share of $4.23. The remainder of this section is based on the assumption that the number of shares of common stock outstanding at the beginning of the year is the same as the number of shares outstanding at the end of the year—that is, no shares were issued or reacquired during the year.

To illustrate the computation for earnings per share, we will assume that Marvel Company's capital structure consists entirely of 26,000 shares of common stock. Earnings per share for 1980 and 1981 would be computed as follows:

$$1980 \quad \text{EPS—Net income from operations} = \frac{\$52,250}{26,000 \text{ shares}} = \$2.01$$

$$\text{EPS—Extraordinary gain} = \frac{\$12,400}{26,000 \text{ shares}} = \$ .48$$

$$\text{EPS—Net income} = \frac{\$64,650}{26,000 \text{ shares}} = \$2.49$$

$$1981 \quad \text{EPS—Net income} = \frac{\$40,375}{26,000 \text{ shares}} = \$1.55$$

Note that only one EPS number is needed for 1981 because there was no extraordinary gain. Earnings per share would be presented on the Income Statement in the following manner.

	1981	1980
Earnings per Share of Common Stock:		
Income Before Extraordinary Gain	$1.55	$2.01
Extraordinary Gain	0	0.48
Net Income	$1.55	$2.49

Price–Earnings Ratio

Financial analysts use the price–earnings (P/E) ratio in judging the potential value of a company's stock in relation to that of other companies. This is because the P/E ratios of a company over a period of years indicate the trend and the stability of its earnings, and are therefore assumed to reflect the capabilities of management and the growth potential of the company.

The ratio is computed by dividing the market price of a stock by its earnings per share. To illustrate, we will use the figures just calculated for Marvel Company. If the price of the stock was $18\frac{3}{8}$ ($18.375) when earnings were $1.55 per share, the stock would have a price–earnings ratio of 11.9.

$$\frac{\$18.38}{\$1.55} = 11.9$$

A P/E ratio of 11.9 means that the stock is selling for 11.9 times annual earnings. Since the price–earnings ratio for all stocks selling on the New York Stock Exchange has averaged about 8 times earnings in recent years, Marvel's P/E ratio is above average.

Dividend Payout Ratio

dividend payout ratio a measure of earnings paid out in dividends; computed by dividing cash dividends by net income available to each class of stock

The dividend payout ratio indicates the percentage of earnings distributed to stockholders. It is computed by dividing cash dividends by the net income available to each class of stock.

To illustrate, we will assume that Marvel Company had the following dividend payout ratios on its common stock in 1980 and 1981.

	1981	1980
cash dividends / net income available to common stockholders	$\frac{\$25,746}{\$40,375} = 64\%$	$\frac{\$23,452}{\$64,650} = 36\%$

The numerators suggest that the company has a policy of paying a stable dividend. It appears that the amount of the dividend for 1980 was determined without taking into consideration the extraordinary gain. Therefore, the payout ratio based on earnings after the extraordinary gain was relatively low. In 1981 it appears that the board of directors, in keeping with a stable dividend policy, decided not to reduce dividends, despite a poor earnings performance. This resulted in an abnormally large payout ratio.

If an investor is interested in buying stocks that will provide a significant annual cash return, the dividend payout ratio is an important piece of information. A "growth company" usually reinvests a large percentage of its earnings and pays little or no dividends. A more stable, mature company, such as a public utility, is likely to pay out a high percentage of its earnings in dividends.

Book Value per Share

Book value is a measure of a company's net worth. It usually will not reflect the fair market values of assets and liabilities since Balance Sheets generally report only historical costs. Therefore, the book value concept must be used with care in assessing a firm's financial condition.

book value per share a measure of net worth; computed by dividing stockholders' equity for each class of stock by the weighted-average number of outstanding shares for that class

Book value per share is computed by dividing stockholders' equity by the weighted-average number of shares outstanding. If the capital structure contains both preferred and common stock, a portion of stockholders' equity must be assigned to preferred stock before the balance can be used in computing book value per share of common stock.

To illustrate the calculation of book value per share, we will now assume that Marvel Company's financial structure contains both preferred and common stock.

Marvel Company
Stockholders' Equity as of December 31, 1981

Preferred Stock (161 shares issued).................	$ 16,100
Common Stock (26,000 shares issued)	26,000
Paid-in Capital in Excess of Par—Common Stock.....	47,067
Retained Earnings.................................	433,758
Total	$523,809

Less Treasury Stock at Cost:

Preferred Stock (43 shares reacquired)	$3,986	
Common Stock (193 shares reacquired)	5,309	
Total Treasury Stock at Cost		9,295
Total Stockholders' Equity		$514,514

In computing book value, an analyst assigns to preferred stockholders the portion of stockholders' equity that represents the redemption value of the outstanding preferred shares, including any dividends in arrears. Assuming that there are no dividends in arrears on Marvel's preferred stock and that its redemption value is $102.75 per share, the book value for preferred and common shares would be computed as follows:

Total Stockholders' Equity.........................		$514,514
Less Portion of Equity Assigned to Preferred Stock:		
Outstanding Shares	118*	
Redemption Value	$102.75	12,125
Stockholders' Equity Applicable to Common Stock		$502,389

Book Value per Share:

$$\text{Preferred Stock} \quad \frac{\$12,125}{118} = \$102.75 \qquad \text{Common Stock} \quad \frac{\$502,389}{25,807^{\dagger}} = \$19.47$$

* 161 shares of preferred stock issued, less 43 shares in treasury.
† Common stock issued, less 193 shares in treasury.

Care must be taken in assigning the appropriate portion of stockholders' equity to preferred stock. The amount assigned is not identical to the equity accounts that have the word "preferred" in their titles. Rather, preferred stock is assigned that portion of stockholders' equity based on the claims of preferred shareholders in liquidation, including any paid-in capital in excess of par and dividends in arrears on cumulative preferred stock. Thus, the stockholders' equity clearly assignable to preferred stock should be used to compute the book value per share of preferred stock. The rest should be assigned to common stock for the purpose of computing book value per share.

Note that although book value per share may provide some useful information about a company's future, the other measures of overall performance—namely, return on stockholders' equity, earnings per share, dividend payout ratio, and price–earnings ratio—are better indicators of a company's expected performance.

Summary of Analysis of Financial Statements

Exhibit 14-8 summarizes the discussion of financial statement analysis by showing the relationships of various subsidiary ratios to the four key ratios: operating performance, asset turnover, debt–equity management, and overall performance. Because other factors must be considered in analyzing a company, you should be careful not to read too much into the numbers generated.

EXAMPLE 14-8   Summary of Financial Statement Analysis

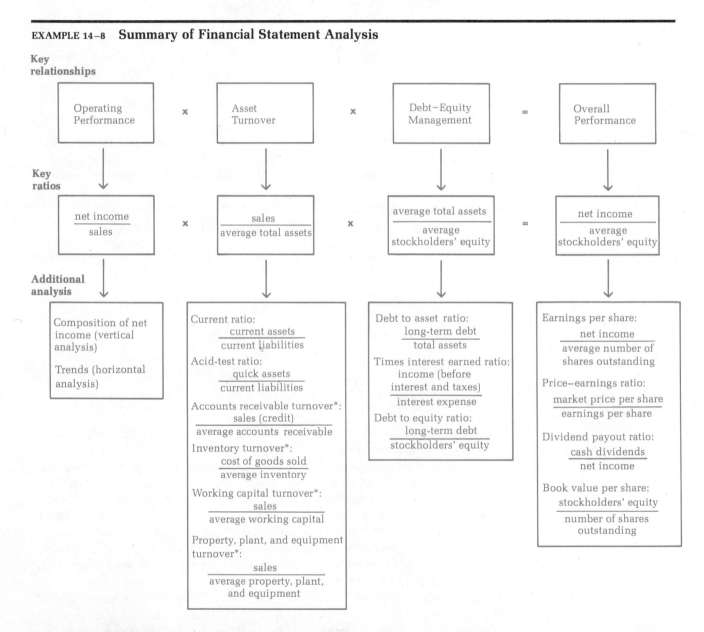

*Can be converted to number of days by dividing number of days in a period by turnover rate.

Limitations of Financial Statement Analysis

Financial statement analysis serves an important function, but it must be used with care. Many people accept numbers computed by an expert without much question. Although ratios may be computed precisely, they are no better than the data on which they are based. Two areas of concern in computing ratios are (1) the use of estimates and judgments in measuring assets, liabilities, and income; and (2) the fact that changing values and price levels are not reflected in the financial statements.

USE OF ESTIMATES

Estimates and judgments are used in allocating costs among periods, such as in measuring depreciation, bad debts, warranty expenses, and prepaid expenses. The allocation judgments made by those who prepare the financial statements may result in different ratios. And, since ratios are only meaningful when compared with similar ratios, care must be taken that the relevant ratios have been computed in the same way, or at least can be translated into common terms. Many analysts attempt to recast statements in order to provide comparable data for financial statement analysis.

CHANGES IN VALUES AND PRICE LEVELS

Financial statements are based on transactions recorded at cost when they were executed. Over time, gains and losses occur as the result of changes in values and changes in the purchasing power of the dollar. However, because no transactions have occurred, these changes in value and price level are not incorporated on a current basis into the primary financial statements and therefore may not be included in the analysis. The fact that unrealized gains and losses are not reflected is one reason that book value figures should be considered with care and in conjunction with other measurements.

RATIOS AS A BASIS FOR COMPARISON

Even if an analyst is able to overcome the measurement problems caused by estimates and value changes, there are pitfalls in the use of ratios. A ratio by itself is neither good nor bad. Before its value can be judged, it must be compared with ratios of other years, other companies, or with a predeter-mined standard. Comparisons with rule-of-thumb guidelines are usually not desirable. Furthermore, ratios may not provide a precise picture of the company's financial situation. More specific analysis may be required.

Financial statement analysis is an important tool in learning about the operations of a firm, but the process of analysis should be performed, and the results evaluated, with its limitations always in mind.

CHAPTER REVIEW

Financial statement analysis provides information about a company's performance that is not readily apparent from a quick reading of the statements themselves. Although the statements are historical in nature, they are often useful in predicting future performance. Investors use financial statement analysis in judging the degree of profitability, liquidity, or solvency of a firm. Management uses it in identifying problems and measuring performance related to operations, asset utilization, and debt–equity management. Regulators use financial statement analysis in assessing operating results and financial status as they relate to taxing income, measuring concentrations of economic power, and so forth.

Four techniques are commonly used in financial statement analysis: vertical analysis, horizontal analysis, common-size statements, and ratio analyses. At the base of these techniques are four key ratios:

Operating Performance		Asset Turnover		Debt–Equity Management		Overall Performance
$\dfrac{\text{net income}}{\text{net sales}}$	$\times$	$\dfrac{\text{net sales}}{\text{average total assets}}$	$\times$	$\dfrac{\text{average total assets}}{\text{average stockholders' equity}}$	$=$	$\dfrac{\text{net income}}{\text{average stockholders' equity}}$

The ratios that measure operating performance, asset turnover, and debt–equity management can be chained together to compute the return on stockholders' equity (which defines overall performance). Use of this approach helps the analyst understand how much each aspect of a company's activity contributed to the overall result.

These basic ratios can be supplemented by vertical and horizontal analyses and the computation of additional ratios. Vertical and horizontal analyses can be applied both to the Income Statement (in measuring operating performance) and to the Balance Sheet (in measuring asset turnover). The additional ratios for measuring asset turnover are the current (working capital) ratio, acid-test (quick) ratio, accounts receivable turnover, inventory turnover, working capital turnover, and property, plant, and equipment turnover. The additional ratios for measuring debt–equity management are the ratio of long-term debt to total assets, times interest earned, and the ratio of long-term debt to stockholders' equity. The additional ratios for measuring overall performance include the return on total assets, earnings per share, price–earnings ratio, dividend payout ratio, and book value per share.

Management and outsiders should recognize that information generated through the use of financial statement analysis has limitations because the underlying data are based on historical costs, estimates and judgments are used in allocating costs, accounting methods are not always comparable, and value and price-level changes may result in unrealized gains and losses which are not reflected in the financial statements.

KEY TERMS AND CONCEPTS

accounts receivable
turnover (469)

acid-test (quick) ratio
(469)

asset turnover ratio
(465)

book value per share
(478)

common-size
statement (464)

current (working
capital) ratio (468)

days sales invested
in working capital
(472)

debt–equity
management ratio
(473)

dividend payout ratio
(478)

earnings per share (476)

horizontal analysis
(463)

inventory turnover
(470)

liquidity (457)

number of days sales in
inventory (471)

number of days sales in
receivables (469)

operating performance
ratio (462)

overall performance
ratio (475)

price–earnings (P/E) ratio
(477)

profitability (457)

property, plant, and
equipment
turnover (473)

return on stock-
holders' equity (476)

return on total assets
ratio (475)

solvency (457)

vertical analysis (462)

working capital
turnover (472)

DISCUSSION QUESTIONS

1. Why is financial statement analysis a desirable approach to studying financial statements?

2. How can the historical data reported by financial statements be used to make decisions affecting the future?

3. Who are the principal users of financial statements?

4. What type of decisions do users make for which information from financial statements is useful?

5. Identify and describe four common techniques of analyzing financial statements.

6. Identify the ratios used to measure overall performance, operating performance, asset turnover, and debt–equity management.

7. What are the components of the asset turnover ratio and what does it measure?

8. Identify the components of the debt–equity management ratio. What does it measure?

9. What is the value of preparing a vertical analysis of an Income Statement?

10. What is the value of preparing a horizontal analysis of comparative Income Statements?

11. What types of financial statement analyses will help explain a trend in the asset turnover ratio?

12. Identify seven ratios that will help explain how efficiently assets were utilized during a given period.

13. Show how the current ratio is computed and explain its significance. What is considered to be an adequate current ratio?

14. Explain the different purposes of the current ratio and the acid-test ratio.

15. How is a firm's number of days sales in receivables computed and what is its significance?

16. How is the inventory turnover ratio computed and what is its significance?

17. Explain the concept underlying property, plant, and equipment turnover. In what way would you expect this ratio to differ among companies in different industries?

18. What ratios might help explain changes over time in debt–equity management?

19. What is meant by the term "leveraging" and what is its relationship to the management of debt?

20. Identify two alternative methods of measuring return on stockholders' equity and indicate the relative significance of each.

21. Before financial statements can be analyzed, what steps should be taken to obtain comparability between years and among companies?

22. What are the limitations of financial statement analysis and how can these limitations be dealt with?

EXERCISES

E14–1   Bad Debt Write-off

North Corporation wrote off a $100 uncollectable account receivable against the $1,200 credit balance in Allowance for Doubtful Accounts. How would this write-off affect its current ratio?

E14–2   Accounts Receivable and Inventory Turnover

Selected data for Delta Corporation are as follows:

Balance Sheet Data

	December 31	
	1982	1981
Accounts Receivable	$500,000	$470,000
Allowance for Doubtful Accounts...	25,000	20,000
Net Accounts Receivable	$475,000	$450,000
Inventories at Cost	$600,000	$550,000

Income Statement Data

Net Credit Sales	$2,500,000	$2,200,000
Net Cash Sales	500,000	400,000
Net Sales	$3,000,000	$2,600,000
Cost of Goods Sold...............	$2,000,000	$1,800,000
Selling and General Expenses......	300,000	270,000
Other Expenses..................	50,000	30,000
Total Operating Expenses	$2,350,000	$2,100,000

What is the accounts receivable turnover for 1982? What is the inventory turnover for 1982?

E14–3   Inventory Turnover

On January 1, 1982, Lake Company's beginning inventory was $400,000. During 1982 Lake purchased $1,900,000 of additional inventory. On December 31, 1982, Lake's ending inventory was $500,000. What is the inventory turnover for 1982?

E14-4   Number of Times Bond Interest Was Earned

The following data were abstracted from the financial records of Gore Corporation for 1982.

Net Sales	$3,600,000
Bond Interest Expense	120,000
Income Tax Expense.......................	600,000
Net Income...............................	800,000

How many times was bond interest earned in 1982?

E14–5   Effect of Transactions on Current Ratio

Company B has a current ratio of two to one. What will be the effect on the current ratio if the company:

1. Receives a 5 percent stock dividend on one of its marketable securities.

2. Pays a large account payable which had been a current liability.

3. Borrows cash on a six-month note.

4. Sells merchandise for more than cost and records the sale using the perpetual inventory method.

E14–6   Price–Earnings Ratio

Information concerning Barnett Company's common stock is as follows:

	Per Share
Book Value at December 31, 1982..............	$12.00
Quoted Market Value on Stock Exchange on December 31, 1982	9.00
Earnings per Share for 1982	3.00
Par Value..................................	2.00
Dividend Declared and Paid in 1982............	1.00

What was the price–earnings ratio on common stock for 1982?

E14-7   Accounts Receivable Turnover and Inventory Turnover

Assuming that a business year consists of 300 days, what was the number of business days sales in average receivables for 1982 and the number of business days sales in average inventories for 1982, respectively, based on the following information.

Net Accounts Receivable at December 31, 1981 ..	$ 900,000
Net Accounts Receivable at December 31, 1982 ..	$1,000,000
Accounts Receivable Turnover	5 times
Inventory at December 31, 1981	$1,100,000
Inventory at December 31, 1982	$1,200,000
Inventory Turnover........................	4 times

E14–8   Acid-Test (Quick) Ratio

Information from River Company's Balance Sheet for December 31, 1982, is as follows:

Current Assets:	
Cash	$ 3,000,000
Marketable Securities, at Cost Which Approximates Market Value..............	7,000,000
Accounts Receivable, Net of Allowance for Doubtful Accounts	100,000,000
Inventories, Lower of Cost or Market	130,000,000
Prepaid Expenses	2,000,000
Total Current Assets	$242,000,000

Current Liabilities:

Notes Payable	$ 4,000,000
Accounts Payable	40,000,000
Accrued Liabilities	30,000,000
Income Taxes Payable	1,000,000
Current Portion of Long-Term Debt	6,000,000
Total Current Liabilities	$ 81,000,000
Long-Term Debt........................	$180,000,000

What is the acid-test (quick) ratio?

E14–9   Dividends and the Current Ratio

Company A has a current ratio of 0.65 to 1.00. A cash dividend was declared last month but paid this month. What is the effect of this dividend payment on the current ratio and on working capital?

E14–10   Calculation of Key Ratios

Olympic Company's 1981 and 1982 financial statements are presented here in summary form.

Olympic Company
Income Statements for the Years Ended December 31, 1982 and 1981

	1982	1981
Net Sales	$260,000	$220,000
Cost of Goods Sold	182,000	165,000
Gross Margin	$ 78,000	$ 55,000
Selling and Administrative Expenses........................	52,000	38,000
Income Before Taxes	$26,000	$17,000
Income Tax Expense	12,000	8,000
Net Income	$14,000	$9,000

Olympic Company
Balance Sheets (condensed) as of December 31, 1982 and 1981

Assets	1982	1981
Current Assets	$30,000	$25,000
Property, Plant, and Equipment	40,000	28,000
Less Accumulated Depreciation	(6,000)	(4,000)
Other Assets	5,000	3,000
Total Assets....................	$69,000	$52,000

Liabilities and Stockholders' Equity	1982	1981
Current Liabilities	$18,000	$14,000
Long-Term Liabilities..............	5,000	0
Capital Stock	25,000	25,000
Retained Earnings	21,000	13,000
Total Liabilities and Stockholders' Equity	$69,000	$52,000

Compute the following ratios for 1982.

1. Net income to net sales.

2. Asset turnover ratio.

3. Average total assets to average stockholders' equity.

4. Net income to average stockholders' equity.

E14–11   Common-Size Statements

On the basis of the information presented for Olympic Company in E14–10, prepare comparative common-size Income Statements for 1981 and 1982.

E14–12   Current Ratio and Return on Total Assets

On the basis of the information presented for Olympic Company in E14–10, answer these questions.

1. How much was declared in dividends during 1982, in dollars and as a percentage of income?

2. What is the return on average total assets for 1982?

3. What was the current ratio in 1981 and in 1982?

E14–13   Asset Turnover Ratio and Inventory Turnover

The following information was taken from the 1981 and 1982 financial statements of Roberts Company.

	1982	1981
Net Sales	$288,000	$225,000
Cost of Goods Sold	172,000	141,000
Average Total Assets...............	180,000	150,000
Average Inventory	40,000	30,000
Average Accounts Receivable........	20,000	15,000
Average Net Working Capital	75,000	60,000

1. Compute the asset turnover ratios for 1981 and 1982.

2. Compute the inventory turnover and the number of days sales in inventory for 1981 and 1982.

E14–14   Accounts Receivable Turnover and Working Capital Turnover

On the basis of the information presented for Roberts Company in E14–13:

1. Compute accounts receivable turnover and the average number of days sales in receivables for 1981 and 1982.

2. Compute the working capital turnovers for 1981 and 1982.

3. What effect did the changes in inventory turnover, accounts receivable turnover, and working capital turnover from 1981 to 1982 have on the total asset turnover from 1981 to 1982?

E14–15   Debt–Equity Management Ratios

The following information was taken from the 1981 and 1982 financial statements of King Company:

	1982	1981
Average Total Assets...............	$300,000	$260,000
Average Stockholders' Equity........	200,000	180,000
Interest Expense....................	11,000	8,000
Net Income After Taxes.............	33,000	24,000
Tax Rate	40%	40%

1. Compute the key ratio of average total assets to average stockholders' equity for 1981 and 1982.

2. Compute the debt–equity management ratio.

3. Compute the number of times interest was earned in 1981 and 1982.

4. Did the company use more or less leverage in 1982 than in 1981?

PROBLEMS

P14–1   Common-Size Income Statement

Presented here are two companies' Income Statements for the year ended December 31, 1982.

	Pinehurst Company	Myrtle Company
Net Sales	$360,000	$500,000
Cost of Goods Sold:		
Beginning Inventory	$ 40,000	$ 80,000
Purchases (Net)	290,000	320,000
Goods Available for Sale	$330,000	$400,000
Ending Inventory.................	60,000	60,000
Cost of Goods Sold	$270,000	$340,000
Gross Margin	$ 90,000	$160,000
Operating Expenses:		
Depreciation.....................	$ 6,000	$ 15,000
Salaries and Wages...............	24,000	40,000
Other Expenses	12,000	30,000
Total Operating Expenses........	$ 42,000	$ 85,000
Income Before Taxes	$ 48,000	$75,000
Income Taxes	18,000	35,000
Net Income......................	$ 30,000	$ 40,000

Required:

1. Prepare common-size Income Statements for the two companies.

2. **Interpretive Question**   Comment on the significant differences between the two companies.

3. **Interpretive Question**   How would your comparison of the two companies be affected if you knew that Pinehurst Company used the FIFO method of inventory costing and Myrtle Company used the LIFO method?

P14–2   Preparing Income Statements from Common-Size Statements

Maddox Company
Common-Size Income Statements for the Years Ended December 31, 1981 and 1980

	1981	1980
Net Sales	100.0%	100.0%
Cost of Goods Sold................	62.5	63.0
Gross Margin	37.5%	37.0%
Selling and Administrative Expenses	23.4	22.2
Interest Expense..................	3.1	1.8
Total Expenses	26.5%	24.0%
Income Before Taxes...............	11.0%	13.0%
Income Taxes	5.5	6.5
Net Income from Operations	5.5%	6.5%

Assume that sales were $800,000 in 1981 and $675,000 in 1980.

Required:
Prepare Income Statements for the two years.

P14–3   Asset Turnover Ratios

Comparative Balance Sheets and Income Statements for Honda Company for the years 1981 and 1982 are as follows:

Honda Company
Balance Sheets as of December 31, 1982 and 1981

Assets	1982	1981
Current Assets:		
Cash	$ 20,000	$ 12,500
Marketable Securities	50,000	37,500
Accounts Receivable	175,000	150,000
Inventories	155,000	125,000
Total Current Assets	$ 400,000	$ 325,000
Investments	$ 150,000	$ 162,500
Property, Plant and Equipment	$1,000,000	$ 950,000
Less Accumulated Depreciation—		
Plant and Equipment	450,000	400,000
Total Property, Plant, and Equipment	$ 550,000	$ 550,000
Intangible Assets	$ 25,000	$ 12,500
Total Assets	$1,125,000	$1,050,000

Liabilities and Stockholders' Equity

	1982	1981
Current Liabilities:		
Accounts Payable	$ 62,500	$ 50,000
Notes Payable	125,000	100,000
Accrued Liabilities	100,000	75,000
Total Current Liabilities	$ 287,500	$ 225,000
Long-Term Debt:		
Bonds Payable	362,500	325,000
Total Liabilities	$ 650,000	$ 550,000
Stockholders' Equity:		
Common Stock (15,000 shares)	$ 75,000	$ 75,000
Additional Contributed Capital	275,000	275,000
Retained Earnings	125,000	150,000
Total Stockholders' Equity	$ 475,000	$ 500,000
Total Liabilities and Stockholders' Equity	$1,125,000	$1,050,000

Honda Company
Income Statements for the Years Ended December 31, 1982 and 1981

	1982	1981
Net Sales	$800,000	$675,000
Cost of Goods Sold	500,000	425,250
Gross Margin	$300,000	$249,750
Selling and Administrative Expenses	$187,200	$149,850
Interest Expense	24,800	12,488
Total Expenses	$212,000	$162,338
Income Before Taxes	$ 88,000	$ 87,412
Income Taxes	44,000	43,706
Net Income	$ 44,000	$ 43,706

Required:
Using the foregoing Balance Sheets and Income Statements, calculate the following ratios for 1982.
1. Current ratio.
2. Acid-test ratio.
3. Accounts receivable turnover.
4. Inventory turnover.
5. Working capital turnover.
6. Property, plant, and equipment turnover.

P14–4   Debt–Equity Management Ratios

Refer to the Balance Sheets and Income Statements in P14–3.
Required:
Calculate the following debt–equity management ratios for 1982.
1. Long-term debt to total assets.
2. Times interest earned.
3. Long-term debt to stockholders' equity.

P14–5   Overall Performance Ratios

Refer to the Balance Sheets and Income Statements in P14–3.
Required:
Calculate the following ratios for 1982.
1. Return on total assets.
2. Return on stockholders' equity.
3. Earnings per share.
4. Book value per share (common).

P14–6   Unifying Problem: Key Ratios and Supplementary Ratios

The Balance Sheets and Income Statements for 1981 and 1982 of Britt Auto Supply Company are given below.

Britt Auto Supply Company
Balance Sheets as of December 31, 1982 and 1981
(in thousands)

Assets	1982	1981
Current Assets:		
Cash	$ 275	$ 450
Accounts Receivable	638	330
Inventories	907	660
Prepaid Insurance	1,620	1,590
Total Current Assets	$3,440	$3,030
Plant and Equipment	$2,350	$2,250
Less Depreciation	910	780
Total Property, Plant, and Equipment	1,440	1,470
Total Assets	$4,880	$4,500

Liabilities and Stock-holders' Equity

Current Liabilities:

Accounts Payable	$ 666	$ 450
Notes Payable	460	450
Other Current Liabilities	210	210
Total Current Liabilities	$1,336	$1,110
Long-Term Debt	270	240
Total Liabilities	$1,606	$1,350
Common Stock	$1,140	$1,140
Retained Earnings	2,134	2,010
Total Stockholders' Equity	3,274	3,150
Total Liabilities and Stockholders' Equity	$4,880	$4,500

Notes: The company paid $50,000 in dividends in 1981 on 100,000 shares of common stock outstanding. The common stock price at December 31, 1981, was $20\frac{1}{4}$.

Britt Auto Supply Company
Income Statements for the Years Ended December 31, 1982 and 1981 (in thousands)

	1982	1981
Sales*	$8,746	$7,950
Cost of Goods Sold	7,258	6,600
Gross Margin	$1,488	$1,350
Expenses:		
Operating Expenses	$962	$735
Depreciation Expense	130	120
Interest Expense	48	45
Total Expenses	1,140	900
Income Before Taxes	$ 348	$ 450
Income Taxes (50%)	174	225
Net Income	$ 174	$ 225

* Assume that all sales were made on credit.

Required:

1. Calculate the key ratios for measuring operating performance, asset turnover, and debt–equity management for 1982.

2. Using the ratios computed in part 1, assess the overall performance of the company from a stockholder's point of view.

3. Compute the following additional ratios to further analyze asset turnover, debt–equity management, and overall performance of the company.
   (a) current ratio
   (b) quick ratio
   (c) accounts receivable turnover
   (d) number of days sales in receivables
   (e) inventory turnover
   (f) numbers of days sales in inventory
   (g) working capital turnover

   (h) property, plant, and equipment turnover
   (i) long-term debt to total assets
   (j) times interest earned
   (k) long-term debt to stockholders' equity
   (l) return on total assets
   (m) earnings per share
   (n) price–earnings ratio
   (o) dividend payout ratio
   (p) book value per share

P14–7   Vertical and Horizontal Analyses

Mr. Dills, manager of Milton's Pickle Company, is pleased to see a substantial increase in 1982 sales. However, he has asked you, as the company's financial analyst, to evaluate the effects of this increase in sales on company operations and earnings. Following are the company's Income Statements for 1981 and 1982.

Milton's Pickle Company
Income Statements for the Years Ended December 31, 1982 and 1981

	1982	1981
Net Sales	$110,000	$80,000
Expenses:		
Cost of Goods Sold	$ 60,000	$48,000
Selling Expenses	22,000	16,000
General and Administrative Expenses	10,000	8,000
Interest	2,000	2,000
Total Expenses	$ 94,000	$74,000
Income Before Taxes	$ 16,000	$ 6,000
Income Taxes (20%)	3,200	1,200
Net Income	$ 12,800	$ 4,800

Required:

1. Perform a vertical and a horizontal analysis of the company's Income Statement.

2. **Interpretive Question**   Note any significant changes that should be brought to Mr. Dills' attention.

P14–8   Horizontal Analysis

On January 1, 1981, Z. N. Miller, sales manager for Petro-Chemical Products Corporation, decided to discontinue the 1980 discount policy of 2/10, n/30. He believed that the company's cash flow and sales levels would not be affected by eliminating the discount. Selected data for 1980 and 1981 are as follows:

	1981	1980
Net Sales	$1,310,000	$1,250,000
Cash on Hand	475,000	625,000
Average Accounts Receivable for the Year	89,726	41,200

Required:

1. Perform a horizontal analysis as a starting point for analyzing the effects of Mr. Miller's decision.

2. **Interpretive Question**   Assume that all sales discounts in 1980 were taken by customers and that all sales were made on credit in both 1980 and 1981. What effect on accounts receivable can you see from discontinuing the discount policy? (Hint: What has happened to the turnover rate and the collection period?)

3. **Interpretive Question**   Using the same assumptions as in 2, what was the effect of Mr. Miller's decision on net sales?

P14–9   Selected Profitability Ratios

The following are selected financial data for Erkes Rental Company for 1981 and additional information about industry averages.

Financial Data for Erkes Rental Company

Earnings	$ 145,000
Preferred Stock (5,500 shares at $100 par, 4%)	$ 550,000
Common Stock (25,000 shares at $1 par, market value $55/share)	25,000
Paid-in Capital in Excess of Par—Common Stock	400,000
Retained Earnings	468,750
Total	$1,443,750

Less Treasury Stock:		
Preferred (500 shares)	$45,000	
Common (1,000 shares)	20,000	65,000
Total Stockholders' Equity......		$1,378,750

Note: Dividends in arrears on preferred stocks, $20,000: redemption value of preferred stock, $101.25/share.

Industry Averages

Earnings per Share	$ 5.00
Price–Earnings Ratio	9.0
Return on Stockholders' Equity	10.0%

Required:

1. Calculate the earnings per share, price–earnings ratio, book value per share, and return on stockholders' equity ratio for Erkes.

2. **Interpretive Question**   Would you want to invest your money in the common stock of this company?

P14–10   Unifying Problem: Alternative Financing Plans

Pearl Company's Balance Sheet and additional information as of December 31, 1981, are presented here.

Pearl Company
Balance Sheet as of December 31, 1981

Assets

Current Assets:		
Cash	$	30,000
Accounts Receivable (Net)		150,000
Notes Receivable		65,000
Inventories		245,000
Prepaid Expenses		10,000
Total Current Assets	$	500,000
Operational Assets:		
Land	$	20,000
Building (Net)		155,000
Equipment (Net)		325,000
Total Operational Assets	$	500,000
Total Assets		$1,000,000

Liabilities and Stockholders' Equity

Current Liabilities:		
Accounts Payable	$	80,000
Taxes Payable		60,000
Accrued Liabilities		30,000
Total Current Liabilities	$	170,000
Long-Term Bank Loan (10%)................		150,000
Total Liabilities	$	320,000
Stockholders' Equity:		
Common Stock ($10 Par)	$	400,000
Retained Earnings.........................		280,000
Total Stockholders' Equity	$	680,000
Total Liabilities and Stockholders' Equity ...		$1,000,000

Additional information: Net income for 1981—$54,400. Effective tax rate—40%.

The company's board of directors is considering several alternative plans for expanding its operations. It has been estimated that an additional investment of $500,000 will make it possible to increase the volume of operations by 60 to 75 percent. The $500,000 would be used to expand the present building, buy additional equipment, and increase working capital. Of the $500,000 needed, $200,000 would be used to increase working capital.

The two most viable alternatives are

a. Sell $500,000 of 20-year bonds at an estimated interest rate of 9 percent.

b. Sell 15.625 shares of common stock at an estimated average price of $32 per share.

Required:

1. Assuming that one of these two alternatives was implemented in late 1981, prepare a Balance Sheet for each alternative as of December 31, 1981.

2. If net income before interest expense and income taxes was expected to be $190,000 for the year 1982, what would be the earnings per share for each alternative?

3. Compute the rate of return on stockholders' equity for 1982 under each alternative and compare these with the 1981 return. Assume that no dividends are paid in 1982.

4. Compute the debt–equity management ratio for each alternative and compare it with 1981.

5. **Interpretive Question**   Which alternative would you recommend to the board of directors? Why?

CHAPTER 15

Financial Reporting for Not-for-Profit Organizations

Most organizations sell products or provide services at prices that are expected to result in a reasonable net return to the owners, that is, generate profits. This book is primarily concerned with financial reporting concepts and procedures for such profit-oriented organizations. The financial reporting standards for business firms are relatively well developed. Their application is carefully monitored through the work of company accountants and independent auditors who render an opinion as to whether the statements present fairly the company's operating results and financial status.

not-for-profit organization
an entity without a profit objective, oriented toward accomplishing nonprofit goals in an efficient manner

The financial reporting concepts and methods applicable to not-for-profit organizations are less well developed. Nonprofit, or nonbusiness, organizations are essentially economic entities that supply goods or services to society without seeking to provide a profit to their owners or founders. They receive their resources from a variety of contributors, who may or may not have an ownership or other equity interest in the entity. These contributors usually do not have the opportunity to sell, trade, or otherwise transfer their interest.

There are a number of reasons why the principles underlying financial reporting for not-for-profit organizations are relatively undeveloped, including

1. The lack of a unified and clearly defined objective that applies to all not-for-profit organizations—for example, whether emphasis should be placed on service to clientele or on responsibility to contributors (dollar accountability).

2. A corresponding absence of well-defined uses for, and users of, not-for-profit financial statements.

3. The relatively minor influence of the nonprofit sector in our society until fairly recently.

It is only in the past few years, in fact, that considerable attention has been directed toward financial reporting concepts and techniques for not-for-profit organizations. One reason for the current interest is that the not-for-profit sector, made up of such areas as local, state, and federal governments, health care, and education, has become a major force in the United States. It now accounts for 20 to 25 percent of the national income. Society is understandably becoming more interested in whether these entities are operating efficiently and effectively, and the accounting profession is responding to the public's concern.

If accountants are to attest to the fairness of certain methods of compiling and presenting financial information, they must be able to relate them to some body of generally accepted accounting principles. Unfortunately, the principles that have been developed for not-for-profit organizations are not always uniformly applied, primarily because of the differing objectives of the various types of organizations in the not-for-profit sector.

In order to identify objectives and to develop concepts that can serve as a basis for nonprofit accounting standards, the FASB commissioned a research study, the goal of which was to identify the key issues that face not-for-profit accounting.[1] In this chapter we describe not-for-profit organizations in general, the current status of accounting for these organizations and the conceptual issues identified in the FASB study.

Ways of Classifying Not-for-Profit Organizations

Not-for-profit organizations may be classified by their size, by the functions they perform (education, health care, religious practice, and so on), and by the sources of their financial support. The FASB study classifies not-for-profit organizations by the sources of their financial support. Thus, it designates Type A and Type B organizations. Type A organizations obtain their financial resources almost entirely from selling goods or rendering services. Included in this category are schools and colleges, hospitals, mutual savings banks and insurance companies, credit unions, and co-operatives. Type B organizations obtain most of their financial resources from taxes, donations, and grants or appropriations from other entities. This category includes most government agencies and those colleges and hospitals that receive large appropriations from state governments.

By basing its classification on sources of financial support, the FASB study has departed from the systems presently in use, which are based on the functions performed by the organization. Thus, the American

---

[1] *Objectives of Financial Reporting by Nonbusiness Organizations*, FASB Exposure Draft, March 14, 1980.

Hospital Association has developed accounting guidelines for hospitals; the National Association of College and University Business Officers, for colleges and universities; and the National Council of Governmental Accounting and the Municipal Finance Officers Association, for governmental units. At the same time, the American Institute of Certified Public Accountants has developed auditing guidelines (but not financial reporting principles) for hospitals, colleges and universities, governmental units, and other not-for-profit organizations. In some states, financial accounting principles for governmental units are prescribed by statute.

Because so many organizations have been involved in the development of not-for-profit accounting principles, the use of accounting and reporting concepts and terms has been inconsistent. Obviously, the FASB, whose goal is to organize and coordinate the divergent procedures of not-for-profit entities, needs to continue its research. Later in this chapter we will discuss the conceptual issues raised in the study we have referred to, but keep in mind that it was only an initial attempt to identify the problems—the solutions are yet to be considered. In order to appreciate the significance of these conceptual issues, however, you should be familiar with the recording principles and financial reports generally used by not-for-profit organizations. Because accounting for governmental units is reasonably well developed and provides a good example of an application of "fund accounting," we will focus initially on the accounting concepts and procedures used by state and local governments.

TO SUMMARIZE   Accounting for not-for-profit organizations lacks a cohesive set of generally accepted accounting principles. This is primarily because the various types of organizations in the not-for-profit sector have different objectives. Traditionally, not-for-profit organizations have been classified by function, although size and source of financial support can also be used.

Fund Accounting

In profit-oriented businesses, the unit accounted for is the entity. All relevant economic events are recorded as a basis for developing operating statements and statements of financial position for the entity as a whole, whether it is a proprietorship, a partnership, or a corporation. This orientation enables users of statements to judge the overall results of operations and the financial status of an entity.

In contrast, not-for-profit accounting, especially for governmental units, is usually organized and operated on a fund basis. The procedures are therefore referred to as fund accounting. A fund is a separate accounting entity within the governmental unit, with a self-balancing set of accounts that reflect only the activities of that entity. The accounts are self-balancing because they reflect all assets, liabilities, revenues, expenses, and an amount needed to bring the fund into balance. This fund balance serves the same purpose as the Retained Earnings account in bringing the equation A = L + OE into balance. A not-for-profit organization is likely to have a number of funds, each of which carries on specific activities designed to achieve one of the objectives of the organization.

fund accounting *an accounting system that involves the use of a group of self-balancing accounts, called funds, for each activity of the not-for-profit organization*

fund *a separate accounting entity that contains a self-balancing set of accounts reflecting only the activities of that entity*

TYPES OF FUNDS

A not-for-profit organization is likely to have the number and types of funds that are uniquely appropriate to its size and functions. For example, the National Council on Governmental Accounting lists the following as common funds for governmental units.

1. General fund
2. Special revenue funds
3. Capital projects funds
4. Special assessment funds
5. Debt service funds
6. Enterprise funds
7. Internal service funds
8. Trust and agency funds

Similarly, the National Association of Colleges and Universities lists the following funds for a typical college.

1. Current fund (general fund)
2. Loan funds
3. Endowment funds
4. Annuity and life income funds
5. Plant funds
6. Agency funds

THE GENERAL FUND

general fund   *the primary fund of a not-for-profit organization; it includes accounts for all transactions that do not fit into more specialized funds*

general fixed asset account group   *a group of accounts used for recording the property, plant, and equipment of the general fund and certain other funds*

general long-term debt account group   *a group of accounts used for recording long-term debt, such as bond issues, for the general fund and certain other funds*

expendable fund   *a fund in which the capital resources are available to carry out the specific objectives of the fund*

nonexpendable fund   *a fund in which the capital resources must be preserved*

All not-for-profit entities usually have a general fund, a catch-all set of accounts for transactions that do not fit any of the specific funds. Additional funds are established as needed. Thus, a governmental unit might maintain only a general fund or it might have all eight of the funds listed above.

The National Council on Governmental Accounting further recommends that two self-balancing groups of accounts be established—the general fixed asset account group and the general long-term debt account group. These two groups are used to account for fixed assets and long-term debt not assigned to other funds. For example, fixed assets acquired by the general fund are recorded as expenditures in the general fund, but it is only in the general fixed asset account group that such information as original cost and major improvements is recorded.

Each fund may be classified as expendable or nonexpendable. An expendable fund consists of capital resources available for carrying out the objectives of that fund. The revenues may come from taxes, fees, assessments, bond issues, or transfers from other funds. Examples of expendable funds are the general fund, special revenue funds, capital projects funds, and debt service funds. A nonexpendable fund is one in which the capital resources must be preserved. This is possible because such funds usually generate sufficient revenues to cover their operating expenses. A trust fund is a typical nonexpendable fund. If money were donated to a trust fund for use in purchasing books for the town library, for example, the nonexpendable capital contribution would be invested, and the income from the investments would pay for the books.

Since governmental units typically have more expendable funds than nonexpendable funds, attention will be restricted here to the general fund as an example of an expendable fund.

Accounting for the General Fund

budgetary accounts *a self-balancing set of accounts that constitute a formal record of a fund's financial plan*

Profit-oriented companies use budgets only for planning and control purposes. Governmental units incorporate budgets into their formal accounting systems. The budget of a fund is initially an estimate of planned expenditures. Once the budget is approved, it becomes an authorization for expenditures and a control device. Each fund has a set of self-balancing budgetary accounts that constitute a formal record of the fund's financial plan.

appropriations *formal authorizations to spend up to specified amounts in carrying out the specific objectives of a fund*

To illustrate, we will assume that the general fund for the town of Carol Woods has an approved budget for the fiscal year beginning July 1, 1980, in which revenues are estimated to be $465,000 and authorized expenditures (called appropriations) are $460,000. This budget information would be recorded in the fund accounts as follows:

Estimated Revenues—Property Taxes	425,000	
Estimated Revenues—Licenses and Fees	40,000	
Appropriations		460,000
Fund Balance.		5,000

To record the budget for the year.

Several aspects of this entry are important to note. First, the budget limits only the total expenditures; it does not identify specific costs. These must be set out separately as the basis for comparing planned with actual costs. Second, the Appropriations account specifies the maximum amount of spending formally authorized during the period. Third, the excess of estimated revenues over appropriations constitutes the expected increase in the fund balance at the end of the accounting period.

proprietary accounts *separate fund accounts for recording actual transactions, that is, actual revenues and expenditures*

Actual fund transactions—actual revenues and expenditures—are recorded in accounts separate from the budgetary accounts. These are called proprietary accounts and are the subject of the next two sections.

ACCOUNTING FOR REVENUES

For governmental units, the revenues of a general fund normally come from taxes, fees, and licenses. In the following example, we will assume that these are the sources of revenue for the general fund of the town of Carol Woods.

To illustrate the recording of revenues, we will assume that property taxes in the amount of $434,000 are assessed by Carol Woods. On an accrual basis, the property taxes would be recorded in the general fund at the time of assessment. At the same time, uncollectable taxes would be estimated and recorded in an Allowance for Uncollectable Taxes account. If uncollectable taxes are expected to amount to $4,000, the entry would be

Taxes Receivable	434,000	
Tax Revenues		430,000
Allowance for Uncollectable Taxes—Delinquent		4,000
To record the expected tax revenues.		

The asset account, Taxes Receivable, is reduced as the taxes are collected. Any taxes not received by the designated due date are transferred to Taxes Receivable—Delinquent. The entry to record the collection of $424,000 in taxes and the transfer of uncollected taxes to a delinquent account would be

Cash	424,000	
Allowance for Uncollectable Taxes	4,000	
Taxes Receivable—Delinquent	10,000	
Taxes Receivable		434,000
Allowance for Uncollectable Taxes—Delinquent		4,000
Collected taxes and transferred uncollected taxes to a delinquent account.		

Assuming that $5,000 of the delinquent taxes were later collected and $3,000 were written off, the entries would be

Cash	5,000	
Taxes Receivable—Delinquent		5,000
Collected delinquent taxes.		
Allowance for Uncollectable Taxes—Delinquent.	3,000	
Taxes Receivable—Delinquent		3,000
To write off delinquent taxes that are not collectable.		

Other revenues, such as fees and licenses, are recorded on a cash basis, that is, only when they are received. For example, if Carol Woods collects $46,000 in licenses and fees, total actual revenues amount to $476,000 ($430,000 in tax revenues + $46,000 in licenses and fees). The entry to record the collection of these other revenues would be

Cash	46,000	
Other Revenues		46,000
Collected revenues for licenses and fees.		

The budgeted revenues for the town of Carol Woods were $465,000 and actual revenues were $476,000. When actual revenues are over budget, the excess is usually recorded in a separate revenue account in order to distinguish it from budgeted revenue.

ACCOUNTING FOR ENCUMBRANCES AND EXPENDITURES

*encumbrance a formal
record of commitments made
now for expenditures to be
made later; usually set up
when a significant period of
time is expected to elapse
between the date of commitment and the time of the
expenditure*

*Reserve for Encumbrances
an account credited at the
time a commitment is made
for an expenditure*

The budget entry for Carol Woods provided for authorized expenditures (appropriations) up to $460,000. To be certain that actual expenditures will not exceed authorized expenditures, governmental units use an encumbrance, a formal record of the commitments made now for later expenditures. An Encumbrances account is used only when a significant period is expected to elapse between the date of the commitment and the time of the expenditure. The Encumbrances account and a related Reserve for Encumbrances account are opened as soon as orders are placed or contracts have been executed.

To illustrate, we will assume that on July 15, Carol Woods orders a new fire truck at a cost of $30,000 and related equipment for $14,000. The truck is to be delivered in six months and the other equipment will arrive in about nine months. The entry to record this commitment would be

Encumbrances	44,000	
Reserve for Encumbrances		44,000
Ordered a fire truck and related equipment.		

When the fire truck is delivered six months later, with an invoice for $29,700, the entry to record its payment is

Expenditures	29,700	
Cash		29,700
Paid for fire truck.		

Once the fire truck has been paid for, $30,000 in the Encumbrances account is no longer necessary and must be reversed.

Reserve for Encumbrances	30,000	
Encumbrances		30,000
To reverse the encumbrance for the fire truck.		

Only the amount encumbered is reversed, whether the actual expenditure is more or less than this amount. If all the encumbrances are not spent by the end of the fiscal year, the Reserve for Encumbrances account remains open and is shown on the Balance Sheet of the general fund as a continuing commitment.

ACCOUNTING FOR RECURRING EXPENDITURES

Expenditures for such recurring items as salaries, interest, and supplies are not usually encumbered. A voucher (a signed document authorizing payment) is prepared and recorded in anticipation of payment in the near future. For example, if the normal expenditures for recurring items in June were expected to be $22,000, vouchers would be prepared and the entry to record their existence would be

Expenditures	22,000	
Vouchers Payable		22,000
To record the liability for June expenditures.		

If $13,000 of the vouchers were paid by June 30, the entry would be

Vouchers Payable   13,000
  Cash   13,000
Paid $13,000 of the June expenditure vouchers.

The remaining vouchers usually will be paid early in the next month.

ACCOUNTING FOR TRANSFER PAYMENTS

transfer payment   *a payment by one fund to another*

Another type of expenditure by the general fund is a transfer payment to another fund. To illustrate, we assume that the general fund of Carol Woods provides $25,000 to the debt service fund so that it can pay principal and interest on general obligation bonds. The entries to record the obligation and the actual transfer of funds would be

Transfer to Debt Service Fund   25,000
  Due to Debt Service Fund   25,000
To record the obligation to transfer $25,000 to the debt service fund.

Due to Debt Service Fund   25,000
  Cash   25,000
To record the transfer to the debt service fund.

CLOSING THE GENERAL FUND ACCOUNTS

The closing process at the end of an accounting period is the same for a general fund as it is for a profit-oriented company. To illustrate, we will assume that the general fund has the following trial balance at the end of the fiscal year, June 30, 1981.

	Debit	Credit
Cash	$ 70,000	
Expenditures.	417,000	
Estimated Revenues	465,000	
Taxes Receivable—Delinquent	2,000	
Encumbrances.	14,000	
Transfer to Debt Service Fund	25,000	
Reserve for Encumbrances		$ 14,000
Vouchers Payable		9,000
Appropriations		460,000
Allowance for Uncollectable Taxes—Delinquent		1,000
Fund Balance		33,000
Revenues		476,000
Totals	$993,000	$993,000

The accounts in the trial balance are of two types—permanent and temporary. The permanent accounts are Balance Sheet accounts, and they will remain open for future accounting periods. They include Cash, Taxes

fund balance *the excess of a fund's assets over its liabilities and reserves; the balancing account in the Balance Sheet of a not-for-profit organization*

Receivable, Vouchers Payable, Allowance for Uncollectable Taxes, and Fund Balance. The temporary accounts appear on the Statement of Revenues and Expenditures. These accounts are closed at the end of the accounting period, so that they have zero balances and can be used to accumulate revenue and expenditure information during the next accounting period. On the basis of the information in the trial balance, the entries to close the general fund's temporary accounts would be

Revenues.............................	476,000	
Estimated Revenues		465,000
Fund Balance..................................		11,000

To close the revenue accounts.

Appropriations............................	460,000	
Expenditures.................................		417,000
Encumbrances................................		14,000
Transfer to Debt Service Fund		25,000
Fund Balance..................................		4,000

To close the expenditure, encumbrance, and transfer accounts.

As these closing entries show, actual revenues were greater than estimated revenues by $11,000, and expenditures, encumbrances, and transfers were less than appropriations by $4,000. Accordingly, during the year the fund's balance increased by $15,000 more than was planned when the budget was established at the beginning of the year.

Fund Balance, Beginning of Year		$28,000
Estimated Revenues in Excess of Estimated		
Appropriations.................................		5,000
Fund Balance on Trial Balance		$33,000
Excess of Actual Revenues Over Actual Expenditures,		
Encumbrances, and Transfers ($476,000 − $456,000)..	$20,000	
Less Planned Excess	5,000	
Increase Above Plan.............................		15,000
Fund Balance, End of Year		$48,000

We know that revenues were $476,000 and that total expenditures ($417,000), encumbrances ($14,000), and transfers ($25,000) were $456,000; so the revenue excess amounted to $20,000. However, the planned excess of $5,000 must be deducted; otherwise, it would be counted twice. With this understanding of the change in fund balance and of the nature of the accounts in the trial balance, the financial statements for Carol Woods can be prepared.

PREPARING THE FINANCIAL STATEMENTS

Three key financial statements would be prepared for the general fund at the end of the fiscal year: the Statement of Revenues and Expenditures, the Balance Sheet, and the Statement of Changes in Fund Balance. Some not-for-profit organizations also prepare a Funds Statement (see the Supplement to this chapter).

EXHIBIT 15–1   Town of Carol Woods

Statement of Revenues and Expenditures—General Fund for the
Fiscal Year Ended June 30, 1981

	Estimated	Actual
Revenues:		
Property Taxes	$425,000	$430,000
Other Revenues	40,000	46,000
Total Revenues	$465,000	$476,000

	Appro-priations	Actual Expenditures and Encum-brances
Expenditures and Transfers:		
General Government	$178,000	$175,000
Police Services	85,000	90,000
Sanitation Services	118,000	110,000
Street Maintenance	44,000	43,700
Capital Expenditures	10,000	11,500
Supplies	25,000	25,800
Total Expenditures and Transfers	$460,000	$456,000
Change in Fund Balance	$ 5,000	$ 20,000

Statement of Revenues and Expenditures

Statement of Revenues and Expenditures *a formal statement prepared for a not-for-profit organization that shows the relationship between actual revenues and expenditures; it may also include the budgeted amounts*

The Statement of Revenues and Expenditures for a general fund shows the relationship between actual revenues and expenditures. In addition, it may have a column identifying budgeted revenues and appropriations so that readers can compare planned and actual results. Exhibit 15–1 is a Statement of Revenues and Expenditures based on information in the trial balance presented earlier.

Note that the Statement of Revenues and Expenditures indicates only the flow of funds and does not identify the causes of the differences between expected and actual results. In other words, it does not explain how efficient the revenue collection process was or how much benefit was realized from the expenditures. In order to measure whether the expenditures achieved adequate benefits, Carol Woods would have to prepare a cost–benefit analysis and compare budgeted expenses with actual expenses on an accrual basis. Cost–benefit and expense-control analyses are appropriate subjects for a course in managerial accounting. At this point, it is sufficient to keep in mind that the usual operating statement of a not-for-profit organization reflects resource flows and expenditure control, but it does not indicate how efficiently resources were used.

Balance Sheet

The Balance Sheet for a general fund reflects the resources available to pay current vouchers and encumbrances as well as the amount in the

---

EXHIBIT 15–2   Town of Carol Woods
Balance Sheet—General Fund as of June 30, 1981

Assets

Cash		$70,000
Taxes Receivable—Delinquent	$2,000	
Less Allowance for Uncollectable Taxes—Delinquent ..	1,000	1,000
Total Assets		$71,000

Liabilities, Encumbrances, and Fund Balance

Vouchers Payable	$ 9,000
Reserve for Encumbrances	14,000
Fund Balance	48,000
Total Liabilities, Encumbrances, and Fund Balance ..	$71,000

---

fund balance available for appropriation in the coming period. The Balance Sheet for Carol Woods, based on the trial balance prepared earlier, would be as shown in Exhibit 15–2.

As you will notice, the fire truck acquired by Carol Woods is not shown on the Balance Sheet of the general fund. The cost of the fire truck would be recorded as follows in the general fixed assets account group:

Fire Equipment	29,700	
Investment in General Assets—General Fund		29,700
Purchased a fire truck.		

Similarly, the amount transferred from the general fund to cover debt service would be recorded in the debt service fund as follows:

Cash	25,000	
Transfer from General Fund		25,000
Transferred cash from the general fund for debt service.		

The fact that fixed assets are recorded in the general fixed asset account group and funds for debt service are transferred to a debt service fund illustrates the fragmented nature of fund accounting. Each fund has a separate set of self-balancing accounts. To get a clear picture of a governmental unit's entire operation, you should obtain a Statement of Revenues and Expenditures, a Balance Sheet, and a combined Statement of Changes in Fund Balances for each fund. Thus, you should view the general fund's financial statements in their proper perspective—as reflecting the general operations of a governmental unit, not its special activities.

EXHIBIT 15–3 **Town of Carol Woods**
Statement of Changes in Fund Balance—General Fund for the
Fiscal Year Ended June 30, 1981

Fund Balance, July 1, 1980		$28,000
Revenues	$476,000	
Expenditures and Encumbrances	456,000	
Excess of Revenues Over Expenditures and Encumbrances..................................		20,000
Fund Balance, June 30, 1981.......................		$48,000

Statement of Changes in Fund Balance

A Statement of Changes in Fund Balance serves the same function as the Statement of Changes in Owners' Equity (see page 42) for a profit-oriented business. It identifies the reasons for the difference between the beginning and ending fund balances. Exhibit 15–3 is a Statement of Changes in Fund Balance for Carol Woods, based on data from the trial balance presented earlier.

The budget for the fiscal year ending June 30, 1981, had projected an increase of $5,000 in the fund balance. That projected $5,000 increase would have been added to the $28,000 shown on the Balance Sheet at June 30, 1980, thus accounting for the $33,000 shown in the trial balance. The fund balance increased another $15,000 because actual revenues exceeded estimated revenues by $11,000 and actual expenditures and encumbrances were less than appropriations by $4,000. The general fund balance of $48,000 on June 30, 1981, reflects the amount that could be available for appropriations by the town governing board in the next fiscal year unless it is retained as a reserve.

TO SUMMARIZE Fund accounting, involving a group of self-balancing accounts for each major activity of the entity, is used by most not-for-profit organizations. The general fund is primary to all such entities, although funds with narrower focuses also may be needed. Both budgetary expectations and actual transactions are recorded in the general fund accounts and are reflected in the three primary statements of a not-for-profit organization: the Statement of Revenues and Expenditures, the Balance Sheet, and the Statement of Changes in Fund Balance.

Fund Accounting for Nongovernmental Organizations

The preceding discussion of the general fund reflects the current state of the art in governmental accounting. A more complete understanding would require a study of the other seven funds plus the general fixed asset and the general long-term debt groups of accounts.

Although other not-for-profit organizations—for example, colleges and universities, hospitals, pension funds, churches, and credit unions—are quite different from governmental units and from each other, the accounting procedures used for the general fund provide a realistic perspective of not-for-profit accounting. The financial statements for a college, for example, are shown as a supplement to this chapter. The three financial statements presented are:

1. Statement of Revenues and Other Additions, Expenses, and Changes in Fund Balance (Exhibit 15–4).
2. Balance Sheet (Exhibit 15–5).
3. Statement of Changes in Working Capital (Exhibit 15–6).

A careful study of Exhibit 15–4 will reveal the sources of funds received by the college and how they differ from those of a governmental unit. The other fund statements have been condensed into only two categories, unrestricted and restricted, to provide you with a summary of the financial operations and status of the college on an aggregate basis. These statements should be studied carefully in connection with the following discussion of key issues in not-for-profit accounting.

Key Issues in Not-for-Profit Accounting

At the beginning of this chapter, we noted that the FASB commissioned a study of the conceptual issues related to financial accounting for not-for-profit organizations. This was an important first step in the process of developing generally accepted accounting principles for not-for-profit organizations. The study identified 15 issues to be resolved in order for uniform reporting standards to be developed. We consider the following questions to cover the most significant issues.

1. Who are the primary users of financial information about not-for-profit organizations?
Comment: Identifying the users of financial information is a first step in determining the type of information needed. Five primary users were named: governing bodies, investors and creditors, resource providers, oversight bodies, and constituents.

2. What type of information is needed by users?
Comment: Although the answer to this question depends on the decisions to be made, the FASB study suggests that the following information is most likely to be useful: financial viability, fiscal compliance (adhering to expenditure policies), managerial performance, and cost of services provided.

3. What types of financial statements would provide the most useful information about not-for-profit organizations?

operating flows *the revenue inflows and operating (expense) outflows of a fund*

capital flows *the sources and uses of funds for long-term assets, such as buildings, land, and equipment*

Comment: To answer this question, a number of subissues first need to be resolved. For example:

(a) Do users need a Revenue and Expenditure Statement?

(b) Should operating flows be separated from capital flows?

(c) Should encumbrances as well as expenditures be reported?

(d) Do users need an overall set of financial statements for the organization rather than separate financial statements for each fund?

These types of questions demonstrate that although accounting for certain types of not-for-profit organizations (such as governmental units) is fairly standard, some fundamental issues need to be reexplored before generally accepted accounting principles can be established.

Other questions raised by the FASB study include the following.

1. When should the depreciation of capital assets be recorded in the accounts of a not-for-profit organization?

2. Should donated or contributed services be reported as expenses at their fair value?

3. How does the revenue recognition principle apply to nonrenewable operating inflows such as contracts and investment earnings?

If you are planning to pursue a career in accounting, we encourage you to study accounting for not-for-profit organizations, not only because of the growing importance of this segment of our society but also because of the need for more uniformity in reporting and for a higher level of reporting standards than now exists.

CHAPTER REVIEW

Financial reporting standards for not-for-profit organizations have developed more slowly than comparable standards for businesses. The primary emphasis has been on the accountability for funds received and spent rather than on how *efficiently* the funds were spent to achieve *effective* results. The accounting profession is paying greater attention to this area of accounting today because not-for-profit organizations are becoming a larger force in our financial affairs, particularly in such areas as government, education, and health care.

Not-for-profit organizations can be classified by their size, by the functions they perform, or by the sources of their financial support. Until now, function has served as the basis for developing the accounting procedures used. Accordingly, there is one set of reporting principles for governmental units, another set for colleges and universities, and yet another for hospitals. Due to widespread concern about this diversity, the FASB has published a research report that explores the conceptual issues related to financial accounting and reporting for nonprofit organizations.

Accounting for not-for-profit organizations is generally based on fund accounting. This means that a separate self-balancing set of accounts is created for each activity of the organization. A governmental unit may have as many as eight types of funds and two account groups for fixed assets and long-term debt. The most commonly used fund is the general fund, which collects information on all activities not recorded in the special-purpose funds.

The number of funds depends on the number of activities an organization engages in. The transactions for a particular activity are recorded in a designated fund, and at the end of the accounting period they are summarized into three primary financial reports: Statement of Revenues and Expenditures, Balance Sheet, and Statement of Changes in Fund Balance. In some cases, the statements for individual funds are aggregated into a statement for the entity as a whole.

As a first step in developing more uniform reporting standards for not-for-profit organizations, the FASB has identified a number of fundamental issues. These issues revolve around the following questions: Who are the users of financial information for nonprofit organizations? What types of financial information do they need? What types of financial statements will provide the desired information? To what extent should the reporting standards for not-for-profit organizations be different from those for profit-oriented companies? Related and more specific issues involve depreciation, contributed services, and the recognition principle with regard to non-revenue inflows.

KEY TERMS AND CONCEPTS

appropriations (495)
budgetary accounts (495)
capital flows (504)
encumbrance (497)
expendable fund (494)
fund (493)
fund accounting (493)
fund balance (499)
general fixed asset account group (494)
general fund (494)

general long-term debt account group (494)
nonexpendable fund (494)
not-for-profit organization (491)
operating flows (504)
proprietary accounts (495)
Reserve for Encumbrances (497)

Statement of Changes in Fund Balance (502)
Statement of Revenues and Expenditures (500)
transfer payment (498)

DISCUSSION QUESTIONS

1. Distinguish between a not-for-profit organization and a business enterprise.

2. Why have the financial reporting concepts and procedures for not-for-profit organizations developed more slowly than those for profit-oriented companies?

3. Why is it difficult for accountants today to attest to the fair presentation of the financial statements of not-for-profit organizations?

4. In what ways can not-for-profit organizations be classified?

5. What is a fund? How many funds is a not-for-profit organization likely to have?

6. Distinguish between an expendable and a non-expendable fund.

7. How is budgetary information accounted for differently in a not-for-profit organization, as compared with a profit-oriented company?

8. What is the purpose of the Appropriations account in the general fund of a governmental unit?

9. If tax revenues of a municipality are not collected by the required due date, what journal entries are made to reflect delinquent taxes and uncollectable taxes?

10. What is an encumbrance system?

11. When is an Encumbrances account set up? What is the usual journal entry if $80,000 is encumbered to buy a piece of snow-clearing equipment for a municipality?

12. What happens to the Encumbrances account when an actual expenditure is made?

13. If an actual expenditure has not been made by the end of the accounting period, what disposition is made of the Encumbrances account and the Reserve for Encumbrances account?

14. Prepare typical entries to close the following general fund accounts: Estimated Revenues, Revenues, Appropriations, Expenditures, and Encumbrances. (Use x's for numbers.)

15. Identify and briefly describe the three primary financial statements prepared for the general fund of a governmental unit at the end of a fiscal year.

16. Do the financial statements of the general fund of a municipality reflect how efficiently resources were utilized? Explain.

17. What are the shortcomings of the general fund's financial statements in providing readers with a clear picture of the operations of a governmental unit?

18. What is the purpose of the Statement of Changes in Fund Balance?

19. Who are likely to be the primary users of the financial statements of (a) a governmental unit, (b) a college, (c) a revenue fund, and (d) a church?

20. Why would financial statement users want to know how much it costs for a not-for-profit organization to provide its services?

21. Do users need an overall set of financial statements for not-for-profit organizations or are separate statements for individual funds sufficient?

22. Should a not-for-profit organization account for donated or contributed services? Explain.

23. (a) What is the difference between an operating flow and a capital flow?
(b) Why might it be desirable to separate the operating flows of a nonbusiness organization from its capital flows?

EXERCISES

E15–1 Budgetary Accounts and Proprietary Accounts

Identify the following accounts as budgetary accounts (B) or as proprietary accounts (P).

1. Appropriations
2. Fund Balance
3. Estimated Uncollectable Property Taxes
4. Encumbrances
5. Expenditures
6. Taxes Receivable
7. Estimated Revenues

E15–2 Recording the Budgetary Accounts

The annual budget of the general fund of a city shows estimated revenues of $875,000 and appropriations of $850,000. Prepare the journal entry to record this budgetary information in the fund accounts and reflect the excess estimated revenue.

E15–3 Recording an Encumbrance

Prepare the journal entry in the general fund to earmark a fund balance for $17,500 of goods ordered but not yet received.

E15–4 Relationships Among Accounts

For each situation below, describe in lay terms the action taken by a town board.

1. Appropriations exceed estimated revenues.
2. Actual expenses exceed estimated expenses.
3. Estimated revenues exceed appropriations.

E15–5 Paying Expenditures and Eliminating Encumbrances

Prepare the journal entries in the general fund to pay for the purchase of supplies costing $12,000 and to eliminate a previously established encumbrance account for these supplies in the amount of $11,500.

E15–6 Closing Entries

The trial balance of the town of Rio Hondo's general fund for the fiscal year ended June 30, 1981, is shown on the next page.

Prepare all entries necessary to close the temporary accounts.

	Debit	Credit
Cash............................	$ 60,000	
Expenditures	230,000	
Estimated Revenues...............	275,000	
Taxes Receivable	40,000	
Encumbrances	25,000	
Reserve for Encumbrances		$ 25,000
Vouchers Payable..................		8,000
Appropriations....................		260,000
Revenues........................		282,000
Fund Balance		55,000
	$630,000	$630,000

E15−7 Statement of Revenues and Expenditures

Refer to Rio Hondo's trial balance in E15−6 and prepare a Statement of Revenues and Expenditures for the fiscal year ended June 30, 1981.

E15−8 Preparing a Balance Sheet

Refer to Rio Hondo's trial balance in E15−6 and prepare a Balance Sheet as of June 30, 1981.

E15−9 Preparing a Statement of Changes in Fund Balance

The fund balance in the general fund of the town of Rio Hondo was $40,000 on July 1, 1980. Prepare a Statement of Changes in Fund Balance for the fiscal year ending June 30, 1981, using appropriate information from the trial balance presented in E15−6.

PROBLEMS

P15−1 Recording Budget and Revenue Transactions

Required:

Prepare the General Journal entry that properly records each of the following events. (Omit explanations.)

1. The city of Salisbury adopted the following budget: estimated revenues—$2,890,000; appropriations—$2,750,000.

2. A tax levy of $2,000,000 was recorded; it is estimated that 1 percent of the levy will be uncollectable.

3. $500,000 was collected in licenses and fees.

4. $1,975,000 was collected on the tax levy. Uncollected taxes were transferred to a delinquent account.

P15−2 Recording Expenditures

Required:

Prepare the General Journal entry that properly records each of the following events. (Omit explanations.)

1. A purchase order for $150,000 for a fleet of 25 police cars was issued.

2. Fifteen cars are received with an invoice for $93,000. The invoice was paid.

3. Salaries were $37,000. This item had not been encumbered.

4. A total of $35,900 was transferred to the Debt Service Fund.

P15−3 General Fund Closing Entries

The following is a trial balance of a city's general fund.

	Debit	Credit
Cash............................	$ 33,500	
Taxes Receivable—Delinquent.......	2,500	
Allowance for Uncollectable Taxes— Delinquent		$ 500
Reserve for Encumbrances		7,000
Vouchers Payable..................		4,500
Fund Balance		16,500
Expenditures	208,500	
Estimated Revenues...............	232,500	
Encumbrances	7,000	
Transfer to Special Fund	12,500	
Appropriations...................		230,000
Revenues........................		238,000
	$496,500	$496,500

Required:

Prepare all entries necessary to close the temporary accounts. (Omit explanations.)

P15−4 Statement of Changes in Fund Balance

The following entry was made to record the budget of a general fund.

January 1, 1981

Estimated Revenues...............	500,000	
Appropriations...........................		490,000
Fund Balance		10,000

Additional Information:

Fund Balance January 1, 1981 (before above entry).........	$ 16,000
Actual Revenues	480,000
Encumbrances	20,000
Expenditures	450,000

Required:

Prepare a Statement of Changes in Fund Balance.

P15–5 Unifying Problem: Adjusting and Closing Entries and Terminology

The controller of the municipality of Cornwallis Island developed the following trial balance of the general fund.

	Debit	Credit
Cash	$ 2,500	
Expenditures	79,500	
Estimated Revenues	129,600	
Taxes Receivable—Delinquent	65,400	
Transfer to Debt Service Fund	1,900	
Reserve for Encumbrances		$ 31,400
Vouchers Payable		7,800
Appropriations		124,000
Allowance for Uncollectable Taxes—Delinquent		13,000
Fund Balance		11,000
Revenues		123,100
Encumbrances	31,400	
	$310,300	$310,300

She was about to close the temporary accounts when one of her assistants told her that a previously recalcitrant taxpayer had just paid $1,300 in taxes that had been written off. In addition, wages of $1,550 were still due the town manager.

Required:

1. Incorporate the above information in the trial balance. (Ignore payroll taxes.)

2. Prepare the appropriate journal entries to close the temporary accounts and explain why you are making them.

3. **Interpretive Question** None of the town council members has a background in not-for-profit accounting. Explain what each of the budgetary accounts is used for.

4. **Interpretive Question** Explain the difference between actual revenues and estimated revenues.

P15–6 Unifying Problem: Assessment of Operational Efficiency

The Senate minority leader of Costa Linda has confronted the executive branch, armed with comparative Statements of Revenues and Expenditures for the National Water Authorities of Costa Linda and Sable Island. Sable Island is a neighboring country with a population, climate, and geography similar to Costa Linda.

Water Authorities of Sable Island and Costa Linda
Comparative Statements of Revenues and Expenditures for the Fiscal Year Ended December 31, 1980 (in thousands)

	Costa Linda		Sable Island	
	Estimated	Actual	Estimated	Actual
Revenues:				
Commercial	$277	$274	$534	$510
Residential	568	575	213	292
Total Revenues	$845	$849	$747	$802

	Appropriations	Actual Expenditures and Transfers	Appropriations	Actual Expenditures and Transfers
Expenditures and Transfers:				
Administration	$114	$179	$166	$185
Maintenance	337	367	19	95
Supplies	97	99	424	415
Capital Improvements	212	215	138	23
Debt Service	85	85		2
Total Expenditures and Transfers	$845	$945	$747	$720
Change in Fund Balance	$ 0	$ (96)	$ 0	$ 82

The senator made several charges based upon a comparison of the figures in these two statements.

a. Costa Linda citizens are paying too much for water.

b. Administration costs are higher in Costa Linda than they were expected to be.

c. Capital spending is too ambitious.

d. Maintenance costs are higher than they need to be.

e. Government inefficiency in Costa Linda has resulted in a heavy debt burden due to continued deficit spending.

Required:

1. The executive branch thought it had administered the water fund properly. Is it possible that the senator had arrived at inappropriate conclusions?

(a) List the facts from the statements above that support the senator's criticisms.

(b) What are some acceptable reasons for the differences between operations in Costa Linda and in Sable Island?

2. **Interpretive Question** Are lower capital and maintenance expenses always better? Explain.

3. **Interpretive Question**   The senator implied that Sable Island has a better water authority than Costa Linda. Do you agree?

4. **Interpretive Question**   The executive branch pointed out that fire insurance rates were lower in Costa Linda because there were more fire hydrants. Who benefits from the lower insurance? Is this relevant to the National Water Authority? Comment.

5. **Interpretive Question**   Unemployment is lower in Costa Linda than in Sable Island because business taxes in Costa Linda are lower. Should this information be considered by the National Water Authority? Comment.

6. **Interpretive Question**   Under what circumstances could deficit spending be considered similar to debt-funded capital expansion in a company operating for profit? Could there be other reasons for deficit spending?

P15—7   Efficiency of Fund Raising

A recent college graduate decided to take a job as fund raiser for a not-for-profit charitable organization. However, he found it difficult to choose between two charities, Alpha and Beta. To help in the decision, he thought he would look at how each charity spent the revenues it raised. The Alpha Charity sent him the following statement of revenues and expenditures for the previous fiscal year.

Alpha Charity
Statement of Revenues and Expenditures for the Fiscal Year Ended June 30, 1981

Revenues:

Corporate Donations	$123,700
Individual Contributions	81,400
Total Revenues	$205,100

Expenditures and Transfers:

Toxin Research	$ 11,900
Heart Disease Research	27,800
Cancer Research..........................	28,900
Hematological Studies	24,600
Research on Children's Diseases..............	35,300
Birth Defects Research	10,600
Fund Raising.............................	40,800
General Administration	36,400
Total Expenditures and Transfers..........	$216,300
Decrease in Fund Balance	($ 11,200)

Beta Charity sent him a brochure stating that its total revenues for the year ending December 31, 1981 were $163,123. The brochure also contained a diagram that showed how every dollar was spent during the preceding fiscal year.

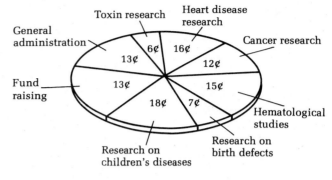

Required:

1. Prepare a Statement of Revenues and Expenditures for the Beta Charity. The increase in the fund balance was $16,167 (rounded to nearest whole dollar).

2. Which charity spent less on fund raising in absolute terms? In relative terms?

3. **Interpretive Question**   The fund raisers for Alpha Charity feel that the increased revenue is worth the extra amount spent for fund raising. What do you think?

4. **Interpretive Question**   The management of Beta Charity is proud that it spends most of its revenues for charitable purposes. Do you think this pride is justified?

5. **Interpretive Question**   Which charity would you want to work for? Why?

P15—8   Statement of Changes in Financial Position

In 1982 the Museum of Modern Art bought several new paintings at a cost of $30,800. During the same period, some paintings that had been acquired for $43,100 were sold for $45,200. Negotiations with the Metropolitan Parks Authority have been completed and an unneeded portion of the Museum's grounds has been sold for $18,800, representing a gain of $17,600 over the price paid in 1925 when the museum was first established. The museum retired $1,600 of long-term debt and issued $83,300 of notes due in the year 2000. (Financial statements appear on the next page.)

Required:

The museum's trustees have asked you to:

1. Prepare a Statement of Changes in Financial Position using working capital as the concept of funds.

2. Prepare another Statement of Changes in Financial Position using cash as the concept of funds.

3. Comment on the similarities and differences between the statements.

4. Describe the museum's financial situation.

The Museum of Modern Art
Statement of Revenues and Expenditures
for the Year Ended December 31, 1982

Revenues:

Gift Shop Sales	$ 18,700
Admissions	9,400
Gain on Sale of Land	17,600
Gain on Sale of Paintings.	2,100
Donations and Membership Dues	64,800
Public Grants	55,300
Total Revenues	$167,900

Expenditures and Transfers:

Cost of Gift Shop Goods Sold	$ 4,700
Salaries and Wages	96,500
Fuel Oil	33,200
Electricity.	11,900
Janitorial Supplies	1,300
Fund Raising Expenses	32,600
Depreciation of Buildings and Physical Plant	9,400
Interest Expense	5,100
Other Expense Items	700
Total Expenditures and Transfers.	$195,400
Decrease in Fund Balance.	($ 27,500)

The Museum of Modern Art
Balance Sheets as of December 31, 1982 and 1981

Assets	1982	1981
Cash.	$ 75,500	$ 78,400
Long-Term Investments	36,900	36,900
Land.	16,900	18,100
Buildings and Physical Plant	236,500	153,800
Less Accumulated Depreciation	(57,400)	(48,000)
Works of Art	331,900	344,200
Industrial Designs	5,300	5,300
Total Assets.	$645,600	$588,700

Liabilities, Encumbrances, and Fund Balance	1982	1981
Accounts Payable.	$ 3,400	$ 3,100
Current Debt.	11,800	10,800
Long-Term Debt	186,900	105,200
Memberships: Initial Contributions . . .	31,900	30,500
Fund Balance (including Grants, Donations, and Membership Fees) . . .	411,600	439,100
Total Liabilities, Encumbrances, and Fund Balance.	$645,600	$588,700

SUPPLEMENT

The Primary Financial Statements of a College

EXHIBIT 15–4   ABC College
Statements of Revenues, and Other Additions, Expenses, and Changes in Fund Balance for the Years Ended June 30, 1981 and 1980

	1981 Unrestricted	1981 Restricted*	1981 Total	1980 Total
Revenues and Other Additions:				
Tuition and Fees	$ 2,964,000		$ 2,964,000	$ 2,550,000
Governmental Appropriations	700,000		700,000	600,000
Governmental Grants and Contracts	20,000	$ 500,000	520,000	410,000
Private Gifts, Grants and Contracts, Other Than Endowment	650,000	415,000	1,065,000	680,000
Endowment Gifts		1,850,000	1,850,000	600,000
Investment Income	734,000	563,000	1,297,000	995,000
Realized and Unrealized Appreciation (Depreciation) of Investments	(100,000)	(415,000)	(515,000)	385,000
Auxiliary Enterprises	1,910,000		1,910,000	1,650,000
Total Revenues and Other Additions	$ 6,878,000	$ 2,913,000	$ 9,791,000	$ 7,870,000
Expenditures and Transfers:				
Instruction	$ 3,491,000	$ 489,000	$ 3,980,000	$ 3,625,000
Research	149,000	400,000	549,000	910,000
Public Service	140,000	25,000	165,000	125,000
Student Services	91,000		91,000	65,000
Scholarships	150,000	50,000	200,000	190,000
Auxiliary Enterprises	1,347,000		1,347,000	1,441,000
Operation and Maintenance of Plant	220,000		220,000	200,000
General and Administrative	691,000		691,000	649,000
Fund Raising	226,000	12,000	238,000	180,000
Total Expenditures and Transfers	$ 6,505,000	$ 976,000	$ 7,481,000	$ 7,385,000
Excess of Revenue and Other Additions Over Expenses:				
Unrestricted (Available for Current Operations)	$ 373,000		$ 373,000	$ (215,000)
Restricted (Increases in Endowment and Other Restricted Funds)		$ 1,937,000	1,937,000	700,000
Fund Balances, Beginning of Year	43,232,000	12,017,000	55,249,000	54,764,000
Interfund Transfers	322,000	(322,000)		
Fund Balances, End of Year	$43,927,000	$13,632,000	$57,559,000	$55,249,000

* Represents receipts and expenditures applied to specifically designated purposes.

EXHIBIT 15–5   ABC College
Balance Sheets as of June 30, 1981 and 1980

| | 1981 | | | 1980 |
Assets	Unrestricted	Restricted	Total	Total
Current Assets:				
Cash....................................	$ 810,000	$ 125,000	$ 935,000	$ 760,000
Short-Term Investments	900,000		900,000	1,391,000
Accounts Receivable (Net).........................	228,000		228,000	178,000
Student Loans (Net, Current).......................		80,000	80,000	50,000
Inventory	352,000		352,000	272,000
Prepaid Expenses.............................	60,000		60,000	44,000
Total Current Assets	$ 2,350,000	$ 205,000	$ 2,555,000	$ 2,695,000
Investments (at Market).........................	4,100,000	12,977,000	17,077,000	14,632,000
Student Loans, Net, Long-Term		550,000	550,000	400,000
Land, Buildings, and Equipment, at Cost, Less				
Accumulated Depreciation of $9,610,000 and				
$8,790,000, respectively	40,410,000		40,410,000	39,305,000
Total Assets.................................	$46,860,000	$13,732,000	$60,592,000	$57,032,000
Liabilities and Fund Balances				
Current Liabilities:				
Accounts Payable..............................	$ 583,000	$ 100,000	$ 683,000	$ 483,000
Accrued Expenses	150,000		150,000	100,000
Portion of Long-Term Debt Due Within One Year	100,000		100,000	50,000
Total Current Liabilities.........................	$ 833,000	$ 100,000	$ 933,000	$ 633,000
Long-Term Debt	2,100,000		2,100,000	1,150,000
Total Liabilities..............................	$ 2,933,000	$ 100,000	$ 3,033,000	$ 1,783,000
Fund Balances:				
Available for Current Use—				
Unrestricted	$ 1,317,000		$ 1,317,000	$ 1,027,000
Restricted		$ 531,000	531,000	400,000
Board-Designated Endowment.....................	4,200,000		4,200,000	4,000,000
Other Designated Funds	200,000		200,000	100,000
Invested in Plant Assets	38,210,000		38,210,000	38,105,000
Endowment Funds.............................		11,230,000	11,230,000	9,667,000
Other Restricted Funds		1,871,000	1,871,000	1,950,000
Total Fund Balances...........................	$43,927,000	$13,632,000	$57,559,000	$55,249,000
Total Liabilities and Fund Balances	$46,860,000	$13,732,000	$60,592,000	$57,032,000

EXHIBIT 15–6   ABC College

Statements of Changes in Working Capital for the Years Ended June 30, 1981 and 1980

	1981			1980
	Unrestricted	Restricted	Total	Total
Sources of Working Capital:				
Excess of Revenue and Other Additions Over Expenses ..	$ 373,000	$1,937,000	$2,310,000	$ 485,000
Add (Deduct) Items Not Affecting Working Capital:				
Depreciation	820,000		820,000	765,000
Unrealized (Appreciation) Depreciation of Investments ..	200,000	265,000	465,000	(470,000)
Working Capital Provided By Operations for the Year . . .	$1,393,000	$2,202,000	$3,595,000	$ 780,000
Issuance of Long-Term Debt	1,000,000		1,000,000	
Proceeds from Sales of Long-Term Investments	400,000	2,180,000	2,580,000	1,070,000
Total Sources of Working Capital	$2,793,000	$4,382,000	$7,175,000	$1,850,000
Uses of Working Capital:				
Purchases of Buildings and Equipment	$1,925,000		$1,925,000	$ 150,000
Reduction of Long-Term Debt	50,000		50,000	50,000
Purchase of Long-Term Investments	1,100,000	$4,390,000	5,490,000	1,180,000
Increase in Long-Term Student Loans		150,000	150,000	50,000
Transfers Between Funds	(322,000)	322,000		
Total Uses of Working Capital	$2,753,000	$4,862,000	$7,615,000	$1,430,000
Increase (Decrease) in Working Capital	$ 40,000	($ 480,000)	($ 440,000)	$ 420,000
Changes in Working Capital:				
Increase (Decrease) in Current Assets:				
Cash	$ 100,000	$ 75,000	$ 175,000	($ 75,000)
Short-Term Investments	119,000	(610,000)	(491,000)	250,000
Accounts Receivable	50,000		50,000	25,000
Student Loans		30,000	30,000	175,000
Inventory	80,000		80,000	(10,000)
Prepaid Expenses	16,000		16,000	10,000
	$ 365,000	$ (505.000)	$ (140,000)	$ 375,000
(Increase) Decrease in Current Liabilities:				
Accounts Payable.	(225,000)	25,000	(200,000)	50,000
Accrued Expenses	(50,000)		(50,000)	(5,000)
Portion of Long-Term Debt Due Within One Year	(50,000)		(50,000)	
	$ (325,000)	$ 25,000	$ (300,000)	$ 45,000
Increase (Decrease) in Working Capital	$ 40,000	($ 480,000)	($ 440,000)	$ 420,000

CHAPTER 16

Internal Control

Roswell Steffen, chief teller at the Park Avenue branch of the Union Dime Savings Bank in New York City, earned a salary of $11,000. A quiet, modest man, he was well liked by his fellow workers and spent most evenings at home with his wife and two teenaged daughters in their $275-a-month garden apartment in New Jersey. An investigation by federal, state, and local authorities into a large-scale, illegal bookmaking operation revealed that Steffen had another side. He had been betting thousands of dollars a day on horse races and professional sports. Because of the size of the bets, the investigators consulted with officials of the Union Dime Bank, who conducted an extensive review of their records and found that Steffen had embezzled $1,500,000 over a 3- to 4-year period. Steffen, a compulsive gambler, admitted that he had lost the entire sum.

When asked how he had embezzled the money, Steffen explained that he had been given daily, unregulated access to the cash vault and that many of the tellers he supervised were inexperienced. As part of his supervisory duties he also had access to the computer terminals and the authority to modify the computerized data. This combination of circumstances allowed Steffen to take cash from deposits and manipulate computer inputs in order to conceal any shortages.

Steffen was not a computer "genius" and the mechanics of his crime were fairly simple. As the supervisor of tellers, he could override many of the basic controls on the bank's computerized accounting system. When a customer brought in a large deposit, Steffen would enter the amount in the customer's passbook. On the computer, however, he would record the deposit under the account number of a second passbook, which he later destroyed. Money was withdrawn periodically by Steffen from the second passbook account.

Steffen kept careful track of the fictitious deposits and constantly made corrections to juggle the more than 50 accounts he was manipulating. When this system became too complicated and time-consuming, he switched to 2-year certificates of deposit, which only required manipulation every 24 months. Occasionally, customers would discover an error in their accounts and march into the bank demanding a correction. The tellers would naturally refer these irate customers to Steffen, the chief teller, who would explain the difficulty as a computer error or a new teller's misposting. He would then make corrections, altering some other account to compensate for the "error."

These "errors" went undetected for almost four years because Steffen, who was not authorized to use the computer terminal except for administrative and clerical procedures, was in fact using it to enter transactions and manipulate the accounts so that they appeared to be correct. More important, Roswell Steffen was able to perpetrate this fraud because there was a serious breakdown of internal controls at the Union Dime Savings Bank.[1] Although the bank had most of the features of a good accounting system (sound reporting practices, timely data, and so on), it lacked strength in an essential area: internal control.

Chapter 8 briefly discussed the controls needed for cash and cash transactions. This chapter explains internal control in more detail. Because of the nature of the subject, the chapter presents information in a more conceptual and less procedural manner than preceding chapters.

What Is Internal Control?

internal control *an organization's methods and procedures for safeguarding its assets, checking on the accuracy and reliability of accounting data, promoting operational efficiency, and encouraging adherence to managerial policies*

The American Institute of Certified Public Accountants has defined internal control as "the plan of organization and all the coordinate methods and measures adopted within a business" to ensure that (1) its resources are protected against waste, fraud, inefficiency, and unauthorized use; (2) its accounting data are accurate and reliable; (3) its performance is evaluated periodically; and (4) its policies and procedures are followed.[2]

Although a good system of internal control would probably have prevented the fraud perpetrated by Roswell Steffen, fraud prevention is not its main purpose. The real purpose of internal control is to promote efficient operations. In fact, the concept of internal control is so basic that it affects every aspect of the organization, including the efficient acquisition, utilization, and conservation of all resources.

In a small coffee shop, for example, questions relating to internal control would include: Have the personnel been adequately trained? Is there a good refrigeration system to keep the food fresh? Do the waiters and waitresses have order booklets with serialized, preprinted numbers on them? Is there a cash register with an internal tape? Does the building

[1] Russell, Harold F., *Foozles and Frauds* (Altamonte Springs, Fla.: Institute of Internal Auditors), 1977.

[2] Statement on Auditing Standards No. 1, "Codification of Auditing Standards and Procedures" (American Institute of CPAs, 1973), Section 320.

have a fire sprinkler system? Is there good supervision of personnel? Are the duties of the cashier and of the waiters and waitresses adequately separated? Who makes the bank deposit of the day's receipts? Who has responsibility for the accounting records? In other words, internal control goes beyond the control of cash receipts and disbursements and the results of transactions as summarized in accounting reports; it extends to all phases of the operations of a business.

BASIC CATEGORIES: ADMINISTRATIVE AND ACCOUNTING CONTROLS

administrative controls *procedures that deal primarily with operational efficiency and employees' compliance with authorized policies and procedures*

Typically, there are two broad categories of internal control. Administrative controls deal primarily with operational efficiency and compliance with an organization's policies and procedures. Management establishes objectives and policies, and then sets up administrative control procedures to ensure that its objectives are being fulfilled.

A typical administrative control is the requirement that all new employees submit to a physical examination. Another might be the requirement that any capital expenditure exceeding $1,000 be approved by the controller. Still another is the design of security procedures to ensure that only certain authorized employees are allowed access to the computer. Other administrative controls are effected through the use of budgets, quality control reports, personnel evaluations, computer logs, statistical analyses, daily absentee records, market research, and periodic performance evaluations.

Thus, administrative controls are designed to achieve management's objectives. As such, they have little or no direct bearing on the accuracy and reliability of the financial statements and, therefore, are not of particular interest to the external auditor (that is, the independent certified public accountant). Because they deal primarily with operational efficiency and authorization, administrative controls are more the concern of the internal auditor, who is often a part of the management team.

accounting controls *the plan of organization and the procedures and records that are concerned with safeguarding the assets and assuring the reliability of the financial records*

In contrast, accounting controls "comprise the plan of organization and the procedures and records that are concerned with the safeguarding of assets and the reliability of financial records."[3] The separation of the custody of assets from the accounting for those assets is an example of an accounting control. Thus, the cashier receiving payments from customers should not also have the responsibility for recording those receipts in the journals. This fundamental control was violated in the case of Roswell Steffen, who not only had access to the cash vault but also to the computer terminals, where he was free to enter transactions and manipulate accounts. Another example is the separation of the authority to approve transactions from the custody of related assets. The person who authorizes the payment of a bill should not be the same person who signs the check that pays the bill. Obviously, that individual could authorize payments to himself or herself. Similarly, the person who distributes checks to employees should not have the authority to add new employees to the payroll, or to delete employees who have been terminated. Why? Because that person could then fire an employee and leave the person's name on the payroll, or hire a

[3] Statement on Auditing Standards No. 1, Section 320.28.

EXHIBIT 16–1   **Internal Accounting Control Objectives**

Control	Description
Authorization	Transactions are executed in accordance with management's general or specific instructions.
Recording	Transactions are recorded as necessary to (1) permit preparation of financial statements in conformity with generally accepted accounting principles or any other criteria applicable to such statements, . . . and (2) maintain accountability for assets.
Access to Assets	Access to assets is permitted only in accordance with management's authorization.
Asset Accountability	The record of assets is compared with the existing assets at reasonable intervals and appropriate action is taken with respect to any differences.*

* Exhibit 16–5 on page 526 provides more details on this important control.

Source: Statement on Auditing Standards No. 1, Sections 320.27–320.28.

fictitious employee and pocket the checks. Still another example: It is not wise to allow programmers unrestricted access to the computer because, with such access, they might be able to manipulate the computer programs for their own benefit.

Accounting controls are the direct concern of external auditors (CPAs), who seek assurance that a firm's accounting system is functioning properly. As a result, CPAs focus on a firm's ability to achieve the four basic categories of accounting control: authorization, recording, access to assets, and asset accountability. The objective for each category is explained briefly in Exhibit 16–1.

MANAGEMENT'S RESPONSIBILITY AND THE FOREIGN CORRUPT PRACTICES ACT

Foreign Corrupt Practices Act (FCPA) of 1977 *legislation that requires all companies registered with the Securities and Exchange Commission to keep accurate accounting records and maintain an adequate system of internal control*

The independent auditor will always review a company's system of internal control to make sure that it meets the four objectives presented in Exhibit 16–1. However, management is directly responsible for establishing and maintaining that system. Until recently, management's responsibility to maintain an adequate internal accounting control system was only implied. There was no formal legal requirement. However, in the wake of illegal political campaign contributions, business frauds, and numerous illegal payments to foreign officials in exchange for business favors, Congress passed the Foreign Corrupt Practices Act of 1977 (FCPA). Portions of the FCPA were then incorporated by amendment into the Securities and Exchange Act of 1934. The result of this legislation is that all companies registered with the Securities and Exchange Commission (SEC) are required by law to keep records that represent the firm's transactions accurately and fairly. In addition, they must maintain systems of internal accounting control that meet the four objectives set forth in Exhibit 16–1.

Note that the law did not create any new responsibilities for management. However, it makes mandatory requirements that had been only implied previously. New SEC regulations are being considered that would legally require a periodic review of internal controls by external auditors. Such regulations would require CPAs to report to management, the SEC, and the public on the internal control systems of the companies they audit and offer judgments as to whether or not the companies are in compliance with the law. For now, the SEC is merely encouraging rather than mandating such a review of internal control by external auditors.

COST-BENEFICIAL CONTROLS

cost-beneficial controls controls that benefit a company to an extent that outweighs their costs

In exercising its responsibility for maintaining adequate internal controls, management will want to be sure that the controls are cost beneficial. This means that the benefits must be greater than the costs. In designing a system that is cost beneficial, management evaluates a number of factors. Among them: The size and complexity of the business, the diversity of its operations, the degree of centralization of its financial and operating management, the types and values of its assets, its personnel policies, and even the prevailing political climate and the degree of economic stability. It would be ridiculous, for example, to hire armed guards for $10,000 a year to watch over a $500 petty-cash fund.

A company could install a system of internal controls that would prevent 99.9 percent of all errors in its accounting system, but it might not be cost beneficial. There is always some level of control that is adequate but not excessive, so management must weigh the potential benefits of having certain controls against the costs of providing them.

TO SUMMARIZE Internal control is the plan of organization and all other measures that a business uses to safeguard its resources, ensure that its accounting data are reliable, reduce irregularities, and detect errors (accounting controls). Internal control also includes those measures used to promote operational efficiency and to encourage adherence to managerial policies (administrative controls). The FCPA and the related amendment to the Securities and Exchange Act of 1934 now require management to take the responsibility for maintaining good internal controls. Management will also want to see to it that these controls are cost beneficial.

Characteristics of an Effective System of Internal Control

There is no "perfect" system of internal control. Each organization is unique, which makes it literally impossible to spell out a system of internal control that is appropriate for all conditions and circumstances. We can, however, identify some general characteristics that, if implemented, would help a firm achieve the four basic objectives of internal control. The AICPA has suggested that a satisfactory system of internal control is one with the following characteristics.

1. A sound plan of organization, including appropriate segregation of functional responsibilities.

2. A system of authorization and recording that provides adequate accountability and control over assets, liabilities, revenues, and expenses.

3. Sound practices and procedures.

4. Competent and trustworthy personnel.

These characteristics are not separate and distinct. Considerable overlap exists, for example, between a system of authorization and recording and the sound practices that must be followed to ensure that authorization and recording are proper. In the same way, a sound plan of organization will be most effective where the company is staffed with competent and trustworthy personnel. In the following discussion of the four basic characteristics of internal control, you should keep in mind that each characteristic interconnects and overlaps with the others to form an efficient and effective total system.

PLAN OF ORGANIZATION

A sound plan of organization has two important characteristics: (1) well-defined lines of authority, and (2) segregation of functional responsibilities. The degree to which these characteristics are applied depends, of course, on a number of considerations. Among them: The nature and size of the business, the style and philosophy of its management, the size and geographical distribution of its units, the variation in its product lines, and political and behavioral considerations. It is impossible, to use an extreme example, for the local Mom & Pop grocery store to have the same segregation of accounting duties as General Motors. Similarly, a small business where members of the family share in the financial duties would not have the same type of organizational structure as a large corporation with well-defined lines of authority and segregation of responsibilities. A sound plan of organization depends on a number of internal and external factors and any internal control system must be designed with these factors in mind.

Lines of Authority

Theoretically, only one person in a department should be responsible for each function, such as cash receipts, cash disbursements, purchasing, payroll preparation, or credit approval. It takes little imagination to envision the confusion that would result if a business gave every employee unlimited purchasing authority. There would be overstocking, duplication of orders, loss of quantity discounts, and tremendous waste. By designating responsibility for the purchasing function, or any other function, the organization runs more smoothly and control is maintained.

Normally, each company will have an organizational chart that not only specifies the formal lines of authority but also indicates departmental responsibilities. Exhibit 16—2 shows how the various functional areas of a typical organization might be separated, each with its respective lines of authority.

EXHIBIT 16–2 Organization Chart

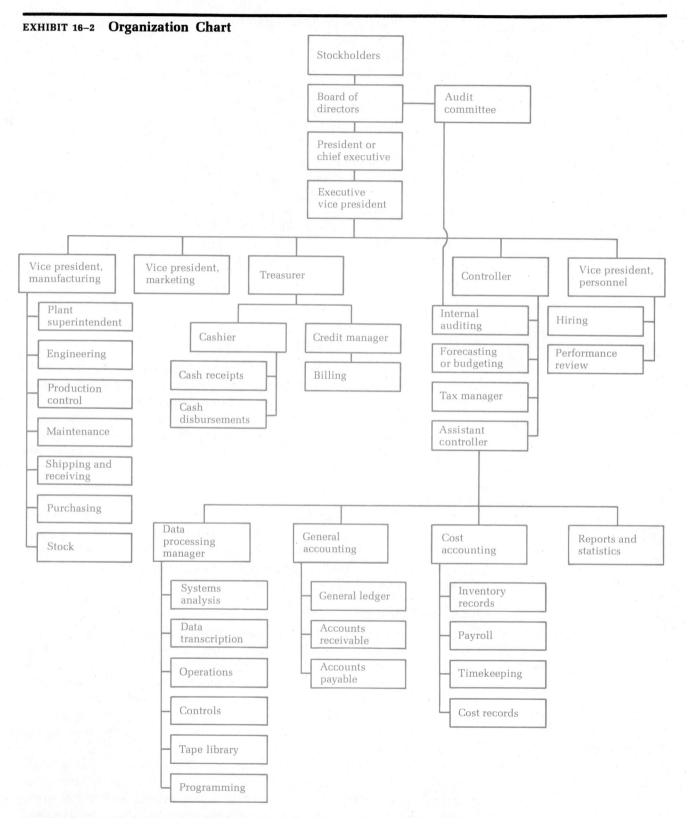

Note: The "bump" in the line from internal auditing to the audit committee indicates a direct reporting relationship.

Segregation of Functional Responsibilities

A sound plan of organization should provide for the appropriate segregation of functional responsibilities. This means that no department should be responsible for handling *all* phases of a transaction. In some small businesses, of course, this segregation is not possible. However, there are three functions that should be performed by separate departments, or at least by different people.

1. *Authorization:* authorizing and approving the execution of a transaction; for example, approving the sale of a building or land.
2. *Record Keeping:* recording the transaction in the accounting journals.
3. *Custodial:* having physical possession of or control over the assets involved in the transaction, including operational responsibility—for example, having custody of cash or marketable securities, or having control over the production function.

By separating the responsibilities for these duties, a company realizes the efficiencies derived from specialization and also reduces the errors, both intentional and unintentional, that might otherwise occur.

Separating operational or custodial duties from record keeping helps ensure that reports are unbiased. For example, having the general accounting department prepare an analysis of accounts receivable for the credit manager helps ensure the objectivity and independence with which this information is compiled, and thereby enhances its usefulness. Separating the custody of assets from record keeping also protects against embezzlement or fraud. By giving custody of the asset to one person and control over the asset's records to another, a company reduces the risk that the asset will be used by an employee for personal gain. If Roswell Steffen, for example, had not had access to the record-keeping function, he would have had to conspire with the person in charge of the records in order to manipulate the customer deposits to his advantage. With these duties separated, the employee who has custody of an asset will be less inclined to steal because another person is accounting for the asset.

Separating the custodial responsibility from the authorization and approval function is also desirable, to the extent that it is possible. For example, a warehouse manager who has custody of scrap materials should not be able to authorize the sale of that scrap. Otherwise, the manager could authorize the sale of, say, 500 pounds of aluminum scrap, but actually sell 2,000 pounds and pocket the difference.

Exhibit 16–3 describes one internal control system—the segregation of duties related to cash receipts.

SYSTEM OF AUTHORIZATION

A strong system of internal control requires proper authorization of every transaction. In the typical corporate organization, this authorization originates with the shareholders. It is then delegated from the board of directors to upper-level management and eventually throughout the organization.

EXHIBIT 16–3   Segregation of Duties Related to Cash Receipts

A mail clerk, in the presence of another employee, opens the day's mail. The mail clerk prepares a list of receipts in triplicate, including the name of the payer and the amount of each remittance and whether it was cash or a check. The receipts are then totaled. This remittance list is given to a cash receipts clerk, who makes entries in the Cash Receipts Journal, debiting Cash and crediting Accounts Receivable for each entry. Totals in the Cash Receipts Journal must agree with the total on the remittance list.

An accounts receivable clerk also receives a copy of the remittance list. The clerk posts the individual accounts to the Accounts Receivable Ledger, checking to be sure that the total agrees with the total cash receipts, as reported by the mail clerk.

The mail clerk hand-carries the day's receipts to the cashier. The cashier counts the money and compares the total with the total on the remittance list. Assuming that the amounts agree, the cashier signs a copy of the remittance list and returns it to the mail clerk as a receipt. The cashier then prepares a deposit slip in duplicate and deposits the money in the bank. One copy of the deposit slip is kept by the cashier and one is given to a supervisor.

The supervisor compares the total on the remittance list with the total on the bank deposit slip (making certain that the bank has validated the deposit slip) to be sure that the day's receipts were actually deposited in the bank. The supervisor also periodically compares the totals in the Cash Receipts Journal and the Accounts Receivable Ledger to ensure that the amounts are credited to the proper accounts.

This segregation of duties related to cash receipts ensures the integrity of the records and the control over cash. The cashier could pocket some of the receipts, but the discrepancy would be discovered when the supervisor compared the remittance list with the deposit slip. Likewise, the mail clerk could steal receipts but it would be more difficult in the presence of another person. In addition, the clerk eventually would be caught when a customer complained that a payment had not been credited. Since the cash receipts clerk and accounts receivable clerk have no access to the cash, falsifying records would do them no good. And finally, the supervisor, who has control over the records, has no control over the cash. If two or more employees were in collusion to defraud, these controls would obviously break down. No controls can provide absolute protection against widespread collusion.

Whereas the board of directors and upper-level management possess a fairly general power of authorization, a clerk usually has limited authority. Thus, the board would authorize dividends, a general change in policies, or a merger, whereas a clerk would be restricted to the authorization of credit or a specific cash transaction.

Authorization, which enhances control by making individuals accountable for their actions, is closely tied to sound organizational policies. That is, if the methods of dealing with transactions are consistent with organizational policies, including proper lines of authority and segregation of duties, then the authorization of any transaction will be monitored and reviewed at various points in the operating cycle. For example, the approval of a cash disbursement for repair work requires several levels of authorization. Before the accounts payable clerk okays the disbursement, the work order should be checked to make sure it was properly authorized. In addition, the work order should be reviewed to verify that the repair was completed satisfactorily. This overlapping process significantly strengthens the internal control system.

Adequate Documentation and Recording

A key to proper authorization is an adequate system of documentation and recording. As explained in Chapter 3, documents are the physical, objective evidence of accounting transactions. Their existence allows management to review any transaction for appropriate authorization. Documents are also the means by which information is communicated throughout an organization. In short, adequate documentation provides evidence that the recording, classifying, and summarizing functions are being performed properly.

A good system of documentation has several characteristics.

1. *Simplicity.* Documents should be as uncluttered as possible, so that they can be easily interpreted and understood.

2. *Multiple Use.* Documents should be designed with all possible uses in mind. There should be enough copies of a sales invoice, for example, so that it can be used for recording sales in the Sales Journal, for calculating commissions, for authorizing credit terms, for authorizing shipments, and as a back-up document for computing sales by sales representatives, territories, products, and other relevant categories.

3. *Good Forms Design.* Forms should be prepared with speed and efficiency in mind. The following are basic requirements: proper size for ease in filing and mailing, adequate room for handwritten notes, left-to-right and top-to-bottom design for ease in filling out, and the right grade, size, weight, and color of paper.

4. *Prenumbering.* Documents should be prenumbered. This facilitates identification of missing documents and filing of material for later reference.

5. *Timely Preparation.* Forms should be prepared as the transaction takes place in order to reduce the chance of unintentional error and/or manipulation. Computers can be used to speed up the preparation and processing of transactions.

Documentation with these features enhances a company's control over its transactions.

Chart of Accounts

chart of accounts *a systematic listing of all accounts used by a company*

A related but separate feature of sound documentation is a chart of accounts. As shown in Chapter 3 (page 78) and repeated here in Exhibit 16–4, this is a written classification of a company's accounts. Typically, the accounts are grouped by type in the order of their appearance on the financial statements and other reports. Each group of accounts is assigned a sequence of numbers. The individual accounts are then given numbers, with gaps left in the sequence for accounts that may be added as the business grows.

The chart of accounts helps to organize the accounting records. In so doing, it contributes to the consistent reporting of similar transactions and to the proper presentation of information on a company's financial statements.

EXHIBIT 16–4   Chart of Accounts for a Merchandising Business

Assets (100–199)

Current Assets (100–120):
100   Petty Cash
101   Cash
102   Marketable Securities
103   Notes Receivable
105   Trade Accounts Receivable
106   Allowance for Doubtful Accounts
107   Inventory
108   Prepaid Rent
109   Prepaid Taxes
110   Prepaid Insurance
111   Other Prepaid Expenses

Funds and Investments (121–140):
121   Bond Sinking Fund
131   Investment in Stock of X Co.

Long-Term Operational Assets (141–160):
141   Land
142   Buildings
143   Accumulated Depreciation—Buildings
144   Store Equipment
145   Accumulated Depreciation—Store Equipment
146   Delivery Vehicles
147   Accumulated Depreciation—Delivery Vehicles
148   Office Furniture
149   Accumulated Depreciation—Office Furniture

Intangible Assets (161–180):
161   Patents
162   Franchises
163   Trademarks
164   Goodwill

Other Assets (181–199)

Liabilities (200–299)

Current Liabilities (200–219):
201   Notes Payable
202   Accounts Payable
203   Salaries Payable
204   Interest Payable
205   Payroll Taxes Payable
206   Income Taxes Payable
207   Rent Payable
219   Other Current Liabilities

Long-Term Liabilities (220–239):
221   Notes Payable
222   Bonds Payable
223   Mortgage Payable
224   Other Long-Term Liabilities

Stockholders' Equity (300–399)

301   Common Stock
302   Paid-in Capital in Excess of Par—Common Stock
303   Preferred Stock
304   Paid-in Capital in Excess of Par—Preferred Stock
310   Treasury Stock
330   Retained Earnings

SOUND PROCEDURES

A well-designed system of internal control, complete with all the appropriate safeguards, will be ineffective unless the organization implements sound procedures. The strength of controls depends on the degree to which they are put into effect with proper procedures.

There is considerable overlap between this accounting characteristic and those just discussed: segregation of responsibilities, authorization, and proper documentation. However, sound procedures include several other elements, such as accounting and procedures manuals, physical safeguards, and internal auditing.

Accounting and Procedures Manuals

Large, complex organizations require a sophisticated accounting system. To ensure that the system is understood and properly used by all per-

Sales (400–499)

400	Sales
402	Sales Returns and Allowances
404	Sales Discounts
450	Purchases
451	Purchase Returns and Allowances
452	Purchase Discounts
453	Freight-In

Operating Expenses (500–599)

Selling Expenses (500–549):

501	Sales Salaries
505	Sales Commissions
510	Freight-Out
520	Payroll Taxes
521	Sales Supplies Expense
522	Fuel Expense
523	Utility Expense
524	Postage Expense
525	Travel Expense
526	Depreciation Expense—Delivery Vehicles
527	Equipment Rent Expense
528	Advertising Expense
529	Display Materials Expense
530	Sales Office Repair Expense
531	Depreciation Expense—Store Equipment

General and Administrative Expenses (550–599):

551	Officers' Salaries
552	Office Salaries
553	Administrative Salaries
570	Payroll Taxes
571	Office Supplies Expense
572	Fuel Expense
573	Utility Expense
574	Postage Expense
575	Travel Expense
576	Depreciation Expense—Buildings
577	Depreciation Expense—Office Furniture
578	Office Equipment Rent Expense
579	Legal Fees
580	Accounting Fees
581	Building Repair and Maintenance Expense
582	Charitable Contributions
583	Bad Debt Expense
584	Amortization of Goodwill
585	Amortization of Patents

Other Expenses (600–699)

601	Interest on Notes
602	Interest on Bonds
603	Interest on Mortgage

Other Income (700–799)

701	Interest Revenue
702	Revenue from Investments
703	Rental Income
704	Miscellaneous Income

accounting manual   *a document that lists all accounts and describes the proper bookkeeping for transactions likely to be processed through each account*

procedures manual   *a document that identifies the general policies of a company*

sonnel, an accounting manual is created. Such a manual lists and describes each account and potential transaction and sets forth the proper bookkeeping procedures. Employees thus can check to be sure that they are handling transactions correctly. For example, suppose a clerk has to account for the purchase of $1,000 of cleaning solution. Should the amount be treated as an expense or as an asset? The answer can be found by looking in the accounting manual for a similar transaction.

A procedures manual, which may be combined with the accounting manual, describes the general policies of a company. For example, it would describe the firm's credit policy and the policy on sales returns, as well as the reports to be prepared by each department. This manual would also include job descriptions that outline the duties, responsibilities, and authority of each position.

Physical Safeguards

Some of the most crucial policies and procedures involve the use of adequate physical safeguards to protect resources. Obviously, a bank would not allow significant amounts of money to be transported in a regular car. In the same way, a company should not leave its valuable assets unprotected. Examples of physical security systems are fireproof vaults for the storage of classified information, currency, and marketable securities, and guards, fences, and remote control cameras for the protection of equipment, materials, and merchandise.

Records and documents are also important resources and must be protected. Recreating lost or destroyed records can be costly and time-consuming. The high cost of back-up records (often on microfilm) is usually more than justified in protecting such valuable resources.

Internal Auditing

A major concern of management and auditors is how well the system of internal control is functioning. That brings us to the fourth basic objective of internal accounting control: "The record of assets is compared with the existing assets at reasonable intervals and appropriate action is taken with respect to any differences" (see Exhibits 16–1 and 16–5). In a large firm, operating results and adherence of employees to management's policies are generally under constant surveillance by a staff of internal auditors. By reviewing the system of internal controls and making a periodic audit of operations, the internal audit department functions as an arm of management.

internal audit *an appraisal by internal accountants of employee performance and adherence to company policies, and an assessment of the reliability of the information system*

An important characteristic of such a department, however, is its independence. To function properly, the internal audit staff should not be subordinate to any operating department; instead, it should report directly to top management. In most large companies the internal audit department is a functional part of the controller's office, but it reports directly to an audit committee composed of outside members of the board of directors (see Exhibit 16–2). This committee's responsibilities include nominating the independent auditors, reviewing their work, and acting as a liaison for the internal audit staff in protecting and safeguarding the assets of the organization.

EXHIBIT 16–5 **Physical Comparison of Assets**

Category	Description
Cash and Checking	Count petty cash and receive bank reconciliations regularly.
Accounts Receivable	Send audit letters to customers, asking them to confirm their accounts receivable balances.
Inventory	Perform periodic physical spot check counts in addition to annual full count.
Long-Term Operational Assets	Count these assets and compare to the company's records.

COMPETENT AND TRUSTWORTHY PERSONNEL

The most important characteristic of a satisfactory system of internal control is the most difficult to evaluate. The best structured system will fail if the company's employees are incompetent or dishonest. People are an organization's most important resource, and for this reason good personnel policies are essential in achieving a good system of internal control. Perhaps the most important areas to consider in assuring that an organization has competent and trustworthy personnel are employee selection, employee training, employee supervision, performance review, and fidelity bonding.

Employee Selection

Prospective employees should be carefully screened. This process may include interviews, aptitude tests, background checks, and the evaluation of references from past employers. Once the person's qualifications are confirmed, great care should be taken in matching jobs with talents. A disgruntled or frustrated employee can do considerable damage to an organization, and the selection process should be thorough enough to minimize this risk.

Employee Training

Programs for training employees should be designed to accelerate employee development and to increase the number of competent individuals available to assume the various levels of responsibility. In addition, employees should be trained to perform a variety of jobs, so that vacations and absenteeism will not cause major disruptions in the company's operations. Such training procedures should also allow for the periodic rotation of assignments, a key element in internal control. Employees who know that someone else may soon be taking over their position usually perform better and are more conscientious in following the established policies and procedures. Rotation of employees also may reveal errors and irregularities that would otherwise go unnoticed.

In a parallel procedure, employees should be required to take vacations. This has the same effect as a periodic rotation of duties. Take the classic example of the bank clerk who had not taken a vacation in 20 years. Everyone thought that she was a most dedicated and efficient employee. An illness forced her to take a few weeks off and her work was performed by another clerk. As a result, it was discovered that for a number of years she had been embezzling large sums of money. She had been able to cover up the fraud only because she was always present. Rotation of employees and mandatory vacations would have prevented this fraud.

Employee Supervision and Performance Review

Even the most carefully selected and trained individuals need to have their work monitored. A qualified supervisor performs this role by assisting in the day-to-day activities and by conducting periodic performance reviews. These reviews, conducted at all levels of the organization, help identify both the strengths and the weaknesses of the employees' performance. A performance review also forces workers to account for the assets under their control. The system whereby employees are held directly responsible for the resources entrusted to their care is called "responsibility accounting."

Fidelity Bonding

Another important aspect of sound personnel policies and procedures is fidelity bonding. No system of internal control is foolproof, and losses can occur if employees who handle cash or other liquid assets are dishonest. As a result, employees in charge of easily converted assets may be bonded. A fidelity bond is simply an insurance contract whereby a bonding company agrees to reimburse the employer for any theft, embezzlement, or fraud perpetrated by an employee covered by the agreement. Its purpose is really twofold: (1) The company is insured against the misappropriation of assets by its employees, and (2) employees, realizing that the bonding companies generally prosecute to the fullest extent to recover losses, are more hesitant to commit dishonest acts.

fidelity bond *an insurance contract whereby a bonding company agrees to reimburse an employer for any theft, embezzlement, or fraud perpetrated by an employee covered by the bonding agreement*

TO SUMMARIZE An effective system of internal control must have a sound plan of organization, with clear lines of authority and adequate segregation of functional responsibilities. Its system of authorization and documentation must provide for accountability and control over resources. A chart of accounts is useful in this regard. In implementing sound procedures, companies use accounting and procedures manuals, establish physical safeguards over assets, and rely on internal auditors to monitor the practices being followed. Finally, a company must have competent and trustworthy personnel, developed by proper employee selection, employee training, and employee supervision and review. In addition, fidelity bonding helps protect against losses.

The Effects of Computers on Internal Control

Computers have contributed greatly to the speed and accuracy with which data are processed. And, because they reduce the amount of human intervention, they are consistently objective and reliable. When data are processed in accordance with the system's design and programs, very few mathematical or procedural errors will occur. Thus, as noted in Chapter 3, computers tend to enhance the overall effectiveness and efficiency of accounting systems.

The elements of internal control discussed in this chapter apply equally to a computerized accounting system. Computer operators are usually bonded, duties are generally rotated and segregated where possible, and physical safeguards are maintained. In addition, computers are valuable assets that require environmental controls, such as sprinkler systems, climate control, guards or restricted access, and fireproof libraries.

For all its benefits, however, the computer can also be a source of problems in internal control, in the following ways.

1. Although the decrease in human involvement with the data will eliminate many mechanical or mathematical errors, it may also obscure errors that would otherwise be discovered in manual systems. For exam-

ple, two identical refunds from one company may go unnoticed by a computer. A person, on the other hand, might become suspicious and, in checking into the matter, discover that an error had been made.

2. Because computer systems require such specialized skills, it may be difficult for a company to achieve the degree of segregation of duties necessary for sound internal control. For example, programmers in a small company may be asked to operate the computer system, making it possible for them to manipulate their own programs for personal benefit.

3. Data must be converted to tape, punched cards, or other media, and so errors are likely to be introduced into the system during the data-conversion process.

4. Less documentary evidence usually remains after certain functions have been performed by the computer. This means that the internal controls that rely upon a review of documentation may be less meaningful. Computers may destroy or conceal much of the "audit trail."

5. Because management, and even auditors, may not thoroughly understand the computer, dishonest employees can take advantage of this ignorance. People can steal with the aid of a computer without actually having to carry away goods or cash.

Due to these factors, internal checks and controls must be adapted to and built into computer systems. Computer-based internal control systems are often complex and may be difficult for management and auditors to work with, but they are necessary in large companies.

CHAPTER REVIEW

Management needs assurance that the company's assets are being properly safeguarded, that reliable financial information is being generated, that operations are running efficiently, and that its policies and directives are being carried out. A good system of internal control helps provide this important assurance. The controls that are implemented to accomplish this goal should be cost beneficial; that is, the benefits of the controls should exceed the costs.

External auditors will want to make sure that a sound system of internal control exists in an organization. If controls are strong, then they can be more confident that the financial picture is accurate and reliable. If controls are weak, the external auditor will need to perform a much more detailed review.

Internal auditors are also concerned with the adequacy of internal controls. Where strong internal controls exist, the chances are greater that operations are functioning efficiently, that management's policies and procedures are being followed, and that assets are being properly protected.

Perhaps the best way to summarize the concepts discussed in this chapter is to use a checklist. Although the following questions are by no means all-inclusive, they do provide guidelines for evaluating a company's internal control system.

1. Does the organization have reliable and trustworthy personnel?

2. Is there adequate rotation of personnel, including mandatory vacations?

3. Are there adequate procedures for the physical protection of assets (that is, security systems, guards, safety deposit boxes, and so on)?

4. Are the controls cost beneficial?

5. Is the system of controls current?

6. Is there adequate separation of authority?

7. Has responsibility for various operations and functions been adequately defined?

8. Have company policies been put in writing and are these policies adhered to?

9. Are employees who work with highly liquid or sensitive assets bonded?

10. For a large firm, is there an adequate and independent internal audit department?

11. Are the accounting and record-keeping responsibilities adequately separated from the custodianship over the respective assets?

12. Is there a good system of employee selection? Of training? Of review and performance evaluation?

13. Are there adequate records and documentation?

14. Does a system of authorization and verification exist?

15. Does the organization have review procedures to evaluate efficiency as well as effectiveness?

16. Have controls been adapted to protect the organization that uses a sophisticated computer system?

KEY TERMS AND CONCEPTS

accounting controls (516)

accounting manual (525)

administrative controls (516)

chart of accounts (523)

cost-beneficial controls (518)

fidelity bond (528)

Foreign Corrupt Practices Act (FCPA) of 1977 (517)

internal audit (526)

internal control (515)

procedures manual (525)

DISCUSSION QUESTIONS

1. Why is internal control a critical element in accounting?

2. "Internal control refers only to those measures taken to prevent fraud and embezzlement." Do you agree? Explain.

3. Distinguish between accounting and administrative controls.

4. List and discuss four objectives of internal accounting controls.

5. Who has primary responsibility for establishing and maintaining the internal control system within an organization? Discuss.

6. What is the significance of the Foreign Corrupt Practices Act of 1977 with respect to internal accounting controls?

7. Internal controls should be cost beneficial. Explain.

8. What are the principal characteristics of an effective system of internal control?

9. The general principle of adequate segregation of duties recognizes that three basic functions should be segregated by department, or at least be performed by separate people. What are those three functions? Why is it important to separate them?

10. Adequately segregating functions and responsibilities provides several benefits. What are they?

11. A good system of internal control includes proper documentation, which has several desirable characteristics. Discuss each.

12. The internal audit department in a large corporation should always report to the treasurer or to the vice president of production. Do you agree? Explain.

13. With respect to internal control, identify the three most important areas to consider in evaluating a firm's personnel.

14. A fidelity bond protects a business from losses by dishonest employees in more than one way. Explain.

15. Computerized accounting systems have had a tremendous impact upon internal accounting controls. Although they increase the speed and accuracy of data processing and enhance the overall efficiency of the accounting information system, computers also have some negative effects upon internal control. Discuss.

EXERCISES

E16-1   Purposes of Internal Control

People often feel that the main purpose of internal accounting control is to prevent fraud, or at least to make it easier to detect. Other purposes of internal control are often overlooked. What other specific purposes does a system of internal control accomplish? Discuss.

E16-2   Administrative and Accounting Controls

Classify each of the following as either an administrative or an accounting control.

1. Potential employees are required to have a complete physical examination.

2. A computer is used to store payroll records and prepare paychecks.

3. The cashier has no access to the accounting journals.

4. The computer programmer does not operate the computer.

5. A record is kept of employee absences.

6. A study is conducted to determine the amount of time required to make one unit of product.

7. The bank statement is reconciled by someone who neither handles the cash nor maintains the accounting records.

8. A feasibility study is conducted before a new computer system is implemented.

9. An independent CPA audits the company records annually.

10. Company procedures and policies are put in writing and made available to employees.

E16-3   Auditor's Review of Internal Control

A CPA typically reviews a client's system of internal accounting control to ascertain the degree of reliance that can be placed on the client's records. The CPA then plans the audit on the basis of this review of the internal control system. Explain why this procedure is followed.

E16-4   Internal Accounting Control Objectives

For each of the following, list the objective of the internal control procedure.

1. An annual physical inventory is taken, although the perpetual inventory method is used by the company.

2. The purchasing department must approve all machine repairs.

3. Only the cashier is authorized to make disbursements from the petty-cash fund.

4. A prenumbered receipt is prepared in duplicate for each cash payment received from a customer.

5. All supplies must be purchased through the purchasing department.

6. The petty-cash fund is audited by the company's internal auditor at irregular, unannounced intervals.

7. All cash disbursements are made by check.

8. All proposed acquisitions of heavy machinery must be approved by the operations vice president.

E16-5   Cost-Beneficial Systems

Sharpshooter Gun Company has grown dramatically in recent years. As a result, its labor force has increased from 100 to 175 workers. The payroll officer,

Monica Bradley, cannot handle the increased workload. Obviously, something must be done, or the employees will not receive their checks on time. The company has two alternatives: It either can hire an assistant to work with Monica, or it can install a small computer to perform some of the routine tasks. Before making its decision, what factors must Sharpshooter's management consider?

E16−6   Separation of Duties

The city of Wadsworth can afford to hire only one employee to give out parking tickets. This employee is also responsible for collecting fines and money from parking meters, as well as for keeping records for all monies collected.

1. What are the control weaknesses of this arrangement?

2. If two employees are available, what arrangements might be made for better control?

E16−7   Internal Control of Assets and Records

For each of the following assets or records, give an example of a physical safeguard.

1. Raw materials inventory.

2. Marketable securities.

3. An inventory of small, expensive electronic components.

4. Perishable goods.

5. Petty cash.

6. Cash received through the mail.

7. Cash received by clerks in a retail operation.

8. Magnetic tapes with accounts receivable information stored on them.

9. Scrap aluminum or other metals used in making a product.

10. Office supplies and small office equipment.

E16−8   Reasons for Internal Control

Discuss the reasons for each of the following control procedures.

1. Before the treasurer of Kane Candy Company signs disbursement checks, she reviews the supporting data. Afterwards, the supporting data are returned to the accounting department, and the checks are mailed by the treasurer's secretary.

2. Each clerk in a department store has a separate cash drawer and does not have access to the cash drawers of other clerks.

3. The ticket-taker at Nemrow Theatre is required to tear each admission ticket in half. He drops half in a box, and presents the stub to the patron.

4. At Lewis Widget Company four copies of each purchase order are prepared. The fourth and final copy is sent to the receiving department. The form is designed in such a way that the quantity ordered does not appear on the fourth copy.

5. Volunteers who solicit contributions for a local charity are required to issue a receipt for any cash contributions. The receipt book is serially prenumbered and has a single carbon copy for each receipt.

6. Richard Jones, the cashier for Allen & Allen Manufacturing Company, is required to keep copies of all voided (invalidated) receipts.

E16−9   Accounting Manual and Chart of Accounts

You have been hired to audit Cockroach Pest Control Company, which performs exterminating services in sixteen cities of the Southwest. You notice that the company has no accounting manual or chart of accounts. When you mention this to the manager, he responds that such documents would not be helpful in his business. Respond to this comment.

E16−10   Audit Committee

Holly Halstorm, the major stockholder of Halstorm Corporation, has decided that the corporation needs an internal audit committee. She proposes a five-member committee composed of herself, the manager of the accounts receivable department, the head cashier, the manager of the sales department, and the chief computer operator. You, as the independent external auditor, must advise her on the formation of this committee. What would you recommend?

E16−11   Employee Fraud

I. B. Call was a respected and competent employee of Highwater Sales, Inc., a person who had shown exceptional devotion and had been rewarded with increased responsibility. Call never took a vacation and had held his current position for over 10 years. President Dan Barnez was shocked, therefore, when he discovered that Call had embezzled approximately $200,000 over the past decade. Call was able to steal the money because he had access to the Sales Journal and to cash receipts. Thus, he would not record some invoices in the Sales Journal, and would pocket the respective amounts. What major weaknesses of internal control allowed this fraud to go undetected?

E16–12   Responsibility Accounting

Under a system of responsibility accounting, individuals are held accountable for the assets and resources placed in their care. Refer to Exhibit 16–2 and match the following activities with the appropriate position of responsibility (for example, review of operations is performed by an internal auditor).

1. Care of raw materials.
2. Signing checks.
3. Authorization for purchasing raw materials.
4. Care of petty-cash fund.
5. Supervision of workers.
6. Care of plant machinery.
7. Design of internal control system.

E16–13   Internal Control for a Small Business

Most small businesses do not have a staff of internal auditors. Instead, the internal audit functions are performed by managers or owners. Suggest and discuss several internal audit steps that an owner or manager might perform to ensure that the company's policies and procedures are being carried out.

PROBLEMS

P16–1   Control of Cash Receipts

Helpful Charities solicits contributions and then distributes the monies to a number of local nonprofit and charitable organizations. The officers and directors are local clergymen, bankers, lawyers, and doctors, all leaders of the community. A clerk and cashier constitute the only full-time salaried employees. The records of Helpful Charities are limited to a Cash Receipts Journal and a checkbook, which is used to maintain a record of all disbursements.

Volunteers from other organizations solicit contributions during fund-raising campaigns. The volunteers are not assigned any specific areas and tend to solicit primarily from friends, relatives, neighbors, and other acquaintances. New volunteers are constantly sought from among church groups, business and professional organizations, local PTAs, and other community groups.

Typically, contributions are collected in the form of cash and checks. The solicitors collect the donations, fill out receipts, and give them to the donors. They then complete the accompanying stub, noting the donor's name, address, and the amount of the contribution. There are no carbon copies of the receipts and no system for accounting for every receipt. Periodically, the volunteers submit the stubs and the contributions to the cashier, who then deposits the money. Donors may also mail their contributions directly to the cashier. (*AICPA adapted*)

Required:

Discuss the procedures that should be implemented by Helpful Charities to improve internal control over donations. Specifically, discuss what controls would ensure that all monies collected by the solicitors are turned over to the cashier.

P16–2   Internal Control Techniques

A company's overall internal control system is strengthened by each control procedure that is well thought out. Thus, printing checks on special paper so that amounts cannot be erased without detection is one safeguard against theft. And a voucher system that provides for all invoices to be properly authorized, checked for accuracy, and recorded before being paid reduces the likelihood that an invoice will be misplaced, a discount lost, or improper or unauthorized disbursements made. (*AICPA adapted*)

Required:

Discuss the purposes of the following procedures and explain how each helps strengthen internal control.

(a) Fidelity bonding of employees.
(b) Budgeting for capital expenditures (such as the purchase of land).
(c) Listing of remittances (cash received) when the mail is first opened.
(d) Maintaining a ledger for plant and equipment purchases and depreciation expenses.

P16–3   Unifying Problem: Design of Internal Control and Separation of Responsibilities

Newton Drug Company has come to your accounting firm with the following problem. Three employees—Norm Needles (the owner's son), Craig Spackman, and Dale Johnson—must perform the following functions.

a. Receive and deposit all cash receipts.
b. Reconcile the bank account.
c. Prepare checks and the accompanying voucher documents for signature.

d. Maintain a General Ledger.

e. Maintain an Accounts Payable Ledger.

f. Maintain an Accounts Receivable Ledger.

g. Maintain a Cash Disbursements Journal.

h. Issue credits for all returns and allowances.

You are told that all three employees are capable of performing any of these tasks and that they will have no other duties.

Required:

1. Assign the functions to the three employees in such a manner as to ensure the highest degree of internal control. Assume that, except for the routine jobs of bank reconciliation and the issuance of credits, all jobs require an equal amount of time and labor.

2. List at least four specific combinations of these functions that would be unsatisfactory.

P16–4   Examination of an Internal Control System

Assume that you are a member of the internal audit staff of Valdez Company. The controller asks that you review the company's cash payroll system. (*AICPA adapted*)

Required:

What questions might you ask as you review the system of internal control relative to payroll procedures? Include questions having to do with each of the following categories.

   (a) Reliable personnel.

   (b) Separation of responsibilities.

   (c) Supervision.

   (d) Responsibility.

   (e) Document control.

   (f) Bonding, vacations, and rotation of employees.

   (g) Independent checks.

   (h) Physical safeguards.

P16–5   Improvement in an Internal Control System

The town of Commuter Park operates a private parking lot near the railroad station for the benefit of town residents. The guard on duty issues annual pre-numbered parking stickers to commuters who submit an application form and show evidence of residency. The sticker is affixed to the auto and allows the resident to park for up to 12 hours at a price of 25 cents per 3-hour period. Applications are maintained in the guard's office at the lot. The guard checks to see that only residents are using the lot and that no resident has parked without paying the required meter fee.

Once a week the guard, who has a master key for all meters, empties the meters and places the coins in a locked steel box. The guard delivers the box to the town hall, where it is opened, and the coins are manually counted by a storage department clerk who records the transaction on a "Weekly Cash Report." This report is sent to the town accounting department and the cash is placed in a safe in the storage department. The cash is picked up the next day by the town's treasurer, who manually recounts the cash, prepares the bank deposit slip, and delivers the deposit to the bank. The deposit slip, authenticated by the bank teller, is sent to the accounting department where it is filed with the Weekly Cash Report. (*AICPA adapted*)

Required:

Describe weaknesses in the existing system of internal control over the parking lot cash receipts and recommend one or more improvements for each weakness. Organize your answer sheet as follows:

Weakness	Recommended Improvement(s)

P16–6   Unifying Problem: Control Procedures for Hiring Personnel and for Payroll

Kowal Manufacturing Company employs about 50 production workers and has the following hiring practices and payroll procedures.

The factory foreman interviews applicants and either hires or rejects them. When hired, a person fills out a W-4 form (Employee's Withholding Exemption Certificate) and gives it to the foreman. The foreman writes the hourly rate of pay for the new employee in the corner of the W-4 form and then gives the form to a payroll clerk as notice that the worker has been employed. The foreman verbally advises the payroll department of any hourly rate adjustments.

A supply of blank time cards is kept in a box near the entrance to the factory. Each worker takes a time card on Monday morning, fills in his or her name, and notes in pencil the daily arrival and departure times. At the end of the week the workers drop the time cards in another box, also near the entrance to the factory.

The completed time cards are taken from the box on Monday morning by a payroll clerk. Two payroll clerks divide the cards alphabetically between them, one taking A to L and the other M to Z. Each clerk is responsible for his or her section of the payroll. The clerk computes the gross pay, deductions, and net pay; posts the amounts to the employee's earnings records; and prepares and numbers the payroll checks. Employees are automatically removed from the payroll when they fail to turn in a time card.

The payroll checks are signed by the chief accountant and given to the foreman. The foreman distributes the checks and arranges for the delivery of checks to workers who are absent. The payroll bank account is reconciled by the chief accountant, who also prepares the various quarterly and annual payroll tax reports. (*AICPA adapted*)

Required:

List your suggestions for improving the Kowal Manufacturing Company's system of internal control for hiring practices and payroll procedures.

P16−7 Unifying Problem: Deficiencies in Internal Control

The cashier of Easy Company is custodian of the petty-cash fund. At the beginning of July he intercepted a $500 check from customer A and deposited it in a bank account that was part of the company petty-cash fund. He then wrote himself a $500 check from the petty-cash fund, which he cashed. At the end of the month, while processing the monthly statements to customers, he changed the statement to customer A, showing that A had received credit for the $500 check. Ten days later he made an entry in the Cash Receipts Journal that purported to record receipt of a remittance of $500 from customer A. Thus, he restored A's account to its proper balance, but overstated cash in the bank. He covered the overstatement by omitting two checks, worth a total of $500, from the list of outstanding checks in the bank reconciliation. (*AICPA adapted*)

Required:

Discuss briefly what you regard as the more important deficiencies in Easy Company's system of internal control. Include what you consider to be a proper remedy for each deficiency.

CHAPTER 17

The Impact of Income Taxes on Business Decisions

THIS CHAPTER EXPLAINS   Some basic corporate tax terminology.

The different tax treatment of each form of business organization.

Tax-planning guidelines.

Capital gains and ordinary income.

The tax effects of investments in current and operational assets.

The federal tax rate for corporate taxable income of more than $100,000 is 46 percent. This means that for every dollar of ordinary income above $100,000 earned by a corporation, the federal government takes 46 cents. Many states also levy an income tax. Obviously, taxes are an important consideration in business decisions. If management plans wisely, taking taxes into account, the company's effective tax rate usually can be reduced.

In this chapter we examine the major provisions of the federal income tax law and the related tax-planning opportunities that give managers some flexibility in making decisions that will lessen the company's tax liability. In fact, managers are expected to use whatever legitimate means are available to avoid, reduce, or postpone taxes. Although many of the tax-planning opportunities presented here are applicable to all types of businesses, we focus on those most appropriate for corporations, and restrict the discussion to federal income taxes unless otherwise noted.

As you read this chapter, bear in mind that this introduction to income taxes is limited by three factors. First, although the basic principles should have relevance for years to come, tax laws change frequently, and these changes may have an important effect on a company's strategies for limiting taxes. Second, these principles are generalizations and may not apply equally well to all situations. Third, the illustrations presented here are far from exhaustive; they provide only a sampling of the tax situations that are possible.

Income Taxation: An Overview

The first federal income taxes on corporations in the United States were levied in 1908, although similar taxes had been levied by the states during the previous century, and before that by the colonies. Then, as now, these taxes based on income seemed to be the fairest measure of a company's ability to pay to support government functions. Today, the federal income tax has such a large impact on corporations, and is so complex, that very few business decisions should be made without first considering their income tax consequences.

BASIC CORPORATE TAX TERMINOLOGY

The subject of income taxes brings with it a whole new vocabulary. This section is intended to serve as a brief introduction, beginning with an overview of the general process for computing a tax liability and concluding with a discussion of key concepts.

The income tax law outlines the following procedure for calculating tax liability. The flow chart in Exhibit 17–1 provides a more explicit guide to the determination of a corporation's federal income tax liability.

gross income the portion of a company's gross receipts less cost of sales that is subject to taxation

1. Identify gross income. This includes all taxable receipts, most of which are sales, less the cost of sales. Also included are cash receipts other than sales, property received for services rendered (at fair market value), gains on sales of operational assets, and benefits received indirectly (that is, through a third party). An example of a nontaxable receipt, or exclusion, is interest income on state and local government bonds.

exclusions gross receipts that are not subject to tax and are not included in gross income, such as interest on state and local government bonds

deductions business expenses or losses that are subtracted from gross income in computing taxable income

2. Identify the expenses to be deducted from gross income. These deductions include all business expenses that are ordinary and necessary, reasonable in amount, and paid or incurred. Deductions should not always be equated with "expenses" in the accounting sense, for two reasons: (a) accounting principles usually stipulate that expenses are recorded on an accrual basis, whereas in certain cases an expense is not deductible for tax purposes until paid, such as expenditures in connection with product warranties; and (b) expenses related to tax-exempt income are not considered deductions for tax purposes. Note also that the tax law imposes some limitations on the amount deductible for certain expenses of corporations, such as for charitable contributions.

business expenses expenses incurred in the course of business that are ordinary and necessary, reasonable in amount, and have been paid or incurred

taxable income the income remaining after all exclusions and deductions have been subtracted from gross income

3. Subtract the total deductions from gross income to arrive at the tax base (taxable income). Taxable income is generally not the same as accounting income before federal income taxes because many of the tax rules for measuring revenues and expenses are different from the generally accepted accounting principles for measuring accounting income.

gross tax liability the amount of tax computed by multiplying the tax base (taxable income) by the appropriate tax rate

4. Multiply the tax base by the appropriate tax rate to arrive at the gross tax liability. The tax rate is a percentage that increases with the level of taxable income.

net tax liability the amount of tax computed by subtracting tax credits from the gross tax liability

tax credit a direct reduction in the tax liability, usually granted to encourage a particular action or to provide tax relief for certain classes of taxpayers

5. Where applicable, reduce the gross tax liability by tax credits to arrive at the net tax liability. A tax credit is a benefit granted to taxpayers

EXHIBIT 17–1   Steps for Calculating the Federal Income Tax Liability of a Corporation

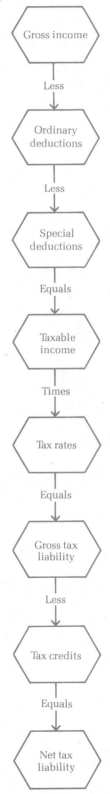

Net receipts or sales less cost of sales; dividends, including nontaxable portion; interest on U.S. obligations (including government bonds); other interest, excluding nontaxable interest; gross rents and royalties; capital gain net income; other income, such as lease income.

Salaries and wages, repairs, bad debts, rent, taxes (other than federal income tax), interest expense, contributions (limited), amortization, depreciation, depletion, advertising, contributions to employee pension and profit-sharing plans (limited), and other "ordinary" expenses.

Net operating loss carryforward from previous year (limited), 85% of dividends received from a domestic corporation subject to federal income tax, 85% of dividends received from certain foreign corporations doing business in the U.S.

Note that taxable income is generally not the same as net income for financial reporting purposes because many income tax regulations are different from generally accepted accounting principles.

The present corporation income tax rate on ordinary taxable income is: 17% on the first $25,000 of taxable income, 20% on the next $25,000 of taxable income, 30% on the next $25,000 of taxable income, 40% on the next $25,000 of taxable income, and 46% on taxable income over $100,000.

This is the amount a corporation would pay if there were no special tax credits.

Special tax credits include foreign tax credit, investment tax credit (ITC), work incentive (WIN) credit, targeted jobs credit.

All corporations must make installment payments of their estimated net tax liability for the coming year if the amount is expected to be $40 or more. The date the corporation can reasonably expect its tax to be $40 determines the number of installments, due dates, and amounts.

that directly reduces the gross tax liability. For example, a business taxpayer may be entitled to an investment tax credit, which would reduce the gross tax liability by up to 10 percent of the cost of certain machinery and equipment purchased and used in a tax year. Note that since a tax credit is a direct reduction in the tax liability, its tax impact is greater than that of a deduction. If a corporation is in the 46 percent tax bracket, a $100 deduction will reduce the tax liability by $46, but a $100 tax credit will reduce the tax liability by $100.

The following example should help clarify the procedure for calculating the tax liability of a corporation.

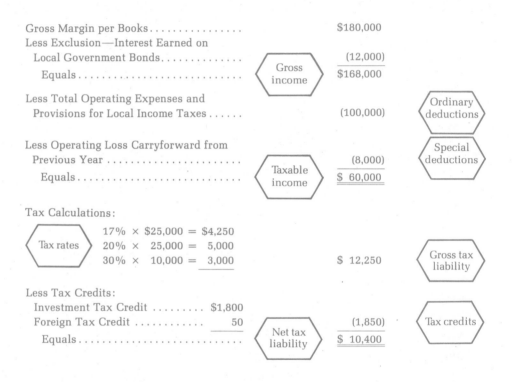

In the above illustration, the company's effective tax rate is only 13 percent, as follows:

$$\frac{\text{net tax liability}}{\text{net book income } (\$180,000 - \$100,000)} = \frac{\$10,400}{\$80,000} = 13\%$$

Taxable income was only $60,000 because, in addition to the ordinary deductions, there was an exclusion of $12,000 of tax-exempt interest on local government bonds and a special deduction for an operating loss carryforward of $8,000. The gross tax liability of $12,250 was reduced by a $1,800 tax credit and a $50 foreign tax credit. The highest tax rate was 30 percent, but the average tax rate was only 20.4 percent ($12,250 ÷ $60,000).

SOME MAJOR CONSIDERATIONS

The first two steps in computing a tax liability involve the identification of gross income and deductible expenses. Since gross income for income tax purposes may not be the same as the accounting gross margin and since not all accounting expenses are deductible for income tax purposes (or are deductible in a different period), these steps require calculations separate from those used to prepare financial statements. Certain concepts and considerations are central to the calculation of gross income and deductible expenses.

The Realization Principle

Gross income includes all taxable receipts less any exclusions. However, amounts received are not considered gross income until they are realized. Realization usually means that a transaction has taken place in which cash and/or other assets have been received in exchange for the assets given up. A realization may also occur when property is exchanged. For example, if an operational asset (land, building, or equipment) is exchanged for inventory, the fair market value of the operational asset would be realized.

Cash- Versus Accrual-Basis Accounting

Identification of gross income also depends on whether the taxpayer is using cash- or accrual-basis accounting. With a cash-basis system, gross income is reported in the year in which it is received. With an accrual-basis system, gross income is reported when it is earned, regardless of when it is received. Note that "receipt of cash" is defined somewhat differently for tax and accounting purposes. That is, the tax law employs the constructive receipt rule, which states that cash is considered to have been received when the taxpayer can exercise control over it, whether or not the cash has been actually received. For example, interest deposited by a bank in a cash-basis taxpayer's savings account before year-end is considered to be gross income in the year of deposit, even if the taxpayer does not withdraw it until the next year.

constructive receipt rule *the idea that cash has been received when the taxpayer can exercise control over it, whether or not the cash has been physically received*

The type of accounting system—cash or accrual—also affects the timing of a business expense as a deduction. That is, with a cash-basis system an expense is recognized and deducted when it is paid. With an accrual-basis system, an expense is recognized when it is incurred, which may be before or after the period in which it is paid. For example, employees' wages are expenses in the period in which they are earned. An insurance premium paid in advance is an expense in the period or periods in which the insurance policy provides protection.

The government allows companies to use either system, except where inventories are a significant item in the measurement of income. Then, the taxpayers must use accrual-basis accounting for inventories. The following simplified situation should illustrate the reason for this. Suppose that Ernie's Machine Company is in its first year of operation. During the year, management pays cash for 100 widgets at $10 each. By the end of the first year Ernie's has sold 90 widgets and has 10 in inventory. On a cash basis the company would show revenues for the 90 widgets sold and expenses for the 100 widgets purchased; income therefore would be understated by $100, which is significant in this case. The ending inventory of 10 units would have a zero cost. Since it is misleading to match expenses for 100 widgets with revenues for 90 widgets, Ernie's should use accrual-basis accounting, which matches expenses for 90 widgets with revenues for 90 widgets. This more appropriately measures income for the period and automatically provides for an ending inventory of 10 units at $10 each. In this example, accrual-basis accounting is not only appropriate for financial reporting purposes, but also is required for income tax purposes.

Other Considerations

As we have indicated, not all expenses are deductible for corporate federal income tax purposes. Expenses that are directly related to the operation of a company are deductible from gross income if ordinary and necessary, reasonable in amount, and paid or incurred. Another category of deductible expenses involves certain types of losses. These would include sales and exchanges of assets at a loss, bad-debt losses, and casualty losses. Losses from sales or exchanges of assets held purely for personal use are not deductible.

TO SUMMARIZE   A corporation pays taxes at rates that increase with the level of taxable income (up to $100,000). Business and special deductions are subtracted from gross income to arrive at the tax base (taxable income). The tax rate multiplied by the tax base gives the gross tax liability, from which tax credits are subtracted to determine the net tax liability. The time of recognition of gross income and expenses depends on whether the cash or accrual basis is used. A company can choose either method, except that the accrual basis must be used when inventories are a significant factor in computing income.

How Each Form of Business Is Taxed

The three basic types of business organizations—proprietorships, partnerships, and corporations—are treated differently from a tax point of view. In fact, the income tax consequences to the company and its owners are usually a key consideration in selecting which type of organization a new business is to be. Of course, other factors, such as the desire for limited liability and the ability to raise capital, are essential considerations as well.

conduit principle   *the idea that all income earned by an entity must be passed through to the owners and reported on their individual tax returns; applicable to proprietorships, partnerships, and, in a modified form, Subchapter S corporations*

PROPRIETORSHIPS

Because a proprietorship is not considered a separate legal entity, it is taxed under the conduit principle. This means that all income earned by the proprietorship is reported on the owner's personal income tax return. The owner lists the revenues and expenses of the business on Schedule C, which is attached to the tax return. The income reported on this schedule is added to other income (salary, interest, and such) and is taxed as personal income, whether or not any of the income is withdrawn for personal use. Since the owner of the proprietorship is not considered an employee of the business, his or her salary cannot be deducted from gross income on Schedule C.

Besides having to report all business income as personal income, owners of proprietorships are considered to be self-employed and so cannot take advantage of tax-free fringe benefits in the form of group life insurance, medical expense reimbursement, certain death benefits to surviving relatives, and stock option plans. However, a self-employed proprietor now has the opportunity to create a pension plan in the form of a Keogh Plan. Basically, the law provides for self-employed individuals to contribute to a retirement plan up to 15 percent of their earned income, or $7,500 per year, whichever is less, and to deduct this amount from their gross income. A minimum contribution of up to $750 can be made and deducted regardless of the 15 percent limitation, provided the contribution does not exceed the individual's earned income.

The primary advantage of a proprietorship is its ease of formation and the fact that its income is taxed only once, to its owner and not to a separate legal entity.

PARTNERSHIPS

Like a proprietorship, a partnership is taxed under the conduit principle. Each partner's personal tax return includes that person's share of partnership income. Unlike a proprietorship, a partnership is required to file an annual tax return. However, since the partnership is not required to pay a tax on its income, this return is for information purposes only.

The partnership return includes a Schedule K, which shows the breakdown of income, expenses, and credits by type: ordinary income, capital gains and losses, dividends from domestic corporations, charitable contributions, investment credit, and tax-preference income. These items are divided between or among the partners and are reported on a Schedule K-1 for each partner. The individual can then report the items in appropriate categories on his or her personal tax return.

Like a proprietorship, the primary advantages of a partnership are the ease of formation and the avoidance of double taxation.

CORPORATIONS

The tax law recognizes three types of corporations: regular corporations, Subchapter S corporations, and tax-exempt corporations. Although we focus on the impact of income taxes on regular corporations, we also discuss the other two types briefly.

Regular Corporations

A regular corporation is a separate legal entity and, as such, is required to file its own tax return and to pay its own taxes. Because dividend payments to stockholders are not allowable deductions for federal income tax purposes, these taxes are calculated on income before dividend distributions. In effect, then, earnings are taxed at the corporate level and distributed earnings become taxable income to stockholders. As a result, dividends are taxed twice, first as corporate income and again as dividend income to the stockholder. To limit the amount of double taxation, the government allows the individual taxpayer to exclude from income the first $200 of interest and dividends received.

This double taxation of a portion of earnings is a characteristic that makes the corporation less attractive than proprietorships or partnerships. However, other elements of the corporate form of organization provide important tax advantages. For example, owner–managers are considered employees and so their salaries are deductions from the corporation's gross income. In addition, owner–managers may receive tax-free fringe benefits that are not available to proprietors and partners.

In general, the key advantages of the corporate form of organization are the tax advantages of fringe benefits and such nontax benefits as limited liability, ease of raising capital, and ease of ownership transfer.

Subchapter S Corporations

Subchapter S corporation *a domestic corporation that is recognized as a regular corporation under state law, but is granted special status for federal income tax purposes*

A Subchapter S corporation is a regular corporation in all respects, except for its special tax status. Most of the income of a Subchapter S corporation is not taxed to the corporation but passes through to the individual stockholders in a manner that is similar to the conduit principle applied to proprietorships and partnerships. Thus, the owners of such a corporation have the advantage of limited liability, while avoiding the problem of double taxation. If the owners are also employees, they receive many of the tax-free fringe benefits mentioned earlier. However, their pension and profit-sharing opportunities are limited to plans that are no better than the retirement plans available to proprietorships and partnerships.

Only certain companies qualify as Subchapter S corporations. Some of the governing rules are

1. The corporation must elect to be taxed as a Subchapter S corporation.
2. A Subchapter S corporation must be a domestic corporation.
3. It can have only one class of stock outstanding.
4. It cannot have more than 15 stockholders. Note that this may involve as many as 30 individuals, since spouses are considered to be one stockholder, without regard to the manner in which the stock is held.
5. All stockholders must be U.S. citizens or resident aliens.
6. The income from investments (dividends, interest, rents, and so on) cannot exceed 20 percent of gross receipts in any one year.
7. The company's income from foreign sources cannot exceed 80 percent of gross receipts in any one year.
8. All new shareholders are considered to have consented to the election to be a Subchapter S corporation, if they do not formally refuse within 60 days after the stock is acquired.
9. Subchapter S status is automatically terminated if any event occurs that would have prevented the corporation from qualifying in the first place—for instance, if a sixteenth stockholder (other than a stockholder's spouse) is added.

As we have indicated, the stockholders of a Subchapter S corporation can avoid double taxation on corporate income. The taxable income of a Subchapter S corporation is reported proportionately on the tax returns of the individual stockholders. Cash dividends paid within $2\frac{1}{2}$ months after the close of the taxable year are considered to have been paid out of the taxable income of the year just ended. If all the taxable income is not distributed to stockholders within $2\frac{1}{2}$ months after the close of the taxable year, the undistributed portion is referred to as previously taxed income, since stockholders are taxed on it even though they did not receive it. It is usually desirable for a Subchapter S corporation to avoid previously taxed income since it cannot be distributed tax-free in a subsequent year until all income of the subsequent year's distribution has been paid out.

One of the most important benefits of the Subchapter S corporation is that operating losses are passed through to the stockholders, thus offsetting other types of personal income. This is especially likely to occur in the corporation's formative years when profits are less probable.

Tax-Exempt Corporations

tax-exempt corporation a legal entity chartered by a state for scientific, religious, educational, charitable, and similar purposes

Corporations that are formed for scientific, religious, educational, charitable, and similar purposes are eligible for tax-exempt status if they meet certain conditions. In general, they must be operated for the benefit of society and no part of their net income may accrue to the benefit of an individual.

CHOOSING THE FORM OF ORGANIZATION

A number of factors must be considered in the process of choosing the form of organization that will minimize a business entity's income taxes. These include:

Nontax factors:

1. Ease of raising new capital.
2. Extent of owners' liability.
3. Transferability of ownership.

Tax factors:

1. Whether tax-free fringe benefits are available.
2. Ease of disposing of the business. The tax effect of selling shares of corporate stock is different from that of selling an interest in a proprietorship or partnership.
3. Disposition of net operating losses. Net operating losses pass through to the owners of proprietorships, partnerships, and Subchapter S corporations. They do not pass through in regular corporations.
4. Special characteristics of income, such as how long-term gains are passed through the entity to the owners. For example, in a partnership, capital gains pass through to the owners as capital gains and are taxed at lower rates. In regular corporations, capital gains pass through as dividend income. (See further discussion of capital gains income on page 547.)

TO SUMMARIZE The IRS recognizes three forms of business organizations: proprietorship, partnership, and corporation (regular, Subchapter S, and tax-exempt). Careful tax planning when selecting the form of organization will ensure that a company, the owners, and the employees (including owner–employees) can maximize tax benefits. Several tax factors, including the availability of tax-free fringe benefits, and nontax factors, such as the extent of owners' liability, should be considered in determining the form of organization.

Tax-Planning Guidelines

Tax consequences continue to be an important consideration after a business has been established. To the extent that management has some control over the timing of a tax liability, its objective is to pay the least legal tax at the latest possible time. In essence, management should take advantage of all legal approaches to avoiding a tax and, if the tax cannot be avoided, then all legal means should be used to postpone its payment as long as possible. Judge Learned Hand expressed it well: "Nobody owes any duty to pay more than the law demands. . . ."

To accomplish the "least and latest" objective, management should follow a number of tax-planning guidelines in executing transactions that may have tax consequences.

1. *Know the tax law.* Only through knowledge of the law can management take advantage of its favorable provisions. If a company cannot afford a full-time tax adviser, management should ask a CPA or a tax lawyer for advice on special transactions and for help in preparing the tax returns.

2. *Keep adequate records.* Adequate records are necessary to justify the deduction of legitimate expenses and the exclusion of receipts that are not taxable. They not only provide proof that the expense was incurred, but also ensure that the taxpayer does not overlook deductible expenses.

3. *Know in advance the tax effect of planned transactions.* The tax impact of a transaction is often determined by how it is executed, because the method chosen may determine when or how the transaction will be reported. For example, if a used operational asset is sold at a gain or loss and a new operational asset of like kind is purchased, the gain or loss is included in income in the year of sale. However, if the old asset is traded for a similar asset, some or all of the gain or loss may be postponed to future years.

These examples make it clear that once a transaction has been executed, the tax consequences will have been determined. Therefore, in order to meet the objective of paying the least tax at the latest time, management must know in advance the tax consequences of alternative ways of executing a transaction.

Capital Gains and Ordinary Income

capital gain *the excess of proceeds over costs from the sale of a capital asset, as defined by the Internal Revenue Code*

All net income of a business entity is taxed either at regular rates as ordinary income or at special rates as a capital gain. Because of these differences, management should plan its investments so that, whenever possible, capital gains tax rates will apply. Generally, income from the sale of an asset is classified as a capital gain if the following conditions are met.[1]

1. The asset disposed of is a capital asset.
2. The asset was held for longer than one year.
3. The asset was sold or exchanged.

Capital assets are all assets except real and depreciable property used in a trade or business, accounts and notes receivable created in a trade or business, inventories, and certain other assets. In a positive sense, capital assets are primarily investment assets (stocks, bonds, and real estate).

Section 1231 *a provision in the tax law that allows businesses to report as capital gains, real and depreciable property that is used in the business for more than 12 months and that is sold, exchanged, or involuntarily converted, and whose selling price exceeds its original cost*

There is an exception to this, in Section 1231 of the tax law, which outlines the treatment of gains on the sale of certain business property as capital gains.

Although it is beyond the scope of this text to discuss Section 1231 in any detail, we can say that it permits capital gains treatment for business properties that meet the following conditions.

1. They are real or depreciable properties used in a trade or business.
2. They are held for more than one year.
3. They are sold, exchanged, or involuntarily converted.

Before Section 1231 can be applied, the gain must be treated as ordinary income to the extent of depreciation taken (recaptured). To illustrate, we will assume the following data.

Sales Price (Machine)		$80,000
Original Cost	$60,000	
Accumulated Depreciation	35,000	
Remaining Book Value		25,000
Gain on Sale		$55,000
Depreciation to Date		35,000
Remaining Section 1231 Gain		$20,000

Thus, $20,000 is treated as a capital gain and $35,000 is an ordinary gain. Note that since depreciation is not used in calculating the capital gain, the only time there can be a Section 1231 gain is when the selling price exceeds the original cost.

---

[1] A corporation may elect to have its gains from the sale or exchange of capital assets held for more than one year taxed at the normal corporate rates or at a 28 percent rate. Individuals may deduct 60 percent of the gain from the sale or exchange of such assets. Capital losses are treated differently for individuals and corporations.

The application of Section 1231 suggests the possibility of tax-planning opportunities. If the combined result of all similar transactions that qualify for Section 1231 is a net gain, the gain is taxed as a capital gain. If the result is a net loss, the loss is treated as a deduction from ordinary income. Suppose, for example, that a firm expects one of its investment transactions to result in a loss and another in a gain. In order to meet the least and latest tax objective, management would probably want to execute these transactions in different years. A loss reported by itself in one year would be an ordinary loss and a gain reported by itself in another year would be a capital gain (over and above the depreciation taken). If the two transactions were executed in the same year, the ordinary loss would offset the capital gain in whole or in part and so would minimize the tax benefit of the capital gain.

Investments in Current Assets

We have discussed investments in capital assets such as stocks, bonds, and real estate. But investments in two types of assets—accounts receivable and inventories—also have significant tax ramifications. The fact that there are alternative methods of accounting for accounts receivable and inventories suggests that careful tax planning is needed.

ACCOUNTS RECEIVABLE

The main tax question concerning accounts receivable is determining how and when to recognize losses due to bad debts. For tax purposes, a company generally has a choice of using the direct write-off method or the allowance method. Under the direct write-off method, accounts receivable that are determined not to be collectable are written off at the time they become uncollectable. No special attempt is made to estimate the amount of bad debts that may result from credit sales, as is required for financial reporting. Thus, costs and revenues are not closely matched nor is the bad debt written off in the earliest possible period.

Under the allowance method, however, an estimate of the dollar amount of accounts receivable expected to be uncollectable is made at the end of each year. That amount is an expense of the period, even though the specific bad debts cannot be identified at that time. The allowance method thus provides a better matching of costs with revenues, as well as an expense deduction at an earlier date. Although the direct write-off method is simpler to administer, it is less consistent with the principle of paying the least tax at the latest time.

INVENTORIES

For the first period in which inventories become a material factor in the determination of net income, the taxpayer is permitted to select among a number of alternative inventory costing methods (see Chapter 6).

Cost Methods:
First-in, first-out (FIFO)
Last-in, first-out (LIFO)
Weighted-average
Specific-identification

Once an inventory costing method has been selected and used, however, the taxpayer must stay with that method until the Internal Revenue Service grants permission to make a change.

If LIFO is used in calculating income taxes, it must also be used for financial reporting to stockholders. If any other method is chosen for income taxes, the taxpayer is free to use any method for financial reporting.

Choosing an inventory method is a form of tax planning because each method has a different impact on the income tax liability of a firm. The FIFO and LIFO methods generally produce the highest and the lowest taxable income, while the weighted-average method usually results in a taxable income figure somewhere in between. Whether FIFO or LIFO will result in the lowest or highest taxable income depends on the pattern of replacement prices over a period of time. During periods of rising prices, LIFO will result in the lowest taxable income. During periods of falling prices, FIFO will produce the lowest taxable income.

The following example presents the effects of FIFO, LIFO, and weighted average on taxable income.

	Units	Unit Cost	Total Cost
Facts: Beginning Inventory	10	$10	$100
Purchases (in chronological order)	10	11	110
	10	12	120
	10	13	130
	10	14	140
Total Purchases..............	40	$12.50	$500
Inventory Available for Sale ...	50	$ 12	$600

Ending inventory: 10 units
Selling Price per Unit: $18

	FIFO	LIFO	Weighted Average
Sales Revenue (40 × $18)	$720	$720	$720
Cost of Goods Sold:			
Beginning Inventory (10 at $10)	$100	$100	$100
Purchases (40)........................	500	500	500
Cost of Goods Available for Sale	$600	$600	$600
Less Ending Inventory:			
FIFO (10 at $14)	140		
LIFO (10 at $10)		100	
Weighted Average (10 at $12)...........			120
Cost of Goods Sold	460	500	480
Gross Margin......................	$260	$220	$240

As you can see, the LIFO method shows the lowest income during a period of rising prices, FIFO shows the highest income during that period, and the weighted-average method shows income that falls between FIFO and LIFO. This pattern is reversed when costs are falling.

For the best tax situation, a company should only switch from FIFO to LIFO when prices are at a low point and are expected to rise. A substantial number of companies shifted to LIFO in 1976, for example, when the United States was in an economic recession. Despite the potential savings, some companies chose not to make the shift because they would be required to use LIFO for financial reporting as well. This would result in the reporting of lower earnings, and hence of lower earnings per share.

If prices rise for one or more periods and then fall to their original level in subsequent periods, FIFO and LIFO will result in the same total taxable income over the entire span of time, assuming that sales remain the same each year. For example, suppose that prices are rising in 1985 and 1986. LIFO will produce the lowest taxable income and FIFO the highest. If prices fall in 1987 and 1988, FIFO will produce the lowest income and LIFO the highest. Over the 4-year period, the total taxable income will be the same under either method, *if* the price in 1988 returns to its 1985 level and *if* the same number of units are sold each year. Note, however, that the taxpayer using LIFO will be better off than the one using FIFO because the former paid lower taxes in the earlier years and thus had use of the tax savings during that time.

Two other observations are significant regarding the choice of an inventory costing method. First, if prices rise because of inflation and do not return to earlier levels, the firm using LIFO will pay less total taxes over a long period of time. Second, if prices fluctuate without any identifiable pattern of increases or decreases, the weighted-average method of valuation may be the most useful method for smoothing out the price fluctuations.

TO SUMMARIZE To meet the "least and latest" objective, companies should follow basic tax guidelines: know the tax law, keep adequate records, and know in advance the tax effect of planned transactions. Investments in capital assets, accounts receivable, and inventories have significant tax ramifications. Income from the sale of capital assets is taxed at the lower capital gains rates. Through the application of Section 1231, income from the sales of certain business property may also be taxed as capital gains. The major tax consideration for accounts receivable is whether to use the direct write-off or the allowance method of accounting for bad-debt losses. The allowance method usually is consistent with the goal of paying the least tax at the latest possible time. The choice of an inventory costing method primarily affects the timing of income taxes. When prices are rising, LIFO produces the lowest income and the lowest tax. When prices are falling, FIFO produces the lowest income and lowest tax.

Investments in Long-Term Operational Assets

A company's income tax liability is affected by the way long-term operational assets are acquired, by the way they are depreciated, and by the way they are disposed of. These assets, as you know, include plant and equipment, land, patents, and goodwill. In this section, we focus first on the methods of acquiring long-term operational assets, then on the ways of calculating depreciation, and end by reviewing the methods of disposal.

TAX EFFECTS OF THE WAYS IN WHICH LONG-TERM OPERATIONAL ASSETS ARE ACQUIRED

Operational assets may be acquired directly by cash purchase, by issuing securities, by leasing, or by construction. Or they may be acquired indirectly by buying the stock of a corporation. Each of these types of transactions has a different tax effect.

Acquisition by Purchase

When an operational asset is acquired by direct purchase, two important tax-related questions are: (1) What should be included in the cost of the asset? (2) Does the asset qualify for an investment tax credit? In principle, the cost of the asset should include all costs incurred to prepare the asset for its intended use—for example, the invoice cost, sales tax, freight, installation, and start-up costs. To qualify for the investment tax credit, assets generally must be tangible, personal, depreciable business property.[2] Whether the taxpayer is entitled to the full credit depends on the expected life of the asset, which must be the same as its depreciable life for tax purposes.

tangible, personal, depreciable business property   *property used in a business that is not considered to be real estate*

Asset's Life	Investment Tax Credit
1–2 years	none
3–4 years	$(33\frac{1}{3}\% \times 10\%) = 3.333\%$
5–6 years	$(66\frac{2}{3}\% \times 10\%) = 6.667\%$
7 years or more	$(100\% \times 10\%) = 10.000\%$

The investment tax credit provides a direct reduction in tax liability of up to 10 percent of the cost of a qualifying asset in the year it is put into service. Note that the credit is for the year the asset is put into service, not when it is purchased or paid for. Only $100,000 of *used* property is eligible for the credit in any one year; there are also certain factors that limit the total amount of investment credit in any one year. Any credit not used in any one year because of this limitation may be carried back three years and forward seven years. If the asset is not held as long as originally planned, any excess credit taken in the first year of the asset's use must be repaid as additional tax in the year in which the asset is disposed of.

The purpose of the investment tax credit is to stimulate economic activity in eligible assets by reducing the cost of those assets. The availability of the investment credit provides management with some tax-planning alternatives. For example:

---

[2] In business law, all property is classified as personal or real (land and buildings).

1. Management must decide whether to select a longer life, which will give a larger investment credit, or a shorter life, in order to increase the depreciation deduction. Other things being equal, management should choose the longer life and take the maximum credit. Some of the credit may be recaptured if the asset does not last as long as planned, but no additional credit is allowed if a short life is planned initially and the asset actually lasts for a longer period.

2. Management must decide when to put the asset to use. Since the taxpayer is eligible to take the investment credit in the year the asset is put in service, maximum benefit would be achieved by buying and using an asset before the end of a current tax year rather than waiting until after the beginning of the next tax year.

3. Where applicable, management must decide whether to purchase and put into use eligible used property that is worth more than $100,000. Since a greater credit will be earned if less than $100,000 of used property is put into use in any one year, the purchase of used property should be spread over several years if it exceeds $100,000.

4. Since buildings and most of their structural components are not eligible for a tax credit, management must decide whether a new asset can be installed in such a way as to be considered tangible personal property rather than as part of a building. The use of movable partitions rather than stationary interior walls is an example.

Acquisition by Issuing Securities

Assets acquired by issuing stocks or bonds are usually major assets, such as a building or another company. When such assets are acquired, a key question is: At what cost should the asset be recorded? Generally, the asset should be recorded at its fair market value or at the fair market value of the securities traded for the asset. The fair market value assigned to the asset would then be used as the basis for calculating depreciation if the asset is a depreciable asset—and for determining the investment credit if the asset qualifies.

Acquisition by Leasing

A company may choose to lease assets rather than buy them, possibly because the company does not want its capital tied up in operational assets. Leasing may have important tax ramifications as well. For example, the rental payment for the use of leased land is a deductible expense, whereas land that is owned cannot be depreciated for tax purposes. In addition, leased property may qualify for the investment credit, which may be taken by the lessor or passed through to the lessee. Usually, the disposition of the investment credit is an important factor in determining the rent on the property. If the lessor takes the credit, the rent will probably be lower than if the credit is passed on.

The tax situation is somewhat different for a lease arrangement that is in substance an installment purchase of an asset. With this type of lease arrangement, at the end of the lease term title may pass to the lessee without any payment beyond the final period's rent. Or, the lessee may have the option to buy the asset for substantially less than its estimated fair market value. In such cases, the lease payments cannot be treated as

EXHIBIT 17–2   **A Lease as an Installment Purchase**

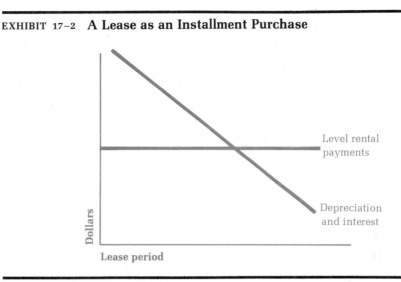

rental expense. Instead, the asset must be recorded in the company's books at its fair market value with a related liability shown for the future rental payments. This provides an annual tax deduction for the depreciation of the asset and for the interest on the installment loan. Usually, the sum of the depreciation and interest expenses will be larger in the early years of the lease than the rental payment, and smaller in the later years, as Exhibit 17–2 indicates.

Acquisition by Construction

When a company constructs its own assets, such as a building, the primary tax consideration is: Which costs must be recorded as part of the building and which can be written off as an expense immediately? For instance, should interest expense and the property taxes incurred during the construction period be allocated to the building cost, as generally accepted accounting principles suggest, or can they be deducted as normal operating expenses? Likewise, must overhead costs be allocated to the construction activity or can they be assigned to work-in-process as costs of producing goods for sale? In general, when an asset is constructed, costs such as these may be expensed as they occur rather than after the building is completed as part of its annual depreciation expense. This approach of taking expense deductions at the earliest possible time is usually consistent with the overall tax-planning objective of paying the least tax at the latest possible time. An exception may exist when the investment tax credit exceeds the benefits of early expensing.

TAX EFFECTS OF THE WAYS IN WHICH LONG-TERM OPERATIONAL ASSETS ARE DEPRECIATED

The primary tax consequence of using an operational asset is the amount of depreciation expense the taxpayer is allowed to deduct. As you recall from Chapter 10, there are several methods of calculating depreciation.

EXHIBIT 17-3 **Maximum Allowable Depreciation Methods[3]**

Depreciation Method	Type of Asset	New or Used	Asset Life
Straight-line	All depreciable assets	New or used	Longer than 1 year
Straight-line	Residential rental property	Used	Less than 20 years
Double-declining-balance	Equipment	New	Three years or more
	Residential rental property	New	Three years or more
Declining-balance at 150 percent	Commercial real estate	New	Longer than one year
	Machinery and equipment	Used	Longer than one year
Declining-balance at 125 percent	Residential rental property	Used	Twenty years or more

[3] The taxpayer may select a depreciation method that results in a lower initial depreciation deduction than the maximum amount provided in the table.

The taxpayer's choice of method will be based on the type of asset, its expected life, and whether it was acquired new or used. Exhibit 17-3 lists the most commonly allowed methods and indicates when each can be used. The exhibit shows, for example, that the maximum accelerated depreciation a taxpayer can take for used equipment is 150 percent declining balance. For new equipment, however, double (200 percent) declining balance is allowed.

Although taxpayers may use one method of depreciation for income tax purposes and another for financial reporting, for tax purposes they must stick with the same method throughout the life of the asset—unless the Commissioner of Internal Revenue gives permission to change the method.

For each depreciation method, the taxpayer may ignore salvage value up to 10 percent of the cost of tangible, personal business property. In applying the straight-line method or the sum-of-the-years'-digits method, the salvage value to be taken into account is subtracted from the asset's cost in determining the annual depreciation expense. In applying the declining-balance method, the appropriate depreciation rate is multiplied by the book value of the asset (cost minus any accumulated depreciation) and, at this point, salvage value is ignored. However, the total depreciation taken over the life of the asset cannot reduce the book value below the salvage value (after the salvage value has been reduced by 10 percent of the asset's initial cost in the case of tangible personal property).

To illustrate these rules, we will assume that a company paid $12,000 for a new machine with a useful life of five years and a salvage value of $2,000. Since salvage value of up to 10 percent of the asset's original cost

($12,000 × 0.10 = $1,200) can be ignored, only $800 of the salvage value must be recognized. The depreciation expense each year under the straight-line, double-declining-balance, sum-of-the-years'-digits, and 150 percent declining-balance methods would be as follows:

Year	Straight-Line	Double-Declining-Balance	Sum-of-the-Years'-Digits	150 Percent Declining-Balance
1	$ 2,240	$ 4,800	$ 3,733	$3,600
2	2,240	2,880	2,987	2,520
3	2,240	1,728	2,240	1,764
4	2,240	1,037	1,493	1,235
5	2,240	622	747	864
	$11,200	$11,067*	$11,200	$9,983*

Calculations:

$\dfrac{\$12,000 - \$800}{5}$	Book value (starting with $12,000) × 40%, down to $800	$\dfrac{x}{15} \times \$11,200$	Book value (starting with $12,000) × 30%, down to $800

* If an asset is worn out or discarded, the remaining book value is written off as a loss.

Of the four depreciation methods listed, the double-declining-balance method provides the largest depreciation expense deduction in the early years. It also has the advantage of allowing taxpayers to shift to the straight-line method without permission from the Commissioner of Internal Revenue. Usually, this is a worthwhile practice for long-lived assets any time after the midpoint of their lives.

Twenty Percent First-Year Depreciation Allowance

20 percent first-year depreciation allowance *a provision in the tax law that allows corporations (and other businesses) to take a deduction of 20 percent of the cost of an asset (up to $10,000) in addition to regular depreciation*

If a company purchases new or used tangible personal property, such as furniture or equipment, that has a useful life of six years or more, it is allowed to take a special "bonus" depreciation deduction in the first year equal to 20 percent of the asset's acquisition cost (up to $10,000[4]). This 20 percent first-year depreciation allowance is in addition to regular depreciation, even if the taxpayer elects to use an accelerated method. The bonus depreciation is calculated without considering salvage value.

To illustrate, we will assume that Ronald Corporation purchased equipment with a useful life of 10 years for $12,000 on January 2. The company elects to use the double-declining-balance method of depreciation for tax purposes. (Bear in mind that salvage value is not considered at this point when the declining-balance method is used.)

First-Year Bonus Depreciation [20% × $10,000 (limitation)] $2,000
First-Year Regular Depreciation at Double-Declining-Balance Rate
   [20% × ($12,000 − $2,000 Bonus Depreciation)]   2,000
     Total Depreciation Deduction in Year of Acquisition $4,000

[4] Individuals filing a joint return can deduct up to $20,000.

As a tangible personal business asset, the new equipment would probably also qualify for the investment credit. This credit would entitle the taxpayer to a $1,200 (10 percent × $12,000) reduction in income taxes. So, assuming that the taxpayer paid cash to acquire the asset and is in a 46 percent tax bracket, net cash outflow applicable to the year of acquisition of the asset would be

Cost of Asset		$12,000
Less (1) Tax Savings from Depreciation (46% × $4,000)	$1,840	
(2) Tax Savings from Investment Credit	1,200	
		(3,040)
Net Cash Outflow Applicable to Year 1		$ 8,960

As you can see, the special first-year allowance, the regular depreciation deduction under the double-declining-balance method, and the investment credit together "save" the taxpayer $3,040 in taxes in the year the asset is purchased, if it is used for the entire year. These provisions obviously encourage the purchase of new equipment.

Selecting the Useful Life of an Asset

In choosing a useful life for depreciable assets, the taxpayer has two options: (1) to select a number of years that reflects how long the asset actually will take to wear out, or (2) to adopt the Class Life System. Under the first approach, the taxpayer picks a useful life on the basis of experience and other known facts about the use of the asset. With the second approach, the taxpayer selects a useful life according to criteria established by the Internal Revenue Service. If the taxpayer uses the Class Life System,

1. The Commissioner of Internal Revenue will not challenge the life selected.

2. The life selected for the asset may be as much as 20 percent longer or shorter than the designated class life.

3. The taxpayer can select a depreciation convention related to when the asset is purchased, as follows:

> a. Half-year convention. A half year's depreciation can be taken on all assets put into service that year regardless of when they were purchased during the year.
>
> b. Modified half-year convention. All assets put into service before midyear are assumed to have been purchased on the first day of the year. All assets put into service after midyear are assumed to have been purchased on the first day of the next year.

DISPOSAL OF OPERATIONAL ASSETS

Most operational assets are eventually used up, either through natural wear or obsolescence, or as a result of an untimely event, such as a fire. When this happens, the asset must be disposed of, either by sale for cash, by exchange for another asset, by installment sale, by involuntary conversion, or by abandonment.

Class Life System *a system that designates the lives of specified classes of assets and allows a taxpayer to select for depreciation purposes a life that is up to 20 percent shorter or longer than the class life*

half-year convention *under the Class Life System, the practice of allowing a half year's depreciation for all assets put into service any time during the year*

modified half-year convention *under the Class Life System, the practice whereby assets put into service before midyear are eligible for a full year of depreciation, and assets put into service after midyear are not eligible for depreciation until the following year*

Disposal by Sale for Cash

When an operational asset is sold for cash in an arm's-length transaction, a gain or loss is recorded for the difference between the selling price and the book value at the time of sale. If an asset has been held for less than a year, the gain on the sale is considered to be ordinary income. If an asset has been held for more than a year, the income from its sale is ordinary income to the extent of depreciation recapture, as discussed earlier, and any remaining gain is a Section 1231 gain eligible for treatment as a long-term capital gain.

Disposal by Exchange

For financial reporting purposes, if an operational asset is exchanged for another asset of like kind, a loss is recognized on the company's books but a gain is generally not recognized, unless cash is received in the exchange. For income tax purposes, however, the exchange of similar assets is treated as a continuation of the original transaction and is therefore considered to be a nontaxable exchange. Thus, if a taxpayer expects to have a gain on the disposal of an asset, the gain can be postponed by exchanging the asset for a similar one. If the taxpayer expects to incur a loss on the disposal of the asset, the loss can be deducted if the asset is *sold* (rather than exchanged), and a replacement asset is *purchased*.

If, on the other hand, the assets are not alike, the exchange transaction is considered a taxable exchange. In that case, the IRS requires that the gain or loss be recognized in the year of the exchange.

Disposal by Installment Sale

If payments for real estate or tangible personal business property are spread over two or more years, the gain may be reported as the cash is collected in the year or years subsequent to the year of sale. The gain reported each year is treated as ordinary income to the extent of depreciation recapture and the balance is treated as a possible capital gain. The installment sale rules permit the taxpayer to postpone reporting a gain from the year of sale to the year of cash collection.

installment sale *a transaction that involves a down payment and a series of payments over a period of two or more years*

Disposal by Involuntary Conversion

An asset is involuntarily converted when it is damaged beyond use or destroyed due to fire, storm, shipwreck, or other casualty, or theft, or if it is surrendered as a result of condemnation proceedings by the federal, state, or local government. A loss due to an involuntary conversion is either an ordinary loss or a capital loss in the year incurred. The type of loss depends on the type of involuntary conversion and on the amount of the loss in relation to other involuntary conversions by the same taxpayer.

It would seem that irreparable damage to an asset would always result in a loss. However, sometimes there is a gain, as, for example, when the insurance proceeds are greater than the asset's book value. If there is a gain, the taxpayer can elect to report it in the year it occurs or to postpone all or a portion of the gain by adjusting the cost (basis) of the replacement

involuntary conversion *a transaction in which an asset is destroyed (for example, by fire or storm) or is taken by a government agency through condemnation proceedings*

asset acquired. This election to postpone the gain is allowed only if the converted asset is replaced with a like asset within two calendar years after the year in which any proceeds from the conversion are received. The total gain is postponed only if the cost of the new asset equals or exceeds the proceeds received from the old asset. A gain must be recognized to the extent that the cost of the new asset is less than the proceeds from the converted asset, but not more than the total gain.

Disposal by Abandonment

If the asset has no value at the end of its economic life, or if the cost of disposal will exceed the fair market value, a taxpayer may choose to abandon the asset and write off the remaining book value as an ordinary loss. The taxpayer has control over the timing of the loss deduction by choosing when to abandon the asset.

TO SUMMARIZE A taxpayer has a variety of tax-planning opportunities with respect to the purchase, use, and disposal of long-term operational assets. The timing and method of executing a transaction can affect when a gain is reported and whether it is considered ordinary income or a capital gain. An asset can be exchanged or sold, depending on whether it is more desirable to postpone the gain or to deduct the loss. A gain from an involuntary conversion can be reported or postponed, depending on which approach is most advantageous to the taxpayer.

CHAPTER REVIEW

The basic objective of tax planning is to pay the least amount of tax at the latest possible time. Three important tax guidelines that will help management meet this objective are: (1) knowing the law, (2) keeping good records, and (3) knowing in advance the tax effects of planned transactions.

Tax consequences are an important consideration in selecting the form of a business organization. Proprietorships and partnerships are not taxed as separate entities; their income is taxed to the proprietor or to the partners under the conduit principle. Because corporations are separate legal entities, corporate earnings are taxed to the corporation and then the distributed portion of the earnings is taxed as dividends to the stockholders. Income from Subchapter S corporations, whether distributed or not, is taxed to stockholders only. Both regular corporations and Subchapter S corporations provide special tax benefits to employees in the form of tax-free fringe benefits that are not available to the owners of partnerships or proprietorships.

The manner in which an accounting transaction is executed may determine whether income is to be reported as ordinary income or as a capital gain, and when that income is to be reported. The methods selected for measuring bad-debt losses and the cost of inventory will influence the amount of profit reported and taxes paid in any one year. The method of recording the acquisition of a long-term operational asset affects the amount and timing of expenses to be charged for the purchase of the asset.

Similarly, the depreciation method selected to measure the use of an operational asset will affect the timing of the write-off of the asset's cost to expense. And finally, the method of disposing of an operational asset will determine the timing of the recognition of the gain or loss.

KEY TERMS AND CONCEPTS

business expenses (538)
capital gain (547)
Class Life System (556)
conduit principle (542)
constructive receipt
  rule (541)
deductions (538)
exclusions (538)
gross income (538)
gross tax liability (538)
half-year convention
  (556)

installment sale (557)
involuntary conversion
  (557)
modified half-year
  convention (556)
net tax liability (538)
Section 1231 (547)
Subchapter S
  corporation (544)
tangible, personal,
  depreciable business
  property (551)

taxable income (538)
tax credit (538)
tax-exempt corporation
  (545)
20 percent first-year
  depreciation
  allowance (555)

DISCUSSION QUESTIONS

1. Distinguish between the following terms as they are used for tax purposes.
  (a) Gross receipts and gross income.
  (b) Exclusions and deductions.
  (c) Deductions and credits.

2. What characteristics of a business expense would allow it to be a deduction in arriving at taxable income?

3. Distinguish between revenues per the Income Statement and gross income per the tax return.

4. What is meant by the constructive receipt rule in measuring taxable income?

5. What are the two major categories of income with respect to determining tax rates? Give the rates currently applicable to corporations.

6. What types of losses are deductible for tax purposes?

7. From a tax point of view, what are the three types of business organizations?

8. Describe the philosophy of the conduit principle as it relates to the taxation of proprietorships, partnerships, and Subchapter S corporations.

9. What are the key tax and nontax factors to consider in choosing the appropriate form of business organization?

10. What is the objective of following good tax-planning guidelines?

11. What are three tax-planning guidelines? Can you identify any additional tax-planning guidelines?

12. Why is it important to keep good records as a basis for preparing a tax return?

13. What is a capital asset, as defined by the tax laws, and how are capital gains and losses taxed to corporations?

14. Describe the two acceptable methods of accounting for bad debts for tax purposes.

15. In a period of rising prices, which inventory valuation method will result in the lowest taxable income for a business? Why?

16. What effect does the investment tax credit have on the decision to acquire a depreciable asset?

17. What factors should be considered in choosing the depreciation method to be used for an operational asset?

18. Explain the tax effects of the choice between selling an old asset and buying a new one versus trading an old asset for a new one.

EXERCISES

E17–1 Computation of Tax Liability

Evergreen Corporation files its tax return on a calendar year basis. Its gross revenues for 1981 were $140,000 and its deductible business expenses were $80,000. Compute the corporation's tax liability for 1981 using the tax rates in Exhibit 17–1 on page 539.

E17–2 Individual Income—Subchapter S Corporation

A Subchapter S corporation reported taxable income of $75,000 on its 1981 calendar year tax return. During 1981 and prior to March 15, 1982, the corporation had distributed $40,000 in dividends to its stockholders. If the corporation has five stockholders, each owning 20 percent, how much income must each stockholder report on his or her 1981 individual income tax return?

E17–3 Deductible Losses

James Gregory operates a plumbing business as a sole proprietor. During the calendar year 1981 one of the trucks used in his business was involved in a wreck and was totally demolished. The truck had a book value of $1,800 at the time of the accident. Gregory collected $1,300 in insurance and immediately purchased a new truck for $7,000. Gregory also owned a sailboat, which he sailed occasionally on weekends. He decided that he did not get to use it often enough so he sold it during 1981. The boat originally cost $3,300 and he sold it for $2,000. How much is Gregory's deductible loss for 1981 in connection with the truck and the sailboat?

E17–4 Bad-Debt Expense

Roberts Corporation uses the allowance method of accounting for bad debts for financial reporting and the direct write-off method for tax purposes. In 1981 the corporation added $4,800 to Allowance for Doubtful Accounts and wrote off $6,000 of uncollectable accounts receivable. Allowance for Doubtful Accounts had a balance of $1,500 on January 1, 1981.

1. What is the bad-debt deduction allowed on the corporation's 1981 tax return?
2. What is the balance in Allowance for Doubtful Accounts on December 31, 1981, for financial reporting purposes?
3. Which method of accounting for bad debts is more consistent with the tax-planning objective of paying the least tax at the latest possible time? Why?

E17–5 Type of Taxable Gain

During 1981, Fowler Corporation sold some machinery that was no longer needed in its business. The selling price was $18,000. The machinery had been purchased several years ago for $42,000 and its book value at date of sale was $12,000. How much is the gain on the sale and what type of gain is it?

E17–6 Alternative Methods of Recording Depreciation Expense

George Company purchased a new machine for $25,000 that had a useful life of 10 years and a salvage value of $3,000. Compute the depreciation expense for the first three years of the asset's life using each of the following methods: straight-line, double-declining-balance, and sum-of-the-years'-digits. Consider salvage value only to the extent required. For each of the depreciation methods, explain when its use is most advantageous to taxpayers. (Ignore the 20 percent first-year depreciation allowance.)

E17–7 Casualty Loss

Regal Manufacturing Company used a special furnace in its cooking process. Due to an unexpected defect, the furnace exploded and was destroyed. The book value of the furnace was $8,000. Insurance proceeds amounted to $11,000 and a new furnace was purchased for $12,000.

1. What was the taxable gain or loss on the old furnace?
2. If the accumulated depreciation on the old furnace amounted to $5,000, how would the gain be recognized as income?
3. What would be the basis of the new asset for tax purposes?

E17–8 Partner's Share of Profits

Roger Redding and Beth Hasler formed a partnership to operate a flower center in the local mall. For the calendar year 1982, the net income of the partnership amounted to $30,000. If Roger and Beth share profits and losses on a 70–30 percent basis, what amount would each report as income for the year 1982, if Roger withdraws $500 per month and Beth withdraws $300 per month for each month during 1982?

E17–9   Depreciation Expense

On July 1, 1982, Chris Company paid $6,000 for a new truck to be used to deliver merchandise to customers. The truck has a life of six years with no salvage value. If the company takes the 20 percent first-year depreciation allowance, and uses double-declining-balance depreciation, how much is the total depreciation deduction for 1982?

E17–10   Depreciation Expense Under Alternative Methods

Stevens Mills acquired a textile machine in early January at a cost of $42,000. The machine is expected to have a useful life of 10 years with a salvage value of $2,000. Assuming that the company will not apply the 20 percent first-year depreciation allowance to this machine, how much depreciation expense is allowable for the calendar year under each of the following methods: straight-line, double-declining-balance, and sum-of-the-years'-digits? The company deducts all salvage value in computing depreciation for tax purposes.

E17–11   Gain on Involuntary Conversion

Green Chemical Company purchased land and a building on July 1, 1982. The land cost $50,000 and the building cost $360,000. The building had a useful life of 30 years. On December 30, 1982, the building was completely destroyed by fire. The insurance proceeds amounted to $375,000. If the building was depreciated on a straight-line basis, what was the gain from the involuntary conversion of the building?

E17–12   Basis of Replacing Property from Involuntary Conversion

Refer to E17–11 and assume that Green Chemical Company elects to postpone the gain on the conversion of the building destroyed by fire. If Green purchases a new building (within 2 years) for $400,000, what is its depreciation basis for tax purposes?

PROBLEMS

P17–1   Inventory Valuation Methods

For 1982, its second year of operation, Richard Company had revenues of $300,000 from the sale of 600 mopeds at an average price of $500 per unit. Inventories and purchases of mopeds for the year were as follows:

Beginning inventory	60 units at	$300
Purchases: January, 1982	130 units at	300
March, 1982	150 units at	310
July, 1982	140 units at	315
October, 1982	170 units at	320
Ending inventory	50 units	

Required:

1. Compute the cost of goods sold and the total cost of the ending inventory using the FIFO, LIFO, and weighted-average inventory methods. (Round weighted average to two decimal places.)

2. Which method shows the highest profit in a period of rising prices?

3. **Interpretive Question**   If a company has been using the FIFO inventory method, when should it consider converting to the LIFO method in order to get the most benefit from the tax laws?

P17–2   Unifying Problem: Depreciation Expense and Investment Credit

On January 2, 1982, Rolex Company purchased a truck for $12,000. The truck has an 8-year life and a $2,000 salvage value. The company plans to take maximum advantage of the tax law in computing depreciation and using the investment tax credit.

Required:

1. What is the maximum depreciation deduction allowed in the year of acquisition?

2. If the truck was purchased for cash, how much of the initial outlay was recovered in the form of tax savings in the first year by means of the maximum depreciation deduction and the investment tax credit? (Assume an effective tax rate of 40 percent.)

P17–3   Unifying Problem: Partnerships and Subchapter S Corporations

Marjorie Habstrum is a partner in a venture that reports net income for the current taxable year of $60,000. Her share is 30 percent. Her withdrawals from the partnership during the year were $15,000.

Required:

1. In preparing her income tax return for the year, what amount is Marjorie required to report as income from the partnership?

2. **Interpretive Question** What are the income tax advantages of a Subchapter S corporation over a partnership? What are the disadvantages?

P17-4 Subchapter S Corporation

Marlboro Corporation was organized on January 2, 1980, as a Subchapter S corporation. Its taxable income for calendar year 1981 was $24,000 and its dividends distributed to stockholders in the same year were $20,000, as shown below. Its taxable income in 1980 had been $18,000, of which $15,000 had been distributed to its stockholders. The corporation made the following distributions during 1981 and early 1982.

March 1, 1981	$ 3,000
June 15, 1981	11,000
November 10, 1981	6,000
March 15, 1982	2,000

Required:

1. How will these distributions be treated by shareholders on their 1981 income tax returns?

2. Assuming the March 15, 1982, distribution has taken place, compute the amount of previously taxed income that has not been distributed and show the year to which it is attributable.

P17-5 Investment Tax Credit

Rio Trucking Company acquired the following assets in 1982. All of the assets, except the used equipment, were placed in service in 1982. The used equipment was first placed in service in 1983.

Asset	Estimated Life	Cost	Salvage Value
Truck (new)	10	$14,000	$2,000
Truck (used)	5	9,000	1,000
Truck (used)	2	4,000	500
Equipment (new)	7	10,000	1,200
Equipment (used)	4	3,000	500
Building (new)	25	60,000	4,000

Required:

1. Compute the amount of the investment tax credit for which the company is eligible in 1982.

2. **Interpretive Question** What effect does the investment tax credit have on management's decisions about replacing assets?

P17-6 Unifying Problem: Depreciation and Salvage Value

Required:

1. Refer to Rio Trucking Company in P17-5. For each asset listed, which allowable depreciation method provides the maximum tax deduction in the year of acquisition?

2. For each asset listed, how much salvage value must be taken into account in computing the tax deduction for depreciation?

3. **Interpretive Question** Explain the advantage to a taxpayer of ignoring part or all of the salvage value in computing the depreciation deduction.

P17-7 Type of Gain on Sale of Machinery

On December 1, 1982, Parker Company sold a machine for $8,000 that it had purchased in 1972 for $27,000. Depreciation expense from the date of purchase to the date of sale amounted to $23,000.

Required:

1. What is the amount of gain on the sale?

2. How is the gain reported for tax purposes?

3. **Interpretive Question** If the company had preferred to postpone the gain, how should the asset have been disposed of?

P17-8 Unifying Problem: 20 Percent First-Year Depreciation, Regular Depreciation, and Investment Credit

Circle Corporation acquired a machine on January 3, 1982, for $60,000. Assume that the machine has a life of eight years and no salvage value. The company has an effective tax rate of 40 percent.

Required:

1. What is the maximum tax saving in 1982 if the corporation utilizes the 20 percent first-year depreciation allowance to the extent eligible, uses the sum-of-the-years'-digits depreciation method, and takes the investment tax credit.

2. If the company elected the Class Life System and the life of the machine is listed as 8 years, what is the shortest life it could have elected for depreciation without expecting any dispute from the Internal Revenue Service?

3. **Interpretive Question** Under what circumstances would it be to the company's advantage not to elect the 20 percent first-year depreciation allowance and not to use an accelerated depreciation method?

P17–9   Partnership Income

X, Y, and Z are partners in Letters Company. They share profits in the ratio of 6:3:1, respectively. This past year, the partnership income totaled $92,000; X withdrew $20,000, Y withdrew $10,000, and Z withdrew no funds during the year.

Required:
What taxable incomes will the partners be required to report on their individual tax returns?

P17–10   Inventory Valuation Methods

Cream Typewriter Company was established this year. Management has asked you to determine which inventory system would result in the lowest taxable income: LIFO, FIFO, or weighted average.

Purchases during the year:		
20 typewriters at $385 =	$ 7,700	
42 typewriters at $375 =	15,750	
49 typewriters at 370 =	18,130	
63 typewriters at 365 =	22,995	
12 typewriters at 395 =	4,740	

Total purchases: 186 typewriters $69,315
Ending inventory   29 typewriters
Average selling price: $450

Required:
1. Assuming no other receipts, what is the gross income using each of the three inventory methods? (Round weighted average to two decimal places.)

2. **Interpretive Question**   If a company has been using the LIFO inventory method during a period of rising prices, what will be the effect on the company's profits in a year in which the ending inventory is substantially less than the beginning inventory?

3. **Interpretive Question**   Under what circumstances would the weighted-average inventory method be more desirable than either the LIFO or the FIFO method?

EPILOGUE

Throughout this book we have tried to show the relationship of accounting to business and to society in general. As a product of its environment, accounting is continually changing, although sometimes not as rapidly as many people in business and government would like. In this epilogue on the current environment of accounting, we begin by describing the organizations that influence accounting and conclude by noting some of the challenges facing the profession.

Organizations That Influence Accounting Practice

Various groups have been influential in the development of accounting practices. Among the most prominent are the American Accounting Association (AAA), the American Institute of Certified Public Accountants (AICPA), the Cost Accounting Standards Board (CASB), the Financial Accounting Standards Board (FASB), the Financial Executives Institute (FEI), the National Association of Accountants (NAA), and the Securities and Exchange Commission (SEC).

AAA

The American Accounting Association has more than 15,000 members; one-third of them are educators and most of the others work for large industrial and CPA firms. Although accounting professors constitute less than half of the membership, they control the organization through an elected, nonpaid executive committee and an extensive volunteer committee system. The AAA emphasizes educational developments and research.

The Accounting Review, which the AAA publishes quarterly, is considered one of the major academic journals in accounting.

AICPA

More than 150,000 CPAs belong to the American Institute of Certified Public Accountants. Established in 1887, the AICPA has served as the focal point for the development of public accounting and auditing procedures. Although CPAs are licensed by individual states, there is close cooperation between the states and the AICPA, which biannually makes available to each state a national, uniform CPA examination. An individual must pass this exam as well as meet state licensing requirements in order to become a CPA and qualify for membership in the AICPA.

The *Journal of Accountancy* is published monthly by the AICPA. This magazine is designed to help CPAs keep abreast of current developments in accounting.

CASB

The Cost Accounting Standards Board was established by legislation as an agency of Congress in 1970. It was given the authority and the responsibility to set cost accounting standards for prime contractors and subcontractors in the pricing, administration, and settlement of negotiated defense contracts in excess of $100,000. The CASB has a five-member, part-time, appointed board, assisted by a full-time paid staff. Congress is currently debating the value of the CASB and there is a chance that it may be phased out.

FASB

As we explained in Chapter 1 and its Supplement, the Financial Accounting Standards Board is the primary accounting standard-setting body in the private sector and has some jurisdiction in setting standards in the not-for-profit area. It deals with a much broader scope of standards than the CASB because it is charged with the task of establishing generally accepted accounting principles for organizations.

FEI

The Financial Executives Institute, formerly known as the Controllers' Institute, is a national organization comprised of financial executives of large corporations. Its members include treasurers, controllers, financial vice presidents, and other individuals who hold important positions in the financial community. The FEI has been involved in sponsoring research projects on a wide variety of important business topics.

The *Financial Executive* is published monthly by the FEI. This magazine contains articles on financial management as well as on technical accounting topics.

NAA

The National Association of Accountants is probably the largest accounting group in the United States. Most of its members are engaged in managerial accounting. Consequently, the NAA concentrates on budgeting, cost accounting, and information systems more than on external financial accounting issues. Research sponsored by the NAA has traditionally dealt with the uses of accounting data within business organizations, although several recent studies have addressed external reporting considerations.

The NAA's monthly publication is *Management Accounting*, which focuses on issues related to the accountant's role in the decision-making process and the specific functions of planning and control.

SEC

With the possible exception of the FASB, the Securities and Exchange Commission has the greatest influence on accounting principles and practices. The SEC was created in 1934 and administers both the 1933 and the 1934 Securities and Exchange Acts. It is a quasi-judicial, quasi-legislative, governmental body that regulates the issuance and trading of corporate securities and attempts to ensure full and fair disclosure to the public of all material facts concerning those securities. In order to perform its "watchdog" role, the SEC was given statutory power to prescribe accounting principles and reporting practices. Except in a few instances, the SEC has not exercised that power, but relies instead on the FASB and the AICPA. Nevertheless, the direct and subtle pressure of the SEC has significantly influenced existing accounting practices.[1]

Challenges Facing the Profession

Accounting is faced with many complex challenges. One of the most important challenge is for accountants to perform better in leadership roles within organizations. Accountants are no longer simply a source of financial data; they are also asked to interpret the data and to assist directly in the decision-making process. In increasing numbers, accountants are becoming a part of the management team charged with making the economic decisions needed to accomplish organizational objectives.

The continuing development of generally accepted accounting principles provides another important challenge for the profession. As explained in Chapter 1, this task was assumed by a committee of the AICPA—the Accounting Principles Board (APB)—in 1959. Later, in 1973, the responsibility for establishing accounting principles was given to the FASB, an

---

[1] For an expanded discussion of the nature and workings of the SEC; see K. Fred Skousen, *An Introduction to the SEC*, 2nd ed. (Cincinnati: South-Western Publishing Co., 1980).

independent body. Some of the same criticisms leveled at the APB are now being directed toward the FASB. Congressional hearings in 1977, for example, criticized the FASB for allowing so many alternative accounting principles to exist. However, as the FASB explains, it is extremely difficult to establish generally accepted accounting principles that are sufficiently flexible to allow for the complexity of U.S. business and yet uniform enough to provide comparability for investors and other users of accounting data.

And still other challenges are facing the accounting profession. For example, what modifications are needed in accounting to keep pace with new technological developments, such as electronic funds transfers and minicomputers? Should auditors be expected to detect fraud? What is the auditor's responsibility in terms of illegal payments? What are the limits of an accountant's legal liability? What responsibilities do managers and accountants have with respect to establishing adequate internal controls? Should accounting continue to be based on transactions recorded at historical costs, or should some other method of valuation be used in the primary financial statements? How should we account for inflation?

For the accounting profession, the next several years are of particular significance. This is especially true with respect to potential governmental influence on accounting. During the mid-1970s, the late Senator Lee Metcalf conducted an extensive study of the "Accounting Establishment." The resulting staff report contained several serious allegations. In essence, the report said that the accounting profession lacks independence, that it is self-serving and not in the public interest and therefore contributes to certain social ills, such as the misallocation of resources, fraud, and illegal payments. The problem, according to Metcalf's staff, is that the so-called "Big 8" public accounting firms control the AICPA, and indirectly the FASB, which sets flexible accounting and auditing standards. This, in turn, helps the clients of the large accounting firms—and these are, of course, the major corporations in the United States. The report further suggested that the SEC, by delegating its standard-setting authority to the FASB, was failing to protect the public and to fulfill its congressional mandate, and so was condoning this "conspiracy" within the accounting profession. Metcalf's staff concluded that the only way of improving accounting practices would be for the government to set the standards and thus regulate the profession.

It is an understatement to say that Metcalf's report created considerable excitement within the accounting profession as well as the business community. Eventually, Senate committee hearings were held and a final report was issued in November 1977.[2] This report concluded that improvements were needed in the accounting profession, but that self-reform, not governmental regulation, was appropriate at the present time. If the accounting profession, working with the SEC, was unwilling or unable to make needed changes, the report continued, then additional congressional action was likely to be forthcoming.

---

[2] *Improving the Accountability of Publicly Owned Corporations and Their Auditors* (Washington, D.C.: Government Printing Office, 1977).

During the late 1970s, Representative John E. Moss also conducted an investigation of the accounting profession. However, Representative Moss went further than Senator Metcalf and introduced a bill, the Public Accounting Regulatory Act, which called for the establishment of a National Organization of Securities and Exchange Commission of Accountancy (NOSECA). This regulatory agency would monitor the activities of the accounting firms that furnish audit reports and documents that are filed by companies in registering with the SEC. Fortunately, in our opinion, this bill was not passed by the 95th Congress. However, it may have set a precedent for future legislation.

Partially because of these pressures and partially because of a self-determined need, the accounting profession has conducted its own studies, which will greatly influence the future development of generally accepted accounting principles. As a result of one of these studies, the FASB was made completely independent of the AICPA, and an SEC Practices Division of the AICPA was established. Public accounting firms that have clients who report to the SEC belong to this division. These CPA firms are required to submit to an annual "peer review," a study by another firm to ensure a high quality of practice. A Public Oversight Board for the accounting profession was also established.

In another study, the responsibilities of auditors were outlined. Several recommendations of this study—for example, the establishment of a full-time audit committee as a means of improving the process of setting auditing standards—have been implemented.

These and other efforts by the profession have helped accounting to grow and develop. Problems that seemed troublesome in the past have now been solved. Progress is being made. However, new problems arise to take the place of old ones. Finding solutions to these new problems presents a continuing challenge. It will take the combined efforts of a great many accountants, working through and with all the organizations mentioned here, including perhaps the Congress, to ensure that future accounting principles and practices will be founded in good accounting theory, and that they will meet the demands of the various users of accounting information.

GLOSSARY

A

account: An accounting record in which the results of similar transactions are accumulated; shows increases, decreases, and a balance. (3)

accounting: A service activity designed to accumulate, measure, and communicate financial information about organizations for decision-making purposes. (17)

accounting concepts and assumptions: Fundamental ideas that provide the foundation upon which the principles and procedures of accounting theory rest. (22)

accounting cycle: The sequence of procedures in the accounting process that includes analyzing business documents, journalizing, posting, balancing the accounts and preparing a trial balance and worksheet, journalizing and posting adjusting entries, preparing financial statements, closing nominal accounts, and balancing the accounts and preparing a post-closing trial balance. Interpretation of reports, while not usually considered a routine step in the accounting cycle, is a vital function of accountants. (71)

accounting equation: An algebraic equation that expresses the relationship between assets (resources), liabilities (obligations), and owners' equity (net equity, or the residual interest in a business after all liabilities have been met). It is: Assets = Liabilities + Owners' Equity. (21)

accounting information system: A subset of the managerial information system whereby the financial data derived from recorded transactions are collected, processed, and reported. (68)

accounting manual: A document that lists all accounts and describes the proper bookkeeping for transactions likely to be processed through each of these accounts. (525)

accounting model: The basic accounting concepts and assumptions that determine the manner of recording, measuring, and reporting an entity's transactions. (18)

accounting principles: Broad guidelines that identify the procedures to be used in specific accounting situations. (22)

Accounting Principles Board (APB): The organization established by AICPA between 1959 and 1973 to set standards for financial accounting and reporting. (24)

accounting procedures: Specific rules or methods for applying accounting principles. (23)

accounting process: The means of transforming accounting data into accounting reports that can be interpreted and used in decision making; often used interchangeably with accounting cycle. (67)

accounts payable: Money owed to creditors; a current liability. (269)

accounts receivable: Money due from rendering services or selling merchandise on credit; a current asset. (263)

accounts receivable turnover: A measure of a company's average collection period for receivables; computed by dividing net sales (or net credit sales) by average accounts receivable. (469)

accrual-basis accounting: A system of accounting in which revenues and expenses are recorded as they are earned and incurred, not necessarily when payments are received or made; *compare* cash-basis accounting. (106)

accrual-basis historical cost method: The method of measuring income whereby income is defined as revenues earned minus expenses incurred during a period without regard to changes in the values of assets or liabilities or in the general price level. (165)

accrued liability: An obligation for benefits received but not yet paid for. (270)

accumulated depreciation: The total depreciation charged on an asset since acquisition; a contra account deducted from the original cost of an asset on the Balance Sheet. (244, 330)

acid-test (quick) ratio: A more precise measure of a firm's ability to meet current liabilities than the current ratio; computed by dividing net quick assets (all current assets except inventories and prepaid expenses) by current liabilities. (274, 469)

adjusting entries: Entries required at the end of each accounting period to recognize on an accrual basis all revenues and expenses for the period and to report proper amounts for assets, liabilities, and owners' equity accounts. (107)

administrative controls: Procedures that deal primarily with operational efficiency and employees' compliance with the authorized policies and procedures. (516)

aging accounts receivable: The process of categorizing each account receivable by the number of days it has been outstanding. (174)

all-financial-resources concept: A concept used in preparing a Funds Statement that reflects all financing and investing activities for a period as sources and uses of funds, whether or not they increase or decrease cash or working capital. (420)

Allowance for Doubtful Accounts: A contra account deducted from Accounts Receivable that shows the estimated losses from uncollectable accounts. (172)

allowance method: The recording of estimated losses due to uncollectable accounts as expenses during the period in which the sale occurred; *compare* direct write-off method. (172)

American Accounting Association (AAA): The national organization representing accounting educators and practitioners; it serves as a forum for the expression of accounting ideas and encourages accounting research. (24)

American Institute of CPAs (AICPA): The national organization representing certified public accountants (CPAs) in the United States. (24)

amortization: The process of cost allocation that assigns the original cost of an intangible asset to the periods benefited. (344)

amortization of bonds: The systematic writing off of a bond discount or premium over the life of the bond. (310)

appropriations: In not-for-profit accounting, formal authorizations to spend up to specified amounts in carrying out the specific objectives of a fund. (495)

arm's-length transactions: Business dealings between independent and rational parties who are looking out for their own interests. (20)

articles of incorporation: *See* charter.

asset approach: A way of accounting for prepaid expenses in which these expenses are originally debited to an asset account. A year-end adjustment is required to record the asset value used up as an expense of the period and to adjust the related asset account to its proper balance; *compare* expense approach. (115)

assets: Economic resources that are owned or controlled by an enterprise, as a result of past transactions or events, and that are expected to have future economic benefits (service potential). (34)

asset turnover ratio: An overall measure of how effectively assets are used during a period; computed by dividing net sales by average total assets. (465)

audit report: A statement issued by an independent certified public accountant that expresses an opinion on the company's adherence to generally accepted accounting principles. (42)

authorized stock: The number of shares and type of stock that may be issued by a company, as specified in its articles of incorporation. (387)

automated accounting system: A system in which most of the data processing is performed by machines. (67)

B

bad debt: An uncollectable account receivable. (171)

Balance Sheet (Statement of Financial Position): The primary financial statement that shows the financial resources of an enterprise at a particular date and the claims against those resources, and therefore the relationships of assets, liabilities, and owners' equity. (37, 236)

bank reconciliation: The process of systematically comparing the cash balance as reported by the bank and as recorded on the company's books and explaining any differences. (262)

bank service charge: A bank's fee for servicing an account, usually charged monthly. (260)

board of directors: Individuals elected by the shareholders to govern a corporation. (385)

bond: Document evidencing a long-term obligation of a company or government agency; bonds bear interest at stated rates, mature at specified future dates, and are usually issued in units of $1,000. (305)

bond discount: The difference between the face value and the sales price of a bond when it is sold below its face value. (309)

bond indenture: A contract between a bond issuer and a bond purchaser that specifies the terms of the bond. (366)

bond maturity date: Date at which the bond principal becomes payable. (305)

bond maturity value: *See* face value of a bond.

bond premium: The difference between the face value and the sales price of a bond when it is sold above its face value. (309)

bond principal: *See* face value of a bond.

bond sinking fund: An interest-bearing investment account, usually managed by an independent trustee, in which periodic deposits are made and interest accrues to retire bonds at maturity. (376)

book value: The net amount shown in the accounts for an asset, liability, or owners' equity item. (330)

book value of accounts receivable: The net amount that would be received if all collectable receivables were collected; equal to total accounts receivable less the allowance for doubtful accounts. (173)

book value per share: A measure of net worth; computed by dividing stockholders' equity for each class of stock by the weighted-average number of outstanding shares for that class. (478)

budgetary accounts: In not-for-profit accounting, a self-balancing set of accounts that constitute a formal record of a fund's financial plan. (495)

business documents: Records of transactions used as the basis for recording accounting entries; includes invoices, check stubs, receipts, and similar business papers. (75)

business entity: An organization with a profit objective, deriving its earnings by providing goods or services to society. (16)

business expenses: Expenses incurred in the course of business that are ordinary and necessary, reasonable in amount, and have been paid or incurred. (538)

C

calendar year: An entity's reporting year, ending on December 31 and covering twelve months. (105)

callable bonds: Bonds for which the issuer reserves the right to retire the obligation before its maturity date. (368)

capital flows: Term used in not-for-profit accounting to describe the sources and uses of funds for long-term assets, such as buildings, land, and equipment. (504)

capital gain: The excess of proceeds over costs from the sale of a capital asset, as defined by the Internal Revenue Code. (547)

capitalization: The recording of an expenditure expected to benefit more than the current period as an asset. (337)

capital stock: The portion of owners' equity contributed by investors (the owners) through the issuance of stock. (38, 387)

cash-basis accounting: A system of accounting in which transactions are recorded, and revenues and expenses are recognized, only when payments are received or made; *compare* accrual-basis accounting. (105)

cash-basis method: The method of measuring income whereby income is defined as cash receipts less cash disbursements during an accounting period. (164)

cash concept of funds: A concept used in preparing a Funds Statement that reflects transactions in which cash is either received or paid. (420)

cash discount: *See* sales discount.

cash dividend: Pro rata cash distribution of earnings to shareholders. (393)

Cash Over and Short: An account used to record overages and shortages in petty cash. (259)

certified public accountant (CPA): A designation given to an accountant who has passed a national uniform examination and has met other requirements in order to be registered or licensed as a public accountant; CPA certificates are issued and monitored by state boards of accountancy or similar agencies. (43)

charter: A document issued by a state that gives legal status to a corporation and details its specific rights; also called articles of incorporation. (385)

chart of accounts: A systematic listing of all accounts used by a company. (78, 523)

classified Balance Sheet: A Balance Sheet on which assets, liabilities, and owners' equity are subdivided by age, use, and source. (241)

Class Life System: A system that designates the lives of specified classes of assets and allows a taxpayer to select a life for depreciation purposes that is up to 20 percent shorter or longer than the class life. (556)

clearing account: A temporary account, such as Income Summary, that is used at the end of an accounting period to collect the debit and credit balances from other accounts as they are closed. The clearing account balance is then closed to a permanent account. (123)

closing entries: Entries that reduce all nominal, or Income Statement, accounts to a zero balance at the end of each accounting period, transferring their preclosing balances to permanent, Balance Sheet accounts. (82)

common-size statement: An Income Statement or Balance Sheet providing percentage relationships or ratios of individual items to the total. (464)

common stock: The class of stock most frequently issued by corporations; it usually confers a voting right in the corporation; its dividend and liquidation rights are usually inferior to those of preferred stock. (387)

compound interest: Interest calculated on the principal amount plus any previously earned interest. (296)

compound period: Period of time for which interest is calculated. (296)

computerized accounting system: A system in which most of the data processing is performed by computers. (68)

conduit principle: The idea that all income earned by an entity must be passed through to the owners and reported on their individual tax returns; applicable to proprietorships and partnerships, and, in a modified form, to Subchapter S corporations. (542)

consignee: A vendor who sells merchandise owned by another party, known as the consignor, usually on a commission basis. (207)

consignment: An arrangement whereby merchandise owned by one party (the consignor) is sold by another party (the consignee), usually on a commission basis. (207)

consignor: The owner of merchandise sold by someone else, known as the consignee. (207)

consolidated financial statements: Statements that show the operating results and financial position of two or more legally separate but affiliated companies as if they were one economic entity. (43)

constructive receipt rule: The idea that cash has been received when the taxpayer can exercise control over it, whether or not the cash has actually been received. (541)

contingent liability: A potential obligation, dependent upon the occurrence of future events. (273)

contra account: An account that is offset or deducted from another account. (170)

contributed capital: That portion of stockholders' equity provided by the owners of a business, usually through the purchase of stock. (245, 387)

control account: A summary account in the General Ledger that is supported by detailed individual accounts in a subsidiary ledger. (196)

convertible bonds: Bonds that can be exchanged for or converted to capital stock after a specified period of time. (368)

corporation: A legal entity chartered by a state with ownership represented by transferable shares of stock. (19)

cost-beneficial controls: Controls that benefit a company to an extent that outweighs their costs. (518)

cost method of accounting for investments in stocks: Accounting for an investment in the stock of another company, usually where less than 20 percent is owned, by recording the initial acquisition at cost and recognizing dividends as revenue earned; *compare* equity method. (302)

cost of goods sold: The expense incurred for purchased or manufactured merchandise sold during a period; equal to beginning inventory plus cost of goods purchased or manufactured less ending inventory. (176)

coupon bonds: Bonds for which owners receive periodic interest payments by clipping the coupon from a bond and sending it to the issuer as evidence of bond ownership. (367)

credit: An entry on the right side of an account. (72)

cumulative-dividend preference: The right of preferred shareholders to receive dividends for all past years in which no dividends were paid before common shareholders receive any dividends. (396)

current assets: Cash and other assets that may reasonably be expected to be converted to cash within one year or during the normal operating cycle. (241)

current-dividend preference: The right of preferred shareholders to receive current dividends before common shareholders receive dividends. (395)

current liabilities: Debts or other obligations that will be paid or otherwise discharged within one year or the normal operating cycle. (244)

current-value method: Approach whereby income is defined as the excess of revenues over expenses, plus the net increases or decreases in the values of specific assets and liabilities during a period. (167)

current values: The amounts that assets or liabilities are presently worth in the marketplace; generally equal to the replacement costs, net realizable values, or net present values of items. (240)

current (working capital) ratio: A measure of liquidity that represents a margin of safety for meeting current liabilities; computed by dividing current assets by current liabilities. (273, 468)

D

data: Inputs to the accounting system that are derived from transactions. (67)

date of record: The date selected by a corporation's board of directors on which dividend-receiving shareholders are identified. (394)

days sales invested in working capital: An alternative measure of the amount of working capital used in sustaining the sales of a period; computed by dividing 365 days by the working capital turnover. (472)

debentures: Bonds on which no collateral has been pledged; also called unsecured bonds. (367)

debit: An entry on the left side of an account. (72)

debt–equity management ratio: A measure of the relative utilization of debt and equity; computed by dividing average total assets by average stockholders' equity. (473)

debt financing: Raising money, or capital, by borrowing; *compare* equity financing. (356)

declaration date: The date on which a corporation's board of directors formally decides to distribute a dividend to shareholders. (393)

deductions: Business expenses or losses that are subtracted from gross income in computing taxable income. (538)

deferred income taxes: The difference between income tax expense, calculated as a function of accounting income based on generally accepted accounting principles, and current taxes payable, calculated as a function of taxable income based on the Internal Revenue and other tax codes. (363)

depletion: The process of cost allocation that assigns the original cost of a natural resource to the periods benefited. (343)

depreciation: The process of cost allocation that assigns the original cost of plant and equipment to the periods benefited. (244, 329)

direct write-off method: The recording of actual losses from uncollectable accounts as expenses during the period in which accounts receivable are determined to be uncollectable; *compare* allowance method. (171)

discount: The amount paid to a bank when selling, or discounting, a note receivable; calculated as maturity value times discount rate times discount period. (266)

discounting a note receivable: The sale by a payee of a note to a financial institution for less than the maturity value. (265)

discount period: The time between the date a note is issued or sold to a financial institution and its maturity date. (266)

discount rate: The interest rate charged by a financial institution for lending money or for buying a note receivable. (266)

dividend payout ratio: A measure of earnings paid out in dividends; computed by dividing cash dividends by net income available to each class of stock. (478)

dividends: The periodic distribution of earnings in the form of cash, stock, or other property to the owners (stockholders) of a corporation. (41, 393)

dividends in arrears: Missed dividends for past years that preferred shareholders have a right to receive under their cumulative-dividend preference, when dividends are declared. (396)

double-declining-balance depreciation method (DDB): The accelerated depreciation method in which book value is multiplied by a constant depreciation rate (double the straight-line percentage); also called 200 percent declining balance depreciation. (333)

double-entry accounting: A system of recording transactions in which the equality of the accounting equation is maintained. (21)

Doubtful Accounts Expense: An account that represents the current period's receivables estimated to become uncollectable. (172)

Drawings: A temporary account for recording withdrawals of cash or other assets from a partnership or proprietorship by the owner(s). (402)

E

earnings (loss) per share (EPS): The amount of net income (earnings) related to each share of stock; computed by dividing net income by the weighted-average number of shares of stock outstanding during the period. (39)

earnings potential: The ability of a company to generate positive future net cash flows from operations. (33)

effective-interest amortization: A method of systematically writing off a bond premium or discount that takes into consideration the time value of money; results in an equal rate of amortization for each period; *compare* straight-line interest amortization. (312, 370)

effective interest rate: The actual rate of return earned on a bond. (370)

encumbrance: In not-for-profit accounting, a formal record of commitments made now for expenditures to be made later. (497)

entity: An organizational unit (a person, partnership, or corporation) for which accounting records are kept and about which accounting reports are prepared. (18)

equity financing: Raising money, or capital, by issuing stock; *compare* debt financing. (356)

equity method of accounting for investments in stocks: Accounting for an investment in the stock of another company, where significant influence can be imposed (presumed to exist when there is 20 or more percent ownership), by recording the acquisition at cost but recognizing dividends as return of investment and the proportionate share of earnings as revenue; *compare* cost method. (304)

exclusions: Gross receipts that are not subject to tax and are not included in gross income, such as interest on state and local government bonds. (538)

expendable fund: In not-for-profit accounting, a fund in which the capital resources are available to carry out the specific objectives of the fund. (494)

expense approach: A way of accounting for prepaid expenses in which these expenses are originally debited to an expense account, even though future benefits exist. A year-end adjustment is required to record the actual expense incurred during the period and to establish a companion asset account equal to remaining future benefits; *compare* asset approach. (115)

expenses: Costs of assets used up or additional liabilities incurred in the normal course of business to generate revenues. (36)

extraordinary items: Special nonoperating gains and losses that are unusual in nature, infrequent in occurrence, and material in amount. (187)

F

face (maturity) value of a bond: The amount that will be paid on a bond on the maturity date; also called principal or par value. (305, 368)

FICA: *See* social security taxes.

fidelity bond: An insurance contract whereby a bonding company agrees to reimburse an employer for any theft, embezzlement, or fraud perpetrated by an employee covered by the bonding agreement. (528)

FIFO (first-in, first-out): An inventory cost flow assumption whereby the first goods purchased determine the cost of goods sold and the last goods purchased determine the ending inventory. (212)

financial accounting: The area of accounting concerned with measuring and reporting on a periodic basis the financial status and operating results of organizations to interested external parties; *compare* managerial accounting. (17)

Financial Accounting Standards Board (FASB): The private organization in the United States responsible for establishing the standards for financial accounting and reporting. (24)

finished goods: Manufactured products ready for sale; includes all manufacturing costs assigned to products that have been completed but not yet sold. (207)

fiscal year: An entity's reporting year covering a 12-month accounting period. (105)

FOB (free-on-board) destination: Business term meaning that the seller of merchandise bears the shipping costs and maintains ownership until the sales destination is reached. (207)

FOB (free-on-board) shipping point: Business term meaning that the buyer of merchandise bears the shipping costs and acquires ownership at the point of shipment. (207)

Foreign Corrupt Practices Act (FCPA) of 1977: Legislation that requires all companies registered with the Securities and Exchange Commission to keep accurate accounting records and maintain an adequate system of internal control. (517)

franchise: An exclusive right to sell a product or offer a service in a certain geographical area. (244, 345)

freight-in: The costs of transporting into a firm all purchased merchandise or materials intended for resale; added to purchases in calculating cost of goods sold. (180)

fund: In not-for-profit accounting, a separate accounting entity that contains a self-balancing set of accounts reflecting only the activities of that entity. (493)

fund accounting: An accounting system that involves the use of a group of self-balancing accounts, called funds, for each activity of a not-for-profit organization. (493)

fund balance: The excess of a fund's assets over its liabilities and reserves; the balancing account for the Balance Sheet of a not-for-profit organization. (499)

funds: Measures of the flow of financial resources, usually defined as working capital or cash. (420)

future amount of an annuity of $1: The amount to which a series of equally spaced payments of $1 will accumulate if invested for a certain number of periods at a specified interest rate. (299)

future amount of $1: The amount to which $1 will increase if invested for a certain number of periods at a specified interest rate. (296)

G

gains (losses): Net increases (decreases) in an entity's resources derived from peripheral activities or associated with nonrecurring, unusual events and circumstances. (36)

general fixed asset account group: A group of accounts used for recording the property, plant, and equipment costs of the general fund and certain other funds in a not-for-profit organization. (494)

general fund: The primary fund of a not-for-profit organization; it includes accounts for transactions that do not fit into more specialized funds. (494)

general long-term debt account group: A group of accounts used for recording long-term debt, such as bond issues, for the general fund and certain other funds in a not-for-profit organization. (494)

generally accepted accounting principles (GAAP): Guidelines that authoritatively define accounting practice at a particular time. (23)

general price-level-adjusted historical cost method: The method of measuring income that defines it as: revenues less expenses as adjusted by a general (economy-wide) price index, plus any purchasing power gains or losses from holding monetary assets and liabilities as changes occur in the general price level. (165)

general price-level adjustments: Restatement of historical costs based on a general price-level index that represents the impact of inflation. (239)

general-purpose financial statements: The primary financial statements intended for general use by a variety of external groups. The primary statements include an Income Statement (Statement of Earnings), Balance Sheet (Statement of Financial Position), and a Statement of Changes in Financial Position (Funds Statement). (33)

going-concern assumption: The idea that an accounting entity will have a continuing existence for the foreseeable future. (21)

goodwill: An intangible asset showing that a business is worth more than the fair market value of its net assets because of strategic location, reputation, good customer relations, or similar factors; equal to the excess of cost over the fair market value of the net assets purchased. (345)

gross income: The portion of a company's gross receipts less cost of sales that is subject to taxation. (538)

gross margin: The excess of net sales revenues over the cost of goods sold. (38)

gross margin method: A procedure for estimating the dollar amount of ending inventory; the relationship of cost of goods sold to sales is determined and used in computing ending inventory; *compare* retail inventory method. (222)

gross tax liability: The amount of tax computed by multiplying the tax base (taxable income) by the appropriate tax rate. (538)

H

half-year convention: Under the Class Life System, the practice of allowing a half year's depreciation for all assets put into service any time during the year; *compare* modified half-year convention. (556)

historical costs: The acquisition costs of assets; equal to current values at the dates of acquisition.

horizontal analysis: A technique for analyzing the percentage change in individual Income Statement or Balance Sheet items from one year to the next. (463)

I

imprest petty-cash fund: A petty-cash fund in which all expenditures are documented by vouchers and vendors' receipts or invoices. (258)

Income Statement (Statement of Earnings): The primary financial statement that summarizes the revenues generated, the expenses incurred, and any gains or losses of an entity during a period of time. (38)

Income Summary: A clearing account used to close all revenues and expenses at the end of the accounting period. The balance of the Income Summary account before it is closed represents the operating results (income or loss) of a given accounting period. (123)

information: Data organized by the accounting system. (67)

installment sale: A transaction that usually involves a down payment and a series of payments over a period of two or more years. (557)

intangible assets: Long-lived assets that do not have physical substance and are not held for resale. (244, 344)

interest: The amount charged for using money. (264)

interest rate: The cost of using money expressed as an annual percentage. (264)

internal audit: An appraisal by internal accountants of employee performance and adherence to company policies, and an assessment of the reliability of the information system. (326)

internal control: An organization's methods and procedures for safeguarding its assets, checking on the accuracy and reliability of its accounting data, and promoting operational efficiency and adherence to managerial policies. (69, 515)

inventory: Goods held for sale; refers to both the number of units involved and the dollar amount of inventory. (164)

inventory cutoff: The determination of which inventory items are to be included in the year-end inventory balance. (206)

inventory turnover: A measure of the efficiency with which inventory is managed; computed by dividing cost of goods sold by average inventory for a period. (470)

investment: An expenditure to acquire assets that are expected to produce future earnings. (291)

involuntary conversion: A transaction in which an asset is destroyed (for example, by fire or storm) or is taken by a government agency through condemnation proceedings. (557)

issued stock: Authorized stock originally issued to stockholders, which may or may not still be outstanding. (387)

J

journal: The accounting record in which transactions are first entered; provides a chronological record of all business activities. (76)

L

lapping: A procedure used to conceal the theft of cash by crediting the payment from one customer to another customer's account on a delayed basis. (257)

lease: A contract whereby the lessee (user) agrees to pay the lessor (owner) for the use of an asset. (364)

lease obligations: Net present value of all future lease payments discounted at an appropriate rate of interest. (364)

ledger: A book or grouping of accounts in which data from transactions recorded in journals are posted and thereby classified and summarized. (76)

legal capital: The amount of contributed capital not available for dividends as restricted by state law for the protection of creditors; usually equal to the par or stated value or the contributed amount of issued capital stock. (388)

lessee: An entity that agrees to pay periodic rents for the use of leased property. (364)

lessor: Renter or owner of leased property. (364)

leveraging: The advantage (or disadvantage) obtained from using borrowed money to finance a business when the net interest rate of the borrowed funds is less (more) than the company's earnings rate. (357)

liabilities: Obligations of an enterprise to pay cash or other economic resources in return for past or current benefits. They represent claims against assets. (35)

liability approach: A way of accounting for unearned revenues in which revenues are originally credited to a liability account. A year-end adjustment is required to record the revenues earned during that period and to reduce the companion liability account; *compare* revenue approach. (112)

LIFO (last-in, first-out): An inventory cost flow assumption whereby the last goods purchased determine the cost of goods sold and the first goods purchased determine the ending inventory. (212)

limited liability: The legal protection given stockholders whereby they are responsible only for the debts and obligations of a corporation to the extent of their capital contribution. (385)

line of credit: An arrangement whereby a bank agrees to loan an amount of money (up to a certain limit) on demand for short periods of time. (292)

liquidating dividend: Distributions of a firm's assets when a corporation is permanently reducing its operations or going out of business. (393)

liquidity: A company's ability to meet current obligations with cash or with other resources that can be quickly converted to cash. (33, 457)

long-term investment: An expenditure for nonoperational assets that a business intends to hold for more than a year or the normal operating cycle. (243, 301)

long-term liabilities: Debts or other obligations that will not be paid for or otherwise discharged within one year or the normal operating cycle. (245)

long-term operational assets: Long-lived assets acquired for use in the business rather than for resale; includes (1) property, plant, and equipment; (2) natural resources; and (3) intangible assets. (326)

lower-of-cost-or-market rule: A basis for valuing certain assets at the lower of original cost or market value (current replacement cost). (220)

M

maker: A person (entity) who signs a note to borrow money and who assumes responsibility to pay the note at maturity. (264)

management: Individuals who are responsible for overseeing the day-to-day operations of a business and who are the "internal" users of accounting information. (17)

managerial accounting: The area of accounting concerned with assisting managers in decision making, specifically with planning, budgeting, and controlling costs and revenues. (17)

managerial information system: The system whereby all information used by management is collected, processed, and reported. (68)

marketable securities: Short-term investments that can be readily sold in established markets. (293)

market rate of interest: The prevailing interest rate in the marketplace applicable to individual categories and grades of securities. (367)

matching principle: The idea that all costs and expenses incurred in generating revenues must be recognized in the same reporting period as the related revenues. (172)

materiality: The concept that accounting should disclose only those events important enough to have an influence on the decision maker. (43)

maturity date: The date on which a note or other obligation comes due. (264)

maturity value: The amount of an obligation to be collected or paid at maturity date; equal to principal plus any interest. (265)

modified half-year convention: Under the Class Life System, the practice whereby assets put into service before midyear are eligible for a full year of depreciation, and assets put into service after midyear are not eligible for depreciation until the following year; *compare* half-year convention. (556)

monetary items: Those assets or liabilities fixed either by nature or contract as to the amount of future dollars they can command in the marketplace. (238)

money measurement concept: The idea that money, as the common medium of exchange, is the accounting unit of measurement, and that only economic activities measurable in monetary terms are included in the accounting model. (20)

mortgage amortization schedule: A schedule that shows the breakdown between interest and principal for each payment over the life of a mortgage. (361)

mortgage payable: A written promise to pay a stated amount of money on or before specified future dates, secured by the pledging of certain assets as collateral. (361)

moving average: A perpetual inventory cost flow assumption whereby the cost of goods sold and the ending inventory are determined to be a weighted-average cost of all merchandise on hand after each purchase. (218)

N

natural resources: Assets, such as minerals, oil, timber, or gravel, that are extracted or otherwise depleted. (343)

net assets: Total assets less total liabilities; equal to owners' equity. (71)

net income (earnings): A measure of the overall performance of a business entity; equal to revenues plus gains for a period minus expenses and losses for the period. (36)

net realizable value: The selling price of an item less reasonable selling costs. (219)

net tax liability: The amount of tax computed by subtracting tax credits from the gross tax liability. (538)

nominal accounts: The accounts appearing on the Income Statement, which are closed to a zero balance at the end of each accounting period; also called temporary accounts. (82)

noncurrent accounts: All operational asset, long-term investment, long-term liability, and owners' equity accounts; all accounts except for working capital accounts. (421)

nonexpendable fund: In not-for-profit accounting, a fund in which the capital resources must be preserved. (494)

nonmonetary items: Those assets or equities that are not fixed as to the amount of future dollars they can command and hence fluctuate in value according to their demand in the marketplace. (238)

no-par stock: Stock that does not have a par value printed on the face of the stock certificate. (388)

note payable: A debt owed to a creditor, evidenced by an unconditional written promise to pay a sum of money on or before a specified future date. (269, 359)

note receivable: A claim against a debtor, evidenced by an unconditional written promise to pay a sum of money on or before a specified future date. (264)

notes to financial statements: Explanatory information considered an integral part of the primary financial statements. (42)

not-for-profit organization: An entity without a profit objective, oriented toward accomplishing nonprofit goals in an efficient manner. (16, 491)

NSF check: A check that is not honored by a bank because of insufficient cash in the customer's bank account. (260)

number of days sales in inventory: A measure of how well inventory is being managed; computed by dividing 365 days by the inventory turnover. (471)

number of days sales in receivables: A measure of the average number of days it takes to collect a credit sale; computed by dividing 365 days by the accounts receivable turnover. (469)

O

operating cycle: The general pattern of business activity whereby cash and other resources are converted to inventory and operational assets and eventually into a product or service that can be sold and for which cash and other resources are received. (69, 237)

operating expenses: Costs incurred in the course of the day-to-day, operating cycle, activities of a firm.

operating flows: In not-for-profit accounting, a term used to describe the revenue inflows and operating (expense) outflows of a fund. (504)

operating income: A measure of the profitability of a business from normal operations; equals revenues minus operating expenses. (37)

operating performance ratio: An overall measure of the efficiency of operations during a period; computed by dividing net income by net sales. (462)

ordinary annuity: A series of equal amounts to be received or paid at the end of equally spaced time intervals. (298)

outstanding stock: Issued stock that is still being held by investors. (387)

overall performance ratio: A measure of overall performance, including management of operations, use of assets, and management of debt and equity; computed by dividing net income by average stockholders' equity. (475)

owners' equity (stockholders' equity): The ownership interest in the assets of an enterprise; equals net assets (total assets minus total liabilities). (35)

P

par: The nominal value printed on the face of a bond or a share of stock. (346)

parent company: A company that owns or maintains control over other companies, known as subsidiaries, which are themselves separate legal entities. Control generally refers to ownership of 50 percent or more of the stock of another company. (43, 302)

participating-dividend preference: The right of preferred shareholders to receive equal distributions of dividends on a proportionate basis with common shareholders. (396)

partnership: An unincorporated business owned by two or more individuals or entities. (19, 403)

partnership agreement: An agreement between partners that usually specifies the capital contributions required by each partner, the ratios in which partnership earnings will be distributed, the management responsibilities of partners, and the partners' rights to transfer or to sell their individual interests. (403)

par-value stock: Stock that has a nominal value assigned to it in the corporation's charter and printed on the face of each share of stock. (388)

patent: An exclusive 17-year right to make, sell, and use an invention granted by the federal government. (244, 344)

payee: The person (entity) to whom payment on a note is to be made. (264)

payment date: The date on which dividends are paid by a corporation to its shareholders. (394)

periodic inventory method: A system of recording inventory in which cost of goods sold is determined and inventory is adjusted at the end of the accounting period, not when merchandise is purchased or sold. (179)

permanent accounts: See real accounts.

perpetual inventory method: A system of recording inventory in which detailed records of the number of units and cost of each purchase and sales transaction are prepared throughout the accounting period. (177)

petty-cash fund: A small amount of cash kept on hand for making miscellaneous expenditures. (258)

post-closing trial balance: A listing of all real account balances after the closing process has been completed; provides a means of testing whether debits equal credits for all real accounts prior to beginning a new accounting cycle. (83)

posting: The process of classifying, grouping, and recording similar transactions in common accounts by transferring amounts from the journal to the ledger. (76)

preferred stock: A class of stock issued by corporations, usually having dividend and liquidation preferences over common stock. (387)

premium on stock: The excess of the issuance (market) price of stock over its par or stated value. (388)

prepaid expenses: Payments made in advance for items normally charged to expense; also called expenses paid in advance. (115)

present value of an annuity of $1: The value today of a series of equally spaced payments of $1 to be paid or received in the future, given a specified interest, or discount, rate. (300)

present value of $1: The value today of $1 to be received at some future date, given a specified interest, or discount, rate. (297)

price—earnings (P/E) ratio: A measure of growth potential, earnings stability, earnings trends, and management capabilities; computed by dividing market price per share by earnings per share. (477)

principal: The face amount of a note; the amount (excluding interest) that the maker agrees to pay the payee. *See also* face value of a bond.

prior-period adjustments: Adjustments made directly to Retained Earnings, which are required to correct errors in the financial statements of prior periods. (400)

procedures manual: A document that identifies the general policies of a company. (525)

profitability: A company's ability to generate revenues in excess of costs incurred in producing those revenues. (33, 457)

property dividend: Distributions to shareholders of assets other than cash or company stock. (393)

property, plant, and equipment: Tangible, long-lived assets acquired for use in the business rather than for resale. (244, 327)

property, plant, and equipment turnover: A measure of how well property, plant, and equipment are being utilized in generating sales; computed by dividing net sales by average property, plant, and equipment. (473)

proprietary accounts: In not-for-profit accounting, separate fund accounts for recording actual transactions, that is, actual revenues and expenditures. (495)

proprietorship: An unincorporated business owned by one person. (18)

pro rata: A term for an allocation that is based on a proportionate distribution of the total. (393)

purchase discount: A reduction in the purchase price, allowed if payment is made within a specified period. (180)

Purchase Returns and Allowances: A contra-purchases account in which the returns of, or allowances for, previously purchased merchandise are recorded. (180)

Purchases: Under a periodic inventory system, the account in which all inventory purchases are recorded. (179)

R

raw materials: Goods purchased for use in manufacturing products. (207)

real accounts: The accounts appearing on the Balance Sheet, which are not closed to a zero balance at the end of each accounting period; also called permanent accounts. (82)

receivables: Claims for money, goods, or services. (263)

recourse: The right to seek payment on a discounted note from the payee if the maker defaults. (266)

registered bonds: Bonds for which the names and addresses of the bondholders are kept on file by the issuing company. (367)

Reserve for Encumbrances: In not-for-profit accounting, an account credited at the time a commitment is made for an expenditure. (497)

residual value: *See* salvage value.

retail inventory method: A procedure for estimating the dollar amount of ending inventory whereby the ending inventory at retail is converted to a cost basis by using a ratio of the cost and retail amounts of goods available for sale; *compare* gross margin method. (223)

retained earnings: The accumulated portion of owners' equity that has been earned and retained from profitable operations and not paid out in dividends or restricted for some other use; equal to owners' equity less contributed capital. (38, 245)

return on total assets ratio: A measure of operating performance and efficiency in utilizing assets to generate a return for both creditors and owners; computed in its simplest form by dividing net income by average total assets. (475)

revenue approach: A way of accounting for unearned revenues in which these revenues are originally credited to a revenue account, even though the amount is not yet earned. A year-end adjustment is required to record the revenue actually earned during the period and to establish a corresponding liability for the amount not earned at year-end; *compare* liability approach. (112)

revenue recognition principle: The idea that revenues should be recorded when (1) the earnings process has been substantially completed, and (2) an exchange has taken place. (168)

revenues: Resource increases from the sale of goods or services derived from the normal operations and from other activities of a business. (35)

S

sales discount: A reduction in the sales price, allowed if payment is received within a specified period; also called cash discount. (170)

Sales Returns and Allowances: A contra-sales account in which the returns of, or allowances for, merchandise previously sold are recorded. (171)

salvage value: Estimated value or actual price of an asset at the conclusion of its useful life, net of disposal costs; sometimes called residual value. (329)

Section 1231: A provision in the tax law that allows businesses to report as capital gains, real and depreciable property that has been used in the business for more than 12 months and that is sold, exchanged, or involuntarily converted and whose selling price exceeds its original cost. (547)

secured bonds: Bonds for which there are pledged assets to guarantee repayment. (367)

Securities and Exchange Commission (SEC): The governmental body responsible for regulating the financial reporting practices of most publicly owned corporations in connection with the buying and selling of stocks and bonds. (24)

serial bonds: Bonds that mature in a series of installments at specified future dates. (368)

short-term investment: An expenditure for nonoperating assets that a business enterprise intends to hold only for a short period of time, usually less than a year. (242, 292)

simple interest: Interest calculated only on the principal amount each period. (296)

social security (FICA) taxes: Federal Insurance Contributions Act taxes imposed on employee and employer; used mainly to provide retirement benefits (270)

solvency: A company's long-run ability to meet all financial obligations. (33, 457)

Sources and Uses of Cash: A summary account used in preparing a Funds Statement based on the cash concept of funds. (435)

Sources and Uses of Working Capital: A summary account used in preparing a Funds Statement based on the working capital concept of funds. (424)

Source of Cash from Operations: A subsidiary account used in preparing a Funds Statement based on the cash concept of funds. (435)

Sources of Working Capital from Operations: A subsidiary account used in preparing a Funds Statement based on the working capital concept of funds. (424)

special journals: Books of original entry for recording similar transactions that occur frequently. (196)

specific identification: A method of valuing inventory and determining cost of goods sold whereby the actual costs of specific inventory items are assigned to those items of inventory on hand and to those that have been sold. (214)

stated value: The nominal value assigned to no-par stock by the board of directors of a corporation. (388)

Statement of Changes in Financial Position (Funds Statement): The primary financial statement that shows an entity's major sources and uses of financial resources (funds) during a period of time. (39)

Statement of Changes in Fund Balance: A formal statement prepared for a not-for-profit organization that shows how the fund balance has changed from the beginning to the end of the period. (502)

Statement of Changes in Owners' Equity: A report that shows the total changes in owners' equity (including retained earnings) during a period of time. (41)

Statement of Partners' Capital: A partnership report reconciling the balances in the partners' equity accounts from year to year. (405)

Statement of Retained Earnings: A report that shows the changes in the Retained Earnings account during a period of time. (40, 400)

Statement of Revenues and Expenditures: A formal statement prepared for a not-for-profit organization that shows the relationship between actual revenues and expenditures; it may also include the budgeted amounts. (500)

stock certificate: A document issued by a corporation to a shareholder evidencing ownership in the corporation. (385)

stock dividend: A pro rata distribution of additional shares of stock by a corporation to its shareholders. (393)

stockholders' equity: The ownership interest in an enterprise's assets; equals net assets (total assets minus total liabilities). (245)

stockholders (shareholders): Individuals or organizations that own a portion (shares of stock) of a corporation. (19, 385)

stock split: An action by a corporation's management that proportionately increases the number of shares outstanding either by reducing the par or stated value of its stock or by issuing a large stock dividend. (399)

straight-line depreciation method: The depreciation method in which the cost of an asset is allocated equally over the periods of the asset's estimated useful life. (330)

straight-line interest amortization: A method of systematically writing off a bond premium or discount in equal amounts each period until maturity; *compare* effective-interest amortization. (310)

Subchapter S corporation: A company legally organized as a corporation in which income or loss is passed through and taxed to individual stockholders. (386, 544)

subsidiary company: A company owned or controlled by another company, known as the parent company. (43, 302)

subsidiary ledger: A grouping of individual accounts that in total equal the balance of a control account in the General Ledger. (196)

sum-of-the-years'-digits depreciation method (SYD): The accelerated depreciation method in which a declining depreciation rate is multiplied by a constant balance (cost minus salvage value). (332)

T

T-account: A simplified depiction of an account in the form of a letter T, showing debits on the left and credits on the right. (72)

tangible, personal, depreciable business property: property used in a business that is not considered to be real estate. (551)

taxable income: The income remaining after all deductions have been subtracted from gross income. (538)

tax credit: A direct reduction in the tax liability, usually granted to encourage a particular action or to provide tax relief for certain classes of taxpayers. (538)

tax-exempt corporation: A legal entity chartered by a state for scientific, religious, educational, charitable, and similar purposes. (545)

temporary accounts: *See* nominal accounts.

term bonds: Bonds that mature in one lump sum at a specified future date. (368)

time-period assumption (periodicity concept): The idea that the life of a business is divided into distinct and relatively short time periods so that accounting information can be timely. (105)

transaction analysis: The procedures for analyzing, recording, summarizing, and reporting the transactions of an entity. (66)

transactions: Exchanges of goods or services between entities (whether individuals, businesses, or other organizations), as well as events having an economic impact on an entity. (20)

transfer payment: In not-for-profit accounting, a payment by one fund to another. (493)

treasury stock: Issued stock that has subsequently been reacquired and not retired by a corporation. (387)

trial balance: A listing of all account balances; provides a means of testing whether debits equal credits for the total of all accounts. (79)

20 percent first-year depreciation allowance: A provision in the tax law that allows corporations (and other businesses) to take a deduction of 20 percent of the cost of an asset (up to $10,000) as depreciation in the first year the asset is put into service. (555)

U

unearned revenues: Amounts received before they have been earned. (111)

units-of-production depreciation method: The depreciation method in which the cost of an asset is allocated to each period on the basis of the productive output of that asset during the period. (331)

unrecorded expenses and accrued liabilities: Expenses not previously recognized, and companion payable accounts incurred during a period but not paid for by the end of that period. (110)

unrecorded revenues and accrued assets: Revenues not previously recognized, and companion receivable accounts earned during a period but not received by the end of that period. (109)

unsecured bonds: *See* debentures.

V

vertical analysis: A technique for analyzing the relationships among items on a particular year's Income Statement or Balance Sheet by expressing all items as percentages of some total, for example, net sales or total assets. (462)

W

weighted average: A periodic inventory cost flow assumption whereby the cost of goods sold and the ending inventory are determined to be a weighted-average cost of all merchandise available for sale during the period. (213)

working capital: The funds (or resources) available to finance current operations; equal to current assets minus current liabilities. (245, 255)

working capital concept of funds: A concept used in preparing a Funds Statement that reflects transactions that increase or decrease current assets or current liabilities. (420)

working capital turnover: A measure of the amount of working capital used in sustaining the sales of a period; computed by dividing net sales by average working capital. (472)

work-in-process: Partially completed units in production; includes all manufacturing costs assigned to products that are in process but have not been completed. (207)

worksheet: A columnar schedule used to conveniently summarize accounting data. (119)

INDEX